Educational Psychology

with

Virtual Psychology Labs

Bruce W. Tuckman
The Ohio State University

David M. Monetti
Valdosta State University

 **WADSWORTH**
CENGAGE Learning

Australia • Brazil • Japan • Korea • Mexico • Singapore • Spain • United Kingdom • United States

WADSWORTH
CENGAGE Learning

Educational Psychology with Virtual Psychology Labs
Bruce W. Tuckman and David M. Monetti

Senior Publisher: Linda Schreiber-Ganster

Education Editor: Christopher Shortt

Executive Editor: Mark Kerr

Developmental Editor: Robert Jucha

Associate Development Editor: Caitlin Cox

Assistant Editor: Genevieve Allen

Editorial Assistant: Greta Lindquist

Senior Media Editor: Ashley Cronin

Marketing Manager: Kara Kindstrom

Marketing Assistant: Dimitri Hagnere

Marketing Communications Manager:
    Heather Baxley

Marketing Coordinator: Klaira Markenzon

Content Project Manager: Tanya Nigh

Creative Director: Rob Hugel

Art Director: Maria Epes

Print Buyer: Paula Vang

Rights Acquisitions Account Manager, Text:
    Margaret Chamberlain-Gaston

Rights Acquisitions Account Manager, Image:
    John Hill

Text Designer: Marsha Cohen

Photo Researcher: Raquel Sousa,
    PreMediaGlobal

Cover Designer: Bartay Studio

Cover Image: © LWA-Sharie Kennedy/Corbis,
    © Masterfile Royalty Free

Compositor: PreMediaGlobal

For product information and technology assistance, contact us at
Cengage Learning Customer & Sales Support, 1-800-354-9706.

For permission to use material from this text or product,
submit all requests online at **www.cengage.com/permissions.**
Further permissions questions can be e-mailed to
permissionrequest@cengage.com.

Library of Congress Control Number: 2011939702

ISBN-13: 978-1-133-30926-0

ISBN-10: 1-133-30926-7

Wadsworth
20 Davis Drive
Belmont, CA 94002-3098
USA

Cengage Learning is a leading provider of customized learning solutions with office locations around the globe, including Singapore, the United Kingdom, Australia, Mexico, Brazil, and Japan. Locate your local office at **www.cengage.com/global.**

Cengage Learning products are represented in Canada by Nelson Education, Ltd.

To learn more about Wadsworth, visit **www.cengage.com/wadsworth.**

Purchase any of our products at your local college store or at our preferred online store **www.cengagebrain.com.**

Printed in the United States of America
1 2 3 4 5 6 7 15 14 13 12 11

Brief Contents

Contents

CHAPTER 4

Learner Diversity   134

CHAPTER 5

Learners with Exceptionalities   **180**

CHAPTER 6
Behavioral Approaches to Learning   224

CHAPTER 7
Cognitive Approaches to Learning   270

CHAPTER 12
The Design of Instruction 472

CHAPTER 13
Classroom Assessment of Student Learning   514

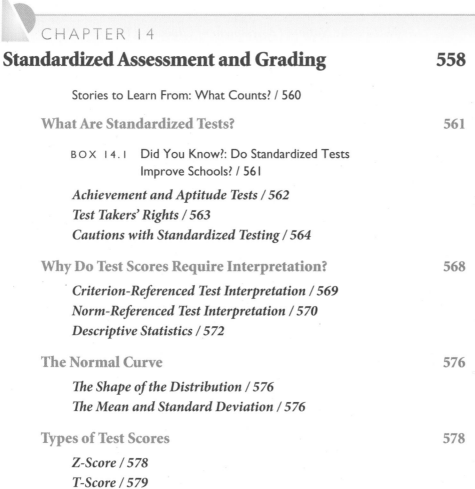

CHAPTER 14

Standardized Assessment and Grading   558

Preface

Introduction

Students in educational psychology courses often begin their exploration of the teaching profession looking for answers to immediate classroom problems; that is, they want to know *"what"* to do in various classroom settings. They are focused on the immediacy of teaching and want to develop knowledge and skills that will directly improve their teaching practice. As instructors of educational psychology, we want to help future teachers understand not only what effective teachers do in specific day-to-day classroom settings, but also *"why"* they are doing it. The *why* is important because modern learning environments do not always conform to the implementation of pre-established and ready-made methods and practices. The effective teacher must use his or her understanding of theory and best practice to meet the diverse learning, social, and cultural needs of the learners and caregivers he or she will serve in the future.

Why We Wrote the Book

Our goal for writing this book is to help students learn about theories and practices which will help them become effective teachers. In order to accomplish this, we have focused on ways prospective teachers can apply psychology to education, how to employ models of effective teaching, and how to be reflective teachers. This text was designed to be accessible to students and written in a manner that will help them succeed in the educational psychology course and in their teaching. We believe that through the instructional design features and content of our book, students will be more able to understand and apply the concepts and skills that the instructor determines as critical to success in teaching. We seek to help students consider numerous alternative solutions to educational issues by providing specific examples, "stories," theories, best practices, models, research findings, and pictures. We also see the students' and instructor's role in learning about educational psychology as a creative one that which requires *inquiry* and *discovery,* and to encourage that process we have included significant information about *creativity* and the nurturance of creativity within the book.

While there are many fine Educational Psychology textbooks an instructor may choose from, none offers what we have done here in terms of content, features, and examples. We think instructors and students want to read a book that offers learning objectives that are meaningfully integrated throughout the text and a book that gets students to think critically about schooling practices.

Major Themes

Overall, our text is **theme-based** and attempts to help students hang concepts and best practices on big ideas that resonate with individuals studying to be teachers. Our five major themes are (1) Exploring Psychology's Role in Education—Chapter 1, (2) Developmental Trends and Learner Diversity—Chapters 2–5, (3) Learning Approaches and Applications—Chapters 6–8, (4) The Teaching-Learning Environment—Chapters 9–12, and (5) Appraisal of Learning—Chapters 13 and 14.

Our overall approach emphasizes important educational **theories** and **best practices** as the building blocks for effective learning and teaching. This emphasis extends through all of our chapters. In addition, like a good teacher, the book practices throughout what it preaches. For example, in Chapter 7—on Cognitive Approaches to Learning—the uses of **abstracting, elaborating, organizing, questioning, advance organizers**, and **adjunct questions** are described as techniques that students can use to understand what they are reading. In other words, we are turning the text we wrote into a lesson in the very principles of why we wrote the book.

Outline of Chapters

Chapter 1—The Study of Educational Psychology

This introduction to educational psychology provides the reader with important foundational concepts such as what educational psychology is, why it is studied, and how it can be applied to education. It also helps the reader see how educational psychology relates to the role of the teacher and what the characteristics of an effective teacher are. In addition, it helps the reader understand how educational psychology relates to the study of human behavior, how the teacher can function as a researcher, and which research methods can be used to inform teachers and enable them to enhance student learning.

Chapter 2—Cognitive and Language Development

This initial chapter on development presents important concepts and models such as principles of cognitive development, brain physiology, and brain-based learning and teaching. Also covered are the developmental approaches of Jean Piaget and Lev Vygotsky and how they can be applied to educational practice. Finally, there is a section on the main aspects of language and how language development can be facilitated in the classroom.

Chapter 3—Moral, Personal, and Psychosocial Development

This second chapter on development focuses primarily on moral and personal aspects and presents important concepts such as Piaget's stages of moral judgment, Kohlberg's stages of moral reasoning, and Erikson's stages of psychosocial development, followed by a segment on how to enhance moral development. In addition, four aspects of personal development are described, as are the characteristics of racial identity.

Chapter 4—Learner Diversity

This engaging chapter describes various aspects of diversity, including social class differences, differences in ethnicity and culture, critical pedagogy, and the impact of multicultural education. Also covered in this chapter are diversity of language and sexual orientation and gender differences. The chapter ends with coverage of diversity in intelligence and factors that affect it, such as ability grouping, and differences in learning styles.

Chapter 5—Learners with Exceptionalities

This important chapter opens with a description of classifications, laws, and special education, followed by a description of the intellectual exceptionalities of giftedness and mental retardation. This is followed by coverage of the important behavioral exceptionalities of learning disabilities, ADHD, emotional and behavior disorders, communication and sensorimotor exceptionalities of hearing and visual impairment, and physical disabilities. Finally, a segment on autism and Asberger's Syndrome includes an analysis of the movie *Rainman*.

Chapter 6—Behavioral Approaches to Learning

This chapter begins the section on learning approaches and applications. It covers classical conditioning—based on learning by association—and operant conditioning—based on consequences. Also described are types of reinforcers, perspectives on punishment, and methods of modifying behavior. A section on applying operant conditioning to the classroom then follows. The final section of this chapter focuses on social-cognitive learning, with an emphasis on observation.

Chapter 7—Cognitive Approaches to Learning

This second chapter on learning approaches starts out with a comparison between the behavioral approach and the cognitive approach, and then covers an information processing model that includes semantic encoding, factors affecting memorizing, cognitive strategies affecting meaningful learning, instructional techniques to enhance the meaningfulness of text, metacognitive strategies, and study skills. This chapter also includes "The Memory Experiment: An Activity You Can Learn From" that enables students to directly engage in the process of memory.

Chapter 8—Constructivism, Problem Solving, and Creativity

The third and final chapter on learning approaches covers the three topical areas listed in the title: first, constructivism and constructivist-based teaching and learning (constructivism is when people create their own meaning of the experiences and thoughts they have rather than having that meaning provided by someone else), as well as the dilemmas of constructivism. The second topical area is problem solving, from general to expert, including problem solving in reading, social studies, and math. The third topical area is creativity, starting with its properties and ending on how it can be increased.

Chapter 9—Group Processes in Instruction

This chapter is critical because of the importance of collaboration and communication in modern classrooms. The senior author of this text is an expert in this area and has published a well-known theory of stages of group development known as "forming, storming, norming, and performing." This also is the first chapter focused on the theme of teaching-learning environment. Starting out with a model of group dynamics, this chapter proceeds to cover how expectations influence the behavior of teachers and students, the norms or rules followed by groups, the important and timely topic of cooperative learning or learning in groups, the teacher as leader in the classroom, and communication between teachers and students. The chapter closes with a discussion of friendship, liking, and classroom climate and a description of how groups grow.

Chapter 10—Motivating Learners

This major chapter in the book covers seven approaches to motivating learners in classrooms. The first three are the social-cognitive approach or self-reflection, self-efficacy or the belief in oneself (including self-efficacy in school), and self-regulation or the control of oneself, including how to teach students to self-regulate. The fourth approach is attribution or the identification of causes, including taking responsibility and acting with intentionality, which includes the teacher's role. The fifth focuses on needs and goals as motivators while the sixth focuses on incentives and values as motivators. Lastly, the self-determination approach to motivation is described.

Chapter 11—Effective Learning Communities

This essential chapter on the teaching-learning environment covers the following topics: creating and maintaining an effective learning community (including classroom rules), teacher interventions for responding to misbehavior, how to deal with bullying in school (including cyberbullying), how to apply culturally responsive classroom management and other management paradigms such as assertive discipline.

Chapter 12—The Design of Instruction

This final chapter on the teaching-learning environment introduces the reader to the conditions of learning and instruction and the outcomes of learning (from Gagné), an instructional planning model for teachers, the mastery learning and teaching model, the direct instructional model—covering behavior and thinking skills, and discovery learning and teaching. It also provides students with an opportunity to discover their own instructional preferences.

Chapter 13—Classroom Assessment of Student Learning

This first chapter on the appraisal of learning covers steps in the classroom assessment process, such as constructing and scoring essay items, as well as short-answer items, constructing and scoring performance assessments, including portfolios, and evaluating the validity and reliability of classroom assessments, as well as building more reliable tests. While challenging, this is an essential topic for prospective teachers to master.

Chapter 14—Standardized Assessment and Grading

This second chapter on the appraisal of learning also covers important and challenging topics, including knowing what standardized tests and test-takers' rights are, knowing how to interpret criterion-referenced and norm-referenced test scores, and knowing the meaning of descriptive statistics. This includes the normal curve and types of test scores, such as the z-score and percentile rank. This also includes the highly important activity of converting and explaining test scores and score reports to students and their parents, as well as practicing meaningful and fair grading and recognizing national trends in standardized assessment. The chapter ends with a segment on preparing students for tests by reducing their test anxiety.

Features of the Book

The features of the book are divided into two categories: (1) Student Learning Aids and (2) Special Features (boxes). Each is described below.

Student Learning Aids

Learning Objectives

When you begin reading a chapter, the first learning aid you will encounter is a series of integrated **Learning Objectives**, each matched to **Chapter Contents**, to alert readers to what they need to know in order to process and understand information presented in that chapter. It is important to note that these learning objectives are created to prompt higher-order thinking in addition to knowledge and comprehension of educational psychology topics. To assist the student in making the connection between the learning objectives and what they are reading in the chapter, the color-coded objective will also appear in the margin of the text where the concept is discussed in the chapter.

Learning objectives also appear at the end of each chapter, in conjunction with a summary of the chapter (as described below). By seeing the objective before, during, and after the chapter, the reader is able to consider the degree to which he or she understands and can apply the concepts he or she read about.

Stories to Learn From

This feature provides a compelling story or anecdote that engages readers in the topic of the chapter right from the beginning. There is a rich tradition of oral storytelling in cultures around the world. These stories are often able to teach important lessons and dispositions in ways that lectures cannot. We use narratives as a way to think about concepts from the chapter in very applied and meaningful ways and then directly connect the stories to the chapter by asking linking questions immediately following the story.

Each chapter opens with a different story that relates to the chapter's content and includes questions to answer, followed by a paragraph on "lessons we can learn from the story." Some of the stories have to do with famous educators, such as Albert Einstein, Susan B. Anthony, and John Dewey, while others describe classroom events, such as "Mr. Sachs Forms Classroom Groups" or "Honesty Is the Best Policy."

Think It Over

Another student learning aid, called **Think It Over**, reflects the dual role of those who will be using the book: namely learner and teacher. During their use of the book, students will be learners, and later teachers. This feature gives students an opportunity to answer questions that reflect as learners their understanding of what they are reading, and then as teachers how they can connect what they are reading to its applications in the classroom.

Concept Review Tables

Each chapter in the book has from one to six concept review tables that are designed to help students review important concepts after having read about them in the text. The tables help students organize and remember information about which they have read, thus facilitating their use of cognitive processes as described in Chapter 7. For example, Concept Review Table 2.1 (in Chapter 2) deals with Piaget's adaptive processes of intellectual development. In the first column of the table, the six concepts (adaptation, assimilation, accommodation, equilibration, intelligence, and operations) are listed. In the second column, the definitions of each of the six concepts are provided, and in the third column, examples are listed. Students, who have already been exposed to the concepts, are able to review and remember them by studying the information in the concept review table.

Glossary

A running **glossary** is a feature that appears in the margin throughout the book to help students identify the most critical concepts from each chapter. These entries are indexed by page number so that if a student is unfamiliar with the concept, he or she can quickly find the information in the chapter.

Summing It Up (connected with Learning Objectives and Key Concepts)

At the end of each chapter, students will see a brief but detailed summary, along with page references, called **Summing It Up**, providing them with a study guide built right into the text. In addition, these summaries are directly linked to the learning objectives detailed at the beginning of the chapters. At the end of each summary paragraph, a list of key concepts related to that paragraph is provided, along with the page number in the text where each key concept can be found.

Special Features (Boxes)

Our book also contains five special features to help engage students in the text material and process it more thoroughly. Each of them, described below, plays a different, but very significant, role in the book.

Discourse on Diversity

To complement the text's focus on diversity, each chapter includes a boxed feature called **Discourse on Diversity**. This feature is designed to present to the reader up-to-date research that shows the valuable connection between student diversity and the topic of the chapter. For example, the Discourse on Diversity for Chapter 11—Effective Learning Communities, titled *Understanding the Discipline Gap Through a Cultural Lens: Implications for the Education of African American Students,* is based on a study by Monroe (2005) about how African American students are disciplined in America's public schools. The study found that African American students are overrepresented in school discipline, resulting in what has been called the "discipline gap."

An Example to Aid Understanding

Each chapter in our book also contains a boxed feature called **An Example to Aid Understanding**. In Chapter 7—The Cognitive Approach to Learning, we talk about "Cognitive Strategies Affecting Meaningful Learning." One of the most important and useful of these strategies is called *elaboration*, a strategy that helps students understand and remember what they read by them adding additional information to what appears in the book. The best way to elaborate is to come up with examples because examples aid understanding. For example, the Chess Masters Study in Box 7.1 helps readers understand that knowledge is the key ingredient of memory as evidenced by the example that chess masters were able to remember the location of the chess pieces on a dozen chess boards as a result of actual moves, but were unable to remember the location of the pieces when they were placed randomly.

Did You Know?

The largely interactive boxed material provided to students under the heading of **Did You Know?** elicits students' responses as *learners*, the role with which they are most familiar, and thereby helps them gain insight into the perceptions and reactions of students, while improving their own learning and motivation skills. For example, in Chapter 1—The Study of Educational Psychology, students are introduced in Box 1.3 to the idea that *Expectations Can Affect Outcomes*, something they more than likely did not know as learners until reading the contents of the box, but that will be important for them to know as teachers.

Take It to the Classroom

We know those students who enroll in the educational psychology course are anxious to take what they have learned and apply it in the classroom. That is why we created the feature called **Take It to the Classroom**. It elicits students' responses as *teachers*, the role for which they are preparing. Once entering the teaching profession, they will be well-served in their reflective processes by being able to see things not only through their own eyes, but through the eyes of their students as well. For example, in Chapter 9—Group Processes in Instruction, the topic of expectations is examined in Box 9.1 from the teacher's perspective rather than the student's by providing a series of recommendations on how teachers can break the cycle of negative expectations in the classroom group.

TeachSource Video Cases

We know many students are visual learners and that is why we created this feature. It appears in each chapter and provides information that prospective teachers can use to improve and increase their teaching skills. Each video case shows a teacher teaching a lesson to a class of his or her elementary, middle, or high school students that relates to the chapter topic. After observing the teacher in action, the prospective students are presented with some useful questions to answer. For example, in Chapter 4—Learner Diversity, the teacher models culturally responsive teaching techniques in teaching a multicultural lesson for her elementary school students. Questions are then posed that ask prospective teachers to react to the teaching strategies that were demonstrated and to the teacher's own cultural background.

Ancillaries

For the Student

Education CourseMate with Virtual Psychology Labs

Cengage Learning's Education CourseMate brings course concepts to life with interactive learning, study, and exam preparation tools that support the printed textbook. Access the Virtual Psychology Labs, an integrated eBook, learning tools including flashcards, quizzes, TeachSource Video Cases, and more, in your Education CourseMate, accessed through CengageBrain.com.

Virtual Psychology Labs

Virtual Psychology Labs is a virtual laboratory experience designed to illustrate key experiments in psychology which are not easily demonstrated in the classroom. The Virtual Psychology Labs takes your experience beyond the book and the classroom allowing you to experience the research method first-hand, with immediate explanations and assessment following each completed experiment. The labs also help you to understand the significance of these classic experiments and offer insight into how students learn.

TeachSource Video Cases

The Video Cases are 4- to 6-minute video modules presenting actual classroom scenarios, supported by viewing questions, teacher interviews, artifacts, and bonus videos. The Video Cases let students experience the complex and multiple dimensions of true classroom dilemmas that teachers face every day.

Education CourseMate also includes access to InfoTrac® College Edition, an Online Research and Learning Center featuring 24/7 access to over 20 million full-text articles from nearly 6,000 journals.

Go to CengageBrain.com to register your access code. If an access card was not included with the text, students can go to CengageBrain.com to obtain an access code.

For the Instructor

Education CourseMate with Virtual Psychology Labs

Cengage Learning's Education CourseMate brings course concepts to life with interactive learning, study, and exam preparation tools that support the printed textbook. CourseMate includes access to the Virtual Psychology Labs, an integrated eBook, quizzes, flashcards, TeachSource Video Cases, and more, and EngagementTracker, a first-of-its-kind tool that monitors student engagement in the course. The accompanying instructor website offers access to password-protected resources such as an electronic version of the instructor's manual and PowerPoint® slides. Go to login. cengage.com to access these resources.

Virtual Psychology Labs

Virtual Psychology Labs is a virtual laboratory experience designed to illustrate key experiments in psychology which are not easily demonstrated in the classroom. The Virtual Psychology Labs takes a student's experience beyond the book and the classroom allowing them to experience the research method first-hand, with immediate explanations and assessment following each completed experiment. The labs also help students to understand the significance of these classic experiments and offer insight into how students learn.

Intstructor's Manual with Test Bank

The Instructor's Manual with Test Bank contains resources designed to streamline and maximize the effectiveness of your course preparations. The contents include a sample syllabus, chapter summaries, objectives, lecture suggestions or concepts to focus on, discussion questions, assignments, test bank, and additional resources.

WebTutor for Blackboard and WebCT with Virtual Psychology Labs

Jumpstart your course with customizable, rich, text-specific content within your Course Management System. Whether you want to Web-enable your class or put an entire course online, WebTutor™ delivers. WebTutor™ offers a wide array of resources including videos and other media, the eBook, quizzes, web links, and access to the Virtual Psychology Labs.

PowerLecture DVD with ExamView and JoinIn

This one-stop digital library and presentation tool includes preassembled Microsoft® PowerPoint lecture slides, an image library with graphics from the text, and videos. It also includes a full Instructor's Manual and Test Bank and Exam View testing software with all the test items from the printed Test Bank in electronic format, enabling you to create customized tests in print or online. You'll also find JoinIn™ Student Response System content (for use with most "clicker" systems), which allows instant classroom assessment and active learning.

Acknowledgments

We wish to express our thanks to the following individuals who helped with the development and production of this book. Lauren Hensley, Coordinator of Learning Services, Walter E. Dennis Learning Center, The Ohio State University, for her help with acquiring the necessary permissions. Cengage Learning publishing professionals aided us at each step of the way. Mark Kerr was our able executive editor. Caitlin Cox, development editor, for the major role she played in bringing our writing project to fruition by guiding our efforts. Kara Kindstrom, Marketing Manager for Education, helped introduce *Educational Psychology* to the college community. The following individuals earned our thanks through their valued contributions: Marie Desrosiers, Content Project Manager; Ashley Cronin, Media Editor; and Greta Lindquist, Editorial Assistant.

Reviewers of Educational Psychology

We are grateful for the participation of the reviewers who read and reviewed portions of our manuscript throughout its development, and for those who gave us valuable insights through their responses to the e-survey.

We greatly appreciate how much you helped us improve our book. We look forward to your continued constructive criticism so that we can provide you and your students with a textbook that will contribute to the important work of teaching children, adolescents, and adults.

Manuscript Reviewers for Educational Psychology

Jane Abraham, Virginia Tech University

Frank Adams, Wayne State University

William Bart, University of Minnesota

Kathryn Biancindo, California State University at Fresno

Ty Binfet, Loyola-Marymount University

Joy Brown, University of North Alabama

Bruce Burnam, California State University at Los Angeles

Jerrell Cassady, Ball State University

Shane Cavanaugh, Central Michigan State University

Linda Chiang, Azusa Pacific University

Steve Cockerham, East Tennessee State University

Larry Cross, Governors State University

Gregory Cutler, Bay de Noc Community College

Debra Defoor, Purdue North Central University

Felicia Dixon, Ball State University

Robert Faux, University of Pittsburgh

Jennifer L. Fisler, Messiah College

Barbara Fuller, Northeastern State University

Judith Geary, University of Michigan

Monica Glina, Montclair State University

Bill Goodwin, University of Colorado at Denver

Mary Hancock, University of West Georgia

Brian Harper, Cleveland State University

Robert Harrington, Kansas University

Huio-Ju Huang, California State University at Sacramento

Laura Hughes, Georgia Perimeter College

John Hummel, Valdosta State University

Virginia Johnson, Biola University

Kristopher Kimbler, Florida Gulf Coast University

Elaine Koffman, Northeastern Illinois University

Nancy Flanagan Knapp, University of Georgia

Pamela Manners, Troy University

Chogollah Marouf, California State University at Northridge

Mary Misevich, Sacred Heart College

Karen Moroz, Concordia University St. Paul

Steven Pulos, University of Northern Colorado

Robin Rackley, Texas A&M University

Elizabeth Reynolds, University of Idaho

Laura Reynolds-Keefer, University of Michigan at Dearborn

Angelia Ridgway, University of Indianapolis

Lawrence Rogien, Boise State University

Pearl M. Rosenberg, Muhlenberg College

Jeff Sandoz, University of Louisiana at Lafayette

Rolando Santos, California State University at Los Angeles

Zsuzsanna Szabo, Southern Illinois University

Yen To, Texas Tech University

Diane Webber, Curry College

Patricia Willems, Florida Atlantic University

Aaron Yarlas, Grand Valley State University

Ronald Zigler, Penn State Abington

We also thank those who took the time to respond to our survey on the needs of the educational psychology instructor.

Wallace M. Alexander, Thomas College

Eric Anderman, The Ohio State University

Greg Anderson, Indiana University— Purdue University Fort Wayne

Amy Bender, University of Wisconsin at Milwaukee

Renee Berg, California State University at Northridge

John Charlesworth, University of West Georgia

Sheila Clonan, Colgate University Barbara Cockroft, Walsh University

Suzy Cox, Utah Valley University

Mary Lee Danielson, Carroll College

Ann Diver-Stamnes, Humboldt State University

Preston D. Feden, La Salle University

Suzanne G. Fegley, University of Pennsylvania

Lucia Flevares, The Ohio State University

Steven Frye, Tennessee Tech University

William Fullard, Temple University

Richard L Gibson, Friends University

Anisa Goforth, Michigan State University

Korrine Gust, Manchester College

Joyce Hemphill, University of Wisconsin at Madison

Karen Hizer, St. Louis Community College

Wanda S. Ingram, Providence College

Nancy Johnson, Geneva College

Sue Kelewae, Kent State University

Catharine C. Knight, University of Akron

Carol B. Lane, Coastal Carolina University

Kimberly Lawless, University of Illinois at Chicago

Barry S. Markman, Wayne State University

John Mascazine, Ohio Dominican University

Joyce Moore, University of Iowa

Katharyn E. K. Nottis, Bucknell University

Mary Seaborn, Indiana Wesleyan University

Donna Seagleq, Chattanooga State Technical Community College

Sonya K. Sedivy, University of Wisconsin at Milwaukee

Diane Simpson, Waubonsee Community College

Karen A. Siska, Columbia State Community College

Curt Visca, Saddleback College

Stewart Wood, Madonna University

Message to Students

This book was designed to be a learning and teaching tool that will help you gain meaning from your experience with the discipline of educational psychology. We value and seek feedback from you to ensure that this textbook is preparing you to effectively work with students you will eventually serve.

Bruce W. Tuckman
David M. Monetti

About the Authors

Bruce W. Tuckman, Ph.D., is Professor of Educational Psychology in the College of Education and Human Ecology at The Ohio State University and Founding Director of the Walter E. Dennis Learning Center, providing students with training in learning and motivation strategies that has been shown to increase their GPAs, retention and graduation rate. He earned his B.S. in Psychology from RPI and his M.A. and Ph.D. in Psychology from Princeton University. He has authored 18 books including *Conducting Educational Research* and *Learning & Motivation Strategies: Your Guide to Success*. He has also authored more than 100 articles in such areas as motivation, cognition, instructional design, measurement, and group development ("forming," "storming," "norming," and "performing"). He served for six years as Executive Editor of the *Journal of Experimental Education*. He is a Fellow of both the American Psychological Association and the American Educational Research Association, based on his contributions to educational research.

David M. Monetti, Ph.D., is Professor of Educational Psychology in the Dewar College of Education at Valdosta State University. He teaches courses in educational psychology, learning theory, and measurement and evaluation. He earned his Ph.D. in Educational Psychology at Florida State University and bachelor's and master's degrees from the University of South Florida. David completed his teaching internship in secondary English and remains actively involved with the public schools as a researcher and evaluator of school improvement practices. His research interests include service learning, Response to Intervention, and epistemology of learning. He is past president of the Georgia Educational Research Association.

To Our Wives: Tracy Cooper-Tuckman and Whitney Monetti

Susan B. Anthony—"A Woman for All Seasons"

Most people know about Susan B. Anthony as a leader of the Women's Suffrage Movement, a movement that fought for women in America to have the right to vote. What most people don't know about her is that she was a teacher and an educational reformer. She was born in 1820, learned to read and write at the age of 3, attended a boarding school in Philadelphia, took her first teaching position at the age of 15 for $1.50 a week plus board, and in 1846 became head of the girl's department at Canajoharie Academy in upstate New York. All told, she spent 15 years as an effective teacher while continually arguing for the need for improvement in then current teaching methods, after which time she directed her energy toward gaining women the right to vote.

In 1853, she attended the state teacher's convention in her hometown, Rochester, N.Y., and campaigned for better pay for women teachers, for their right to be admitted to the professions, and for their right to have a voice at the convention. In 1859, she spoke at two other state teachers' conventions on behalf of coeducation and argued that the intelligence of men and women were the same. She also called for equal educational opportunities for all people, no matter their race, and argued that all schools at every academic level admit women, ex-slaves, and the children of ex-slaves.

In the 1890s, she served on the Board of Trustees at Rochester's State Industrial School and campaigned for coeducation and equal treatment regardless of gender. She also raised $50,000 in pledges to try to ensure women's admission to the University of Rochester. In addition, she put up the cash value of her life insurance policy. Her efforts forced the University to admit women for the first time in 1900.

In 1920, fourteen years after Susan B. Anthony's death, American women finally won the right to vote with the passage of the 19th Amendment. Congress honored her in 1979 by putting her portrait on a new, one-dollar coin.

- What have you learned from this story?
- How do you see this story relating to you as a prospective teacher?

Lessons We Can Learn from the Story It takes a lot to be a good teacher. Not only are many skills required, but attitudes and feelings also make a difference. A teacher's calling includes accepting and believing in his or her students and valuing and advocating for them—regardless of students' gender, race, and ethnicity. The purpose of this book is to help you become an effective teacher, and part of that is learning how to teach students from diverse backgrounds. Indeed, student diversity is a major theme of this book.

We started this book with a story about Susan B. Anthony, an effective teacher and a great educational reformer who continues to serve as a role model for today's teachers and students from every possible background.

In this chapter, you begin your journey to becoming an effective teacher by becoming familiar with its terrain. Important features—which are sometimes like beaches, sometimes gravel roads, sometimes wooded paths, and sometimes paved streets or highways—are explored in subsequent chapters. Here, we present you with an overview of the setting, resources, and tools you will master in your understanding of human behavior and its practical applications in your future classrooms. This chapter is the staging ground for your continuing growth and experience. It covers the fundamentals of the study of educational psychology.

What Is Educational Psychology?

Psychology is the scientific study of human behavior and mental processes. **Educational psychology** is the science of human behavior applied to the teaching and learning processes. Like general psychology, educational psychology is a science; therefore, its findings are generated through research that relies heavily on the scientific method. However, its purpose in study is to produce practical knowledge about educational settings and behaviors.

Educational psychology helps teachers understand issues such as how students learn, what motivates students to learn, how to design instruction that maximizes learning, and how to assess student learning and curricular effectiveness. It also can assist teachers to become more aware of their thoughts and actions and understand the effects these thoughts and actions have on others.

Why Study Human Behavior?

Human behavior is an individual's action in a given situation. It is not random, it follows patterns, and, in many cases, is predictable. Behavior may be predicted as a reaction to external events; in turn, it may precipitate other behaviors. For example, when someone is yelled at, he or she will often yell back, and may feel hurt or hold a grudge. Teachers who attempt to manage a learning environment through yells and threats quickly isolate their students. An expert teacher knows that, when students begin to elevate their voices, it is preferable to talk softly to diffuse the situation rather than to raise his of her voice and escalate the classroom disturbance. We often know what is likely to result from our behavior. For example, when an idea is explained well to someone, she will understand it. When a child cries, someone who cares for that child will often console him to stop the crying.

Some of these regularities in behavior are known to most people based simply on their experiences. As children grow up, they naturally learn these things. However, some of these regularities are not necessarily noticed because (1) they are subtle, (2) it is hard to behave and analyze what is going on at the same time, or (3) most people have not learned to attend to behavior and its causes. In addition, many factors that help explain behavior occur internally, based on experiences people have already had, rather than externally where they can be observed at that moment. Often, what is observed is not necessarily an accurate reflection of what is going on inside a person. Many people smile even though they are sad, or laugh even when they do not find something funny. Therefore, the science of psychology helps us to systematically notice and explain behavior.

While most behavior has patterns, it is complex. Experts may not always have an explanation for a particular behavior. Behavior is dynamic, has many variables, and occurs at a rapid and continuous pace. People sometimes are naive about their own feelings and motives, to say nothing of the feelings and motives of others. Because some feelings and motives are covert or hidden inside, you may not know how your behavior affects other people, even after you perform it. As a result of this lack of knowledge or awareness, people may affect others in unintended ways, and may fail to affect them in desired ways.

Learning Objective 1

Define educational psychology and its application in the classroom, including practical and intellectual reasons for studying human behavior.

educational psychology
the science of human behavior applied to the teaching and learning processes

human behavior
an individual's action in a given situation

The Teacher Practitioner

Knowing psychology is particularly valuable for anyone whose profession involves frequent interaction with others, where one has some degree of responsibility for others' outcomes that confronts them with the sometimes difficult task of managing the interaction. The role of teacher clearly fits this description. Doyle (1986) identified six characteristics of the classroom environment and the teacher's role in it.

- **Multidimensionality:** A teacher has to deal with many aspects and types of behavior, including scheduling, observing, recording, and reacting to and evaluating it for a sizeable number of students, many of whom may be doing different things.
- **Simultaneity:** All of these types of behavior may be occuring at the same time.
- **Immediacy:** A teacher's reactions must occur when the student behavior occurs.
- **Unpredictability:** A teacher cannot always anticipate what will happen.
- **Public nature of the classroom:** Every student gets to see what a teacher does, even if only with another student.
- **History:** Students often anticipate and react to a teacher's prior behavior in a situation similar to one in the past.

With so much happening so quickly and so many students involved, a teacher may inadvertently hurt a student's feelings when he really wants to make her feel better, or may fail to help a student understand something even though she is trying hard to convey the information necessary to make him understand. Knowledge of psychology can help you become more aware of and sensitive to student behavior in the complex environment of the classroom.

A teacher's job is very rewarding, but it is not without challenge. Educational psychology is intended to help teachers meet the challenges of the classroom and be more effective practitioners. Teachers wish to help students learn and understand subject matter ideas while simultaneously helping them feel good about themselves and about the experience of learning. Teachers also attempt to motivate students to want to learn; to do so, teachers must communicate with students and create the necessary experiences in order for students to learn. Teachers have to do all this in ways that make students feel positive about their attitudes or feelings toward learning as well as their capabilities as learners. A student's attitude or belief about the nature of knowledge and learning is referred to as a student's **epistemology**. To maximize student learning, teachers need knowledge and awareness, which are the products of studying human behavior and knowing what to do (and not do), what to look for, and where to look.

Along with the practical side discussed above, there is also an intellectual side to knowing educational psychology, as there is to knowing anything. Such knowledge expands a person's capabilities for thinking and knowing, and it enhances mental discipline and problem-solving skills. In a very real sense, it makes teachers better decision makers. One of the greatest concerns of the new teacher is how to create and maintain a classroom environment that maximizes student learning. This is one area in which findings from educational psychology can be of great benefit.

epistemology

a student's attitude or belief about the nature of knowledge and learning

Knowledge and skills gained through the study of educational psychology will help the new teacher foster an atmosphere conducive to student success. Essentially, educational psychology will give teachers information and skills that will help them maximize educationally fitting behavior, such as motivation to study, specific use of effective learning strategies, and appropriate interpersonal classroom behavior.

Applying Psychology to Education

Learning Objective 2

Describe three applications of psychology to education: (1) a model of the teaching-learning process, (2) principles of classroom management, and (3) perspectives on the causes of behavior.

It is important to realize that the relationship between knowledge of educational psychology and either the practical or intellectual skills of teaching is not a perfect one. Just as get-rich-quick schemes advertised on late night infomercials rarely lead to real financial stability, the study of educational psychology will not provide quick and certain recipes for being either a scholar or a successful teacher. For teachers to be successful, they will not only have to have significant knowledge, but always be experimenting to determine what works best in their classrooms.

A Transactional Model of the Teaching-Learning Process

Educational psychology can provide teachers with frameworks for combining psychology and education. One such framework, a **transactional model of the teaching-learning process**, appears in Figure 1.1. It illustrates the many factors that combine to influence student achievement, including the characteristics and behaviors of students

transactional model of the teaching-learning process
illustrates the many factors that combine to influence student achievement, including the characteristics and behaviors of students and teachers

FIGURE 1.1

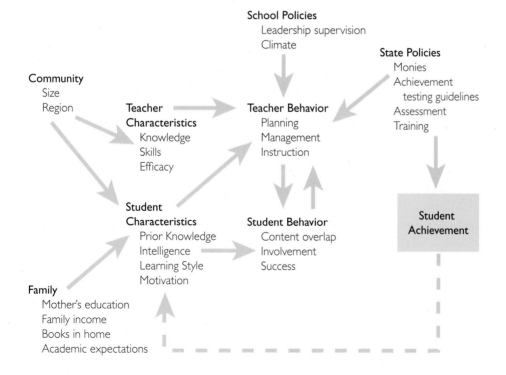

MODEL OF THE TEACHING-LEARNING PROCESS

A Transactional Model of the Teaching-Learning Process (Huitt, 2003)

and teachers. As you will see throughout this book, this is largely the subject with which educational psychology is concerned.

A similar approach is offered by Mayer (1999). He identifies the following factors in the teaching-learning process: (1) instructional manipulations, such as group work or conducting a discussion; (2) learner characteristics, such as the strategies used for learning; (3) learning processes, such as organizing information; (4) learning outcomes, such as memorization; and (5) outcome performance, such as retention as reflected on a test. You will encounter these factors in the teaching-learning process in a number of the chapters in this book.

Classroom Management

Educational psychology considers more than just the teaching-learning process. It also deals with motivation, development, classroom management, and other social processes. These have frameworks as well. For example, Tuckman (1999a) proposed that motivation was comprised of three components: (1) attitude, such as beliefs about one's ability to carry out a particular task; (2) drive, or the desire to achieve a particular outcome; and (3) strategy, or the way one goes about gaining one's ends. These ideas will be further described in subsequent chapters.

Box 1.1

TAKE IT TO THE CLASSROOM

A New Teacher Applies Educational Psychology in His High School Classroom

Mr. Harper was 24 when he entered a 12th-grade English literature classroom at an inner-city high school to begin his first day of teaching. Fresh from a rigorous undergraduate program that emphasized a thorough knowledge of subject matter as the key to good teaching, he arrived with a highlighted and dog-eared textbook, carefully printed overhead slides, and a thorough lesson plan. Dressed smartly in a conservative dark suit, he cleared his throat, smiled at his students and launched right into his prepared monologue: introduction, outline of the course, and the day's lesson.

He was very taken aback by the reaction he received from the 30 or so 17- and 18-year-olds in the room. Several quickly put their heads down on their desks, as if sleeping. Others turned and began to converse with their neighbors. None seemed to be terribly interested in what he had to say. This pattern continued throughout the first month; no matter how much time Mr. Harper spent on his lesson plans or how thoroughly he understood his subject matter, his student's did not seem to stay on task for very long, and no amount of yelling or threatening on his part seemed to change the situation. Worse still was the reaction he received from several of his colleagues when he reported on what was taking place each day. Many responded that the school district was populated with students who "did not care" or "did not want to learn." This added to the anxiety and depression he felt concerning the situation.

After about a month of ineffective teaching, Mr. Harper reflected on what was taking place and what he had learned in his teacher education program—particularly in his Educational Psychology course—and recognized the need for a change in the way he approached teaching. First and foremost, he realized that he must accept responsibility for classroom control, rather than merely conceding that his students were not interested in learning, and then change the way he did things.

When he returned to school, he began his lesson by admitting his difficulties and stressing to his students that he would work with them to establish a classroom environment that was more conducive to learning. In addition, he began to implement more solution-oriented strategies, such as integrating a token reward system and using more encouraging phrases to build his students' self-esteem rather than yelling and using punishments as short-term deterrents. These changes alone reduced many of the occurrences of problem behavior. In an effort to redirect those few students who still insisted on exhibiting disruptive behavior during the lesson, he made contact with parents, coaches, other teachers, and school counselors to identify underlying problems that may have caused the undesirable behavior. Over time, he found that his students were able to complete far more work for him than for other teachers in his department whose classrooms were dominated by yelling and threats of punishment. For the first time that year, Mr. Harper began to enjoy teaching.

- What did you learn about effective teaching strategies from Mr. Harper's experiences?

Hill Street Studios/Harmik Nazarian/Blend Images (RF)/Jupiter Images

The teacher in this example carefully analyzed what was not working and with the help of his class developed a new approach to classroom management. Reflecting over and modifying your teaching practices can help you increase student learning.

In the Box 1.1 story, Mr. Harper reminded himself of four basic assumptions on which good classroom management is built (Good & Brophy, 2003, p. 119):

- Students are likely to follow rules they understand and accept.
- Discipline problems are minimized when students are engaged in meaningful activities geared to their interests and aptitudes.
- Management should be approached with an eye toward establishing a productive learning environment, rather than from a negative viewpoint that stresses control of misbehavior.
- The teacher's goal is to develop inner self-control in students, not merely to exert control over them.

Many educational psychology frameworks such as the ones above will be provided throughout this book to help students gain the knowledge to be effective teachers.

Two Ways of Viewing the Causes of Behavior

Many of the behaviors carried out in schools and elsewhere can be explained on the basis of their consequences. Getting out of bed when the alarm goes off may be explained by the consequence of getting to school on time. Wearing a heavy coat in the winter provides more warmth and comfort than not wearing one. Paying attention in class results in good grades. Watching your step when you cross the street enables you to avoid being hit by a car. Because of these naturally occurring consequences, people perform many behaviors like these on a regular basis without even thinking about them. Explaining behavior on the basis of its consequences has come to be known as the **behavioral approach**. You will encounter this concept in some of the chapters of this book.

All behavior, however, cannot be explained on this basis. Often, we go through a thinking process before we carry out a behavior, and then think about that behavior again after we have carried it out. We think about whether or not we are likely to be successful before we undertake a difficult task such as climbing a rock wall or taking a college course, and then decide what we will do. After we do something we regret, like not studying for a test, we think about how foolish we were to have done that in the first place, or we may think about how it was acceptable under the circumstances. Explaining behavior on the basis of thinking is called the **cognitive approach**. This concept also appears frequently in this book.

Is one of these approaches correct and the other incorrect? Absolutely not! Which type of explanation is more accurate typically depends on the circumstances. When we are given two simple numbers to multiply, and we have learned our multiplication tables, we can come up with the answer without even thinking; but if the problem is more difficult, prolonged thinking may be required before we can arrive at an answer. In our own small neighborhood where everything is familiar to us, we usually find a way to a desired location without thinking, but in an unfamiliar neighborhood, especially a busier one, we may find it necessary to think out our route before we start. In addition, when we use trial-and-error

behavioral approach

explaining behavior on the basis of its consequences

cognitive approach

explaining behavior on the basis of thinking

to figure something out, because we see no other way of proceeding, we are using the behavioral approach. When we use logic to figure something out, we are using the cognitive approach. Each may lead to the same result.

Learning Objective 3

Explain educational psychology and the role of the teacher regarding the constraints to applying new knowledge and how school learning can be more like real-world learning.

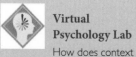

Virtual Psychology Lab

How does context affect the decisions that teachers make? When you go to the *Decision Making Virtual Psychology Lab*, you will have an opportunity to participate in a classic psychology experiment. The original study found that the way a problem is stated (or 'framed') has a strong impact on the decisions that individuals make. Go to CengageBrain.com to access this Virtual Psychology Lab in the Education CourseMate.

Educational Psychology and the Role of the Teacher

Teachers may be confronted with limitations in their application of educational psychology, but they must use their teaching skills to overcome them as best they can. Two common categories of such limitations are described below.

Some Constraints to Applying New Knowledge

A teacher operates within very real restrictions. Groups of students are organized into classes, which often are large, with teaching and learning confined to classrooms. The subject matter to be taught usually is prespecified in the form of a curriculum or a course of study. The amount of time designated for teaching and learning is further delimited by the clock to distinct class periods and by the calendar to days, weeks, semesters, and school years.

Given all these restraints, even if there were a formula for successful teaching, it would be hard to follow. Imagine if educational psychology taught that people learned better when there was a practical problem to solve rather than for its own sake or for the purpose of passing a course or getting a degree. If that were true, it might be hard for a teacher to apply educational psychology when the course was one like history or algebra, with a seeming lack of practicality. A history teacher or a math teacher would still have to teach the concepts of these courses, even if they were inherently hard to teach. But knowledge of educational psychology may yield some insight into how to go about teaching these difficult concepts.

Similarly, a teacher may learn from educational psychology that she can best teach certain concepts by allowing students to experiment with them directly and discover how they can be applied. However, the teacher may be teaching a class of 35 students in a lecture room for one hour a day, and the material in question may constitute only a small part of the curriculum for that course. Under these conditions, a hands-on discovery approach to teaching may be highly impractical. Yet, knowing what she knows, the teacher may still elect to slant her approach to make great use of question-asking in preference to straight lecturing, thus putting her knowledge of educational psychology to use.

Educational psychology is not studied to discover the formulas or recipes for success because such formulas or recipes do not exist; even if they did, however, they would be impossible to apply in the real world. Educational psychology is studied to learn principles and theories of human behavior because these may help teachers determine the best way to behave in different situations or may help them figure out how to determine what the best way is.

School Learning versus Real-World Learning

There is a difference between the way learning typically takes place in school and the way it occurs in the "real world." Resnick (1987) pointed out that school learning focuses on individual performance because students are evaluated as individuals and most often learn by themselves. Real-world learning, by comparison, focuses on socially shared performance because people work in teams and contribute to only a portion of the final outcome. Knowing about educational psychology research on the advantage of having students work in groups should help teachers include opportunities for socially shared performance in their teaching approach.

Resnick (1987) also suggests that school learning typically fosters unaided thought, or thought done entirely in the head, while real-world learning involves the use of cognitive tools such as books or calculators. Moreover, schools primarily attempt to cultivate symbolic thinking, while in the real world people engage directly with objects and situations. In other words, school problems are more abstract—that is, students try to solve them because teachers pose them—while in the real world people solve problems because they must be solved to accomplish some purpose. In the real world, people work with the problem itself, rather than with a representation of it as in school. However, recent advances in teaching problem-solving skills provide students with a more tool-based, concrete, real-world view of problems and their potential solutions (see Chapter 8).

Resnick (1987) also sees school learning as focusing on general skills and knowledge in contrast to the situation-specific competencies of the real world. Horticulturalists, for example, would need to know a lot about which plants grow best under which conditions, but would not necessarily need a great knowledge of general biology. Yet, the general biology teacher can apply some of the techniques of expert systems to teaching many aspects of biology (see Chapter 8).

Again, within the limits of the nature of school learning, educational psychology can provide some broad strategies or approaches for the classroom teacher. Specific facts or details about learning and school performance may be most difficult for teachers to remember and use because these may be hard to fit into the classroom situation. Broader, more flexible representations of psychological processes that apply to the educational setting are needed. An example of how this could be done is illustrated below.

Juan was a 10th grader in a large urban high school that had recently decided to divide itself into four small high schools, each with a central theme. One of the new high schools, the one Juan opted for, was organized around the theme of applied science and technology. All of the subjects taught related to the application of scientific processes and technology in the real world. Juan was really interested in science and technology applications and found himself highly motivated to come to school every day. He liked the idea of learning by working on group projects under

In school, children are grouped by age, but in the "real world," younger children frequently learn from older ones. What other differences do you see between school learning and real-world learning?

the guidance of teachers. He found it particularly challenging and engaging to learn science—not just as a bunch of abstract concepts that he might have to struggle to understand, but as an approach to solving concrete problems in the real world. Not only did it help him learn, it also gave him a real sense of the types of careers he might want to pursue.

After reading about Juan, it would be helpful for you to think about school experiences you had that involved learning by doing and how those experiences made you feel about school.

Learning Objective 4

Discuss characteristics of the effective teacher, including (1) an ecological model and (2) reflective teaching.

Characteristics of the Effective Teacher

Because a primary reason for studying educational psychology is to become an effective teacher, a natural question is "what makes a teacher effective?" or "what are the characteristics of an effective teacher?" In the field of education, a significant amount of research has been conducted with the intent to identify the personality, beliefs, and behavioral characteristics of effective teachers. What is the "magic" that makes some individuals exceptional teachers and others less effective?

An Ecological Model

Consider the following as a possible list of the characteristics of an effective teacher:

- concern for student learning;
- ability to communicate clearly;
- ability to create a positive learning environment;
- knowledge of the content;
- skills in teaching;
- ability to organize and plan effectively; and
- high expectations for oneself and students.

You may wonder if any of these characteristics can be learned; and if so, how? One of the major themes throughout this book is that recipes for guaranteed success in teaching do not exist. Therefore, a static list of characteristics would do little to prepare prospective teachers to be successful in their careers without discussing teacher characteristics in the context of the school setting. Yet, some teacher characteristics tend to yield success in multiple educational settings.

Think It Over

as a LEARNER   Think of a teacher you have had who has been effective. What were some of the characteristics of that teacher? Which, if any, of these characteristics appear in the above list?

as a TEACHER   Which two of the characteristics of effective teachers do you feel would be most important to you, and how might you go about developing them in yourself?

John Dewey (1859–1952) was one of the earliest advocates for considering the effects of the environment on a given behavior. Dewey thought it was not only important to study the individual to understand his or her behavior, but also to study the individual's behavior within the context of his or her environment. This is referred to as an **ecological approach**. The focus on the educational setting as an important variable of study was a significant strength of Dewey's work.

Thus, to understand what makes teachers effective, it is necessary to look at more than just their characteristics and to examine the complicated interaction between the internal beliefs and competencies and the external educational setting. By examining both the characteristics of a teacher and the setting, the ecological approach will help teachers succeed in diverse educational settings.

Internal characteristics identified as typical of excellent teachers include: knowledge of and interest in subject matter, effective communication skills, cognitive flexibility, fairness, and expression of care and concern for students. However, the specific criteria for what makes a teacher effective will depend, to some extent, on the educational setting. Characteristics of the educational setting that could influence the effectiveness of the teacher include: classroom size, number of students in a classroom, heterogeneous or homogeneous class grouping, organization of classroom, age and needs of students, classroom behavior of students, group cohesion, and interest and motivation of students. An ecological model for interpreting the characteristics of an effective teacher is depicted in Figure 1.2. Another model of effective teaching is described in Box 1.4 (on page 36).

Danielson (1996) developed a *framework for teaching* that identifies the competencies required of teachers to demonstrate expertise. She identified 22 activities and clustered them into the following four domains:

- Planning and preparation—how a teacher designs instruction and develops and organizes the content of lessons; this requires that teachers know the content they teach, the techniques for teaching that content, the goals and objectives they hope to attain, methods for designing instruction, and methods for assessing what students have learned.

ecological approach

studying an individual's behavior within the context of his or her environment

---

FIGURE 1.2

INTERNAL CHARACTERISTICS   EXTERNAL CHARCTERISTICS

Knowledge
Attitudes/ Beliefs
Skills
Pedagogy

Behavior of Students
# of Students in Class
Size of Classroom
Organization of Classroom

Ecological Model for the Characteristics of the Effective Teacher

- The classroom environment—how a teacher manages the noninstructional interactions in the classroom; this requires the ability to establish rapport between teacher and students as well as among students, managing classroom procedures and student behavior, and organizing physical space.
- Instruction—engaging students in learning, using a variety of instructional techniques, communicating clearly, and providing feedback.
- Professional responsibilities—maintaining records, communicating with families, contributing to the school, and developing professionally.

Teachers can use this framework to identify and discuss what excellent teaching requires, and use it as a guide to achieve excellence in teaching.

Teachers, especially new ones, often are confronted with challenging situations that differ from what they have experienced either as a student or as a student teacher. Here is an example: Mrs. Foster, a new fourth-grade teacher, was having a bad day. Her own children had been sick, and she felt like she was catching whatever they had. On top of that, she had trouble starting her car that morning and was late for school, which the principal did not particularly appreciate. Still, Mrs. Foster knew she had to make it through the day. As she presented an assignment to the class, one student asked what she regarded as an irrelevant question. She lost her temper and scolded the child. A couple of weeks later, when Mrs. Foster was feeling better and was more relaxed, she was again presenting a lesson to her class and accidentally omitted an important detail. Many of her students realized they had not been given all the necessary information to complete the task, but did not ask a question for fear of being scolded in front of the class by Mrs. Foster.

The purpose of this book is to help you become a good teacher, and part of that is learning to use psychology. In the above example, Mrs. Foster neglected to use educational psychology, and let her temper get the best of her. It may take the rest of the term before her students feel comfortable to ask questions again.

Educational psychology can provide you with theories and understandings about students that will help you empower your students and help them succeed in school.

Think It Over

| as a LEARNER | How would you feel if you were a student in Mrs. Foster's class, and how would you have behaved? |
| as a TEACHER | How could Mrs. Foster have handled the situation better? |

Reflective Teaching

To become an expert teacher, you need to continuously examine your own attitudes, practices, and outcomes. The process of asking questions about your teaching and attempting to identify answers is called **reflective teaching**. Prospective teachers would be well served to begin this process during their preservice training.

Reflection, called *reflection-in-action* by Schon (1987, 1991), is particularly important when you are confronted by something unexpected or out of the ordinary. For example, suppose a child who ordinarily behaves well in class suddenly becomes very angry and starts yelling, throws things, or hits another student. As the teacher, you need to deal with it. You might take the student aside, but be unable to calm her down. The parent is called, comes to school, and takes the child home. Afterward, you might think about how you handled the situation and come up with

reflective teaching
the process of asking questions about your teaching and attempting to identify answers

TeachSource Video Case

Teaching as a Profession: What Defines Effective Teaching?

In this video segment, you'll see what it means to be an effective teacher; examples are provided of the dimensions of teaching excellence (developing command of your subject matter, drawing on your emotional intelligence, and setting up an effective learning environment). Throughout the video, you'll hear from educators who love what they do and take on challenges.

After viewing the video case, consider what you have just watched about effective teaching and answer the following questions:

1. What did you think of the teacher's advice to "know who you are" and "draw on your strengths"? What do you think are your teaching strengths?
2. Based on the experiences you've had as a student, what would you say are the characteristics of an effective teacher?
3. What did you learn from the video about getting to know your students?

You can view the video case at the Education CourseMate. Go to:
CengageBrain.com

some alternative ways you might have handled it better. Perhaps you write about it in a journal. The next time you encounter a similar situation, you will be able to use this past experience and your reflections on it to handle things better than the first time.

To help you develop the habit of reflection, the "Think It Over" feature below offers opportunities to reflect, both *as a learner* and *as a teacher*. In addition, a description of a reflective teacher appears in Box 1.2.

Think It Over

as a LEARNER   What was the last unexpected situation or circumstance in which you had little experience? How did you handle it? What was the result? What did you learn from this experience?

as a TEACHER   How could you put the experience you described above—and its result—to good use in a classroom?

AN EXAMPLE TO AID UNDERSTANDING   **Box 1.2**

A Reflective Teacher

Mrs. Cooper was a Title I reading teacher in an inner-city elementary school. In addition to a variety of other duties, every afternoon Mrs. Cooper worked with small groups of third graders who were reading well below grade level. Her goal was to raise the reading level of these students to help her school ascend from its "academic emergency" status under the "No Child Left Behind" law.

Jeremy, a student in one of Mrs. Cooper's afternoon reading groups, was creating a lot of problems. He lacked patience and often lost focus, becoming disruptive and making it impossible for Mrs. Cooper to teach the other six students in the reading group and making it difficult for them to learn.

Mrs. Cooper was a highly motivated and conscientious teacher, and she spent a lot of time thinking about how she could help Jeremy keep his focus and maintain him as a member of the reading group. After much reflection, she decided that, when Jeremy became disruptive, she would send him

back to his classroom, which resulted in him losing an opportunity to earn special rewards for that lesson. (Students who focused their attention and performed well on the lesson earned "dragon passes" that could be turned in on Fridays for treats, pencils, etc. The more dragon passes earned, the more stuff a student could "buy".) Even though Mrs. Cooper would spend some one-on-one reading instruction with Jeremy, he could not earn dragon passes for those sessions, even if he performed perfectly, because he was not working as part of the group.

Every evening after school, Mrs. Cooper reflected on Jeremy's behavior and performance. She thought about how he rarely made it through a reading group session without becoming disruptive and being sent back to class. On those days when Jeremy was sent back to class and then given the opportunity to spend a little time working one-on-one with Mrs. Cooper, he always would say, quite wistfully, "I guess I'm not going to get any dragon passes, even though I got everything right, am I? And Mrs. Cooper would reply, "To get dragon passes, you have to work with your group." Mrs. Cooper reflected and reflected. She felt sorry for Jeremy, but knew that he might never truly learn to read if he did not participate in group learning activities. And so she continued with her plan.

One day, Jeremy came to class and made it through the entire lesson without becoming disruptive and he got his dragon passes. The next day, the same thing happened. Now, Jeremy makes it through almost every day without becoming disruptive, and he has accumulated a lot of dragon passes for which he is proud. And when Mrs. Cooper reflects on this, which she often does, she is very proud of Jeremy as well.

- Can you describe an experience you've had where you had to reflect on something? How did it turn out?

Educational Psychology and the Study of Human Behavior

Learning Objective 5

Explain the psychological study of behavior, including the four tenets of science; the difference between facts, principles, and theories; the determination of a theory's accuracy; and factors affecting the accuracy of judgments.

Educational psychologists do not rely on intuition and unsystematic observation as a method to study behavior. Instead, they use a very specific way of knowing about the world that has been perfected for thousands of years. That way of knowing is referred to as *science*.

The Tenets of Science

Science is the identification, description, and explanation of naturally occurring phenomena. The specific scientific methods and activities used in educational psychology are detailed later in this chapter. Here it is important to recognize that science is based on four general principles: observation, testability, replication, and parsimony.

Making observations is the foundational property of science. **Observation** is the process of recording something—such as observing student test anxiety, math achievement, or motivation—with reliable and valid instruments. Sometimes scientific observation is referred to more formally as empiricism. One of the main ways that science is different from other ways of knowing things (e.g., intuition, philosophy, expert opinion) is that science relies on direct observation. Observation helps to provide data necessary to answer questions.

However, making observations is not the only requirement of the scientific process. Science requires that research questions be phrased specifically as **testable questions**; in other words, the questions must be falsifiable or capable of being disproved. Because we often seek to confirm our own ideas and beliefs, we naturally search for information that confirms our beliefs while ignoring information that disconfirms them. Thus, science is purposely organized to reduce the bias of confirmation by challenging scientists to disprove their proposed answers or hypotheses instead of attempting to prove them.

Posing research questions that rely on direct observation and are testable in a potentially falsifiable way are two necessary components of the scientific paradigm,

observation

the process of recording something with reliable and valid instruments

testable questions

questions that are falsifiable or capable of being disproved

A *hypothesis* is a proposed answer to a research question. It must be tested more than once for students working as scientists to be confident in its accuracy.

Sean Justice/Photonica/Getty Images

or model. There are two additional necessary conditions of science. Findings from research must be reproducible. That is, if a *hypothesis* or proposed answer to a research question was disproved in one study, it must be disproved in subsequent studies before scientists can have confidence in the results. **Replication** involves conducting numerous, independent studies and collecting information over a period of time to judge whether results are consistent. Replication helps to increase confidence in scientific findings.

The fourth tenet of science is **parsimony**. The odd thing about parsimony is that, in such a complicated world, science strives for an outcome that literally means simplicity. The law of parsimony, often referred to as Ockham's Razor, finds its origin with a Franciscan scholar named William of Ockham. The law of parsimony is the scientific rule that the simpler of two competing theories is the preferable theory. Therefore, contrary to popular misperception, science values simple (parsimonious) explanations over complicated ones. However, scientists try to "make things as simple as possible, but no simpler" as Einstein stated.

In conclusion, psychology is a science based on data. Therefore, the pedagogical, or teaching, principles that are valued and taught in educational psychology are those that have been held up to the rigorous standards of science. These standards are displayed in Figure 1.3.

replication

conducting numerous, independent studies and collecting information over a period of time to judge whether results are consistent

parsimony

the scientific rule that the simpler of two competing theories is the preferable theory

---

F I G U R E   I . 3

The Four Tenets of Science

Observation	Testability
Replication	Parsimony

Facts, Principles, and Theories

The psychological study of human behavior focuses on facts, principles, and theories. **Facts** are disconnected pieces of knowledge and information; for example, it is a fact that expecting to be in a stressful situation makes a person anxious. **Principles** expand on and connect several facts, help create meaning, and establish associations between facts. Gagne (1985; Gagne & Medsker, 1996) used the term *rules* (as an alternative to principles) to describe these connections or associations (see Chapter 12). In his description, they are "if–then" statements, such as: "If you push a round object, then it will roll" (the principle or rule is "round things roll"). In the case of a person expecting to be placed in a stressful situation who was observed to become anxious, the principle or rule would be: "expectations affect emotions" or, more specifically, "expected stress produces anxiety."

For example, imagine that tomorrow is the first day of school at your first teaching job. You are excited and pleased at the thought of the new school year, but this situation is likely to produce a small amount of normal anxiety, a general feeling of apprehension, which helps provide the motivation necessary to be fully prepared. Anxiety can also be provoked if a person is led to expect an unpleasant situation; for example, a trip to the dentist's office could cause some apprehension. When someone experiences anxiety, being with others who share the same expectation is preferable to being alone (i.e., "misery loves company"). Therefore, the principle concerning anxiety is more general and more explanatory than the fact by virtue of including many facts, and so there will be fewer principles than there are facts. Consequently, it will be easier to remember principles and easier to adapt them to a variety of situations.

Theories are collections of principles (which are based on facts) and are even more general and more inclusive than principles. They may be called comprehensive because their scope and range are inclusive enough to enable people to use them to better understand the world around them.

The theory that people use others to help them judge and understand their own capabilities and feelings, particularly in uncertain settings (called *social comparison theory* by Festinger, 1954; Buunk & Mussweiler, 2001) would help teachers comprehend the relationship between perceived student stress and students' desire to be with others. By watching others' reactions and sharing their feelings with them, students in a stressful situation can determine either that there is nothing to worry about or that it is all right to be worried and avoid comparing themselves to others who are worse off (Gibbons et al., 2002). Teachers might then be inclined to use a cooperative learning approach when the assigned task is likely to be anxiety-provoking (such as making a class presentation or preparing for a test) so that students would have ready access to others for comparison and support. If teachers knew the power and importance of social comparison, they might be less inclined to ask John why he could not do his work as well as Joan.

Sometimes there is a tendency to hear the word theory and think "useless" or "abstract" or "irrelevant" because it is part of the word theoretical. But theoretical means speculative, that is, explanatory of why a particular fact or set of facts

facts
disconnected pieces of knowledge and information

principles
expand on and connect several facts, help create meaning, and establish associations between facts

theories
collections of principles (which are based on facts); even more general and more inclusive than principles

occurs. In other words, theories are not only comprehensive, they are also speculative. They attempt to explain the *why* of something, not merely to note its existence. Students sometimes get anxious––this is a fact. They often get anxious when they expect something they do not like (like a test)—this is another fact. When students get anxious, many of them like company—third fact. Why do people like company when they get anxious? Perhaps because they can see then whether it is okay to be anxious—they can use social comparison. This last statement is not a fact. It is an attempt at an explanation. It is speculative. It is theoretical.

But is this theoretical explanation useless and irrelevant? The answer is *no*—if it helps teachers know how to handle stressful situations in their classrooms. If the theory can be translated into action, then it becomes practical. What is also practical is that there will be much fewer theories than facts, because theories both subsume, or include, facts as well as explain them. Facts fill encyclopedias while theories only fill college textbooks. Through an understanding of a small number of theories, most of the behavior that goes on in classrooms (and probably in life as well) can be explained.

Hence, the focus on theories has three bases. First, theories are comprehensive or inclusive, and so each one can subsume a lot of facts. Second, because they are so broad-based, only a small number of theories need to be learned. Third, theories are speculative, or explanatory, and can be used to explain—in a wide variety of situations—what will happen, why it will happen, and how to to deal with it when it happens. Learning about theories, therefore, helps learners organize information better and use it more easily than simply learning a collection of facts. See Table 1.1 for a *Concept Review* of the relationship between facts, principles, and theories.

In this book, a number of theories and explanatory principles relevant to education will be presented—all unique in what they address and how they attempt to do so. The explanations vary because, depending on your viewpoint, there are

By learning about educational psychology theories and thinking about how they could be put into action in the classroom, educational psychology students will be better prepared for the type of problem solving they will have to do as a teacher.

Ellen B. Senisi/The Image Works

CONCEPT REVIEW TABLE 1.1

What We Know: Facts, Principles, and Theories

FACTS	PRINCIPLES	THEORIES
Based on observation	Based on inference	Based on speculation (about facts)
Discrete, specific and numerous	Fewer in number than facts	Comprehensive and fewest in number
Elemental and unitary	Made up of connected facts	Made up of connected principles
Actual behavior that can be seen	Help relate behaviors to one another	Help explain behavior

always different ways to describe an outcome or a phenomenon. They vary in what they try to explain because no theory, and especially no single principle, is likely to apply equally well to all aspects of behavior, nor is any one model likely to be universally useful. Remember: There are no quick fixes and simple recipes in educational psychology.

Some theories fit certain aspects of behavior better than others. As each of the following aspects of educational psychology is covered, the theories and explanatory principles that help make that aspect understandable, and the models that help make it most manageable, will be explored. After finishing this book, you will have much of the prerequisite knowledge of how it can be applied to help you become an expert teacher. An **expert teacher** is an individual who plans effective instruction, maintains an effective learning atmosphere, and anticipates and reflects on how classroom issues are handled.

How Do We Know if a Theory Is Accurate?

Because theories are based on facts, we can test theories by gathering facts that relate to the theory. On the basis of theories, hypotheses or predictions are made about what is expected to happen or which facts are expected to be observed in a given situation. We can then test these hypotheses by making the necessary observations (i.e., by collecting the necessary facts). The pattern looks like this:

expert teacher
an individual who plans effective instruction, maintains an effective learning atmosphere, and anticipates and reflects on how classroom issues are handled

Induction   Deduction

Known facts → Principles → Theories → Hypotheses → Expected facts

Research

When specific facts are used to create more general theories that explain those facts, the process is called **induction**. Taking a variety of facts about how people are observed to behave in classroom situations and then coming up with the explanation that their behavior is based on a particular theory is an example of induction.

When general theories are used to create specific facts that will help test those theories, the process is called **deduction**. Using a particular theory to make a hypothesis or prediction is an example of deduction. We induce theories from facts, and then we deduce what new facts are needed to test their accuracy.

Research is the process to test whether or not the facts that theories tell us to expect are actually accurate. Doing research means making observations or collecting data; by contrast, induction and deduction are modes of thinking. The purpose of this research is to test the hypotheses or hunches about what will happen in a given situation based on the explanatory power of a theory. Supportive evidence collected by research helps validate or invalidate the theory tested.

The approach used to test a theory is called a **paradigm**—a design or framework that can be used repeatedly for testing the relationships within a set of variables or factors that affect behavior. Later in this chapter, four research paradigms are described: experimental research, single-subject research, correlational research, and qualitative or observational research.

Teachers are expected to interpret and apply some of the research they learn about in courses such as educational psychology, and perhaps to do some research of their own. In evaluating knowledge, it is helpful for teachers to know how it was discovered and if it is likely to apply under the circumstances in which they may use it. Teachers are also likely to draw their own conclusions about students as well as about the circumstances of their behavior, and so it is important that they realize what factors affect the validity of these conclusions.

Two Factors That Affect the Accuracy of Judgments

Two factors that affect the accuracy of judgments are called internal and external validity, or certainty and generality (Tuckman, 1999b). **Internal validity** refers to the confidence held in the conclusion that a teacher's or researcher's action, rather than some other variable, has caused a student to behave or perform differently. For example, suppose a teacher is trying a new program for teaching reading for the first time. If the students taught by this program perform better on a subsequent reading test than last year's students did on the same test after being taught by the old program, can the teacher conclude with certainty that the new program works? Perhaps not! Perhaps this year's students were brighter or more motivated than last year's. Perhaps the teacher was more enthusiastic about the new program and devoted more effort to teaching it. Perhaps the teacher expected it to work better (see Box 1.3). The new program may indeed work better than the old one, but it is difficult to be certain about that conclusion under the given circumstances. Therefore, the internal validity, or certainty, of the research is questionable.

induction

when specific facts are used to create more general theories that explain those facts

deduction

when general theories are used to create specific facts that will help test those theories

paradigm

a design or framework that can be used repeatedly for testing the relationships within a set of variables or factors that affect behavior

internal validity

the confidence held in the conclusion that a teacher's or researcher's action, rather than some other variable, has caused a student to behave or perform differently

BOX 1.3

Did You Know?

Expectations Can Affect Outcomes

In a classic experiment, Rosenthal and Fode (1963) told half of their student experimenters that the rats they were to study had been selectively bred to be bright. The other half were told that their rats were dull. In fact, the two groups of rats were identical. Each student experimenter was instructed to train his or her rats, bright or dull, to run through a maze as fast as they could to get a bit of food. The timing device on the maze was completely automatic. It went on automatically when the rat left the start box and went off automatically when the rat entered the goal box; there was no way to artificially influence the timing. Nevertheless, the "smart" rats ended up outperforming the "dull" ones. And the "smart" ones were liked more by their student experimenters. Get the picture? Somehow the experimenters must have treated the "smart" rats better.

Rosenthal and Jacobson (1968) then tried the same thing with school children. They circulated to teachers a list of names of students who were expected to "bloom" that year, based on results of an IQ test. In fact, the children on the list were no different from their classmates. However, teachers must have believed they were and changed their expectations because those children gained more in IQ over the course of the year than their classmates did. As the children on the list improved, their teachers reported them to be more interesting and better adjusted. When other children improved—those who were not expected to (their names were not on the list)—they still were seen by their teachers as being less interesting and less well adjusted. Something expected to happen is indeed more likely to happen than something that is not expected to happen. This is called the *self-fulfilling prophecy*.

● What effect do you see the self-fulfilling prophecy having on the behavior of teachers?

In addition to wanting to be certain about conclusions, we also want them to apply again, under other circumstances—that is, to have **external validity**, or generality. If a teacher concludes that the new reading program works better than the old one, should other teachers try it? Can they conclude that it is likely to work for them, too? What if they are not as enthusiastic as the original teacher, or what if their students are not as bright or as motivated? Is it accurate to say that the judgment of program superiority can be made again? If not, then there is no point in training teachers to use the new program or in having them use it to teach students.

Educational psychology, as previously stated, focuses on attempting to discover and transmit knowledge about student behavior and performance. That means transmitting information about factors that affect student behavior and performance for which there is a high degree of certainty and generality. To understand if the findings on which educational psychology theories are based have adequate certainty and generality, it is useful to examine the manner in which these findings are determined.

external validity

the ability to have conclusions apply again under other circumstances

Using Research to Inform Teachers and Enhance Learning

There are a number of ways to do research, each of which has its own specific purposes and its own set of operations and methodology. In this section, we will describe four widely-used methods for testing a hypothesis about student learning and performance. Over the course of your career, you will likely be a consumer of research, and may even have opportunities to contribute your own research.

Experimental Research

In **experimental research**, the impact or effect of one variable or factor on another variable or factor is studied. By conducting an experiment, the researcher attempts to maximize certainty in the outcome by controlling what people experience. The researcher does not wait for the causative or *independent variable* to occur naturally or under its own initiative. Instead, the researcher makes the independent variable happen by imposing (by manipulation) a treatment or intervention.

For example, to be certain about whether the intervention caused the outcome or *dependent variable*, the researcher must provide the treatment for only some of the students rather than for all of them. In this way, two groups—those receiving the intervention and those not—can be compared to see whether the manipulation or treatment has actually caused a change in the outcome. In evaluating a new reading program, for example, not all of the students should be given the new program.

In addition, as much as possible, everything must be exactly the same for and about both groups—the one that receives the treatment and the one that does not. If any aspect of the experience (other than the presence or absence of the treatment) differed between groups, the researcher would not know which aspect had caused the difference in the outcome. Additional possible causes would then "confound" the relationship between the independent and dependent variables and reduce internal validity or certainty.

In determining which students should be given the treatment and which ones should not, the researcher should pick the names out of a hat, to randomize the assignment to groups and ensure that one group is not smarter or more motivated than the other. **Random assignment** is important because it increases the likelihood that one group will not be different from the other to begin with. If students are permitted to pick their own groups, then the groups might not start out on an equal footing.

Let us consider a reading program example. Comparing two classes—one that uses a new program and one that uses an old one—would not result in an accurate or certain conclusion if the students in one class were brighter or already had better reading skills than the students in the other class. In this case, one program might appear more effective than the other, but only because the students who used it were more capable; those students would probably do well regardless of

experimental research

studying the impact or effect of one variable or factor on another variable or factor

random assignment

increases the likelihood that one group will not be different from the other to begin with

which reading program was used. It is better to assign students to the two classes on a random basis so that they are likely to be the same mix of capabilities, or to assign the new program to half of the students in each class, chosen by chance, with the remaining halves using the old program. In this way, any disparities in outcome would more certainly be a function of program differences than of student differences.

It is also important, especially for generality, that students are unaware of anything out of the ordinary when a treatment is tried. That lack of awareness is called being *blind* to the treatment. When people realize they are given special treatment, they often respond differently than they ordinarily would. The teacher using the new reading program in the above example would be advised to avoid having the students respond to their treatment as being new or special.

In summary, the requirements of experimental research are: (1) make the independent variable happen by manipulation, (2) include a control group, (3) except for the treatment, treat the experimental and control groups the same, (4) assign subjects randomly to experimental and control groups, and (5) keep participants unaware of what group they are in (Tuckman, 1999b).

Single-Subject Research

Although the majority of educational studies involve groups of participants, there are situations in which the use of groups is neither appropriate nor possible. Examples include situations in which there are not enough participants to use a group approach and situations where intensive data collection on one or a small number of participants is necessary, such as in special education. Here, the small number and uniqueness of students—as well as the nature of the data to be collected—make **single-subject research** the better choice. Lacking numbers of students with highly similar characteristics, in the single-subject approach participants are compared with themselves rather than with members of a control group as described above.

Single-subject research involves a minimum of two necessary phases: the baseline phase and the treatment phase. During the **baseline phase**, the researcher measures the subject's behavior under typical, or ordinary, circumstances. Everything remains the same as it would if no research were taking place. During the **treatment phase**, the researcher measures the subject's behavior under the special circumstances that the researcher is interested in studying. The baseline condition, for example, could be *punishing unacceptable behavior*, while the treatment condition would be *ignoring unacceptable behavior*, but *rewarding acceptable behavior*. Because the same participant or participants will be subjected to both conditions, only one condition can be studied at a time.

There are many variations of the single-subject approach, but only the three most common ones will be described here. In the first, the simplest, the participant experiences the baseline (A) and the treatment (B) once each, creating the A-B version of the design. What this means is that after experiencing the normal or typical situation, and having measures taken, the participant then experiences the new or

single-subject research

participants are compared with themselves rather than with members of a control group

baseline phase

the researcher measures the subject's behavior under typical circumstances

treatment phase

the researcher measures the subject's behavior under the special circumstances that the researcher is interested in studying

trial situation, and has the measures taken again. Results following the treatment are compared to those following the baseline. In the A-B-A version, the baseline is experienced before *and* after the treatment to see if any treatment effect persists after completion. Finally, the A-B-A-B version represents the simpler A-B version done twice in succession, primarily to see if the results are stable enough to occur a second time.

An example of the use of the A-B approach is shown in Figure 1.4. It involved a single participant or subject, a seventh-grade boy in a class for emotionally handicapped students, and took 16 weeks to complete. The first 10 weeks were used to establish the baseline ("A" in the design); the remaining six weeks were used to test the treatment or trial program ("B"). During this time, two measures that reflected disruptive behavior were taken each week—the first was *rate of chair time out* (CTO), represented in the figure by the solid line. After the student committed three disruptive behaviors, he had to sit in a chair at the back of the classroom for five minutes. The second measure was *rate of escalated chair time out* (ETO), the dashed line in the figure. If the disruptive behavior continued, not only did the student have to remain seated in the back of the classroom, but, after the second ETO, he lost the privilege of participating in a special end-of-week activity.

The treatment consisted of rewarding the student subject with bonus points for no CTOs and ETOs for an entire day. The bonus points could be exchanged for prizes during the special weekly activity. As shown in Figure 1.4, the treatment was accompanied by a reduction in disruptive behavior.

The single-subject approach is also experimental, only with a sample of one person participating in both the control and experimental condition (called baseline and treatment). Because of the small sample, the single-subject approach lacks the generality of experiments done with more participants.

FIGURE   1 . 4

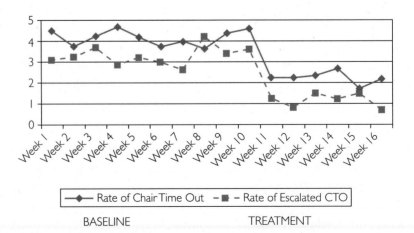

Baseline and Treatment Incidence of Disruptive Behavior (Tuckman, 1999b)

Correlational Research

In the **correlational research** paradigm, a researcher collects two or more sets of data from a group of participants for analysis and then attempts to determine the relationship between them. The data are based on test scores or observational measures, and their relationship is determined using a statistic called a **correlation coefficient**. For example, to determine the relationship between *time spent studying* and *grades*, a group of students could be asked to report the number of hours they spent studying per week over the course of a school term, and then those data could be related to the average of the grades (GPA) they earned that term in school.

The correlation coefficient is a measure of the degree of relationship between two scores, or the extent to which one score predicts the other. It is represented as a number between –1 and 1, with both extremes reflecting a perfectly overlapping relationship or complete predictability. By comparison, a correlation coefficient of 0 indicates a total lack of relationship, or no predictability. Therefore—other than the improbability of a perfect overlap—the correlation coefficient will be a decimal, the size of which reflects the magnitude of the relationship between the variables. A positive correlation indicates the two variables vary in the same direction (e.g., more studying, higher grades/less studying, lower grades), while a negative correlation means that the variables covary in the opposite direction (e.g., more studying, lower grades/less studying, higher grades).

An important rule in research to be aware of is that *correlation does not necessarily imply causation*. In other words, just because two variables are highly correlated does not necessarily mean that one *causes* the other. For example, the amount of time spent watching violence on TV tends to correlate highly with the extent of a person's own aggressiveness, but it does not necessarily mean that watching violence on TV causes one to become violent. An alternative explanation would be that people who are aggressive are attracted to violent TV shows. A correlation between variables A and B is as likely to mean that B causes A as that A causes B. There is also the possibility that both are caused by a third variable, C. For example, a high correlation between infant mortality and a high amount of required road repairs does not necessarily mean that potholes in the road cause infants to die or that infants dying ruins the roads. What the correlation may mean is that heat, a third variable, causes both.

A major difference between correlational research and experimental research, therefore, is in the idea of internal validity—the confidence we have that one variable causes another. Because correlational research data are collected after the fact, there is no avoiding the old "which came first, the chicken or the egg?" problem. On the other hand, it is much easier and more convenient to measure the degree of something than to create and implement a treatment that will cause that something to happen.

AP Photo/Mark Gilliland

What began as a class research study of the holocaust at Whitwell Middle School became a well known 2004 movie called *Paper Clips*. In this picture you see some of the 30 million paper clips that students have collected.

correlational research

a researcher collects two or more sets of data from a group of participants for analysis and then attempts to determine the relationship between them

correlation coefficient

a measure of the degree of relationship between two scores, or the extent to which one score predicts the other

Let's look at an actual example of a correlational study, one particularly relevant to teaching. Tuckman & Kennedy (2009) studied the relationship between the grade point averages of students taught study skills during their first term in school and the grade point averages earned by those same students at the end of their second and their third year in school, to see if the initial gains were carried over in time. They found the correlation between first term and second year academic performance to be .82 and between first term and third year performance .74. These high positive correlations indicated that first term results following study skills instruction were associated with, but did not necessarily cause, high academic performance two and three years later. Since correlations of .40 and higher may be considered to have theoretical or practical value (Fraenkel and Wallen, 2006), these results would be considered exceptional.

Overall, correlational studies—in and of themselves—are not adequate for identifying causal relationships between variables, but they can be highly useful steps in that direction. They often do suggest causal links because, while correlation does not necessarily imply causation, causation does necessarily imply correlation. Subsequent studies can then be undertaken to attempt to establish cause and effect.

Observational/Qualitative Research

While the formal tests of our theories may come in the form of experiments, the foundations on which theories are built often are based on less formal, **observational/qualitative research**. Merely observing behavior in various naturally occurring situations is less precise and more subjective than conducting controlled experiments, but it is accomplished more easily. If such observations can be made without altering the behavior observed, then the researcher can be confident that the behavior is real and not staged for his or her benefit (or detriment). Unlike experimental research, where subjects may behave differently because they know they are part of an experiment (see Box 1.3 on the effect of expectations), observational/qualitative research provokes no such effect if the researcher is sufficiently unobtrusive. Thus, observational/qualitative research is less intrusive—but more subjective—than experimental research.

In addition, observational/qualitative research often does not utilize quantitative data, that is, numerical data, and therefore does not employ statistics to help understand the meaning of the data as does experimental or correlational research. Instead, it utilizes qualitative, or descriptive, data and employs the perceptions and judgments of the researcher to help understand the meaning of the data. Nevertheless, both types of research are planned and conducted systematically.

Consider the classic observational work of Smith and Geoffrey (1968) in an inner-city school where Geoffrey was a teacher. Smith spent every day of the whole school year sitting in Geoffrey's classroom observing what went on. Their purpose was to develop a model of the classroom and to learn more about how a middle-class teacher would cope with a group of children from a lower socioeconomic status. They tested a number of hypotheses, such as:

observational/qualitative research

observing behavior in various naturally occurring situations

As amount of personalized interaction increases, then both pupil satisfaction and esteem for teacher increase; and as pupil satisfaction and esteem for teacher increase, then classroom control increases. (Smith & Geoffrey, 1968, p. 19)

Both men kept detailed field notes, one as a participant and the other as a nonparticipant. They then compared and combined their notes to produce their research results. When a researcher participates in observational research, the individual is termed **participant observer**.

Their analysis of the field notes (Smith & Geoffrey, 1968, p. 15) consisted of: (1) reading them through, looking for "insightful" comments; (2) abstracting the incident that precipitated the comment and elaborating on its significance; (3) showing the teacher, Mr. Geoffrey, the report of the incident and asking him to explain it and to react to the elaboration; (4) rereading one another's comments and generating new interpretations; and (5) including occasional insignificant incidents "to keep the other honest!"

To produce pupil enthusiasm and the joy of knowing, they discovered teaching techniques such as: (1) teaching a lesson that has content low enough in difficulty for all students to understand, but at the same time making sure that the content is both clear and important; (2) using a variety of activities that include pupils actually doing things that will provoke their interest and that have a game-like quality; and (3) keeping the frequency of teacher interaction with pupils high and including banter (personal, humorous conversation or byplay).

In a lesson dealing with making compound words out of simple ones (one of the simple words was "girl"), Smith and Geoffrey (1968) recorded the following incident:

participant observer
when a researcher participates in observational research

Much insight into student behavior can be gained through observational research, like this researcher studying playground behavior at a school.

webphotographeer/istockphoto.com

Geoffrey sends Elma to the board to call on people and write down their answers. She's highly embarrassed about calling on people at first but Elma soon finds this is fun and calls on them by pointing. There is much humor as they call out particulars. Joe K. suggests "Tom girl!" This brings down the house. They list some more. Billy suggests "sexy girl" and Elma with big chuckle writes it on the board. Geoffrey finally says "enough of that nonsense" and has Elma erase it—along with the rest. (p. 196)

See Table 1.2 for a *Concept Review* of the different types of research.

CONCEPT REVIEW TABLE 1.2

Different Types of Research

TYPE OF RESEARCH	HOW IT WORKS
Experimental	Two groups, one receiving an intervention, the other not, are compared on outcomes. Ideally, students are assigned at random to one of the two groups.
Single Subject	The behavior of one student is measured in its original state (baseline) and again after having received an intervention or treatment.
Correlational	Two or more sets of data, based on test scores or observations, are compared statistically to see if there is a relationship between them.
Observational	Behavior is observed in naturally-occurring situations, and those observations and resulting conclusions are reported.

Learning Objective 7

Explain the role of the teacher as researcher and provide an example of teacher research.

The Teacher as Researcher

Educational research, much of it done by university researchers, represents a rich body of information that can be very helpful to classroom teachers in influencing their practice of teaching. This information is accessible to teachers, but its value depends on the ability to interpret and critically appraise it. However, many contend that, in addition to this body of work, research by teachers can be an equally significant way of knowing about teaching. Lytle and Cochran-Smith (1992), for example, argue that teacher research is a way for classroom teachers to generate knowledge useful not only for themselves and their immediate communities, but for the larger school and university communities as well.

Teacher research has been defined as *systematic, intentional inquiry by teachers about their own school and classroom work* (Cochran-Smith and Lytle, 1990). *Intentional* indicates planned rather than spontaneous. *Inquiry* suggests that it "… stems from or generates questions and reflects teachers' desires to make sense of their experiences" (Lytle and Cochran-Smith, 1992, p. 450).

The kind of research that teachers typically do is observational/qualitative. Single-subject and correlational research are possible, but less common. In addition, experiments can be done under certain circumstances, as the example below illustrates. Observational/qualitative research has the following features: (1) it is done in a natural setting, (2) the researcher is the key data collection "instrument," (3) it is concerned as much or more with events that transpire than with product or outcome, (4) data are "analyzed" inductively by trying to make sense of what they mean, (5) the focus is on *why* events occur as well as *what* happens (Bogdan and Biklen, 2003).

The four kinds of research data collection or documentation you might conduct as a teacher are: (1) field notes and journals that describe and reflect on *observations* of classroom events, interactions, or other class-related activities; (2) notes, audiotapes or transcripts of *interviews* with students, other teachers, or conferences with parents; (3) classroom *documents* such as students' seatwork, homework, test papers and scores, teachers' plans or handouts; and (4) *tapes* (audio and video) of ongoing class activities, extracurricular activities, or presentations.

An example of teacher research is a study by Fecho (1998) of teacher-student writing conferences. The research is based on videotapes he made in his classroom. In trying to understand direct conversations about writing between a teacher and an individual student in an urban high school, Fecho gained insight from a student who liked the idea of being his own critic, meaning he could be "mean and sensitive" to himself. Fecho realized that a key to his own role as teacher of writing was to be "mean" enough to get his students to become more self-reliant, while continuing to be "sensitive" to their needs.

An Example of Teacher-Initiated Research

A second-grade teacher had been reading about self-efficacy theory (as you will too in Chapter 10). At the time, she just began teaching her 20 second graders to write in cursive. Because they had just started, there were few individual differences between them. She decided to compare two somewhat different approaches in reacting to her students' cursive writing attempts.

One of the approaches was based on reinforcement theory (covered in Chapter 6), the technique she had already established in her classroom. This technique involved giving each student a happy face sticker for each line of practice writing that contained at least one perfectly formed letter, and telling them "good" or "perfect" for their work. The stickers could be traded in for weekly treats, and

teacher research

systematic, intentional inquiry by teachers about their own school and classroom work

contains a **Take It to the Classroom** box that illustrates the application of educational psychology.

Diversity

In education as in life, it has become increasingly important as teachers to understand, relate to, and teach persons from different cultural and ethnic backgrounds as well as those with different physical and mental capabilities. As we become a global, multicultural society, we need to be aware of and appreciate the many differences among people. Particularly as a teacher, with a classroom of students who do not all speak the same native language or have the same beliefs or customs, or the same skills and abilities, it is imperative to be sensitive to the differences among cultures, cultural practices, and abilities/disabilities. To help prospective teachers and others learn about these differences that make us a diverse society, each chapter of this book includes a feature called **Discourse on Diversity** (an example follows).

D I S C O U R S E   O N   D I V E R S I T Y

Core Values in the Latino/Latina Culture   BOX 1.4

The distribution of ethnic groups in the United States is constantly shifting based on birth and death rates, immigration, and other factors. One ethnic group increasing in population is Latinos. In fact, it has been estimated that "by the year 2010, one in five Americans will identify as Hispanic—with cultural ties to Spanish-speaking countries such as Mexico, Cuba, and El Salvador" (Dingfelder, 2005, p. 58). This means school teachers all over the United States can expect to have a growing number of Latino/Hispanics in their classrooms and would be well-served to develop some understanding of their culture.

Although considerable diversity exists within the Latino population in the United States, there is also significant communality. One area of communality across Latino subcultures is in core values, that is, essential beliefs and corresponding behaviors. Arredondo, Santiago-Rivera, & Gallardo Cooper (2007; see also Fraga, Atkinson, & Wampold, 2004) identify the following four Latino core values that counselors, or teachers, would benefit from a familiarity with:

- *Familismo.* Coming typically from tight-knit families, Latinos tend to feel uncomfortable, and even disloyal, discussing family matters with "outsiders." However, teachers can draw on the family as a support system in helping Latino students succeed in school.

- *Simpatia.* Students from Latino cultures are more likely to place a greater value on being in harmony with others than to aggressively express their issues and problems as is characteristic of the mainstream culture in the United States. Teachers need to be aware of the stress that Latino students are likely to experience when they are confronted.

- *Respeto.* The tendency exists in Latino cultures to express more respect and even deference to persons in positions of authority, such as teachers, than is typical of the mainstream culture in the United States. Teachers need to be aware of the degree of authority they are afforded by Latino students, and to use it mindfully.
- *Personalismo.* Teachers acting in a detached, professional manner with their students may seem quite strange, even alien, to Latino students in whose culture close interpersonal relationships are valued. Teachers may be able to make Latino students feel more comfortable by sharing information about themselves with their students.

Think It Over

as a LEARNER

Think about how it might be different to tutor a student one-on-one as opposed to teaching a multicultural group of 35. In what ways would you expect students' behavior to differ in these two settings?

as a TEACHER

What strategies might you employ to maximize learning in both settings?

SUMMING IT UP

Define educational psychology and its application in the classroom, including practical and intellectual reasons for studying human behavior.

Learning Objective 1

Key Concepts:
educational psychology, human behavior (p. 5); epistemology (p. 6).

Educational psychology, the science of human behavior applied to the teaching and learning process, helps teachers to understand issues such as how students learn, what makes students want to learn, how to design instruction that maximizes learning, and what are ways of assessing student learning. **Human behavior** follows patterns, many of which are subtle or escape our notice because people are too busy behaving to also be observers. Moreover, what goes on inside people does not necessarily show on the outside. By not being aware of behavioral patterns, teachers may affect students in ways other than those intended. Studying educational psychology can help increase our awareness of how certain behaviors affect others. In addition to this practical reason, there is also an intellectual reason—namely, to expand our knowledge and awareness of the world around us.

Learning Objective 2

Key Concepts:

transactional model of the teaching-learning process (p. 7); behavioral approach, cognitive approach (p. 11).

Describe three applications of psychology to education: (1) a model of the teaching-learning process, (2) principles of classroom management, and (3) perspectives on the causes of behavior.

Many factors combine to influence student achievement, the principal ones are the characteristics and behaviors of students and teachers. Specific factors in **the teaching-learning process** include instructional manipulations, learner characteristics, learning processes, learning outcomes, and outcome performance. Assumptions underlying good classroom management include getting students to understand and accept rules, engaging them in meaningful activities, and helping them develop inner self-control. Two perspectives on the causes of behavior are: (1) explaining it on the basis of its consequences (the **behavioral approach**), and (2) explaining it on the basis of thinking (the **cognitive approach**).

Learning Objective 3

Explain educational psychology and the role of the teacher regarding the constraints to applying new knowledge and how school learning can be more like real-world learning.

A teacher operates within real constraints, including the organization of students into typically large *classes* confined to *classrooms*, a predominantly preset *curriculum* or course of study, and a limitation in class time based on the *clock* and the *calendar*. School learning differs from real-world learning in that it focuses on *individual performance* rather than *socially-shared performance*, it fosters *symbolic thinking* or thought done entirely in the head rather than using *cognitive tools* and dealing directly with objects and situations, and it focuses on *general skills and knowledge* rather than *situation-specific competencies*. Educational psychology can help teachers create opportunities for real-world learning in the classroom.

Learning Objective 4

Key Concepts:

ecological approach (p. 15); reflective teaching (p. 17).

Discuss characteristics of the effective teacher, including (1) an ecological model and (2) reflective teaching.

Characteristics of effective teachers are important and useful to know in order to help preservice teachers develop into expert teachers. However, it is also important to look at the interaction between the teacher characteristics and the characteristics of the educational setting. John Dewey was one of the earliest researchers to place a value on studying the impact of the educational setting. This is known as the **ecological model**. The competencies required of teachers to demonstrate expertise fall into the following domains: planning and preparation, the classroom environment, instruction, and professional responsibilities. **Reflective teaching** is the process of asking yourself questions about your teaching and attempting to identify answers. It can help you become an expert teacher.

Explain the psychological study of behavior, including the four tenets of science, the difference between facts, principles and theories, the determination of a theory's accuracy, and factors affecting the accuracy of judgments.

Learning Objective 5

Psychologists study behavior using the scientific method. The scientific method is based on four principles: **observation, testability, replication,** and **parsimony.** In this book, the approach is to focus on principles and theories rather than on discrete facts. **Principles** are more general than the **facts** that make them up, and theories, by combining principles, are more comprehensive yet. **Theories** are speculative: They attempt to explain the *why* of something and help to organize information and to apply it in a variety of situations (unlike facts, which simply represent information). In order to determine whether theories are accurate, we can deduce hypotheses or predictions from them and then test these by doing research. The models used to do research or collect data are called **paradigms**.

Key Concepts:

observation, testable questions (p. 19); hypothesis, replication, parsimony (p. 20); facts, principles, theories (p. 21); induction, deduction, paradigm, certainty, generality (p. 24).

Describe four types of research (experimental, single-subject, correlational, and observational) that can be used to inform teachers and to enhance learning.

Learning Objective 6

Some of the specific research methods that educational psychologists utilize include experimental, single-subject, correlational, and observational research. **Experimental research** is used to determine the effectiveness of different instructional methods. **Single-subject research** is used when one is lacking numbers of students with highly similar characteristics. In the single-subject approach, participants are compared with themselves rather than with members of a control or comparison group as in experimental research. In **correlational research**, a researcher collects two or more sets of data from a group of participants for analysis and then attempts to determine the relationship between them. The data are based on test scores or **observational** measures, and their relationship is determined using a statistic called a **correlation coefficient**. Finally, **observational research** involves observing behavior in various naturally occurring situations, while trying to be as unobtrusive as possible, and recording one's observations.

Key Concepts:

experimental research, random assignment (p. 26); single-subject research (p. 27); correlational research, correlation coefficient (p. 29); observational research (p. 30); participant observer (p. 31).

Explain the role of the teacher as researcher and provide an example of teacher research.

Learning Objective 7

Teacher research has been defined as systematic, intentional inquiry by teachers about their own school and classroom work; "intentional" indicates it is planned rather than spontaneous; "inquiry" suggests it stems from or generates questions and reflects teachers' desires to make sense of their experiences. The kind of research that teachers typically do is observational research (usually referred to as qualitative research). The four sources of data or documentation common to research by teachers are observations, interviews, documents, and tapes.

Key Concepts:

teacher research (p. 33).

Visit the Education CourseMate for *Educational Psychology* to access study tools and resources including the Virtual Psychology Labs, TeachSource Video Cases, chapter web links, tutorial quizzes, glossary flashcards, and more. Go to CengageBrain.com to register using your access code.

2 | Cognitive and Language Development

Banana Stock/PhotoLibrary

After reading this chapter, you should be able to meet the following learning objectives:	Chapter Contents
LEARNING OBJECTIVE 1 Explain general principles of development and the relationship between the brain and cognitive development.	Cognitive Development and the Brain • General Principles of Cognitive Development • Physiology of the Brain • The Cerebral Cortex • Brain-based Learning and Teaching
LEARNING OBJECTIVE 2 Describe intellectual development according to Piaget as the process of adaptation, featuring the schema; the processes of assimilation, accommodation and equilibration; and the four factors that influence cognitive development.	The Developmental Psychology of Jean Piaget • The Basic Structure of Cognitive Organization: The Schema • Intellectual Development as Adaptation • Developmental Factors
LEARNING OBJECTIVE 3 Explain and illustrate the four stages of Piaget's model of cognitive development: (1) sensorimotor, (2) preoperational, (3) concrete operational, and (4) formal operational.	Piaget's Four Stages of Cognitive Development • Sensorimotor Stage (Infancy-Toddlerhood) • Pre-operational Stage (Early Childhood-Early Elementary) • Concrete Operational Stage (Elementary-Middle) • Formal Operational Stage (High-College)
LEARNING OBJECTIVE 4 Apply Piaget's conception of cognitive development to the process of education.	Applying Piaget to Educational Practice • Learning by Exploration • Learner-Centered Orientation • Use of Themes • Focus on Development of Schemata
LEARNING OBJECTIVE 5 Recognize criticisms and limitations of Piaget's theory.	A Critique and Updating of Piaget's Theory
LEARNING OBJECTIVE 6 Explain and apply to teaching Vygotsky's theory of cognitive development in terms of its main concepts and characteristics: sociocultural perspective, social construction of meaning, internalization, zone of proximal development, and scaffolding.	The Developmental Psychology of Lev Vygotsky • Social Interaction: Its Critical Role in Acquiring Meaning • Internalization: Evolving of Social Activities into Mental Activities • The Role of Language and Other Cultural Tools • Zone of Proximal Development and Scaffolding • Applying Vygotsky to Teaching
LEARNING OBJECTIVE 7 Describe language development, including the concepts of phonology, meaning, grammar, and communication, and illustrate how language development can be facilitated in the classroom and English language learners accommodated.	Language Development • Four Main Aspects of Language • Language and Thinking • Is Language Special? • Facilitating Language Development in the Classroom

Infinity

One day, I visited a private elementary school in Amherst, Mass. called the Common School. It was started by a seasoned teacher, Mrs. Johnson. As I entered the building, I saw four fourth- graders in a small room with a large scroll of paper. One student appeared to be writing out numbers while the others watched intently. It was clear a large part of the scroll was full of numbers. Each number being written appeared to have about 25 digits, and each successive number was an increment of one over the previous number. The students were absolutely transfixed. I watched for a few more minutes and then set off to find Mrs. Johnson.

I found Mrs. Johnson and introduced myself. I mentioned the four students writing out numbers and asked whether she knew what they were doing. She said she did, and explained that their teacher, two days previously, during their math period, had been talking about the concept of *infinity*. It seems some of the students indicated they did not "get it" and argued that numbers had to end somewhere. Infinity, as the teacher was talking about it, did not make any sense to the students. During the discussion, several students suggested that they could write out all the numbers and get to the end. They asked to try. The teacher produced the scroll of paper and sent them off to try. They had been at it for days when I arrived. They actually had teams of students spelling each other every few hours. Later I found out that they kept it up for another day and decided to stop.

- Was this a worthwhile use of the students' time? Did they learn something about infinity? If so, what?

Adapted from Wadsworth, B.J. (2004). *Piaget's theory of cognitive and affective development* (5th ed.; p. 167. Boston: Allyn and Bacon).

Lessons We Can Learn from the Story According to Wadsworth, the teller of the story— and an expert on Piaget's theory of cognitive development—this was a worthwhile use of the students' time. Because they were actively engaged in constructing knowledge, the activity was interest-driven, and their actions were autonomous and cooperative. The students ended up learning that infinity has no end. The activity was an example of a teacher's positive response to spontaneous interest and natural curiosity.

This chapter deals with the development of thinking skills and language among children and adolescents. Your understanding of how the capacity for thinking grows and develops as children mature makes it possible to provide instructional experiences for your students. They will be able to understand the subject matter and enhance their own developmental process through their engagement. Jean Piaget and Lev Vygotsky have provided us with frameworks for understanding the process of cognitive development. Piaget provided a detailed and far-reaching model, extensively covered in this chapter. We begin this chapter, though, with a brief examination of general cognitive development and the functions of the brain.

Cognitive Development and the Brain

We begin with a description of four general principles of cognitive development. Then we acquaint you with the functions of the brain and the relationship of these functions to learning and teaching. At this time, much more is unknown than known in this area. It is a developmental topic that may increase in interest and insights over time.

Learning Objective 1

Explain general principles of development and the relationship between the brain and cognitive development.

General Principles of Cognitive Development

1. *All children do not develop at the same rate.* Although average ages have been identified for the attainment of various developmental milestones (for example, puberty for boys begins at age 11 ½ and for girls at age 10; McDevitt & Ormrod, 2007), some children achieve these milestones sooner than others. Age alone is not a sufficient basis for judging individual performance. As a teacher, you will notice differences among your students on many variables such as height, learning ability, and ease in working with others. Such differences are within the normal range of development.

2. *Development as a process is continuous and relatively orderly.* Though there are occasionally spurts and plateaus, that is, periods of more rapid or less rapid growth, for the most part children's growth is continuous rather than spasmodic or "jumpy" (Berk, 2006). For example, as we shall see when we examine Piaget's four stages of development, children invariably learn how to master less complex ideas before they can comprehend more complex ones, just as they learn how to crawl before they learn how to run and how to do algebra before they do calculus.

3. *Learning, experience, and social interaction all contribute to development.* This is clearly illustrated by the work of both Piaget and Vygotsky, the two important researchers in the study of children's cognitive development covered in this chapter. When children interact with one another by doing group work in school, are exposed to experiences like libraries and museums, and are read to by their parents, there is an impact on their cognitive development beyond that of children who lack the same opportunities (Siegler & Alibali, 2005).

4. *Development is affected by both heredity and environment.* The environment, which includes school, home, family, and culture, interacts with a child's genetic predispositions to influence development (Gottlieb, 2000). For example, a child's high level of intelligence—a genetic factor—can enhance development, while a poor diet—an environmental factor—can retard development. Because environmental factors are easier to control than genetic factors, they should be given the greater focus in the classroom.

Physiology of the Brain

The brain and the nervous system are composed of different types of cells, but the primary cell is the **neuron**. It is estimated that between 100 billion and 200 billion neurons occupy the brain (Berninger & Richards, 2002). All sensations, movements, thoughts, memories, and feelings are the result of signals that pass through neurons.

The neuron consists of three parts: (1) the **cell body**, which contains the nucleus that manufactures most of the molecules the neuron needs to survive and function; (2) **dendrites**, which extend out from the cell body like the branches of a tree and receive messages from other nerve cells; and (3) **axons**, which receive signals from the dendrites and transmit them to other neurons in the brain or to cells in some other organ (Craig, 2003).

When a neuron's dendrites are stimulated, the dendrites become "electrically charged," and if the charge is sufficient, the neuron will "fire" resulting in an "electrical impulse" sent to the axon (actually to its tips, or **terminal buttons**). Neurons do not touch one another; they are separated by tiny spaces called **synapses**. When an "electrical impulse" travels along a neuron's axon, it causes the terminal buttons at the end of the axon to release **neurotransmitters**—chemicals that traverse the synapses and stimulate the dendrites of adjacent neurons. A single neuron may have synaptic connections to a very large number of other neurons. However, neurons that are not used because there are more than are necessary will be removed or "pruned," which facilitates cognitive development (Bransford, Brown, & Cocking, 2000). Stimulating environments may facilitate the pruning process in early life and lead to increased synapse production in adulthood (Cook & Cook, 2005).

The changing of the interconnections among neurons may be an important basis for cognitive development because it involves strengthening or eliminating existing synapses or forming new ones. Though not yet proven, neuron formation may be stimulated by new learning experiences (Lichtman, 2001).

The Cerebral Cortex

The **cerebral cortex** is part of the brain itself. It is made up of four parts, or *lobes*: the frontal lobe, at the front of the cortex; the parietal lobe, at the top of the cortex; the occipital lobe, at the back of the cortex; and the temporal lobe, at the bottom of the cortex. Some of the major functions controlled by the cerebral cortex are body movement and coordination, body sensation, vision, hearing, language, behavior, and complex thinking.

The cortex is divided into two halves, or hemispheres. The **left hemisphere** is involved primarily with language and thinking, while the **right hemisphere** is associated with vision, spatial relations, and emotions (Byrnes, 2001). This specialization of each of the two hemispheres is referred to as **lateralization**, with each half of the brain controlling the opposite side of the body. When one part of the cortex is damaged (as perhaps the result of an automobile accident), other parts of the cortex tend to compensate by taking over the functions of the damaged area. Moreover, no

---

neuron

the primary cell of the brain and the nervous system; all sensations, movements, thoughts, memories, and feelings are the result of signals that pass through neurons

cell body

contains the nucleus that manufactures most of the molecules the neuron needs to survive and function

dendrites

extend out from the cell body like the branches of a tree and receive messages from other nerve cells

axons

receive signals from the dendrites and transmit them to other neurons in the brain or to cells in some other organ

terminal buttons

the tips of axons, which receive the signals from neurons

synapses

tiny spaces separating neurons

neurotransmitters

chemicals that traverse the synapses and stimulate the dendrites of adjacent neurons

cerebral cortex

part of the brain itself; made up of four lobes: the frontal lobe, the parietal lobe, the occipital lobe, and the temporal lobe

left hemisphere

the half of the cortex involved primarily with language and thinking

right hemisphere

the half of the cortex associated with vision, spatial relations, and emotions

lateralization

the specialization of each of the two hemispheres

mental activity is exclusive to a specific part of the brain, so the potential for retaining a specific function remains intact.

Brain-based Learning and Teaching

Brain-based learning, or brain-based education, has been described as a "combination of brain science and common sense." Caine and Caine (1994) identified the following 12 mind/brain learning principles:

1. The brain is a complex adaptive system.
2. The brain is a social brain.
3. The search for meaning is innate.
4. The search for meaning occurs through patterning.
5. Emotions are critical to patterning.
6. Every brain simultaneously perceives and creates parts and wholes.
7. Learning involves both focused attention and peripheral attention.
8. Learning always involves conscious and unconscious processes.
9. There are at least two ways of organizing memory.
10. Learning is developmental.
11. Complex learning is enhanced by challenge and inhibited by threat.
12. Every brain is uniquely organized.

The same authors also identified conditions needed for complex learning to occur: (1) relaxed alertness—a low threat, high challenge state of mind; (2) orchestrated immersion—a multiple, complex, authentic experience; and (3) active processing—creating meaning through experience processing.

Kovalik & Olsen (2007) identified nine brain-compatible elements in their Integrated Thematic Instruction model: absence of threat, meaningful content, choices, movement to enhance learning, enriched environment, adequate time, collaboration, immediate feedback, and mastery at the application level.

The principles offered in these models, and others like them, seem very similar to the principles of constructivism (covered in Chapter 8). They clearly are learner-centered and experiential and include ideas like those proposed by Vygotsky (covered later in this chapter). However, these "brain-based" approaches have aroused considerable controversy. Based on what we currently know, brain structure and physiology do not provide specific guidance for facilitating either cognitive development or learning. More particularly, it does not provide evidence that

- early life skill-intensive experiences enhance brain power (Thompson & Nelson, 2001);
- special developmental periods occur in brain activity when learning subjects like reading and mathematics (Bruer, 1999; Geary, 1998); and
- certain teaching strategies are most conducive to the facilitation of mental growth in the brain (Byrnes, 2001).

Most psychologists believe what we know about learning and development is the result of research studies on actual behavior rather than on neurological studies of the brain.

brain-based learning

a "combination of brain science and common sense"

Two theories of cognitive development—Piaget's and Vygotsky's—each depict a version of how children's thought processes develop.

Describe intellectual development according to Piaget as the process of adaptation, featuring the schema; the processes of assimilation, accommodation and equilibration; and the four factors that influence cognitive development.

Knowledge of Jean Piaget's work helps teachers consider how knowledge changes and grows in children over time.

The Developmental Psychology of Jean Piaget

Swiss biologist Jean Piaget made a major contribution to our understanding of cognitive, or intellectual, development (and even moral development, as will be shown in the next chapter). Piaget, who died in 1980 at age 84, spent 60 years observing children and reporting on their growth in more than 200 books and articles. Although trained in biology and philosophy, Piaget turned to psychology to try to understand the development of intelligence in children. In this chapter, Piaget's major concepts and principles for explaining the behavior he observed are examined first, followed by the four developmental stages he hypothesized to exist. Next, some of Piaget's experiments are described, and last, his principles are applied to education.

It is important to point out that Piaget's method of doing research was to make meticulous observations and then report on what he observed (a technique called *observational research* in Chapter 1). He began with observations of his own three children and then expanded to observe many other children and young adults as they engaged in a variety of tasks, many of which he posed for them to deal with. From his extensive observations, he fashioned the detailed theory of development described in this chapter and the next.

The Basic Structure of Cognitive Organization: The Schema

Piaget, and others who followed him, perceived the **schema** to be the basic unit necessary for mental organization and mental functioning (see Chapters 7 and 8 for further discussion of the schema). Piaget (1952; also Flavell, 1963) defined a schema as "*a cohesive, repeatable action sequence possessing component actions that are tightly interconnected and governed by a core meaning.*" Wadsworth (2004) suggests that schemata (the plural of schema) be thought of as "index cards" filed in the brain, each one telling an individual how to identify and react to incoming stimuli or information. An infant has a small number of small index cards, all of which represent reflexive schemata such as grasping or sucking. Adults, by comparison, have large numbers of large index cards. They need to be large to keep track of the experiences associated with each schema and the refinements that might result from some of those experiences.

Farrell Grehan/Historical/Corbis

Schemata help people classify or categorize an object or event and decide how to act toward that object or react to that event. Often, the initial necessary act is to label or recognize a situation so that the appropriate response can be made. When you are given a list of grocery items and the cost of each and are asked what the total cost will be, you have a schema that enables you to recognize that addition is the appropriate arithmetic process and another schema that enables you to carry out the addition process to arrive at a solution.

When Piaget talked about the development of a person's mental processes, he was referring to increases in the number and complexity of the schemata that a person had learned. Once learned, those schemata were available for the person to use to deal with, or identify and react to, whatever objects and events he or she encountered.

Intellectual Development as Adaptation

The basic tenet of Piaget's theory of development is that the organism interacts with the environment in a relationship called **adaptation**. In adaptation, the organism develops schemata that enable it to continue to function in that environment. The very essence of life is a continuing and repeatable interaction between the organism and its environment that enables the organism to function.

Think of the giraffe. It has evolved a long neck that enables it to feed on the leaves of very tall trees. For the giraffe, the long neck is an environmental survival adaptation. Of course, physical adaptations of this sort take longer than intellectual ones. You learn quickly to use a ladder when you want something stored on the top shelf. Even before learning about ladders, you may have learned to pile up boxes or to use a chair to climb up on the kitchen counter.

Assimilation and Accommodation

Piaget (1952; see also Wadsworth, 2004) posited two mechanisms to carry out adaptation. The first, **assimilation**, is a process used *to incorporate new information into existing schemata that are sufficient to understand it.* In other words, when someone encounters something new, he or she will try to deal with it (i.e., recognize it or react to it) by using an existing schema or action plan. As a result, the schema is not changed essentially, but it is expanded to include the new experience and the result of the reaction to it.

Assimilation is somewhat similar to the behavioral concept of stimulus generalization (discussed in Chapter 6), in which students, after having learned to respond to one stimulus, such as the teacher clapping her hands to get attention, respond similarly to other stimuli similar to the original, such as the teacher holding up her hand. This tendency increases if the outcome of responding to the new but similar stimulus is as satisfactory (students give their attention to the teacher) as it was when they responded to the original.

Suppose you are teaching and a student who has not completed her work gives you an excuse you have never heard before. You already have a schema to deal with incomplete work, and you assimilate this experience into it and react to the student by giving her an additional assignment—as you would any other noncompleter, regardless of the circumstances. You have adapted to the new situation by using an

schema

the basic unit necessary for mental organization and mental functioning

adaptation

how an organism interacts with the environment in a relationship

assimilation

a process used to incorporate new information into existing schemata that are sufficient to understand it

existing plan to deal with it. You have not added a new schema; you have simply made an existing one fit.

By contrast, **accommodation**—Piaget's second adaptive mechanism—is a process used *to modify an existing schema in order to be able to understand information that would otherwise be incomprehensible with existing schemata*. This time, the person having the new experience cannot deal with it by using an existing schema; none fits it closely enough. That person must change an existing schema to create an essentially new schema in order to make an adaptive response. This is like concept learning or problem solving in Chapter 8. When what is known does not work in a given situation, something new must be tried.

To continue the earlier illustration likening schemata to index cards, accommodation means that a person adds new index cards by finding the closest existing one and then modifying it. As a new teacher, you may not have a schema for dealing with a student's incomplete work, but you might remember how your supervising teacher dealt with this issue and then modify that approach to fit your situation. Once you have done this, you will have a schema for dealing with incomplete work and will probably use it to assimilate future instances of the problem. Assimilation and accommodation are processes that enable children to grow and adapt to their environment continually. Assimilation helps children make better use of their schemata, and accommodation helps them alter their schemata to fit new situations. In assimilation, the situation is made to fit existing schemata; in accommodation, existing schemata are changed or new ones developed to fit the situation. **Play**, according to Piaget (1952; Wadsworth, 2004), is an example of essentially pure assimilation in that something is done as it always has been, that is, as a simple, repetitive activity. By comparison, **imitation** is an example of essentially pure accommodation in that a child does something never done before by watching and copying it from someone else. All other experiences would fall somewhere in between.

According to Piaget, a balance must exist between assimilation and accommodation as well as between an individual and the environment. Life cannot be all play, because then nothing new would be learned. Neither can it be all imitation, because then there would be no self or stability. There must be enough accommodation to meet and adapt to new situations and enough assimilation to use one's schemata quickly and efficiently. In other words, a state of equilibrium must exist between these two processes, which, in turn, make possible a state of equilibrium between an individual and the environment. When equilibrium or balance does not exist, something must be done to achieve it. That something is either accommodation or assimilation, depending on the circumstances. Carrying out these processes in an effort to restore equilibrium is called **equilibration**, and it represents the major source of motivation in Piaget's system.

The basis for development of the increasing intellectual capacity of a child is equilibration. As new experiences occur, the young child is motivated to develop new schemata to deal with them through accommodation. Once these new schemata are developed, the young child is then motivated to use them through assimilation. The "index card file" is continually expanding, with each new development laying the foundation for subsequent developments in an orderly and progressive

accommodation

a process used to modify an existing schema in order to be able to understand information that would otherwise be incomprehensible with existing schemata

play

something is done as it always has been, that is, as a simple, repetitive activity

imitation

a child does something never done before by watching and copying it from someone else

equilibration

carrying out processes in an effort to restore equilibrium; the major source of motivation in Piaget's system

way. Because equilibrium is always only momentary and each new encounter creates disequilibrium, the process of equilibration or trying to attain equilibrium serves as a constant motivator of intellectual development throughout childhood.

Intelligence

To Piaget, **intelligence** is a combination of all of an individual's schemata (Siegler & Alibali, 2005). These schemata enable an individual to maintain equilibrium with the environment—to adapt to and deal with circumstances as they arise. Intelligence, therefore, is the regulating or adapting force, and as such is the result of assimilations and accommodations between a person and the surrounding world. Moreover, to Piaget intelligence does not represent content or the amount of knowledge a person has. Rather, it represents *structure,* or how what is known is organized, so that it can be used. The particular organizational structures of intelligence are schemata—structures formed as the result of assimilation and accommodation.

This view of intelligence as adaptability or capability of dealing with a changing environment is quite different from the more common view of intelligence (to be described in Chapter 4) as either general or specific knowledge. To Piaget, intelligence is more like procedural knowledge, or knowing what to do, than declarative knowledge, or simply knowing facts. (These types of knowledge will be described in Chapter 7).

Because intelligence is both the result of and the basis for assimilation and accommodation, it can be expected to vary considerably from age to age. As children have more and more experiences, they develop the structures, or schemata, that help them adapt to their environment. Piaget divides the development of intelligence into discrete stages, each with its own intellectual challenges to equilibrium.

Operations

What is intelligence used for? In other words, what are its outputs? For Piaget, the answer is **operations**, that is, *systems or coordinated sets of actions* for dealing with objects or events. *Identification, addition,* and *classification* are examples of operations. In addition, all of the actions a person can take within the systems of logic or mathematics constitute operations (Piaget, 1950; Wadsworth, 2004). As children mature, their thinking gets organized into more and more well-defined systems, that is, as children grow, they can perform increasingly more operations that become increasingly more complex.

A *Concept Review* of Piaget's adaptive processes of intellectual development is shown in Table 2.1.

Developmental Factors

Piaget's theory is a theory of development, or a theory of changes in intelligence over time. These changes, as we will see in the next section, are represented by stages children go through that are characterized by different adaptations as a function of existing schemata and the development of new schemata. Before these stages are described, it is useful to examine the four factors Piaget (1961; Wadsworth, 2004) cites as contributing to cognitive development.

The first factor is **heredity**, or inheritance, which affects a child's rate of *maturation*. According to Piaget, maturation does not cause cognitive structures to develop.

intelligence
a combination of all of an individual's schemata

operations
systems or coordinated sets of actions for dealing with objects or events

heredity
inheritance

CONCEPT REVIEW TABLE 2.1

Piaget's Adaptive Processes of Intellectual Development

CONCEPT	DEFINITION	EXAMPLE(S)
Adaptation	Developing schemata that enable one to function in the environment	Using a ladder to get something on a high shelf
Assimilation	Incorporating new information into existing schemata	Play
Accommodation	Creating an essentially new schema to understand inform-ation otherwise incomprehensible	Imitation
Equilibration	Carrying out assimilation and accommodation to restore equilibrium	Motivation
Intelligence	A combination of all of a person's schemata	Adaptability; knowing what to do
Operations	Coordinated sets of actions for dealing with objects or events	Addition; classification

Think It Over

as a LEARNER   When was the last time you engaged in accommodation, and what was the situation? (Hint: Think of the last time you had to deal with a very unfamiliar situation.) How did you deal with the situation, that is, what exactly did you do?

as a TEACHER   How would you get your students to engage in accommodation in a subject area you were teaching?

Rather, it determines the range of possibilities at a specific stage, that is, whether a particular structure can possibly develop at a specific stage, not necessarily whether it will. Hence, maturation places broad constraints on cognitive development. It provides the potential for the appearance of specific structures; but whether or not they do in fact appear depends on the next three factors.

The second factor is **active experience**, or the child's actions in his or her environment. These actions can be physical or mental and they can involve objects or people. Children who have a childhood rich in active experiences are more likely to develop the structures that characterize each stage and to proceed through all four stages than children whose experience base is limited or impoverished. Early school programs such as Head Start and participation or imitation-type television programming such as "Sesame Street" serve to increase the active experiences of children, especially those who may lack the opportunity for such experiences in their everyday lives.

The third factor is **social interaction**, or the exchange of ideas among people. This is especially important in the development of ideas that do not have a physical referent, that is, cannot be seen or heard—like the idea of *freedom* or *fairness*. Socially defined concepts depend heavily on social interaction for their development. (This aspect of development will be covered in the next chapter.)

The fourth factor, equilibration, has already been introduced and, according to Piaget (1977), accounts for the coordination between the other three factors. Beyond this, however, equilibration serves as a self-regulating device that enables the child to process new information through either assimilation or accommodation and to always be moving toward a balance with the environment.

Taken together, these four factors account not only for the continuous process of development, but also for the dramatic changes that occur from one period or stage of development to another.

Piaget's Four Stages of Cognitive Development

Learning Objective 3

Explain and illustrate the four stages of Piaget's model of cognitive development: (1) sensorimotor, (2) preoperational, (3) concrete operational, and (4) formal operational.

The four stages of development are not absolute in either their timing or their characteristics. Rather, they represent a set of tendencies brought about by the four developmental factors described in the previous section. Each of the stages is described below; their classroom applications are then explored in the following section, which includes a *Concept Review* in Table 2.2. Both sections are devoted to these concepts because they are an important aid to your recognition and interpretation of, and response to, student behaviors. In this and subsequent chapters, these concepts can be recognized as underpinning both pedagogic and classroom management applications.

Sensorimotor Stage (Infancy–Toddlerhood)

This stage of development extends from birth to the acquisition of language. At inception of this stage, the newborn does not distinguish him- or herself from surrounding objects; at the end of this stage, the young child recognizes him- or herself as one part of a much larger world (Piaget, 1967). The major themes of

active experience
the child's actions in his or her environment

social interaction
the exchange of ideas among people

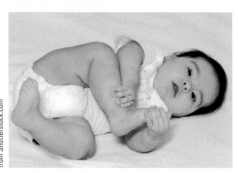

How does this image of an infant illustrate the primary circular reaction?

this stage relate to the progressive growth of the child's concepts of *object* (things outside of oneself) and *causality* or cause-and-effect relationships. Piaget divides this stage into six periods, each of which features the appearance of more complex behaviors involving the connections between the *senses* (seeing, hearing, touching) and actual movements, or *motor* behavior.

The major assimilation activity of this stage is what Piaget (1952) calls the **circular reaction**, in which the infant tries to reproduce interesting events or make interesting sights last. This repetition of events enables the infant to assimilate experience and to make new adaptations, such as increasing awareness of the existence of specific objects and understanding the relationship between cause and effect. Up to the fourth month of age, the **primary circular reaction** appears, with its focus on the infant's own body and directed toward the manipulation of some object.

Piaget's method for discovering the characteristics and features of this stage was to observe his own children—Laurent, Lucienne, and Jacqueline—and report on their behavior at different ages. From about four to eight months of age, the **secondary circular reaction** appears and is a clear illustration of what Piaget calls **reproductive assimilation**, or making interesting sights last. A familiar example is the infant throwing a toy out of the crib, entreating someone to give it back; when the toy is returned, it is immediately tossed out again. The whole sequence is repeated over and over until it becomes tiresome.

Following a period (age 8–12 months) that features the coordination of schemata and the appearance of intentionality of action, the **tertiary circular reaction** is exhibited (age 12–18 months), evidenced by the invention of new means—through active experimentation—to accomplish ends. The child now intentionally varies the repetitions to see if similar actions have the same effect. He may, for example, drop a rubber object and then wait for it to bounce. The child has discovered that people as well as objects can cause outcomes completely independent of his own actions.

When the sensorimotor stage ends (age 18–24 months), the child begins to learn how to talk and is able to represent objects and events mentally—by thinking about them. New learning can now be accomplished without active physical experimentation but by the representation of action through thinking.

A major capstone of the sensorimotor stage, representing an important state of equilibrium, is the emergence of schemata that make possible the realization of **object permanence**, even when the objects are out of sight and hearing. Heretofore, the child was unable to represent objects in the mind; hence, when no longer seen or heard, they did not exist. Now, with the emergence of the ability to store ideas, object permanence becomes a reality. The same is true for **causality**. The availability of thought makes possible the awareness of causality. (See Box 2.1 for examples of object permanence and causality.)

The child has now reached age 2 and is quite different from the newborn infant. As the infant has proceeded through the six sensorimotor periods, new and more sophisticated capabilities have emerged, each making the child better equipped to

circular reaction

the infant tries to reproduce interesting events or make interesting sights last

primary circular reaction

the focus is on the infant's own body and directed toward the manipulation of some object

secondary circular reaction or **reproductive assimilation**

making interesting sights last

tertiary circular reaction

evidenced by the invention of new means—through active experimentation—to accomplish ends

object permanence

recognizing that objects exist, even when out of sight and hearing

causality

cause-and-effect relationships

BOX 2.1

Concepts That Develop During the Last Period of the Sensorimotor Stage, Based on Observations by Piaget (Preschool)

Object Permanence

Observation 64.—At 1;7(20) Jacqueline watches me when I put a coin in my hand, then put my hand under a coverlet. I withdraw my hand closed; Jacqueline opens it, then searches under the coverlet until she finds the object. I take back the coin at once, put it in my hand and then slip my closed hand under a cushion situated at the other side (on her left and no longer on her right); Jacqueline immediately searches for the object under the cushion. I repeat the experiment by hiding the coin under a jacket; Jacqueline finds it without hesitation.

II. I complete the test as follows: I place the coin in my hand, then my hand under the cushion. I bring it forth closed and immediately hide it under the coverlet. Finally I withdraw it and hold it out, closed, to Jacqueline. Jacqueline then pushes my hand aside without opening it (she guesses that there is nothing in it, which is new), she looks under the cushion, then directly under the coverlet where she finds the object…

I then try a series of three displacements: I put the coin in my hand and move my closed hand sequentially from A to B and from B to C; Jacqueline sets my hand aside, then searches in A, in B, and finally in C.

Lucienne is successful in the same test at 1;3(14). (Piaget, 1954, p. 79).

Causality

At 1;4(4) … Laurent tries to open a garden gate but cannot push it forward because it is held back by a piece of furniture. He cannot account either visually or by any sound for the cause that prevents the gate from opening, but after having tried to force it he suddenly seems to understand; he goes around the wall, arrives at the other side of the gate, moves the armchair which holds it firm, and opens it with a triumphant expression. (Piaget, 1954, p. 296).

In a general way, therefore, at the sixth stage the child is now capable at causal deduction and is no longer restricted to perception of sensorimotor utilization of the relations of cause to effect. (Piaget, 1964, p. 297).

● Can you describe the concepts of object permanence and causality in your own words?

---

deal with life's demands. The development and use of each new schema through assimilation and accommodation is a reflection of the adaptive process that Piaget viewed as the development of intelligence.

Preoperational Thought Stage (Early Childhood–Early Elementary)

The ability to represent ideas in the form of symbols and signs, such as words and numbers, makes its appearance during this stage and helps distinguish the actual thinking of this stage from the mere sensory and physical coordinations of the preceding one. Piaget describes the four essential features of preoperational thought (Piaget, 1951, 1952; Piaget & Inhelder, 1969).

When teachers provide students with opportunities to explore concrete objects, students are able to modify their schemata.

Egocentrism

Egocentrism is a preoccupation with oneself and one's own particular point of view. Egocentric preoperational children cannot take another's point of view; they believe that everyone sees and thinks the same as they do. Moreover, preoperational children do not question their own thoughts, even when presented with evidence to the contrary. They believe, although not intentionally, that their ideas and perceptions are right. Hence, reasoning with them ranges from difficult to impossible. It is not uncommon for preoperational children to talk to themselves and to fail to listen to someone who is speaking to them.

Egocentrism is a factor that acts to limit development, and it manifests itself in some form in every stage. Just as the sensorimotor child initially is egocentric in failing to distinguish himself or herself as an object from other objects, the preoperational child is at first egocentric in failing to differentiate between his or her own thoughts and the thoughts of others. This tendency lessens as the child proceeds through this stage.

Centration

Centration occurs when the preoperational child, presented with a visual stimulus, tends to focus or *center* all of his attention on only one aspect or dimension of the stimulus at a time. Any thinking task is dominated by perception, or what things look like, since it is appearance on which the child is focused. Consider the following two arrays.

Array 1   Array 2

egocentrism

a preoccupation with oneself and one's own particular point of view

centration

when the preoperational child tends to focus or center all of his attention on only one aspect or dimension of a visual stimulus at a time

nontransformational reasoning

when the preoperational child focuses on the elements in a sequence or each successive state, not on the changes that have occurred between states or the final state

When asked which array has more objects, the preoperational child typically picks Array 2, even though it has fewer objects and she "knows" that. Array 2 is seen as having more because the child is centered on the appearance or length of the two arrays, that is, Array 2 *looks* longer.

Nontransformational Reasoning

The preoperational child does not focus on the transformation of an object from an original state to a final state. Instead, she focuses on the elements in the sequence or each successive state, not on the changes that have occurred between states, hence **nontransformational reasoning**. For example, when four-year-olds were shown a glass of water that was then poured into another glass hidden behind a screen, many correctly realized that the unseen glass had as much water in it as the original glass. However, when the water in the first glass was poured into a smaller glass that the children could see, they all said that the second, shorter glass held less water than the original (Bruner, 1964). The preoperational children focused only on the original state and the final state, disregarding the transformation between them. Nontransformational reasoning makes logical thinking impossible.

Irreversibility

According to Piaget (1954), **irreversibility**, the inability to reverse thought or follow a line of reasoning back to where it started, is one of the most important characteristics of this stage. In order to realize that something has changed in appearance but has not changed in amount, a child must be able to reverse the operation of change in his mind and mentally restore that object to its original appearance. If someone runs into your car and dents it, you can still tell that it is your car and you can still visualize what it looked like without the dent. This is because operational thinking enables you to reverse an event, to think backward. Preoperational thinking does not. For a preoperational child, thinking is irreversible. Once something has changed, it is a "new" thing, different from the original.

For example, if a preoperational child is given two equal rows of eight coins each, he or she will recognize that the two rows are equal. If one of the rows is lengthened while the child is watching, the child will perceive that the lengthened row has more coins (Wadsworth, 2004). The preoperational child cannot reverse or undo the lengthening in her mind to "see" that it still contains the same number of coins as *before*, only now they are further apart. The child at this stage cannot reverse an action, and so depends solely on perception or appearance to make judgments.

Piaget's four concepts of egocentrism, centration, nontransformational thinking, and irreversibility are closely related. When a child focuses on himself, judges things by a single dimension, and ignores the transformations or actions that cause things to change, it surely follows that he will be unable to do reverse thinking or to visualize something as it once was. Because physical reality usually goes in one direction only—forward—the preoperational child lacks physical models for reverse thinking. It is only when maturation and experience combine to help the child overcome these egocentric, centered, nontransformational patterns that the mental capability for reverse thought becomes possible.

irreversibility
the inability to reverse thought or follow a line of reasoning back to where it started

---

A Party for Children in the Preoperational Stage (Elementary School)

A group of high school students who were members of the student council in a K–12 school gave a small party for some kindergarten students. First, they played games, such as pin-the-tail-on-the-donkey and show and tell, which were supervised by the older students. The games made everyone hungry and thirsty, even the high school students, so next they prepared the table for refreshments.

The 15 high school students poured punch into different shaped glasses. There were 15 very wide glasses and 15 narrow glasses. They filled them so that the narrow glasses were filled just a bit higher

(Continued)

than the wide ones. When the kindergarten students went up to the table to get food and punch, they checked out the level of each glass. The kindergarten students quickly reached for the narrower glasses, laughing and saying that they had more punch than any of the high school students.

The high schoolers also served apples, and one of the kindergarten students wanted one. When asked whether he wanted it cut into six pieces or eight, he replied that he'd rather have it cut into *six* pieces because he "wasn't hungry enough to eat eight." To a kindergarten child, an apple cut into eight pieces represented more fruit than an apple cut into six pieces, just as a narrower, taller glass appeared to contain more punch than a wider, shorter glass.

Conservation: Three Different Types

Conservation is the development of a schema that enables a child to realize or recognize that the amount or quantity of something stays the same even when its shape or arrangement is changed, that is, regardless of changes in any dimension irrelevant to the amount or quantity (Wadsworth, 2004). (See Box 2.2.) *Conservation marks the transition from preoperational to concrete operational thought.* A child can conserve when he or she can recognize that the number of pennies or dots in each of two rows is the same, even when those in one row are further apart than those in the other row (as shown below). This is called **conservation of number.**

A child can also conserve when he or she recognizes that the area within two shapes is the same, even if the shapes are arrayed differently (as shown below). This is called **conservation of area.**

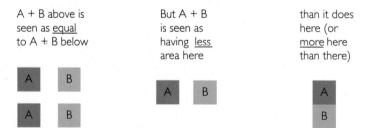

Finally, a child can conserve when he or she recognizes that the amount of water in two glasses of different shapes is actually the same, even though the level of one is higher (as shown below). This is called **conservation of volume.**

As the transition occurs from preoperational thought to concrete operational thought, the ability to conserve appears. It is not likely to appear while the child's thinking is strongly characterized by egocentrism, centration, nontransformational thinking, and irreversibility. This is because these patterns are antithetical to

conservation

the development of a schema that enables a child to realize or recognize that the amount or quantity of something stays the same even when its shape or arrangement is changed

conservation of number

recognizing that the number of objects are the same, even when those in one row are further apart than those in the other row

conservation of area

recognizing that the area within two shapes is the same, even if the shapes are arrayed differently

conservation of volume

recognizing that the amount of water in two glasses of different shapes is actually the same, even though the level of one is higher

These two look the same.

This one (tall glass) looks like more than this (wide glass) and this one (wide glass) looks like less than this (tall glass).

performing a mental operation like conservation, which is both logical and independent of the way things look. Therefore, the ability to conserve does not appear until near the end of the preoperational stage and does not become developed until the child enters the stage of concrete operations.

Thus, the emergence of conservation is a gradual process. It stretches from ages of about 5 to 6 when conservation of number appears to ages of about 11 or 12 when conservation of solid volume appears. Within this period, conservation of area and liquid volume appears (ages 7 to 8). Hence, conservation somewhat overlaps two developmental stages.

Also, Piaget contends that conservation ability cannot be taught directly and cannot be acquired until the child is ready developmentally. He believes that development of conservation depends on a combination of maturation and relevant direct experience that enables it to evolve spontaneously. However, others have shown that the mastery of conservation skills can be accelerated somewhat through teaching (Pasnak, Brown, Kurkjian, Triana, & Yamamoto, 1987; Halford & Andrews, 2006).

Think It Over

as a LEARNER What experience have you had with one or more children between the ages of 2 and 7 that illustrated the characteristics of the preoperational stage? How did you react to and feel about what the child or children did? Now that you have read about Piaget, what do you understand about the behavior you observed that you did not necessarily understand at the time?

as a TEACHER How would you go about teaching your developmentally ready students the concept of conservation?

Concrete Operational Stage (Elementary–Middle School)

This is the stage in which a child develops the capacity for logical operations, or thinking characterized by mental actions or internalized thoughts that are reversible and therefore allow a child to arrive at logical conclusions.

According to Piaget (1970), logical operations have four characteristics: (1) they are actions that can be carried out in the head, (2) they are reversible, (3) they assume some invariance or conservation, and (4) they are part of a system.

Up until this stage, the child's thinking has been rooted in the visible or perceptual world. *Any* discrepancy between perception and logic has been resolved in favor of perception. In this stage, thinking shifts to the cognitive, logical realm, enabling the child to solve concrete problems in his head. Concrete operational thinking is less egocentric and less centered than preoperational thinking. Moreover, it is both transformational and reversible, enabling the child to solve all varieties of conservation problems.

Clearly, concrete operational thought is more advanced and logical than preoperational thought. However, it still has its limitations. Its logic can be successfully applied only to real, observable objects in the immediate present (Piaget, 1972; Inhelder & Piaget, 1958). Its logic cannot be applied with the same degree of success to solve problems that are hypothetical or abstract, such as those that involve both multiple variables and the application of abstract principles.

Inversion and Compensation

One form of reversibility used by concrete operational children Piaget (1967) called **inversion**. Inversion is the application of reversibility to problems of order or sequence. Wadsworth (2004) reports on a study in which three Ping-Pong balls were put in a tube: first a black ball, then a white ball, then a striped ball. Both preoperational and concrete operational children realized that the balls would both exist within the tube and exit the tube in the same order in which they entered: (1) black, (2) white, and (3) striped. Then, the tube was inverted, turned upside down. Now, while the preoperational children still thought the balls would exit in the order they entered, the concrete operational children realized that because of inversion, the bails would exit in the opposite order: (1) striped, (2) white, and (3) black.

Concrete operational thinking also features a second kind of reversibility called **compensation**, which reflects the logic of one dimension compensating equally for another. When the liquid is poured from the short, squat container into the tall, thin one (as on page 57), the concrete operational child realizes that the amount of water is the same because the increased height of the container is compensated for by its narrowness. There is a relationship between height and width as they affect volume. If height goes up and width compensates for it by going down, then volume can remain the same.

Seriation

Seriation is the ability to mentally arrange a set of elements in increasing or decreasing order along some dimension such as size, weight, or volume. Researchers typically test this by having children arrange a set of sticks in order of length.

inversion

the application of reversibility to problems of order or sequence

compensation

reflects the logic of one dimension compensating equally for another

seriation

the ability to mentally arrange a set of elements in increasing or decreasing order along some dimension such as size, weight, or volume

Preoperational children, because of their inclination toward physical centering, tend to align the sticks according to the heights of their tops, with little regard to the alignment of their bottoms, as shown below.

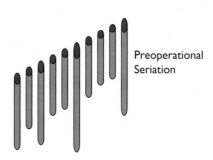

Preoperational
Seriation

Children at the stage of concrete operation order the sticks correctly by maintaining an equal alignment at the bottom, as shown below.

Concrete Operational
Seriation

To perform seriation correctly, children must understand the principle of *transitivity*. Transitivity, as illustrated in Figure 2.1, is the realization that if *B* is greater than *A* and *C* is greater than *B*, then *C* is greater than *A*. Using transitivity, a child would recognize in the example in the figure that the correct increasing order of the three quantities would be *A*, *B*, *C*.

FIGURE 2.1

Here is stick A ➡️   ⬅️ Here is stick B

1. Which one is longer, A or B?

Here is stick B ➡️   ⬅️ Here is stick C

(Cover up stick A.)

2. Which one is longer, B or C?

3. Which one is longer, A or C?

(Transitivity is required for students to be able to answer question 3.
Preoperational children are not likely to answer it correctly.)

Demonstrating the
Principle of Transitivity in
Solving Seriation Problems
(Concrete Operational
Stage)

Classification

Classification is the ability to put together objects that are alike, such as geometric shapes (Piaget, 1972; Piaget & Inhelder, 1969). To accomplish this task, children must understand the principle of *class inclusion,* namely, that objects of the same class or overlapping classes can be combined, and that a class includes all possible subclasses. Using a concept to label things that are alike in some respect—say, all kinds of fish—is an example of classification. Gagné (Chapter 12) included both concrete and defined concepts as categories of intellectual skills.

Consider this experiment by Piaget (1952): A child is given 20 brown wooden beads and two white wooden beads and is asked, Are there more wooden beads or more brown beads? Concrete operational children realize that the class "wooden beads" includes the classes of brown beads and white beads. There are 22 wooden beads (20 brown beads plus 2 white beads) compared to just 20 brown beads. The number in a total class includes the sum of the numbers in all of its distinct subclasses. This is class inclusion. Without this capability, preoperational children believe that brown beads outnumber wooden beads because they compare brown beads to white beads, not to total beads.

The concrete operational stage also features the development of the ability to combine dimensions such as time and distance, as illustrated in Figure 2.2.

F I G U R E 2 . 2

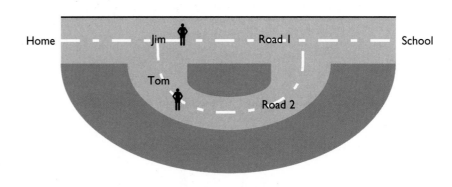

Demonstrating the Principle That Distance = Speed × Time (Concrete Operational Stage)

Tom and Jim are brothers. They leave home at the same time and arrive at school at the same time even though Jim takes Road 1 and Tom takes Road 2. Did they travel at the same speed? If not, which boy traveled faster? (Preoperational children are not likely to answer this correctly.)

Formal Operational Stage (High School-College)

In this stage, the student is able to reason in a logical manner using abstract schemata and can use this reasoning power to solve scientific problems (Moshman, 1998). However, not all students reach this stage of logical reasoning. Only about half of the U.S. student population attain this level of formal operations; the remainder stays in the preceding stage of concrete operations (Schwebel, 1975).

classification

the ability to put together objects that are alike

Whereas concrete thought is limited to solving tangible problems in the present, formal thought makes it possible to go beyond experience to solve complex, hypothetical problems like the ones illustrated later in this chapter. Using formal operations, a student can make hypotheses about what is going to happen based on general or abstract principles and then can test those hypotheses in a scientific manner.

According to Inhelder and Piaget (1958), formal operational schemata enable students to engage in (1) hypothetical deductive reasoning, that is, reasoning in which specific inferences or conclusions are drawn from a set of general premises; (2) scientific-inductive reasoning, or reasoning in which general conclusions are drawn from a set of specific facts; and (3) combinatorial reasoning, or reasoning about a number of variables at the same time. These processes cannot be carried out with concrete operational schemata.

Some of the formal operations of this stage are described below in the context of specific experiments conducted by Piaget and his coworkers to illustrate these operations (as reported by Inhelder & Piaget, 1958). These experiments can be recreated by both elementary and secondary school teachers in their classrooms to help their students discover and develop concrete and formal operations. (The discovery learning approach is also discussed in Chapter 12.)

The development of formal operational thinking brings with it the capacity to think abstractly and deductively.

Reciprocal Implication

The principle of compensation has already been introduced in conjunction with concrete operational thought. In solving conservation problems, the concrete operational child realizes that quantities can remain the same even though one dimension increases if a second dimension *compensates* for it by decreasing to the same degree. In formal thought, the conservation principle can be extended to more complex relationships in which one dimension is the reciprocal of the other, being equal to and opposite from it. This is illustrated in the billiard game experiment shown in Figure 2.3.

Balls are shot from a plunger and banked off a cushion in an effort to hit balls already positioned on the table. The operating principle, which the children must discover, is that the angle at which the ball hits the cushion (or angle of incidence) is equal to the angle at which the ball comes off the cushion (or angle of reflection). Each angle implies or leads to its own reciprocal or exact opposite. Preoperational children, in this as in all the experiments, can describe only what they see or what they do. For example, they say: "I think it works because it's in the same direction!" or "It always goes over there."

Concrete operational children discover the **concrete correspondence** between what they do and what results from their action. For example, they say: "The more I move the plunger this way—to the left—the more the ball will go like that—on

concrete correspondence

the correlation between what is done and what results from the action

FIGURE 2.3

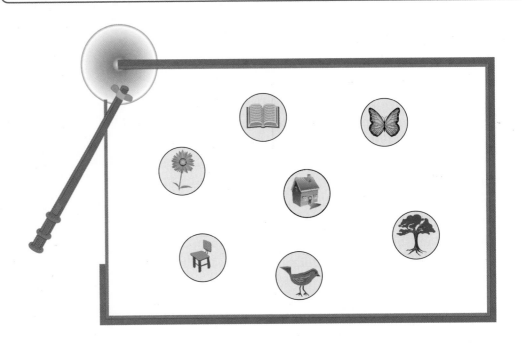

The Billiard Game

The principle of the billiard game is used to demonstrate the angles of incidence and reflection. The tubular spring plunger can be pivoted and aimed. Balls are launched from this plunger against the projection wall and rebound to the interior of the apparatus. The circled drawings represent targets placed successively at different points.

that sharp angle." It is only at the stage of formal operations that students discover and report that the two angles, the one striking the cushion and the one coming off it, are in fact, the same. They see the necessary reciprocity between the inclination of the plunger and the angle made by the trajectory of the ball off the cushion.

Separation of Variables

The flexibility experiment is used to illustrate the ability of formal operational students to separate out the independent effect of a number of variables at the same time. The idea is to control the effects of all of these variables at the same time, except one—the *independent variable*. The apparatus is shown in Figure 2.4. The rods can be (1) extended in length (long) or retracted (short); (2) thick or thin; (3) round or square in cross-section; (4) wood or metal; or (5) a light or heavy object at the unattached end. The objective is to determine which combination of these five variables yields the greatest flexibility, or bend. If each rod is thought of as a "diving board," the question becomes: "Which combination of variables would make a diving board that bends the most toward the water when jumped on?"

Again, preoperational children try random combinations and report what they see regardless of contradictions. For example, they say: "It doesn't work because it's too high!" Concrete operational students try different combinations but fail to see how one dimension compensates for another because they vary more than one dimension at a time. If the rods are made longer and thinner at the same time, it is impossible to tell whether both dimensions contribute to flexibility or if only one does. If a rod is made longer and thicker at the same time, and there

FIGURE 2.4

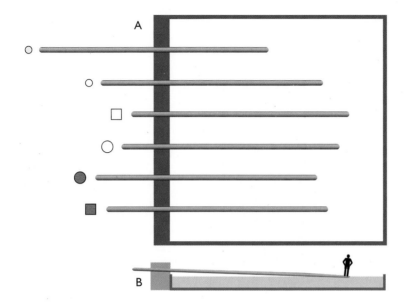

A

B

The Flexibility Experiment

Diagram A illustrates the variables used in the flexibility experiment. The rods can be shortened or lengthened by varying the point at which they are clamped (see A for apparatus used). Cross-section forms are shown at the left of each rod; shaded forms represent brass rods, unshaded forms represent nonbrass rods. Dolls are used for the weight variable (see B). These are placed at the end of the rod. Maximum flexibility is indicated when the end of the rod touches the water.

is no change in bend, the concrete operational student might think that neither matters; in fact, both do matter, but the changes actually are compensating for one another.

The key to solving this experiment is discovered by formal operational students. They see that the key is to separate variables by testing or *varying one variable or dimension at a time while holding all the others constant* (as in the description of experimental research, in Chapter 1). In this way, they can discover, for instance, that "a rod made of the same material as another thicker rod may bend an equal amount providing it is lengthened" (Inhelder & Piaget, 1958, p. 63). By being systematic and separating variables, these students figure out the extent to which one dimension can compensate for another.

Exclusion

The principle of exclusion is illustrated by the pendulum problem, shown in Figure 2.5. To create a pendulum, the teacher or researcher simply suspends a weight from a string. The student then causes the weight to move back and forth, or oscillate, by pulling it back and applying a force. The variables that can be changed are (1) the length of the string; (2) the amount of weight at the end; (3) the height of the dropping point, that is, the distance the weight is pulled back

FIGURE 2.5

The Pendulum Problem

The pendulum problem utilizes a simple apparatus consisting of a string, which can be shortened or lengthened, and a set of varying weights. The other variables that at first might be considered relevant are the height of the release point and the force of the push given by the subject.

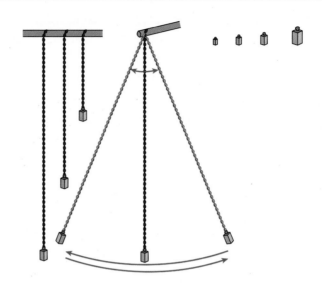

(see the dashed lines in the figure); and (4) the force with which the weight is pushed forward. The objective is to determine which variables affect the number of times the pendulum will swing back and forth (the frequency of oscillations is the number of swings per minute, not the size of the swing or how far the weight swings).

Think of the pendulum as a child's swing in the park. A parent is pushing the swing and wants to push it so that it swings back and forth the most number of times during the next full minute. The parent can vary (1) the length of the swing, by picking a short one or a long one; (2) the weight of the child (perhaps putting one child or two on the swing); (3) how far the swing is pulled back; and (4) how hard the swing is pushed forward. Which combination should the parent choose?

In this experiment, as in the preceding one with the bending rods, it is important that the student vary only one of the variables at a time, to avoid being misled by compensating relationships between variables. If length was increased and weight decreased, and length and weight happened to compensate for one another, the relationship would never be discovered because the result would be no change. Weight, pull distance, and push force must all be held constant while length is varied. Then length, pull distance, and push force must all be held constant while weight is varied, and so on, until each variable has been tested by itself, independent of the others. Only then can the effect of each variable be discovered. (Again, this is the basic principle of *experimental research* described in Chapter 1.)

The preoperational child cannot separate or dissociate the force he or she applies from the motion of the pendulum, which is independent of his or her action. For example, they say: "If you put it very high, it goes fast." The concrete operational student varies several variables at the same time and hence cannot separate those that have an effect from those that do not. For example, they say: "You have to try to give it a push, to lower or raise the string, to change the height and the weight."

It is only at the stage of formal operations that students realize they must vary only one variable at a time while holding the others constant. By so doing, they discover the principle of exclusion: that only the length of the string, not any of the other variables, affects the frequency of oscillations. For example, they are able to provide explanations such as: "When the string is short, the swing is faster." Three of the variables, or factors, must be excluded from the explanation because only the fourth variable—length of the string—affects the outcome, and this discovery can be made only if factors are tested one by one.

Piaget's four stages of development provide a model that can be used by teachers who teach students ranging from early childhood through elementary, middle, and high school (and even college). Piaget's ideas and experiments can help increase one's understanding of how students learn and grow.

A *Concept Review* of Piaget's four developmental stages appears in Table 2.2.

CONCEPT REVIEW TABLE 2.2
Piaget's Four Cognitive Development Stages

STAGE	APPROXIMATE AGE	OVERVIEW
Sensorimotor	0–2	Behavior is primarily motor, involving action schemata such as reaching and grasping. Circular reactions feature learning by repetition. Preverbal and prethinking. Ends with object permanence.
Preoperational	2–7	Development of language and prelogical thought. Focuses on self and own perspective with no ability to vary one's point of view. Unable to reverse operations.
Concrete Operations	7–11	Development of ability to apply logic on basis of concrete correspondence between event and explanation. Ability to conserve is developed.
Formal Operations	11–15	Thinking structures reach their highest level of development, making possible the use of logical reasoning. Can think out explanations for events by considering combinations of variables.

Think It Over

as a LEARNER   Do you feel you have attained the stage of formal operations? On what do you base your judgment?

as a TEACHER   What kinds of experiences, particularly in school, would you as a teacher be inclined to use in helping students reach this stage?

Applying Piaget to Educational Practice

If you were asked to derive some practical characteristics of the schooling process from the work of Piaget, what might they be? This section will be your guide.

Learning by Exploration

According to Piaget (1973), intellectual development depends on constructive activity, with all the errors that may result and the extra time that may be required. Assimilation and accommodation require an active learner, not a passive one, because problem-solving skills cannot be taught, they must be discovered (Piaget, 1958). Hands-on classroom activities are recommended for teaching students the operations appropriate to their level of development because they increase the likelihood that students will develop necessary problem-solving skills (Kamii and DeVries, 1978; Wadsworth, 2004).

Exploration also means experimentation. Building things, using things, trying them out, making them work, "playing" with them, and trying to answer questions

The Piagetian inspired classroom is divided into learning centers where students explore individual or small-group work on specific projects with various learning materials and activities.

Ariel Skelley/Blend Images/Jupiter Images

about how and why they work is the essence of Piaget's approach to development. The opposite of his approach is simply transmitting knowledge to students verbally in lecture or "cookbook" form.

Lesson plans based on Piaget's work would not be simple summaries of content to be transmitted. They would include activities for children to engage in, demonstrations for them to watch, and questions for them to answer. Student roles would be both active and self-directed, much more like the model of discovery learning than the model of direct instruction or most of the other models described in Chapter 12. Because of its emphasis on active learning and the construction of knowledge, Piaget's approach can best be described as an example of constructivism (Wadsworth, 2004). We will have more to say about constructivism in Chapter 8.

Learner-centered Orientation

In this teaching approach, the learner—rather than the curriculum or any national testing program—would be the basis for devising classroom instruction. Instructional choices, rather than a strictly defined or prescribed set of skills to be mastered, would reflect where the individual learner was in the developmental sequence. The learner-centered orientation would also be reflected in the approach to evaluation, which would be individualized and based primarily on observation rather than on any large-scale or lockstep testing program. Much learning would take place individually or in small groups engaged in different learning activities or tasks rather than through whole-class instruction, with the teacher available to answer individual questions and to function as a guide.

Kevin Summers/Photographer's Choice/Getty Images

The process of educating children would be oriented toward their self-controlled engagement with learning materials, and the physical structure of the classroom would be designed to enhance student activity and self-direction. The learner-centered classroom would be divided into learning centers where students would interact directly with a set of specific learning materials. Students would move from center to center to be exposed to and learn about different ideas.

One way to provide students with activities in conjunction with learning centers is to provide **task cards**. Each task card presents students with a concrete activity that enables them to apply many of the Piagetian processes appropriate to their grade level. Tasks should be relevant to the children's experiences, inherently motivating to do, and connected to topics and content important for the children to learn. Examples of task cards are shown in Box 2.3.

A learning center might be a place where a student can listen to a favorite story—learning to connect the words he hears with the words he sees.

Use of Themes

Applying Piaget to educational practice produces a curricular emphasis less on discrete subject matter knowledge and more on integrated, interdisciplinary topics or themes. Themes like probability, trees, ecology, the family, and the automobile provide vehicles for learning about and using science, mathematics, social science, and language arts in an integrated way. With a thematic approach, it is the process of acquiring information, rather than the information itself, that takes on

task cards

activity cards that provide students with activities in conjunction with learning centers

Box 2.3

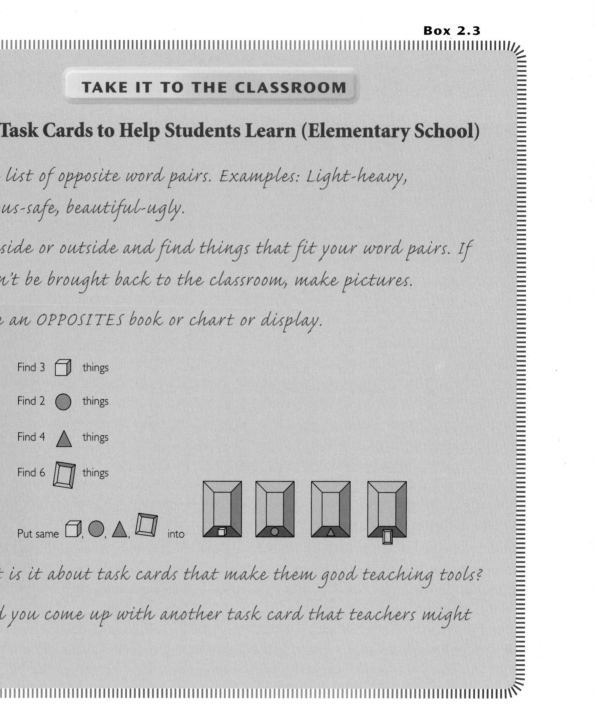

TAKE IT TO THE CLASSROOM

Using Task Cards to Help Students Learn (Elementary School)

Make a list of opposite word pairs. Examples: Light-heavy, dangerous-safe, beautiful-ugly.

Go inside or outside and find things that fit your word pairs. If they can't be brought back to the classroom, make pictures.

Make an OPPOSITES book or chart or display.

Find 3 ☐ things

Find 2 ● things

Find 4 ▲ things

Find 6 ▱ things

Put same ☐, ●, ▲, ▱ into

- What is it about task cards that make them good teaching tools?

- Could you come up with another task card that teachers might use?

the greatest importance. In other words, the important skills become the "how-to" skills. Figure 2.6 shows a flowchart for a unit on the theme of family.

Focus on Development of Schemata

At the appropriate time developmentally, instruction in mathematics and science in particular would focus on helping children develop and use schemata to aid their problem solving (see Chapter 8). In the early and middle elementary grades,

FIGURE 2.6

Flowchart for the Theme "Family"

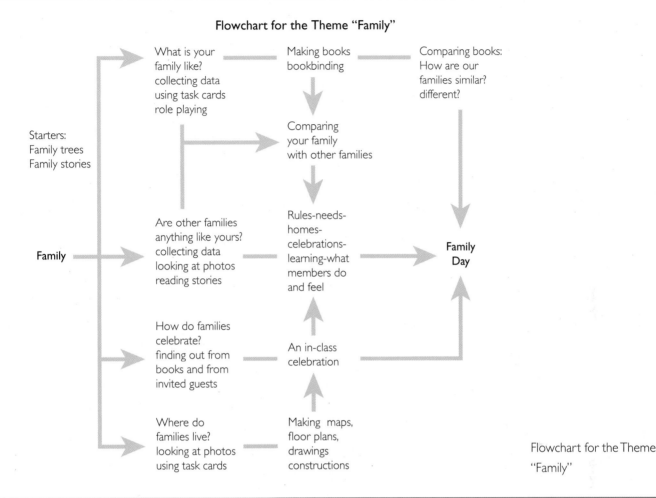

Flowchart for the Theme "Family"

for example, children could be taught to solve conservation problems correctly (Gelman & Gallistel, 1978), or even problems involving proportional reasoning (Fujimora, 2001). In the late elementary and early middle grades, the conceptual focus would be on tasks involving seriation, classification, inversion, compensation, and the use of concrete correspondence. Starting in the final grades of middle school and extending through high school, the emphasis would be on teaching logical reasoning and critical thinking rather than on rote memorization of facts and formulas. In every instance, the teaching focus would be on helping students to develop schemata that would enable them to understand and explain phenomena in the world around them.

Some examples of teaching concrete correspondence through measurement and comparison in the elementary grades are shown in Figure 2.7. Such measurement activities help children develop the various schemata required for concrete operations. For the development of formal operational schemata, experiments patterned after those described on the preceding pages can be used.

FIGURE 2.7

Examples of Teaching Concrete Correspondence
Through Measurement and Comparison

Make a list of things
that appear to be
impossible to count...
then count one of
them.

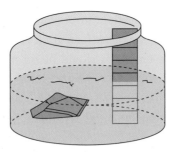

Volume of stone (a) is 3 "spinks"

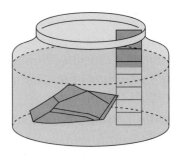

Volume of stone (b) is 4½ "spinks"

Stone (b) is larger — 4½ : 3
4½ − 3 = 1½

FIGURE 2.7

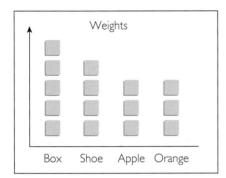

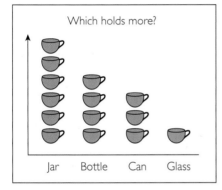

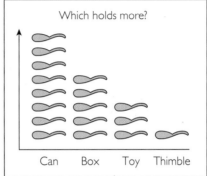

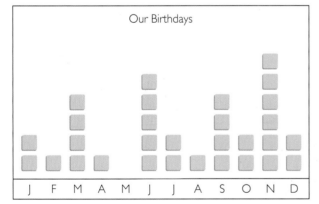

Examples of Teaching Concrete Correspondence Through Measurement and Comparison

Think It Over

as a LEARNER Can you think of a recent educational experience you have had that illustrates some aspect of Piaget's theory? How does thinking of and remembering the experience better help you understand Piaget's theory?

as a TEACHER Can you think of one or two ways that you would use Piaget's theory in your instruction?

A Critique and Updating of Piaget's Theory

Piaget's theory of cognitive development is rich in descriptive detail and deals with a wide array of situations. Its conception of developmental stages has survived scrutiny for many decades. Many of its concepts are currently in use today, and many of its findings have been supported by more recent research (Siegler & Alibali, 2005).

One aspect of Piaget's theory, however, has been contradicted by new studies, namely descriptions of the cognitive capabilities of infants and young children. Work from Baillargeon (2004), Cohen & Cashon (2006), and Gelman (1990) and others show that aspects of concepts such as object permanence and conservation appear earlier than proposed by Piaget. While accurately describing these concepts, Piaget's observations reflected a tendency to underestimate their age of origin.

Clear demarcation between the stages is another aspect of the theory that has not been entirely supported by newer studies. For example, Siegler & Alibali (2005) report findings that search skills required for locating lost or hidden objects develop over a long period, stretching from ages 1 to 4. On more advanced conservation tasks, while characteristic ways of reasoning have been associated with specific narrow age ranges, ages at which specific problems are solved tend to vary more than suggested by Piaget's work. Moreover, some research suggests that children can learn more than supposed by Piaget, depending on the task and the nature of the instruction provided (Beilin, 1977). A review of studies showed that when a task is simplified, some students at the elementary school level are able to solve relatively abstract problems (Metz, 1995).

Research also suggests that today's high school students may not demonstrate **formal operational thinking skills** comparable to those reported by Piaget (Kuhn & Franklin, 2006). However, if training in these skills is provided, students have been found to reach higher levels of reasoning at a faster rate than reported by Piaget (Kuhn, 2006).

Finally, Piaget has been criticized for failing to consider the **influence of culture** on development, since culture has a pervasive effect on children's language, experience, and interactions (Halford & Andrews, 2006; Rogoff, 2003). Vygotsky's theory, covered in the next section, makes up for this with its heavy emphasis on cultural factors.

Despite these shortcomings, Piaget's theory still merits our close attention because it provides a clear, overall view of how children think. It also helps to identify questions about children's cognitive development that remain to be answered.

Extensive work to update Piaget's theory was done by Case (1985). His description of the four stages is similar to Piaget's but with the preoperational stage renamed "representational operations" and the concrete operational stage renamed "logical operations." His view of the developmental sequence is also similar to Piaget's. However, he differs somewhat in his idea that children's thinking is organized into three central conceptual structures or internal networks of concepts that focus on numbers, space, and stories (Case & Griffin, 1990). The greatest difference between Case and Piaget is Case's incorporation of the information-processing approach (which you will

formal operational thinking skills

ability to reason in a logical manner using abstract schemata, and to solve scientific problems

influence of culture

the effect that culture has on children's language, experience, and interactions

encounter in Chapter 7). Case (1985) proposes that working memory functions with increasing efficiency as children develop, based on amount of practice and biological maturation, the latter resulting in changes in electrical activity in the brain (Case, 1992).

The Developmental Psychology of Lev Vygotsky

Lev Vygotsky studied the development of children's thinking from the 1920s until his death in 1937 from tuberculosis at age 37. His work ultimately became well known in the 1970s and 1980s when it was translated into English from Russian (Vygotsky, 1978; 1987a; 1987b). He proposed that adults contribute to the cognitive development of children by helping them perform challenging tasks, and then talking with them about the experiences. In particular, Vygotsky emphasized the importance of society and culture in promoting children's cognitive growth, thus leading his approach to be regarded as a **sociocultural perspective**. His main ideas are described in the following sections.

Social Interaction: Its Critical Role in Acquiring Meaning

Social interaction with adults, such as parents and teachers, was proposed by Vygotsky (1978) as the way children learn about the meanings and cultural interpretations associated with objects, events, and experiences. In particular, language—either spoken or written—is what mediates between the situations encountered and the meanings they convey, but music, art, or various kinds of symbols can help play that role as well. This is regarded as the **social construction** (or co-construction) **of meaning**, and represents the foundation of Vygotsky's approach.

For example, when an adult reads a book to a child, explaining and answering questions as he or she goes along, certain aspects of the book—such as situations, characters, actions, and consequences—take on meaning to the child in his or her social and cultural context. This represents an informal way to provide information and interpretations, in contrast to the formal ways used by teachers through lessons and projects and other classroom-related activities. A teacher bringing her collection of Mexican art to class to illustrate aspects of Mexican life and culture, for example, can help to convey meaning to her students of the relation between art and the values and interests of the people who make it.

Internalization: Evolving of Social Activities into Mental Activities

In addition to learning meaning, according to Vygotsky the **cognitive tools** for acquiring meaning also come from the social interaction process, through the process of **internalization**. As a result of internalization, children begin to give themselves the instructions to guide their behaviors that heretofore have been provided by others. Thought and language, to Vygotsky, start out as independent functions in young children, but eventually become intertwined. In other words, what started as **social speech** (talking to others) is transformed into **self-talk** or **private speech** (talking aloud to oneself), and ultimately into **inner speech** ("talking" to oneself mentally rather than aloud).

sociocultural perspective
the importance of society and culture in promoting children's cognitive growth

social construction of meaning
what mediates between situations encountered and the meanings they convey

cognitive tools
tools used to acquire meaning

internalization
children begin to give themselves the instructions to guide their behaviors that heretofore have been provided by others

social speech
talking to others

self-talk or private speech
talking aloud to oneself

inner speech
"talking" to oneself mentally rather than aloud

The Role of Language and Other Cultural Tools

According to Vygotsky, in addition to social interaction, human behavior is affected by culture, the context in which development occurs (Glassman, 2001). Culture provides **cultural tools**, including technical tools (that act on the environment) and psychological tools (that facilitate thinking) passed on from generation to generation. Cultural tools help children make sense of the world.

An important cultural tool proposed by Vygotsky is language, which can be used by children for a variety of mental functions such as regulating behavior, solving problems, and understanding the world around them. Language, particularly talking to themselves, gives children a means for reflecting on their own thinking (Winsler & Naglieri, 2003). When children articulate their experiences or explain the actions of other children, both their learning and development are positively affected (Pine & Messer, 2000). Vygotsky (1978) claimed that the time when language and action are integrated "is the most significant moment in the course of intellectual development" (p. 24).

Additional psychological tools that have evolved include maps, number systems, programming languages, calendars, and clocks, which help children organize and remember information. Material artifacts, such as books, abacuses, rosary beads, and Lego blocks, represent other psychological tools available to children (Siegler & Alibali, 2005).

We will discuss the development of language further in the last section of this chapter.

Zone of Proximal Development and Scaffolding: Role of Others in Facilitating Independent Performance

Vygotsky distinguished between the level of tasks children can perform without any help (*actual development*) and the level of tasks they can perform with assistance from someone more competent, either adult or peer (*potential development*).

cultural tools

technical tools (that act on the environment) and psychological tools (that facilitate thinking) passed on from generation to generation

The range of tasks between actual development and potential development is called the zone of proximal development (ZPD). This teacher is helping a student progress through the ZPD by providing support called scaffolding.

Nicola Armstrong/Alamy

The range of tasks that lie between these two levels was labeled by Vygotsky as the **zone of proximal development**. The very basis of cognitive development, in Vygotsky's view, is social collaboration between adults and children, or children and more competent peers, in enabling children to successfully complete tasks that lie within the their zone of proximal development.

The concepts of the zone of proximal development and the social collaboration that helps students to constantly move through it can play an important role in designing school environments.

Scaffolding to Help Children Grow

The key to enabling children to continually proceed through their zone of proximal development, which advances every time the next level of potential is reached, is assistance provided by others—namely adults such as teachers or more competent peers. This often is provided by a technique referred to as **scaffolding**. (This, and the other techniques briefly described in this section, will be covered in more detail in Chapter 8.) You may be familiar with this term in another context. In building construction, painting, and window cleaning, workers gain access to otherwise inaccessible parts of the structure by standing on wooden frames called "scaffolding." As sections of the building are completed, scaffolding are taken down. When

zone of proximal development

the range of tasks that lie between *actual development* and *potential development*

scaffolding

assistance provided by others that enables children to proceed through their zone of development

TeachSource
Video Case

Vygotsky's Zone of Proximal Development: Increasing Cognition in an Elementary Literacy Class

In this video segment, you'll be introduced to the concept of the "zone of proximal development" and how it can be used in the classroom. You'll see how a teacher uses this approach to support students' abstract thinking in a lesson on poetry, and experience their writing samples.

After viewing the video case, consider what you have just watched about Vygotsky's zone of proximal development and its impact on cognition and answer the questions below:

1. Did the video help you understand the concept of the zone of proximal development? In what way did it help?
2. How did the pieces of poetry the teacher selected help the students understand the concepts she was trying to teach them?
3. How might you use poetry and the zone of proximal development to help your students develop cognitively?

You can view the video case at the Education CourseMate. Go to:
CengageBrain.com

a teacher helps students recognize shapes, solve a puzzle, or complete some other task, the teacher is providing scaffolding. When students reach the point where they can recognize the shapes, solve the puzzle, or complete the task, the teacher no longer provides help, hence the scaffolding "comes down." See Table 2.3 for a *Concept Review* of Vygotsky's theory of development.

CONCEPT REVIEW TABLE 2.3
Vygotsky's Theory of Development

MAJOR CONCEPTS	WHAT IT MEANS
Social Construction of Meaning	Teachers, parents, and peers interact with children to help them learn and develop.
Internalization: Changing Social Activities into Mental Activities	Children giving themselves instruction to guide their own behavior. Transforming social speech into inner speech.
Language and Other Cultural Tools	Using language and cultural context as psychological tools for problem solving, reflection, and understanding.
Zone of Proximal Development (ZPD)	The range of tasks that lies between those children can perform on their own and those they can perform only with assistance.
Scaffolding	Adults and/or peers helping children proceed through their ZPD.

Applying Vygotsky to Teaching

Below is a list of techniques for teaching and working with children and adolescents that are suggested by Vygotsky's ideas.

1. *Provide learners with challenging tasks.* Students will not be placed in a zone of proximal development, nor scaffolding made possible, if they are not confronted by tasks that initially require assistance to perform.
2. *Have learners work cooperatively on tasks.* In this way, more competent peers will be able to assist those with less competence. (We will encounter this again in Chapter 9.)
3. *Provide learners with cognitive models.* These models can be teachers or peers who can be observed performing the task while providing verbal instructions. Learners can internalize these instructions and give them to themselves. (This will come up again in Chapter 6.)

4. *Provide learners with opportunities to work on tasks likely to be encountered in the real world* (such as planning a budget or repairing a broken toy). These opportunities help learners relate what they are learning in school to real life situations, and provide additional opportunities for scaffolding.

5. *Relate your instructional style to the cultural background of learners.* Vygotsky emphasizes the relevance of the learner's cultural context, since learning does not occur in isolation from it. Tharp (1989) has shown, for example, that Hawaiian, Anglo, and Navajo students react differently to various styles of instruction: Hawaiian children prefer collaborative activities while Navajo children prefer to wait their turn.

A comparison of the application of Piaget's and Vygotsky's theories appears in Table 2.4.

Think It Over

as a LEARNER
What are some specific ways you have been taught that reflected Vygotsky's ideas about development?

as a TEACHER
In what way do you see yourself applying Vygotsky's approach as a teacher? Think of some specific examples.

CONCEPT REVIEW TABLE 2.4
Comparing the Application of Piaget's and Vygotsky's Theories in the Classroom

APPLYING PIAGET	APPLYING VYGOTSKY
Provide opportunities for play and communicating through symbols (e.g., writing, drawing).	Use guided participation, apprenticeship, modeling, and verbal cues.
Use actual experiences and concrete objects as tools for learning concepts.	Give students increasing responsibility for doing activities on their own.
Encourage students to follow their interests and experiment (i.e., hands-on learning).	Use peers as role models and promote collaboration in exploring ideas.
Provoke students to examine alternative explanations for their experiences and to share feedback with peers.	Provide instructional support within the zone of proximal development and then gradually reduce such support.

Learning Objective 7

Describe language developement, including the concept of phonology, meaning, grammer, and communication, and illustrate how language developement can be facilitated in the classroom and English language learners accommodated.

Language Development

Children engage in a wide variety of mental activities that help them produce and understand speech. Based on what they hear, they are able to divide speech into individual words. Hearing other people talk and having the ability to imitate what they hear enables children to learn how to pronounce words correctly. Moreover, children pay attention to what they hear and can remember the order of words in particular phrases. Most particularly, children attend to the meanings of words, both the meanings they want to convey and the meanings other people are trying to convey to them. Phrases become expanded into sentences and gradually language, a tool for functioning in a social world, is acquired. This process is facilitated by others: parents, siblings, other children, teachers, and other adults.

Four Main Aspects of Language

We now examine the four main aspects of language: phonology, meaning, grammar, and communication. (See Table 2.5 for a *Concept Review* of these four aspects.)

CONCEPT REVIEW TABLE 2.5

The Four Main Aspects of Language

ASPECT	WHAT IT MEANS
Phonology	The production and comprehension of speech sounds in a language, and the tacit or unstated rules governing pronunciation; it represents the knowledge of how words are pronounced.
Meaning	The relationship between words and what they describe; what a person is trying to express; understanding and producing words; acquiring a vocabulary.
Grammar	The ordering of words into sentences (also referred to as **syntax**), and the specification of tense and number; the sentences themselves are the basic unit of grammar.
Communication	The ultimate purpose of language; using phonology, meaning, and grammar to impart information, interchange thoughts and opinions, express intentions or needs, and elicit reactions.

Phonology

Phonology deals with the distribution and patterning of speech sounds in a language and the tacit, or unstated, rules governing pronunciation. In other words, phonology represents the knowledge of how words are pronounced. Turning sounds into language is affected by the difficulty in making particular sounds. The progression of sounds made by babies follows a typical pattern (Kent & Miulo, 1995): (1) crying (from birth), presumably to communicate that they want something, with parents attempting to infer what it is they want (usually from the context); (2) cooing (between 1 and 2 months); resembles the *uh* sound (as in the word *fun*); (3) simple articulation (at about 3 months), increase in consonant sounds; (4) babbling (at about 6 months), production of syllables (e.g., bababba); (5) patterned speech (at about 1 year), less babbling, first words.

Achieving phonological competence requires considerable practice; usually, it is not achieved until school age. Before that, pronunciation is inconsistent, in that the same words may sometimes be pronounced correctly and other times incorrectly. Some sounds, like *sh* and *th,* are difficult to make. Leonard (1995) reports that toddlers with small vocabularies, when choosing a word from among options, tend to select words that are easiest to pronounce. But once children are able to make a particular sound, they tend to use words that include that sound (Vihman, 1992). Rvachew, Chiang, and Evans (2007) found that children who enter kindergarten with age-appropriate pronunciation skills also achieve age-appropriate phonological skills, that is, the ability to distinguish and blend parts of speech by sound. They recommend that teachers monitor children who enter kindergarten with delayed pronunciation skills to ensure age-appropriate development of phonological awareness, a predictor of literacy.

Meaning

Between 12 and 18 months of age, children acquire a small vocabulary of single words; the most common are *dada, mama, juice, milk, cookie, water, dog, cat, shoes, ball, car, bottle,* and *more* (Nelson, 1996). Because the difficulty of pronunciation limits the **meaning** that they express, toddlers usually speak in single words. But the single words usually convey meanings beyond the word itself. The single words are called *holophrases,* since they have extended meanings. If the toddler wants *juice,* for example, he or she will simply say *juice* rather than *I want juice* (Greenfield & Smith, 1976). The word *juice,* by itself, conveys the meaning of what the toddler wants.

Children's vocabulary more than doubles between the ages of 18 and 21 months, and doubles again between 21 and 24 months. By first grade, a typical child understands at least 10,000 words; and by fifth grade, 40,000 words (Anglin, 1993). Learning at such a fast pace means that children must determine the meanings of new words on the basis of being exposed to them a relatively small number of times, for example, only 10 times for a one-year-old (Woodward, Markman, and Fitzsimmons, 1994).

Markman (1992) hypothesized that children's guesses as to the meaning of a word are based on the belief that when told the name of an object, the name refers to the whole object rather than one of the object's features or properties

Polka Dot/Jupiter Images

Teachers help students to develop phonemic awareness, which will help them attain literacy.

Virtual Psychology Lab

What is it like to be a struggling reader? In your career as a teacher you will work with students who will struggle with literacy. When you go to the *Stroop Effect Virtual Psychology Lab,* you will have an opportunity to participate in a classic experiment in psychology where you can see the direct impact of cognitive mechanisms like attention and automaticity. It is interesting to note that only experienced readers exhibit the Stroop Effect. Why do you suppose that is? Go to CengageBrain.com to access this Virtual Psychology Lab in the Education CourseMate.

phonology

the distribution and patterning of speech sounds in a language and the tacit, or unstated, rules governing pronunciation

meaning

the relationship between words and what they describe; what a person is trying to express

(e.g., color). She called this the *whole-object constraint*. She also hypothesized that children's judgment of the meaning of a word is based on the belief that when a new word is used to label an object, for example, a German Shepard called a "dog," the word also applies to other objects of the same class, for example, a collie called a "dog." Markman termed this the *taxonomic constraint*. Finally, she hypothesized that when children hear an unfamiliar word that might refer to one of two objects, and they already know a name for one of them, the first guess they tend to make is that the unfamiliar object word applies to the object whose name they do not know. She called this the *mutual-exclusivity constraint*. For example, if three-year-olds already know the word *plate* but not the word *platter* and are asked "Point to the platter," more often than not they point to the platter (Markman & Wachtel, 1998).

As students become more proficient in language skills, they become capable of thinking about the nature of language itself; this is called **metalinguistic awareness**. An example of this would be understanding the nonliteral meanings of words and expressions and the symbolism associated with them.

Grammar

Grammar represents rules for forming sentences (also referred to as **syntax**); in most of the world's languages, these rules are highly complex. The sentences themselves, therefore, are the basic unit of grammar. Examples of two grammatical conventions are to form past tenses and to ask questions. For most verbs in the English language, the past tense is produced by adding *ed* to the infinitive, for example, *carried*, *spilled*, *helped*. But there are many exceptions such as *eaten*, *heard*, *went*, *ran*. Once children learn the *ed* rule, they tend to use it not only in cases where it fits, but also in cases where it does not fit, for example, *eated*, *runned* (Marchman & Bates, 1994). The ability to use the correct past-tense form appears at about age 7 (Kuczaj, 1978).

After children start using two-word phrases, they begin to learn common grammatical forms for asking questions, often beginning with the question: "What dat?" (Reich, 1986) and following soon after with "where" questions ("Where shoe?"), yes–no questions ("Go home?"), and questions involving doing ("What Nanny doing?"). Abbreviated questions grow over time into more grammatical ones.

Pinker (1984) proposed that children's learning of grammar is based on what may be called **semantic bootstrapping**. That is, children first identify the person or thing that produces the action, then the name of the action, and lastly the person or thing affected by the action. They then use these common categories of meanings in the sentences they hear to form rules for ordering words in sentences. This works because grammatical categories tend to be associated with particular meanings. For example, names are nouns, actions are verbs, and attributes or properties are adjectives. In sentences such as "Mrs. Prim opened the door" the actor is named at the beginning of the sentence, the action is in the middle, and the recipient of the action is at the end. This agent-action-recipient framework enables children to order words in sentences.

metalinguistic awareness
being capable of thinking about the nature of language itself

grammar or syntax
rules for forming sentences

semantic bootstrapping
first identifying the actor, then the action, and lastly the person affected by the action to form rules for ordering words in sentences

Communication

At about the age of 8 or 9, the majority of students have mastered the sounds of English, but not necessarily the idea of the listener's point of view as compared to their own (McDevitt & Ford, 1987). The latter is especially important in communicating effectively. Equally important are the social conventions or rules of etiquette as applied to carrying out conversations, called **pragmatics**. Some examples include not interrupting someone when they are talking and knowing how to change the topic of conversation and how to present an argument. A lack of these skills can affect a student's relationships with teachers and peers. As students develop, though, they become more aware of taking into account those with whom they are communicating (Sonnenschein, 1988).

Communication is also affected by visual access to one's communication partner. Alibali and Don (2001) found that kindergartners use more gestures when speaking to someone face-to-face than to someone sitting behind a curtain. As more and more communication is done by cell phone, visual access may become an important factor.

Language and Thinking

Siegler (1998) raises the following question about the relationship between language and thinking: "Does children's learning of new words trigger the formation of new concepts, or does ability to understand new terms demand that the relevant concepts already be in place?" (p. 169) In other words, do you need the words to learn the concepts or do you need the concepts to learn the words? Three alternative positions present themselves.

The first alternative explanation is that *language shapes thought*, that a culture's language shapes the way members of that culture interpret information about the

pragmatics
the social conventions or rules of etiquette as applied to carrying out conversations

Students' language develops through experience with teachers and peers.

Chris Cheadle/Stone/Getty Images

world, and that cultural differences produce differences in the way members of each culture view the world (Sapir, 2004).

The second possible explanation is just the reverse; that *thought shapes language*. Piaget (1926) proposed that representational ability—the ability to represent objects and events at the beginning of the preoperational stage—makes possible the development of language. Thus, Piaget believed that language development required the necessary cognitive development rather than cognitive development requiring the necessary language development.

Finally, the third possible explanation is a combination of the first two, that is, *language and thought influence each other*. According to Vygotsky (1962), at first language and thought develop independently, but then they begin to influence each other. The child's thoughts become expressed in language, and language begins to influence thoughts and actions with thought becoming internalized language. The evidence tends to favor the third explanation (Siegler, 1998).

Is Language Special?

Siegler and Alibali (2005) raise the question "Is language special?" and indicate that it is based on the fact that "the vast majority of children learn language rapidly and well" (p. 186). But the question of *why* still remains. An answer proposed by noted linguist Chomsky (1972) was that we have a *language organ* that facilitates language acquisition. Without a language organ, it seems inconceivable that children could learn something as complicated as language just based on hearing it from others. Chomsky further argued that the language organ enables children to recognize the type of grammar, that is, rules for forming sentences, of their native language, and, despite its complexity, learn it fairly easily. MacWhinney (2002) agreed with Chomsky's claim that language was special, not because learning grammar is innate, but because of neutral, cognitive, and social factors that have evolved over time.

Siegler and Alibali (2005) identify three types of evidence to support the claim that learning language differs from other forms of learning and hence is special. First, acquiring language is *universal*; it occurs across a variety of environments, at a rapid rate, and in a wide variety of cultures ranging from those where children are encouraged to converse with adults to those where such conversing is not customary or even acceptable. Second, in comparison to other comparable skills, language learning is *self-motivating*, that is, virtually all children are interested enough in language to master it, primarily in order to communicate. The desire to learn language seems inherent in people. Third, a comparison of children with Down Syndrome and Williams Syndrome, disorders that affect thinking in general, reveals that the language skills of children with Williams Syndrome tend to be much greater than those of children with Down Syndrome, while the reverse is true for thinking skills (Vicari et al., 2002). This suggests that language development is independent of other aspects of cognitive development.

Facilitating Language Development in the Classroom

The American Speech-Language and Hearing Association recommends the following techniques for improving children's language abilities (De Maio, 2000; Evans, 2007):

- Modeling—you can restate a child's comment by adding words to make the child's comment more mature and grammatically correct. For example, if a child says: "Him talking," you can model: "Yes, he is talking."
- Expansion—you can add information to a child's comment, thus showing the child how to use more advanced vocabulary and language structures. For example, if a child says: "The ball is rolling," you can expand by saying: "Yes, the red, rubber ball is rolling very quickly."
- Self-Talk—you can talk about what you are doing at the same time you are doing it. For example, you put a jigsaw puzzle together and say: "First, I pick up a puzzle piece and try to fit it into the pieces of the puzzle that have already been put together. If it doesn't fit, I'll try another piece. Now let's see if we can fit this piece I am holding in my hand into the puzzle."
- Parallel Talk—you can talk about what the child is doing while she is involved in an activity. For example, as the child puts the next piece in the puzzle, you can say: "You just picked the large blue piece with a part of the moon on it and tried to see if it fit into the other part of the moon, which is already in the puzzle! Yes, it did fit in, right!"

It has also been suggested that teachers can promote students' language development by (1) encouraging them to describe verbally what they are learning, particularly in mathematics and science (Gauvain, 2001) and (2) creating a supportive emotional climate to help them articulate what they are learning (Kuhn & Dean, 2004).

DISCOURSE ON DIVERSITY

Facilitating Language Development for Inner-City Children (Elementary)

BOX 2.4

A deficiency in language has been overwhelmingly reported by kindergarten teachers as the problem that most restricts children's school readiness (Boyer, 1991). To overcome this deficiency among inner-city children, Hadley, Simmerman, Long, & Luna (2000) completed a study to determine whether kindergarten and first-grade children enrolled in two English-language-enriched (experimental) classrooms designed to enhance the development of vocabulary and phonological awareness skills would show greater vocabulary development and phonological awareness and letter-sound associations than children enrolled in two standard practice (control) classrooms.

There were 46 students distributed among the two experimental classes and 40 students distributed among the two control classes. Overall, 83 percent of the students were economically disadvantaged, that is, they qualified for free or reduced school lunches. The participants' ethnicities included 56 percent Hispanic Americans, 28 percent Caucasians, 3 percent African Americans, 7 percent Native Americans, and 6 percent Asian Americans. The native languages of the students were 37 percent English and 47 percent Spanish, with the remainder divided up among eight different languages; 41 percent had limited English proficiency.

Each of the four classrooms had a regular education teacher. In addition, each of the two experimental classrooms had a certified speech-language pathologist for 2 ½ days per week while each of the control classrooms had a paraprofessional for 2 ½ days per week. The two experimental classrooms used a collaborative service delivery model, including joint curriculum planning with a language focus on a weekly basis between the two teachers and the speech-language pathologist. Most importantly, teachers in these two classrooms focused on strategies to increase students' vocabulary and phonological awareness while teachers in the two control classrooms followed their existing curricular plans.

The results showed that, at the end of the six-month period, children in the experimental classrooms showed significantly greater gains in vocabulary, beginning sound awareness, and letter-sound associations than children in the control classrooms. These results demonstrate that the use of a collaborative teaching model with a focus on improving vocabulary and phonological awareness indeed facilitate the language abilities of inner-city children at risk for academic difficulties in the early elementary grades.

SUMMING IT UP

Learning Objective 1

Key Concepts:

axon, cell body, neuron, synapse, terminal button, neurotransmitter, left and right hemisphere of brain, lateralization (p. 44); brain-based learning (p. 45).

Explain general principles of development and the relationship between the brain and cognitive development.

Development is a continuous and relatively orderly process, affected by both heredity and environment and contributed to by learning, experience, and social interaction; all children do not develop at the same rate. The primary cells of the brain are **neurons** that consist of the **cell bodies**, **dendrites**, and **axons** (the tips of the latter are called **terminal buttons**). When dendrites are stimulated, the neuron fires, causing an impulse to traverse the space called a **synapse**, resulting in the terminal buttons of the axon transmitting the impulse to other neurons. The cerebral cortex is made up of four parts or *lobes*—the frontal lobe, the parietal lobe, the occipital lobe, and the temporal lobe—and two hemispheres: the **left hemisphere**, which governs language and thinking, and the **right hemisphere**, which governs spatial relations, vision, and emotions (**lateralization**). The **brain-based learning** model includes the following elements: (1) absence of threat, (2) meaningful content, (3) choices, (4) movement to enhance learning, (5) enriched environment, (6) adequate time, (7) collaboration, (8) immediate feedback, and (9) mastery at the application level, although it has engendered considerable controversy.

Describe intellectual development according to Piaget as the process of adaptation, featuring the schema; the processes of assimilation, accommodation and equilibration; and the four factors that influence cognitive development.

Learning Objective 2

Key Concepts:

schema, assimilation, accommodation (p. 47); imitation, play, equilibration (p. 48); intelligence, operations, heredity (p. 49); active experience, social interaction (p. 51).

Piaget formulated a theory of cognitive development with the **schema**, a repeatable action sequence governed by a core meaning, as the basic unit. He theorized that the basis for intellectual development is **adaptation** (being able to function in a given environment) with two adaptive mechanisms: **assimilation**, or incorporating new information into existing schemata, and **accommodation**, or modifying an existing schema when new information cannot be understood with existing schemata. To ensure that a balance or equilibrium exists between an individual and the environment, people **equilibrate**, that is, they sometimes assimilate and sometimes accommodate in dealing with the situations they encounter. This force toward attaining and maintaining equilibrium is what motivates the developmental process. What develops are schemata, the organizational structures that represent **intelligence**, used to carry out **operations** or coordinated sets of actions for dealing with objects and events. This development is based on four factors: heredity (which affects **maturation**), **active experience**, **social interaction**, and **equilibration**.

Explain and illustrate the four stages of Piaget's model of cognitive development: (a) sensorimotor, (b) preoperational, (c) concrete operational, and (d) formal operational.

Learning Objective 3

Key Concepts:

circular reaction, causality, object permanence, primary, secondary, and tertiary circular reaction, reproductive assimilation (p. 52); centration, egocentrism, nontransformational reasoning (p. 54); irreversibility (p. 55); conservation, of area, number, volume (p. 56); inversion, compensation, seriation (p. 58); reciprocal implication, concrete correspondence (p. 61); separation of variables (p. 62); exclusion (p. 63).

The first stage, the **sensorimotor** stage (0–2 years of age), is characterized by the appearance of progressively, more complex behaviors involving the connections between the senses and motor behavior. By the end of this stage, the child has developed sufficient schemata to recognize objects in their absence (i.e., **object permanence**) and **cause and effect**. The second stage, **preoperational thought** (2–7 years of age), is characterized by four features of prelogical thinking: (1) **egocentrism**, a preoccupation with oneself and one's own point of view; (2) **centration**, the focusing of all of one's attention on only one aspect or dimension of a stimulus at a time; (3) **nontransformational reasoning**, focusing only on the successive states in a sequence while ignoring the transformations that caused them; and (4) **irreversibility**, the inability to reverse thought or follow a line of reasoning back to where it started. By the time this stage ends, children are able to do **conservation** of number, with conservation of area and of volume soon to follow. The stage of **concrete operations** (7–11 years of age) is characterized by logical operations. They represent thinking, are reversible, assume conservation, and are part of a system, but are still limited to what can be perceived. In other words, there is a **concrete correspondence** between thoughts and external, observed reality. In the final stage, **formal operations** (11–15 years of age), logical reasoning appears without concrete limitations, enabling students to solve both hypothetical–deductive and scientific–inductive problems. To describe this stage, Piaget used a series of experiments involving *reciprocal implication,* the equal and opposite relationship between two dimensions; (2) *separation of variables,* varying one variable at a time while holding the others constant; and (3) *exclusion,* that some variables could be excluded from the solution because their variability did not affect the outcome.

Learning Objective 4

Key Concepts:

learning by exploration (p. 66); learner-centered instruction, task card, themes (p. 67); development of schemata (p. 68).

Apply Piaget's conception of cognitive development to the process of education.

To apply Piagetian principles to educational practice, teachers would adopt the processes of (1) **learning by exploration**—by active engagement with learning materials; (2) **use of themes** or integrated, interdisciplinary topics for teaching subject matter skills; (3) **learner-centered instruction,** making use of both individual and small-group instruction, and learning centers; and (4) **focus on the development of schemata** such as seriation, conservation, and classification in the elementary and middle grades and formal, abstract problem solving in the high school grades.

Learning Objective 5

Key Concepts:

object permanence, conservation, formal operational thinking skills, cultural influence (p. 72).

Recognize criticisms and limitations of Piaget's theory.

Current research suggests that **object permanence** and **conservation** tend to appear earlier than Piaget proposed, that the four stages are not as clearly differentiated as he proposed, that the ages at which specific types of problems are solved, particularly with regard to **formal operational thinking skills,** tend to vary more than he proposed, that he ignored **cultural influences,** and that children's capacity to learn is greater than he proposed.

Learning Objective 6

Key Concepts:

sociocultural perspective, social construction of meaning, social collaboration, cognitive and cultural tools, inner and private speech, internalization, self-talk (p. 73); zone of proximal development, scaffolding (p. 75).

Explain and apply to teaching Vygotsky's theory of cognitive development in terms of its main concepts and characteristics: sociocultural perspective, social construction of meaning, internalization, zone of proximal development, and scaffolding.

Vygotsky's theory represents a **sociocultural perspective**; he viewed social interaction and cultural context as playing a critical role in the social construction of meaning. He saw thought and language becoming intertwined through the process of **internalization,** enabling children to function cognitively in the world around them. He labeled the range of tasks that lie between what students can do on their own and with help as the **zone of proximal development.** He viewed **social collaboration** between children and adults or more competent peers as the basis of cognitive development in enabling children to successfully complete tasks that lie within the their zone of proximal development. To facilitate the above process, teachers are encouraged to use **scaffolding** (ways of helping students use new skills), challenging tasks, cooperative groups, real-world tasks, and be sensitive to the role of cultural factors.

Describe language development, including the concepts of phonology, meaning, grammar, and communication, and illustrate how language development can be facilitated in the classroom.

Language development includes learning **phonology** (pronunciation of words), **meaning** of words, **grammar**, and **communication**, within the framework that language and thought influence each other. Teachers can help children's language development by using **modeling**(restating a child's comment), **expansion** (adding information to a child's comment), **self-talk** (talking about what you're doing at the time you're doing it), and **parallel talk** (talk about what the child is doing when he or she is doing it).

Learning Objective 7

Key Concepts:

phonology, meaning (p. 79); metalinguistic awareness, grammar, syntax, semantic bootstrapping (p. 80); communication, pragmatics (p. 81); model, expansion, self-talk, parallel talk (p. 83).

Visit the Education CourseMate for *Educational Psychology* to access study tools and resources including the Virtual Psychology Labs, TeachSource Video Cases, chapter web links, tutorial quizzes, glossary flashcards, and more. Go to CengageBrain.com to register using your access code.

3 | Moral, Personal, and Psychosocial Development

After reading this chapter, you should be able to meet the following learning objectives	Chapter Contents
LEARNING OBJECTIVE 1 Explain Piaget's three stages of the development of moral judgment—moral realism, mutuality, and autonomy—including his concepts of justice and punishment.	Piaget's Developmental Stages of Moral Judgment • Stage 1: Moral Realism (ages 2–7) • Stage 2: Mutuality (ages 7–11) • Stage 3: Autonomy (ages 11–15) • A Related Approach
LEARNING OBJECTIVE 2 Explain Kohlberg's six stages of moral development—punishment-obedience, personal reward, good person, law and order, social contract, and universal ethical principle—within three levels: preconventional, conventional, and postconventional.	Kohlberg's Developmental Stages of Moral Reasoning • Level 1: Preconventional Moral Reasoning • Level 2: Conventional Moral Reasoning • Level 3: Postconventional Moral Reasoning
LEARNING OBJECTIVE 3 Describe the limitations of Kohlberg's model, including Gilligan's criticism based on gender differences and her proposed alternative model for women.	Some Limitations of Kohlberg's Theory • Three Often-Cited Limitations • The Issue of Gender: Gilligan's Alternative
LEARNING OBJECTIVE 4 Discuss and illustrate procedures for enhancing moral development.	Enhancing Moral Development • Training • Classroom Applications
LEARNING OBJECTIVE 5 Describe and explain personal development, including social cognition, the self, friends' influence/peer pressure, and parenting.	Personal Development • Social Cognition • The Self • Friends' Influence/Peer Pressure • Parenting
LEARNING OBJECTIVE 6 Outline Erikson's eight stages of psychosocial development in terms of the developmental crises faced in each, and summarize procedures for building initiative, industry, and identity in the school context.	Erikson's Stages of Psychosocial Development • Infancy: Basic Needs (Trust vs. Mistrust) • Toddlerhood: Self-Control (Autonomy vs. Shame and Doubt) • Early Childhood: Purpose (Initiative vs. Guilt) • School Age: Productivity (Industry vs. Inferiority) • Adolescence: Self-Discovery (Identity vs. Confusion) • Young Adulthood: Sharing (Intimacy vs. Isolation) • Adulthood: Parenting (Generativity vs. Stagnation) • Old Age: Self-Acceptance (Integrity vs. Despair) • Applying Erikson in the Classroom
LEARNING OBJECTIVE 7 Illustrate the characteristics and categories of a model of African American racial identity.	Racial Identity

Honesty is the Best Policy

Ms. Williams is a third-grade teacher at an elementary school in an upper-middle-class suburb. She has a class of 24 students, half girls, half boys. For today's lesson that centers on writing and sharing, Ms. Williams has asked her students to bring in an action figure, or if they don't have an action figure, a picture of one of their favorite cartoon characters. Each student is then given the chance to present and talk about his or her action figure or picture to the class. Sherman, the first student to go, comes up to the front of the room, takes his action figure out of the box, and holds it up for the class to see. It's a very lifelike GI Joe wearing military fatigues and carrying a slick rifle. All the boys respond, especially Craig, who indicates he thinks the figure is "cool," and gets out of his seat to get a closer look. When Sherman is finished with his presentation, he puts it back in the box and puts the box on the teacher's desk.

When the school day is about to end, Sherman goes looking for his box on the teacher's desk, but it has disappeared. Ms. Williams asks her students to help Sherman find his box, and all chip in, but with no success. The box is nowhere to be found. But Ms. Williams spots Craig stuffing what looked like a box into his book bag. She asks Craig to stay in the classroom while the other students exit, and then asks Craig to tell her where Sherman's box with the GI Joe action figure is. Craig says he doesn't know; he insists he looked all over the classroom with the rest of the kids and couldn't find it. Ms. Williams then asks him if he would mind letting her look in his book bag, and his face turns red as he nods his head. She opens his book bag, and indeed there is the box. She reminds him that she gave him a chance to return it, so that now he has not only stolen, but also lied. She reminds him of the Golden Rule, and Craig appears quite contrite, and blurts out, "I just wanted it real bad."

The next morning Ms. Williams takes Craig to the principal's office and Craig's parents are summoned to come to school, which they do. Craig's father, an attorney, is mildly upset by his son's behavior, but declares that "boys will be boys," and offers to reimburse Sherman for the cost of the action figure. (Adapted from Greenwood, G.E. & Fillmer, H.T. (1999). *Educational psychology cases for teacher decision-making.* Upper Saddle River, NJ: Merrill, pp. 68–76.)

- If you were the teacher, how would you have dealt with Craig?
- How do you see this story relating to this chapter's topic, moral development?
- What do you think teachers can do to keep these types of incidents from happening or at least minimize their occurrence?

Lessons We Can Learn from the Story In the previous chapter, the focus was on the development of cognitive functioning: thinking, learning, and problem solving. Now, the focus shifts to different aspects of human functioning: moral, personal, and psychosocial. Moral development represents the mechanism for children and adolescents to learn the difference between right and wrong, that is, morality. Thus, they become able to evaluate their own and others' actions (Turiel, 1998). In the above story, Craig's behavior reflects a low level of moral development. You will learn more about moral development and how a teacher can affect it in the sections that follow. Personal development refers to the way young people interact with their environment and the learning experiences that result, particularly as influenced by teachers, parents, and peers (Coolahan, Fantuzzo, Mendez, & McDermott, 2000).

Psychosocial development is the process by which a person's sense of self emerges as the result of the interaction between his or her *social* and *personal* side, meaning that individual development takes place in a social context. This includes the development of *feelings, attitudes, beliefs,* and *values* that manifest themselves as morality and identity. These are important human qualities that, like the cognitive qualities described in the previous chapter, follow a pattern of development as people grow and mature.

These moral, personal, and psychosocial qualities are also important determinants of how people function and perform in various situations, such as school. As a teacher, not only must you deal with students as learners, thinkers, and problem solvers, you must also deal with them as social and emotional beings, possessors of feelings and values. In this chapter, you will learn to be aware of elements in the nature of students' social interactions, moral characteristics, and sense of self. Student behaviors and expressions will depend on their moral, personal, and psychosocial development.

Described here are three general approaches to explaining the development of this moral, personal, and **psychosocial** side of people's being. The first of the three approaches was developed by Piaget and represents a counterpart of his theory of cognitive development covered in the preceding chapter.

psychosocial development

the process by which a person's sense of self emerges as the result of interactions between his or her social and personal side

Piaget's Developmental Stages of Moral Judgment

Piaget's focus in affective development was primarily on **moral development**, or the development of **moral judgment**. This refers to children's conceptions of rules and the respect that children acquire for these rules (Piaget, 1932). To discover what children's conceptions of rules are at different ages, Piaget (1932) studied the game of marbles, the most popular children's game of his day, and questioned children about their perceptions of the rules by which the game is played.

He also constructed stories that contained an immoral act, such as a lie, but varied in their degree of **intentionality**, or whether or not the immoral act was intended to deceive someone. He asked children to tell him which child (in each story) was naughtiest and why. Consider these two sample stories:

A. *A little boy (or a little girl) goes for a walk in the street and meets a big dog who frightens him very much. So then he goes home and tells his mother he has seen a dog that was as big as a cow.*

B. *A child comes home from school and tells his mother that the teacher had given him good marks, but it was not true; the teacher had given him no marks at all, either good or bad. Then his mother was very pleased and rewarded him.* (Piaget, 1932, pp. 144–145.)

moral development

the mechanism by which children and adolescents learn the difference between right and wrong

moral judgment

children's conceptions of rules and the respect that children acquire for these rules

intentionality

whether or not an immoral act was intended to deceive someone

Finally, Piaget (1932) studied children's ideas about justice and punishment by telling children stories like the one below and asking them whether the child in the story should be punished and how.

> *A little boy is playing in his room. His mother asks him to go and fetch some bread for dinner because there is none left in the house. But instead of going immediately, the boy says that he can't be bothered, that he'll go in a minute, etc. An hour later, he has not gone. Finally, dinnertime comes, and there is no bread on the table. The father is not pleased, and he wonders which would be the fairest way of punishing the boy. He thinks of three punishments. The first would be to forbid the boy to go to the Round-abouts [fair] the next day. The second punishment the father thought of was not to let the boy have any bread to eat. (There was a little bread left from the previous days.) The third punishment the father thinks of is to do to the boy the same thing as he has done. The father would say to him, "You wouldn't help your mother. Well, I am not going to punish you, but the next time you ask me to do anything for you, I shall not do it, and you will see how annoying it is when people do not help each other." (The little boy thinks this would be all right, but a few days later, his father would not help him reach a toy he could not get by himself. The father reminded him of his promise.) Which of these three punishments was the fairest? (Piaget, 1932, pp. 200–201).*

Based on the pattern of responses by children of different ages to questions about rules, intentionality, and justice taken from the game of marbles and the two types of stories, Piaget (1932) identified the stages of moral development described below.

Stage 1: Moral Realism (ages 2–7)

In the stage of **moral realism**, rules are taken literally and absolutely and must be respected. The child believes in **objective responsibility**, or being responsible for one's transgressions, regardless of the intentions behind them. The child also believes that the severity of a transgression is directly proportional to its superficial magnitude. In other words, the bigger the lie, the worse it is. Rules are a reality of the outside, adult world, and the child has a sense of duty in following them.

Furthermore, according to Piaget (1932), children regard moral rules as sacred and fixed, as being created and handed down by authority figures, and as being alterable only by authority figures. Piaget referred to this as **heteronomous morality**. Consider the following examples.

In playing the game of marbles, each child plays for himself rather than competing with his companions and sharing a set of common rules. Each rarely looks at the other and each simultaneously follows his own conception of the rules of the game. Each strives to imitate an elder model rather than engage in a socially interactive activity. Two children play two separate games, reflecting the egocentricity that has already been encountered at this age.

In evaluating a lie, as reflected in stories A and B above, the child at this stage reacts not to the intentions of the liar, but to the likelihood that the lie might be

moral realism

stage in which rules are taken literally and absolutely and must be respected

objective responsibility

being responsible for one's transgressions, regardless of the intentions behind them

heteronomous morality

morals are regarded as sacred and fixed, as created and being handed down by authority figures, and as being alterable only by authority figures

true. In other words, the more outrageous the lie, the worse it is, regardless of the intention of the liar to deceive. So the little girl who said she saw a dog as big as a cow is naughtier than the one who said her teacher had given her good marks, because it (a dog as big as a cow) "could never happen," or "there's no such thing," or it is "the biggest lie." The child who told that lie should, in the judgment of children at this stage, be punished the most.

Moreover, in the stage of moral realism, actions are evaluated in terms of the material result and independently of motives. That means the worse the result, the worse the crime—as illustrated in Box 3.1, where the greater number of items broken, even by clumsiness, the naughtier the act. This carries over to the idea of justice in which the moral realist believes that the worse the crime, the more severe the punishment should be. The moral realist hands out what Piaget (1932) calls **expiatory punishment**, which is strong and arbitrary and thereby allows the wrongdoer to expiate or pay penance for the wrongdoing. Painful punishment is expected to deter further rule-breaking. So, for the story of the child who would not get the bread (page 92), children in the stage of moral realism choose the only punishment of the three they regard as at all severe, namely, not allowing the child to go to the fair. Punishment is morally necessary to make up or pay for the transgression and thus to prevent a relapse.

expiatory punishment
punishment that is strong and arbitrary and thereby allows the wrongdoer to expiate or pay penance for rule-breaking

---

BOX 3.1

Did You Know?

Moral Realism and the Punishment for Clumsiness

(Elementary/Middle School)

The two stories of the broken cups were used to evaluate a child's level of moral development.

A. *A little boy who is called John is in his room. He is called to dinner. He goes into the dining room. But behind the door there was a chair, and on the chair there was a tray with fifteen cups on it. John couldn't have known that there was all this behind the door. He goes in, the door knocks against the tray, bang go the fifteen cups, and they all get broken!*

B. *Once there was a little boy whose name was Henry. One day when his mother was out he tried to get some jam out of the cupboard. He climbed up onto a chair and stretched out his arm. But the jam was too high up and he couldn't reach it and have any. But while he was trying to get*

it he knocked over a cup. The cup fell down and broke. (Piaget, J., 1932. *The moral judgment of the child.* New York: Harcourt, Brace & World, p. 118.)

The basis for punishment in moral realism—the magnitude of the crime (objective responsibility)—is revealed in the response of George, age 6:

C. Have you understood these stories, George? —*Yes.* —What did the first boy do? —*He broke eleven cups.* —And the second one? —*He broke a cup by moving roughly.* —Why did the first one break the cups? —*Because the door knocked them.* —And the second? —*He was clumsy. When he was getting the jam the cup fell down.* —Is one of the boys naughtier than the other? —*The first is because he knocked over twelve cups.* —If you were the daddy, which one would you punish most? —*The one who broke twelve cups.* —Why did he break them? —*The door shut too hard and knocked them. He didn't do it on purpose.* —And why did the other boy break a cup? —*He wanted to get the jam. He moved too far. The cup got broken.* —Why did he want to get the jam? —*Because he was all alone. Because his mother wasn't there.* —Have you got a brother? —*No, a little sister.* —Well, if it was you who had broken the twelve cups when you went into the room and your little sister who had broken one cup while she was trying to get the jam, which of you would be punished most severely? —*Me because I broke more than one cup.* (Piaget, J., 1932. *The moral judgment of the child.* New York: Harcourt, Brace & World, pp. 120–121.)

The basis for punishment in later stages, intent, is revealed in the response of Nuss, age 10:

D. *[The naughtiest is] the one who wanted to take the jam.* — Does it make any difference the other one having broke more cups, Nuss? —*No, because the one who broke 15 cups didn't do it on purpose.* (Piaget, J., 1932. *The moral judgment of the child.* New York: Harcourt, Brace & World, p. 125.)

George, the younger one, would punish the child who had, however unintentionally, broken the most cups, while Nuss, the elder one, would punish the child who broke only a single cup but did it while trying to do something bad.

● How might you apply these findings to the teaching of students?

This view of justice is termed **retributive justice** ("an eye for an eye, a tooth for a tooth"), and it is based, according to Piaget (1932), on the child's perception that adult authority imposes respect for given orders and rules and that the laws themselves must be avenged when broken (Piaget calls this **adult restraint**).

Developmentally, in between retributive and distributive justice is **immanent justice**. This is the idea that if you do something bad, something bad will happen to you. In other words, there are automatic punishments that emanate from the events or acts themselves. Getting a stomach ache from eating candy you were not supposed to have is an example.

Stage 2: Mutuality (ages 7–11)

Mutuality means *equality* or following the "golden rule" of doing unto others as you would have them do unto you. Mutuality also means *reciprocity* or taking turns or sharing equally. If the ball goes over the fence, then each of the players should take turns retrieving it rather than the same one getting it every time. Hence, mutuality means *mutual respect*. It means sharing when only one has something or when everybody but one has something. If there is a chocolate bar to be divided between two sisters, each should get half.

When it comes to following rules, mutuality means *cooperation*. Cheating is bad because it is not fair to others. In regard to justice, one person who wrongs another must be punished or made to give back what he or she has taken: This reflects reciprocity. In the game of marbles, the boy who cheats is excluded from the game for a time. Marbles unlawfully won are restored to their rightful owner or distributed

retributive justice
punishment is morally necessary to make up or pay for the transgression and thus to prevent a relapse ("an eye for an eye, a tooth for a tooth")

adult restraint
the child's perception that adult authority imposes respect for given orders and rules and that laws themselves must be avenged when broken

immanent justice
the idea that if you do something bad, something bad will happen to you

mutuality
equality, reciprocity, and cooperation between people

Jupiter Images

among the other players. When the strong exploit the weak, they must be forced to make restitution. Punishment is neither automatic and absolute nor a means of making one pay for one's sins, as in retributive justice. Instead, it is a way of treating everyone the same and restoring equality; it is called **distributive justice**.

If a misdeed occurs and the perpetrator is unknown, as when someone throws something in class but the teacher cannot tell who, then mutuality dictates that no one be punished because it cannot be done fairly. On the other hand, moral realism requires that everyone be punished because there must be a punishment at all costs, even if it strikes the innocent as well as the guilty.

When it comes to lying, children in the stage of mutuality take into account the notion of fairness or the effect on other people, which makes them sensitive to intentionality. In response to the stories about lying on page 91, the "big dog" versus the "good marks," the worse lie to children in this stage is the one about the "good marks" because it was intended to mislead and gain something to which the liar was not entitled. Such deceit is not in keeping with the spirit of mutuality.

In the stories on clumsiness in Box 3.1, older children choose to punish an act of destruction, however small, if the child performs it while trying to take advantage of someone or something unfairly; they forgive an act of destruction of larger magnitude if it occurs accidentally.

Finally, in meting out distributive justice, children in this stage believe there should be reciprocity between the punishment and the crime. In the story about the child who would not help his mother by going out to pick up the bread, the punishment of choice is to not help the child when he asks for it, because he was not willing to help when asked. The punishment is designed to "fit the crime," showing that children at this stage realize the social consequences of their actions.

distributive justice

a way of treating everyone the same and restoring equality; punishment is neither automatic and absolute nor a means of making one pay for one's sins

Stage 3: Autonomy (ages 11–15)

In the stage of **autonomy**, rules are seen as social conventions, set by mutual agreement and changeable through mutual agreement. There is an interest in rules, in an abstract or formal sense, as a code of conduct, and in codifying all possibilities. The rules serve to accomplish more than just guaranteeing cooperation; they maintain the spirit of the game or, in the case of marbles, ensure insofar as possible that outcomes will be a function of skill rather than luck. Hence, the young adult of this stage has been freed from or has become autonomous of the constraints of either adult-imposed reality or peer-imposed mutuality. Rules have become entities unto themselves; they are made by people and can be changed by people through mutual consent. The enforcement of rules has passed from constraint to cooperation to mutual consent. The rule has become the rational rule as part of a system of legality involving rationally interlocking rules. Piaget (1932) referred to this as **autonomous morality**, contrasted with the heteronomous morality of the moral realism stage.

In the case of justice, the principle of equality, or "the same for all," gives way to the principle of **equity**. Equity means not automatically treating everyone exactly the same but rather taking into account each individual's particular circumstances. In equity, there are shades of equality depending on factors such as age, size of contribution, need, and so on. Consider the following question (Piaget, 1932, p. 287): "Why must you not copy from your neighbor?" Moral realists answer, "Because you get punished!" Those in the stage of mutuality answer, "Because it isn't fair!" Those in the stage of autonomy answer, "It isn't fair for those who can learn, but those who can't learn ought to be allowed to have a little look" (Piaget, J. (1932). *The moral judgment of the child*. New York, Harcourt, Brace & World, pp. 287–288). Here is another example relating to the idea of justice (Piaget, J. 1932). *The moral judgment of the child*. New York, Harcourt, Brace & World, pp. 309–311).

> *Two boys, a little one and a big one, once went for a long walk in the mountains. When lunchtime came they were very hungry. But when they took their food out of their lunch bags, they found that there was not enough for both of them. What should they have done? Given all the food to the big boy, all to the little one, or the same to both?*

Moral Realism: *"The big boy should have had most."* Why? *"Because he's the eldest."*
Mutuality (Equality): *"Each must be given the same. It would be fair."*
Autonomy (Equity): *"The little boy should have had more because be was smaller."*

So we see that the idea of *unfairness* develops from:

1. moral realism, or behavior forbidden by either adults or the rules of the game, to
2. mutuality, or behavior that goes against equality, to
3. equity, or acts of economic or political injustice connected with adult society.

autonomy

stage in which rules are seen as social conventions, set by mutual agreement and changeable through mutual agreement

autonomous morality

morals are regarded as rational parts of a system of legality and are seen as made by people and able to be changed by people

equity

not automatically treating everyone exactly the same but rather taking into account each individual's particular circumstances

To the moral realist, some forbidden acts are lying, stealing, fighting, and breaking things. In the mutuality stage, the inequalities might be giving something better to one than to the other, punishing one worse than the other, and hitting someone who has done nothing to you. In the autonomy stage, inequities or social injustices include a teacher preferring a student because she is more clever than others, or students leaving other students out of their games because they are not well-dressed enough.

Hence, justice goes from *retributive* or requiring punishment to stamp out disobedient or unjust acts, to *distributive* or considering equality by treating everybody the same and maintaining harmony as the primary consideration, to *equity*, in which attenuating circumstances are taken into account.

See Table 3.1 for a *Concept Review* of Piaget's stages of affective development.

CONCEPT REVIEW TABLE 3.1

Piaget's Three Stages of Moral Development

STAGE	RULES	ACCIDENTS	LYING	JUSTICE
Moral Realism (2–7 years)	Games played in isolation; no cooperation or social interaction	Intentions not considered. Children do not take the view of others. Judgments are based on effects of actions.	Punishment is the criterion for a lie. No punishment = no lie. Lying is being "naughty."	Submission to adult authority. Arbitrary, expiatory punishments are considered just.
Mutuality (7–11 years)	Rules observed, though children lack agreement as to what the rules are.	Intentions begin to be considered. Children begin to take the view of others	Lie = not true. Unpunished untruths are lies.	Justice is based on reciprocity. Equality is more important than authority.
Autonomy (after 11–12)	Rules known to all; agreement as to what the rules are; rules can be changed by consensus; rules are of interest for their own sake.		Intentions decide whether a false statement is not a lie. Truthfulness is viewed as necessary for cooperation.	Equality with equity. Reciprocity considers intent and circumstances.

Source: Adapted from Wadsworth, B.J. (1996). *Piaget's theory of cognitive and affective development* (5th ed., p. 132). New York: Longman.

Think It Over

as a LEARNER   Suppose one of the students in a high school class you were in took a pen that belonged to another student and, while using it, broke it. According to Piaget's theory, based on the stage of development, how would the other students in the class react?

as a TEACHER   Think of the grade level in school you plan to teach. Suppose one of the students in your class took a pen that belonged to another student and, while using it, broke it. How would you react? How does your reaction relate to Piaget's theory based on the stage of moral judgment of your students?

A Related Approach

Selman (1980; Selman & Schultz, 1990) described a sequence of levels of social thought that parallels Piaget's stages of logical thought (described in Chapter 2). At the lowest level, Level 0 (ages 3–6), children confuse their own perspectives with those of others. They are, therefore, egocentric, as were Piaget's preoperational children. At Level 1 (ages 5–9), children realize that other children have social thoughts and feelings different from their own, but are unable to understand them. At Level 2 (ages 7–12), they consider and reflect on others' attitudes and feelings, but are unable to consider their and other's feelings at the same time. At Level 3 (ages 10–15), they view their own and other children's thoughts and feelings mutually and simultaneously, and at Level 4 (adolescence–adulthood), they recognize a general social viewpoint exists that goes beyond the perspectives of the individual child. These stages also parallel Piaget's affective stages.

By asking children to solve social dilemmas, Selman helps them consider more social perspectives than just their own. One such dilemma is whether to buy a dog for a close friend for his birthday to replace his recently lost dog, even though the friend does not want a new dog. In this dilemma, the choice of buying the dog for the friend as a way of helping is a more socially advanced response than not doing it for fear of losing a friend. The choice of buying the dog takes into account the friend's needs even beyond what the friend himself has acknowledged. It is based on the recognition that people's needs can be changed through acts of friendship.

Before considering the classroom implications of Piaget's theory of moral development, we will describe Kohlberg's theory of moral development—a refinement and expansion of Piaget's.

Kohlberg's Developmental Stages of Moral Reasoning

Learning Objective 2

Explain Kohlberg's six stages of moral development—punishment-obedience, personal reward, good person, law and order, social contract, and universal ethical principle—within three levels: preconventional, conventional, and postconventional.

Lawrence Kohlberg (1969, 1975, 1981) took Piaget's ideas about the development of the conception of justice in children and expanded them into a six-stage theory of **moral reasoning**. He determined the characteristics of moral reasoning in children by presenting them with **moral dilemmas**, or situations, in which they had to choose between two desirable or two undesirable alternatives (where no choice is either absolutely right or wrong), and explain the reasons behind their choice. The above story about the dog is an example of a dilemma. Another example, used by Kohlberg, is this:

> *A man's wife is dying. There is one drug that could save her, but it is very expensive, and the druggist who invented it will not sell it at a price low enough for the man to buy it. Finally, the man becomes desperate and considers stealing the drug for his wife. What should he do, and why?*

How do children of different ages respond to a situation like this, and is there a pattern? Are there stages at which children say it is absolutely wrong to steal the drug and stages at which it may be acceptable—but with qualifications? Kohlberg answered these questions by identifying three levels of progressive moral reasoning, each with two stages. Descriptions follow. (See Table 3.2 on page 100 for a *Concept Review* of Kohlberg's stages.)

Level 1: Preconventional Moral Reasoning

This level of moral reasoning conforms closely to Piaget's stage of moral realism and is typical of young preoperational children. Because of their egocentricity, or their focus on their own interests to the exclusion of the interests of others, young children's judgment of right and wrong is based on doing what is good for them. And what is good for them is primarily avoiding punishment. Young children acquiesce to the power of the rule-givers if they fear the consequences; if they do not fear the consequences, their behavior is likely to be relatively uncontrolled by moral considerations. In response to the drug story, children at Level 1 are likely to say it is wrong to steal the drug because you might get caught (or, alternatively, that it is OK to steal the drug if you think you can get away with it).

Preconventional moral reasoning is divided into two stages:

Stage 1: Punishment-Obedience Orientation

In this stage, individuals are limited in their own actions only by the fear of punishment. They do not act out of a sense of duty or because of personal values or ideals. They defer to power because to do otherwise is to risk punishment. Of course, when the likelihood of punishment is perceived to be slight, Stage 1 individuals will do most anything that pleases them.

moral reasoning

stages of reasoning achieved by encountering moral dilemmas

moral dilemmas

situations in which a choice must be made between two desirable or two undesirable alternatives where no choice is either absolutely right or wrong

CONCEPT REVIEW TABLE 3.2

Kohlberg's Stages of Moral Reasoning

LEVEL 1: PRECONVENTIONAL MORAL REASONING

Basis for judgment: rules and personal needs

Stage 1: Punishment-Obedience Orientation

Rules are obeyed to avoid punishment. Actions are judged "good" or "bad" by their physical consequences.

Stage 2: Personal-Reward Orientation

"Right" and "wrong" are determined by personal needs. Favors are paid back as in "you do something good for me and I'll do something good for you."

LEVEL 2: CONVENTIONAL MORAL REASONING

Basis for judgment: traditional values, approval of others, loyalty, expectations, laws of society

Stage 3: Good-Person Orientation

"Good" is determined by what is approved of or by what pleases others.

Stage 4: Law-and-Order Orientation

Laws are absolute. Social order and authority must be respected and maintained.

LEVEL 3: POSTCONVENTIONAL MORAL REASONING

Basis for judgment: social standards, individual rights, conscience, human dignity

Stage 5: Social-Contract Orientation

"Good" is determined by socially agreed on and mutually acceptable standards of individual rights.

Stage 6: Universal-Ethical-Principle Orientation

"Good" is a matter of universal standards and is based on abstract concepts of human dignity, justice, and fairness.

Source: Adapted from Kohlberg, L. (1975). The cognitive-developmental approach to moral education. *Phi Beta Kappan*, 56, 271.

In the normal course of development, most young children go through this stage. However, without appropriate role models and socializing agents, some children may never leave this stage. Their behavior will remain relatively uncontrolled except by the threat, and subsequent realization, of severe punishment. They will continue to believe that "good" means what you can get away with and "bad" means what you cannot get away with. They will lack any moral criteria for judging "right" and "wrong."

Stage 2: Personal-Reward Orientation

At this slightly more advanced, preconventional stage, some limited sense of reciprocity emerges, as in: "You scratch my back and I'll scratch yours." Good is still defined as "what's good for me"—that is, personal need satisfaction. But morality at this stage has become a very practical morality, a kind of "honor among thieves!" In other words, a Stage 2 individual might try to strike up some sort of a deal with the druggist or else make a deal with a law enforcement officer to "look the other way" while he or she steals the drug. While this is a perfectly natural stage for children to pass through, those who never progress beyond it may well choose to spend their lives engaged in organized crime or in a career considered to be without "scruples."

Level 2: Conventional Moral Reasoning

At this level, moral reasoning is reasoning with a focus on the social perspective in that the child takes into consideration the viewpoints of others. The result is doing what is expected of her, doing her duty, doing what will please other people, and consequently gaining social acceptance. Conventional morality is an adherence to: traditional values, law and order, loyalty to others, and society. This level corresponds roughly to Piaget's stage of mutuality and is characteristic of children in the upper elementary and middle grades but, for many people, represents the limit of their moral development.

In the conventional stage, individuals look beyond personal benefits and consider the effects of their actions on other people. Approval of one's beliefs, actions sought, and laws are considered of paramount importance.

Stage 3: Good-Person Orientation

In this first conventional stage, the emphasis is on (1) being nice, (2) being approved of, (3) pleasing others, (4) performing "appropriate" behavior, (5) fulfilling mutual expectations, and (6) conforming. This and loyalty are important virtues, and the "golden rule" is observed. In response to the drug story, the Stage 3 individual would say it is all right for the man to steal the drug because he is trying to help his wife. In other words, his intention is honorable, and to the Stage 3 moral reasoner, intentions are of great importance. Stealing the drug, therefore, is justified by the man's good intentions based on loyalty to his loved ones.

Stage 4: Law-and-Order Orientation

In this second conventional stage, morality is oriented toward (1) respecting authority, (2) doing one's duty, and (3) maintaining the social order for its own sake. The concern enlarges to an awareness of societal, national, and religious values that extend beyond the immediate primary groups of family and friends. However, a tendency toward conformity remains, along with a sense of duty and a belief in "doing the right thing." Laws and rules are upheld to fulfill one's responsibility to keep the system as a whole going. In response to the drug problem posed on page 99, law-and-order moralists would say that stealing the drug is wrong under any circumstances because it is wrong to steal.

Level 3: Postconventional Moral Reasoning

This third and highest level features a more abstract, principled, and individual view of rules and morals, not attained until the high school years and even then not attained by many. It corresponds to Piaget's stage of autonomy. Moral principles are defined independently of either authority or group identification conditions, as in the preceding two levels. A Level 3 moral reasoner might say that stealing the unaffordable drug to cure one's dying wife is not wrong as long as the man is willing to suffer the consequences of his act and go to jail. However, the Level 3 person would also see a need to protect the right of the druggist, and so a better solution might be gained through legal recourse.

Stage 5: Social-Contract Orientation

The belief here is that while laws are necessary, they are relative rather than absolute. Laws are perceived to reflect a social consensus, or agreement, among people to maintain social standards and to protect individual rights. Because laws are consensual rather than handed down, they may be changed democratically if they no longer meet society's needs. In other words, Stage 5 moralists believe that laws are not "carved in stone" but serve to protect individual rights in the society. The purpose of laws is to enable people to live in harmony and maintain a sense of community while not transcending such individual liberties as set forth in the Bill of Rights. When a law is unjust, it is changed or discarded in order to help regulate society better. Laws serve people, rather than vice versa, and must not interfere with higher-order rights such as individual liberties.

Stage 6: Universal-Ethical-Principle Orientation

The few who reach this stage (epitomized by Jesus, Gandhi, and Martin Luther King, Jr.) have a clear vision of abstract moral principles such as justice and fairness. They not only teach these principles to others but sacrifice their lives, if necessary, to stand up for them. Right is defined not by convenience or by mutual consent but by universal standards of justice. Right is abstract and ethical (such as the dignity of human beings) rather than concrete and moralistic. The right to equality is a major belief.

Stage-specific responses to the resolution of another moral dilemma are shown in Box 3.2.

Think It Over

as a LEARNER	What stage do you see yourself fitting in? What is the value to a learner of knowing Kohlberg's theory? How would you use this theory in a practical way?
as a TEACHER	What is the value of knowing Kohlberg's theory? How would you use it in a practical way?

AN EXAMPLE TO AID TO UNDERSTANDING · Box 3.2

Resolving a Moral Dilemma (Elementary/ Middle/ High School)

A firefighter in the midst of fighting a fire in an occupied building hears that his own house is on fire. Should the firefighter leave his post to help his own family members who may be in danger, or should he stay where he is and help others?

Level 1: Preconventional

Stage 1: *Punishment-obedience orientation:* The firefighter should stay, or else he will be punished or fired by the head of the fire department.

Stage 2: *Personal-reward orientation:* The firefighter should go to his own family, or else he'll never stop worrying about what's happened to them.

Level 2: Conventional

Stage 3: *Good-person orientation:* He had better go to his own family because good parents care about their families.

Stage 4: *Law-and-order orientation:* He should stay where he is because that's exactly what the rules say he should do.

Level 3: Postconventional

Stage 5: *Social contract orientation:* He probably should stay because that's what he agreed to do, but if he hears his family is in real danger, that might justify his leaving.

Stage 6: *Universal-ethical-principle orientation:* He should stay because it is right and ethical to put the welfare of the many above that of the few—regardless of who they are. The people he is helping are someone's family members too, and he is bound to take care of them. To do less would be to sacrifice self-respect.

Some Limitations of Kohlberg's Theory

Learning Objective 3

Describe the limitations of Kohlberg's model, including Gilligan's criticism based on gender differences and her proposed alternative model for women.

Like all theories, Kohlberg's has its limitations, and they are important to recognize before you use his theory in the classroom. Such limitations do not negate a theory; they just help us put it in perspective. Let us look at what some of these limitations are.

Three Limitations

First, it is important to recognize that moral reasoning and behaving morally are not the same thing. Kohlberg's is a theory of moral reasoning and so, even though moral reasoning has been associated with moral behavior (Miller, Eisenberg, Fabes, & Shell, 1996; Arnold, 2000), it does not guarantee that moral behavior will occur. There are other factors (e.g., inconvenience, personal risk, gender role-orientation, perspective taking) that enter into moral decisions (Eisenberg, Zhou, & Koller, 2001).

Second, as is true in all stage theories, there is an inevitable overlapping between stages, as well as the occasional tendency to appear to move in a backward direction.

Again, the complexity of moral decision making based on the number of factors involved, may lead to the kind of inconsistency and unpredictability for which a systematic theory of discrete stages has difficulty accounting.

A third limitation relates to the universality or generality of Kohlbergs' stages. It has been argued that the theory is biased in favor of Western cultures, and particularly among the highest social and educational levels of Western culture (Shweder et al., 1990). These authors contend that in Eastern, more traditional cultures, the universal moral principles of postconventional moral reasoning often are based on traditional and religious beliefs, while Kohlberg's model classifies moral reasoning based on such beliefs as conventional. As a result, few people outside the Western part of the world would be classified as having reached the highest level of moral development.

The Issue of Gender: Gilligan's Alternative

The major criticism of Kohlberg's theory of moral development has been offered by Carol Gilligan in her book: *In a Different Voice* (1982; see also Gilligan, Hamner, & Lyons, 1990). Based on interviews, she contends that women and men use fundamentally different approaches to making moral decisions. The male approach to morality, often referred to as the "Morality of Justice," is that because individuals have certain basic rights that have to be respected, morality imposes moral restrictions on what a person can do. On the other hand, while the female approach to morality, often referred to as the "Morality of Caring," is that because people have responsibilities toward others, morality makes it imperative for people to care for others. Gilligan, a Harvard professor, further contends that traditional male dominance over discussions of morality causes the female perspective to be considered less developed and less sophisticated.

In a Morality of Caring, students have responsibilities toward others. For example, helping one another to understand a challenging class assignment.

Gilligan further distinguishes three stages in the moral development of women, different from the stages proposed by Kohlberg. The first stage is the **selfish morality** stage where female children focus exclusively on themselves. This is followed by the stage of **conventional morality** where they progress from selfish to **social morality**, believing it is wrong to act in their own interests rather than in the interests of others. Finally, in the third, or postconventional, stage they turn to a **principled morality**, wherein they learn that neither their own nor others' interests should be ignored. This belief grows out of a concern with connecting with others; for example, if either person in a relationship is viewed as slighted, it is believed that the relationship is harmed. This is summed up by Gilligan, as follows:

> *The moral imperative that emerges repeatedly in interviews with women is an injunction to care, a responsibility to discern and alleviate the "real and recognizable trouble" of this world. For men, the moral imperative appears rather as an injunction to respect the rights of others and thus to protect from interference the rights to life and self-fulfillment ... For women, the integration of rights and responsibilities takes place through an understanding of the psychological logic of relationships ... by asserting the need of all persons (including themselves) for care. For men, recognition [is] through experience of the need for more active responsibility* (Gilligan, 1982, p. 100).

Gilligan further contends that the basis for this gender difference in moral development is that girls are parented by a person of the same gender, leading them to perceive themselves as less differentiated than boys and more continuous with and related to the external world. While masculinity is defined through separation and independence, femininity is defined through attachment. Accordingly, males are more likely to be threatened by intimacy and have problems with relationships, while females are more likely to be threatened by separation and have problems with individuation. Women's failure to separate, according to Gilligan, is seen by "men's psychology" as a failure to develop.

In responding to the moral dilemma posed earlier in this chapter of the man caught between the druggist and his dying wife, Gilligan finds that girls are puzzled by the failure of the druggist to respond to the wife as a comember of a network of relationships (the female "care" perspective), as opposed to an opponent in a conflict of rights (the male "justice" perspective). While boys seem confident that "the judge would agree that stealing is the right thing," girls seem confident that the husband and the druggist "could figure out a way rather than stealing," such as giving the wife the drug and having the husband pay back the money later.

Gilligan (1982) also claimed that, in adolescence, girls lose their willingness to express their views in settings where students of both genders are present. This claim is supported in a study by Russell (2007) that showed that, while girls at young ages were comfortable expressing their moral views, as they grew older they experienced ridicule from boys and thereafter tended to avoid or withdraw from expressing their views publicly in settings that included boys.

selfish morality
stage in which female children focus exclusively on themselves

conventional morality
transition stage where female children progress from selfish to social morality

social morality
stage in which female children believe it is wrong to act in their own interests rather than in the interests of others

principled morality
stage in which female children learn that neither their own or others' interests should be ignored

Children operate on all three levels of moral development, not only in the United States, but in other cultures as well.

Tim Graham/Tim Graham Photo Library/Getty Images

In examining gender differences in moral development, along with their causes and effects, Gilligan also looked at the differences between the kinds and operations of games, played essentially by same sex groups (see Table 3.3).

TABLE 3.3
Comparing Boy's and Girl's Games

BOY'S GAMES	GIRL'S GAMES
Out-of-doors (public)	Indoors (private)
In large groups	In small groups
In mixed age groups (casual)	Often best friend dyads (more intimate)
Competitive	Turn-taking
Lasts longer	Lasts shorter
Fascinated with rules	More tolerant toward rules
Like to resolve disputes	Avoid disputes by making exceptions, innovating
Resolve disputes when they occur	End game when disputes occur

While Gilligan's critique of Kohlberg's theory is well-made, and highlights some important distinctions, research studies have not tended to find major differences in moral reasoning between males and females by late adolescence (Eisenberg, Martin, and Fabes, 1996). Research has not yielded differences between males and females in the area of moral maturity (Bee & Boyd, 2003). The moral judgments made by males and females appear to reflect elements of both justice and care, with relative amounts of each depending on the specific situation, a result that has been acknowledged by Gilligan herself (Brown, Tappan, and Gilligan, 1995).

Think It Over

as a LEARNER Do you agree with Gilligan that moral development is different in men and women? Why or why not? Have you experienced that difference?

as a TEACHER Would you use Gilligan's ideas about moral development in your classroom? If yes, how? If no, why not?

Enhancing Moral Development

Learning Objective 4

Discuss and illustrate procedures for enhancing moral development.

As a result of normal socialization and development, preconventional moral reasoning (Level 1) characterizes almost all children at age 7, about a quarter of all 13-year-olds, and slightly less than a quarter of all 16-year-olds. Conventional moral reasoning (Level 2) characterizes only a small number of 7-year-olds, but more than half of all 13- and 16-year-olds. Postconventional moral reasoning (Level 3) is virtually unseen among 7-year-olds, while it characterizes about one quarter of all 16-year-olds. Thus, 7-year-olds are primarily preconventional, while about half of 13- and 16-year-olds are conventional, and the remaining half are split between preconventional and postconventional. This is true for children not only in the United States, but in such diverse places as a Malaysian aboriginal village, a Turkish village, a Mexican city, and a Mayan village (Turiel, 1998). Do you think this can be changed? Or, as a teacher, are these generalities to be used by you as guidelines to making classroom judgments about student behavior?

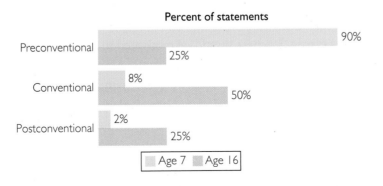

Training

Schlaefli, Rest, and Thoma (1985) examined 55 studies that attempted to enhance moral development through training. These studies used a test called the *Defining Issues Test*, or DIT, in which students were given moral dilemmas to resolve. Instead of making up their own answers, they were required to choose given answers representative of the different stages of moral reasoning. Test-takers were given a score that placed them on the moral reasoning scale somewhere between the low end (preconventional or personal-consequences reasoning) and the high end (postconventional or principled reasoning).

Studies using the DIT have shown that (1) older people score higher than younger ones, (2) better-educated people score higher than less-well-educated people, (3) children of parents who use democratic yet warm childrearing practices score higher than children of parents who use dictatorial childrearing practices, (4) children of parents who practice rational behavior themselves score higher than children of parents who do not, and (5) there are no differences between major religious groups in level of moral reasoning.

In the studies reviewed, when students in junior and senior high school discussed the moral dilemmas and their resolutions in a supervised class setting, the tendency to use principled reasoning increased significantly in comparison to students not participating in these discussion sessions. According to Oser (1986), what makes these discussions of morality effective in raising the level of moral reasoning is that they provide students with an opportunity to (1) focus on moral conflict in an effort to stimulate higher moral thought, (2) analyze their own moral beliefs and reasoning, (3) undertake moral role-playing and experience moral empathy, (4) understand shared norms and the meaning of community, and (5) directly consider moral action in relation to moral choice.

In addition, the use of three teaching strategies—active learning, reflection, and teacher-student interaction—was related to positive change in moral reasoning while negative interactions with other students was likely to have the opposite effect (Mayhew & King, 2008). Finally, Strain (2005) argued that service-learning courses could be powerful instruments for cognitive, affective, and moral transformation. (Note: Service-learning activities teachers can use for each of the chapters in this book are available on the companion Web site.)

Classroom Applications

Geiger and Turiel (1983) have found that students who score especially low in moral judgment are particularly likely to exhibit disruptive behavior in the school setting. For this reason, teachers should be motivated to stimulate moral growth and encourage moral development in their students. Along with this, teachers should help their students attain related affective goals, such as interpersonal skillfulness, self-discipline, independence, and enthusiasm for learning. Developing these skills will enable students to participate cooperatively and enthusiastically in classroom life. To teachers, having students develop good moral behavior in the classroom should be every bit as important as having them acquire knowledge. So, stimulating personal growth among students is as significant a classroom goal as teaching them facts and concepts.

How can teachers help students grow morally and emotionally? The answer lies in formal and informal efforts at **moral education**. Eisman (1981) suggests having *classroom discussions* of the kinds of *dilemmas* students encounter in their lives, such as sibling rivalry, teasing, and prejudice among elementary grade students and cheating, drinking and drugs, conformity, and unpopularity among high school students. To aid you in carrying out such discussions, Eisman (1981) further suggests the following:

- Encourage students to see others' perspectives, perhaps by switching roles.
- Help students connect values and actions, and see inconsistencies where they arise.
- Make sure students listen to one another by having them acknowledge what others are saying.

These sound like the advanced stages described by Selman on page 98.

It is essential that the teacher allow students to remain silent, if they so choose, and protect their right to privacy. It is also important that students learn to distinguish between administrative rules, such as coming to class on time, and more basic, moral rules, such as respecting another person's right to privacy.

Another classroom approach is for teachers to recognize the level or stage of moral reasoning of their students from a discussion of high school problems. For example, you might ask "What was the worst thing that happened in school this week?" Then you can present conflicting arguments representative of the next higher stage. This technique is called **plus-one matching** (Lickona, 1991), and it is based on the premise that people cannot skip a stage in their moral development. Therefore, by provoking disequilibrium and stimulating change, the teacher can enhance a student's moral development from one stage to the next. Teachers can help students develop their character by helping them recognize that moral development is composed of three distinct components: (1) moral knowing, (2) moral attitudes, and (3) moral behavior (Lickona, 2001).

Alternatively, teachers may choose simply to guide a discussion of students' moral issues and record on the blackboard the reasons students give for behaving as they did. Students can then be called on to provide illustrations of the various stages of moral reasoning. A sample classroom activity for moral development is shown in Box 3.3 (on pages 110–111).

Antes and Norton (1994) provide the following suggestions for moral education:

- You should provide opportunities for students to be responsible for each other by providing cross-age grouping and cross-age tutoring. The older will benefit by being a role model and by developing patience and tact. The younger will benefit by being helped academically and witnessing a caring, helping relationship.
- You can relate educational experiences to students' lives, providing opportunities for students to share their points of view.

moral education
formal and informal efforts to help students grow morally and emotionally

plus-one matching
argument presentation technique based on the premise that people cannot skip a stage in moral development

You can develop cooperative activities in the community with service projects to help students develop a sense of responsibility and connection to the community as a whole.

- You can encourage discussions with and among students concerning aspects of school life and how to interact with other people in the appropriate manner.
- You can guide children in playing a role in decision making in the classroom and school.
- You might provide for forms of student self-government in public schools as a means of helping students contribute to others and develop critical thinking and interaction skills.
- You might use day-to-day activities and events happening in the students' lives as opportunities to deal with values and ethics.
- You can encourage students to think in complex ways about moral issues in life as they appear in the curriculum.
- You can use reading and writing activities to encourage moral and ethical thought.
- You might structure the learning environment so that it models democratic values and provides a safe environment for learning, sharing, and cooperating.
- You can encourage self-discipline through cooperative interaction between persons in the learning environment.
- You might use discussion, role-playing, and analytical and creative projects as a basis for critical thinking about values, attitudes, character traits, and moral issues.
- You can use cooperative learning activities to help students develop social interaction skills.
- You might establish parent support groups to develop a moral consensus.

The school environment itself can play a significant role in the creation of moral identity. As a teacher, you can serve as a model of behavior. You can guide students to discover morality in real life applications. The school as a whole can implement a model of a democratic society. Each student in the school community can play an active role in helping to develop a moral environment (Atkins, Hart, & Donnelly, 2004).

Think It Over

as a LEARNER   Can you describe a classroom you have been in where a teacher engaged students in activities or discussions related to their moral development? How did it work out?

as a TEACHER   For the grade level you plan to teach, would you engage your students in activities or discussions to enhance their moral development? Why or why not? If yes, what are some ways you might go about it?

Personal Development

Learning Objective 5

Describe and explain personal development, including social cognition, the self, friends' influence/peer pressure, and parenting.

Now that we have covered moral development, we look at another aspect of development: personal development. **Personal development** refers to the way young people interact with their environment, and the learning experiences that result, particularly as influenced by teachers, parents, and peers (Coolahan, Fantuzzo, Mendez, & McDermott, 2000). We will look at four important aspects of personal development: social cognition, the self, friends' influence/peer pressure, and parenting. As with moral development, as you study these ideas, you should be forming strategies for guiding your students.

Social Cognition

Social cognition represents the way we think about ourselves and other people, which is influenced by our social institutions, and in turn, influences our social relationships. We will examine a number of aspects of social cognition that will better help you understand personal development and its impact in social and educational settings.

Perspective Taking

Perspective taking is the ability to understand the thoughts and feelings of others (Arnett, 2007). Selman (1980) describes four levels among school-aged children:

Level 1—differentiated (ages 5–9): children recognize that others may see things differently than they do, but their understanding is one-way; that is, making another person happy is not seen as leading that other person to make you happy in return.

Level 2—reciprocal (ages 7–12): children can put themselves in another's shoes and realize that others can do the same.

Level 3—mutual (ages 10–15): children can see their own and another's perspective from the viewpoint of a third person such as a teacher, parent, or peer.

Level 4—in-depth (ages 12 and up): children can see that a person's perspective may represent a larger, societal viewpoint such as different beliefs for different generations or different cultures.

Perspective-taking abilities can play an important part in gaining popularity with peers and making new friends (Vernberg et al., 1994). Adopting another person's perspective may prompt perceivers to consider that person using the same cognitive processes as those normally used for self-introspection (Ames et al., 2008), suggesting that perspective taking can be learned and taught. Perspective taking also has been associated with **prosocial behavior,** or kind and considerate behavior (Eisenberg, Zhou, & Koller, 2001), suggesting that people who are good at perspective taking are also likely to be good at making new friends (Berk, 2006).

Perspective taking also contributes to **social problem solving,** or helping students solve interpersonal problems. Berk (2006) identifies four steps students can take for accomplishing this: (1) observe and interpret social cues, for example, someone is not willing to cooperate because she is not taken seriously; (2) identify social goals, for

personal development
the way young people interact with their environment and the learning experiences that result

social cognition
the way we think about ourselves and other people as influenced by social institutions

perspective taking
the ability to understand the thoughts and feelings of others

prosocial behavior
kind and considerate behavior

social problem solving
solving interpersonal problems

example, if we want to work together, we have to cooperate; (3) generate strategies, for example, having each of us take on a specific task; and (4) implement and evaluate the strategies, for example, everybody tried that and it seemed to work out well.

Adolescent Egocentrism

During early adolescence, I got it into my head that I was a great basketball player in the making. I pretended that there were baskets all over my house, my neighborhood, and even my school and everywhere I went I mimicked a jump shot, or a hook shot, or dribbling or slamming the ball through the hoop. People would give me all kinds of strange looks, but I thought I looked pretty cool. (Ben, age 14)

Adolescents, in particular, often find it difficult to distinguish between their own thoughts and the thoughts of others. They are self-centered, as reflected in Ben's story, hence **adolescent egocentrism**. It has three aspects, described below (Elkind, 1985).

The **imaginary audience** represents those people, often peers, who adolescents believe are thinking about them as much as they are thinking about themselves. This makes them very self-conscious about their appearance and their behavior. An example would be spending a lot of time examining yourself in the mirror to be sure your outfit conformed to the expected mode of dress and thereby avoid embarrassment in the eyes of all your peers who you view as having nothing better to do than look at you.

Kelly, Adams, & Jones (2002) concluded that imaginary audience experiences have more to do with social anxiety than cognitive development, while Bell & Bromnick (2003) found that adolescents are concerned with what other people think because real personal and social consequences exist. In this case, concerns can be regarded as based in social reality rather than imaginary.

adolescent egocentrism
when adolescents find it difficult to distinguish between their own thoughts and the thoughts of others

imaginary audience
the people that adolescents believe are thinking about them as much as they are thinking about themselves

Adolescents are often self-conscious about their appearance and behavior.

The **personal fable** is the belief that something special or unique about you causes others to be preoccupied with you. It can make you think no one understands you or that you have a unique destiny to fulfill (e.g., famous athlete, rock star). It can also make you think you can take risks without endangering yourself (Arnett, 2007).

Related to the personal fable is the **optimistic bias**—judging your own risk as less than the risk of others (Helweg-Larsen & Shepperd, 2001). It assumes that mishaps and misfortunes, such as having an accident while driving intoxicated, are more likely to happen to other people. A study about giving up smoking revealed that 60 percent of adolescent smokers believe they could smoke for a few years and then give it up, thus justifying to themselves the lack of danger associated with their current smoking behavior (Arnett, 2000).

The Self

How do I see myself? I'm pretty serious and I take things to heart, so my feelings often get hurt. I'm pretty much an introvert; I keep to myself so I don't have a lot of friends, maybe two or three at the most. I get along really well with my parents, but that's mostly because they don't tell me what to do. I tend to be anxious around boys. In school, I'm pretty outspoken, even sometimes obnoxious, because I like to be the one with the right answers. (Darlene, age 17)

Self-Concept

The **self-concept**, one's view of oneself, tends to develop more in adolescence than in pre-adolescence because of the greater use of abstractions in describing oneself, for example, as serious, introverted, outspoken, or obnoxious as in Darlene's story. This enables a person to distinguish between a number of different selves such as **actual self** (how you see yourself), **possible self** (what you could become), **ideal self** (what you would like to be), **feared self** (what you dread becoming), and **false self** (what you present to others, while realizing it doesn't represent what you are) (Whitty, 2002). Harter (1999) found that recognizing contradictions in your own behavior and personality creates confusion in terms of separating "the real me" from a variety of aspects of yourself as they appear in a variety of situations.

Self-Esteem

At breakfast I wanted waffles and not eggs, and I wanted to wear my football jersey to school so I ended up having a shouting match with my Mom and left the house feeling miserable. When I got to school, I met up with my buddies and had fun; that made me feel good. Later, I got my science test back with a grade of C- and that made me feel real bad. But when school let out, I got a real nice smile from this girl I like, and I felt great. (Lester, age 12)

Self-esteem is a person's overall sense of worth and well-being (Arnett, 2007). Rosenberg (1986) identified two aspects of self-esteem: **baseline self-esteem**, a person's stable, enduring sense of worth and well-being, and **barometric self-esteem**, a sense of worth and well-being that fluctuates as a person reacts to variations in thoughts, experiences, and interactions over the course of a day. Variations in

personal fable
the belief that something special or unique about you causes others to be preoccupied with you

optimistic bias
judging your own risk as less than the risk of others

self-concept
one's view of oneself

actual self
how you see yourself

possible self
what you could become

ideal self
what you would like to be

feared self
what you dread becoming

false self
what you present to others, while realizing it doesn't represent what you are

self-esteem
a person's overall sense of worth and well-being

baseline self-esteem
a person's stable, enduring sense of worth and well-being

barometric self-esteem
a sense of worth and well-being that fluctuates as a person reacts to variations in thoughts, experiences, and interactions over the course of a day

barometric self-esteem can be especially intense in early adolescence (Rosenberg, 1986), as Lester's story illustrates.

Harter (2003) lists the following eight domains of self-image:

- scholastic competence
- social acceptance
- athletic competence
- physical appearance
- job competence
- romantic appeal
- behavioral conduct
- close friendship

Ferkany (2008) suggests that self-esteem is crucially linked to the confidence and motivation needed by children to participate in and achieve educational pursuits. In addition, Ferkany suggests that it can be facilitated socially through interactions between the teacher and the student and between the student and the school's social environment. Manning (2007) contends that self-esteem is enhanced by teachers promoting competence in domains important to the student, and using interventions based on an accurate assessment of the student's deficits and targeted to the student's individual needs. Encouraging support from significant others is also recommended.

Social and Emotional Loneliness

"A substantial amount of adolescents' time is spent in their bedrooms with the door closed" (Arnett, 2007, p. 188). This does not necessarily mean they are lonely all the time. Some of the time they spend listening to music, talking on the telephone, watching TV, or even fantasizing. But those who spend a large amount of their time alone also have more school problems, more depression, and various other psychological difficulties (Larson & Richards, 1994).

Weiss (1973) distinguished between **social loneliness**, occurring when people lack social contacts and relationships, and **emotional loneliness**, when relationships lack closeness and intimacy. The first is lacking in quantity of contact while the latter lacks quality of contact. While the group most affected by loneliness is "emerging adults" (ages 19–24; Iacovou, 2002), it can also be experienced by children as young as kindergartners. Coplan, Arbeau, & Closson (2007) found that overall loneliness in kindergarten-aged children was associated with greater anxiety, aggression, and peer exclusion. Gender differences in behaviors associated with loneliness were also found, with girls more likely than boys to experience it. Moreover, the experience of emotional problems is more likely to be based on loneliness than on rejection (Qualter & Munn, 2002).

At the other end of the age distribution, college freshmen were found to experience less loneliness when they received more social support from their peers, which also increased their academic persistence. This was particularly true for women (Nicpon, Blanks, & Huser, 2006). In general, though, emotional loneliness is more common than social loneliness. In either case, the best antidote for loneliness is social support.

social loneliness
this occurs when people lack social contacts and relationships

emotional loneliness
this occurs when relationships lack closeness and intimacy

Friends' Influence/Peer Pressure

Friends, people with whom one has mutual relationships, and **peers**, people who share a common status, contribute to personal development in both positive and negative ways. Berndt (2004) describes the following four **types of support** that friends may provide to one another:

- **informational support:** guidance and advice in solving personal problems (such as those that arise from school or romantic relationships);
- **instrumental support:** helping with tasks such as homework or money management;
- **companionship support:** being with one another in social situations such as dances, sports events, eating lunch together, or sitting together on the school bus;
- **esteem support:** offering congratulations for successes and commiseration for failures; being there for one another.

Friends and peers usually congregate in **cliques**, small groups made up of people who know one another well, or **crowds**, larger groups who do not necessarily spend much time together (Brown & Klute, 2003). Arnett (2007) identifies the following eight **crowd labels** found in high schools:

- **populars** or **preppies:** those with the highest social status in the school;
- **jocks:** athletes on school teams;
- **brains, dweebs, nerds,** or **geeks:** socially inept students who strive for high grades;
- **druggies** or **burnouts:** alleged drug users who are aliens from the school environment;
- **dirties:** grunge-style clothing wearers; smart but academically disengaged;

friends

people with whom one has mutual relationships

peers

people who share a common status

types of support

ways in which people offer guidance, assistance, companionship, or emotional support to others

cliques

small groups made up of people who know one another well

crowds

larger groups who do not necessarily spend much time together

crowd labels

categories applied to different social groups

Sometimes in an effort to develop a separate identity, teenagers take on highly distinctive styles of appearance.

Ladi Kirn/Alamy

- **gothics** (or **goths**): wearers of black clothes who engage in deviant behavior and listen to heavy metal music;
- **nobodies:** those low in social skills and typically ignored;
- **normals:** these are students who blend in with the school environment.

Larson & Crouter (2002) report that the happiest moments students experience take place with friends (more so than with parents) because they mirror one another's emotions, and can talk about their deepest feelings with one another. At the same time, they worry about whether their fiends like them and whether they are popular enough (Larson & Richards, 1994). In addition, friends can push you into doing things you shouldn't be doing and into things you should be doing (usually referred to as **peer pressure**; Brown, 2004).

Many interactions between friends are not smooth. They can be antagonistic in order to keep people in line. To accomplish this, **ridicule** (making fun of or embarrassing someone) is a common technique. In its extreme form, this becomes **relational aggression**, defined as gossiping, spreading rumors, snubbing, and excluding. This is most common among girls, whose gender role prohibits more direct, physical conflict (Underwood, 2003).

When it comes to choosing friends, the major basis for choice tends to be similarity in gender, age, ethnicity, leisure preferences, and participation in risk behavior (Sampter (2003). This is referred to as **selective association** (Rose, 2002).

Social Skills and Popularity

Social skills are the key to popularity (Nangle et al., 2002). Well-liked people are those who are friendly, sensitive to others, good listeners, and good communicators. They often are the leaders of and eager participants in group activity. They manage to draw people in without appearing arrogant. Unpopular people often lack social skills. They suffer from either rejection, due to their quarrelsome and belligerent behavior, or neglect, because of their shyness and withdrawal (Prinstein & La Greca, 2004).

Weissberg, Kaplan, and Harwood (1991) designed a program for teachers to help rejected students learn how to control anger and aggressiveness, by following six steps when they began to lose self-control:

- Stop, calm down, think before you act.
- Go over the problem and say or write down your feelings.
- Set a positive goal for the outcome of the situation.
- Think of positive solutions that will lead toward that goal.
- Try to anticipate the consequences of the possible solutions.
- Choose the best solution and try it out.

It has been found that elementary school teachers stress the importance of social skills, particularly cooperation and self-control, which they regard more highly than assertiveness (Meier & DiPerna, 2006). Moreover, teachers who take classroom time to teach students to manage their emotions and to practice caring, empathy, and cooperation can expect to see a consequent improvement in their students' academic achievement (Viadero, 2007).

peer pressure

friends pushing one another to do things they should or should not be doing

ridicule

making fun of or embarrassing someone

relational aggression

conflict in the form of gossiping, spreading rumors, snubbing, and excluding

selective association

the tendency for people to choose friends based on gender, age, ethnicity, leisure preferences, and participation in risk behavior

social skills

interpersonal skills that affect an individual's ability to interact with others

Parenting

My parents are very laid back, at least in terms of the way they treat me. They pretty much let me make my own decisions, because I get good grades in school and also manage to stay out of trouble. I guess they figure that I can manage my life so they cut me a lot of slack, which is what I like. This makes me the envy of all my friends! (Bernard, age 15)

Above and beyond friends and peers, parents have the potential to provide the strongest influence on children and adolescents. A major factor that affects personal development is the **parenting style** of the parents, which is described in terms of two dimensions: **demandingness**, the degree to which parents set down rules and expectations for their children's behavior and require their children to comply with them, and **responsiveness**, the degree to which parents are sensitive to their children's needs and express love, warmth, and concern for their children (Steinberg & Silk, 2002). These two dimensions have been combined to yield the four distinct parenting styles described below (Baumrind, 1991, Steinberg & Silk, 2002).

1. **Authoritative parents** are high in both demandingness and responsiveness. They set clear rules and expectations, which they explain, discuss, and negotiate with their children; indicate the consequences for noncompliance; and enforce those consequences when it becomes necessary. At the same time, they are loving and warm toward their children, and provide for their desires and their needs.
2. **Authoritarian parents** are high in demandingness and low in responsiveness. They require obedience from their children and provide punishment for its nonoccurrence. There is no give-and-take as is true for authoritative parents. In addition, they show little warmth or love toward their children. They act with seeming emotional detachment.
3. **Permissive parents** are low in demandingness but high in responsiveness. They have limited expectations for their children and rarely discipline them. At the same time, they provide their children with unconditional love and give them considerable freedom to do what they want (as illustrated in Bernard's story).
4. **Disengaged parents** are low in both demandingness and responsiveness. They require little of their children and thus devote the minimum amount of time, effort, and emotion into parenting them. They impose few limits on their children, require little of them, show them little love or concern, and seem to have little if any emotional attachment to them.

According to data provide by Steinberg et al. (1994), 35 percent of parents are authoritative, 18 percent are authoritarian, 12 percent are permissive, and 35 percent are disengaged. Of the four parenting styles, authoritative parenting appears best for adolescents, because while they have become capable of exercising more autonomy and self-regulation than previously in their lives, they still need the balance provided by authoritative parenting to act responsibly.

Table 3.4 provides a *Concept Review* of the aspects of personal development.

parenting style

the level of demandingness and responsiveness that parents display in raising their children

demandingness

the degree to which parents set down rules and expectations for their children's behavior and require their children to comply with them

responsiveness

the degree to which parents are sensitive to their children's needs and express love, warmth, and concern for their children

authoritative parents

parents that are high in demandingness and responsiveness

authoritarian parents

parents that are high in demandingness and low in responsiveness

permissive parents

parents that are low in demandingness but high in responsiveness

disengaged parents

parents that are low in both demandingness and responsiveness

CONCEPT REVIEW TABLE 3.4
Aspects of Personal Development

ASPECT	COMPONENTS	WHAT IT MEANS
Social Cognition	Perspective taking	Understanding others' thoughts and feelings
	Adolescent egocentrism	Cannot distinguish between one's own and others' thoughts
The Self	Self-concept	How you think of yourself
	Self-esteem	Your sense of self-worth
	Loneliness	Lacking personal contact and intimacy
Friends' Influence/Peer Pressure	Support	Ways friends help one another
	Crowd labels	Ways of categorizing types of students
	Social skills	Making others like you
Parenting	Authoritative	Demanding and responsive
	Authoritarian	Demanding but not responsive
	Permissive	Not demanding but responsive
	Disengaged	Neither demanding nor responsive

Think It Over

as a Learner   How would you describe your social skills and self-esteem, and the role your parents have played in your development?

as a Teacher   How would you go about enhancing the social skills and self-esteem of the students you are, or will be, teaching?

Learning Objective 6

Outline Erikson's eight stages of psychosocial development in terms of the developmental crises faced in each, and summarize procedures for building initiative, industry, and identity in the school context.

Erikson's Stages of Psychosocial Development

Erik Erikson was particularly interested in how people developed their **ego identity**, or their sense of who they really are. He saw ego identity as the essence of a person's individuality, within the context of society and the demands of the culture. His view was that a person's identity is formed as the result of a series of developmental crises that occur naturally within the social environment at different stages of life.

In dealing with each of these crises and attempting to master the challenges they pose, individuals either grow toward greater **self-actualization** (greater mastery, unity of personality, and accuracy of perception), or regress toward a more infantile resolution (Erikson, 1968). It is important that youth achieve a sense of self, and develop their own beliefs and perspectives (Johnson, Buboltz, & Seemann, 2003).

Crisis, to Erikson, represented "a turning point or a crucial period of increased vulnerability and heightened potential" (Erikson, 1968, p. 96) rather than a threat or catastrophe. Each crisis, in each stage, represented an opportunity for a person to develop another aspect of self or identity in either a healthy or an unhealthy way. It is to each of these eight stages (Erikson, 1963, 1968) that the discussion now turns. (The desire for self-actualization as a motivational force will be encountered again in Chapter 10.)

Infancy: Basic Needs (Trust versus Mistrust)

Infancy is a time of dependency on others, particularly on the mother, for the satisfaction of basic needs. Food, shelter, security, and care must be provided by another person. When these basic needs are fulfilled, infants learn to trust others as well as develop a fundamental sense of their own trustworthiness. When an estrangement or a distance exists between parent and child such that basic needs are not adequately met, infants develop a sense of mistrust, often accompanied by a tendency to withdraw into themselves. Hence, we can "regard basic trust as the cornerstone of a vital personality" (Erikson, 1968, p. 97).

It is true that newborns live through their mouths. To live, therefore, they must be met by the coordinated ability and intention of their mothers to feed them. But the infant's need to incorporate or take into itself soon extends to sensory and social stimuli as well. It is through such receiving and accepting that infants first encounter their culture. It is also by "getting what is given" that a person develops the inclination to be a giving person. Erikson (1968) refers to the relationship between mother and infant as mutuality, a term already introduced by Piaget.

In the latter part of infancy, the need to incorporate manifests itself as taking and holding onto things. As the mother begins to withdraw as part of weaning and becomes less involved in child care, the infant may feel abandoned. This feeling may produce a sense of mistrust. It is at this point that young children must begin to learn to depend on, or trust, themselves. Although the quantity of maternal care may be reduced, if the quality is maintained, the sense of trust is likely to survive this crisis.

Traditional child care, Erikson (1968) believes, is likely to produce the least conflict and hence the most trust. And with trust comes a gain in psychosocial strength, along with the origin of later feelings of faith, hope, and optimism.

Toddlerhood: Self-Control (Autonomy versus Shame and Doubt)

As children grow, their needs grow too, along with new possibilities for satisfaction and frustration. At the same time, two other factors increase in children's lives: the number and kind of people to whom they can respond, and their capacities and skills for dealing with their physical and social environment. *It is the experience with new encounters and the necessity to manage them, coupled with the sense of having to do it more and more alone, that evokes the developmental crisis of each period.*

ego identity
a person's sense of who they really are

self-actualization
individual growth achieved through dealing with developmental crises

At this stage of life, the need to successfully manage the combined acts of holding on and letting go, associated with such tasks as toilet training and self-control, are critical to the child's development of an autonomous or independent will.

It is during the toddler period that children learn to delineate their world into "me" and "you," and "mine" and "yours." According to Erikson (1968, p. 109), "the matter of mutual regulation between adult and child now faces its severest test!" If the parent is overcontrolling, overdemanding, or overprotective, the child will be faced with defeat—represented by feelings of doubt and shame. The creation of these feelings now is often accompanied in later life by an excessive degree of conscience or compulsiveness. If the child is allowed to experience a sense of self-control without loss of self-esteem, feelings of free will or autonomy will be the positive result. The child will become convinced that she is a person in her own right. However, positive resolution at this stage, as at all others, presupposes positive resolution at all preceding stages. Hence, trust is a prerequisite for the development of autonomy or free will.

Early Childhood: Purpose (Initiative versus Guilt)

Three relevant developments occur in early childhood that support the potential emergence of a realistic sense of ambition and purpose in the young child. These are (1) the opportunity for greater freedom of movement; (2) the development of language, making it possible for the child to question; and (3) an expansion of imagination and dreams (Erikson, 1968, p. 115). Out of this develops the anticipation of adult roles and the possibility of a sense of initiative, a vitality to explore and try new things. The child's learning leads away from the child's own limitations and into his or her future possibilities.

This is the stage of play and curiosity, of powerful impulses to explore and express. If these impulses are thwarted, frustrated, or condemned by adults, the result will be guilt—the pangs of conscience and self-condemnation. And the morality of guilt can, according to Erikson (1968, p. 119), "become synonymous with vindictiveness and with the suppression of others" when it grows out of experiences with a parent who tries to get away with the very transgressions the child has been told are unacceptable. In later life, the absence of initiative will be represented by self-restriction and self-denial.

The necessary adult role is to offer children of this age models for action by example. Successful models offer children appropriate avenues for exploration and mastery rather than providing them with an endless stream of "don'ts." The heroes of children's fantasies must gradually be replaced with realistic role models such as a parent or teacher who can function more like a companion than an overseer. Only then can the child establish the "steadily growing conviction, undaunted by guilt, that 'I am what I can imagine I will be'" (Erikson, 1968, p. 122). (Models and their effects will be explored further in Chapter 6.)

School Age: Productivity (Industry versus Inferiority)

When children enter elementary school, they usually are ready to learn to perform, share obligations, apply discipline, work cooperatively, and imitate. Each child is ready to make things and make them well, become a worker, and develop

Play satisfies impulses to explore, and satisfies the child's growing curiosity. The development of initiative is the result.

Creatas/PhotoLibrary

what Erikson (1968) called a sense of industry. At this age, children seek to win recognition by producing and accomplishing things.

If a child (1) is not prepared by family life to take on the responsibility of productiveness, (2) still wants to be a "baby," or (3) has had his will to learn thwarted by criticism and lack of opportunity, then a sense of inferiority or unworthiness will develop at this stage. This is the feeling that he will never be any good. It is an important time for teachers to emphasize what children can do rather than what they cannot do, to help them avoid or overcome this feeling. Teaching children to set challenging yet attainable goals helps them learn how to achieve success (Dweck, 1999).

The child's optimal environment at this stage is one that features neither the extreme of restraint and the strict imposition of duty nor the extreme of autonomy and its total lack of structure. In other words, for industriousness to develop as part of a child's identity, the environment must fall somewhere in between total work and total play. Given the guided opportunity for learning the necessary skills to function in a school setting, a child can come to believe that "I am what I can learn to make work" (Erikson, 1968, p. 127).

Adolescence: Self-Discovery (Identity versus Confusion)

Ranny replaced her alcoholic, sexually promiscuous mother as the responsible one in the family. She was her highly moral father's favorite, and before she left for college, they had long intellectual discussions. During her first year in college, Ranny was a serious, dedicated science student. The next year, she acquired a reputation as a brilliant but erratic student, one who almost failed courses but always rescued herself at the last moment. She was known as a drinking "party girl" who dated only athletes; she pretended to be promiscuous, although she graduated still a virgin. Finally, in her senior year, Ranny became a serious student in a useful but not especially intellectual field. And she kept her fun-loving personality. During her first year in college, Ranny slavishly imitated her father. In the next few years, she blindly mimicked her mother by living out a "party" life. But throughout, she remained true to some inner voice and pulled it all together in her final year.

We form our adult consciousness slowly during our adolescent years. Step by step, we abandon our parents as models and begin to construct our own identities. By about age 22, we have to leave the half-child, half-adult world in which we can be anyone and settle into being someone. Each time we replace a piece of childhood consciousness with adult consciousness, we become our own someone. The process is painful—but also exciting and rewarding. (Gould, R.L. (1978). *Transformations: Growth and change in adult life*. New York: Simon & Schuster, pp. 68–69.) How can the above description of Ranny's life and the message it contains help you become a more effective teacher of adolescents?

All preceding development seems to coalesce in the period of adolescence. If everything has gone well thus far, adolescents, such as Ranny, will possess (1) trust in themselves and in others, (2) a sense of autonomy or free will in choosing their life directions, (3) the initiative and imagination to focus on what they might become, and

(4) the industry to work in order to meet their goals. Taken together, these qualities create the potential for the self-discovery of a sense of identity if they are present in an environment where expression is permitted, choices are available, and recognition and acceptance are forthcoming. Without these qualities or the opportunity to express them, the question of identity or "who I am" will become cloudy and confused.

Identity represents the image persons have of who they are, defined in terms of their abilities, likes and dislikes, hopes, and expectations. Career choices, sexual choices, and beliefs about the surrounding world all grow out of the sense of identity. Integrating their intellectual, social, moral, and sexual aspects of themselves helps adolescents develop a unified self-identity (Harter, 1998).

How confident are adolescents of their identity? How confused are they? Are they committed to an identity, or searching for one? Some, though not many, according to Marcia (1980, 1988, 2002), have reached a state of **identity achievement**. They have experimented and explored and know, at least for now, what they want out of life. They have set their goals and have a plan for achieving them. Later in life, there may be detours or reversals, but at this point they have made some carefully planned choices.

Other adolescents have chosen **identity foreclosure**. Rather than explore the possibilities, they have simply chosen a predetermined path—often the career of a parent—and are committed to that choice. They have taken on or borrowed an identity and may experience much confusion in the future if that identity does not work. Students need guidance and support from teachers and families that help them prevent foreclosing on identity options (Kerka, 2003).

Many adolescents experience **identity diffusion**. Some have thought about their future but reached no conclusion; others have avoided making choices at all. These are the confused ones. Should I go to college or work? What should I major in? What school should I go to? Should I get married or stay single? They have many questions and few answers.

Finally, some adolescents are in a state of **moratorium**. They are struggling to find the best occupational and ideological directions to follow by exploring and trying out new things. Although this may cause them to postpone their final decisions, it is a necessary and positive step for them, one that may result in identity achievement. They may be leaning in a certain direction, but they are not ready to firm up that choice.

Research shows there is a relationship between adolescent identity status and other developmental characteristics (Berzonsky & Adams, 1999). Adolescents in both the achievement and moratorium statuses are more likely to be self-directed, good at problem solving, and cooperative than those in the other two categories; those in moratorium status are understandably more indecisive than those in achievement status. Alternatively, adolescents classified in the diffusion category are lower in self-control and self-esteem than those in achievement and moratorium statuses. Diffusion status is considered the least favorable by virtue of its link to poorer relationships with parents, anxiety, apathy, and other psychological problems (Berzonsky & Adams, 1999). Adolescents in foreclosure status show more conventionality, conformity, and obedience to authority than those in the other three statuses (Phinney,

identity achievement

adolescents that know what they want out of life

identity foreclosure

adolescents choose to follow a predetermined path, rather than explore their possibilities

identity diffusion

confusion adolescents may feel when considering their future

moratorium

a state in which adolescents struggle to find the best occupational and ideological directions to follow

Angela Hampton/Alamy

Some adolescents use volunteer activities, like helping in a hospital, to find the occupation that best fits them and helps them get out of their state of moratorium.

2000). Not surprisingly, they also show strong parental attachment that may account for their choice to limit exploration and follow their parents' guidance.

Another important finding is that identity achievement is not nearly complete by the end of high school, with only about one-quarter of students reaching this status (Waterman, 1999). For many adolescents, the path to identity achievement extends well into college and even beyond, meaning a postponement of entrance into full adulthood. Ranny, in the previous story, is an example of this.

How can the problems of adolescence be dealt with in ourselves, our children, and the students we teach? As in many of the preceding stages, a balance must be struck between too little and too much freedom, too much and too little structure. Neither total control nor total autonomy is conducive to resolving the identity crisis of adolescence. External control and externally imposed structure must gradually be decreased so that adolescents can set their own standards based on who they are. But adults must still help provide adolescents with some sense of limits and support for efforts gone awry as the process of identity formation begins to gel. The adolescents' transition to adulthood must be made possible, yet neither the adolescents nor their parents should expect their childhood to be instantaneously and totally abandoned.

Young Adulthood: Sharing (Intimacy versus Isolation)

Intimacy represents a fusing of identities, a joining together or sharing by two people. It goes beyond sexual intimacy, because it includes sharing in many regards—combining sexual intimacy with friendship. Those choosing impersonal or highly stereotyped interpersonal relationships over genuine sharing develop or retain a deep sense of isolation or separation. The manner in which adolescent romantic couples resolve disagreements affects the longevity of their relationships. Research reveals that couples who either minimize problems or use direct conflict to resolve problems tend to have less enduring relationships than couples who utilize integrative strategies to solve their disagreements (Shulman, Tuval-Mashiach, Levran, & Anbar, 2006).

T e a c h S o u r c e
V i d e o C a s e

Social and Emotional Development: Understanding Adolescents

In this video segment, you'll see how adolescent boys deal with their anger and how they can be helped to devise ways to deal with their emotions. The video shows a group of seventh-grade boys discussing their feelings with a guidance counselor and coming up with a list of coping strategies. You'll also see the counselor sharing her ideas with another teacher.

After viewing the video case, consider what you have just watched about boys' anger management issues and answer the questions below:

1. The video deals with anger management in adolescent boys. What do you think of the strategies for anger management that the boys identify and those that the counselor encourages them to use?

2. In what ways do you feel the discussion benefits the boys, and is it likely to lead them to manage their anger?

3. As a classroom teacher, how might you facilitate the social and emotional development of your adolescent male students in general, and specifically learn how to control their anger?

You can view the video case at the Education CourseMate. Go to:
CengageBrain.com

Shared intimacy defines the meaning of love, according to Erikson (1968), and the result is shared identity between two people. Where individual identities have not yet developed, love is impossible. People who attain the stage of intimacy together believe that "we are what we love" (Erikson, 1968, p. 138).

Young adults can also avoid isolation by becoming involved with others through social activities and memberships in clubs and organizations. Foubert & Granger (2006) report that involved college students are more likely to move through autonomy toward interdependence and establishing and clarifying purpose than uninvolved students.

Adulthood: Parenting (Generativity versus Stagnation)

Generativity refers to a "concern for establishing and guiding the next generation" (Erikson, 1968, p. 138). It represents the parenting not only of children but of ideas. Its byproduct is productivity and the capability to live a satisfying and useful life. A lack of generativity yields boredom, dissatisfaction, even apathy, and a pervading sense of stagnation. Adults who are able to attain a sense of generativity through family and career represent caring, self-fulfilled, and contributing members of society.

Old Age: Self-Acceptance (Integrity versus Despair)

By accepting yourself, your life as it has been lived, and those people who played a significant role in it, you develops a sense of integrity, of wholeness. Self-acceptance carries with it an acceptance of fate, lifestyle and life cycle, and of the people and institutions in an individual's world. Those who lack this self-acceptance or acceptance of old age and its circumstances experience disgust and a sense of despair. It often is hidden behind cynicism, hostility, displeasure, and contempt. Erikson (1968) calls the strength born of integrity "wisdom." And it manifests itself at this stage by the belief that "I am what I am." (See Table 3.5 for a *Concept Review* of Erikson's eight stages of psychosocial development.)

CONCEPT REVIEW TABLE 3.5

Erikson's Stages of Psychosocial Development

PSYCHOSOCIAL STAGE	PERIOD OF LIFE	CHARACTERISTICS
Trust vs. Mistrust	Infancy	Fulfillment of basic needs leads to trust in self and others, along with a sense of faith and hope, rather than mistrust.
Autonomy vs. Shame	Toddlerhood	Opportunity for self-control leads to a sense of autonomy rather than doubt of selfhood.
Initiative vs. Guilt	Early childhood	Opportunity to play and explore leads to learning initiative within limits rather than feeling guilty about one's behavior.
Industry vs. Inferiority	School age	Opportunity to perform and succeed at "work" tasks yields a sense of industriousness, not inferiority.
Identity vs. Confusion	Adolescence	Opportunity for expression, choice, and acceptance leads to the development of a sense of who one is rather than to confusion over identity.
Intimacy vs. Isolation	Young adulthood	Accepting the opportunity for openness and sharing with others results in intimacy and love rather than separation and isolation.
Generativity vs. Stagnation	Adulthood	Choosing to become the parent of children or the producer of a career represents the generative sense; to do otherwise is to stagnate.
Integrity vs. Despair	Old age	Accepting oneself and one's life gives a sense of wholeness and completion rather than of disgust and despair.

Source: Adapted from Erikson, E.H. (1968). *Identity: Youth and crisis*. New York: Norton.

Applying Erikson in the Classroom

Teachers need to create classroom environments that relate to the psychosocial stage of their students. This means helping preschoolers build initiative; helping elementary and middle schoolers build identity; and helping adult, returning students build generativity. Some specific suggestions for how to accomplish this are given in Table 3.6.

T A B L E   3 . 6

Helping to Build Initiative, Industry, Identity, and Generativity

Building Initiative in Preschool

- Let children make choices for themselves (especially of learning activities they want to engage in).
- Help children succeed at the activities they choose.
- Create activities that enable children to play different roles.
- Don't use adult standards to evaluate what children do.
- Be supportive of what children try to do even if it does not come out perfectly.
- Make children take responsibility for some aspect of their learning and play environment.

Building Industry in Elementary and Middle School

- Increase the amount of responsibility students must take for their learning and play environment.
- Expose students to realistic occupational models.
- Identify positive aspects of the performance of each student.
- Provide students with encouragement regarding their ability to succeed.
- Give recognition for jobs well done.

Building Identity in High School

- Create a climate of trust and acceptance.
- Help students become aware of their values
- Help students build their self-concepts.
- Give students the opportunity to set goals.
- Build choices for students into the curriculum.
- Exhibit patience and understanding when dealing with behavior.

Building Generativity in Returning Students

- Show respect for a student's "adultness."
- Build on the many experiences of adult students.
- Recognize the other skills adults bring to the classroom.
- Relate to the adult student as a person.
- Help the adult student feel comfortable in the classroom context.
- Give the adult the opportunity to make a productive contribution.

Think It Over

as a LEARNER   What stage of psychosocial development do you expect the students to be in that you plan to teach? Why are you planning to teach students at this level?

as a TEACHER   Will you engage your students in activities intended to facilitate their psychosocial development, and if so, what activities might you use?

racial identity

a sense of group or collective identity based on one's perception that he or she shares a common racial heritage with a particular racial group

Racial Identity

As we have already seen, Erikson (1968) viewed identity development as a central issue of adolescence. It is during this period of life when children seek to define themselves based on characteristics such as personality, interests, physical attributes, ethnic orientation, and other distinct traits (Moshman, 1999). While participation in the exploratory behaviors and experimentation that contribute to identity development is typical of virtually all adolescents, it has been proposed that this developmental process has a somewhat different focus for persons of different races and ethnicities as compared to American Caucasians. In particular, for African Americans, the focus is reflected in a search for **racial identity** that carries with it a sense of belongingness and pride (Cross, 1998), and that is represented by a "sense of group or collective identity based on one's perception that he or she shares a common racial heritage with a particular racial group" (Helms, 1990, p. 3). This perception of communality among African Americans is based on recognition of "a common thread of historical experience and a sense that each member of the collectivity, regardless of how distinct he or she may be, somehow shares in this historical experience" (ibid, p. 4). (A model of racial identity appears in Box 3.4.)

Kris Timken/Blend Images/Jupiter Images

Students develop racial identity by sharing interests and belongingness with other members of a group.

DISCOURSE ON DIVERSITY

A Model of African American Racial Identity

BOX 3.4

While early research on racial identity showed that African American children preferred to be like Caucasian dolls—a reflection of a negative self-image based on living in a society that "consistently labels them as inferior" (Clark, 1989, p. 128)—the Civil Rights and other consciousness movements led to the "redefinition of the constituent groups' identities and political consciousness" (Cole and Stewart, 1996, p. 99). This resulted in a considerable increase in positive self-perceptions by African Americans.

Dimensions of Racial Identity

A comprehensive model of African American racial identity that reconciles Dubois' (1903) concepts of the "African self" and "American self" has been proposed by Sellers et al. (1998). It addresses two important questions: "How important is race in the individual's perception of self?" and "What does it mean to be a member of this racial group?" (Sellers et al., 1998). It assumes that perception of racial identity is a valid indicator of identity and that individual differences exist in what it means to be African American. Rather than introduce a developmental sequence or stages, it considers individuals based on the significance and qualitative meaning of race to them at that point in their life.

The model incorporates three dimensions: (1) racial centrality, or how central an African American feels race is to his or her self-concept (i.e., whether an individual chooses to define him- or herself as an African American); (2) private regard, or how positive or negative the attitudes are that an African American holds about him- or herself (i.e., the level of esteem one affords to being African American); (3) public regard, or one's assessment of others' perceptions of African Americans as a whole (i.e., the perceived level of acceptance by Caucasians).

Profiles of Racial Identity

To apply this model as a basis for classification, Chavous et al. (2003) conceived of racial identity profiles that simultaneously consider the three dimensions described above. This has yielded the following four profiles: (1) Idealized—high on all three dimensions (race is central; high racial self-esteem; high perceived esteem by Caucasians); (2) Buffering/Defensive—high on centrality of race and racial self-esteem, but low on perceived esteem by Caucasians; (3) Low Connectedness/High Affinity—low on centrality of race and perceived esteem by Caucasians, but high on racial self-esteem; (4) Alienated—low on all three dimensions.

Chavous et al. (2003) report findings suggesting that those African American students classified as Idealized (high on all three dimensions) are the most successful students of the four groups, while those classified as either Alienated (low on all three dimensions) or Low Connectedness/High Affinity (low on two of the three dimensions) are the least successful academically, with the Buffering/Defensive group (high on two of the three dimensions) in between. In contrast, Harper and Tuckman (2007) report findings that students classified as Alienated are the most successful academically, rather than the least, suggesting that some African American students, particularly males, deliberately reject academic achievement as "acting white" and, thus, distance themselves from behaviors that would ensure educational success (Fordham & Ogbu, 1986; Ogbu, 2003).

SUMMING IT UP

Explain Piaget's three stages of the development of moral judgment—moral realism, mutuality, and autonomy—including his concepts of justice and punishment.

Piaget's conception of **moral development** focuses on three stages of how children learn to make **moral judgments**, based on the concepts of **justice** and **punishment**. The first stage, **moral realism**, is characterized by a belief in **objective responsibility**: believing (a) one must take responsibility for one's transgressions, regardless of the intentions behind them, and (b) the magnitude of the punishment should fit the magnitude of the crime. In this stage, children evaluate outcomes in terms of the material result rather than the motive. Evaluation results in **expiatory punishment**: penance paid for wrongdoing, and **retributive justice**, or "an eye for an eye," and **adult restraint** is what controls children's behavior. The second stage is **mutuality** or "doing unto others as you would have them do unto you," using shared rules enforced by mutual consent; and judging wrongdoing by means of **distributive justice**, or treating everyone the same (equality). The child applies the principle of **reciprocity**, meaning the punishment should fit the spirit of the crime. In the third stage, **autonomy**, the more abstract notion of **equity**, judging everyone on an individual basis as a function of circumstances, replaces the peer-imposed constraint of equality as the basis for judgment. This means accepting some behaviors from some people, based on their unique unmet needs, but not from others.

> **Learning Objective 1**
>
> **Key Concepts:**
>
> moral development, moral judgment, intentionality (p. 91); moral realism, objective responsibility, heteronomous morality, expiatory punishment (p. 93); retributive justice, adult restraint, immanent justice, mutuality, reciprocity, distributive justice (p. 95); autonomy, autonomous morality, equity (p. 96).

Explain Kohlberg's six stages of moral development—punishment-obedience, personal reward, good person, law and order, social contract, and universal ethical principle—within three levels: preconventional, conventional, and postconventional.

Kohlberg elaborated on Piaget, converting his stages into levels—preconventional, conventional, postconventional—and dividing each level into two stages of **moral reasoning**. He detected these stages by posing **moral dilemmas**, situations in which children must choose between undesirable alternatives (e.g., letting a loved one die versus stealing to save her), and examining their responses. The preconventional level is akin to moral realism, wherein children base their judgment of what is "wrong" on what they will get punished for doing (in Stage 1, the punishment-obedience orientation) and what is "right" on what is materially good for them (Stage 2, personal-reward orientation). In Level 2, or conventional moral reasoning, the emphasis is on doing one's duty—that which is expected or that which will please other people (Stage 3, good-person orientation)—or on respecting authority and maintaining the social order for its own sake (Stage 4, law-and-order orientation). In Level 3, or postconventional moral reasoning, laws are taken as relative, reflecting a social consensus to

> **Learning Objective 2**
>
> **Key Concepts:**
>
> moral reasoning, moral dilemma (p. 99).

maintain social standards and protect individual right (Stage 5, social-contract orientation) or as abstract, ethical principles, defined not so much by mutual consent as by "conscience" (Stage 6, universal-ethical-principal orientation).

Learning Objective 3

Key Concepts:

selfish morality, conventional morality, social morality, principled morality (p. 105).

Describe the limitations of Kohlberg's model, including Gilligan's criticism based on gender differences, and her proposed alternative model for women.

Kohlberg's theory has been criticized as confounding moral reasoning and moral behavior and having an overlap between the stages, but most importantly, for not adequately explaining moral development in women. Gilligan's work suggests that women, in contrast to men, are less influenced in their moral judgments by abstract notions of justice and influenced by more immediate consideration of responsibility and caring. While the sequence of stages has been found to occur in many diverse cultures, the transition between stages is far from complete, with twice as many people ending up with conventional morality as with either pre- or postconventional levels. Moral development has been shown to relate to age, education level, and parents' childrearing practices, but not to religious affiliation.

Learning Objective 4

Key Concepts:

moral education, plus-one matching (p. 109).

Discuss and illustrate procedures for enhancing moral development.

Moral education, that is, discussions of moral dilemmas in junior and senior high school classrooms have been found to stimulate moral thought and produce moral empathy. Ignoring moral development may be the same as ignoring disruptive behavior. Classroom discussions of relevant issues are encouraged to help students exchange perspectives, connect values and actions, and learn to listen to one another. Teachers can help by presenting conflicting arguments at the next higher stage of moral reasoning, a technique called **plus-one matching**.

Learning Objective 5

Key Concepts:

perspective taking (p. 113); adolescent egocentrism (p. 114); self-concept, self-esteem (p. 115); social and emotional loneliness (p. 116); types of support, crowd labels (p. 117); social skills and popularity, authoritative, authoritarian, permissive, and disengaged parenting (p. 118).

Describe and explain personal development, including social cognition, the self, friends' influence/peer pressure, and parenting.

Personal development includes (1) social cognition or understanding, with two components: **perspective taking** (understanding the thoughts and feelings of others) and **adolescent egocentrism** (not distinguishing between self thoughts and others' thoughts; (2) the self, with three components: **self-concept** (how you think of yourself), **self-esteem** (your sense of self-worth), and **social and emotional loneliness** (lacking personal contact and intimacy); (3) friends' influence/peer pressure, with three components: **support** (ways that friends help one another), **crowd labels** (how different types of students are categorized), and **social skills/popularity** (ways of interacting with others to make them like you); (4) parenting, with four components: **authoritative** (both demanding and responsive), **authoritarian** (demanding but not responsive), **permissive** (not demanding but responsive), and **disengaged** (neither demanding nor responsive).

Outline Erikson's eight stages of psychosocial development in terms of the developmental crises faced in each, and summarize procedures for building initiative, industry, and identity in the school context.

In *infancy*, the crisis is over satisfaction of one's basic needs, such as food and shelter; need fulfillment is accompanied by a sense of *trust* in others as well as in oneself; weaning too soon or too late provokes instead a sense of *mistrust*. The *toddler* faces a crisis over who is in control: child or parent, particularly regarding toilet training. Experiencing a sense of self-control without loss of self-esteem develops *autonomy*, while overdemanding or overprotective parents cause the child to feel *shame and doubt*. The preschoolers of *early childhood* must learn a realistic sense of purpose and ambition through play and curiosity, exploration, and expression to develop *initiative*, while frustration and condemnation by adults provoke a sense of *guilt*. *School age* brings on the need to perform, share tasks, and apply discipline. Given the opportunity and stimulus to be productive yields a sense of *industry*, a belief that one can learn to make things work, while too much restraint or too little structure results in a sense of *inferiority*. In *adolescence*, if all has gone well thus far and choices are available and expression encouraged, a sense of **ego identity**, rather than *confusion*, will result. Optimally, **identity achievement**, or knowing what you want out of life, will develop—as opposed to **identity foreclosure** (automatically following a prescribed plan), **identity diffusion** (not knowing what you want to do), or **moratorium** (postponing your decisions). In *young adulthood*, choosing to share yields *intimacy*, while choosing impersonal relationships yields *isolation*. In *adulthood*, the choice is between parenting of family and ideas, which yields *generativity*, and following a narrower, more fixed path into *stagnation*. Finally, *old age* offers the choice between self-acceptance or *integrity* and disgust or *despair*. Building initiative requires letting children make choices, play different roles, take responsibility, observe occupational models, receive performance feedback, encouragement, and recognition for jobs well done, experience a climate of trust and acceptance, become aware of their values, build their self-concepts, set goals, and exhibit patience and understanding.

Learning Objective 6

Key Concepts:
ego identity, self-actualization (p. 121); identity achievement, identity foreclosure, identity diffusion, moratorium (p. 124).

Illustrate the characteristics and categories of a model of African American racial identity.

A model of African American **racial identity identifies** three dimensions of importance to development: (a) *centrality*, or importance of race to one's self-concept; (b) *private regard*, or the level of self-esteem one affords to one's racial identity; (c) *public regard*, or the perceived level of esteem afforded by Caucasians to African Americans. Combinations of these dimensions affect academic success rates.

Learning Objective 7

Key Concepts:
racial identity (p. 129); racial centrality, private regard, public regard, racial identity profiles (p. 130).

4 | Learner Diversity

After reading this chapter, you should be able to meet the following learning objectives	Chapter Contents
LEARNING OBJECTIVE 1 Illustrate how social class relates to experiences that students may have in school and discuss the importance of social justice practices like critical pedagogy that a teacher can employ to insure all students have an opportunity for a quality education.	Social Class Differences • Critical Pedagogy • Differentiated Instruction • Class Size
LEARNING OBJECTIVE 2 Support how students' experiences in school are influenced by their ethnicity and culture and tell some of the history of what African American students went through during the desegregation movement.	Differences in Ethnicity and Culture • Ethnic Identity Development • School Desegregation • Multicultural Education
LEARNING OBJECTIVE 3 Describe the different demographic and language patterns in America's public schools and discuss approaches to assisting English language learners.	Language Diversity • English Language Education Approaches • Accommodating English Language Learners
LEARNING OBJECTIVE 4 Explain how schooling can be biased towards students based on gender and orientation and discuss methods a teacher could implement to insure an equitable and safe classroom environment.	Gender Differences • Gender Bias • Sexual Orientation
LEARNING OBJECTIVE 5 Distinguish between the different definitions of intelligence and generalize about how the definition a teacher chooses impacts how they teach students.	Diversity in Intelligence • Intelligence as a General Mental Capability • Sternberg's Triarchic Theory of Intelligence • Gardner's Theory of Multiple Intelligences • Measuring Intelligence • Influences on Intelligence • Ability Grouping
LEARNING OBJECTIVE 6 Conceptualize learning style as an educationally relevant type of individual difference between students and consider ways of matching instructional and learning style.	Learning Style Differences • Match/Mismatch: The Fit Between Instructional Style and Learning Style • Adapting to a Mismatch

"Little Rock Nine"

On September 4, 1957 nine African American students attempted to attend school at the all-white Central High School in Little Rock, Arkansas. Unfortunately, they found their way blocked by Arkansas National Guard Troops, who were ordered by the then governor Orval Faubus (Joiner, 2007). These nine brave students were attempting to desegregate Central High School, in compliance with the historic 1954 Brown V. Board of Education Supreme Court ruling that all segregated schools were unconstitutional. The opening photo for this chapter is of a monument found at the capital of Arkansas that was erected to honor the bravery of the "Little Rock Nine."

As the nine students again entered the school, enraged white students and parents yelled racial slurs and threatened lynching (Boyd, 2007). Fearful that the mob would get out of control, school administration decided to remove the nine from school and return them home. In response to this incident, President Eisenhower federalized the National Guard and sent in the U.S. Army's 101st Airborne Division to escort the "Little Rock Nine" into Central High School (Hendrickson, 1993).

Even with their military escort, the "Little Rock Nine" experienced frequent psychological and physical abuse. Without the military presence some white students intensified their assaults in an effort to drive them out of Central High. One of the nine students fought back and subsequently moved away from the community. The remaining eight stayed through the school year. One of the remaining eight, Ernest Green, became Centrals' first black graduate. (See Box 4.3, Discourse on Diversity, for more on Ernest Green.) Unfortunately, the other seven had to move elsewhere to attend other schools the following year, because citizens voted to close all four of Little Rock's High Schools rather than desegregate them!

- What thoughts and feelings does this story provoke in you?
- To what extent do you think today's public schools are more or less integrated than they were in 1957?

Lessons We Can Learn from the Story Children are different from one another in a variety of ways. It might seem that many of these ways, such as how tall they are, how wealthy their parents are, what colors they like to wear, what color their skin is, and what country their ancestors came from, ought not to have very much to do with how they learn or how they behave in school. However, the evidence suggests that these variables have some direct and indirect effects on how children perform in school, and what schools children are permitted to attend, as reflected in the story of the "Little Rock Nine". Other differences, such as how smart they are, how much they have already learned, how they learn best, and how they feel about themselves and school, are more typically expected to affect their school behavior and performance.

This chapter will deal with some of the ways school children are different and, equally important, how these differences are determined. We will pay particular attention to social class differences, ethnicity and culture, language, gender differences, diversity in intelligence, achievement, and learning style. You will want to focus on how you might minimize negative attitudes students have toward individuals who are different and ways to support student interactions that are enriched by differences. (Because test scores are used and interpreted in determining some of these differences, the reader is also referred to Chapters 13 and 14 on the appraisal of learning.)

Social Class Differences

Learning Objective 1

Illustrate how social class relates to experiences that students may have in school and discuss the importance of social justice practices like critical pedagogy that a teacher can employ to insure all students have an opportunity for a quality education.

Mrs. Cooper taught reading and math to third graders in a big city public elementary school. She had students of different genders, cultures, and ethnicities who spoke different languages, but the one thing her students had in common was that they were all children from families who were poor. It was hard for her to imagine their lives and the many disadvantages they faced, through no fault of their own, in stark contrast to kids who lived in the suburbs. Mrs. Cooper worked very diligently on giving her students two very important gifts, stability and acceptance. She tried to provide a caring supportive environment where things were based on mutual respect and support.

Social class or **socioeconomic status (SES)** is a function of parents' *education level* and *occupational status* with higher SES being associated with higher *income level* and *prestige*. Based on this definition, children with college-educated parents who are engaged in professional occupations have higher SES, hence greater prestige, than children with uneducated parents who are engaged in unskilled jobs or are unemployed. Social class, because it is based entirely on parental attainments, is wholly beyond a child's control.

Of what consequence is social class to education? Research shows that high SES parents tend to be actively involved in the education of their children, not only in the home environment (Hickman, Greenwood, & Miller, 1995) but also in their interactions with their children's schools (Feuerstein, 2000). Low SES parents may value education for their children, but they are less comfortable than their high SES counterparts in dealing with the authority structure of the schools (Feuerstein, 2000). It is not that low SES parents do not value education as much as high SES parents, but instead they have less access to school involvement than higher SES parents (Gorski, 2008).

About one out of five persons in the United States lives either on welfare or on an income that is below the subsistence level. An increasingly high percentage of low-income people are homeless. It is hard for people living with the disadvantage of poverty to provide for the basic needs of their children, much less their social and educational needs. Children of poverty frequently lack the educational stimulation and opportunity characteristically provided to children of higher social class by their parents. Moreover, many poor children are members of single-parent families and that single parent works, reducing even further the opportunities for educational stimulation in the home.

When looking at data on student academic achievement, the measure of SES usually used is eligibility for free and reduced meals in school. Students' eligibility is based on the income level of their family, hence those eligible represent low SES and those ineligible, high SES. A comparison of high and low SES students based on meal eligibility is shown in Table 4.1. This data is from the beginning of the decade.

socioeconomic status

social class; a function of education level and occupational status

CONCEPT REVIEW TABLE 4.1

Percent of Students at or above Basic Level of Proficiency on the National Assessment of Educational Progress (National Center for Education Statistics (2003). Washington, DC: U.S. Department of Education, Institute of Education Sciences.)

		MATHEMATICS			READING		
YEAR	GRADE	NOT FREE	FREE LUNCH	DIFFERENCE	NOT FREE	FREE LUNCH	DIFFERENCE
2003	4th	88	59	29	76	42	34
2003	8th	79	44	35	82	54	28
2000	12th	69	37	32	76	58	18

Results shown in Table 4.1 indicate high SES students ("Not Free") score considerably higher than their low SES counterparts ("Free Lunch") in both math and reading at all three tested grade levels. It is interesting to look at patterns of data over time. Table 4.2 shows more recent results from toward the end of the decade revealing a similar achievement disparity between students from low and high SES families.

What can be done to improve the plight of low SES children? While not the panacea originally thought, early childhood enrichment programs for low income children provide many benefits, not the least of which are health and nutritional benefits such as good meals (Lazar & Darling, 1982). They can also help to offset any lack of early stimulation in the home by providing the conversation, books, and educational toys that might otherwise be missing (Hess, 1970). As a teacher, you cannot fix student poverty. You can, though, encourage students as learners and empower them to help themselves. Here we acquaint you with some actions you might take to accomplish this.

Critical Pedagogy

critical pedagogy

an approach to education that emphasizes the importance of giving a voice to students who are typically powerless or minimized in the classroom due to being a member of a minority group or being from a less advantaged background

Critical pedagogy is an approach to education that emphasizes the importance of giving a voice to students who are typically powerless or minimized in the classroom due to being a member of a minority group or being from a less advantaged background. This approach emphasizes innovative practices to help empower students. Specific practices may take the form of asking students to provide input into the curriculum regarding topics that a given class might study, how that content might be examined, and how the learning should be evaluated.

CONCEPT REVIEW TABLE 4.2

Percent of Students Eligible for Free/Reduced-Price Lunch on the National Assessment of Educational Progress (National Center for Education Statistics, 2007; Washington, DC: U.S. Department of Education, Institute of Education Sciences.)

YEAR	GRADE	CONTENT AREA	ELIGIBLE FOR FREE/REDUCED-PRICE SCHOOL LUNCH				
			ELIGIBLE		NOT ELIGIBLE		Average Scale Score Difference Between Eligible and Not Eligible Students
			% of Students	Average Scale Score	% of Students	Average Scale Score	
2007	4th	Mathematics	46	227	53	249	22
2007	4th	Reading	45	205	54	216	11
2007	8th	Mathematics	41	265	58	291	26
2007	8th	Reading	40	247	58	271	24

Critical pedagogy's historical background comes from a critique of the "banking" concept of education, an approach to education that "…leads students to mechanically memorize the narrated content. Worse yet, it turns them into 'containers,' into 'receptacles' to be 'filled' by the teacher. The more completely she fills the receptacles, the better teacher she is. The more meekly the receptacles permit themselves to be filled, the better students they are" (Freire, 2000, p. 71–72).

A central value of the critical pedagogy approach is equality and democracy. Critical pedagogy examines the impact of a standardized educational system, paying particular attention to who and what political and economic interests are protected (Kincheloe, 2008). The goal of critical pedagogy is for future educators to transform schools into places where students are intrinsically motivated and democratically guided. Public schools should emphasize social change and social justice through empowerment of students. **Social justice** is the fair distribution of advantages and benefits across members of a given society. For educators to be successful in the twenty-first century, they must seriously consider how the role and purpose of schools will be influenced by globalization, technology, and racial diversity (Giroux, 1994).

A specific example of critical pedagogy used in school and community settings is called **Theatre of the Oppressed**, a drama technique developed by Augusto Boal. It is intended to help people learn how to deal effectively with social problems,

social justice

the fair distribution of advantages and benefits across members of a given society

Theatre of the Oppressed

a drama technique intended to help people learn how to deal effectively with social problems, combat injustice, and encourage social change

Paulo Freire's book *Pedagogy of the Oppressed* helps teachers look critically at the experiences that disadvantaged students have in school.

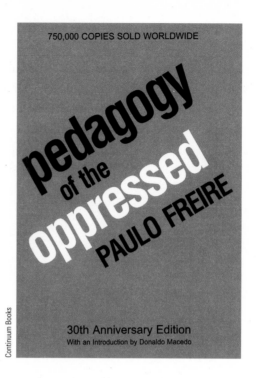

750,000 COPIES SOLD WORLDWIDE

pedagogy of the oppressed PAULO FREIRE

Continuum Books

30th Anniversary Edition
With an Introduction by Donaldo Macedo

combat injustice, and encourage social change. One gifted and talented summer school program used this teaching method in Cleveland, Ohio (Sanders, 2004). The students served by this program, called Urban Odyssey, were primarily minority, inner city students. In the program, the students were able to write and perform in their own short plays that touched on various social ills. The students were given the opportunity to think about and discuss potential solutions to these social problems. The Urban Odyssey project is an excellent example of critical pedagogy because its methodologies empower students to think about concepts they are learning in a reasoned way and also gives the students a voice as to what they will learn, how they will learn, and how the learning will be assessed.

Differentiated Instruction

Rather than expecting students to adapt themselves to the instruction, why should the instruction not be flexible enough to be effective for all students? **Differentiated instruction** is a method of teaching that allows students alternate ways to understand concepts and to provide evidence that they have learned. To use this model effectively, teachers should be flexible enough to adjust the curriculum and its presentation to students, rather than the other way around. While differentiation seems to be something that an effective teacher could hardly do without, there are often barriers to differentiation that can limit how often it is actually implemented in the classroom. Unfortunately, differentiation is sometimes viewed as another bureaucratic burden (Everest, 2003). In order to learn how to effectively differentiate teaching to meet the needs of diverse

differentiated instruction

a method of teaching that allows students alternate ways to understand concepts and to provide evidence that they have learned

learners, teachers need to be able to observe real teachers using differentiation strategies effectively (Carolan & Guinn, 2007).

Tomlinson (2001) identifies three elements of the curriculum that can be differentiated: (1) *content*, by being aligned to learning goals, focused on concepts, and driven by principles; (2) *process*, by using flexible grouping and key strategies for classroom and lesson organization and instructional delivery; and (3) *products*, by continually assessing student readiness and growth, challenging students to be active and responsible explorers, and varying expectations and requirements for student responses.

According to Tomlinson (2001), to use differentiation in your classroom you should:

- Clarify key concepts and generalizations that serve as a foundation for learning
- Use assessment as a teaching tool to extend versus merely to measure instruction
- Emphasize critical and creative thinking as a goal in lesson design
- Develop lessons that are engaging and motivating for a diverse class of students; that is, vary instructional activities
- Provide a balance between teacher-assigned and student-selected tasks.

Tomlinson (2001) provides an excellent example of one way in which Mrs. Riley, a third grade teacher, used differentiated instruction effectively in her class. Mrs. Riley created two different areas where students work on understanding the concept of biography. The students in Mrs. Riley's class have the freedom to choose between the two areas and they also have the choice of whether they prefer to work alone or with other students. In the first area, Mrs. Riley's students create a timeline of the person they read about in the biography and explain that timeline by acting it out, drawing it, or creating a paper describing it. In the second area, her students demonstrate reoccurring themes involved in growing up that were presented in a biography they read, a fictional story they read, and from written accounts of their own life experiences. Mrs. Riley demonstrated elements of differentiated instruction in her class by providing students with the opportunity to master the concept of biography by using different processes and by allowing them to create different products that demonstrate their learning.

Think It Over

as a LEARNER   Have any of your teachers ever differentiated the content, process, or products they used to teach you? How did they do this?

as a TEACHER   What is one barrier to differentiated instruction that you anticipate in your classroom? How can you overcome it?

Class Size

There has been much discussion on the effect of class size on student learning and performance, particularly among students with low socioeconomic status. In addition to trying to improve student learning by using different forms of instruction (such as differentiated instruction described above), many have argued that simply reducing the number of students in the class, thereby giving each student more access to the teacher, will result in improved student academic performance. Because a history of poor academic performance has been shown to be one of the three leading school-related characteristics associated with dropping out (National Research Council, 2001), it would not be unreasonable to suspect that smaller class size might increase the possibility of increased graduation rate.

To determine whether class size did indeed contribute to graduation rate, Finn, Gerber, & Boyd-Zaharias (2005) studied students in the early grades, K–3, who participated in Project STAR, Tennessee's class size experiment. They discovered that a relationship existed between graduating and K–3 achievement, and furthermore that attending small classes for three or more years increased students' likelihood of graduating from high school. Of particular interest was their finding that the relationship between attending small classes and likelihood of graduation occurred especially among students of low socioeconomic status, that is, students who were eligible for free lunch. These authors also report that "the odds of graduating after having attending small classes for four years were increased by about 80%" (p. 220).

The earlier that learning problems are identified, the more likely they are to be overcome. Maintaining a small class size appears to be an excellent strategy to accomplish this.

Differences in Ethnicity and Culture

SES is not independent of ethnicity. Not surprisingly, minority students like African Americans and Hispanics are highly overrepresented among the group eligible for free lunches while White students are highly overrepresented among those ineligible. Moreover, White students are more likely than either African American or Hispanic students to (a) live with both parents, (b) have more educated parents, (c) attend private or more advantaged schools, (d) and take more advanced courses (Byrnes, 2003), all of which may be primarily a function of SES rather than ethnicity.

Byrnes (2003) has proposed that the three factors most responsible for the enhancement of academic skills are *exposure* to opportunities to enhance these skills, *motivation* to take advantage of these opportunities, and having the initial *skill level* to take advantage. He found that up to half of the variation in 12th-grade math performance was accounted for by these three factors, represented by specific variables such as parent education, high school program, coursework, and perceptions of one's own ability in math. Among high scorers in math, ethnic differences were not a factor when students were matched on variables such as those listed above. This suggests that SES may be more influential than ethnicity in affecting academic growth. On the other hand, Ogbu (2003) has observed that African American students continually fall below White students academically, even when comparisons are made *within* social classes.

Another aspect of ethnicity that relates to academic performance is culture. Ogbu (2003) distinguishes between the "caste-like" culture of people who through slavery, conquest, or colonization have been involuntarily incorporated into a society, and consequently view major changes in political power and economic opportunity as necessary ingredients for improvement, and immigrants who have entered a new cultural milieu and view education as the route to political and economic advancement. African Americans fit the first group and Hispanics the second.

A third aspect of ethnicity that relates to academic performance is called **stereotype threat**, the effect of a stereotype about one's ethnicity on one's own behavior and performance (Steele, 1997; Steele & Aronson, 1995). The person need not believe the stereotype is true, only that it exists, and feel some concern that he or she may self-fulfill it, that is act as if it were true. An example would be the ethnic stereotype that African Americans are intellectually inferior to Whites, a belief that may cause African American students to perform more poorly on academic tasks than comparable White students.

Steele and Aronson (1995) compared the performance of African American and White students with comparable SAT scores on a subset of highly difficult items from the Graduate Record Exam (GRE). Half of each group of students was told the GRE items represented a test of intellectual ability; the other half were told it was a laboratory problem-solving task unrelated to ability. When told it was a test of intellectual ability, African American students scored significantly lower than Whites. When told it was a problem-solving task unrelated to ability, both groups scored the same. The same pattern of results was obtained when participants recorded their race on a form prior to taking the test, namely reduced performance by African Americans relative to Whites.

Steele (1997) advocates "wise" schooling. That is, you can employ situational changes to reduce the influence of stereotype threat. For example,

- You might provide challenge rather than remediation because remediation reinforces the stereotype while challenge mitigates it;
- You can offer statements that reflect a belief in a student's potential when providing critical feedback on their work;
- You can offer the kind of mentoring and encouragement that helps students learn to believe in themselves (see the discussion of self-efficacy in Chapter 10);
- You might provide role models; that is, people of that ethnicity who have been successful and whose success helps disprove the stereotype and reduce its threat.

Ethnic Identity Development

There is a special focus for groups and cultures who live in societies where they are poorly represented politically and economically and are, at worst, discriminated

stereotype threat

the effect of a stereotype about one's ethnicity on one's own behavior and performance

against (Phinney, 1990). The relationship of such group members with their own group and in relation to the White mainstream group has been labeled **ethnic identity**, and has become of increasing interest and importance as the number and size of ethnic minorities in the United States grows and more ethnic minority children enter the public schools.

In Chapter 3 Box 3.4, we talked about racial identity development. In the next several pages, we will examine an identity model that is representative of different ways of understanding the development of identity from the perspective of culture. While not possible in the scope of this book to examine all ethnic cultures separately, the models can be adapted to fit different non-majority groups.

Phinney (1993) developed a model of ethnic identity, for groups sharing a common and distinctive culture that proposes a sequence of the following three distinguishable stages:

1. *Unexamined Ethnic Identity* – in this stage, individuals do not probe into the concept of ethnicity. Rather, they tend to accept the values and attitudes of the majority culture.
2. *Ethnic Identity Search/Moratorium* – in this stage, individuals are faced with a situation that compels an individual to begin to think about and search for an ethnic identity.
3. *Ethnic Identity Achievement* – in this stage, individuals develop a clear and confident sense of their ethnicity.

A Model of Latino/Hispanic Ethnic Identity

Using Phinney's model as a framework, Torres (1999) validated what he called the *Bicultural Orientation Model* (BOM). This model is focused on identifying the choices that Hispanic students make between their culture of origin (Latino/Hispanic) and the majority culture (Anglo). In the Torres model, the following four cultural orientations distinguish the Hispanic students:

1. *Bicultural Orientation*, which indicates a comfort level with both cultures.
2. *Latino/Hispanic Orientation*, which indicates greater comfort with the culture of origin.
3. *Anglo Orientation*, which indicates a greater comfort with the majority culture.
4. *Marginal Orientation*, which indicates discomfort with both cultures and may indicate conflict within the individual.

Individuals are classified into one of the four stages of the Torres model by determining their degree of **acculturation**, based on the judgments they make about the majority culture, and their degree of ethnic identity, based on the judgments they make about the maintenance of their culture of origin. While the Torres model was developed to describe ethnic development among students living and going to school in the United States whose culture of origin is Latino/Hispanic, it would seem applicable to American students with other cultures of origin (e.g., Russian, Somali, Vietnamese).

ethnic identity

the sense of association and connection an individual has with an ethnic group

acculturation

assimilation with a dominant culture

To apply his model, Torres (2003) studied ethnic identity development among students whose culture of origin was Latino/Hispanic and who were enrolled in their first two years of college in the United States. The two major categories that emerged during the first two years of college to explain the ethnic development process of the students he studied were as follows: Situating Identity (the starting point of identity development in college) and Influences on Change in identity development. In terms of **situating identity**, Torres' data revealed the following three conditions that influenced the different starting points of the students he studied and helped explain their ethnic identity status and development: (1) the environment where they grew up, (2) family influences and generation in the United States, and (3) self-perception of status in society.

Environment where they grew up. The makeup of the environment where the students came from influenced both how they ethnically self-identified and their cultural orientation. The most influential feature of the environment where the students grew up is the degree to which it reflected ethnic diversity. Torres (2003) found that students coming from "areas where Latinos are a critical mass did not see themselves as in the minority until they arrived on the predominantly White campus. This change in their environment prompted a stronger tie to their ethnicity rather than assimilation. On the other end of the dimension are those who came from environments where there was mainly a White European influence. These students tended to define their ethnicity as where they are from—using a geographic definition" (p. 537). In other words, they labeled themselves as "Texans" or "Americans" rather than as "Mexicans" or "Latinos." They tended to associate with the majority culture and found the diversity in the college environment as presenting some conflict for them.

Family influence and generation in the United States. "The most obvious dimension that emerged is that students identified themselves using the same terms and language their parents used." In addition, "the more parents participated in culturally relevant activities, such as speaking Spanish at home and attending Latino social functions, the more students identified with their ethnic identity" (Torres, 2003, p. 538).

The second dimension that emerged is the generational status of the students and their parents. "Students who are the first generation in the United States struggled with the unknown expectations of the college environment. Though all students make some adjustments, first generation in the United States students also struggled to balance the college expectations with those of their parents" (Torres, 2003, p. 538). Torres (2003) found two consequences that resulted from this balancing of acculturation levels. First, students who tried to please their parents ended up feeling a little alienated from their peers, because they would not tell them what they were dealing with. One student, for example, tried to please her parents by being in her room every night when they called. The second consequence was that students kept things from their parents. They felt caught between the two cultures, not completely fitting in with either culture. "These students are caught between the expectations, traditions, and knowledge from the majority culture and their culture of origin. At the other end of the array in this dimension are the students

situating identity

the starting point of identity development in college

who are second and third generation in the United States who assume the mingling of the two cultures. These students tend to have less conflict with parents and are comfortable with the role their parents play in their identification" (Torres, 2003, p. 539).

Self-perception of status in society. This condition is often associated with socio-economic status, such as wealth and education level. But in Torres' study, it is more generally described as students perceiving some advantage or privilege in comparison to others. The basic dimension of this condition is the perception or non-perception of privilege. While those who came from privileged backgrounds recognized the negative stereotypes about Latinos, they did not see the stereotypes as applying to them. Those from non-privileged backgrounds, on the other hand, perceived the stereotypes as racism.

In terms of influences on change in **identity development**, two subprocesses of cultural dissonance and change in relationships within the environment emerged as relevant conditions that influenced change in the students' ethnic identity.

Cultural dissonance. The behaviors that are expressed within this condition refer to the experience of dissonance or conflict between one's own sense of culture and what others expect. "For the students who came from first generation in the United States families, conflicts with parents' cultural expectations led them to desire more association with the majority culture" (Torres, 2003, p. 540).

Change in relationships within the environment. The prominent dimension of this condition is the peer group that the individual student seeks out while in college. "Students who came from diverse environments self-selected the descriptions associated with the Bicultural or Latino Orientations (Torres, 1999). The students who found the college environment as not accepting of diversity would identify with a Latino Orientation wanting to focus their orientation toward those who share their interest in diversity. The other students who acknowledged the lack of diversity, but were not as critical of the environment, would self-select the bicultural description of their orientation" (Torres, 2003, p. 544).

It appeared that students who came from environments where they had been the majority may come to college without ever going through Phinney's stages of Unexamined Ethnic Identity or Ethnic Identity Search, because they had developed their ethnic identity very early in life as the natural result of their culture of origin. The students from majority-White environments, on the other hand, tended to identify with an Anglo orientation or Bicultural Orientation (Torres, 1999) and seemed to fit the description of Phinney's first stage, Unexamined Ethnic Identity.

Although students who are first generation in the United States may have a stronger tie to their country of origin, they are also the ones that tend to experience more dissonance with their culture of origin. This is because of the acculturation level of their parents and their desire to balance their parents' expectations with their own. Moreover, students who were first generation in the United States found it difficult to talk to non-Hispanics about the pressure they feel from their parents.

identity development
two subprocesses of cultural dissonance and change in relationships within the environment emerged as relevant conditions that influenced change in the students' ethnic identity

The level of stress can be an underlying issue for students with academic or social problems. Teachers are encouraged to have sensitivity to these issues when dealing with Hispanic students.

Asian American Identity and Culture in the Classroom

There are over one and a half million Asian American students in public schools in the United States (Fry, 2007). These students include individuals whose families have been here for numerous generations as well as those who are recent immigrants. While you may think that there are only a few countries on the continent of Asia, in fact it is actually composed of over 40 countries, and contains about half of the world's population.

It is important to know something about the culture of the students we teach, but regardless of what we know about a specific culture, it is just as important for teachers to believe that all cultures have important characteristics about which we and our classes can learn. Kelley (2008) argues that reading literature about different cultures is one of the best ways of preparing students to participate in globalization. One thing that multicultural literature can teach us is the defining values that other cultures hold. For example, Kelley (2008) says that critical aspects of Japanese culture, such as harmony and patience, are demonstrated in children's books like *The Way We Do It in Japan* written by Geneva Cobb Iijima and illustrated by Paige Billin-Frye.

One way to understand Asian American culture is look at its beliefs about learning, intelligence, play, and family involvement. For example, Li (2003) conducted a study that compared U.S. and Chinese beliefs about the nature and process of learning. When detailing the process of learning, western students did not list effort or persistence as often as did Chinese students, and Chinese students

Gareth Brown/Comet/Corbis

To work effectively with other cultures, it is important for a teacher to understand the uniqueness and diversity within their own culture.

seemed more likely to view intelligence as something that increases as a function of learning as opposed to the western view that a person is born with a set intelligence. Japanese public schools also emphasize effort over innate ability (Wieczorek, 2008). Wong (2001) offered that educational leaders in China have been influenced by the work of Confucius, who was opposed to a system of class differences and believed that education should be shared by all (Wong, 2001). Additional evidence of sharing success and duty is that in Japanese schools, teachers and students work together on a weekly basis to clean up school property (Lucien, 2001).

The role of play among young children and the role of the family in Asia are also important areas to examine. There is a stereotype that Asian students interact in purely social ways in school with limited independence. However, research has shown this to be inaccurate, in that young Japanese students often participate in social play as well as nonsocial, independent play (Mariano, Welteroth, & Johnson, 1999). Chinese parents are typically less involved in Chinese public schools than western parents are in American schools (Gu, 2008). This information is valuable for American teachers of Chinese students who are new to the west, because it tells them that they may have to make additional efforts to reach out to connect with Chinese parents and make them feel welcome and involved in the American public school process. One way to do this would be through the creation of an active school-based parent group and a parent resource center to help Chinese parents determine how they would like to be involved (Gu, 2008).

Misconceptions about Asian American students abound. One stereotype is that all Asian American students are smarter than other students. There is evidence, however, that when socioeconomic status is removed from the equation, Asian American students perform like other students (Bracey, 1999). Thus Asian Americans, like all other cultural and ethnic groups, present a diverse range of abilities and disabilities. Kember (2000) gave three suggestions for improving how teachers work with Asian American students: (1) make sure the curriculum is focused on higher order thinking as opposed to memorization, (2) create activities that require students to participate in their learning, and (3) make instruction relevant to preparation for future prospective jobs.

Another stereotype that Asian American students are confronted with by the media, public, and public schools is termed the model minority stereotype (Lee, 1996). The **model minority stereotype** is an oversimplification that states that members of a particular group achieve greater success in life than members of a different group. Teachers may find students from Southeast Asia in their classes and Ngo (2006) argues that students from this region tend to come from less advantaged background than other Asian Americans and are often marginalized by the model minority simplification. These are students from countries like Cambodia, Laos, and Vietnam and are distinct from other Asian Americans as they often came to the U.S. as refugees as opposed to coming as immigrants (Ngo & Lee, 2007).

model minority stereotype
an oversimplification that states that members of a particular group achieve greater success in life than members of a different group

Native American Identity and Culture in the Classroom

Like any cultural label, the term Native American or American Indian encompasses many distinct groups of individuals with unique and distinct cultural practices. In fact, the term Native American encompasses over 500 Indian tribes (Horse, 2005). While there are many tribes, the languages of indigenous people of American, such as Alaska Natives, American Indians, and Native Hawaiians are vanishing (National Indian Education Association, 2008). There is some disagreement about which label is most accepted in the Native American community and one resolution offered has been to use the specific name of the tribe whenever possible (Fleming, 2006). For example, instead of using the general label like Native American, a teacher might teach a unit on the heritage of a specific tribe, such as the Seminole Tribe of Florida.

Just like with any cultural group in the world, there are psychosocial similarities and differences between individual members of a group. Each tribe is composed of individuals who each posses their own identity, which Horse (2001) says is shaped by the degree to which the individual: (1) is connected with his or her American Indian language, (2) the nature of the person's genealogy, (3) the degree to which an individual values connection and unity with nature, and (4) a person's membership status in a tribe.

An effective practice would be to include lessons that explore the contributions of indigenous Americans. Montana has taken a lead role in bringing American Indian culture into the classroom. In 1999, the state passed the Indian Education for All Act, which requires students to learn about the contributions and culture of American Indians (Warren, 2006). This type of legislation helps introduce American Indian culture to classrooms in places where it might not have been taught previously. However, as teachers introduce American Indian culture in the classroom, they must be careful to do so in appropriate ways. Moomaw & Jones (2005) discuss inappropriate ways in which American Indian culture is taught in the classroom which includes stereotyping, such as teaching that all American Indians live in teepees or being insensitive, by having students make symbols hallowed in American Indian tradition, like headdresses.

One of the best ways to introduce a specific American Indian culture to a class would be for a teacher to use stories. Reese (2007) has written some guidelines to help teachers evaluate American Indian literature for use in schools. Stories should be specific to a tribe, and if a story is set in a modern setting American Indian should engage in some activities that members of a majority culture would, and the characters should display varied emotional responses that individuals from all cultures might display (Reese, 2007). Additional resources and books that teach about American Indians and recommended by Dr. Reese can be found on the Internet. It is important for teachers to realize that Native Alaskans are also original inhabitants of America and should be meaningfully incorporated in the curriculum. One example of how to bring Native Alaskan culture and tradition into the classroom can be found in an elementary school in Anchorage, Alaska. In that class, the teacher taught a unit about art, writing, and mathematics through the lens of the

Native Alaskan wood carving tradition (Hughes & Forbes, 2007). Learning about and examining a variety of American Indian cultures in the classroom open opportunities for teachers, the majority of whom are female and White, to develop a deeper understanding and respect for the diversity of the students in the classroom. Different cultures have different worldviews that influence what and how they learn (Demmert, 2005). By including information about numerous cultures, including specific American Indian tribes, students can examine their own culture and the culture of other students. Calsoyas (2005) states that respect for the members of their tribe and for the world around them is critical to the development of Native American children. It is important to involve parents/caregivers of all students in the educational process, and American Indian students and families are no exception to this best practice (Gilliard & Moore, 2007).

Think It Over

as a LEARNER   To what extent, if any, has your racial or ethnic identity been an issue with which you have had to deal, and how have you dealt with any conflict it has produced in yourself?

as a TEACHER   How do you expect your interactions with students who do not share your racial or ethnic identity will influence your self-perceptions and helped raise or reduce your own identity conflict?

School Desegregation

Cheryl and her sister Linda Brown, walked by railroad tracks to get to a bus for African American children that would eventually take them to a segregated school further away than the school for White children which was close by their home (Willoughby, 2004). Cheryl and Linda's father, Oliver Brown, in conjunction with other parents and students, filed a suit to reverse the segregation in Topeka, Kansas' schools. **Segregation** is the separation of students into different schools and classes based on their race or ethnic group. The main attorney for Oliver Brown and the other plaintiffs was Thurgood Marshall, who in 1967 became the first African American U.S. Supreme Court Justice.

On May 17, 1954 in a unanimous decision, the U.S. Supreme Court eliminated the practice of school segregation by ruling in the **Brown v. Board of Education of Topeka** case that separate educational systems and facilities resulted in unequal educations. In a later interview about the case, Cheryl Brown Henderson stated that, "We believe the results have been seen more in other areas of society, such as public accommodations, which were some of the most segregated situations. Education has been slow to comply. The greatest improvement is an understanding of all people by learning about cultures different than our own.

segregation
the separation of students into different schools and classes based on their race or ethnic group

Brown v. Board of Education of Topeka
case that eliminated the practice of school segregating by ruling that separate educational systems and facilities resulted in unequal educations

It took significant effort and courage to challenge segregation in the workplace and schools.

Multicultural education was unheard of before this took place" (McConnell & Hinitz, 2005).

While the initial reaction to the judgment was mixed, today, the bulk of American parents support the desegregation efforts of Brown v. Board of Education of Topeka and desire for their students to be prepared to work effectively with individuals from various backgrounds (Orfield & Frankenberg, 2004). This important ruling moved American education toward the critical goal of equal opportunity and integration of all students (Wraga, 2006). There is still much work to be done to ensure that students of all races have the opportunity of a quality education. The desegregation issue is far from resolved, and in fact there is still an achievement gap between students of various racial groups. Table 4.3 highlights some critical steps in integration. Part of that stems from the differential treatment, which children from various groups still receive in schools. Majority students are far less likely to experience discrimination than minority group students. **Discrimination** is the unjust treatment of an individual because of their perceived membership in a particular group or category. In a school setting discrimination can take various forms, for example, teachers may have different expectations of students based on the color of their skin, their gender, sexual orientation, or other characteristics. As research suggests, students tend to live up or down to the expectations of their teachers, parents, and peers.

In response to the death of Dr. Martin Luther King, Jr., Jane Elliott, a third grade teacher in Riceville, Iowa designed a now famous exercise aimed at helping her students understand what discrimination is like. As reported by Bloom (2005), Elliott divided her class by eye color, and told them that brown-eyed students were smarter because they had more melanin. While praising and favoring her brown-eyed students, she marginalized those with blue eyes by having them wear armbands which identified them as different. Being discriminated against, the blue-eyed students began to perform poorly in class, while the brown-eyed students adopted a more superior attitude than their blue-eyed peers. Mrs. Elliott then reversed the roles,

discrimination

the unjust treatment of an individual because of their perceived membership in a particular group or category

CONCEPT REVIEW TABLE 4.3

A Brief Integration Timeline

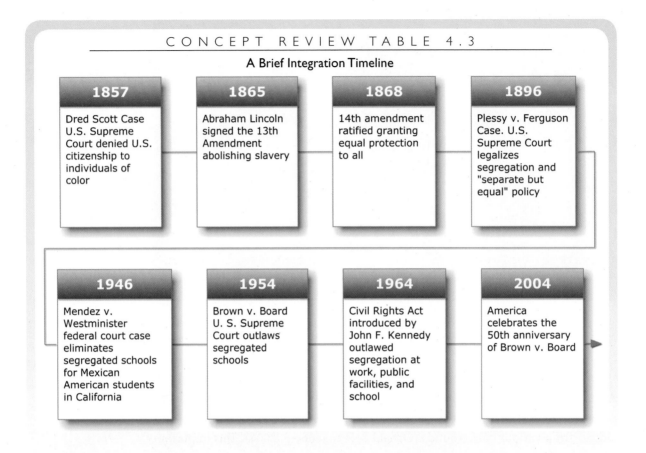

1857	1865	1868	1896
Dred Scott Case U.S. Supreme Court denied U.S. citizenship to individuals of color	Abraham Lincoln signed the 13th Amendment abolishing slavery	14th amendment ratified granting equal protection to all	Plessy v. Ferguson Case. U.S. Supreme Court legalizes segregation and "separate but equal" policy

1946	1954	1964	2004
Mendez v. Westminister federal court case eliminates segregated schools for Mexican American students in California	Brown v. Board U. S. Supreme Court outlaws segregated schools	Civil Rights Act introduced by John F. Kennedy outlawed segregation at work, public facilities, and school	America celebrates the 50th anniversary of Brown v. Board

designating the blue-eyed students as superior and the brown-eyed students inferior. At the conclusion of the exercise, Mrs. Elliott's students expressed an increased understanding of what it's like to be discriminated against. Without having been discriminated against, it is difficult to appreciate the impact of the experience. African-American students are more likely to be placed in general education and vocationally-focused tracks and are underrepresented in challenging, college preparatory, courses (Saddler, 2005). To help reduce the achievement gap, teachers can look at their curriculum materials and activities to ensure that African Americans are included and they can also help match students with same race and gender role models to help increase the students' motivation (Zirkel, 2005).

It is important to note that African Americans were not the only individuals involved in a struggle for equality in America's public schools. Eight years earlier, an important case occurred in Orange County, California. This case was called Mendez v. Westminster (1946), and was the first successful case against segregation and was filed on behalf of 5,000 Mexican American students (Valencia, 2005).

Because of the court systems' significant use of scientific evidence in informing their decisions in the Brown v. Board of Education of Topeka case (Ancheta, 2006) and in the Mendez v. Westminster case (Valencia, 2005), it highlights for the future educator the critical role of educational research to civil rights and social justice.

Think It Over

| as a LEARNER | Does segregation still exist? What evidence can you provide to support your answer? |
| as a TEACHER | How might the classroom experiences of African American and Caucasian students be similar and different? How could you bring more racial integration to your classroom? |

Multicultural Education

How will you approach difference in your classroom? Modern teachers work with students who speak different languages, have different cultures and ethnicities, come from advantaged and disadvantaged backgrounds, have different gender and sexual identities and orientations, and come from urban, rural, and suburban settings. This presents a significant challenge to a new teacher, but when approached from a perspective of knowledge and understanding, the diversity that your students come to you with is a significant opportunity and will help you make the classroom an exciting and motivating learning environment. One way to effectively work with diverse students is an approach called multicultural education. **Multicultural education** is an approach to teaching that asks students to examine concepts and skills that are being taught from diverse perspectives. Banks (1995) has proposed the following five dimensions of multicultural education:

- Content integration – teachers using examples and content from a variety of cultures to illustrate key concepts and issues within their subject matter;
- Knowledge construction process – teachers helping students to understand and determine how the frames of reference and biases within a discipline influence the way it constructs knowledge;
- Prejudice reduction – teachers using lessons and activities to help students develop positive attitudes toward different ethnic and racial groups;
- Equity pedagogy – Teachers modifying their teaching to facilitate academic achievement of students from diverse racial, cultural and ethnic groups;
- Empowering school culture and social structure – Teachers and administrators transforming the culture and organization of the school to enable students from diverse racial, cultural, and ethnic groups to experience equality and equal status.

Banks (1995) is critical of the *Contributions Approach* whereby teachers integrate racial, ethnic, and cultural content into the curriculum by merely celebrating ethnic holidays, and the *Additive Approach* of adding isolated units about racial or ethnic culture or history to the curriculum. He recommends the *Transformation Approach* in which the perspectives of the curriculum are changed to allow students to view events and information from a variety of ethnic and cultural perspectives, not just their own. Examples of this would be viewing the history of American westward expansion during the latter half of the

multicultural education

an approach to teaching that asks students to examine concepts and skills that are being taught from diverse perspectives

In classrooms that value multicultural education, students look at events and content from numerous cultural perspectives.

Jose Luis Pelaez Inc/Blend (RF)/Getty Images

nineteenth and early twentieth century not only from the perspective of Whites, but from American Indian culture as well, and of the history of American industrialization during this same period from the perspective of African Americans as well as Whites.

To further enable students of minority ethnic and cultural groups to achieve the benefits of education, Tharpe (1989) has proposed the *cultural compatibility hypothesis,* namely "when instruction is compatible with natal-culture patterns, improvements in learning, including basic skills, can be expected" (p. 350). For the majority culture, compatible instruction structure is whole class with rank-and-file seating and a teacher who instructs the whole group, followed by individual practice and teacher-organized individual assessment. For non-majority cultures, compatible instruction features collaboration, cooperation, and assisted performance using small-group organization, where the teacher works intensively with one small group at a time while the others work in small groups utilizing peer teaching-learning interaction. Tharpe (1989) reports considerable success in using the non-majority compatible model with classes of ethnic and cultural minority students.

Educators who adopt the idea of multicultural education advocate for the educational empowerment of all of their students. Unfortunately, not all individuals training to become teachers value multicultural education or see how the concepts can help motivate their students to learn. Hill-Jackson, V., Sewell, K. L., and Waters, C. (2007) studied the belief systems of individuals training to be teachers and found that they tend to either be advocates of multicultural education or resisters of multicultural education. They found that the advocates of multicultural education in their study tended to have more nuanced thinking about diversity

TeachSource Video Case

Culturally Responsive Teaching: A Multicultural Lesson for Elementary Students

In this video segment, you'll see how Dr. Francis Hurley models a culturally responsive approach to teaching a classical topic, the five paragraph essay. In this video you will see seamlessly integrates multiculturalism into her literacy lesson.

After viewing the Video Case, consider what you have just watched about classroom management and answer the questions below.

1. What teaching strategies demonstrated by Dr. Hurley in this Video Case would help you work with students from different cultures?

2. In the Video Case, Dr. Hurley shared her own culture and how she came to America then she asked the students to share. Do you think this was an effective approach? Why?

You can view the video case at the Education CourseMate. Go to:
CengageBrain.com

issues, tried to look at issues from numerous perspectives, were empathic and ethical, and believed that they could help all of their students learn.

If you as a teacher make the decision to value multicultural education, what are some concrete steps you could take in your classroom? It is highly recommended that you incorporate as many as you can of the instructional techniques compatible with your students from non-majority cultures. For example, you can include

Think It Over

as a LEARNER | What experiences have you had that illustrate one or more of Banks' five dimensions of multicultural education, and what experiences have you had that illustrate Tharpe's cultural compatibility hypothesis, and how would you evaluate those experiences?

as a LEARNER | In what ways would you teach in order to provide students with the opportunity to view things from a cultural perspective other than their own?

CONCEPT REVIEW TABLE 4.4

Why a student's ethnicity/culture might place them at risk and what a teacher can do to support all learners.

CONCEPT	FINDING(S)	WHAT A TEACHER CAN DO TO ENHANCE EQUITY
Socioeconomic Differences	• In general, students from minority groups come from less advantaged backgrounds (Brynes, 2003)	• Create class activities and homework assignments that do not give advantage to students with access to more resources. For example, if requiring a science diorama make sure the students use similar materials to construct it which are available in the classroom
Institutionalized Racism	• Throughout American history, society at large and educational institutions in particular have not treated all racial ethnic groups equally (Ogbu, 2003)	• Encourage students to believe in themselves in order to help the students develop academic self-efficacy
Stereotype Threat	• Stereotypes about one's ethnicity can negatively impact school performance (Steele, 1997)	• Provide examples and role models who represent minority groups to demonstrate that all students have the capacity to learn
Multicultural Education	• Celebrating ethnic holidays is not sufficient to promote diversity in the classroom (Banks, 1995)	• Provide classroom examples that view topics that are being studied from different cultural perspectives. For example, look at the current war in Iraq from the perspective of civilians in Iraq.
Cultural Compatibility Hypothesis	• Pedagogy of classroom often is compatible with majority groups (Tharpe, 1989)	• Increase the usage of small group activities and peer interaction

small-group, hands-on activities as a part of every lesson rather than relying exclusively on lectures and worksheets. Table 4.4 summarizes some of the risks that students from various cultures face in schools and some ideas for how teachers can enhance equity for all students.

Language Diversity

Learning Objective 3

Describe the different demographic and language patterns in America's public schools and discuss approaches to assisting English language learners.

The demographics of America's public schools and the languages our students speak at home have changed over the past three decades. Based on data from the National Center for Educational Statistics (2008), from 1979 to 2006, the number of students aged 5–17 years who used a language other than English in their homes increased from 3.8 to 10.8 million children. The majority of those students, approximately 72%, are speaking Spanish at home (NCES, 2008). Many of the children who immigrate to this country are referred to as English Language Learners. **English language learners** are students who are in the process of learning to communicate in English.

These changing language and immigration patterns bring many advantages to the public school classroom in terms of broader perspectives and first-hand learning about different cultures and languages. At the same time, children with limited English skills are at higher risk for school failure (Lopez & Tashakkori, 2004). In fact, a majority of students with limited English proficiency did not meet various state progress goals in mathematics and language arts during the 2003–2004 school year (Ashby, 2007). Teachers who are effective at working with English language learners often ask the students to share their experiences while making an effort to become aware of the cultures of their students (Mays, 2008). Teachers with strong organizational skills who make significant use of cooperative learning strategies and differentiated instruction tend to be successful with English language learners (Garcia & Jensen, 2007). Here we acquaint you with strategies for incorporating these learning techniques into your classroom.

English Language Education Approaches

There are different perspectives on what is the best way for teachers to provide a quality education to English Language Learners. One approach is called bilingual education. **Bilingual education** is teaching students in their native

English language learners
students who are in the process of learning to communicate in English

bilingual education
teaching students in their native language and over time shifting to teaching the students in English

Changing demographics will make it likely that you will have one or more students in your class learning to speak English. How will you help those students succeed?

AP Photo/Manuel Balce Ceneta

language and over time shifting to teaching the students in English. Another type of innovative approach to bilingual education is called two-way bilingual education. In **two-way bilingual education**, students receive content instruction and language arts instruction in two languages. Parent evaluations of English/Spanish two-way bilingual education programs have been quite positive (Ramos, 2007).

Another approach to teaching English language learners is termed immersion. **Immersion** is when the English language learner is taught only in English. There is disagreement as to which instructional method is more successful. However, the evidence seems to suggest that the quality of the instruction the students receive is actually more important than whether they receive the bilingual or immersion instruction (Hamilton, 2006). In 1998, proponents of the immersion approach found support when Proposition 227 was passed by a majority of California voters. **Proposition 227** requires that all public school instruction be in English and that English language learning students be given up to a year of additional support before being transitioned into a mainstream English speaking classroom. While immersion champions were pleased with the results of Proposition 227, supporters of bilingual education argue that if children are taught all of their content using a language they do not speak, they risk falling further behind.

Think It Over

as a LEARNER	What do you think it would be like to try to learn a new subject in a classroom where the teacher and students spoke a language that you did not?
as a TEACHER	How might you help an English Language Learner be successful in a class that you teach?

two-way bilingual education

students receive content instruction and language arts instruction in two languages

immersion

when the English language learner is taught only in English

Proposition 227

requires that all public school instruction be in English and that English language learning students be given up to a year of additional support before being transitioned into a mainstream English speaking classroom

Accommodating English Language Learners

Learners who come to the United States from other countries and who speak only their native language, are at a major disadvantage when they enter schools in the United States where instruction is offered only in English. Ideally, the transition to English should be gradual, but for the most part, that is unlikely to be the case. Even knowledge of conversational English is not sufficient for reading textbooks and understanding lectures, which has been known to require from five to seven years (Cummins, 2004). A small sampling of the fifty strategies proposed by Herrell & Jordan (2008) to help English-speaking teachers teach English language learners are listed below. In your classroom, you can

- use visual aids and realistic examples that students can see and manipulate
- involve students actively in the learning process using kinesthetics and games (like "Simon Says")

- use bilingual textbooks when possible and, when not possible, use materials outside the textbook
- use the dual-method of giving both oral and written directions
- use modes of teaching that do not rely so heavily on language to convey information (e.g., graphic organizers, "buddy reading," role playing, cooperative learning, working in pairs)
- provide direct teacher modeling
- speak slowly and clearly and repeat instructions as often as needed
- use prompts for clarification (see more on prompting in Chapter 6)
- create opportunities for students to present and celebrate their cultures in school
- focus on what students can do rather than what they cannot do.

Gender Differences

Learning Objective 4

Explain how schooling can be biased towards students based on gender and orientation and discuss methods a teacher could implement to insure an equitable and safe classroom environment.

Gender differences in school achievement have been closely examined over the years. In reading, consistent differences favoring girls over boys have been found. Girls tend to display higher reading scores on the *National Assessment of Educational Progress* from seven scale points on average in 4th grade to 16 scale points in 12th grade. Girls also receive higher school grades in reading throughout elementary school and into the adolescent years (Dwyer & Johnson, 1997). In addition, there are a significantly higher number of boys than girls in remedial reading classes (Alloway & Gilbert, 1997).

While boys still outperform girls in the mathematics portion of the National Assessment of Educational Progress, the difference is quite small. However, girls still tend to feel less confidence in themselves than boys in math (Vermeer, Boekaerts, & Seegers, 2000), suggesting that girls may still believe the long-standing stereotype that they are less able than boys in math.

Achievement differences between the genders may be in part the results of gender differences in socialization. Tannenbaum & Leeper (2003) found that parents were more likely to believe that science, for example, was less interesting and more difficult for their daughters than their sons, and used more cognitively demanding language when teaching it to their sons than to their daughters. This would be likely to lead girls to believe that careers in science may not necessarily be for them. The influence of teachers on these self-perceptions must be considered as well. Altermatt, Javonovic, & Perry (1998) report that science teachers in their study called on male students more frequently to answer questions than female students. This tendency may be responsible for their finding that male students were more likely than female students to answer questions in science.

That some of the gender differences in school achievement are accompanied by differences in behavior is suggested by the fact that the ratio of boys to girls is 4:1 in favor of boys in learning disabled programs (Vogel, 1990), and 2:1 in favor of boys in referrals to school psychologists (Vardill, 1996). The nature of the school environment is more verbal than physical. With the restraints imposed by teachers and classrooms, the school environment may pose a greater behavioral challenge for boys than girls, leading them to have greater need for special programs and services related to behavior management.

In spite of their tendency to get better grades than boys in language arts, social studies, science and math, girls were found to be more vulnerable than boys to internal distress (Pomerantz, Altermatt, & Saxon, 2002). This was particularly true among the girls that performed poorly. Girls tended to evaluate themselves more negatively, worried more about their performance, and experienced more general anxiety and depression. This may be due to the fact that girls tend to be more concerned than boys with pleasing adults, such as parents and teachers (Pomerantz, Saxon, & Kenney, 2001). While this motivation may improve their performance, it may also lead to the distress brought on by not wanting to disappoint adults.

It has been suggested by Roberts (1991) that girls are more likely than boys to view their performance as a reflection of their abilities, and hence view evaluative feedback as informational and diagnostic. This may lead to both improved performance and increased distress. As a teacher, you would do well to be aware of the welcome but potentially distressing effect of your negative performance feedback on students. While most noticeable among girls, distress undoubtedly applies to many boys as well. You should try to deliver it in the most supportive ways possible. (Refer to the section on Congruent Communication in Chapter 9.)

Gender Bias

Gender bias is the different treatment of girls and boys and is a problem in schools. According to Sadker and Sadker (1994), while girls get better grades and require less frequent discipline than boys (as described above), they receive less time, attention, help, encouragement, challenges and feedback from teachers than boys. They learn to defer to boys, be less assertive, avoid math and science, and hide their intelligence, becoming what Sadker and Sadker (1994) refer to as "educational spectators" rather than "players." This affects their self-esteem and motivation, and reduces their academic opportunities.

Knowing about some of the different tendencies of girls and boys may be helpful in some respects, but as a general rule, teachers need to avoid any tendency toward stereotyping students by gender, and as a result, treating them differently. Such treatment will tend to reinforce the stereotypes and cause students to believe them more than they may already. As described in a previous section, Steele (1997) has identified a phenomenon that he calls stereotype threat, where people tend to believe the stereotypes that others hold toward them, and in so doing, act in a way to fulfill them (that is, act as if they were true!). Telling girls that "girls are not good at math," or boys that "boys don't know how to behave," would be examples of statements that would reinforce gender stereotypes and activate stereotype threat.

gender bias
the different treatment of girls and boys

Think It Over

as a LEARNER	What experiences have you had (or observed) about dealing with stereotypes regarding who is expected to be good or poor in a particular subject such as science, and what have you learned from these experiences?
as a TEACHER	How can you deal with or help the person experiencing it overcome a stereotype?

Sexual Orientation

Sexual orientation is one of the many ways that students can be diverse. **Sexual orientation** represents the direction of an individual's sexual preference. This preference can take the form of heterosexual (opposite sex), homosexual (same sex), or bisexual (both sexes) preference. Students' sexual orientation has historically been thought of as being fixed and stable over the course of a lifetime, however recent research has suggested the flexibility of sexual attraction over the course of an individual's lifetime (Diamond, 2008)

The cause of differences in students' sexual orientation has been a controversial yet often asked question. Essentially, research has pointed to a several factors such as biological differences and environmental factors (Baldwin & Baldwin, 1998). While the cause(s) of sexual orientation is not understood with certainty, it is almost certain that you will interact with students, teachers, and parents/caregivers who fall in various places on the sexual orientation continuum.

sexual orientation

represents the direction of an individual's sexual preference

Proposition 8 was passed in California on November 4, 2008, which took away the right of same-sex couples to marry. How might legislation like this impact your students who have diverse sexual orientations?

AP Photo/Gary Kazanjian

How you work with diverse students, teachers, and parents/caregivers of all varieties, including those with differing sexual orientation will have an impact on how effectively you can help your students develop academically and socially. Being a supportive professional to all of your students is a disposition that will help ensure that your classroom is the kind of environment where students, co-teachers, and parent/caregivers can comfortably interact. **Dispositions** are beliefs that a teacher has that influence his or her actions and reactions in a classroom. Teacher's dispositions have an impact on student learning (Eberly, Rand, & O'Connor, 2007), and believing that all students can learn and seeing the importance of having sensitivity when working with diverse students will help educators create a space conducive to their students' development.

Learning Objective 5

Distinguish between the different definitions of intelligence and generalize about how the definition a teacher chooses impacts how they teach students.

Diversity in Intelligence

Bobby Fischer learned to play chess when he was six years old from the instructions that came with a chess set sold in a candy store. For more than a year he played chess on his own, before joining the Brooklyn Chess Club at the age of seven and being tutored by the Club president. He attended Erasmus Hall High School, but later dropped out. School records showed him having an IQ of 184 and an incredible memory.

At the age of 13, Bobby won the U.S. Junior Chess Championship. A year later, at the age of 14, he became the youngest person ever to win the invitational U.S. Championship. He also earned the title of Grandmaster, making him at that time the youngest grandmaster in history. At the age of 19, Bobby established himself as the strongest non-Soviet player in the world. In 1972, still in his twenties, Bobby beat Boris Spassky of Russia and became the 11th World Chess Champion.

dispositions

beliefs that a teacher has that influence his or her actions and reactions in a classroom

America's most gifted chess player, the late Bobby Fisher, dropped out of high school. How can we make our classroom a place that none of the students want to leave?

Pictorial Parade/Getty Images

Intelligence or mental ability is a concept used for explaining individual performance and performance differences in the school setting. **Intelligence** is defined as the ability to solve problems and adapt to the environment. Another way to view intelligence is as a reflection of the process of *learning.* In other words, intelligence is one's teachability or one's ability to learn. Feuerstein, Rand, Hoffman, and Miller (1980) determine intelligence by teaching someone how to do something and then measuring how much better he or she can do it after being taught than before. Feuerstein et al. (1980) call this process **mediated learning** or learning that is assisted by the teaching process. The question of how intelligent a person is then becomes a matter of how readily that person can learn as a result of being taught.

There is considerable disagreement and controversy about the nature and measurement of intelligence, but Anastasi and Urbina (1997) offer the following five points on the way that intelligence may best be viewed by educators:

1. as a descriptive rather than an explanatory concept, meaning as an expression of an individual's ability at a given point in time, in relation to current age norms (intelligence tests cannot indicate the reasons for someone's performance);
2. able to be modified by experience and education instead of being thought of as fixed and unchanging;
3. as the end product of a vast and complex sequence of interactions between hereditary and environmental factors;
4. as a composite of several functions rather than a single, unitary ability, meaning the combination of abilities required for survival and advancement within a particular culture;
5. as a relative ability or one that will tend to increase with age in those functions whose value is emphasized in the culture or subculture, and will tend to decrease in those functions whose value is deemphasized.

Intelligence represents another aspect of student diversity. Individuals who do not have significant experience working in schools might not see this aspect of diversity, but experienced teachers know that students bring very different approaches, ways of thinking, and cognitive styles to the classroom. To teach students effectively, you need to have a sense of how they organize and understand the world. To guide your consideration of what intelligence is and how it develops to different degrees in different students, we will look at different conceptions of intelligence and at how intelligence testing first developed.

Intelligence as a General Mental Capability

Alfred Binet, a French psychologist, was asked to identify schoolchildren in Paris who required special educational treatment, so that they could be separated from those who did not. To identify these children, he decided that first he needed to determine the *intelligence* or *general mental capability* of all schoolchildren. He defined intelligence as a combination of the following abilities: (1) reasoning and judgment, (2) comprehension, (3) maintenance of a definite direction of thought, (4) adaptation of thinking to the attainment of a desirable end, and (5) finding

intelligence
the ability to solve problems and adapt to the environment

mediated learning
learning that is assisted by the teaching process

one's own mistakes (Binet & Simon, 1908; Binet, 1916). Despite the fact that he defined intelligence in terms of components, he believed that intelligence was a single, complex process and not a set of separate elements. Thus, he measured intelligence as a single score across a set of 30 different tasks that he believed reflected the process of intelligence. (These tasks, grouped by age level, are shown in Box 4.1.)

Binet's original conception of intelligence as a single process was later supported by Spearman (1927), who found an overlap between individual performances on a variety of intelligence subtests. He concluded that this reflected a common or general factor of intelligence, defined as a shared requirement of all the subtests. Beyond the general factor, Spearman (1927) also posited the existence of specific factors, unique to each mental activity that combined with the more important general factor to constitute intelligence. Intelligence, therefore, was largely viewed as a general ability to solve mental problems.

Sternberg's Triarchic Theory of Intelligence

Sternberg (1985, 1988) has proposed a **triarchic theory of intelligence** that includes three related aspects: analytic, creative, and practical abilities. Understanding and using this theory as a frame of reference will enable you to look at your students in new ways. For example, you might find in a student that does not perform exceptionally well in comparing the properties of elements in the periodic table might excel when given an opportunity to describe why having a periodic table is necessary and why a chemist would actually want to refer to the table.

The first aspect of this theory is componential intelligence, which represents the analysis and reasoning skills traditionally valued in school that would be used to solve a geometry proof or analyze a piece of poetry. The second aspect is experiential intelligence, which represents creative ways students solve problems or look at situations. The third type of intelligence is contextual, which deals with students' ability to deal with practical day to day issues and concerns effectively. A student who uses practical intelligence is able to deal with one's environment by a) adapting to it, b) shaping it to fit themselves, and c) selecting alternative environments when current ones can be neither adapted to nor sufficiently shaped to meet one's needs.

According to this view of intelligence, helping students learn means teaching them how to execute, perform, and learn in a wide variety of content areas. It also means that measuring how intelligent they are requires that they be tested to see how well they solve problems in practical as well as academic areas, using their analytical, creative and practical skills rather than testing only what they already know. It is a markedly different approach to intelligence than the one proposed by Binet, and it is more likely than Binet's to stimulate a broad conception about the kinds of things students should learn in school.

triarchic theory of intelligence

theory that includes three related aspects: analytic, creative, and practical abilities

The triarchic theory of intelligence should be of interest to teachers because it helps us to see intelligence in students who might not ordinarily be labeled as smart in school. The theory is also useful to teachers because, by knowing that students can be intelligent in three different ways, it helps a teacher create lessons that

BOX 4.1

"The First Intelligence Test: The Binet-Simon Scale of 1908"

The grouping of items at the appropriate age levels is shown below. Items are included that about 75% of the children of that age group could pass. Many of the items still appear in current intelligence tests.

Age 3

- Points to nose, eyes, mouth
- Repeats sentences of six syllables
- Repeats two digits
- Enumerates objects in a picture
- Gives family name

Age 4

- Knows own sex
- Names certain family objects shown to him (key, knife, penny)
- Repeats three digits
- Perceives which is the longer of two lines 5 and 6 cm. in length

Age 5

- Indicates the heavier of two cubes (3 and 12 grams; 6 and 15 grams)
- Copies a square
- Constructs a rectangle from two triangular pieces of cardboard, having a model to look at
- Counts four coins
- Repeats a sentence of ten syllables

Age 6

- Knows right and left; indicated by showing right hand and left ear
- Repeats sentence of sixteen syllables
- Chooses the prettier in each of three pairs of faces (aesthetic comparison)
- Defines familiar objects in terms of use
- Carries out three direct instructions
- Knows own age
- Knows morning and afternoon

Age 7

- Perceives what is missing in unfinished pictures
- Knows numbers of fingers on each hand and on both hands without counting
- Copies a written model ("The Little Paul")
- Copies a diamond
- Describes presented pictures
- Repeats five digits
- Counts thirteen coins
- Identifies by name four common coins

Age 8

- Reads a passage and remembers two items
- Adds up the value of five coins
- Names four colors; red, yellow, blue, green
- Counts backwards from 20 to 0
- Writes short sentences from dictation
- Gives differences between two objects

Age 9

- Knows the date: day of week, day of month, month of year
- Recites days of week
- Makes change: four cents out of twenty in play store transaction
- Gives definitions that are superior to use; familiar objects are employed
- Reads a passage and remembers six items
- Arranges five equal-appearing cubes in order of weight

Age10

- Names the months of the year in correct order
- Recognizes and names nine coins
- Constructs a sentences in which three given words are used (Paris, fortune, gutter)
- Comprehends and answers easy questions

Comprehends and answers difficult questions (Binet considered item 5 to be a transitional question between ages 10 and 11. Only about one-half of the ten-year-olds got the majority of these correct.)

Age 11

- Points out absurdities in statements
- Constructs a sentence, including three given words (same as number 3 in age 10)
- States any sixty words in three minutes
- Defines abstract words (charity, justice, kindness)
- Arranges scrambled words into a meaningful sentence

Age 12

- Repeats seven digits
- Gives three rhymes to a word (in one minute)
- Repeats a sentence of twenty-six syllables
- Answers problem questions
- Interprets pictures (as contrasted with simple description)

Age 13

- Draws the design made by cutting a triangular piece from the once-folded edge of a quarter-folded piece of paper
- Rearranges in imagination the relationship of two reversed triangles and draws results
- Gives differences between pair of abstract terms: pride and pretension.

It is interesting to speculate on how many of these age-graded tasks from 1908 could be passed by 75% of today's children of those respective ages. More than likely today's 4-year-olds could name objects like a key, a knife, or a penny, but how many 13-year-olds today could distinguish between the terms "pride" and "pretension"? Have we become less bright, or it is simply a matter of changing cultures? Such differences in standards certainly point up the importance of constantly updating tests.

Source: Binet, A., and Simon, T. (1908). Le developpement de l'intelligence chez les engants. *L'Annee Psychologiquie, 14*, 1–94.

emphasize practical and creative intelligence, not just analytical. Sternberg (2006) conducted several studies with native Alaskan, Kenyan, and American students and found that when teachers taught in ways that incorporated a student's type of intelligence they were more likely to see performance increases in the classroom. Thus, the triarchic theory suggests that whenever possible, instead of trying to find and work on areas where a student is weak, a teacher should find out which of the three intelligences students use best and try to teach new concepts and skills through their strong suit (Sternberg, 2006).

Gardner's Theory of Multiple Intelligences

Closely related to the conception of intelligence as a group of traits is the idea of different kinds of intelligence. An Eagle Scout from northeastern Pennsylvania who enjoyed and had a talent for playing the piano, but was not inclined toward athletics (Schaler, 2006), grew to become one of the most influential figures in the modern study of human intelligence. Howard Gardner went from Eagle Scout to Harvard psychologist and developed a model that says that instead of having a single intelligence quotient, students have multiple intelligences. **Multiple intelligences** is a theory about the human mind that proposes that there are eight different areas of intelligence that an individual can possess.

This theory can help educators think about students in different ways. As opposed to a student being "dumb" or "smart", multiple intelligences permits the teacher to look at a number of different strengths and weaknesses that a learner possesses (Moran, Kornhaber, & Gardner, 2006). Because each of your students will have different patterns of intelligence across these eight areas, a great hope for multiple intelligences theory is that schools can support and help students grow in their individual and distinct profile of intelligences (Shearer, 2004). Gardner (1993, 1999) proposed eight different intelligences:

1. *Linguistic* intelligence or the ability to use words (as might a writer),
2. *Logical-mathematical* intelligence or the ability to reason and use symbols (as might a scientist),
3. *Spatial* intelligence or the ability to arrange and rearrange objects in space (as might an architect),
4. *Musical* intelligence or the ability to write music or play an instrument (as might a musician),
5. *Bodily kinesthetic* intelligence or the ability to control one's body (as might a dancer or gymnast),
6. *Interpersonal* intelligence or the ability to function well socially (as might a salesperson or politician),
7. *Intrapersonal* intelligence or the ability to control one's inner thoughts and feelings (as might a spiritual leader),
8. *Naturalist* intelligence or the ability to spot and understand patterns in nature (as might an explorer or meteorologist).

multiple intelligences
theory about the human mind that proposes that there are eight different areas of intelligence that an individual can possess

In Multiple Intelligences, students can be intelligent in many ways. For example, the students performing this intricate dance are demonstrating bodily kinesthetic intelligence.

Tom Carter/PhotoEdit

"Multiple Intelligences in the Classroom"

TYPE OF MULTIPLE INTELLIGENCE	THINGS THAT THIS TYPE OF LEARNER EXCELS IN	EXAMPLE ACTIVITIES THIS TYPE OF LEARNER MIGHT ENJOY	CAREER CHOICE THAT A LEARNER WITH HIGH INTELLIGENCE IN THIS AREA MIGHT FAVOR
Linguistic	Use of words	Keeping a web blog, writing a poem	English teacher, newspaper reporter
Logical-mathematical	Deductive reasoning and use of numbers	Trying to solve brainteasers, hypothesizing about what might happen in an experiment	Engineer, computer programmer
Spatial	Manipulation of images and organizing objects in three dimensional space	Creating an advertising layout for a school periodical, putting together a puzzle	Cosmetologist, artist
Musical	Producing sounds and rhythms	Making a song to help learn and remember content in a class, learn songs from another area in the world	Symphony member, music teacher
Bodily kinesthetic	Graceful movement and balance	Acting out a scene in a play, choreographing a dance	Physical education teacher, chef
Interpersonal	Understanding others' needs, feelings, and thoughts	Having a class discussion about the evidence for and against a particular view, interviewing someone in the community and reporting the results	Psychologist, school counselor
Intrapersonal	Understanding own needs, feelings, and thoughts	Having 15 minutes in class to individually complete seatwork, researching family genealogy	Clergy member, politician
Naturalist	Living harmoniously with the environment	Participating in a service learning activity that volunteers to clean up a local stream, learning to categorize plants and animals	Science teacher, forester

Gardner sees these types of intelligence as being *modular* like the components of a stereo system. Schools often ignore many of these types of intelligence while focusing primarily on linguistic and logical-mathematical types. Instead, teachers should focus on concepts in ways that engage different types of intelligences (Nolen, 2003). By focusing on only linguistic or logical-mathematical intelligence, they may unnecessarily cause some students to feel inferior to others.

Think It Over

as a LEARNER	Which of Gardner's types of intelligence would you consider a personal strength? What experiences have you had that led you to pick those?
as a TEACHER	Do you believe that the students you teach can improve their various intelligences, and if so, how?

Measuring Intelligence

Intelligence is characteristically measured by a test, the first one being the Binet-Simon shown in Box 4.1. The original method for scoring intelligence tests was based on the obvious fact that intellectual performance increases with age (Binet & Simon, 1908). To ensure that intelligence-test scores reflected the age of test-takers, the concept of **mental age** was created. A child's mental age was based originally on the age equivalence of the most difficult items a child was able to get right (see Box 4.1 for item groupings by age). Today, however, a child's mental age is based on the average age of children who get the same number of items right as that child does. For example, if a child, regardless of age, gets 30 items right and the average age of all children who get 30 items right is 6.5, then that child has a mental age of 6.5. This represents a norm-referenced approach to test-score interpretation, as described in Chapter 14.

To convert mental age into a measure of intelligence, researchers created the **intelligence quotient** or **IQ** using the following formula:

$$IQ = \frac{\text{Mental age}}{\text{Chronological age}} \times 100$$

Thus, if the child who has a mental age of 6.5 is also 6 1/2 years old, then that child would have an IQ of 100. Whenever a child scores exactly the same as the average child of his or her own age, then that child has an IQ of 100. Children scoring the same as those older than they are will have IQ's above 100, while children scoring the same as others younger will have IQ's below 100. Nowadays, the IQ score is simply computed on the basis of how a child scores compared directly to children of different ages and is called the **deviation IQ**. (This will be discussed further in Chapter 14.)

mental age

based on the average age of children who get the same number of items right as that child does

intelligence quotient (IQ)

a student's mental age divided by their chronological age and then multiplied by 100

deviation IQ

computed on the basis of how a child scores compared directly to children of different ages

Intelligence can be described as a general mental ability or as a set of more specific mental abilities or traits. How, then, does it differ from achievement as measured by achievement tests? Perhaps we can best answer this question by looking at what it is that achievement tests measure and then contrasting that with the content of intelligence tests.

Achievement tests generally measure *reading skills,* such as (1) vocabulary or identifying a synonym of a word or a word that fits a given definition, (2) word analysis or identifying the sound of a word or a part of a word, and (3) reading comprehension or answering a question based on a story or reading passage. Achievement tests also tend to measure *language skills,* like (1) spelling, (2) punctuation, (3) capitalization, and (4) grammar or word usage.

Mathematics is another area covered by achievement tests. It is usually divided into (1) computation, (2) concepts or basic rules, and (3) applications or solving problems. Achievement tests also cover *social studies, science,* and, occasionally, *study skills.*

The content of achievement tests is not very dissimilar from that of intelligence tests. Both seem to measure what students have learned, but intelligence seems to be less dependent upon specified prior experiences than does achievement (Anastasi & Urbina, 1997). Also, intelligence tests often include the measurement of nonverbal skills, while achievement tests do not. Cronbach (1984) saw ability as a spectrum or continuum ranging from the broad ability to transfer what has been learned from one situation to another (or *intelligence)* to crystallized or specific learning resulting from direct training and instruction (or *achievement).* Intelligence, therefore, looks forward toward possible future learning, while achievement looks backward toward the measurement of past learning. Nevertheless, the overlap between the two concepts of intelligence and achievement, and the tests that measure them, is considerable, especially as reflected by an overall correlation between scores on standardized achievement tests and intelligence tests that range between 0.5 and 0.7 (Sattler, 2001).

Influences on Intelligence

The two potential sources of influence on intelligence are heredity and environment. Heredity refers to the extent to which a person's intelligence is based on the intelligence of his or her parents. The environment represents the contribution to intelligence of a person's experiences, both at home and in school.

There is clear evidence to suggest that while heredity is a highly influential factor on intelligence, it is not the only factor (Grigorenko, 2000). The level of intelligence of identical twins, born from the same egg, who are reared together in the same home at the same time by the same parents has been compared to the level of intelligence of identical twins reared apart, individuals separated at birth and then reared by different "parents" in different homes. The influence of heredity on a zero to one scale, called the heritability coefficient, goes from 0.86 in the first instance to 0.76 in the second (Bouchard, 1997; Scarr; 1997). In other words, twins who have the same heredity have very similar IQ's regardless of whether they have the same environment. Moreover, identical twins reared apart, meaning siblings with the same heredity but different environments, have IQ's much more similar to one another than ordinary siblings reared together; their heritability index is 0.47. The latter have a similar environment but a somewhat different heredity.

LITTLE ROCK CENTRAL HIGH

RAY   ROBERTS   PATTILLO   THOMAS   WALLS

MOTHERSHED   BROWN   ECKFORD   GREEN

AP Photo/File

Here are the nine members of the Little Rock Nine that were discussed in the opening story to this chapter. You can read about one of the members, civil rights pioneer Ernest Green, in the Discourse on Diversity for this chapter. You can also watch the 1993 Walt Disney Television film about his life called *The Ernest Green Story.*

These findings, of course, do not suggest that the impact of home environment and school on intelligence is inconsequential. No matter how great a child's inborn intellectual capacity is, that capacity will not be realized or actualized unless the home and school environments are reasonably supportive and stimulating. While teachers must recognize that each child has his or her own intellectual level, that level may represent only a partial degree of that child's potential. The teacher still has the opportunity to help all children reach their potential. School experiences, therefore, should not be discounted. To put this issue into perspective, see Box 4.3: Discourse on Diversity.

There is little certainty about exactly what intelligence is, what its properties are, how best to measure it, or what it should be a prerequisite for. One controversy is whether intelligence, as it is presently used, is universally applicable (as it might be if it were based on heredity) or culturally bound (as a result of environmental influences that vary from culture to culture). Using intelligence test scores as a basis for life decisions for children, or even for adults (see Box 4.3), in all but extreme cases, may be unwise and unfounded. Another controversy is whether the results of testing should be used to place students in different groups. This controversy is the topic of the next section you will read, and you will be exposed to some information that will help you to think about the potential uses and misuses of ability grouping in schools.

Ability Grouping

Ability grouping or homogeneous grouping means classifying pupils in terms of factors presumed to affect learning, such as intelligence or mental ability or achievement, and then forming instructional groups made up of pupils who are highly similar on these factors. Many elementary schools have school-wide gifted, remedial, and special-education classes, and in-class reading and mathematics groups. Many high schools have honors, college preparatory, and special education classes, and/or academic, vocational, and general tracks. In every instance, students of common ability or achievement level are grouped together, separate from students of either greater or lesser ability or achievement level. The rationale is that instruction will be more efficient if all students are equally capable than if the level of capability varies

DISCOURSE ON DIVERSITY

"Cultural Bias in Intelligence Testing"

BOX 4.3

In the late 1960's, while many civil rights groups focused their efforts on elimination of tests as culturally biased, Ernest Green* of the A. Phillip Randolph Institute took a different approach. He developed a program in Brooklyn's Bedford-Stuyvesant section to train potential apprenticeship candidates to take the screening test. The General Aptitude Test Battery (GATB) is a type of broad-based intelligence test that the United States Employment Service used in screening and counseling job seekers. It was also used as a screening device for apprenticeship training programs. Because in the 1960s blacks tended to score lower than whites on this test, they were eliminated from competition for places in apprenticeship programs. Assuming that white candidates have had more specific training in taking such tests as the GATB, Mr. Green added relevant experience to the culture of minority candidates to overcome the cultural bias. Using mainly self-educated ex-convicts as teachers, he had black candidates spend six to eight weeks learning basic math and English. They practiced on items similar to those found on the current form of the GATB (a review process not unlike the College Board review or the "Regents review" in the New York schools).

Their heads filled with vocabulary words, analogies, and math skills, Ernest Green's first group of graduates from his program took the exams. The results were gratifying: Virtually all the students in the program were above the cut-off scores. "They're beating the system," shouted their critics, who were trying to maintain the status quo. "It's not fair to teach people to take a test." "But," responded Green, "isn't that what the middle-class school experience is all about?" The courts agreed and ruled that those who had never been taught what the test measured were entitled to be given the opportunity to learn it.

Test results may be a cause of school behavior and not just its effect. If children who have higher IQ scores are expected by their teachers to do better in school than children with lower scores (a not unreasonable supposition), and if teachers are nicer to these high-IQ-test-scorers, and help them more than they help the low scorers, it is evident that IQ test scores are not only the effect of school experiences but also their cause. (This effect of expectations, called the self-fulfilling prophecy, is described in Chapter 9.)

One benefit of the debate on intelligence testing in the 1960s and 1970s was to make educators more careful in the use of IQ tests. Clearly, African Americans and Whites as groups do tend to score differently on IQ tests—perhaps, it could be argued, because African Americans have had poorer schooling, rather than the difference being substantially genetic in origin as claimed as recently as 1994 by Hernstein and Murray in *The Bell Curve*. Possibly, then, we should reconsider how tests should be used. Except for the diagnosis of marked deficiency, it would be wiser to focus testing on what children have learned as a result of school experiences and to draw conclusions on this basis rather than on the basis of variations in native intelligence.

*This was the same Ernest Green who in 1957 was one of the "Little Rock 9," a group of nine brave African American students who entered Central High School in Little Rock, Arkansas under military protection, as the first step of school integration in the South.

greatly from student to student. In other words, narrowing the range of capability among students in a class is presumed to improve the effectiveness of instruction and thereby increase achievement.

A major study of 86 fifth-grade classrooms in the New York City Public Schools over a two-year period (fifth grade to seventh grade) revealed that "narrowing the range of ability (on the basis of group intelligence tests) per se, without specifically designed variations in programs for the several ability levels, does not result in consistently greater academic performance for any group of pupils" (Goldberg, Passow, & Justman, 1966, p. 161). In other words, ability grouping was not effective.

One reason for the lack of effectiveness was that most teachers were more successful in teaching a single subject to several ability levels at the same time than in teaching all subjects to narrow-range classes. Moreover, teachers did not necessarily alter what they taught when the range of ability of the students they were teaching changed, especially in the subject areas the teachers felt least competent to teach. Grouping students by ability does not tend to help them learn more *unless* their instruction is specifically designed and fitted to their ability level, a practice that is not typical, except perhaps in special education classes.

A review of ability and achievement grouping studies in elementary schools by Slavin (1987) reached a similar conclusion for **between-class** or self-contained grouping, that it did not enhance achievement. While high-track classes may provide slight benefits, these are far outweighed by the losses experienced by students in low-track classes, who tend to be low income students of color (Oakes & Wells, 1998).

However, when students are assigned to heterogeneous homeroom classes for most of the day, but regrouped based on ability or achievement for reading and/ or mathematics, as occurs in most elementary schools, then achievement can be improved provided the level and pace of instruction is adapted to achievement level. Kulik (1992), in an analysis of the research on ability grouping, found that programs that make only minor adjustments of course content for ability groups have little or no effect on student achievement, while those that make the greatest amount of curricular adjustment typically have the greatest effects on student achievement. Slavin (1987) also found that **within-class** ability or achievement grouping was effective, particularly for teaching *mathematics*, again providing that appropriate curricular adjustments were made from group to group (See Box 4.4).

Opponents of ability grouping, or tracking, have proposed **detracking**; that is., eliminating any form of tracking to ensure that all students have equal access to school resources, particularly the better teachers and more demanding curriculums (Lockwood & Cleveland, 1998; Rubin, 2006). If students in heterogeneous or mixed ability groups need extra help, it can be provided, say detracking proponents, through tutoring or after-school help (Oakes & Wells, 1998). Detracking advocates go on to argue that the tracking process gives a more enriched curriculum to students from advantaged backgrounds (Futrell & Gomez, 2008).

What about the effects of ability grouping on nonacademic variables, such as attitude toward self? Goldberg, Passow, and Justman (1966) found little effect, either positive or negative. The act of being grouped, however, can affect a student's self-expectations as well as the expectations of teachers, resulting in what has been

between-class

grouping students in separate classrooms based on perceived ability

within-class

grouping students within a class into different reading or mathematics groups based on achievement level

detracking

eliminating any form of tracking to ensure that all students have equal access to school resources

BOX 4.4

TAKE IT TO THE CLASSROOM

The Elements of Successful Ability Grouping Plans
(based on Slavin, 1987)

Successful teachers give careful consideration to the question of whether they should use ability grouping, and if they decide that it is in the best interest of the students, they are sure to think about the following five issues:

1. Placing students in heterogeneous classes, and regrouping them into self-contained ability classes only for math or reading instruction (where reducing heterogeneity facilitates learning)

2. Using grouping into self-contained ability classes to reduce heterogeneity only in the specific skill being taught (not in IQ or overall achievement level)

3. Doing frequent reassessment of student placement in these classes, and making reassignments to different groups based on student progress

4. Insuring that teachers vary the level and pace of instruction in regrouped classes to accommodate students' levels of readiness and learning rates

5. When using within-class ability grouping, creating only a small number of groups to make adequate instruction possible for each group

• Do you think you will use ability grouping in your classroom? Why or why not?

called the self-fulfilling prophecy (See Figure 9.2). Ability or achievement grouping would appear, therefore, to be a poor educational strategy except when specific instructional approaches have been designed for a particular group. Alternatively, the cooperative-learning approach would appear to be a good strategy for dealing with students with a range of abilities. (See the section on normative goal structures in Chapter 9, and Box 9.3 in particular.) Having more accomplished students work with less accomplished ones can provide academic and nonacademic benefits to both groups (Webb, 1982).

Learning Style Differences

Learning Objective 6

Conceptualize learning style as an educationally relevant type of individual difference between students and consider ways of matching instructional and learning style.

Quite apart from the question of a person's intelligence is the question of how that person typically goes about thinking and learning. **Learning style** is a student's preferred way of learning concepts and skills. Some people are very organized and structured, for example; others are less organized and more spontaneous. Some people like to work independently while others like to interact and communicate with other people. It is useful for you to be aware of differences in the ways students think and learn. In the classroom, you will need to link these differences to different styles of teaching.

Match/Mismatch: The Fit Between Instructional Style and Learning Style

Students gain more knowledge, retain more information, and perform better when teaching styles match learning styles (Lage, Platt, & Triglia, 2000). Which type of learner is most likely to be taught in a way that is consistent with his or her learning style? Most classrooms and curriculums are structured and controlled by rules and requirements external to the student. Thus, organized learners are most likely to find themselves in learning situations that *match* their style. Because many teachers incorporate interactive processes into their teaching, such as group work or discussions, interactive learners are the next most likely to find matches. Least likely to find matches are spontaneous learners whose needs run counter to the order and structure of most schools. Peacock (2001) found that when there was a mismatch between group and individual styles of teachers and learners, student learning proficiency was affected. It was recommended that teachers teach in a balanced style to accommodate different learning styles.

A famous example of mismatch is the story of Felix Unger and Oscar Madison, characters in a Neil Simon play, movie, and television series, lived together despite the fact that their personal styles were extremely different. Dubbed the "odd couple" because Felix was so neat, organized, and fastidious, while Oscar was rambunctious, spontaneous, and carefree, their oddness or mismatch made for many laughs. Felix, for example, was always concerned that Oscar would miss an appointment or fail to carry out a responsibility, so he left him little notes on his pillow, on the bathroom mirror, on the refrigerator—to name just a few places. Oscar would stumble upon the notes, crumple them up, and throw them

learning style

a student's preferred way of learning concepts and skills

at Felix in a mock rage because he figured that anything he couldn't remember to do wasn't worth doing. Felix, by comparison, would never, knowingly, allow his schedule to be messed up.

When a teacher must deal with students who are very different from him or herself, the result is an "odd couple," a "Felix" and an "Oscar." The teacher may want order and explicit following of directions. The student may be more carefree—not just to give the teacher a hard time, but because that's the way that student is. Oscar and Felix, however, could never manage to avoid fighting with one another over their differences. If Felix cooked a gourmet meal and taunted Oscar about preferring to eat hot dogs, then Oscar would invariably end up throwing the food at Felix, or putting his dirty socks in Felix's bed. All this makes good theater, but it does not make good instruction. Teachers have to learn not only to tolerate their differences with some students but to respect and enjoy them as well. Students also have to be open to differences in the classroom and it is recommended that students try to translate what is covered in a class into a form they can understand, as well as being open to new ways of learning, and be willing to ask the teacher for help (Pace University Counseling Services, 2008).

Adapting to a Mismatch

The choice of an instructional method to match individual learning needs has been referred to by Cronbach and Snow (1977) as the **aptitude-treatment interaction** or **ATI** because the treatment or approach is chosen to match the inclination of the students. How can you implement matching models? Ideally, each student should be allowed to choose his or her preferred form of instruction, but in a class of 20 to 30 students allowing this much choice could be chaotic. A second possibility is for you to vary the instructional model (using a continuum such as that shown in Box 9.3) so that every student would experience times of match and times of mismatch. A third possibility is for you to offer so-called magnet classrooms (similar to magnet schools), in which a particular model of teaching predominates, and let students (and their parents) choose their own match. A fourth possibility would be for you to measure individual style by test or interview and then assign students to class sections taught in a way consistent with that style. This could be called learning-style grouping.

In summary, your alternatives for matching are to

1. provide instructional style choices within a classroom,
2. alter instructional style from unit to unit within a classroom,
3. offer alternative classes or schools with different instructional styles from which students can choose,
4. offer alternative classes with different instructional styles and assign students based on their measured learning styles.

Typically, teachers employ the instructional style they are the most comfortable with or are the most encouraged to use by the principal. Usually, though not exclusively, this is the organized or structured one, where students are assigned to classes without regard to their learning styles. As a result, in every instructional setting, some students are experiencing a match and some a mismatch between their teacher's approach to instruction and the way they learn.

aptitude-treatment interaction (ATI)

the degree to which an instructional strategy may be more or less effective with an individual based on their current level of achievement

How can mismatches be addressed to achieve a successful learning result? Because it may be impossible for you to change the way you teach, what adaptive strategies can your students employ? As the teacher, you can provide guidelines to adaptive behaviors to the students who most need it. Following are suggestions you might use yourself as a pre-service student and then provide to your students in your own future classrooms.

If you are a student who prefers structure and organization in a class where little or none is provided, adaptation will require that you provide your own. This may mean preparing your own worksheets to help you study, outlining your lecture notes and textbook readings, developing your own study schedule and instructional aids, such as flash cards, and talking to your instructor often to clarify topics to be tested and grading standards and expectations.

If you are a student who prefers interaction and class activities and find yourself in a large lecture class, adaptation will require that you provide your own interaction. Some ways to make the learning experience more interactive are to communicate frequently with your instructor before or after class, form or join study groups, team up with classmates before and after class to discuss course topics and assignments, and ask questions in class when opportunities present themselves.

If you are a student who prefers an independent problem-solving approach and find yourself in a class that features frequent group discussions, group projects, and repetition of information, adaptation will require that you establish a role for yourself as leader or resource person. Try taking the initiative to be a leader in group discussions and activities, make every effort to keep group discussions on task, generate your own ideas insofar as possible and look for classmates to piggyback on them, and serve as an information resource for your classmates or group-mates.

Finally, if you are a student who prefers hands-on learning by doing and actual performance opportunities and find yourself in a class that features seemingly endless, boring lectures and frequent writing assignments and tests, adaptation will require that you do something to keep yourself awake and engaged. Try finding connections between what you are being taught and your own interests, tailor writing assignments to topics that you find stimulating and useful, request permission from your instructor to do creative alternatives to papers such as slideshows, construction projects or games, and reward yourself for managing to focus your attention and survive the experience.

Think It Over

as a LEARNER   What is an instructional situation where you would feel the greatest sense of mismatch, and how would you handle it?

as a TEACHER   What would you do differently in your teaching approach if you had a class with a high degree of mismatch?

SUMMING IT UP

Learning Objective 1

Key Concepts:

socioeconomic status (p. 137); critical pedagogy (p. 138); social justice, Theatre of the Oppressed (p. 139); differentiated instruction (p. 140).

Illustrate how social class relates to experiences that students may have in school and discuss the importance of social justice practices like critical pedagogy that a teacher can employ to insure all students have an opportunity for a quality education.

Social class or **socioeconomic status** (SES), is a function of parents' education level and occupational status, and reflection of income level, wholly outside of a child's control. High SES children tend to score considerably higher than low SES children on tests of math and reading achievement. **Critical pedagogy** is one methodology that can be used to counteract the privilege of wealth and insure high quality education for all students.

Learning Objective 2

Key Concepts:

stereotype threat (p. 143); ethnic identity acculturation (p. 144); situating identity (p. 145); identity development (p. 146); model minority stereotype (p. 148); segregation, Brown v. Board of Education of Topeka (p. 150); multicultural education (p. 153).

Support how students' experiences in school are influenced by their ethnicity and culture and tell some of the history of what African American students went through during the desegregation movement.

African American and Latino/Latina students tend to score lower than white students on tests of math and reading achievement. This may be a reflection of low SES, exposure to opportunities, initial skill level, or of **stereotype threat.** Teachers need to employ **multicultural education** principles to eliminate this achievement gap and help all students achieve.

Learning Objective 3

Key Concepts:

English language learners, bilingual education (p. 157); two-way bilingual education, immersion, Proposition 227 (p. 158).

Describe the different demographic and language patterns in America's public schools and discuss approaches to assisting English language learners.

Many of the children who immigrate to this country are referred to as **English Language Learners.** English language learners are students who are in the process of learning to communicate in English. Many of these children with limited English skills are at higher risk for school failure. **Bilingual education** and **immersion** are two approaches to educating English language learners. The quality of the instructional program the children receive seems to be more important than the actual method they receive the instruction in.

Explain how schooling can be biased towards students based on gender and orientation and discuss methods a teacher could implement to insure an equitable and safe classroom environment.

Evidence suggests that girls consistently outperform boys in reading, equal them in math, and receive higher grades in school, yet report more internal distress, perhaps because of their greater desire to please adults and their openness to evaluative feedback. This is due to **gender bias** in the classroom. In addition to being different genders, students also come to the classroom with different **sexual orientations.** Believing that all students can learn and seeing the importance of having sensitivity when working with diverse students is an important teacher characteristic.

Learning Objective 4

Key Concepts:

gender bias (p. 160);
sexual orientation (p. 161);
dispositions (p. 162).

Distinguish between the different definitions of intelligence and generalize about how the definition a teacher chooses impacts how they teach students.

Albert Binet conceived of **intelligence** as a general mental ability, made up of a single, underlying process or general factor. Other researchers defined it as a group of abilities such as linguistic, musical, logical-mathematical, spatial, bodily kinesthetic, intrapersonal, interpersonal, and naturalistic. Researchers originally related intelligence to age, in the form of the **intelligence** quotient or IQ with mental age being based on the age equivalence of the most difficult test items a child was able to get right. Today, however, a child's **mental age** is based on the average age of children who get the same number of items right as that child does. Intelligence is a joint function of a person's heredity and his or her environment. Studies with identical twins reared apart show that heredity is a highly consequential factor. However, the impact of school experiences should not be discounted.

Learning Objective 5

Key Concepts:

intelligence, mediated learning (p. 163);
multiple intelligences (p. 167);
mental age, intelligence quotient, deviation IQ (p. 169);
between-class grouping, within-class grouping, detracking (p. 173).

Conceptualize learning style as an educationally relevant type of individual difference between students and consider ways of matching instructional and learning style.

How a person thinks or learns represents his or her **learning style.** Spontaneous learners prefer real-life experiences and adventure, while organized learners desire highly structured learning environments with routines and explicit instructions; conceptual learners prefer to provide their own structure and control by working independently, and interactive learners like working with peers. To facilitate each group's learning, the type of instruction should be matched to the learning style, as opposed to mismatched, so that structure- or conformity-seekers are taught by formal, teacher-controlled methods and independence-seekers are taught by informal, student-controlled methods. To accomplish matching, teachers must have instructional alternatives available and students must be able to choose between them.

Learning Objective 6

Key Concepts:

learning style (p. 175);
aptitude-treatment interaction (p. 176).

5 | Learners with Exceptionalities

After reading this chapter, you should be able to meet the following learning objectives	Chapter Contents
LEARNING OBJECTIVE 1 Describe learners classified with exceptionalities, the implications of such classifications, and the laws that govern the process.	Background • Who are Learners with Exceptionalities? • Advantages and Disadvantages of Classifying Learners as Exceptional • Laws Governing the Education of Learners with Exceptionalities
LEARNING OBJECTIVE 2 Discuss the process of service provided to exceptional learners, i.e., special education, including Individualized Education Program, least restrictive environment, and inclusion.	Special Education: Service to Exceptional Learners • Individualized Education Program (IEP) • Least Restrictive Environment • Inclusion
LEARNING OBJECTIVE 3 Explain and illustrate intellectual exceptionalities: giftedness/talent and mental retardation, including characteristics, causes, assessment, and educational approaches.	Intellectual Exceptionalities • Giftedness and Talent • Mental Retardation
LEARNING OBJECTIVE 4 Explain and illustrate behaviorally challenging exceptionalities: learning disability, attention deficit/hyperactivity disorder (ADHD), and emotional/behavioral disorder, including characteristics, causes, assessment, and educational approaches.	Behaviorally-Challenging Exceptionalities • Learning Disabilities • Attention Deficit/Hyperactivity Disorder (ADHD) • Emotional and Behavior Disorders
LEARNING OBJECTIVE 5 Explain and illustrate sensorimotor exceptionalities: communication, speech, hearing, and vision.	Communication and Sensorimotor Exceptionalities • Communication Disorders • Hearing and Visual Impairment
LEARNING OBJECTIVE 6 Explain and illustrate physical disabilities, including characteristics, causes, assessment, and educational approaches.	Physical Disabilities
LEARNING OBJECTIVE 7 Explain and illustrate autism.	Autism • Definition and Description • Educational Approach

Making a Difference

Andrew was a student in Mrs. Green's varying exceptionality classroom. He had been diagnosed with emotional/behavioral disorder. He was disrespectful and verbally aggressive, particularly to adults, and most particularly to Mrs. Green who tried to get rid of him and failed. After that, Mrs. Green just "wrote him off" as hopeless and tried her best to ignore him. It was at that point that Amy, a consultant hired by the school system to deal with "problem children," entered the picture and made Andrew her personal mission. Despite the fact that Andrew was the most disruptive student in the classes she worked with, Amy believed she could turn him around.

She began by focusing on how he was disciplined, and rather than doing it hit-or-miss depending on her mood, as Mrs. Green had done, Amy set up a behavioral program for Andrew and, during the periods she was in Mrs. Green's room, she modeled it in hopes that Mrs. Green would follow suit. She was extremely consistent in providing Andrew with consequences for his behavior, but never responded angrily or got fed up. She went out of her way to notice and praise any step he made in the right direction.

Andrew began to be aware of his own inappropriate behavior, and before long, accepted his consequences without backtalk. Amy never belittled him or talked to him like he was a delinquent. He may not have liked her, but he accepted her authority. After Andrew misbehaved and had to serve a time-out, Amy began to sit down with him and identify the events that led up to his behavior. She directed the negative to his misbehavior; everything positive was directed at him. Andrew came to learn where his reaction went wrong and what the appropriate action would have been. He began to learn and practice self-control. He also began to realize that Amy was on his side and so went out of his way to please her. He never acted out when Amy was in the room. Mrs. Green, who is easily overwhelmed and talks to Andrew's face about his incorrigibility, does not receive the same respect from Andrew as Amy does.

- How did Amy make a difference?
- What did you learn from this story about dealing with challenging students?

Lessons We Can Learn from the Story Dealing with the Andrews of this world poses a great challenge. It requires those who teach these special children to possess considerable skills and dedication. The outcome, unquestionably, is well worth the effort.

There is a widely held belief that "individuals with disabilities have the right to as much self-determination as we can help them achieve" (Heward, 2003, p. 3). But as a classroom teacher, like Mrs. Green, you may be easily overwhelmed by these types of students. How do you recognize them? What amount and type of special learning experiences do they need? How do you help them? In this chapter, we will acquaint you with special learning needs students, their descriptions, determinations, and educational interventions.

Background

We will begin with a discussion about students with **exceptionalities**. The term expands the category of "disability" to include "giftedness and talent" by examining who these individuals are, why we classify them as exceptional, and what laws govern their education.

Who Are Learners with Exceptionalities?

Students vary in both their physical attributes and their learning and behavioral abilities. Obvious physical differences can be observed in height, weight, speed, strength, and endurance. More importantly, from an educational point of view, differences can be observed in speech, hearing, vision, and movement. Learning and behavioral differences include the ease with which new ideas are learned and retained, and the extent to which self-control can be maintained. When a student's differences in either category vary enough from the average or norm to require some form of special or individualized programs or services, he or she is considered exceptional. Collectively, these students are known as **exceptional learners**.

While exceptionality may reflect either a disability or a heightened ability, it does not necessarily impose a *handicap*, a term that associates a stigma with learners whose characteristics are indicative of special needs. In K–12 schools, special needs are met by programs identified as **special education**. The availability of special education grew to accommodate approximately 6.3 million children during the 2000–2001 school year (U.S. Department of Education, 2002). The vast majority of special education students are in the learning disabilities category, where the number of students has doubled since the 1976–1977 school year.

Advantages and Disadvantages of Classifying Children as Exceptional

The process of **classification** is key in providing students with assistance. Without recognizing a student's special needs, it would not be possible to undertake the necessary intervention. For example, if no one knew you had a visual problem, no one would think to give you an eye exam or prescribe glasses, if necessary. Classification has the added advantage of bringing issues associated with exceptionality to the public's attention, particularly to those who establish educational policies and provide related program funds.

There are disadvantages of classification, especially the chance of stigmatizing learners by focusing on their deficits and thereby withholding or reducing opportunities to learn. It can also impact negatively on a learner's level of self-esteem. Labels may also have an effect on teachers' perceptions or expectations of learners. Teachers might expect less from them than from other students, or, alternatively more, in the case of the "gifted" label. Thus, teachers might treat these students inappropriately. Additionally, labels can be difficult to "lose." Once classified, a label may predispose teachers and even other children to view classified children in a particular way, regardless of their performance accomplishments.

exceptionalities

expands the category of "disability" to include "giftedness and talent" by examining who these individuals are, why we classify them as exceptional, and what laws govern their education

exceptional learners

when a student's behavior or learning abilities vary enough from the average or norm to require some form of special or individualized programs or services

special education

programs in K–12 schools designed to meet special needs

classification

recognizing a student's special needs

It has been suggested by Steeker and Fuchs (2000) and others that students be classified in terms of the degree to which they are learning specific curriculum content. This approach, called **curriculum-based assessment**, is more specific than the current classification system that relies on comparisons with other students. However, it is not likely to replace the current system in the near future. Instead, this approach is expected to lead to the identification of better instructional programming for children with exceptionalities.

Laws Governing the Education of Learners with Exceptionalities

Prior to the 1970s, laws in some states permitted the exclusion of children with exceptionalities (Murdick, Gartin, & Crabtree, 2002). Indeed, including these children in public schools is a relatively recent occurrence. When those with less extreme problems were accepted into schools, they received no special help and often were labeled "slow learners" or "disciplinary problems."

In 1975, Public Law 94-142 was passed by Congress and changed education in the United States. Originally called the Education for All Handicapped Children Act, it has been reauthorized and amended four times, and had its name changed to the **Individuals with Disabilities Education Act** (IDEA). The purpose of the law is to assure that all children with disabilities have available to them special education and related services designed to meet their needs, and to provide federal funds to cover part of the cost of its mandates.

The law enunciates the following six major principles (Turnbull and Turnbull, 2000):

- zero reject—schools must provide all children with disabilities between the ages of 6 and 17 with special education;
- nondiscriminatory identification and evaluation—testing and evaluation procedures for determining whether a child has a disability that do not discriminate on the basis of race, culture, or native language (indeed testing must be done in the child's native language), and placement decisions may not be made based on only one test score;
- free, appropriate public education—for all children with disabilities regardless of type or severity, and including an individualized education program (IEP), described below;
- least restrictive environment—students with disabilities will not be removed to separate classes or schools, but be educated with and among peers without disabilities to the greatest degree possible and appropriate (described below);
- due process safeguards—to protect the rights of children with disabilities and their parents (e.g., parental consent, confidentially of records, independent evaluation, etc.); and
- parent and student participation in shared decision making—getting input from parents of children with disabilities and the children themselves where appropriate, on the design and implementation of services.

IDEA does not cover gifted and talented children, but the Jacob K. Javits Gifted and Talent Student Education Act, passed in 1988, provides funds for these

curriculum-based assessment

students are classified in terms of the degree to which they are learning specific curriculum content

Individuals with Disabilities Education Act

law passed that is intended to assure that all children with disabilities have available to them special education and related services designed to meet their needs, and to provide federal funds to cover part of the cost of its mandates

children as well as a national research center and position in the U.S. Department of Education.

The Americans with Disabilities Act, passed in 1990, mandates that employers make reasonable accommodations to ensure that persons with disabilities can perform essential job functions, a key to their achievement of self-determination.

Special Education: Service to Exceptional Learners

Educational intervention programs, called **special education**, are designed to teach persons with disabilities the skills required for independent and successful functioning, that is, self-determination. These skills can be academic (e.g., reading), vocational (e.g., job skills), personal (e.g., dressing oneself), or social (e.g., interacting well with others). Special education is distinctive in that its target population is delimited to that subgroup of students who have been classified as students with disabilities. But it can also be described as an approach to instruction that is "individually planned, specialized, intensive, and goal-directed" (Heward, 2003, p. 38). As such, it has some special features; three of the most important are described below. Even if you plan to become a regular classroom teacher rather than a special education teacher, you will likely deal with special needs students in a variety of capacities during your teaching career. To be an effective teacher in any situation, you will need to be acquainted with special education.

> **Learning Objective 2**
>
> Discuss the process of service provided to exceptional learners, i.e., special education, including Individualized Education Program, least restrictive environment, and inclusion.

special education

programs designed to teach persons with disabilities the skills required for independent and successful functioning

Special education is an intervention designed to help students with disabilities participate fully and actively in school and society. It helps them overcome obstacles that may otherwise impede their learning.

Bill Aron/PhotoEdit

Individualized Education Program (IEP)

IDEA very specifically requires that an **Individualized Education Program** (IEP) be developed and implemented for every student with disabilities. The law is equally specific about what an IEP must include and who will be on the team that prepares it. The IEP is a central feature of special education. The team that prepares a child's IEP must include the following:

- the child's parents;
- the child's regular teacher (if he or she has one);
- the child's special education teacher;
- a knowledgeable representative of the school district;
- a person who can knowledgably interpret the evaluation results;
- other individuals having special knowledge of the child, if requested by the parents or school; and
- the child, if 14 or older (or younger, if deemed appropriate).

The IEP itself must include the following components:

- the child's current level of educational performance, including how the child's disability affects that performance;
- measurable goals for the school year across different areas of functioning and benchmarks or objective criteria for measuring progress toward those goals that will enable the child to meet the needs associated with his or her disability in order to make educational progress;
- the special education (and related services and aids, including program modifications) to be provided for the child to meet the above stated goals, and to participate in academic and nonacademic activities with other children (both those with disabilities and those without);
- the reasons, if any, why the child will not participate with nondisabled children in the above activities;
- modifications of state or district-wide assessments of student achievement, if any, that will need to be made for the child; or alternatively, why a particular assessment is not appropriate and how the child will otherwise be assessed;
- when the services and modifications, if any, described in the third bullet will begin, and what their frequency, duration, and location will be; and
- the manner in which the child's annual progress toward the goals listed in the second bullet will be measured, and how the child's parents will be informed on a continuing basis throughout the year (at least as often as parents of nondisabled children are informed of their progress).

Goals are a critical feature of the IEP writing process, reflecting what the team expects the child to accomplish during the year provided that the special services he or she receives are effective. Unfortunately, however, according to Bateman and Linden (1998), all too often the IEP writing process burdens teachers with an excessive amount of paperwork that ultimately provides few benefits for children. The IEP describes what the team hopes to accomplish. Too often, this description contains little indication of what exactly will be done educationally or service-wise to

Individualized Education Program

individual programs developed and implemented for every student with disabilities

help the child meet the goals. An example of the most important part of an IEP form is shown in the *Concept Review* in Table 5.1 (on page 188). This example does, indeed, describe the interventions that will be employed with the student.

The IEP Form

The IEP for a student covers three categories: (1) educational needs, characteristics, and present levels of performance; (2) special education, related services, supplemental aids and services, assistive technology, program modifications, and support for personnel; and (3) measurable goals and short-term objectives (Bateman & Linden, 1998). The first category includes an indication of how the disability affects the student's ability to progress in the general curriculum. The second category includes frequency, duration, and location of services. The third category includes how progress toward goals will be measured.

An Example of an IEP: Curt's Situation

Bateman & Linden (1998) describe the IEP for Curt, a ninth grader with learning disabilities and a history of discipline problems. Regarding educational needs, Curt has difficulties in both learning and behavior. He needs to learn study skills, namely reading text, notetaking, studying notes, and memory work. Behavior-wise, he needs to come to class prepared, improve his attention span, and maintain on-task behavior. At his present level, Curt lacks all of these skills and behaviors.

Curt also needs remedial help in spelling, punctuation, capitalization, and word usage. In these skills, he is currently two grade levels behind his peers. Regarding adaptations to his regular program, it is recommended that Curt sit near the front of the class, be helped in study skills by teachers trained by a spelling/language specialist, called on often to be kept on task, and monitored by the teacher in the early stages of his program.

What can be done about Curt's situation? The answer falls in the area of providing him with special education and other supplemental and assistive services that will enhance his learning and improve his behavior. It is recommended that Curt be provided with direct and specific teaching of study skills by a speech therapist, resource room teacher, and content area teachers; assigned a "study buddy" in each class; be given a motivational plan to lengthen his attention span and time on-task; have an aide teach him self-monitoring techniques and the use of a self-recording form for completion of academic tasks; receive direct instruction in language skills; experience cumulative reviews to help with memory difficulty; and develop a list of commonly used words to improve his vocabulary. Following this plan should help Curt improve.

In addition to needs and services, Curt's IEP also includes goal setting; the ultimate goals include enabling Curt to participate in the general curriculum and meet the needs that result from his disability, and determining how his progress toward meeting these goals will be measured. Some examples of Curt's goals are (1) earning higher grades and learning new study skills by the end of the school year; (2) doubling his on-task behavior by year's end; and (3) improving his written language skills by one-and-a-half or two grade levels. All of this will be monitored by teachers and classroom specialists to increase the likelihood that these goals will be met.

IEPs like Curt's will provide teachers as well as parents with both the opportunity and responsibility to deal with their students' needs and goals in a realistic and creative manner and to help their students advance from their present level of performance to meet future academic goals. It will also serve as a measure of accountability (Heward, 2003). A *Concept Review* of the IEP is shown in Table 5.1.

CONCEPT REVIEW TABLE 5.1
The IEP

EXAMPLES OF EDUCATIONAL NEEDS	EXAMPLES OF INTERVENTIONS & RELATED SERVICES	EXAMPLES OF MEASURABLE GOALS & BENCHMARKS
Improve study skills (e.g., reading, notetaking)	Providing specific teaching of reading and notetaking	Student can take appropriate notes as judged by the teacher and read 10–15 pages of text
Improve attention span and on-task behavior	Developing a motivation plan to lengthen attention span and time on-task	Doubling on-task behavior as measured by a qualified observer at year's end
Improve spelling, punctuation, capitalization, and usage	Provide direct instruction in spelling, punctuation, capitalization, and usage	Given 10 sentences, student can punctuate and capitalize with 90% accuracy
Improve short-term rote memory	Provide continuous review to help short-term memory	Given a list of 10 words to remember, student will perform with 90% accuracy
Improve retention	Provide direct instruction of strategies for reading text to retain information	Given 10–15 pages to read, student will employ an appropriate strategy for retaining information as judged by teacher

Least Restrictive Environment

The concept of **least restrictive environment**, mandated by IDEA, requires that learners with disabilities be educated with nondisabled learners to the extent possible, except in cases where the nature of the disability would not allow satisfactory results to be achieved. This means that students with special needs will be educated in regular school programs and settings to the greatest degree possible, as long as the students' special needs are met.

However, "least restrictive environment" must be regarded as a relative rather than an absolute concept. A range of services, programs, and settings must be available—starting with the regular classroom at one end and hospitals, special schools, or homebound facilities at the other—to accommodate the special needs of students with disabilities. In between these two ends is typically a combination of regular classroom with supplementary services, the latter provided sometimes in the regular classroom but more commonly in a resource room. Beyond that is the wholly separate special education classroom. The decision of which of these alternatives is best for the student is based on the specific services recommended in the IEP.

Inclusion

Inclusion represents the process of educating learners with exceptionalities in regular classrooms. It often is confused with the least restrictive environment, which represents educating learners with exceptionalities in settings as close to the regular classroom as possible and providing the appropriate programs to meet their special needs. Therefore, the least restrictive environment prescribed in IDEA is a broader strategy than inclusion. The policy of inclusion has generated some controversy.

least restrictive environment

requires that learners with disabilities be educated with nondisabled learners to the extent possible, except in cases where the nature of the disability would not allow satisfactory results to be achieved

inclusion

the process of educating learners with exceptionalities in regular classrooms

In *inclusive education*, students with and without disabilities work together in regular classrooms in order to facilitate educational progress.

Bob Daemmrich/PhotoEdit

Merely placing a student with disabilities into a regular classroom, while placing more demands on regular classroom teachers, does not ensure that the child will learn, behave in a proper manner, or gain acceptance by children without disabilities (Freeman & Alkin, 2000). On the other hand, placing a student with disabilities in a more restrictive environment than the regular classroom does lessen the opportunity for these students to interact with students without disabilities. It can, perhaps improperly, become a self-fulfilling way to legitimize the use of restrictive environments. Where inclusion is used, it is recommended that regular classroom teachers be involved in placement decisions and receive supportive services (Kennedy & Fisher, 2001).

M.F. Giangreco, C.J. Cloninger, R.E. Dennis, and S.W. Edelman (2000) list the following five features occurring on an ongoing, daily basis as evidence that inclusive education is in place:

- heterogeneous grouping—all students are educated together in groups where the number of those with and without disabilities approximates the natural proportion;
- a sense of belonging to a group—within the class, all students, both with and without disabilities, are equally welcomed;
- shared activities with individualized outcomes—while learning objectives are individualized and may be different, students with and without disabilities share educational experiences at the same time; within a shared activity, some students' objectives may come from a different curriculum area than others;
- use of environments frequented by persons without disabilities—shared experiences take place in settings typically frequented by students without disabilities, for example, general education classrooms; and
- a balanced educational experience—an individualized balance of aspects of schooling between academic/functional, such as literacy competencies, and social/personal, such as social network.

To encourage and promote the creation of inclusive school environments and to provide the necessary support for inclusive classrooms, the position of "inclusion specialist" was created (Stainback & Stainback, 1991). These persons are the coordinators, developers, and organizers of support for students and teachers in inclusive settings (Stainback & Stainback, 1996). The intent is to have them support all students, rather than just those with special needs, and to help them fit into the mainstream. However, many inclusion specialists see themselves responsible only for the academic and social needs of students with disabilities (Cameron, 1994).

Inclusion is regarded as a "meaningful goal" by the Council for Exceptional Children, but within the context of a continuum of services as reflected by the concept of least restrictive environment. At its best, inclusive education provides a balance on a daily basis between the academic/functional and social/personal aspects of schooling (Giangreco, 1992).

TeachSource Video Case

Inclusion: Grouping Strategies for Inclusive Classrooms

In this video segment, you'll see how a teacher and an inclusion specialist work with an inclusive class of fourth- and fifth-grade students on a curricular topic: the Caribbean. The teacher assigns each student to one of four groups, mixing students with and without special needs. If you look at the interview transcript, you'll see the teacher reflecting on the process.

After viewing the video case, consider what you have just watched about inclusive classrooms and answer the questions below:

1. What were the considerations the teacher took into account in putting together the groups for the lesson?
2. How did the members of a group work together, particulary the typical students and those with special needs?
3. What did you think the inclusion specialist added to the group activity?

You can view the video case at the Education CourseMate. Go to:
CengageBrain.com

Think It Over

as a LEARNER If you were a student in an inclusive classroom, how did the teacher deal with the wide range of individual differences represented by the combination of students with and without exceptionalities? How did you feel about the experience?

as a TEACHER How could you use inclusion specialists to help you provide support for students with the range of differences within your inclusive classroom? How could you use small groups and learning centers as techniques for facilitating inclusive instruction?

Intellectual Exceptionalities

Learning Objective 3

Explain and illustrate intellectual exceptionalities: giftedness/talent and mental retardation, including characteristics, causes, assessment, and educational approaches.

Intellectual exceptionalities include giftedness and talent as one category and mental retardation as the other. By virtue of being at opposite ends of the continuum, students in both categories require specially designed instruction to reach their potential. Here we acquaint you with students in each category to aid in recognizing their important characteristics.

Giftedness and Talent

Bob graduated high school when he was 16. He had the greatest number of items correct on the National Merit Scholarship Test of everyone who took it that year. His score was used as the upper limit for the test that year for purposes of scoring. Upon graduation, he enrolled in one of the top engineering schools in the country and majored in electrical engineering. Initially, his engineering classmates resented his giftedness. In his sophomore year, during the final exam for the most difficult course in the electrical engineering sequence, he turned in his exam paper (which turned out to be perfect) halfway through the time allotted, while everyone else in the room was still hard at work. His classmates jeered and threw wadded pieces of notebook paper at him as he walked out of the room, so great was their resentment, or perhaps jealousy. By his senior year, however, he was constantly requested by his friends and fraternity brothers to run study sessions for them and go over the difficult material that would be on their exams. By then, and to his credit, Bob had figured out how to be both smart and liked at the same time. Think about some of the challenges that gifted students present to teachers.

Children with disabilities are not the only ones who may require a special program to help them reach their potential. The same may be true of students with demonstrated or potentially special capabilities in intellectual and artistic areas, like Bob described above.

Defining Giftedness

The Marland Report (Marland, 1972) was the first to define giftedness and talent. It delineates the following categories:

- general intellectual capability
- specific academic aptitude
- creative or productive thinking
- leadership ability
- ability in the visual or performing arts
- psychomotor ability

In 1991, in a report entitled, *National Excellence: A Case for Developing America's Talent*, an alternative definition was proposed, removing the word "gifted" and replacing it with *outstanding* or *exceptional talent*, to reduce the emphasis on the intelligence test score as the criterion. Nevertheless, the majority of states still consider superior cognitive ability as giftedness, but many also include some of the categories included in the Marland definition as well (Stephens & Karnes, 2000).

Other models of giftedness have had a strong influence on current thinking. Renzulli (1978) proposed a three-component definition of actual or potential ability, shown in Figure 5.1, that combines above-average ability, creativity, and task commitment as they are applied to general (such as mathematics) and specific (such as, playwriting) performance areas. Sternberg (1985) focused on intelligent behavior and identified three components: (1) practical intelligence, (2) creative ability, and (3) executive ability (described in Chapter 4). Gardner (1993) identified seven types of intelligence (described in Chapter 4). Shaklee et al. (1989)

FIGURE 5.1

The Renzulli
Three-Ring Model
of Giftedness

Source: "The Three-Ring
Conception of Giftedness:
A Developmental Model
for Creative Productivity"
(Figure 3.1, p. 66) by J. S. Renzulli
in *Conceptions of Giftedness*, ed.
by R.J. Sternberg and
J.E. Davidson. Copyright © 1996.
Reprinted by permission of
Cambridge University Press.

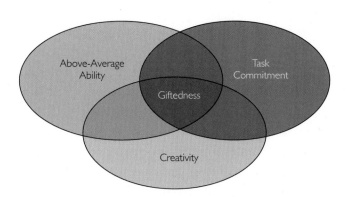

proposed four identifiers of giftedness and talent exceptionality among young children: (1) ability to acquire and retain knowledge, (2) ability to apply and comprehend knowledge, (3) ability to generate knowledge (i.e., creativity), and (4) ability to motivate oneself. The basis for identification of giftedness includes the following (Heward, 2003):

- intelligence tests;
- achievement tests;
- portfolios of student work and achievements;
- teacher nomination (based on reports of student classroom behavior);
- nomination by parent, peer, or self; and
- extracurricular or leisure activities.

Clark (2000) identifies behaviors that can guide you in identifying gifted and talented students in the classroom. Watch for students who:

- seem to understand easily;
- like to solve puzzles and problems;
- want to know why or how something is so;
- show unusual ability in some area;
- show fascination with one field of interest;
- try to do things in different, unusual, imaginative ways;
- have a vivid imagination;
- synthesize ideas and information from a lot of different sources; or
- pick up skills without instruction.

In addition, Calero et al. (2007) found that high-IQ children aged 6–11 have better self-regulatory abilities than a comparable group of average-ability children. For example, high-IQ children take action, motivate themselves, and work efficiently. (We will have more to say about self-regulating abilities in Chapter 10.)

Teaching Gifted Children

One of the more common curricular approaches for teaching gifted children is **acceleration**, or speeding up the pace at which the student moves through the curriculum. Because gifted children typically need less explanation, they can move through the curriculum more quickly. Starting elementary school at an early age, skipping grades, or taking advanced placement courses in high school in order to enter college at a higher level are all examples of acceleration.

A somewhat alternative curricular approach is **enrichment**, that is, adding material to a course's curriculum to go deeper into the material or to make it richer, perhaps with more individualized or independent projects. This enables gifted students to examine topics of interest in more detail than would be possible in the regular curriculum. Ability grouping (described in Chapter 4), of which "honors" classes is an example, illustrates a method of curricular enrichment. Kulik (1992) reported that high-ability students in enrichment programs outperformed their high-ability counterparts in regular programs.

An approach that combines both acceleration and enrichment is **curriculum compacting** (Renzulli, Smith, & Reis, 1982). In this approach, the course curriculum is compressed, or compacted, by removing redundant or previously learned material, leaving more time for students to work on more challenging aspects of the subject. This makes it possible for gifted students to advance more quickly in school, while working at a greater depth than in regular classes.

In elementary schools, the most typical type of enrichment programming for gifted students is the pull-out, or **resource room program**, where gifted students are taken out of their regular classrooms for special instruction, usually by instructors with special training. (We will encounter this approach later on when discussing curricular models for students with disabilities.)

---

acceleration

speeding up the pace at which the student moves through the curriculum

enrichment

adding material to a course's curriculum to go deeper into the material or to make it richer, perhaps with more individualized or independent projects

curriculum compacting

compressing a course's curriculum by removing redundant or previously learned material, leaving more time for students to work on more challenging aspects of the subject

resource room program

where gifted students are taken out of their regular classrooms for special instruction, usually by instructors with special training

Tailoring enrichment activities to students' particular areas of *giftedness* produces outstanding results.

Hill Street Studios/Harmik Nazarian/Blend Images/Corbis

Renzulli & Reis (1997) identified three kinds of enrichment: **Type I**, where students experience a topic in more depth in order to build their interest in it; **Type II**, where students are trained in higher-level thinking skills, along with research, and reference-using skills; and **Type III**, where students work independently or with other students to apply what they have learned to the investigation of real problems. Suppose the students were reading about Louis Pasteur and his work on microbiology in their biology textbook. Type I enrichment might involve having them read some more detailed accounts of this work by Pasteur. Type II enrichment might then direct them to engage in research about the circumstances of life and prevailing health practices before and during Pasteur's time in order to understand the immediate context and impact of his work. Finally, Type III enrichment would have groups of students examining current public health crises such as ebola or AIDs and considering whether problem-solving procedures like those used by Pasteur and his contemporaries could be applied to their solution.

Renzulli (1994) also proposed the *revolving-door model* for identification and instruction of gifted and talented students to be used in combination with the three types of enrichment described above. In it, multiple groups are identified as gifted in different areas and revolve in and out of activities for each of the three types of enrichment. The activities themselves focus on the specific area of giftedness of the group members. It has been shown that tailoring enrichment activities to the students' particular area of giftedness produces outstanding results (Sternberg, Ferrari, Clinkenbeard, & Grigorenko, 1996).

To close out our discussion of giftedness and talent, an ancient story about a gifted child appears in Box 5.1.

Type I

where students experience a topic in more depth in order to build their interest in it

Type II

where students are trained in higher-level thinking skills, along with research, and reference-using skills

Type III

where students work independently or with other students to apply what they have learned to the investigation of real problems

---

AN EXAMPLE TO AID UNDERSTANDING   **Box 5.1**

The Ultimate Gifted Student

As legend goes, when Blaise Pascal was five years old, he began to show an interest in and penchant for numbers, which made his father quite nervous. After all, young Blaise was an aristocrat-in-waiting, so to speak, and numbers, his father believed, were so bourgeois. They were for merchants and accountants, not for the landed gentry. But how was one to keep the small boy from them?

It was time for young Blaise to begin what we now refer to as home schooling, in his case being provided by professional tutors rather than parents. His son, his father decided, would be tutored in the more "high-brow" subjects: philosophy, theology, music, classics, even the fine arts, but most assuredly not in mathematics. In fact, his father would remove all writing materials from the castle-like home they lived in, and have them only made available to his son by the tutors when they came to teach him their subject, and take them back when they were done. "Now let's see if the youngster will turn into an accountant," laughed his father to himself.

Flash forward four years; Blaise Pascal is now nine. As chance would have it, his father was passing through the nursery on his way to fetch a painting from the garret, when he was stopped in his tracks.

(Continued)

The stone walls of the nursery were covered with scrawling, which, upon closer examination, turned out to be some sort of symbols. A little rub of his fingers revealed the symbols to have been written in chalk, something he had not thought to confiscate as a possible writing implement. (Clearly, he had thought only of pen and ink.) Was the child going mad, he wondered, or was it the accursed numbers thing again?

To answer his question, he sent a messenger to nearby Paris, to The Sorbonne, the preeminent university of France, to the attention of the chairman of the Department of Mathematics, asking him to come and examine some markings made by his nine-year-old son. The chairman did indeed come and, once there, made a very careful examination of the wall-markings, keeping Blaise's father waiting a rather long time while he studied them in detail. When he had satisfied himself as to their meaning, he turned to the father and asked him: "Sir, has your son ever studied mathematics? " "No," said the father, mumbling "God forbid" under his breath. Whereupon, the chairman asked: "Sir, have you ever heard of Euclid?" "Some sort of Greek, eh!" the father blustered. "A Greek indeed," the chairman replied, "in fact the very man who invented what is called geometry, the mathematics of plane surfaces. Took him a lifetime to do it," said the smiling chairman, "and it still remains one of the greatest accomplishments of mathematics ever made."

(Now reader, I turn to you for a moment, to discover whether or not you have studied geometry, or suffered through it perhaps, with its axioms and theorems, all 27 of them, and proofs and the like. Surely if you had, you would remember at least a little about it, and I can go on with my story!)

"What you have here, my dear Sir, scrawled out, as it were, in pastel chalk on the four stone walls of this nursery, is the entirety, yes entirety, of Euclidian geometry; axioms, postulates, theorems, all 27 of them worked out, indeed 'invented' by your young son. I say *invented* because, never having been exposed to it, he made it up out of his own head, using only the logic and mathematical implications of the plane surfaces on which he wrote. He started out as did Euclid, realizing that on a plane surface a straight line is the shortest distance between two points, and going on from there."

(Imagine this, dear reader, in four years, between the ages of 5 and 9, this child untrained in mathematics has done what it took a man of genius, a brilliant mathematician, a lifetime to do. Would you call this child gifted? I surely would, and so ultimately did his father, thus opening the door to a career in mathematics for his son. Blaise Pascal studied mathematics at The Sorbonne, indeed became, himself, the chairman of the Department. Before he died, Blaise Pascal made a number of unprecedented mathematical breakthroughs, earning himself the moniker: "Father of Modern Mathematics.")

Think It Over

as a LEARNER How would you describe the most gifted student you have known? How did most of the other students react to this student, and what judgments about gifted students did you make from this experience?

as a TEACHER How would you react to having gifted students in your class? Would you treat them differently than nongifted students, and if so, how?

Mental Retardation

Mental retardation and special education are very closely connected. Indeed, in 1896 the first public school education classes were established just for students with mental retardation. We turn now to take a look at the many aspects of mental retardation and suitable approaches for assisting students with this exceptionality.

Definition and Characterizations

The American Association on Intellectual and Developmental Disabilities (formerly The American Association on Mental Retardation) defines mental retardation as "significantly sub-average general intellectual functioning resulting in or associated with deficits in adaptive behavior and manifested during the developmental period" (Grossman, 1983, p. 11). This definition, essentially the one that appears in the Individuals with Disabilities Education Act (IDEA), provides three distinguishable criteria for identifying mental retardation:

- intellectual functioning significantly below the average level and that typically manifests itself as limitations in memory, learning rate, attention, motivation, and ability to transfer what has been learned to new settings;
- adaptive competence that is low, as typically manifested as limitations in two or more of the following areas: communication, home living, self-care, social skills, self-direction, health and safety, community use, functional academics, work, and leisure; and
- occurrence of the above limitations during the developmental period prior to the age of 18.

Classification

Students are classified as mentally retarded primarily on the basis of scores on tests of intelligence and adaptive behavior. Typically, the intelligence criterion is scoring two or more standard deviations below the average for students of the same age, an outcome achieved by approximately 2 percent of the test takers. (These testing concepts are described in more detail in Chapter 14.) However, a national estimate places the prevalence of people with mental retardation at 0.78 percent (Larson et al., 2001).

This classification process based on IQ score has been further broken down into four categories of mental retardation, shown in Table 5.2.

Approximately 80 to 85 percent of those classified as mentally retarded fall into the "mild retardation" category and 10 percent fall into the "moderate retardation" category, with the remaining 5 percent in the last two categories. Petrus (1997) reports there are four times as many people with IQs between 70–85, just above the cutoff for mild retardation, than those with IQs below 70, all those classified as mentally retarded.

In 1992, the American Association on Intellectual and Developmental Disabilities created a new definition for mental retardation based on the amount of *support*

mental retardation

significantly sub-average general intellectual functioning resulting in or associated with deficits in adaptive behavior and manifested during the developmental period

CONCEPT REVIEW TABLE 5.2

Classification Categories of Mental Retardation Based on IQ Score

LEVEL	INTELLIGENCE TEST SCORE
Mild Retardation	50–55 to approximately 70
Moderate Retardation	35–40 to 50–55
Severe Retardation	20–25 to 35–40
Profound Retardation	Below 20–25

From *Diagnostic and Statistical Manual of Mental Disorders* (American Psychiatric Association, 1994)

an individual needs to function, rather than on a group of traits as in the original definition. Four levels of support are included in the new definition: intermittent, limited, extensive, and pervasive. These are summarized in Table 5.3.

Think It Over

as a LEARNER What are your perceptions and feelings about students with mental retardation, and on what do you believe these perceptions and feelings are based?

as a TEACHER What would you do to help your students with mild mental retardation adjust to an inclusive classroom?

Causes

Causes for mental retardation are generally classified into two categories: *biological* and *environmental*, with about 67 percent of those with the more severe forms of retardation having biological causes (Batshaw, 1997). Biological causes include the following: brain damage from metabolic disorders, such as Tay-Sachs disease or head injuries; inherited disorders or syndromes, such as Down Syndrome; degenerative disorders, such as Parkinson's disease; developmental disorders of brain formation; birth injuries; fetal alcohol or drug conditions; and malnutrition.

In the absence of detectable biological causes, environmental causes are cited that fall under the categorization of psychosocial disadvantage. These include a poor social and cultural environment in early life, often characterized by child

CONCEPT REVIEW TABLE 5.3

Definitions of Intensities of Supports for Individuals with Mental Retardation

Intermittent	Supports on an "as needed basis." Characterized by episodic nature, person not always needing the support(s), or short-term supports needed during life-span transitions (e.g., job loss or an acute medical crisis). Intermittent supports may be high or low intensity when provided.
Limited	An intensity of supports characterized by consistency over time, time-limited but not of an intermittent nature, may require fewer staff members and less cost than more intense levels of support (e.g., time-limited employment training or transitional supports provided during the school to adult period).
Extensive	Supports characterized by regular involvement (e.g., daily) in at least some environments (such as work or home) and not time-limited (e.g., long-term support and long-term home living support).
Pervasive	Supports characterized by their constancy and high intensity; provided across environments; potential life-sustaining nature. Pervasive supports typically involve more staff members and intrusiveness than do extensive or time-limited supports.

Source: Reprinted from the American Association on Mental Retardation (AAMR). (1992). *Mental retardation: Definition, classification, and systems or supports* (9th ed., p. 26). Washington, D.C.: Author. Used by permission.

abuse, neglect, and social or sensory deprivation, and limited opportunities to learn language. Many of these circumstances are byproducts of low socioeconomic status of the parent(s) (McDermott, 1994).

Educational Needs and Strategies

Perhaps the most important questions to answer are what do students with mental retardation need to learn, and what should we teach them? Three areas of need stand out. The first is a **functional curriculum**. From a student perspective, this means spelling out what skills they need in order to function independently when they are 21 (Beck et al., 1994). Functional academics, for example, are defined by Browder and Snell (2000) as the most useful part of the "three R's," that is, the ways students with mental retardation can use reading, writing, and arithmetic in the environments they will face in the future.

functional curriculum

skills students need in order to function independently when they are 21

The second area of need is **life skills**. These are skills students with mental retardation will need to carry out activities in the six domains of adult functioning: employment, home and family life, leisure pursuits, community involvement, emotional-physical health, and personal responsibility relationships (Cronin & Patton, 1993). Examples of applying academic and social skills in these six domains are shown in Table 5.4.

The third area of need is **self-determination**, that is, learning how to take responsibility for one's own learning. One example of this comes from a study of recruiting teacher attention (Craft, Alber, and Heward, 1998). Fourth graders with mental retardation were taught strategies for recruiting teacher attention in their special education classroom. Later, they increased their work completion rate and accuracy in a general education classroom by applying those very same strategies.

Applied behavior analysis (Alberto & Troutman, 2006) is an instructional technique that can be used effectively to teach students with mental retardation. Heward (2003) lists six aspects of this systematic approach you might use in teaching new skills:

- define the new skills precisely and analyze them into sub-tasks;
- measure them directly and frequently in terms of performance;
- provide frequent opportunities for students to respond actively;
- provide immediate and systematic feedback for student performance;
- utilize procedures to enable control of behavior to transfer from instructional cues to naturally-occurring ones; and
- utilize strategies for enabling students to transfer these new skills to situations outside of the training situation.

life skills

skills students with mental retardation will need to carry out activities in the six domains of adult functioning: employment, home and family life, leisure pursuits, community involvement, emotional-physical health, and personal responsibility relationships

self-determination

learning how to take responsibility for one's own learning

applied behavior analysis

an instructional technique that can be used effectively to teach students with mental retardation

Mentally retarded students need to learn how to function independently which involves learning life skills that will help learn how to take responsibility for themselves.

Steve Skjold/Alamy

CONCEPT REVIEW TABLE 5.4

Relationship of Scholastic/Social Skills to Adult Life Skills Domains

	EMPLOYMENT EDUCATION	HOME AND FAMILY	LEISURE PURSUITS	COMMUNITY INVOLVEMENT	EMOTIONAL-PHYSICAL HEALTH	PERSONAL RESPONSIBILITY RELATIONSHIPS
Reading	Reading classified ads for jobs	Interpreting bills	Locating and understanding movie information in a newspaper	Following directions on tax forms	Comprehending directions on medication	Reading letters from friends
Writing	Writing a letter of application for a job	Writing checks	Writing for information on a city to visit	Filling in a voter registration form	Filling in your medical history forms	Sending thank you notes
Listening	Understanding oral directions of a procedure change	Comprehending directions	Listening to a weather forecast to plan an outdoor activity	Understanding campaign ads	Attending lectures on stress	Taking turns in conversation
Speaking	Asking your boss for a raise	Discussing morning routines with family	Inquiring about tickets for a concert	Stating your opinion at the school board meeting	Describing symptoms to a doctor	Giving feedback to a friend

(Continued)

CONCEPT REVIEW TABLE 5.4—(Continued)

Relationship of Scholastic/Social Skills to Adult Life Skills Domains

	EMPLOYMENT EDUCATION	HOME AND FAMILY	LEISURE PURSUITS	COMMUNITY INVOLVEMENT	EMOTIONAL-PHYSICAL HEALTH	PERSONAL RESPONSIBILITY RELATIONSHIPS
Math Applications	Understanding difference between net and gross pay	Computing the cost of doing laundry in a laundromat versus home	Calculating the cost of a dinner out versus eating at home	Obtaining information for a building permit	Using a thermometer	Planning the costs of a date
Problem-solving	Settling a dispute with a coworker	Deciding how much to budget for rent	Role-playing appropriate behaviors for various places	Knowing what to do if you are the victim of fraud	Selecting a doctor	Deciding how to ask someone for a date
Survival Skills	Using a prepared career-planning packet	Listing emergency phone numbers	Using a shopping-center directory	Making a calendar for important dates (e.g., recycling, garbage collection)	Using a system to remember to take vitamins	Developing a system to remember birthdays
Personal-social	Applying appropriate interview skills	Helping a child with homework	Knowing the rules of a neighborhood pool	Locating self-improvement classes	Getting yearly physical exam	Discussing how to negotiate a price at the flea market

Source: Life Skills Instruction for All Students with Special Needs: A Practical Guide for Integrating Real Life Content into the Curriculum (p. 33) by M.E. Cronin and J.R. Patton, 1993, Austin, TX: PRO-ED. Copyright 1993 by PRO-ED. Reprinted by permission.

(You will encounter this behavioral approach to learning and teaching again in Chapters 6 and 11. It is also used in regular classrooms.)

Behaviorally-Challenging Exceptionalities

In this section, we examine three categories of exceptionality that involve difficulty with concentration and behavior management: learning disabilities, attention deficit/hyperactivity disorder, and emotional and behavior disorders. As a classroom teacher, you will be able to observe and describe individual student behaviors that concern you. Thus, your attention is valuable in working with other professionals to appropriately identify the exceptionality and its educational intervention.

Learning Disabilities

In the Individuals with Disabilities Education Act (IDEA), a **learning disability** is defined as a disorder in one or more of the basic psychological processes involved in understanding or using language, spoken or written. It may manifest itself in an imperfect ability to listen, think, speak, read, write, spell, or do mathematical calculations. In general, it is reflected in deficits or problems associated with reading, writing, and spelling, and doing arithmetic or mathematics.

The diagnosis of a learning disability is based on meeting the three following criteria:

- the determination of a severe discrepancy between the student's intellectual ability and academic achievement;
- the absence of any other known condition present in the student that could cause the learning problems; and
- the necessity for special education services.

Of these three criteria, the overwhelmingly defining one is the first, namely substantial deficits in school achievement by a student with adequate intelligence to perform better. By comparing students' performance on standardized intelligence tests with their performance on standardized achievement tests, judgments relative to the defining criterion can be made. Often, observations of student performance in the classroom are used to supplement or reinforce achievement test results.

Since its inclusion in IDEA in 1975, no other area of disability has shown a degree of growth comparable to learning disabilities. Indeed, it is currently the largest of all special education categories, having nearly tripled since 1975, with approximately 50 percent of all special education students and 5 percent of students overall so classified (U.S. Department of Education, 2002). About 90 percent of all children identified as having learning disabilities are referred to special education because of reading problems.

The astronomical growth of this classification has raised a controversy, namely that many students who are merely doing poorly in school have been improperly

Learning Objective 4

Explain and illustrate behaviorally challenging exceptionalities: learning disability, attention deficit/hyperactivity disorder (ADHD), and emotional/behavioral disorder, including characteristics, causes, assessment, and educational approaches.

learning disability

a disorder in one or more of the basic psychological processes involved in understanding or using language, spoken or written

Students with *learning disabilities* can be helped by seeing examples to illustrate what they are learning as well as visual displays that help make concepts more understandable.

Jeff Greenberg/Alamy

identified as learning disabled. That is, the learning disabilities classification has become a catchall for students experiencing learning problems. This may be due to the fact that the causes for learning disabilities are not well understood. They often are traced to environmental influences such as impoverishment of stimulation in the home (Hart & Risley, 1995) or poor instruction in school (Engelmann, 1977).

Given the difficulty of identifying students with learning disabilities, the list of potential signs of learning disabilities shown in Box 5.2 can be most useful to teachers.

Educational Intervention

An instructional technique recommended for use with students manifesting learning disabilities is called **explicit instruction**. As described by Gersten (1998), you would employ explicit instruction by providing students with the following:

explicit instruction

using examples, models, questions, practice, and feedback to help students focus attention and facilitate processing

- examples to illustrate a concept or problem-solving strategy;
- models of successful performance, including step-by-step questions or strategies to help focus attention and facilitate processing;
- opportunities to explain why and how they did what they did;
- frequent, positive performance feedback to motivate persistence; and
- frequent practice opportunities using interesting and engaging activities.

graphic organizers

using outlines and diagrams to help students construct meaning of what they are reading

visual displays

using visual representations of concepts to enhance comprehension

Other useful teaching adjuncts are **graphic organizers** and **visual displays**, in keeping with the still relevant adage that "a picture is worth a thousand words." These help students see the relationships between concepts and often make the abstract seem more concrete and understandable. Figure 5.1 (on page 193) is an example of a visual display, in this case a diagram of three partially overlapping circles that makes it easier to visualize the simultaneous application of three different criteria for classification.

BOX 5.2

Did You Know?

Potential Signs of Learning Disabilities
(Elementary/Middle/High School)

Beginning in Grades 1–4

Gross and Fine Motor Skill

- difficulty with hand-eye coordination (e.g., piano lessons, softball)

Language

- uses vague, imprecise language and has a limited vocabulary
- uses poor grammar or misses words in conversation
- confuses words with others that sound similar
- inserts malapropisms ("slips of the tongue") into conversation
- has trouble understanding humor, colloquialisms, proverbs, idioms (note: consider regional and cultural factors)
- has difficulty with pragmatic skills

Reading

- has difficulty recognizing and remembering sight words
- frequently loses place while reading
- confuses similar-looking words (e.g., beard/bread)
- reverses letter order in words (e.g., saw/was)
- has weak comprehension of ideas and themes
- has significant trouble learning to read
- guesses at unfamiliar words rather than using word analysis skills
- reads slowly
- substitutes or leaves out words while reading

Written Language

- writing is messy and incomplete
- uses uneven spacing between letters and words
- copies inaccurately
- spells poorly and inconsistently
- has difficulty proofreading and self-correcting work

Math

- has difficulty mastering number knowledge (e.g., recognition of quantities without counting)
- has difficulty with learning and memorizing basic addition and subtraction facts
- has difficulty learning strategic counting principles (e.g., by 2, 5, 10, 100)
- has difficulty with comparisons
- has trouble telling time and conceptualizing the passage of time
- has trouble counting rapidly or making calculations

Social/Emotional

- does not pick up on other people's mood/feelings
- may not detect or respond appropriately to teasing
- has trouble knowing how to share/express feelings
- has trouble "getting to the point" in conversation (gets bogged down in details)
- has difficulty dealing with group pressure, and unexpected challenges
- confuses left and right
- often loses things
- is slow to learn new games and master puzzles
- performs inconsistently on tasks from one day to the next
- has difficulty generalizing (applying) skills from one situation to another

Beginning in Grades 5–8

Written Language

- has difficulty preparing outlines and organizing written assignments
- fails to develop ideas in writing so written work is incomplete and brief
- expresses written ideas in a disorganized way

Math

- poorly aligns numbers, resulting in computation errors
- has trouble learning multiplication tables
- has trouble interpreting graphs and charts

Social/Emotional

- has trouble setting realistic social goals
- has trouble evaluating personal social strengths and challenges
- is doubtful of own abilities, and is prone to attribute successes to luck or outside influences rather than hard work (external locus of control)

- has a poor sense of direction; easily lost or confused in unfamiliar surroundings
- finds it hard to judge speed and distance (e.g., play certain games)
- has trouble reading charts and maps
- is disorganized and poor at planning
- has difficulty listening and taking notes at the same time

Source: Learning Disabilities Checklist, National Center for Learning Disabilities (2006), www.ld.org.

- How can a teacher use this information to identify students with potential learning disabilities and to help them deal with their disability?

Finally, the teaching of **learning strategies** such as planning and self-monitoring provide a structure that helps students organize, understand, and retain what they are taught (Hardman, Drew, & Egan, 2005). Indeed, all of the recommended approaches for teaching students with learning disabilities emphasize the idea of and provide a basis for *structure* as a critical requirement for learning.

Think It Over

as a LEARNER	Why do you believe there is such a strong tendency to classify students as having learning disabilities?
as a TEACHER	What do you see as some of the advantages and disadvantages of classifying students as having learning disabilities?

Attention Deficit/Hyperactivity Disorder (ADHD)

As the name implies, **attention deficit/hyperactivity disorder** (ADHD) refers to behavior that reflects an inability to pay attention. It often is combined with excessive and uncontrolled, or impulsive, activity. This pattern of inattention and/or hyperactivity/impulsivity is more persistent, frequent, and severe than is typical of most students (American Psychiatric Association, 2000). It is believed to represent a lack of inhibition or self-control (Mather & Goldstein, 2001). Common manifestations of this disorder by students are fidgeting and restlessness. For example, a student is not able to stay in a seat, and has trouble finishing tasks (see Box 5.3 on pages 207–209). Common results of ADHD are academic and disciplinary problems

learning strategies

planning and self-monitoring to provide structure that helps students organize, understand, and retain what they are taught

attention deficit/ hyperactivity disorder

behavior that reflects an inability to pay attention

in school, particularly among boys, often leading to remediation and repeating of grades (Barkley, 1998). A problem for diagnosis is in drawing the line between high but "normal" levels of activity and inattentiveness and classification as ADHD.

There is considerable controversy associated with ADHD, particularly in terms of cause and treatment. Even though the disorder does not have a clear biological basis, indeed no clear and consistent causes are associated with it, it often is treated with drug therapy. Strangely enough, central nervous system stimulants are prescribed. Jensen (2000) estimated that more than 3 million U.S. schoolchildren received drug therapy in the year 2000, most frequently in the form of Ritalin, Adderall, or Dexedrine. Barkley (1998) summarized studies indicating that about three-quarters of the students diagnosed with ADHD and given Ritalin, or one of the other psychostimulants, showed a reduction in symptoms and an improvement in performance in the short term. However, side effects of the drug such as loss of appetite, irritability, and insomnia are not uncommon. Nevertheless, experts in the field, including Mather & Goldstein (2001), contend the benefits of drug therapy outweigh the liabilities and recommend its continued use.

While ADHD is not included in IDEA, as many as half of the students diagnosed with ADHD receive special education, under a diagnostic category for emotional and behavioral disorders (Reid & Maag, 1998).

Educational Intervention

Behavioral intervention, **applied behavioral analysis** in particular, has been used successfully to teach ADHD students self-control (Flick, 2000). Research has shown that students who receive clear instruction and consistent reinforcement show behavioral improvement (Bicard & Neef, 2004).

applied behavioral analysis
providing clear instruction, well-defined rules, and consistent reinforcement to help students improve their behavior

BOX 5.3

TAKE IT TO THE CLASSROOM

Jesse (Middle School)

Jesse is 11. He is having difficulty in school, primarily in terms of maintaining attention and following through with activities and assignments. He begins an assignment, like a book report, and his mind wanders almost immediately. He gets squirmy and moves around. He fidgets. He drops his pencil or gets up to sharpen it, and then messes around with the pencil sharpener. He manages not to get very much done.

In the classroom, Jesse often busies himself by walking around and talking to other students. He distracts himself from schoolwork by distracting his classmates. Mrs. Gold, Jesse's teacher, is not sure what to do about Jesse. But one thing she knew for sure: She had to do something because Jesse was not learning and he was interfering with other students' learning. So she talked to Jesse about showing greater self-control and he did for the rest of that afternoon, but the next day he was back to his old self. Then she talked to his mother who said that, other than when he was outside playing with his friends, Jesse behaved the same way at home. And she too was at a loss when it came to dealing with it.

Mrs. Gold decided to take the next step. She referred the matter to her school team for **Behavioral Intervention Assistance**, a procedure called for under the Individuals with Disabilities Education Act (IDEA). The school team came up with the idea of having Jesse use a vibrating timer to help him keep on task. Mrs. Gold would set the timer for a certain amount of time, and when the time had elapsed, the timer would vibrate (like those devices in restaurants that vibrate when your table is ready). Jesse's job was to stay on task until the timer vibrated. If he did, he would then get to spend some time on the computer, something he particularly enjoyed. At first, using the timer worked well, but then Jesse began to ignore it and revert to his old behavior. Several other accommodations were made, such as moving Jesse's desk to the front of the classroom and away from distractions of the door and windows. Additionally, his assignments were shortened *to better accommodate his attention span. However, after several weeks of failed attempts to keep Jesse on task, Mrs. Gold returned to the intervention team with the bleak report. The team decided to refer Jesse to the school psychologist for a thorough assessment of his academic and cognitive abilities as well as his socio-emotional skills. The school psychologist found that Jesse's behavior was having a significant impact on his learning, and he qualified for special education services. An IEP was written to accommodate his disability in which Jesse spent part of his school day in the traditional classroom, and part of his time in a resource room.*

- *Have you encountered other students like Jesse? How did they behave?*

- *What would you suggest be done to help them overcome their problem?*

In regular classroom settings, it is important to provide *structure*, particularly for students with ADHD. Clear rules, daily routine, designated places for materials, and overall organization help students function in an orderly manner. It is also important to provide outlets for energy such as learning centers, group activities, and outdoor activities, but even these should be governed by well-defined rules.

Emotional and Behavior Disorders

The Individuals with Disabilities Education Act (IDEA) defines **emotional disturbance** in the following way:

- an inability to learn that cannot be explained by intellectual, sensory, or health factors;
- an inability to build or maintain satisfactory interpersonal relationships with peers and teachers;
- inappropriate types of behavior or feelings under normal circumstances;
- a general, pervasive mood of unhappiness or depression; and
- a tendency to develop physical symptoms or fears associated with personal or school problems (U.S. Department of Education, 1999, p. 12422).

Behavioral Intervention Assistance

a technique to help students stay on task

emotional disturbance

an inability to learn and to maintain satisfactory interpersonal relationships; a general mood of unhappiness and fear

The Council for Children with Behavioral Disorders offers the following definition for **emotional or behavioral disorder**: "A disability characterized by emotional or behavioral responses in school programs so different from appropriate age, cultural or ethnic norms that the responses adversely affect educational performance, including academic, social, vocational or personal skills; more than a temporary, expected response to stressful events in the environment; consistently exhibited in two different settings, at least one of which is school-related; and unresponsive to direct intervention in general education, or the condition of the child is such that general education interventions would be insufficient" (Federal Register, February 10, 1993, p. 7938).

Although the estimated number of students identified as having behavior problems severe enough to require individualized intervention and support ranges between 1 and 7 percent (Sugai, Sprague, Horner, & Walker, 2000), a government report shows that the number classified as emotionally disturbed represented fewer than 1 percent of the school-age population (U.S. Department of Education, 2002). It appears that considerably more schoolchildren have behavioral disorders than are identified and provided with special education.

Behaviors characterizing children with this disorder fall into two categories, **externalizing**, or antisocial, and **internalizing**, or avoidant. Externalizing behaviors include such things as complaining, fighting, moving around the classroom, disturbing other students, arguing, stealing, lying, destroying property, having temper tantrums, ignoring the teacher's instructions, yelling, cursing, and not doing schoolwork (Walker, 1997). Such children, the vast majority of whom are boys, can single-handedly disrupt a classroom, and hence make teachers' lives miserable (Rhode et al., 1998). Moreover, children who show early signs of antisocial behavior patterns do not typically grow out of them and, as adolescents often drop out of school, get in trouble with the law and live marginalized lives (Walker, Colvin, & Ramsey, 1995).

Alternatively, some children with this disorder exhibit internalizing behaviors rather than, and the opposite of, externalizing ones. That is, they exhibit too little rather than too much social interaction that, while not posing a threat to others, interferes with their own development. Their shyness and withdrawal leads them to avoid interacting with others in preference to living in a world of fantasies, often coupled with depression and fear. This internalizing pattern, often referred to as mood or **anxiety disorder**, presents teachers with less difficulty but often fails to be detected. Its seriousness is evidenced by poor educational performance at the least and the possibility of suicide in its most extreme form.

Overall, students with an emotional and behavioral disorder, regardless of its specific form, often experience academic failure as reflected in failing scores on competency tests, poor grades, high absenteeism, and a strong tendency to drop out of school (U.S. Department of Education, 1999). Furthermore, these students are characterized by having low intelligence scores and a lack of high-quality interpersonal relationships.

emotional or behavioral disorder

"a disability characterized by emotional or behavioral responses in school programs so different from appropriate age, cultural or ethnic norms that the responses adversely affect educational performance, including academic, social, vocational or personal skills; more than a temporary, expected response to stressful events in the environment; consistently exhibited in two different settings, at least one of which is school-related; and unresponsive to direct intervention in general education, or the condition of the child is such that general education interventions would be insufficient"

externalizing
antisocial behavior

internalizing
avoidant behavior

anxiety disorder
shyness and withdrawal coupled with depression and fear, resulting in poor educational performance and the possibility of suicide

Classifying a student as having an emotional or behavioral disorder typically requires testing by a school psychologist. However, as a teacher you can detect and document instances of antisocial behavior, and to a lesser extent withdrawal behavior, by observing students' behavior incidents in various educational settings, such as in the classrooms, hallways, playground, or cafeteria. You can use five dimensions to describe the observations in documentation: rate, duration, latency, magnitude, and topography (Heward, 2003). *Rate* refers to the frequency of a particular behavior, like screaming, during a standard unit of time such as one minute, five minutes, or a class period. One outburst in a class period may be tolerable, but one outburst a minute is not. *Duration* refers to how long the behavior lasts. Again, a one-minute tantrum and a 10-minute tantrum are vastly different. *Latency* refers to the amount of time between the precipitating incident and moment the behavior occurs; that is, how little time it takes for something to "set a child off," which effects the teacher's opportunity to respond. *Magnitude* is the strength or intensity of the behavior. *Typography* is the specific form the behavior takes. Frequently occurring, long lasting, intense behaviors—particularly those that affect other people and for which the teacher has virtually no opportunity to respond—pose the greatest problem to teachers and other students and make teaching difficult. It should be the basis for referral to the school psychologist.

Educational Intevention

Is there anything teachers can do to help students control their extreme behaviors? Put another way, the question becomes: What can be done in the area of **behavior management**? (A behavioral approach to learning is described in Chapter 6 and the general application of the behavioral approach to classroom management is described in Chapter 11.) Think about Andrew, described in the story at the very beginning of this chapter, and Amy, the consultant who taught him self-control using the behavioral approach.

The Center for Positive Behavioral Interventions & Supports (2001) lists the following as essential to successful behavioral management at the classroom level:

- state behavioral expectations such as respect the property of others;
- define and teach behavioral expectations such as what is the "right" way to treat the property of others and what is the "wrong" way;
- acknowledge appropriate behaviors with praise, rewards, or special activities; and
- correct behavioral errors proactively. For example, tell students in advance what the consequences of inappropriate behavior will be; tell them when they have behaved inappropriately; and do not reward, however inadvertently, inappropriate behavior.

Imposing behavioral expectations and rewarding students for following them is a much more positive approach than waiting for misbehavior to occur before responding.

behavior management
imposing behavioral expectations and rewarding students for following them

Students with *emotional or behavioral disorders*, the majority of whom are boys, can disrupt a classroom and make teachers' lives miserable. Behavior management techniques can help students control their extreme behaviors.

group contingencies

students behaving appropriately bring rewards to the whole class

differential acceptance

teachers establishing a positive relationship with students; witnessing extreme acts without responding similarly

empathic relationship

understanding a disturbed student's needs and communicating directly and honestly with that student

While the behavioral approach is managed by the teacher, a companion approach is to teach students self-management, using approaches such as self-monitoring and self-evaluating, including providing oneself with consequences. Studies have shown that these techniques help students with behavioral problems to regulate their behavior (Peterson, Young, West, & Hill Peterson, 1999). One can also enlist other students in helping to control the behavior of their peers. Peer tutoring, for example, when used to improve academic skills, can also function to help students with emotional and behavior disorders improve their social skills (Blake, Wang, Cartledge, & Gardner, 2000).

Another group-based approach is to offer incentives to a group of students or the entire class if its collective behavior meets a particular criterion. For example, students who are quiet during the silent reading period, raise their hands before speaking, and turn in classwork on time would bring rewards to the whole class. When this approach, called **group contingencies**, is used, it is important that all group members are accountable to the group, have daily group responsibilities, participate in group meetings focused on group decision making, contribute to the collective performance of the group, and share all major rewards (Barbetta, 2002).

Finally, a critical ingredient to success with students in general, and students with emotional and behavioral disorders in particular, is for teachers to *establish a positive relationship* with them. Morse (1985) identifies two key traits that teachers must display. The first he calls **differential acceptance**, meaning that the teacher can witness students' extreme acts without responding similarly. As the teacher, you must view these acts as resulting from the student's past frustrations. You must try to help him or her learn that he or she is behaving inappropriately and how to behave better. This means understanding and addressing the behavior, without approving or condemning the person.

The second key trait is one Morse (1985) calls **empathic relationship**. This means you are attuned to recognizing the nonverbal cues that help you understand an emotionally disturbed student's individual needs. It also means communicating with that student directly and honestly; students can tell when a teacher is genuinely interested in their welfare. Beyond this, to be successful, you must be a role model by demonstrating the kind of self-control you are trying to instill in the student.

See Table 5.5 for a *Concept Review* of int ellectual and behavioral exceptionalities.

Think It Over

as a LEARNER	What experiences have you had in a classroom where one or more students behaved in the manner described as emotionally or behaviorally disordered? How did the teacher and other students react?
as a TEACHER	How would you as a teacher react? In what ways would your reactions as a teacher be different to the ways you have experienced other teachers reacting, and in what ways similar.

CONCEPT REVIEW TABLE 5.5

Intellectual and Behavioral Exceptionalities

EXCEPTIONALITY	DEFINITION AND DESCRIPTION	EDUCATIONAL INTERVENTION
Giftedness and Talent	Superior cognitive, creative, leadership, psychomotor, or artistic ability as measured by tests, portfolios, or teacher nominations.	Accelerate the pace of instruction or enrich the curriculum or both, via a resource room (pull-out) program.
Mental Retardation	Significantly subaverage intellectual functioning, associated with deficits in adaptive behavior, occurring before age 18.	Instruct in independent functioning, life skills, and taking responsibility for one's own learning, effectively done using applied behavioral analysis.
Learning Disabilities	An imperfect ability to listen, think, speak, read, write, spell, or do math, resulting in large deficits in school achievement with no other bases than the above.	Provide explicit instruction featuring examples, illustrations, frequent feedback, practice opportunities using engaging activities, and structure.
ADHD: Attention Deficit/ Hyperactivity Disorder	Behavior that reflects an inability to pay attention, often combined with uncontrolled, impulsive behavior and academic and disciplinary problems.	Use applied behavioral analysis with well-defined rules and consistent reinforcement to teach self-control. (Drug therapy is often used as well.)
Emotional and Behavioral Disorders	Disrupting a classroom by fighting, yelling, stealing, having temper tantrums, not doing schoolwork. Or withdrawing, fantasizing, experiencing depression.	Teach behavioral expectations and reward students for following them. Teach students self-management. Use peer tutoring. Help teachers cope.

Communication and Sensorimotor Exceptionalities

Learning Objective 5

Explain and illustrate sensorimotor exceptionalities: communication, speech, hearing, and vision.

Communication disorders and hearing and visual impairments are the next category of exceptionalities for you to be alert to in your classroom teaching.

Communication Disorders

A **communication disorder** is defined as "an impairment in the ability to receive, send, process, and comprehend concepts or verbal, nonverbal, and graphic symbol systems; it may be evident in the processes of hearing language and/or speech" (American Speech-Language-Hearing Association, 1993, p. 40). While people normally differ in many aspects of the way they communicate, a communication difference is considered a disability justifying special education when the student is placed at a learning disadvantage (Haynes & Pindzola, 1998). According to IDEA, communication disorders include stuttering and other forms of impaired articulation such as distorting sounds or substituting one sound for another. It also includes language or voice impairments that adversely affect a child's educational performance.

Two types of communication impairments have been distinguished: **speech impairments** and **language impairments**. Speech is considered impaired "when it deviates so far from the speech of other people that it (a) calls attention to itself, (b) interferes with communication, or (c) provokes distress in the speaker or the listener" (Van Riper & Erickson, 1996, p. 110). A speech problem often goes away as a child matures. If it continues and has an adverse effect on the child's interactions with others, the child should be referred to a speech pathologist (Owens, 1999).

Speech impairments include the following disorders:

- speech sound errors—distortions, substitutions, omissions, or additions of sounds in a word; when the basis for the error is that a child is not able to produce a given sound physically, it is called an articulation disorder;
- fluency disorder—an interruption in the flow of speaking, stuttering being the most common example; and
- voice disorder—distortions in the sound of the voice, such as excessively breathy, horse, or strained, or excessively nasal sounding, making it difficult to understand what is being said.

Language impairments involve understanding language or expressing oneself through language. An example of a problem with language reception would be an inability to follow a sequence of commands in the proper order. An example of a problem with language expression might be difficulty with putting the sounds in a word in the proper order ("nucular" instead of "nuclear"). Children with language impairments are less likely to initiate conversations or answer questions in school. They are also likely to have problems in both reading and writing (Westby & Clauser, 1999).

It is important not to confuse dialects with communication disorders, which they are not. **Dialects** are forms of pronunciation associated with different regions. When we refer to a New York or a Boston accent, we are distinguishing dialects.

Because communication disorders typically require special programs to ameliorate, they usually are treated by speech-language therapists. However, relatively common disorders like stuttering often can be helped by classroom teachers who are careful to model good speech, reinforce occurrences of fluency and ignore occurrences of nonfluency, react to what children say more than how they say it, listen attentively, and treat children who stutter the same as children who do not.

communication disorder

an impairment in the ability to receive, send, process, and comprehend concepts or verbal, nonverbal, and graphic symbol systems

speech impairment

when speech deviates so far from the speech of other people that it (a) calls attention to itself, (b) interferes with communication, or (c) provokes distress in the speaker or the listener

language impairment

involves difficulty understanding language or expressing oneself through language

dialects

forms of pronunciation associated with different regions

Hearing and Visual Impairment

According to IDEA, **hearing impairment** represents a hearing loss that adversely affects educational performance, and thus qualifies a student for special education. Children who are hard of hearing usually are able to use a hearing aid to help them understand what others are saying. The effects of hearing loss on a child's academic performance and general functioning vary considerably as a function of the degree of loss, age of onset, and the attitudes of family members, teachers, and other children (Schirmer, 2002). It is important not to generalize across children with this impairment and lock oneself into a specific set of expectations. However, hearing loss, especially at an early age, tends to adversely affect the acquisition of English language skills, speaking skills, academic achievement, and social functioning.

Visual impairment includes total blindness, functional blindness, and low vision. Fewer than 0.2 percent of the school-age population received special education during the 2000–2001 school year on the basis of visual impairment, the vast majority of which were classified as having low vision or functional blindness (U.S. Department of Education, 2002). Special education services for students with visual impairments are often difficult to provide by small schools in rural areas.

Visual impairment often affects a child's learning, motor development, social adjustment, and interaction. To learn concepts, students with visual impairment need repeated, direct contact using primarily nonvisual senses. Children with visual impairment, particularly when severe, often experience delays in motor development (Stone 1997) and in the development of social skills (Skellenger, Hill, & Hill, 1992). The latter is based on the inability of students with this impairment to see and respond to social signals from other students (Frame, 2000).

For students who are blind, Braille is their major means of literacy. This can be supplemented by computer software that uses optical character recognition (OCR)

hearing impairment

hearing loss that adversely affects educational performance, and thus qualifies a student for special education

visual impairment

includes total blindness, functional blindness, and low vision

Hearing loss can affect the acquisition of language skills and affect academic achievement. However, *American Sign Language* can provide students, even young ones, with a pathway to linguistic competence.

Robin Sachs/PhotoEdit

to scan printed texts and read them aloud with synthetic speech. In addition to the common use of glasses and OCR software, partially sighted students are aided by print magnification software that increases the size of the print to a larger type size.

Your teaching materials should not rely exclusively on visuals such as writing on the chalkboard, using overheads, or handing out printed material. You should supplement the visual with simultaneous verbalizing to help low-vision students. You should also give low-vision students extra time for doing assignments that require copying. Finally, you should genuinely encourage students with visual impairment to seek your help, or the help of an aide, rather than merely waiting for it to be offered.

Explain and illustrate physical disabilities, including characteristics, causes, assessment, and educational approaches.

Physical Disabilities

Physical disabilities include **orthopedic impairments** that impair physical movement and mobility and are caused by (1) congenital abnormalities such as being born with a missing portion of a limb, (2) a disease like polio, or (3) other causes such as cerebral palsy or fractures. Orthopedic impairments affect the skeletal system. Physical disabilities also include **neuromotor impairments** that affect the central nervous system, for example, spinal cord injury, often causing similar physical limitations to those caused by orthopedic impairments. Finally, there are **health impairments**, diseases such as cystic fibrosis, diabetes, asthma, and AIDS that impose limitations that affect a student's activities and performance in school. If a child's educational performance is adversely affected by any of these physical and health impairments, then he or she is entitled to special education services under IDEA. The combination of physical and health impairments account for over 6 percent of school-age children receiving special education, out of the approximately 20 percent estimated to have these conditions (Sexson & Dingle, 2001).

The range of physical, behavioral, and social characteristics associated with physical disabilities is quite great, making it difficult to narrow it to a predictable list. Overall, on average, students with physical disabilities and health impairments perform below average academically, in part because of side effects of their treatments and medications, and in part as a result of missing school for prolonged periods for medical treatment or hospitalization (Kline, Silver, & Russell, 2001). These circumstances also make it difficult for these students to develop and maintain relationships with their classmates and teachers.

Within the school environment, assistive technology can help students with physical disabilities function and learn. Assistive technology includes any piece of equipment or system that helps these students improve their functional capabilities. Some low-tech examples are picture books and chalk holders. A high-tech example is a computerized synthetic speech device, which increases a student's access to different activities and educational opportunities, thus increasing the level of independence (Reed & Best, 2001).

It is extremely important to the self-esteem and well-being of students with physical disabilities that their teachers treat them as worthwhile people rather than

orthopedic impairments
physical disabilities that affect the skeletal system

neuromotor impairments
physical disabilities that affect the central nervous system

health impairments
diseases that affect a student's activities and performance in school

as ones with disabilities, that they expect them to meet reasonable standards of performance, and that they help them to experience success and accomplishment. Moreover, they should help them become as independent as possible, hence able to cope with their disability, while comfortable relying on teachers and others for assistance when needed.

Inclusion for these students with physical disabilities is fostered by teachers using tasks that require students to work together, and if possible, treating them in the same manner as children without disabilities. It also helps if teachers assist students without disabilities gain a greater knowledge of impairment and learn how and when to assist those students who have them.

First Light

Insofar as possible, students with *physical disabilities* should be treated in the same manner as students without disabilities.

Think It Over

as a LEARNER | What do you see as the difficulties faced by students with sensory or physical impairments?

as a TEACHER | What are some things you would recommend schools or other teachers do to reduce these difficulties?

DISCOURSE ON DIVERSITY

Race and Special Education (Elementary/Middle/High School)

BOX 5.4

A review of national data from the U.S. Department of Education (2000) for the 1998–1999 school year reveals that African American students, who make up 14.8 percent of the student population, account for 20.2 percent of the students in special education programs. The discrepancies for African American students fall primarily in the categories of mental retardation (for which they are 2.9 times as likely to be labeled), seriously emotionally disturbed (for which they are 1.9 times as likely to be labeled), and learning disabled (for which they are 1.3 times as likely to be labeled as students who are not African American). African American students represent over one-third of all students identified as mentally retarded and one-fourth of those labeled emotionally disturbed.

Ladner and Hammons (2001) found that in Virginia, where African Americans make up 20 percent of the population, they constitute over half of the students in programs for the mildly retarded (EMR), and that Alabama certifies four times as many minorities as EMR than Caucasians. The overwhelming number of African American students identified for special education are males, particularly for the categories of behavioral disorders and mental retardation, with a placement rate over three-and-a-half times that for females (U.S. Department of Education, 1999).

An extensive empirical examination of this phenomenon and its potential causes led Ladner & Hammons (2001) to conclude that "minority students are treated differently in predominantly White districts than in predominantly minority districts. Districts with predominantly Black teachers, for example, have lower special education rates for all students, but particularly for African American and Hispanic students. That is, the data reveal that in districts with a predominantly Black faculty, minority students see a reduction in special education enrollment that is three to four times greater than the reduction seen by White students. ... The percentage of minority students in the district is the strongest driver of special education enrollment in our model. ... The racial composition of the district, therefore, is a key predictor of special education enrollment" (pp. 104–106).

In their final words, Ladner & Hammons (2001) offer two possible interpretations for the disparate rates of special education placement by race. The more positive interpretation is that "minority parents in primarily White districts may be more likely to want their children placed in special education, and they therefore may be receiving the services they want for their children with special needs" (p. 108). The more negative interpretation is that "these findings represent racial bias: that special education is, in part, a de facto method for intra-district and intra-school racial segregation" (p. 108).

Autism

Autism is the fastest-growing category in special education. The Autism Society of America (2000) estimates that it occurs in as many as one in 500 people. Fombonne (1999) estimates that boys are affected about 400 times more often than girls. In its mild forms, it can be difficult to recognize. Your attention and observation skills are important to identifying some of these individuals.

Definition and Determination

Autism is a severe developmental disability characterized by impairments of communication, social, and emotional functioning. According to the Autism Society of America (2000), the distinguishing features of autism generally appear before 30 months of age and include disturbances in (1) developmental rates and sequences; (2) responses to sensory stimuli; (3) speech, language and cognitive capacities; and (4) capacities to relate to people, events, and objects.

Kanner (1985), the first to describe the condition, which he called early infantile autism, lists the following 10 characteristics of autistic children:

- difficulty relating to others in a typical manner;
- extreme aloneness that seemed to isolate the child from the outside world
- resistance to being picked up or held by parents;
- significant speech deficits, including mutism (not speaking) and echolalia (echoing what other people say);
- in some cases, very good rote memory;

autism

a severe developmental disability characterized by impairments of communication, social, and emotional functioning

- early specific food preferences;
- obsessive desire for repetition and sameness;
- bizarre, repetitive behavior, such as rocking back and forth;
- lack of imagination and few spontaneous behaviors; and
- normal physical appearance.

There are five types of what are now referred to as autism spectrum disorders that vary in degree; the mildest is **Asperger Syndrome**, or "high-functioning autism." Asperger Syndrome does not include language delay and does include average or above average intelligence, poor communication and social skills, repetitive and stereotyped behavior, preoccupation with objects (e.g., machines), and difficulty developing friendships (Barnhill et al., 2000).

In the Academy Award-winning 1988 film *Rain Man*, the character played by Dustin Hoffman has a mild form of autism, probably Asperger Syndrome, and displays many of the characteristics associated with this syndrome. The movie tells the story of an abrasive, selfish, yuppie named Charlie Babbitt who discovers that his late father has left his multimillion dollar fortune to his autistic brother, Raymond (who pronounces his name "Rain Man," hence the title of the movie), who Charlie never knew he had. Charlie takes Raymond on what becomes a cross-country trip back to Los Angeles to meet with his attorneys and get custody of him. During the trip, Charlie learns more about his brother's disorder and his sometimes annoying mannerisms. Some of the scenes in the movie, some of which are mind-boggling and comical, are drawn from the kinds of character traits that exist in real-life autistic children and adults. To the film's credit, it did not stray far from the truth regarding autism, specifically Asperger's Syndrome.

Early on, Raymond's mannerisms frustrate Charlie greatly, even leading him to conclude that his brother's "neurological disorder" is part of a scheme to keep him from getting the money to which he believes he is entitled. Able to communicate and possessing an excellent memory, Raymond's thinking was extremely literal and he shows signs of obsessive behavior, such as insisting on flying with QANTAS Airlines, eating only with toothpicks, and getting his underwear from Kmart at 400 Oak Street, Cincinnati. Although Raymond is able to repeat the "Who's on First" routine without flaw, he is unable to comprehend the punchline, therefore stripping it of its comical value. *Rain Man* has long been regarded as the best portrayal of autism to date and remains an important film for its depiction of people with Asperger's Syndrome and our attitudes toward them.

Educational Intervention

A recommended approach for teaching students with autism is the use of applied behavior analysis. In a study by Lovaas (1987), a group of 19 autistic children received an intensive early intervention program of one-on-one behavioral treatment for two years and demonstrated a substantial gain in IQ and educational achievement over and above that of similar children not receiving the intervention. Follow-up evaluations led Lovaas (1994) to conclude that after one year of intensive intervention, half of the children can be integrated into regular kindergarten classrooms.

Starstock/Photoshot

Dustin Hoffman played a character with a mild form of *autism* in the movie "Rain Man." He displayed an excellent memory, but also exhibited obsessive behavior like eating only with toothpicks.

Asperger Syndrome

"high-functioning autism"; includes average or above average intelligence, poor communication and social skills, repetitive and stereotyped behavior, preoccupation with objects, and difficulty developing friendships

A description of applied behavioral analysis can be found in the section of this chapter on mental retardation, because this approach is the primary one used in teaching students with mental retardation.

See Table 5.6 for a *Concept Review* of communication and sensorimotor exceptionalities, physical disabilities, and autism.

C O N C E P T   R E V I E W   T A B L E   5 . 6

Communication and Sensorimotor Exceptionalities, Physical Disabilities, and Autism

EXCEPTIONALITY	DEFINITION AND DESCRIPTION	EDUCATIONAL INTERVENTION
Communication Disorders	Impaired speech that deviates so far from the speech of others that it calls attention to itself, interferes with communication, or provokes distress in the speaker or listener.	These usually are treated by speech-language therapists. Teachers can help by treating children who stutter the same as children who don't.
Hearing and Visual Impairment	Hearing impairment represents a hearing loss that adversely affects educational performance. Visual impairment includes total blindness, functional blindness, and low vision. Visual impairment often affects a child's learning, motor development, social adjustment, and interaction.	Children who are hard of hearing usually are able to use a hearing aid to help them understand what others are saying. To help low-vision students, teachers should not rely exclusively on visual presentation of material, but should supplement it with simultaneous verbalizing.
Physical Disabilities	Physical disabilities include orthopedic impairments that impair physical movement and mobility, neuromotor impairments that affect the central nervous system, and health impairments that impose limitations that affect a student's activities and performance in school.	Within the school environment, assistive technology can help students with physical disabilities function and learn. Assistive technology includes any piece of equipment or system that helps these students improve their functional capabilities.
Autism	It is characterized by disturbances in developmental rates and sequences, responses to sensory stimuli, speech, language and cognitive capacities, and capacities to relate to people, events, and objects.	A recommended approach for teaching students with autism is the use of applied behavior analysis.

SUMMING IT UP

Describe learners classified with exceptionalities, the implications of such classifications, and the laws that govern the process.

Exceptional learners are those whose physical attributes or learning and behavioral abilities vary enough from the norm to require special or individualized programs or services. The advantage of classifying students as exceptional is that it is the key to providing them with services; the disadvantage is that it may be stigmatizing. The primary law governing the classification of and services for exceptional students is the **Individuals with Disabilities Education Act** (IDEA). It calls for **special education**, a program or intervention designed to teach persons with disabilities the skills required for independent and successful functioning.

Learning Objective 1

Key Concepts:
exceptionalities, exceptional learners, special education, classification (p. 183); curriculum-based assessment, Individuals with Disabilities Education Act (p. 184).

Discuss the process of service provided to exceptional learners, i.e., special education, including Individualized Education Program, least restrictive environment, and inclusion.

An **Individualized Education Program** (IEP) is required by IDEA for all students with disabilities. The plan must include measurable performance goals for the school year and criteria for measuring progress toward them, services to be provided for the student to meet those goals, and how progress toward the goals will be measured. A **least restrictive environment** is mandated by IDEA, that is, learners with disabilities must be educated with nondisabled learners to the extent possible, except when it would not allow satisfactory results to be achieved. A combination of special and regular classroom settings may be used. **Inclusion** represents educating learners with exceptionalities in regular classrooms, and hence is narrower in scope than least restrictive environments.

Learning Objective 2

Key Concepts:
individualized education program (p. 186); least restrictive environment, inclusion (p. 189).

Explain and illustrate intellectual exceptionalities: giftedness/talent and mental retardation, including characteristics, causes, assessment, and educational approaches.

Giftedness and talent describes students with demonstrated or potentially special intellectual or artistic capabilities, above-average ability, creativity, and task commitment, combined with practical intelligence and executive ability. Common curricular approaches for teaching gifted students are **acceleration**: speeding up the pace with which they move through the curriculum, or **enrichment**: adding additional material or depth, teaching thinking skills, and including independent projects. **Mental retardation** is intellectual and adaptive competence significantly below the average level during the period prior to age 18, ranging from mild (IQs between 50 and 70) to profound (IQs below 20). Mentally retarded students need

Learning Objective 3

Key Concepts
acceleration, enrichment, curriculum compacting, resource room program, type I enrichment, type II enrichment, type III enrichment (p. 194); mental retardation (p. 197); functional curriculum, life skills, self-determination, applied behavior analysis (p. 199).

a **functional curriculum** that will enable them to function independently in terms of employment, family life, health, and personal responsibility and relationships. An effective instructional approach to teach this curriculum is **applied behavior analysis**.

Learning Objective 4

Key Concepts:

learning disability (p. 203); explicit instruction, graphic organizers, visual displays (p. 204); learning strategies, attention deficit/hyperactivity disorder (p. 206); applied behavioral analysis (p. 207); behavioral intervention assistance (p. 209); emotional disturbance, emotional or behavioral disorder, externalizing, internalizing, anxiety disorder (p. 210); behavior management (p. 211); group contingencies, differential acceptance, empathic relationship (p. 212).

Explain and illustrate behaviorally challenging exceptionalities: learning disability, attention deficit/hyperactivity disorder (ADHD), and emotional/ behavioral disorder, including characteristics, causes, assessment, and educational approaches.

Learning disabilities affect processes involved in understanding or using language that result in deficits associated with reading, writing, spelling, and doing arithmetic. They are diagnosed on the basis of a severe discrepancy between a student's intellectual ability and academic achievement in the absence of any other causal condition, and necessitate special education. It is the largest special education category, leading to accusations that it is a catchall for all students experiencing learning problems. A common intervention is **explicit instruction**, a structured, example-based, step-by-step approach with frequent performance opportunities for practice and feedback, and graphic or visual displays. **Attention Deficit/Hyperactivity Disorder** (ADHD) is characterized by excessive, uncontrolled, impulsive behavior (e.g., fidgeting, leaving one's seat) that reflects an inability to pay attention, and often results in academic and disciplinary problems. It is typically treated by drug therapy, a controversial approach since the disorder does not have a clear biological basis. Recommended classroom treatment includes structure (e.g., daily routines), constructive outlets for energy, and well-defined rules. **Emotional and behavioral disorders** are characterized by the frequent display of inappropriate emotional and behavioral responses that adversely affect educational performance, and require special education interventions. The manifested behaviors can be categorized as either **externalizing** (antisocial acts, e.g., fighting, stealing) or **internalizing** (avoidant acts, e.g., shyness, withdrawal). Students demonstrating the externalizing behaviors (mostly boys) can single-handedly disrupt a classroom. **Behavior management** techniques are recommended for classroom use, i.e., setting expectations, acknowledging appropriate behaviors, proactively correcting errors.

Learning Objective 5

Key Concepts:

communication disorder, speech impairments, language impairments, dialects (p. 214); hearing impairment, visual impairment (p. 215).

Explain and illustrate sensorimotor exceptionalities: communication, speech, hearing, and vision.

Communication disorders are impairments in the ability to send, process, and comprehend concepts and symbol systems, that is, to speak and understand, that place the student at a learning disadvantage. **Speech impairments** include speech sound errors, fluency disorders such as stuttering, and voice disorders or distortions in the sound of the voice. **Language impairments** involve understanding or expressing oneself through language. A **hearing impairment** is a hearing loss that adversely affects educational performance as well as social functioning. **Visual impairment** includes total blindness, functional blindness, and low vision and can affect motor development, social adjustment, and interaction. Teachers should supplement visual presentations with simultaneous verbalizing to help low-vision students.

Explain and illustrate physical disabilities, including characteristics, causes, assessment, and educational approaches.

Learning Objective 6

Key Concepts:

orthopedic impairments, neuromotor impairments, health impairments (p. 216).

Physical disabilities include **orthopedic impairments** (e.g., cerebral palsy) that affect the skeletal system and **neuromotor impairments** (e.g., spinal cord injury) that affect the central nervous system, both of which impair physical movement and mobility. Also included are **health impairments** (e.g., diabetes) that impose limitations on a student's activities and performance in school. Assistive technology can be used to increase the access of students with physical disabilities to different educational activities and opportunities, and thus increase independence. Teachers are admonished to treat students with physical disabilities as worthwhile people, expect them to meet reasonable standards of performance, and help them become as independent as possible.

Explain and illustrate autism.

Learning Objective 7

Key Concepts:

autism (p. 216); Asperger Syndrome (p. 217).

Autism is a severe developmental disability characterized by impairments of communication, social, and emotional functioning that appear before 30 months of age and include disturbances in developmental rates and sequences, responses to sensory stimuli, speech, language and cognitive capacities, and capacities to relate to people, events, and objects. **Asperger Syndrome** is the most mild form of autism. An effective instructional approach to teach pre–K autistic children is applied behavior analysis.

Visit the Education CourseMate for *Educational Psychology* to access study tools and resources including the Virtual Psychology Labs, TeachSource Video Cases, chapter web links, tutorial quizzes, glossary flashcards, and more. Go to CengageBrain.com to register using your access code.

6 | Behavioral Approaches to Learning

After reading this chapter, you should be able to meet the following learning objectives:	Chapter Contents
LEARNING OBJECTIVE 1 Using classical conditioning, explain how your students can have positive and negative emotions associated with experiences in school.	Classical Conditioning-Learning by Association • Pavlov's Famous "Ringing Bell" Example • Educational Implications of Classical Conditioning
LEARNING OBJECTIVE 2 Interpret student behavior through the lens of operant conditioning by modifying student and teacher behavior based on the systematic use of consequences.	Operant Conditioning-Emphasizing Consequences • Positive Behavioral Support • The Process of Operant Conditioning
LEARNING OBJECTIVE 3 Provide classroom examples of different types of reinforcers, including positive and negative; primary and secondary; and consumable, social, activity, exchangeable, and tangible.	Types of Reinforcers • Positive versus Negative Reinforcers • Primary versus Secondary Reinforcers • Schedules of Reinforcement
LEARNING OBJECTIVE 4 Describe the different types of punishment and the effect punishment has on student behavior. Explain how the use of presentation punishment could be detrimental to students.	Perspectives on Punishment • Types of Punishment • The Use of Punishment
LEARNING OBJECTIVE 5 Illustrate how you could help a student learn new behaviors through the classroom use of prompting, chaining, and shaping.	Modifying Behavior • Prompting • Chaining • Shaping
LEARNING OBJECTIVE 6 Show how a classroom teacher could apply operant conditioning to the classroom by specifying desirable behavior, praising those behaviors, and ignoring nontarget behavior.	Applying Operant Conditioning to the Classroom • Establish Classroom Rules • Emphasize Appropriate Behavior
LEARNING OBJECTIVE 7 Evaluate how students learn behaviors in school settings through social learning.	Social Cognitive Learning-Emphasizing Observation • What Do Students Learn by Observing Models? • How Do Students Learn from Models? • What Behaviors Are Students Likely to Model?

Little Albert

John B. Watson (1878–1958) is considered the founder of American behaviorism. His perspective was radical in that he did not accept or acknowledge the influence of internal mental processes on behavior. His extreme position in being able to shape a person's behavior is illustrated in the following quote:

"Give me a dozen healthy infants, well-formed, and my own specified world to bring them up in, and I'll guarantee to take any one at random and train him to become any type of specialist I might select—doctor, lawyer, artist, merchant-chief and yes, even beggarman and thief—regardless of his talents, penchants, tendencies, abilities, vocations, and race of his ancestors." (Watson, 1930, p. 104).

While most behavioral research has been conducted on animals (e.g., rats, pigeons), Watson conducted his most famous experiment on an 11-month-old infant named Little Albert. Watson's purpose in the research was to see if he could condition fear in Little Albert and then get that fear to generalize to other stimuli. His design was to use a loud, startling noise (striking a hammer on a steel bar) as an unconditioned stimulus that automatically provoked fear in Little Albert as evident by his unconditioned response to it (he trembled, cried, and had a fit), and then pair it with another stimulus, a live white rat, that did not initially provoke fear in the infant. Indeed, after seven pairings of the rat with the noise, the rat, by itself provoked the fear response. The rat had become a conditioned stimulus and the resulting fear a conditioned response.

To test for generalization of the conditioned fear response, Watson then presented Little Albert with other stimuli similar to the white rat, namely a white rabbit, a white dog, and a white fur coat. Each, in turn, provoked the fear response, demonstrating that it could be made to generalize to stimuli other than the original conditioned stimulus. In fact, it also generalized to Watson himself, whose hair was in the process of turning white with age. Although Watson's intention was then to attempt to extinguish the conditioned fear response by repeatedly presenting the white "objects" without the presence of the loud noise, Little Albert's mother removed him from the experiment, leaving us to hope that his fears would gradually extinguish themselves over time, lest he spend the rest of life being afraid of white furry objects. While Watson was, however, able to importantly demonstrate a way in which strong fears or phobias could be learned, the manner in which Little Albert was treated would not be tolerated today given current requirements for the protection of human subjects.

- Consider Watson's quote in the story you just read. What elements of Watson's quote reflect beliefs that effective teachers might share?
- How do you see this story about Little Albert relating to the topic for this chapter, behavioral approaches to learning?

Lessons We Can Learn from the Story Little Albert learned to fear a white rat, not because it was a rat, but because its presence was paired with a loud, unpleasant sound. A goal of educational psychology is to explain the many ways that students learn. According to behaviorists, **learning** is a relatively stable and observable change in a learner that is the result of experience. Through our experiences, we learn new information, beliefs, concepts, and proficiencies. Just like Little Albert, our students learn important things from us and one another through association and experience.

Think about the reason you are taking this course. Initially, it might have been because educational psychology is a required course in your path to becoming a teacher. However, as you interact with other members of your class and your instructor, your interest in the course will probably deepen. In part, this is because psychological concepts are interesting to discover and debate. They are all the more fascinating when you look at them at work in educational contexts.

Take for instance the complexity of student behavior in the classroom. At times, students are not fully aware of the reasons for their behavior in various situations, while at other times they give their behavior considerable thought and consideration. The topic of this chapter, behaviorism, provides a rational explanation for why various types of student behaviors happen and why they continue. Behaviorism also tries to address why some student behaviors seldom appear. In the final analysis, the question for educators is how we can learn enough about students from numerous theoretical and applied perspectives to help them increase the quality of their lives. The ideas presented in this chapter represent one method by which you can help the students in your class navigate the difficult change process of adjusting their behavior to ways that will help them attain the goals they have set for themselves.

The concepts discussed in this chapter are important for teachers because they provide teachers with knowledge that will help them to increase the academic success of students while reminding teachers of the detrimental effects of using punishment as the primary means of maintaining a learning environment. While concepts associated with classical and operant conditioning are useful to know and be able to apply in a teacher's professional practice, they certainly are not universally applicable nor are they impervious to misapplication and misuse. It is also important that, with any strategy you use in your classroom, you evaluate the degree to which it impacts students differentially for whatever reason. Kaufman, Conroy, Gardner, and Oswald (2008) describe the importance of cultural sensitivity in education and investigated studies based on behaviorism to determine if behavioral classroom interventions functioned in different ways depending on the ethnic composition, sex, or religious beliefs of the student. They found no evidence that these differences impacted how various students react to principles of operant conditioning, but they point out that just because they did not find differences does not mean none exist. Because of the importance of the issue and the growing diversity of America's schools, they recommended additional studies be dedicated to this important issue.

In this chapter, we turn our attention toward behavioral explanations of learning. Learning will be explored from the classical conditioning, operant conditioning, and social learning theory perspectives. We start with classical conditioning and how your students associate their emotional responses with activities and events that occur at school.

learning
a process that changes knowledge and behavior as a result of past experience

Learning Objective 1

Using classical conditioning, explain how your students can have positive and negative emotions associated with experiences in school.

Classical Conditioning-Learning by Association

Does the name *Ivan Pavlov* ring a bell? Ivan Pavlov (1849–1936) was a Russian physiologist who experimented with dogs in order to study their digestive process (LoLordo, 2000). His study of salivation and identification of the conditioned reflex brought him eminence in the field of psychology and the Nobel Prize in 1904 (The Nobel Foundation, 2008). Pavlov's work was groundbreaking and is still relevant as it helps us to understand test anxiety and phobias in children (King et al., 2000). It also demonstrates the role that learning plays in shaping children's emotional and physiological responses. Additionally, classical conditioning concepts such as generalization and extinction have become vital to contemporary psychology (Windholz, 1997).

Pavlov's Famous "Ringing Bell" Example

In order to study digestion, Pavlov (1927) detached the salivary duct from the inside of a dog's mouth and fastened it to a point in the dog's cheek where a hole had been made. This caused any saliva that was secreted to flow not into the dog's mouth but through the hole in the cheek into a glass bulb that had been attached to the outside of the cheek. The bulb had calibrations on it so that the amount of saliva secreted could be measured.

When food was presented to the dog, it salivated into the glass bulb. Let a hungry dog see or smell food, and it will salivate. The salivation reflex is not learned; it occurs automatically and provides the juices needed in the mouth to chew food so the digestion process can begin. Pavlov called the food the unconditioned stimulus and the salivation the unconditioned response, because the connection between them was reflexive, that is, automatically occurring. Thus, the **unconditioned stimulus** (UCS) is a stimulus that automatically elicits a response without learning and an **unconditioned response** (UCR) is an automatic, unlearned reaction to an unconditioned stimulus.

The connection looked like this (the diagrams are to be read from left to right):

Unconditioned Stimulus (Food) ⟶ **Unconditioned Response (Salivation)**

unconditioned stimulus

a stimulus that automatically elicits a response without learning

unconditioned response

an automatic, unlearned reaction to the unconditioned stimulus

Ivan Pavlov's lab work gave the world the famous example of a dog salivating to a bell. But, his work also helps teachers understand student's emotional reactions to things that happen to them during school.

Snark/Art Resource, NY

In this model, Pavlov (1927) then presented a sound (the ring of a bell or the click of a metronome) before presenting the food. This sound was termed a neutral stimulus. A **neutral stimulus** (NS) is a stimulus that does not initially elicit a response.

Neutral Stimulus (Sound) ⟶ **No Response**

However, something unexpected happened during the experiment. After he presented the sound and food together a few times, the dog later salivated at the sound, even before the food was presented. This pairing of sound and food caused the animal to become conditioned to, or established a connection between, the sound stimulus and the salivation response.

Neutral Stimulus + Unconditioned Stimulus ⟶ **Unconditioned Response**

Thus, the sound eventually yielded a response and was no longer neutral. The sound became the conditioned stimulus. A **conditioned stimulus** (CS) is a previously neutral stimulus that, after association, prompts a conditioned response. The salivation to the sound became the conditioned response. A **conditioned response** (CR) is a learned reaction to a stimulus that was once neutral and after association becomes conditioned. It is important to note that in this example the unconditioned response and the conditioned response actually are the same response; the only difference between them is whether they were elicited by the unconditioned stimulus or the conditioned stimulus. Thus, after conditioning, the sound comes to elicit the salivation all by itself:

Conditioned Stimulus (Sound) ⟶ **Conditioned Response (Salivation)**

This association approach to learning is called classical conditioning. To test whether conditioning has occurred, one should present the sound without the food and see what happens. If the result is salivation, then conditioning has occurred. Table 6.1 defines and provides an example of classical conditioning principles.

Educational Implications of Classical Conditioning

The impact of classical conditioning extends beyond the classic example of a dog's salivation and has real effects in day-to-day school settings. It is important for a person studying to become a teacher to take psychological concepts, such as classical conditioning, and connect them to things that happen to students and teachers in schools. You might encounter a student who has math anxiety or a fear of taking standardized tests, and these types of student responses are common and are rooted in classical conditioning.

To help you start thinking about the application of classical conditioning in education, consider the following example about a student we will call Jamarkus, a student who loves school, except for when he has to change classes. He finds this time harried and stressful and he dislikes being in the large mass of people. He typically is able to relax and enjoy himself in class, but as soon as he hears the signal to transition from one class to the next, he begins to feel a little anxious.

What is the naturally occurring reflex Jamarkus is experiencing? What events in the school have been associated with that natural reflex? Knowing about classical conditioning will help the teacher recognize that the reflex Jamarkus is experiencing is having

Virtual Psychology Lab
Do you think students are judged in schools by their parents or friends? When you go to the *Classical Conditioning Virtual Psychology Lab*, you will have an opportunity to participate in a classic experiment in psychology where you can see how classical conditioning principles can shape our attitudes. Go to CengageBrain.com to access this Virtual Psychology Lab in the Education CourseMate.

neutral stimulus

a stimulus that does not initially elicit a response

conditioned stimulus

a previously neutral stimulus that, after association, prompts a conditioned response

conditioned response

a learned reaction to a stimulus that was once neutral and after association becomes conditioned

CONCEPT REVIEW TABLE 6.1
Classical Conditioning

CONCEPT	DEFINITION	PAVLOV'S CLASSICAL EXAMPLE(S)
UCS	A stimulus that automatically elicits a reflexive response	Food
UCR	An automatic, unlearned reaction to an unconditioned stimulus	Salivation
NS	A stimulus that does not initially elicit a response	Ringing of a bell
CS	A previously neutral stimulus that, after association with the UCS, prompts a conditioned response	Ringing of a bell
CR	A learned reaction to a stimulus that was once neutral and after association becomes conditioned	Salivation

to walk in a crowd (UCS), which then causes him distress (UCR). The originally neutral stimulus that he now begins to dread is the school signal that indicates a class change.

Tables 6.2 and 6.3 provide additional examples of how students learn positive and negative emotional responses in classroom settings through classical conditioning. Now that you have read this section, you have some insight into how a teacher might better understand what Jamarkus is experiencing and be better prepared to brainstorm some concrete suggestions with him to help him adjust to stressful experiences. For example, you might suggest he try walking with a friend from one class to the next. Or you might try having him talk to you about a cherished experience he has had with his family and have him think about that experience when he is feeling stressed during class changes. Knowledge of psychology

Chris Hondros/Newsmakers/Getty Images

Classical conditioning can help teachers understand positive and negative reactions that students have to different occurrences at school.

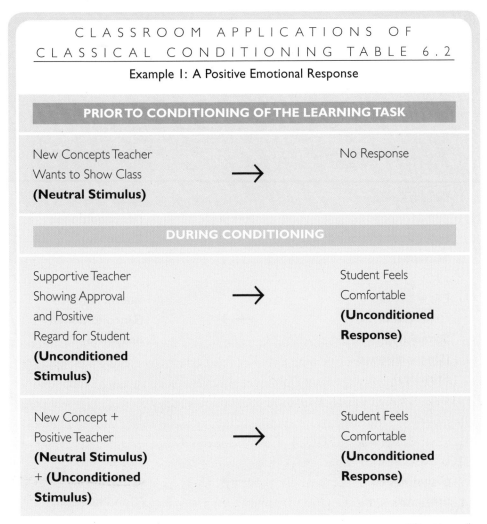

CLASSROOM APPLICATIONS OF CLASSICAL CONDITIONING TABLE 6.2

Example 1: A Positive Emotional Response

PRIOR TO CONDITIONING OF THE LEARNING TASK

New Concepts Teacher Wants to Show Class **(Neutral Stimulus)**	→	No Response

DURING CONDITIONING

Supportive Teacher Showing Approval and Positive Regard for Student **(Unconditioned Stimulus)**	→	Student Feels Comfortable **(Unconditioned Response)**
New Concept + Positive Teacher **(Neutral Stimulus) + (Unconditioned Stimulus)**	→	Student Feels Comfortable **(Unconditioned Response)**

(Continued)

CLASSROOM APPLICATIONS OF CLASSICAL CONDITIONING TABLE 6.2 (continued)

Example 1: A Positive Emotional Response

AFTER CONDITIONING

New Concept **(Conditioned Stimulus)**	→	Student Feels Comfortable **(Conditioned Response)**

CLASSROOM APPLICATIONS OF CLASSICAL CONDITIONING TABLE 6.3

Example 2: A Negative Emotional Response

PRIOR TO CONDITIONING

Bell Signaling the End of the School Day **(Neutral Stimulus)**	→	No Response

DURING CONDITIONING

Student Threatened with an After School Fight **(Unconditioned Stimulus)**	→	Student Feels Fear **(Unconditioned Response)**
End of Day Bell + Threat **(Neutral Stimulus)** + **(Unconditioned Stimulus)**	→	Student Feels Fear **(Unconditioned Response)**

AFTER CONDITIONING

End of Day Bell **(Conditioned Stimulus)**	→	Student Feels Comfortable _Fear_ **(Conditioned Response)**

Typo

concepts, like classical conditioning, will help you think about the psychological dimensions of your students. They are people with feelings and emotions, not just individuals whose achievement scores we are trying to raise.

The most obvious outcome of Pavlov's research was the realization that one way in which learning took place was by forming connections between stimuli and responses. While classical conditioning certainly does not explain all the types of learning, it does offer basic behavioral concepts still in use today. In describing the learning of new feelings and emotions that students have, Pavlov provided a useful framework for explaining how that learning occurs and how it can be varied.

Think It Over

as a LEARNER   Why do you think the neutral stimulus needs to be presented before the unconditioned stimulus for the learning to occur?

as a TEACHER   How might a student develop a classically conditioned fear response to his or her bus ride home from school?

Operant Conditioning-Emphasizing Consequences

A second behavioral approach for learning behaviors is primarily based on the work of psychologist B.F. Skinner (1904–1990). **Operant Conditioning** is a method of learning emphasizing that the consequences of a behavior determine how likely or unlikely it is for the behavior to occur in similar settings in the future. In operant conditioning, a **behavior** is something the student does that is directly measurable and observable. According to the theory, a teacher who systematically uses operant conditioning principles can change the probability of a student's behavior by choosing whether or not to follow that behavior with a positive reinforcer. Hence, the effect or reinforcement becomes *contingent* on, or depends on, whether or not the appropriate behavior occurs (Branch, 2000).

Glenzer (2005) stated that instructional strategies based on operant conditioning include determining a student's prerequisite skills, clearly detailing the behavior to be taught, and creating instruction to teach the behavior in sequential measurable pieces. Examples of this type of instruction can be found in many schools, and even in unexpected places such as popular plays like *My Fair Lady* and popular movies such as *Pretty Woman* (Glenzer, 2005).

Operant conditioning and its role in informing effective instructional practice was obvious in schools and Colleges of Education in the mid-20th century and less so at the end. Some argue that, as public funds become more scarce, a renewed interest in instruction informed by the principles of operant conditioning and powered by the increased capacity of educational technology may occur (Molenda, 2008). There are also researchers who see behavioral research more acceptable in

Learning Objective 2

Interpret student behavior through the lens of operant conditioning by modifying student and teacher behavior based on the systematic use of consequences.

operant conditioning

a method of learning that emphasizes that consequences of a behavior determine how likely or unlikely it is for the behavior to occur in similar settings in the future

behavior

something a student does that is directly measurable and observable

mainstream psychological literature (Overskeid, 2008). Because of the well-known tension between behavioral and humanistic approaches to schooling (Ediger, 2006), you are in an ideal position to select a range of methods from the different approaches to educational psychology that will best serve your students. Out of rich philosophical debate and disagreement come effective solutions to everyday educational problems.

Positive Behavioral Support

One current use of operant conditioning principles in the schools is the positive behavioral support (PBS) program. The Individuals with Disabilities Act (IDEA) requires that students with behavior that interferes with their learning, or that of their peers, be provided with appropriate behavioral intervention (Sugai, 2007). **Positive Behavior Support** is a way of helping students gradually decrease classroom behaviors disruptive to themselves and others. PBS methods can be applied with an individual student, a group of students, a classroom, and throughout a school. To find out more information about PBS, you can visit the U.S. Department of Education-funded Center for Positive Behavioral Interventions and Supports Web site.

The PBS process starts with an analysis of a student or group of student's behavior. This analysis is called a **functional behavioral assessment**, a detailed accounting of the nature and frequency of a student's problem behavior along with a clear description of the setting that prompts and maintains the disruptive behavior. Figure 6.1 is an example of a portion of a functional behavioral assessment created by Horner and Crone (2005) that could be used to interview students. It can be found on the U.S. Department of Education-funded Center for Positive Behavioral Interventions and Supports Web site.

A classroom example of the effective use of positive behavior support principles to help students with deficit hyperactivity disorder (ADHD) is described in Box 6.1.

This decision to reinforce or not reinforce a behavior can be called contingency management. **Contingency management** is altering the likelihood of occurrence of a specific behavior by following it or not following it with a reinforcer. The teacher can be the contingency manager by giving or withholding reinforcers selectively, depending on the student's behavior. Thus, the emphasis is on changing behavior through the use of selective reinforcement. By learning about and methodically employing the principles of operant conditioning, the teacher can optimize the potential learning opportunities in the classroom. Operant conditioning can help students to perform specific behaviors (such as raising your hand in class) based on the occurrence that immediately follows it; that is, its consequences (for example, being recognized by the teacher or peers).

Behaviors followed by positive consequences increase in their frequency and probability of occurrence; they are learned and repeated. People learn to "operate" in their environment because those behaviors have been followed by positive consequences in the past (hence the name "operant conditioning"). This is the most fundamental principle of operant conditioning. The principle of reinforcement is a development and refinement of Thorndike's (1911) law of effect. The **law of effect**

Positive Behavior Support

program designed to help students gradually decrease classroom behaviors disruptive to themselves and others

functional behavioral assessment

a detailed accounting of the nature and frequency of a student's problem behavior along with a clear description of the setting that prompts and maintains the disruptive behavior

contingency management

altering the likelihood of occurrence of a specific behavior by following it or not following it with a reinforcer

law of effect

states that behaviors that lead to positive outcomes are strengthened while behavior that leads to negative outcomes are weakened

FIGURE 6.1

Student Name _____ Age: _____ Grade: _____ Date: _____

Interviewer _____

Student Profile: What are things you like to do, or do well, while at school? (e.g., activities, classes, helping others, etc.)

Description of the Behavior

- What are some things you do that get you in trouble or that are a problem at school? (e.g,. talking out, not getting work done, fighting, etc.)

- How often do you _____ ? (Insert the behavior listed by the student)

- How long does _____ usually last each time it happens?

- How serious is _____? (Do you or another student end up getting hurt? Are other students distracted?)

Description of the Antecedent

Where, when, and with whom are problem behaviors most likely?

Schedule (Times)	Activity	With Whom Does Problem Occur?	Likelihood/Intensity of Problem Behavior	Specific Problem Behavior
			Low High 1 2 3 4 5 6	
			1 2 3 4 5 6	
			1 2 3 4 5 6	
			1 2 3 4 5 6	
			1 2 3 4 5 6	
			1 2 3 4 5 6	
			1 2 3 4 5 6	
			1 2 3 4 5 6	
			1 2 3 4 5 6	
			1 2 3 4 5 6	

Summarize Antecedent (and Setting Events)

- What kinds of things make it more likely that you will have this problem? (difficult tasks, transitions, structured activities, small group settings, teacher's request, particular individuals, etc.)

- When and where is the problem most likely to happen? (days of week, specific classes, hallways, bathrooms)

Description of the Consequence

- What usually happens after the problem occurs? (what is the teacher's reaction, how do other student's react, is the student sent to the office, does the student get out of doing work, does the student get in a power struggle)

Functional Behavioral Assessment Interview Created by Horner and Crone (2005)

DISCOURSE ON DIVERSITY

Efficacy of a Function-Based Intervention in Decreasing Off-Task Behavior Exhibited by a Student with ADHD

BOX 6.1

Brenna Stahr, Danielle Cushing, and Kathleen Lane of Peabody College of Vanderbilt University and James Fox of East Tennessee State are interested in studying and helping students who have attention-deficit/hyperactivity disorder (ADHD) succeed in school settings. They report that the behavior of students with ADHD can be "manifested in classrooms as difficulty in attending to and following instructions, completing instructional activities, and complying with classroom rules" (Stahr et al., 2006, p. 201). These manifestations often result in the student performing poorly in class.

To understand the behavior and achievement of students with special needs, Dr. Stahr and her colleagues conducted research using a single-subject approach. They worked with a student named "Shawn" (the real name was altered to protect the child's identity and confidentiality). Shawn was a 9-year-old African American student who received special services in a fourth-grade, self-contained classroom. Shawn's teacher requested that Shawn participate in the study "due to excessive levels of off-task and anxious behaviors (e.g., rocking, shaking, tapping, and pronounced frowning) that would eventually lead to disruptive behavior (i.e., refusing to do the assigned task, talking back to the teacher, and leaving the assigned instructional area)" (Stahr et al., 2006, p. 202).

Behavior as defined by PBS is observable activity a student engages in and which can be recorded and measured through observation. One of the key ideas is that behavior changes based on its immediate consequences. Therefore, if a behavior is reinforced, it is more likely to be exhibited by a person in the future. If a behavior is punished, it is less likely to be exhibited in the future.

Thus, the authors of the study set out to observe and record Shawn's behavior, figure out consequences the teacher and the class provided for his behaviors, and then determine how to alter the consequences of his behavior in order to make his classroom behavior more conducive to school success. To figure this out, they used a procedure called a functional assessment. It examines "The function of the behavior, be it to obtain something preferred or avoid something nonpreferred, once identified, is used to inform intervention efforts" (Stahr et al., 2006, p. 201).

Based on the results of the functional assessment, a signaling system was developed that enabled Shawn to communicate with the teacher. He was given a green card, a yellow card, and a red card. The green card told the teacher that he was feeling comfortable working on his own and did not need assistance. The yellow card was a signal for the teacher that he was feeling anxious but could wait for teacher assistance. The red card told the teacher that he needed immediate assistance. The results of the study were analyzed by the researchers "marking a tally on a recording sheet taped to Shawn's desk and praised Shawn for using the system correctly. Shawn was also offered a piece of candy after five appropriate uses. The candy was included as a positive reinforcer because Shawn had requested candy as a reinforcer during the student functional assessment interview" (Stahr et al., 2006, p. 206).

The results showed that "the reinforcement system provided positive teacher attention, additional assistance to promote task participation and completion and reduce escape-motivated behaviors, and primary reinforcers in the form of candy. If Shawn did not use the communication system correctly, the teacher provided corrective feedback, reminding him of how to make such a request" (Stahr et al., 2006, p. 206). Thus, by using some of the tools and concepts described in this chapter, the teacher and researcher were able to help Shawn develop skills to successfully and appropriately navigate a classroom environment.

● The researchers had Shawn choose his own reinforcer. How important do you think that was? Why do you think that?

states that behaviors that lead to positive outcomes are strengthened, while behaviors that lead to negative outcomes are weakened.

In operant conditioning, the response is emitted initially on a low-frequency basis; but as it continues to occur and be reinforced, its frequency increases. The cause of the behavior in operant conditioning is the consequence that follows it—the reinforce—rather than some automatic or learned stimulus that precedes it and triggers it (Belfiore & Hornyak, 1998). The reinforcing stimulus, in operant conditioning, is connected to a response. The next section will describe the three phases of operant conditioning: antecedent, behavior, and conse-quences.

The Process of Operant Conditioning

Many behaviors occur without any preceding or triggering stimulus in the class-room. Sometimes, however, a stimulus can serve as a signal or cue in operant conditioning, thereby increasing the likelihood that the operant response will be emitted (Skinner, 1953). The importance of this signal is that, rather than having to wait for a student to perform a behavior a teacher would like to see on a random basis, the teacher can cue students to behave in a certain way and then reinforce those who do. Thus, an **antecedent** is a signal to the students that reveals which behavior will be reinforced. For example, if a teacher and a group of students agree that to get called on the students must wait until a certain point in the lesson where the teacher asks for questions, then that call for questions serves as antecedent. The call for questions does not cause students to raise their hands. It simply directs or signals them to do so at that time if they wish to experience a positive consequence—the attention of their teacher and/or peers. It is important to recognize that, in operant conditioning, the behavior is ultimately contingent on the consequence, not the signal, but the signal helps cue or guide the learner to choose to perform the appropriate response, the one on which reinforcement depends or is contingent. Box 6.2 shows how a teacher can use an antecedent to help make the time the students spend in class more productive.

What happens if a child raises her or his hand at an inopportune time, like when other students are presenting their work and the teacher has not asked for questions? According to the theory, it all depends on what the teacher does

antecedent

a signal to the students that reveals which behavior will be reinforced

Students can be taught to display a behavior like the thumbs up and thumbs down sign to let the teacher know whether they understand a concept or not.

David Butow/Corbis News/Corbis

Box 6.2

TAKE IT TO THE CLASSROOM

Effects of Teacher Greetings on Student On-Task Behavior

You learned in your reading of this chapter that, according to the principles of operant conditioning, an antecedent gives students information about what behaviors are expected in the situation. One of the largest challenges for new teachers is starting a class period effectively, so that the time the students spend in the classroom isn't wasted. Sometimes, confusion, lack of planning, or misbehavior right at the beginning of class can make it very difficult to get your students focused on learning.

Researchers Allday and Pakurar (2007) were interested in helping reduce misbehavior in the beginning of class and they argued that this misbehavior could partly be due to the fact that the students were not provided a clear antecedent at the beginning of class. They studied the impact of having the teacher greet the students at the class door on the on-task behavior of urban middle school students. What the researchers found was that greeting students at the door was an effective practice. In their study, having the teacher greet the student at the door, say the student's name in addition to a positive statement, increased the on-task behavior in the first 10 minutes of class by 27%.

What does this research tell us as future teachers? We need to find ways to make students feel welcome in the classroom and demonstrate to them that we care for them. While saying hello and greeting students seems like an obvious effective practice, in reality you would be surprised to see how infrequently it is actually done. The goal is for you to try to create a positive learning community which will impact the students' motivation to learn. Try the following for a successful start to your classes:

1. Position yourself near the entry of the classroom, but leave enough space for students to comfortably enter.

2. Make eye contact with each student as they enter the room.

3. Smile and say hello.

4. Think of something positive to say as students enter or ask students about activities you know they are interested in.

- Do you recall a teacher ever greeting you at the classroom door? If yes, what effect did that have on you? If no, do you think it would have been beneficial?

Source: Allday, R.A., & Pakurar, K. (2007). Effects of teacher greetings on student on-task behavior. Journal of Applied Behavior Analysis, 40(2), 317–320.

in response to this behavior. If the teacher ignores the hand, the behavior is not provided reinforcement, thus the likelihood of the response is reduced. If the teacher calls on the student even though the antecedent was not presented, the student will be more likely to call out of turn and interrupt other students. According to the theory, the only combination that should yield positive reinforcement is a behavior that is emitted when the correct antecedent is presented. A teacher who wants to use operant conditioning effectively in his or her classroom needs to recognize how using antecedents can have a powerful impact on how the students behave. For example, a best practice of effective teachers is to greet students at the door. Research demonstrates that using an antecedent, like a teacher greeting, produced increases in students' on-task behavior during class (Allday & Pakurar, 2007). Antecedents are also helpful in that they help students recognize when to make a request of their teacher so that it will not disrupt the flow and learning of the class (Cammilleri, Tiger, & Hanley, 2008).

We have explored antecedents and behaviors and hinted at the power that consequences have in impacting people's behavior. Thus, learning the phases of operant conditioning should be like "learning your abc's" (antecedents, behaviors, and consequences).

Antecedent ⟶ Behavior ⟶ Consequences

The next several sections will detail the various types of consequences and how those consequences can be effectively administered. (More explicit information on utilizing the operant conditioning model in the classroom as a management tool will be described at the end of this chapter and additionally in Chapter 10.)

Learning Objective 3

Provide classroom examples of different types of reinforcers, including positive and negative; primary and secondary; and consumable, social, activity, exchangeable, and tangible

Types of Reinforcers

Different types of reinforcers can be used to modify student behavior. Reinforcers can be classified as positive and negative; primary and secondary; and consumable, social, activity, exchangeable, and tangible. In this section, the types of reinforcers are described and compared. It is important to note that a **reinforcer** increases the likelihood of a specific student behavior in the future. According to the theory, if a teacher is administering what he or she believes to be a reinforcer and it is not increasing behavior, then the consequence is by definition not a reinforcer. A teacher who wants to properly use operant conditioning in his or her class needs to recognize that various classroom consequences, like a smile from the teacher, will not be reinforcing for each and every child. Research suggests that it is an effective practice for teachers to assess what individual children in their class find reinforcing and use reinforcers students find interesting and desirable (Cote, Thompson, Hanley, & McKerchar, 2007).

When a teacher provides what he or she considers a reinforcer following desirable student behavior, he or she does so with the belief that desirable student behavior will

reinforcer

something that increases the likelihood of a specific student behavior in the future

Teachers can use smiles to reinforce their students.

increase. Often, teachers guess correctly and provide incentives and reinforcers to students that they find desirable. Research with toddlers has found that teacher selection of reinforcers tend to correlate well with direct assessments of the toddler's preferences for reinforcers (Cote, Thompson, Hanley, & McKerchar, 2007). Research with elementary aged students found that both teacher- and student-generated lists of reinforcers were effective in identifying reinforcers that the students wanted and that also resulted in increases in responding (Mintz, Wallace, Najdowski, Atcheson, & Bosch, 2007).

Despite the finding in the research that teacher selection of reinforcers generally is effective, there are times when a teacher can administer what he or she thinks is a reinforcer but desirable student behavior does not increase. This apparent contradiction is rooted in the idea that a reinforcer is only a reinforcer if it increases the occurrence of a specific behavior. Just because a teacher thinks something is "good" or "desirable" does not necessarily make it so for each and every student. Students are individuals, just like the teachers who serve them. They bring to the classroom unique temperaments, interests, reinforcement histories, and personal histories that make it difficult to create one list of statements or incentives that would motivate all students. If you choose to attempt to systematically use reinforcers in your classroom, an effective best practice would be for you to determine through a questionnaire what types of reinforcers your students value. This will not only provide you with insight into the students you serve, but also allow your students to self-determine what is of value to them.

Positive versus Negative Reinforcers

It is important for the classroom teacher to distinguish between positive and negative reinforcers. While both positive and negative reinforcers can increase the likelihood of a behavior's occurrence, the way in which they do so is different.

Positive reinforcers are stimuli or events presented after a behavior that increase the occurrence of the behavior in the future. When children are given candy, praise, or a fun activity for their behavior, and it increases the occurrence of the targeted behavior, then the candy, praise, or fun activity has served as a positive reinforcer. Thus, when students receive something desirable following a given behavior, they are more likely to repeat that behavior because the response in the past has contingently triggered a positive consequence.

One of the most powerful positive reinforcers a classroom teacher can apply to modify student behavior is praise (Madsen, Becker, Thomas, Koser, & Plager, 1968). **Praise** is a positive statement about another person's behavior or performance. Praise can take the form of a verbal statement or it could take a written form, such as a weekly progress report. Effective teachers use praise with the intention of helping students to increase their academic achievement and to create a classroom environment conducive to the learning of all students. They also might use praise to help a child who does not often play with other children to be more confident. While the use of praise is very common by educators and parents/caregivers, research has presented different viewpoints on the practice of using praise (Henderlong & Lepper, 2002). Some research reveals praise had a positive impact on student interest (Deci, Koestner, & Ryan, 1999), whereas other research has argued that praise has a detrimental impact on student motivation (Kohn, 1993). Kohn (2001) suggests that instead of praise, teachers could "say what they saw." This means that teachers and parents/caregivers could make evaluation-free statements after a behavior; for example a teacher could say "you put your art supplies away by yourself." Kohn (2001) also suggests that teachers "talk less, ask more." This means that instead of praising performance, a teacher could ask questions about student performance. For example, a teacher might say to a student who has just finished a chemistry lab experiment, "What part of the lab was most difficult for you to complete?" and "What portion of your lab are you most proud of? Which would you like to put more time into?"

Negative reinforcers are stimuli or events that are removed following a behavior that increase the likelihood of the behavior in the future. Negative reinforcers can be thought of as those aversive experiences or stimuli people desire to terminate, escape from, or avoid. When children's behavior allows them to escape from a painful, embarrassing, or aversive experience, it is called negative reinforcement and the behavior will also tend to be learned and repeated. As we will see later, negative reinforcement is different from punishment, because negative reinforcement increases the frequency of a behavior, while punishment decreases the likelihood of a behavior. In Skinner's early research, he used an obnoxiously bright light that the rat could turn off by pushing the bar. The bar press response was thus negatively reinforced when the rat terminated the unpleasant brightness of the light. An example of the classroom use of negative reinforcement is allowing students to not have to do (escape) an evening homework assignment, if they appropriately participate in a classroom activity. Another classroom example of a negative reinforcement would be permitting students to be exempt from a test for great class participation.

Negative reinforcement can be a difficult concept to understand. Just think about all the things students do to avoid getting in trouble, and you will have examples of

positive reinforcers

stimuli or events presented after a behavior that increase the occurrence of the behavior in the future

praise

a positive statement about another person's behavior or performance

negative reinforcers

stimuli or events that are removed following a behavior that increase the likelihood of the behavior in the future negative reinforcement. The reinforcers for those behaviors is what students *do not* get rather than what they *do* get. Also remember with reinforcement not to think of positive as "good" and negative as "bad." Instead, think of positive reinforcement as adding a consequence after a behavior to increase the behavior and think of negative reinforcement as taking away a consequence of behavior in order to increase the behavior.

Think It Over

as a LEARNER   Which of the two types of reinforcers, positive or negative, do you consider preferable as a way of conditioning behavior, and why?

as a TEACHER   Can you give an example of a positive and negative reinforcer typically used by teachers? If a teacher commented on a student's minor misbehavior and it increased, what kind of consequence was the comment according to operant conditioning? Why?

Primary versus Secondary Reinforcers

Some reinforcers automatically strengthen behaviors when you are initially deprived of them. For example, if one is hungry and asks for food, asking for food (when one is hungry) will occur more often if the request is contingently followed by receiving food. In the example, one does not have to learn food is a reinforcer, because the food functions automatically as a reinforcer for the request. Those reinforcers that operate automatically in this way are called **primary reinforcers** and they include things such as food and water. The reinforcement value of these things does not have to be learned. Because it would be hard to provide such primary reinforcers in a classroom on a regular basis, teachers have come to rely instead on reinforcers that students have learned to value. These learned preferences are called **secondary reinforcers**, and they include praise, money, and the opportunity to play. Some parents pay their children for good grades on their report card, which is an example of them trying to use a secondary reinforcer. Because of low graduation rates in some of America's largest cities, educational systems are experimenting with the impact on school achievement of providing students secondary reinforcers. Box 6.3 describes a bold plan in New York City public schools to use a powerful positive reinforcer, money, to increase the achievement of students.

Secondary reinforcers have come to have reinforcement value because they have been associated early and often in our lives with other reinforcers. Five kinds of secondary positive reinforcers can be used with reasonable ease in the classroom (Deitz & Hummel, 1978). They are: (1) consumable (candy, gum, popcorn); (2) social (praise, smile, attention); (3) activity (free time, movie, computer time); (4) exchangeable (token, points, money); and (5) tangible (toys, favorite chair, favorite sweater).

The first of these, *consumable* reinforcers, includes both primary and secondary reinforcers. These are termed consumable because they are items that are ingested. However, consumable reinforcers can be of either the primary or secondary variety.

primary reinforcers
stimuli that are a necessity and therefore naturally reinforcing, such as water and food

secondary reinforcers
stimuli or events that we learn to value

BOX 6.3

Did You Know?   Do Incentives Work in School?

A statistic that should alarm future teachers is that about half of America's students in urban public schools fail to graduate. Barring rare exceptions, students who do not graduate from high school have very different opportunities in life than those who do earn their diploma. New York City Mayor Michael Bloomberg and School Chancellor Joel Klein hired a well-known Harvard professor, Dr. Roland Fryer, to help address this problem and improve achievement among urban students from low socioeconomic status backgrounds.

Dr. Fryer proposed a plan to provide urban students incentives to do well in school. This is a very business-oriented approach to changing the performance of children and schools, which was very novel. The plan is in the pilot stage currently and they are experimenting by paying 4th and 7th grade students for performance. Dr. Fryer is convinced that innovation in public schools is necessary because what is currently happening is not working effectively for certain populations of students.

However, the incentive program is actually quite controversial. Some worry that students will become motivated only by the reward as opposed to being motivated by the joy of learning. Also, a critic might argue that by paying only for test performance, we might ignore or minimize the effort that a student puts in and the process that a student goes through who does not reach the test score required to earn an incentive. Thus a student who seldom attended and started attending school consistently might receive no incentive if he or she failed to see test score increases. Other efforts similar to NYC's plans have been attempted; for example, Dr. Fryer is currently evaluating a Dallas, Texas, program called "Earning by Learning" which pays students to read books.

- How do you feel about paying students for grades?
- Does this program reduce children learning for the love of learning, or does success in school, however stimulated, make children love learning even more?
- Do you think the students who are paid for good grades will keep up the performance when and if the incentive is removed?

Source: http://www.nytimes.com/2007/06/21/nyregion/21fryer.html?_r=1

Dr. Fryer is attempting to use operant conditioning principles to help increase graduation rates of disadvantaged and minority students.

Ramin Talaie/Corbis News/Corbis

For example, if one is thirsty, water from a faucet is okay. If one merely wants a drink, an individual might purchase bottled water. Food, when hungry, is a primary reinforcer, but a bag of chips, unnecessary to sustain life, would be considered a secondary reinforcer.

The second of these, *social reinforcers,* represents desirable interactive experiences with other people, usually with either the teacher or other students. Social reinforcers that teachers can use with students include complimenting them, smiling at them, patting them on the back, a head nod, or making eye contact with them. Contingently saying to students "Good work" and "You're working hard" and "Way to go" are all phrases that can serve as social reinforcers.

The third of these, *activity* reinforcers, are desirable things to do, such as going out to play, having recess, being a monitor, going on a field trip, or getting to use a computer. Many activity reinforcers can often be considered an earned privilege. The effective use of activity reinforcers was illustrated by the psychologist David Premack (1965), giving rise to what is formally referred to as the Premack principle. The Premack principle is also referred to as "Grandma's Rule." It is called that because the essence of the principle comes from wisdom doled out by grandmothers throughout time, which is have students complete tasks that involve the most work and challenge before they complete more desirable tasks.

The **Premack principle** states that any high-frequency behavior (something the child likes to do) that is contingent upon (will only be allowed to happen) following the occurrence of a low-frequency behavior (something the child is not likely to do) can be used to increase the occurrence of the low-frequency behavior. Put more simply, Grandma's Rule says children will learn to do things they may not like very much, such as doing their homework, if the consequence of doing these things is to get to do something they like a lot, such as playing with their friends. The more preferred activity thus becomes the reward or reinforcer for carrying out the less preferred activity. It is important for a teacher to recognize that the opposite of the Premack principal is not as effective. Meaning, it would probably not be as effective to say to your students, we will hold the pizza party now, if you each promise to read the three stories later.

Consistent with the Premack principle is the idea that the teacher need not guess at what a more preferred activity or activity reinforcer might be for a child or group of children. The best strategy would be to ask each child what he or she would like to do as a reward for completing the seatwork or reading or other classwork activity. Or, the teacher could provide a list of such activities from which the students could select. In other words, tailor-made or individualized activity reinforcers could be used to reward each child's classroom work. The teacher must be sure, though, that the student likes the "rewarding" activity, because it will be rewarding only if the student perceives it as such. Many individuals select and use "rewards" they believe are positive reinforcers and are upset (and mistakenly conclude that operant conditioning does not work) when the real problem is that the reward presented does not qualify as a reinforcer for the individual. An example of the actual application of the Premack principle in a classroom situation is given in Box 6.4.

Premack principle

states that a teacher can use an activity that a student prefers as a reinforcer to complete a less preferred activity

AN EXAMPLE TO AID UNDERSTANDING   **Box 6.4**

Using the Premack Principle to Get Brian to Do His Schoolwork

Ms. Blake had tried everything she could think of to get second grader Brian to complete his assignments on time, to no avail. This was not a new problem. Brian's first-grade teacher had informed Ms. Blake that she too had tried everything she could think of. Most recently, Ms. Blake had kept Brian in from recess numerous times, thinking this would help. But it turned out that this form of punishment meant nothing to him.

Another approach Ms. Blake tried was contacting Brian's mother about his work not being turned in. This had failed too. Instead of problem solving with Ms. Blake to improve Brian's performance at school, she instead told Ms. Blake of the difficulty and frustration she experienced when she attempted to get Brian to complete any of his responsibilities at home.

Ms. Blake was frustrated; she knew Brian was capable of the work but he just wasn't motivated. A visit to the teacher's lounge one day changed everything. Ms. Grant, the music teacher, made a casual remark about how much Brian loved music. She went on to say that she had no academic or behavioral problems with him during class.

Ms. Blake decided to purchase some popular music compact disks and put them in the classroom learning centers. Only the children who correctly completed their work were permitted to go to any of the learning centers. Up to this point, Brian had never gone to the centers and hadn't seemed to want to. This now changed. Brian was eager to listen to the music, so Ms. Blake made a deal with him: If he would correctly complete his reading activity on time each day, he could go to one of the centers and listen to the music.

The next day, when Brian arrived at class, he immediately went to his seat. It was time for reading. The independent reading activity was about start. To Ms. Blake's delight, Brian correctly completed his assignment. He was then permitted to go to one of the learning centers. He headed to the center, put on the earphones, and gave a wide grin of satisfaction. You would have to know Brian to appreciate that smile.

Brian's story is a perfect example of how the Premack principle can be such an effective tool. Because each child is unique, though, there are no set rules or guarantees. Basically, it takes trial-and-error to find a solution. But for a busy and caring teacher, a solution is well worth the effort.

- Why do you think taking away recess and talking to his parents had no effect on Brian's behavior?
- Instead of punishing what she did not want Brian doing, how did Ms. Blake reinforce the behavior she wanted?
- Did you ever complete a school assignment or task at work as a means to an end? What was the project?

The fourth of these are the *exchangeable* reinforcers. Exchangeable reinforcers are things that can be "traded-in for," or converted to, some other reinforcer. Gold stars and points can work as exchangeable reinforcers. Often, exchangeable reinforcers come to have reinforcement value of their own because of their common association with other reinforcers such as social ones. Money is such a token reinforcer: For many people, it has come to be desirable in its own right, independent of what it might buy.

The last of these is the *tangible* reinforcer. This type of reinforcer involves the presentation of an object that the individual is able to keep. For example, young children often enjoy receiving "happy faces" for academic work well done, and children who earn good grades on their report cards may consequently earn new clothing or a bicycle.

Sometimes, such as when learning or operant conditioning is first taking place, reinforcement must be given every time the operant response occurs. This is called **continuous reinforcement**, and it is necessary if learning is to occur.

If, on the other hand, reinforcement is no longer given after a response that has been reinforced in the past, the response that had been learned will eventually decrease and finally stop occurring. This process is called extinction. *Extinction* is the result of no longer reinforcing a behavior that was reinforced, which leads to the elimination of the behavior. Continuous reinforcement, which produces learning, and no reinforcement, which produces extinction, represent the extreme schedules or patterns of reinforcement. There are other schedules in between (Ferster & Skinner, 1957; Walker & Buckley, 1974), which are called schedules of reinforcement. Table 6.4 reviews ways that teachers can apply reinforcers in their classrooms.

Schedules of Reinforcement

It is possible to provide reinforcement following the performance of the operant response some specific number of times (such as five times) rather than every time. In other words, a child would have to do five problems rather than just one to be reinforced, or an animal would have to push the bar five times rather than just one to get food. The ratio of responses to reinforcements would be five to one (5:1). Whenever the response must occur some number of times before reinforcement is triggered, a **ratio reinforcement** schedule is being used. If the response must occur three times for a reinforcement, then the ratio schedule is 3:1, and so on. Because reinforcement

continuous reinforcement
a particular behavior is reinforced every time it occurs

ratio reinforcement
a type of schedule where reinforcers are delivered based on the number of responses

---

CONCEPT REVIEW TABLE 6.4
Ways Teachers Can Effectively Use Reinforcers

- Provide reinforcers soon after a student behaves in a way that improves their learning or makes the class a better place to learn.

- Let students choose the types of reinforcers they want to receive.

- Use praise or other types of reinforcement to increase the academic performance of students, not just their social behavior in your classroom.

- Instead of evaluative praise, consider clearly describing what you notice students doing in class (Kohn, 2001). For example, instead of saying "good job" to a student, you might say "you put your belongings in your desk without being reminded."

- When using the Premack principle in your class, have the students engage in the less preferred task first. The reverse of the Premack principle (having them engage in the more preferred activity first) is not as effective.

Thinkstock/Jupiterimages

Interval reinforcement has a teacher provide reinforcement to a student after a period of time has elapsed. How frequently do you think you would try to reinforce your students?

interval reinforcement

a type of schedule where reinforcers are delivered after a time interval

fixed schedules

in this type of schedule, the student knows exactly when and how the consequence will be provided

variable schedules

in this type of schedule, the student does not know when and how the consequence will be provided because it changes from situation to situation

is given not for every response but for every *n*th response, a ratio schedule represents intermittent or occasional reinforcement rather than continuous reinforcement. When students read books and are reinforced for that activity, it often occurs on a fixed ratio schedule. For example, a school might give students a card, and the card is punched for each book the student reads. When a student reads a certain predetermined number of books, they get a reinforcer of their choosing.

Another way to give reinforcement intermittently is to give it for the first response that occurs after a given interval of time has elapsed. In this schedule, reinforcement could be given for the first response that occurs after a minute has elapsed or two minutes or three minutes, and so on depending on how the teacher wants to set up the schedule. This is called **interval reinforcement**. For example, the teacher might say that at the end of the 15 minutes of practice time, whichever students are participating will be allowed to use the computer. The problem with an interval schedule is that a child or even an animal quickly learns that the reinforcement will occur only every so many minutes, no matter how many responses are made; so the response rate is low during the beginning and middle of the interval. It is only at the end of the interval, when the reinforcement is provided, that rapid responding is likely to occur.

In order to increase both response rate (the number of responses per minute) and resistance to extinction (the number of responses that will occur with no reinforcement at all), Skinner invented the idea of a variable reinforcement schedule in contrast to fixed ones. **Fixed schedules** are set up so that the student knows exactly when and how the consequence will be provided; in essence, fixed schedules can be thought of as predictable schedules.

In **variable schedules,** the number of times a response must be made before a reinforcement is received, or the interval of time that must elapse before a response produces reinforcement, changes after every reinforcement. In other words, for a variable ratio schedule, the schedule could be two responses followed by a reinforcement, then four responses before the next reinforcement, then three responses, and so on. The average ratio might be 3:1, but the actual ratio would vary each time rather than being fixed or constant. Thus, while there is predictability with fixed schedules, there is no predictability for variable ones.

Similarly, for a variable interval schedule, the first reinforcement might follow the first behavior that occurs after one minute, the second after three minutes, the third after two minutes, and so on. With such a variable schedule, the child or animal could not predict exactly when a response would be followed by a reinforcement, and so would respond at a high rate in order to maximize the possibility of the response being reinforced. (See Table 6.5 for a *Concept Review* of the four kinds of intermittent reinforcement schedules.)

Intermittent reinforcement schedules, particularly variable ones, add a high degree of practicality to the practice or use of reinforcement theory in managing

CONCEPT REVIEW TABLE 6.5

Four Kinds of Intermittent Reinforcement Schedules

TYPE OF SCHEDULE	DESCRIPTION OF SCHEDULE	EFFECTS ON BEHAVIOR	
		SCHEDULE IN OPERATION	SCHEDULE TERMINATED
Fixed Ratio (FR)	Reinforcer given after preset number of responses	High response rate	Irregular responding
Fixed Interval (FI)	Reinforcer given for first response to occur after each preset amount of time	Student stops working after reinforcement; then works hard prior to the time of next reinforcement	Gradual decrease in responding
Variable Ratio (VR)	Reinforcer applied after a random number of responses	Very high response rate.	Very resistant to extinction
Variable Interval (VI)	Reinforcer given for first response to occur after a random amount of time	Steady rate of responding	Very resistant to extinction

behavior. It is neither necessary nor even desirable to give reinforcement after each performance of the operant response, other than when it is being learned in the first place. Once the behavior has been learned, variable ratio or variable interval reinforcement schedules can be used to maintain the performance of the operant response at a high rate of occurrence.

Think It Over

as a LEARNER Why do you think some of the schedules are more likely than others to lead to increases in behavior?

as a TEACHER Which of the four schedules do you think is most typically used in a school setting, and why?

Perspectives on Punishment

According to operant conditioning theory, effective use of reinforcement should make the use of punishment less necessary. The most effective technique for weakening behavior is to use extinction, to ignore it. The next best approach is to use negative reinforcement, to allow punishment to be avoided or escaped if the undesirable behavior is terminated (Skinner, 1953). Punishment is not a preferred method for changing behavior, because punishing a person usually does not totally eliminate the undesirable behavior. Rather, it causes the person to simply resist the punishment, or wait and perform the undesirable behavior at another time, perhaps when the punisher is not around. The behavior is merely suppressed and may reappear later under different circumstance (Skinner, 1953, 1968). Moreover, the punisher may serve as a model for future aggressive behavior on the part of the person punished, and the current situation may turn into a battle of wills between, for example, the teacher and a youthful "offender."

However, there are two circumstances when punishment, as a last resort, may be used effectively. The first is when undesirable behavior is so *frequent* that there is virtually no desirable behavior to reinforce. Extreme aggressiveness in a child sometimes leaves no room for reinforcement. The second is when the problem behavior is so *intense* that someone, including the child himself, may get hurt. Again, aggressiveness can be an example of such intense behavior.

Types of Punishment

There are two types of punishment. **Presentation punishment** involves the presentation or use of aversive or painful events, such as scolding to decrease the incidence of a behavior, that is, "getting something bad." **Removal punishment** involves taking away or stopping positive reinforcers, and is usually referred to as *response cost*. The person's undesirable response costs him or her privileges, for example, play time, which might be described as "avoiding something good." Cutting out a student's potential reinforcers and access to all possible reinforcement by having him or her sit alone, called *time-out*, is an example of Type 2, or removal punishment. Table 6.6 reviews how consequences affect classroom behavior.

The Use of Punishment

Research by Azrin and Holz (1966) has shown that if punishment is used effectively, it can be expected to weaken behavior, just as reinforcement strengthens it. In using punishment effectively, one must *prevent avoidance and escape from the source of punishment.*

Withdrawal of positive reinforcers, as in removal punishment, generally is regarded the more acceptable form of punishment (Burchard & Barrera, 1972) as long as clear-cut steps are provided for earning the reinforcement back. In other words, once a procedure like time-out begins, it cannot be avoided or escaped; but by subsequently behaving properly, the student can earn back the lost rewards and

presentation punishment

the use of aversive or painful events to decrease the incidence of a behavior

removal punishment

taking away a student's access to positive reinforcers to decrease the incidence of a behavior

CONCEPT REVIEW TABLE 6.6
How Consequences Affect Classroom Behavior

EFFECT ON BEHAVIOR	PRESENTATION	REMOVAL
Strengthens Behavior	Positive Reinforcement (being praised for raising one's hand before speaking)	Negative Reinforcement (not being assigned the weekend homework because of appropriate behavior)
Weakens Behavior	Presentation Punishment (being scolded for throwing a pencil)	Removal Punishment (being sent out of the classroom due to threatening another student)

avoid future time-outs. By behaving acceptably, students can avoid time-out and response cost and earn positive reinforcers in its place.

Secondly, it is important to *minimize the need for future punishment.* The teacher can do this by using a warning signal, which, when paired with a punisher, becomes a conditioned punisher, that is, the warning signal alone comes to cause the person to behave properly. Also, reinforcing behavior incompatible with the objectionable behavior will cause the objectionable behavior to be replaced by the desired behavior. In other words, students cannot talk and be quiet at the same time.

Finally, the teacher administering the punishment must be *calm and consistent,* and the punishment must be *matter-of-fact* and *directed at the behavior,* not at the child. And, it must be *immediate.* The punisher must not be angry or aggressive, nor must the punishment function as a retaliation or put-down; otherwise, the receiver will be exposed to an aggressive model who is likely to be imitated (see the discussion of modeling later in this chapter).

Time-out can be an effective punishment, particularly for young children, but it must involve *cutting off access to all sources of reinforcement for a short period of time.* Removing a child from a situation, when the child is misbehaving, does not necessarily constitute a punishment for the child. In fact, it could represent a negative reinforcement and so strengthen the misbehavior that led to the child's removal. For example, sending a child to the principal's office may actually reinforce the behavior that caused the child's ejection if the classroom represents an aversive environment to the child. Objectionable behavior will be weakened by ejection only if the child thereby loses the chance to gain immediate positive reinforcement. For that to occur, the child must want to stay in the classroom.

Learning Objective 5

Illustrate how you could help a student learn new behaviors through the classroom use of prompting, chaining, and shaping.

prompting

the adding of a familiar antecedent that is likely to signal the desired response

Modifying Behavior: Prompting, Chaining, and Shaping

In addition to modifying existing behaviors, operant conditioning can be used to develop new behaviors conducive to learning and to constructive social interaction. Three primary approaches are covered here: prompting, chaining, and shaping. They can be used in combination. You may want to incorporate these processes, to some extent and in some circumstances, into your lesson planning.

Prompting

Prompting means adding a familiar antecedent that is likely to signal the desired response, rather than waiting for the desired response to occur on a chance basis. Prompting may mean, for example, a teacher describing to the class appropriate behavior during a particular moment in a science experiment. He or she might do such prompting when presenting rules for classroom behavior. Prompts are established relationships between antecedents and behaviors that can be used to facilitate learning new ones.

Prompting is commonly used in the teaching of reading. When a child has trouble reading a word, the teacher may help the child sound it out. Giving clues to help the unfamiliar become more familiar represents prompting.

In prompting, there are two important ideas or rules to remember. First, the normal antecedent should occur before the prompting antecedent. In other words, extra help should not be given before the student tries to complete the task without extra help. If the teacher helps or prompts first—by sounding out a word, for example—the student will come to rely on the prompts rather than on the normal antecedent, the appearance of the word on the page. The student will not learn to respond without prompting if it always comes first. This relates to the Vygotskian concepts of scaffolding and zone of proximal development that you have already learned about that suggest how and to what degree we should provide assistance to learners.

Second, prompts should be faded or withdrawn as soon as possible so that the student is able to act without constant help or reminders. Gradual withdrawal is best.

Teachers and peers provide prompts to help other students read new words.

Brand X Pictures/Jupiter Images

Thus, prompting is a way of helping students know what response will be right, and prompting should lead to the correct response in a given situation. Prompts can help increase the likelihood of the student emitting reinforceable responses at the start of learning, but they should be gradually eliminated so that they do not become a necessary element of the performance situation. A main goal of teaching at all levels involves students increasing their self-regulation and decreasing their dependence.

Chaining

Chaining represents a technique for connecting simple responses in sequence to form a more complex response that would be difficult to learn all at one time. In a chain, simple behaviors under the control of an antecedent are joined into a sequence of behavior, which is then reinforced at its completion. A chain might look like this:

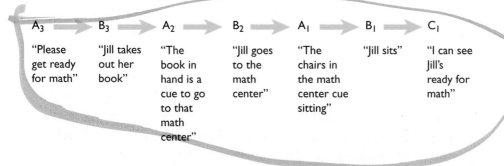

A_3 → B_3 → A_2 → B_2 → A_1 → B_1 → C_1

"Please get ready for math" → "Jill takes out her book" → "The book in hand is a cue to go to that math center" → "Jill goes to the math center" → "The chairs in the math center cue sitting" → "Jill sits" → "I can see Jill's ready for math"

The above example is purposefully simplistic to demonstrate that each antecedent in a behavior chain tends to acquire a reinforcing function for the response that precedes it and a discriminative function for the response that follows it.

The most common method for establishing a behavior chain in the classroom is first to prompt each step in the chain and then to fade the prompts. For example, the chain for preparing for math, shown above, could initially have been made up of three separate instructions:

1. "Everyone, please get out your math books."
   "Good. Everyone has a book out."
2. "Now let's all walk to the math corner."
   "Good."
3. "Let's all sit in our chairs."
   "You are ready. Thank you."

After several repetitions, it would have been unnecessary to say more than "Please get ready for math," because the students would now have known what to do.

Shaping

Shaping is the process of reinforcing each form of the behavior that more closely resembles the final version of the target behavior. Shaping is used when the target or desired response is not one the student can perform already, that is, the desired

chaining

a technique for connecting simple responses in sequence to form a more complex response that would be difficult to learn all at one time

shaping

the process of reinforcing each form of the behavior that more closely resembles the final version of the target behavior

response is not in the student's repertoire or when there is no way to prompt the response.

Skinner (1953) gives the following laboratory example of shaping:

> To get the pigeon to peck the spot as quickly as possible we proceed as follows: We first give the bird food when it turns slightly in the direction of the spot from any part of the cage. This increases the frequency of such behavior. We then withhold reinforcement until a slight movement is made toward the spot . . . We continue by reinforcement of positions successively closer to the spot, then by reinforcing only when the head is moved slightly forward, and finally only when the beak actually makes contact with the spot. We may reach this final response in . . . two or three minutes. (p. 92)

There are two components to shaping. The first is differential reinforcement, or reinforcing only those behaviors that meet a given criterion and not behaviors that fail to meet that criterion. This, of course, is a standard practice in all behavior modification and should be standard practice in a classroom where behavioral learning principles are utilized.

The second component to shaping is to use a shifting criterion for reinforcement, that is, gradually changing the response criterion for reinforcement in the direction of the target behavior. To implement this, the teacher starts shaping by reinforcing any behavior that approximates or is vaguely similar to the target behavior, such as doing one math problem correctly, and ends up reinforcing only the exact target behavior, such as doing 10 math problems correctly. Between start and end, he or she gradually imposes the requirement that the student's behavior must move closer and closer to the target behavior.

Thus, the technique of shaping reinforces successive approximations to the target behavior, each getting closer to it than the one before. Care must be taken not to stay with each new requirement any longer than necessary to meet the criterion, or else the student's behavior will stop there. Consider the following classroom situation where a teacher tries to use shaping and other behavioral principles to help a student behave in ways that made the learning environment safe for all of the students in the class:

The classroom had a few rules to help establish a positive learning environment: speak quietly, remain seated during independent practice time, keep your hands and feet away from others, respect the belongings of others, use language that is respectful of others (no swearing), and do your best work. Dwayne would go down the list and seemingly try to break them all, one or two at a time. For a second grader, he had quite a reputation. He swore, hit other children, was out of his seat most of the time, and his hands were always busy, throwing pencils in the classroom or food in the lunchroom.

Each time he broke a rule, he was sent to a time-out section of the office with his unfinished work. He often had company from other classrooms, and because these children were usually left unsupervised, time-out was a regular treat for Dwayne. It was a reinforcer, rather than the punishment it was intended to be. In the regular classroom, he was always punished for his antics, and the other children shunned him. It was more desirable to him to be sent to the time-out room.

Dwayne's teacher finally realized that her "punishment" was actually increasing Dwayne's inappropriate behavior! She decided something else must be tried. She had read an article on shaping, so she decided to begin such a program for Dwayne. First, she focused on getting him to just remain in his seat. She had a difficult time ever catching him in it, but when she did she reinforced him with praise. To keep his interest, she varied her reinforcement to include stickers and computer time. He seemed to thrive on the attention he received.

Soon, Dwayne began staying in his seat. But he was still continually making contact with the other students by throwing things at them, talking loudly, and swearing at them. So the teacher concentrated next on getting him to not throw things. Here, she used some prompting. She told him that if he wouldn't throw anything at anybody for an hour, she would let him be the official fish feeder the next day. He had never earned this privilege before. He was very excited at the prospect and helped the teacher design and decorate a chart with his name and the days of the week on it. The whole first day, he restrained himself from throwing things, but the next day he forgot. So they started over. This happened for about a week. When the second week began and by Monday afternoon he had not thrown anything at all, the entire class cheered for him. So that whole second week he didn't throw anything, and he sat in his seat most of the time. Imagine his face when he got to feed the fish the next week.

To use shaping in the classroom, like in the situation that describes Dwayne, you would follow these steps: (1) define the target behavior, for example, do 10 math problems independently, without distraction, and correctly; (2) decide what behavior to build from, such as do one math problem with help; (3) establish a reinforcer such as learning points to be used toward a play period; (4) outline the program of steps and explain each new criterion to the students, for example, the sequence of criteria are one math problem with help, one problem without help, two problems with help, two problems without help, five problems without help, eight problems without help, 10 problems without help; (5) start training with the first criterion; (6) decide when to shift to a new criterion; (7) if the criterion is not met, return briefly to an earlier step or add a new step in between and try again; and (8) repeat steps 6 and 7 until the target behavior is achieved. How did the teacher who worked with "Dwayne" implement these procedures?

Applying Operant Conditioning to the Classroom

Learning Objective 6

Show how a classroom teacher could apply operant conditioning to the classroom by specifying desirable behavior, praising those behaviors, and ignoring nontarget behavior.

Skinner (1953, 1968) applied operant conditioning to the process of teaching. There are many times when classroom behavior will be influenced by operant conditioning principles. For example, think about the educational psychology class you are currently taking. Your professor probably asks critical thinking questions. When you decide to raise your hand and provide and answer, the professor provides some sort of reaction. According to Skinner, the nature of this reaction could very well influence how likely you will or will not be likely to volunteer an answer in the future. When your role changes from college student to professional educator, there will be areas of your practice where you can use operant conditioning to positively impact the behavior of others. The seven principles below summarize ways in which operant conditioning can be applied to teaching.

1. Provide for an active *response* by the learner. Merely listening is not enough; the learner must perform a response.
2. Follow the performance of a correct response with *positive consequences* such as "You are correct" or "good answer."
3. Provide optimal *contingencies* of reinforcement for correct performance: positive, immediate, and frequent; initially continuous and then intermittent.
4. Maximize the likelihood of correct responses and minimize the likelihood of errors by *shaping* behavior through the use of small instructional steps.
5. *Avoid* aversive control, that is, the use of the threat of punishment to modify student behavior. Use the promise of reward instead.
6. Use *cues* to signal and *prompt* the correct response.
7. *Reinforce* the exact performance you want the learner to learn.

Establish Classroom Rules

Based on these seven general points, classroom rules could be taught utilizing operant conditioning principles. For example, after discussion and consensus was reached with the students, a teacher wrote the following five agreed upon rules on a corner of the chalkboard for permanent display:

Classroom rules can be created based on what teachers know about operant conditioning principles.

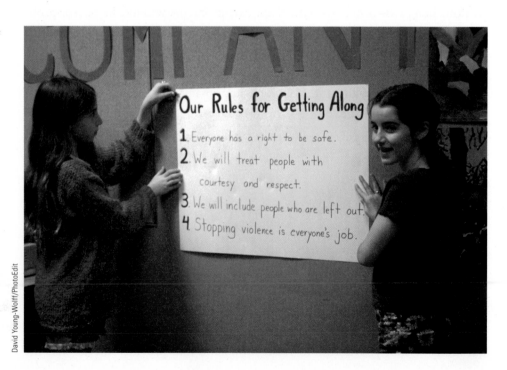

David Young-Wolff/PhotoEdit

1. Please raise your hand when you wish to talk.
2. For your safety, walk in the classrooms and halls.
3. Keep your hands and feet to yourself.
4. Be polite.
5. When your individual activity is finished, please go to the learning center area in the back of the room and select an extension activity.

The teacher reminded the children of the rules by (1) having them read the rules each morning; (2) making praise comments contingent on their being followed and referring to the rule in the praise comment, for example, "I called on Tim because he raised his hand"; and (3) attending to only that behavior within the limits of the rules (Becker, Engelmann, & Thomas, 1975, pp. 117–18). This illustrates some basic strategies for effective classroom management using operant conditioning theory. Regardless of what rules you and your students decide to implement in the classroom, it is still imperative that you remember that how you treat them will have an impact on the degree to which they want to participate in activities that we think would be good for their learning. (This topic of effective classroom management will be discussed again in Chapter 11 from numerous perspectives.) The TeachSource Video Case for this chapter shares perspectives on classroom management from different teachers, counselors, and students.

Emphasize Appropriate Behavior

According to behaviorism, the first principle of effective classroom management is to *specify,* in a positive way, the rules that are the basis for reinforcement. The rules serve as prompts; as children learn to follow them, they can be repeated less frequently (faded). Good classroom behavior, however, should continue to be reinforced. The rules represent the antecedent.

The second principle is to *praise* desirable behavior; teachers should catch children being good rather than waiting for them to misbehave. The focus should be on reinforcing or praising behavior important for the development of social and cognitive skills. Teacher behaviors such as relating children's performance to the rules, being specific, and praising the behavior rather than the child are recommended. Becker et al. (1975) provide these examples of effective praise (p. 120):

> *"You watched the board all the time I was presenting the example. That's paying attention."*
>
> *"That's a good answer. You listened very closely to my question."*
>
> *"Jimmy is really working hard. He'll get the answer. You'll see."*

It is also important that improvement, rather than just the absolute or final level of performance, be rewarded. Students should be praised for doing better as a way of shaping their behavior in the direction of doing well.

Being aware of what you say to students and how you say it is crucial. A teacher can choose to make either positive or negative statements that focus on their students' learning or classroom behavior. Praise has also been shown to be an effective way of changing *teachers'* behavior. Hayes, Hindle, and Withington (2007) conducted research

TeachSource Video Case

Classroom Management: Best Practices

In this video segment, you see how various teachers, a middle school student, and a school guidance counselor discuss their experiences with the best ways to manage a classroom. The video will give you perspectives on classroom management from many viewpoints, student and teacher, elementary and secondary education, different cultural backgrounds, and males and females.

After viewing the video case, consider what you have just watched about classroom management and answer the questions below.

1. Mrs. Ross talks about the community circle. What is she trying to accomplish with this strategy?
2. The most important advice the middle school student, Alan, offered was for teachers to just listen. How could taking Alan's advice help you with classroom management?

You can view the video case at the Education CourseMate. Go to:
CengageBrain.com

in a large secondary school in the United Kingdom and found that, when a school focused on positive behavioral management, the teachers at the school increased the amount of positive statements they made to students and minimized the negative ones. Previous research has found similar findings. For example, Cossairt, Hall, and Hopkins (1973) found that teachers who were praised by an observer for using praise themselves dramatically increased their subsequent use of praise. An example of a positive statement of student learning that a teacher could make is "I really liked the explanation you gave for your answer" and an example of a positive behavioral statement would be "You really are sharing a lot of good ideas with your group today, thank you."

When a behavior problem persists, another student in the class, or the teacher, is inadvertently reinforcing it. Often, the reinforcement comes in the form of giving attention to a student who craves it and attempts to gain it by acting out. Ignoring such minor behavior is preferable to punishing it. For example, Madsen, Becker, Thomas, Koser, and Plager (1968) discovered that the more the teacher said "Sit down," the more children stood up. In other words, the less often teachers ignored students' standing up and instead scolded or criticized them by ordering them to sit down, the more often students stood up. The "sit down" response served as a reinforcement for standing up. Because the children sat down after being told to do so, the teacher thought that the "sit down" response was working, but instead the response was causing more students to stand up. Criticism represents teacher attention being given to off-task behavior, and it is like a trap. The more a teacher criticizes, the more likely the criticized behavior will occur; then the teacher has to criticize even more. A vicious circle has been created.

Also, reinforcement should occur immediately; if it is delayed, it may follow and thereby strengthen behaviors other than the target behavior. Any behavior immediately followed by reinforcement is more likely to occur. Skinner's pigeons sometimes walked around in a circle before pecking the key and getting food. Thereafter, they would always make a circle before pecking even though reinforcement was not contingent on this circling behavior. When a reinforcement occurs accidentally, perhaps when a child finds some money while walking home from school, any behavior that happened to precede this stroke of good luck will be reinforced and is likely to be repeated. The lucky youngster may continue to follow the same route home or may walk looking down, even though finding money was not predictably contingent on either behavior. Skinner (1953) called behavior that occurs in response to accidental reinforcement **superstitious behavior**.

Every instance of the target behavior should be reinforced, known as continuous reinforcement, until it is mastered. Thereafter, intermittent, variable reinforcement schedules can be used.

Finally, teachers must be aware of themselves or else they will not be able to use these principles effectively. Their use of praise must be consistent, as must their inclination to ignore disruptive behavior. A teacher's loss of temper will likely lead to ineffective classroom management. For example, scolding or criticizing might result in an increase rather than decrease of the undesirable behavior.

Social Cognitive Learning-Emphasizing Observation

Learning Objective 7

Evaluate how students learn behaviors in school settings through social learning.

So far in this chapter you have read about how students learn from association (through classical conditioning), how they learn from consequences (through operant conditioning), and now you will read about an approach to learning emphasizing that students learn much of their behavior through observing others. This approach is called **social cognitive learning theory**. You will learn about what students learn by watching others, the process they go through to learn from others, and how likely a student will be to model a behavior.

Social learning is learning by observation, particularly the observation of other people's behavior. It is both a cognitive process and a behavioral one because people often carry their observations around in their heads and do not act on them until a later time. It is for this reason that social learning often is considered a bridge theory between behaviorism and more cognitively oriented learning theories. In developing his theory of social learning, Albert Bandura (1977) began by presenting his case for its cognitive (or indirect) rather than behavioral (or direct) nature, by observing that people usually (1) must learn to manage and control their own behavior, rather than having others do it for them; (2) behave in ways they never have before, rather than always behaving in the same way; and (3) learn a behavior but do not perform it immediately, instead waiting for the appropriate opportunity.

superstitious behavior

behavior that occurs in response to accidental reinforcement

social cognitive learning theory

a theory of learning created by Albert Bandura that emphasizes the cognitive components of social learning

social learning

students learning by observing other people's behavior

Myrleen Ferguson Cate/PhotoEdit

Students learned to mimic aggressive behavior in Bandura's famous Bobo doll study. What other behaviors do you think students learn by watching other people?

The theory of social learning has many educational applications and helps a teacher understand many of the behaviors they will see in and out of the classroom. It explains how a 9th grade language arts student is able to analyze imagery in a poem after watching the teacher model the skill several times for the class. It also explains how students know what type of jeans are popular in their school. Social learning theory also helps explain students' most endearing behaviors, such as helping others, in addition to when they are at their worst behaving in ways that are potentially harmful to others. In a well-known series of studies (Bandura, Ross, & Ross, 1961), children in an experimental group observed an adult behave aggressively with an inflatable toy called a "Bobo Doll." Children in the control group watched an adult play with the toys in a nonviolent manner. The students in the experimental group exhibited considerably more aggressive behavior than the children in the control group during a play period where the adult was no longer present. This gives teachers clear evidence that students are watching their social surroundings carefully and modeling behaviors they observe. You need to be attuned to this dynamic because it can either enhance or inhibit your efforts as a teacher.

What Do Students Learn by Observing Models?

A powerful characteristic of social cognitive learning is that it can be done vicariously, through the observation and modeling of others. A **model** is an individual who is imitated or whose behavior others learn from. By watching, students learn from models' behavior and the consequences of their behavior. Students are paying careful attention to the teacher's social behavior and that of their peers. When the teacher is involved in a stressful situation in the classroom, the other students are paying attention to the action of the teacher. From that they will learn things about how the teacher might respond in the future. Students are looking for consistency in our response; are we treating boys and girls similarly? Are we calling on and praising students in equivalent ways? Students learn an incredible amount through observation. According to Bandura (1986), there are five things observers can learn from models.

1. Observers can learn *new cognitive skills*, such as reading, and *new behaviors*, such as how to operate a new piece of software, by watching others perform.

2. Watching models can *strengthen* or *weaken* observers' previously learned *inhibitions* over their own behavior. In other words, observers can learn what they can and cannot get away with. When observers see models perform an act, they decide (1) whether they too have the ability to perform that act, (2) whether the model was rewarded or punished for performing the act, and (3) whether they are likely to experience the same consequences if they perform the act. If an observer decides not to perform an act after seeing a model perform it and suffer unpleasant consequences, then the modeling effect is known as **inhibition**. If the observer was unlikely to perform the act before, but then becomes less restrained after seeing the model do it and not suffer any adverse consequences, the influence of modeling is known as **disinhibition** and the observer will probably perform the act too. If, for example, one child sees a second child punished for playing with a particular toy, the first child will be inhibited from playing with the toy. But if the second child is seen playing with the toy and not being punished, then the first child will be more likely to want to play with that same toy.

3. Models can also serve as *social prompts* or *inducements* for observers. In other words, observers can learn what the benefits of performing an act are. Sometimes an act is performed not because of any disinhibition not to avoid it, but because it is worth doing. Seeing the gratitude and good feeling someone else provokes by doing a good deed, for example, may stimulate or induce an observer to behave in a similarly altruistic way (Bandura, 1969).

4. From watching models, observers can learn how to *use their environment* and the *objects* in it. An observer might not have thought of using a ladder as a bench, for example, or a shoe as a paper weight, until first seeing a model do it.

5. Seeing models express emotional reactions often causes observers to *become aroused* and *express the same emotional reaction*. Children often display delight, for example, when they see it in others or distress when others display that feeling.

model

an individual who is imitated or whose behavior others learn from

inhibition

deciding not to perform a behavior after seeing a model perform it and suffer unpleasant consequences

disinhibition

becoming more likely to exhibit a behavior after seeing a model do it and not suffer any adverse consequences

How Do Students Learn from Models?

The process of learning by observing others and learning from them is governed by four processes. They are the processes of attention, retention, production, and motivation. When students learn from one another or the teacher, they are watching and remembering and later having the motivation to produce the behavior they observed. For example, in a 6th grade science class, a student might hear a peer at another table explain the phases of the moon and what causes them. Later, the student who was listening to the explanation might choose to create a picture that demonstrates what the moon looks like at different times. Students are also learning from the examples we use as well as the ones we do not present. This is one of the reasons why it is so important to be sure to expose students to books, stories, and events from numerous cultural standpoints. Figure 6.2 details the factors involved in the four observational processes.

Attention

People cannot learn by observation unless they attend to and accurately perceive the modeled activities. This will depend on how *simple* and *conspicuous* are the modeled acts. Simpler and more conspicuous acts are easier to attend to than more obscure ones. It also will depend on whether or not the observer is *set* or *disposed* to look for these acts, especially when many acts are competing for the observer's attention. This will depend, in part, on their *relevance* to the observer. Student teachers, when observing classroom teachers in action, may attend to the less significant teaching acts because there are so many teaching acts going on at the same time, but they may be attending to them all more than the students taught because these acts have great relevance to the future career of these prospective teachers. Finally, attention will depend on what activities and models are most readily available to be attended to. For example, someone is more likely to attend to aggressive acts if constantly surrounded by them than if aggression is rare in the environment (Short, 1968).

Attention is also influenced by whether the observed action produces a noticeable effect (Yussen, 1974). Actions without *functional value*—without apparent results or usefulness for dealing with the environment—often are ignored. People pay little attention to much of what they see everyday because it has no noticeable outcome.

Attractive models, like those in advertisements or on television programs, attract considerable attention. Television, in general, is an effective attention-getting device for modeling purposes, though that is not its prime intention, except perhaps for advertisements.

To gain student attention for observational learning, teachers should try (1) *accentuating* the *essential features* of the performance to be learned, (2) *subdividing* activities into parts, (3) *highlighting* the component skills, and (4) *giving* the students *opportunities between observations* to *practice* what they have seen.

Retention

In order to profit from the behavior of others who are no longer present, observers must remember what they have seen. They must *code* the information into

FIGURE 6.2

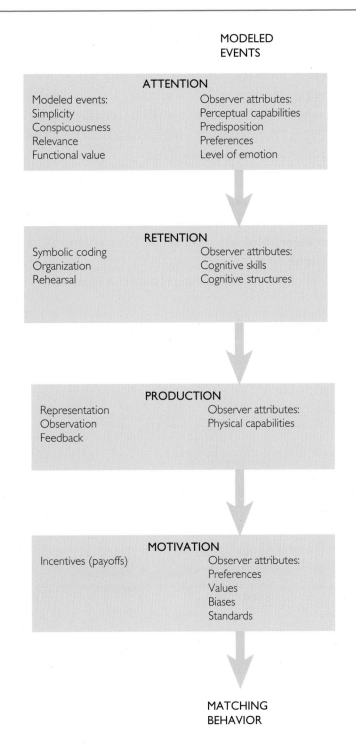

MODELED EVENTS

ATTENTION

Modeled events:
Simplicity
Conspicuousness
Relevance
Functional value

Observer attributes:
Perceptual capabilities
Predisposition
Preferences
Level of emotion

RETENTION

Symbolic coding
Organization
Rehearsal

Observer attributes:
Cognitive skills
Cognitive structures

PRODUCTION

Representation
Observation
Feedback

Observer attributes:
Physical capabilities

MOTIVATION

Incentives (payoffs)

Observer attributes:
Preferences
Values
Biases
Standards

MATCHING BEHAVIOR

Process Governing
Observational Learning
Adapted from Bandura,
1997, p. 89.

images or abstractions such as mental pictures, or into verbal symbols, and then store it in their memories (as described in Chapter 7). It is very helpful if the modeled activities are *rehearsed* or practiced immediately after they are seen (Bandura & Jeffrey, 1973). Rehearsal or practice need not be physical; it can be cognitive, that is, with the person imaging or visualizing the action in contrast to actually doing it.

Production

The third component of modeling is converting the idea, image, or memory into action. **Performance feedback** can be an important aid to this process. Self-observation through videotape replays is one way to accomplish this. Feedback from coaches, teachers, and the models themselves is equally helpful. Most effective is corrective modeling (Vasta, 1976), in which performance problems are identified and the correct performance is then remodeled.

Motivation

People do not enact or carry out everything they have learned from observation. They are more likely to enact a modeled behavior if it results in a valued or desired outcome than an unrewarded or punished one. (Motivation will be dealt with in more detail in Chapter 10.)

The sequence of observational learning is shown in Figure 6.3.

performance feedback
reviewing behavior and evaluating for performance progress

FIGURE 6.3

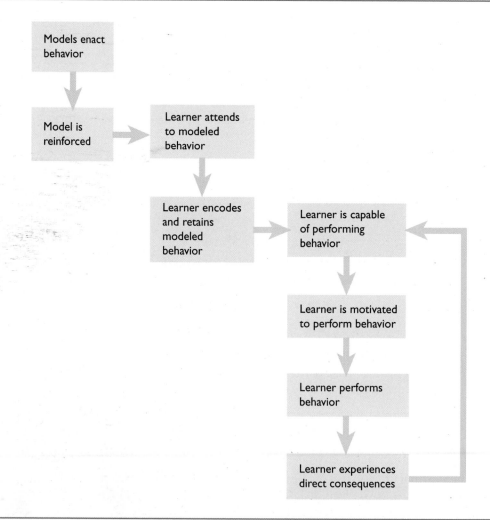

The Sequence of Observational Learning

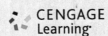
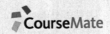

ead individuals
cts will be imi-
. The choice to
he model being

*warded model-
ior.* This effect,
d on what type
nt aspects are
led for doing
ositive. This
ding or effort-
(1972) reported
al information
on about them-
lined to keep it

t in situations
act or behavior.
ket, it is evident
vior is harder to
teacher's ques-
ble information
he model would

ccess." When a
When one tele-
s situation com-
ow suit (Brown,
re to follow.

*tion of others to
mechanism for
ehavior and the
, Herlong, and
ressively in the
acher, but they
their peer went
or punished are
much less likely to act on what they have learned than if they have seen the modeled behavior rewarded or ignored" (Bandura, 1986, p. 288). However, when behavior

is controlled by intimidation, its occurrence varies depending on whether or not the intimidator is present. So, if the only way a teacher maintains their classroom is with fear and intimidation, when the teacher leaves the classroom, taking with her the inhibitory threat of punishment, the effect of vicarious punishment will be minimal and students can be expected to act out.

Students, therefore, can be taught what the classroom prohibitions are by being shown the negative consequences of violating them. It is especially important that forbidden acts not go unpunished, because disinhibition will result and then the acts will be modeled and repeated by others. Children can often get what they want more easily by disregarding prohibitions or rules than by following them. Therefore, it will not require much modeling of successful rule-breaking behavior to disinhibit or reduce vicarious restraints against forbidden but pleasurable activities. In other words, it is easier to get children to break rules as a result of unpunished modeling than to get them to follow rules as a result of rewarded modeling. Generally speaking, children need less influence to pursue enjoyments that their teachers may disapprove of than they need to forsake enjoyments to make their teachers happy (Bandura, 1986). That is why *prohibited or forbidden behavior must be followed by negative consequences*. The absence of punishment conveys the message of social acceptability and so weakens the restraints of observers. Consequently, "weaker inducements are needed to goad behavior that violates social codes but serves one's self-interests" (Bandura, 1986, p. 290).

When aggression goes unpunished, children tend to imitate it. When they are punished aggressively or emotionally, they tend to become aggressive, emotional punishers themselves. Hence, punitive and aggressive parents tend to raise children who become punitive and aggressive parents themselves. In addition, the portrayal of violence in movies and on television as permissible leads children to believe that such behavior is acceptable, and reduces or disinhibits their restraints against it (Larsen, 1968).

Think It Over

as a LEARNER What is a skill or concept you learned by watching someone else? What steps did you go through to learn by watching them?

as a TEACHER As a teacher, how could knowledge of social learning theory make us better "models" for our students?

SUMMING IT UP

Using classical conditioning, explain how your students can have positive and negative emotions associated with experiences in school.

An early behavioral model was classical conditioning as proposed by Ivan Pavlov, a Russian physiologist. Dogs learned (or were conditioned) to salivate at the sound of a tone (the **conditioned stimulus**) when it was paired with food (the **unconditioned stimulus**). Salivation, initially elicited as the **unconditioned response** to the food, came to be elicited as a conditioned response by the sound of the tone alone, after sufficient pairings of tone and food, but only if the tone preceded or overlapped the food in time. After conditioning, repeatedly presenting the tone alone ultimately resulted in the loss of conditioning—called extinction.

Learning Objective 1

Key Concepts:

learning (p. 227); unconditioned stimulus, unconditioned response (p. 228); neutral stimulus, conditioned stimulus, conditioned response (p. 229).

Interpret student behavior through the lens of operant conditioning by modifying student and teacher behavior based on the systematic use of consequences.

Operant conditioning refers to the responses that are emitted and learned because they lead to or are followed by reinforcement. People learn to operate on their environment to gain reinforcement.

Learning Objective 2

Key Concepts:

operant conditioning (p. 233); behavior, positive behavior support, functional behavioral assessment (p. 234); contingency management, law of effect (p. 237); antecedent (p. 240).

Provide classroom examples of different types of reinforcers, including positive and negative; primary and secondary; and consumable, social, activity, exchangeable, and tangible.

There are many types of reinforcement. Some, called primary, have automatic reinforcement value; others, called secondary, must be learned to be valued. Food is a **primary reinforcer**, while money is a **secondary reinforcer**. Positive reinforcement is the contingent application of a stimulus that increases the likelihood of a behavior to occur, while negative reinforcement is the removal of a stimulus that increases the likelihood of a behavior. Once a behavior has been learned, the teacher can maintain its occurrence by reinforcing it intermittently, that is, after so many occurrences (called **ratio reinforcement**) or after so much time has elapsed (called **interval reinforcement**). Moreover, the number of occurrences or the amount of time between reinforcements can stay the same (be **fixed**) or change (be **variable**), with **variable reinforcement** being the more powerful.

Learning Objective 3

Key Concepts

reinforcer (p. 240); positive reinforcer, praise (p. 242); negative reinforcer, primary reinforcer (p. 243); secondary reinforcer, Premack principle (p. 245); continuous reinforcement (p. 246); ratio reinforcement (p. 247); interval reinforcement, fixed schedules (p. 248); variable schedules (p. 249).

Learning Objective 4

Key Concepts:

presentation punishment, removal punishment (p. 250).

Describe the different types of punishment and the effect punishment has on student behavior. Explain how the use of presentation punishment could be detrimental to students.

In extreme cases of unacceptable and potentially harmful behavior, punishment may be explored. However, punishment should take the form of response cost, or the removal of opportunities for reinforcement.

Learning Objective 5

Key Concepts:

prompting (p. 252); chaining (p. 253); shaping (p. 254).

Illustrate how you could help a student learn new behaviors through the classroom use of prompting, chaining, and shaping.

Giving the learner additional signs or signals in the form of more antecedents is called **prompting**. Such prompts should eventually be removed or faded out to avoid the learner becoming dependent on them. Connecting simple responses together to form a complex act is called **chaining**. If a learner cannot initially perform a target behavior according to a particular performance criterion, the teacher can shape that behavior by initially reinforcing approximations of it and, little by little, requiring that the performance attain the final criterion in order to be reinforced. Thus, **shaping** can be used to achieve gradual mastery of a difficult behavior.

Learning Objective 6

Key Concepts:

superstitious behavior (p. 259).

Show how a classroom teacher could apply operant conditioning to the classroom by specifying desirable behavior, praising those behaviors, and ignoring nontarget behavior.

A teacher can utilize operant conditioning principles to be an effective classroom manager. Desired behaviors such as following class rules should be specified in advance, performing these behaviors should be praised, and not performing them should be ignored.

Learning Objective 7

Key Concepts:

social learning (p. 260); model, inhibition, disinhibition (p. 261); performance feedback (p. 264).

Evaluate how students learn behaviors in school settings through social learning.

How do people learn from models? First, they must pay *attention* to what the model is doing (which will be easier if the model's behavior is simple, conspicuous, relevant, and frequent, and if the model is attractive). Second, they must *retain* or remember what they see by coding the information into images and rehearsing. Third, they must convert the information into action, or *produce* it, for which feedback is helpful. Finally, they must be *motivated* to imitate it, because it leads to a desired outcome.

Visit the Education CourseMate for *Educational Psychology* to access study tools and resources including the Virtual Psychology Labs, TeachSource Video Cases, chapter web links, tutorial quizzes, glossary flashcards, and more. Go to CengageBrain.com to register using your access code.

7 | Cognitive Approaches to Learning

Digital Vision/Jupiter Images

After reading this chapter, you should be able to meet the following learning objectives	Chapter Contents
LEARNING OBJECTIVE 1 Distinguish between behaviorism and cognitivism.	Introduction: Comparing Behaviorism and Cognitivism
LEARNING OBJECTIVE 2 Outline and illustrate a three-stage information processing model, including sensory register, short-term memory, and long-term memory.	A Three-Stage Information Processing Model • Sensory Register • Short-Term Memory • Long-Term Memory
LEARNING OBJECTIVE 3 Define and differentiate types of semantic networks that are made up of units of declarative and procedural knowledge, and schemata.	Semantic Encoding • Semantic Networks • Schemata
LEARNING OBJECTIVE 4 Summarize and contrast the factors that affect memorization: meaningfulness, serial position, practice, organization, transfer and interference, and mnemonics.	Factors Affecting Memorizing • Meaningfulness • Serial Position • Practice • Organization • Transfer and Interference • Mnemonic Devices
LEARNING OBJECTIVE 5 Explain the cognitive strategies that affect meaningful learning: abstracting, elaborating, schematizing, organizing, questioning, and notetaking.	Cognitive Strategies Affecting Meaningful Learning • Abstracting • Elaborating • Schematizing • Organizing • Questioning • Notetaking
LEARNING OBJECTIVE 6 Explain three instructional techniques that enhance the meaningfulness of text: advance organizers, signals, and adjunct questions.	Instructional Techniques to Enhance the Meaningfulness of Text • Advance Organizers • Signals • Adjunct Questions
LEARNING OBJECTIVE 7 Outline and illustrate the metacognitive strategies of planning, monitoring, affecting, and evaluating.	Metacognitive Strategies • Goal Setting/ Planning • Monitoring • Affecting • Evaluating
LEARNING OBJECTIVE 8 Describe combinations of the above that constitute study skills.	Study Skills

What a Memory!

Arindam had a very fine memory, especially when it came to numbers. He could read or hear phone numbers once and remember them. You could give him a long list of numbers, he would study them for a few minutes, and then be able to repeat them all from memory in exactly the same order as they had been given to him. He contended that his father could remember numbers even better than he could when he was younger, but now at 17, Arindam claimed he could remember numbers better than his father. He pointed out, though, that his father rarely tried to remember numbers while he, Arindam, had made a hobby of trying to remember them, and practiced remembering them relentlessly. He had a technique he used where he practiced trying to actually see the numbers visually, like they were written on a chalkboard. He said that while he sometimes did it to impress people, he mostly did it for a more practical reason, to do well on tests.

- What do you do to help yourself remember information for a test?
- As a teacher, how would you help your students improve their memories?

Lessons We Can Learn from the Story In this chapter, we will encounter a variety of cognitive approaches to learning, one of which is "factors affecting memorizing." One of the factors affecting memorizing that you will read about later in the chapter is "practice." Arindam, in the above story, had a natural talent for remembering, but he enhanced his talent by doing a considerable amount of practice. Before we get to the topic of memorizing, we will contrast behavioral and cognitive learning and examine some of the basic aspects of cognition.

Learning how to behave in a classroom is based on experiencing or observing the different consequences that result from behaving in different ways, and subsequently behaving in those ways that yield the most desirable consequences. This is the behavioral approach to learning, typically used to manage classroom behavior so that the desired behaviors will occur automatically (Landrum & Kauffman, 2006). In contrast, the cognitive approach typically is used to teach students the thinking, remembering, and self-monitoring skills that enable them to reason and solve problems (Boekaerts, Pintrich, & Zeidner, 2000). In the previous chapter, you learned about the behavioral approach to learning. In this chapter, you will learn about the cognitive approach to learning. You can expect to use both in your future classrooms.

Learning Objective 1

Distinguish between behaviorism and cognitivism.

behaviorism

focuses on teaching behaviors on the basis of the situation in which they will be performed and the consequences that follow

cognitivism

focuses on teaching students the thinking, remembering, and self-monitoring skills that enable them to reason and solve problems

Introduction: Comparing Behaviorism and Cognitivism

It is important to look at **behaviorism**, covered in the preceding chapter, and **cognitivism**, covered in this chapter, as alternative but not necessarily exclusive, ways of learning. In other words, people learn some things better one way than the other. It would not be efficient for all learning to require memorizing or reasoning, cognitive processes, when a learned behavior will be repeated frequently. The behavioral approach focuses on teaching behaviors on the basis of the situation in which they will be performed and the consequences that follow. Students learn, for example, to raise their hands in class and be recognized before speaking, because this behavior results in satisfactorily gaining the teacher's attention. Most students have learned this behavior to a sufficient degree that they do not have to picture it from memory or reason it out every time they want to speak in class. Behavioral learning principles have been shown to be relevant for school learning (Dempster & Corkill, 1999).

On the other hand, some behaviors require students to use memorizing or reasoning. Solving a mathematics problem, for example, requires that students reason out the particular steps they will have to use to solve the problem. They have to think about what kind of a problem it is, and how one goes about solving that kind of problem. Students learn to solve mathematics problems by learning different problem-solving procedures and learning how to determine which one to use to solve a particular problem (Bransford et al., 1996).

Memorizing is another form of cognitive learning. Our consideration of cognitive factors that impact learning will begin with memorizing, or most typically, learning by repetition. For example, saying something over and over to oneself, called *vocalization* or rehearsal, places its greatest reliance on short-term or working memory. Many kinds of information are likely learned this way, especially in preparation for tests. In this chapter, *The Memory Experiment*, an example of learning by memorizing, will be used extensively to illustrate the various factors that affect the ability to learn by this way. You are invited to take *The Memory Experiment* presented in Box 7.1.

AN EXAMPLE TO AID UNDERSTANDING   **Box 7.1**

The Memory Experiment

To illustrate a number of the factors that influence memory, we are going to start out this chapter with an experiment, called "the memory experiment." You need to do this experiment right now, before you read this chapter. It will be referred to in a number of places throughout this chapter. Make sure to keep a record of your results so you can see for yourself how memory works.

To prepare for this experiment, take a piece of paper and write the numbers 1 through 12 down the left side. Draw a vertical line just to the right of the numbers and then draw four more vertical lines so the paper is divided up into four columns. Now you are going to test yourself to see how well you can remember each of four lists of words. Each list has 12 words and you must study each list for exactly *10 seconds*. The lists each appear at the top left-hand margin of each of the next four left-hand pages.

When you are ready to start, turn to page 274 and look at your watch. Then study the list of words at

the top left corner of the page for **exactly 10 seconds**. (You may need to have a friend or roommate do the timing.) At the end of 10 seconds, turn back to this page and, in the first column on your lined sheet of paper, write down as many of the words as you can remember. Then turn to the second list on page 276 and repeat the procedure; do the same with the third list on page 278, and finally the fourth and last list on page 280.

When you have tested yourself on ALL four lists, compare the printed lists to your own, and write down at the bottom of each column on your paper the number of words that you have correctly remembered (regardless of order). Remember, you should do this experiment before you read this chapter. Then, when you read the text, you will realize exactly what this experiment is all about. Are you ready? Have you numbered and lined your paper? Do you have a stopwatch or a timer? OK, GO.

List 1

gis

dep

tir

bez

yad

kol

wuk

jov

puh

hab

mij

lec

Learning Objective 2

Outline and illustrate a three-stage information processing model, including sensory register, short-term memory, and long-term memory.

semantic encoding
storing information in a retrievable form

modal model
(1) entry via a sensory register, which is also referred to as perception; (2) storage in short-term memory; and (3) storage in long-term memory

sensory register
sensory memory

perception
detection

short-term memory
information a person focuses on and chooses to retain at least for a short period of time

A Three-Stage Information-Processing Model

The processing of, or acting on, incoming information to the brain is not a single-step process. The information must first "get into" the brain and then must be kept or stored in the brain through a process called memory. Furthermore, it must be stored in such a way that it can be recalled or retrieved. Storing information in a retrievable form has been called **semantic encoding** by Gagne (1985) and others. "Semantic" refers to words, and "encoding" to classifying or labeling an idea or concept in order to remember it. For example, if you wanted to remember what a reflex is, you could associate it with the words "rubber hammer," based on the doctor making your knee jump by hitting it with a rubber hammer. This would enable you to remember that a reflex was an involuntary action.

Three stages of information processing have been widely proposed. See, for example, Healy & McNamara (1996) who refer to it as the **modal model**. These stages are (1) entry via a sensory register, which is also referred to as perception; (2) storage in short-term memory; and (3) storage in long-term memory. In this section, we will examine each of the three stages.

Sensory Register

The information we attend to and perceive with our eyes and ears is registered or received in our thinking process. It is then stored, temporarily, in our **sensory register**, or sensory memory, before transferred to short-term memory for temporary retention. It is in the sensory register that **perception**, or detection, takes place along with pattern recognition and the assignment of meaning. The first step is detecting the stimulus, that is, seeing and/or hearing it, followed by briefly storing it. Then, based on what information we already possess, we recognize the stimulus and determine what it means. If you carried out *The Memory Experiment* (Box 7.1, on page 273) as you studied each word list you were committing them to your sensory register, or sensory memory, for initial perceptual processing (along with any markings in the book that you or others have made and any background sounds, such as conversation or TV, that might be going on while you study).

We have a visual sensory register and an auditory one, enabling us to register both incoming sights and sounds. Both enable us to retain environmental information, after it has disappeared, for about half a second in the visual register (Chase; 1987) and three seconds in the auditory register (Hawkins & Presson, 1987). This suggests that if we are teaching, we limit the amount of information we present at one time and present that information so that it can be seen and heard. Using visual aids in conjunction with verbal presentation is recommended.

Short-Term Memory

Information a person focuses on and chooses to retain enters into **short-term memory**, at least for a brief period of time. Unfortunately, short-term memory has a limited capacity (though not as limited as sensory memory). If someone is introduced to six people at a party, he or she may remember the names of only a few of

We temporarily store information in our sensory register, the place where patterns are recognized and meaning is assigned.

them. Of course, part of the problem may be attention. George Miller (1956) has shown that the capacity of short-term memory is about seven units of information. Of the twelve "words" on the first list in *The Memory Experiment* (actually they were not words but so-called nonsense syllables—two consonants separated by a vowel), you probably were able to remember about seven of them, the limit of your short-term memory. Even though you may have repeated the list over and over to yourself in the 10-second period—an encoding strategy known as **rehearsal**—this would enable you to reach only the upper limit of your short-term memory, again about seven or eight units of information.

However, people can expand their short-term memory capacity by increasing the size of each unit of information. This involves an encoding strategy called **chunking**. The last list in *The Memory Experiment* is an example of chunking. It combines an entire list of words into a meaningful chunk or sentence, so it can be remembered along with six or seven more chunks, or sentences.

We can store information for longer periods in short-term memory through (1) chunking, that is, by connecting smaller pieces together to make larger pieces; or (2) continuous, or repeated, rehearsal. For example, if you repeat a phone number you heard at a party, you can remember it until you get home and write it down; you can remember phone numbers you call frequently; you can remember phone numbers more easily if you can connect the numbers together.

Short-term memory is called by some researchers **working memory** (Baddeley, 2001). It is the place where newly registered information is mixed with previously learned information during reading, thinking, and problem solving. People with good short-term memories can shift their focus repeatedly from reading to thinking without having to reread the previous material to remember the gist of it. This is a major difference between skilled and unskilled readers (Chall, 1983).

Virtual Psychology Lab

How can a student best use his or her short-term memory, despite its limited capacity? Teachers are also often confronted by this problem. But there are ways that both students and teachers can overcome this problem. Go to the *Memory Span Virtual Psychology Lab* to test your own short-term memory. What memory-enhancing techniques do you use? Go to CengageBrain.com to access this Virtual Psychology Lab in the Education CourseMate.

rehearsal

an encoding strategy utilizing repetition

chunking

combining an entire list into a meaningful chunk, so it can be remembered along with six or seven more chunks

working memory

the place where newly registered information is mixed with previously learned information during reading, thinking, and problem solving

List 2

pen
our
whom
can
has
boy
fast
too
spam
run
foot
wing

Long-Term Memory

Information that must be remembered for longer periods of time is transferred to **long-term memory** where it may remain for most of a person's life. Two types of long-term memory have been distinguished (Tulving, 2002): semantic and episodic. **Semantic memory** is memory of facts, concepts, and principles such as the meanings of words, locations of cities, and formulas for solving physics problems. **Episodic memory**, alternatively, is memory of life experiences such as the clothes you wore yesterday, a particular conversation with your roommate, or what you did on your last birthday. In addition to these **explicit memory** forms, there are **implicit memories** (Schacter, 2000) of which we are not consciously aware but can influence our actions, such as tying our shoes without even thinking about it. Implicit memory represents an additional type of long-term memory, separate from the two explicit types.

Learning Objective 3

Define and differentiate types of semantic networks that are made up of units of declarative and procedural knowledge, and schemata.

Semantic Encoding

The process of long-term memory storage is called **semantic encoding**, because many psychologists believe that what is stored is not the information itself but some more efficient verbal representation of it. Thus, people do not usually store information in long-term memory by rehearsal or repetition, as was true for short-term memory, but by transforming the information into meaningfully and purposefully connected verbal chunks that have been referred to as **semantic networks** (E.D. Gagne, Yekovich & Yekovich, 1993). (An example of such a semantic network is shown in Figure 7.1.) You can learn more about semantic networks in Chapter 12.

FIGURE 7.1

An Example of a Single Propositional Network

(The Network is composed of two propositions that share the element *Ralph*) From E. M. Gagné, C. W. Yekovich, & F. R. Yekovich, 1993, p. 67.

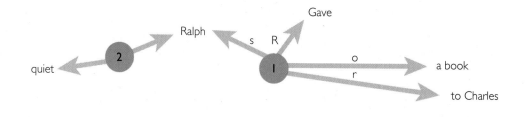

Semantic Networks

A semantic network is a set of interconnected and interrelated ideas in which one idea or element of an idea can trigger the memory of another idea. Entire sets of knowledge can be organized into such networks of ideas with common or shared elements. In this way, all of the ideas do not have to be in short-term or working memory but can still be accessible to it.

The ideas formed into semantic networks may be of three types (E.D. Gagne et al., 1993; Bruning, Schraw, Norby & Ronning, 2004): (1) **propositions**, or units of declarative knowledge, that is, knowledge about facts; (2) **productions**, or units of procedural knowledge, that is, knowledge about operations or how to do something; (3) **conditional knowledge**, that is, knowing when and why to use declarative and procedural knowledge. For example, the knowledge that the words *was* and *were* are verbs is declarative knowledge, whereas knowing which form of the verb to use with the singular pronoun *I* is procedural knowledge, and why to use that particular form of the verb rather than another is conditional knowledge. Verbal statements to describe a skill would be declarative knowledge, while performing a skill without having to verbalize what you are doing would represent procedural knowledge, and when to use the skill, conditional knowledge (Anderson, J.R., 2000). We can represent procedural knowledge as productions that are IF–THEN statements. An example: IF the subject of the sentence is "I," THEN use the verb form "was." If the subject is "you," THEN use "were."

Schemata

So far, only semantic networks of propositions and productions have been described as a means of representing or encoding information in long-term memory. An alternative form of long-term knowledge representation are schemata (the plural of schema). A **schema** is a mental image or code that can be used to organize or structure information and control its encoding, storage, and retrieval (Marshall, 1995; Bruning et al., 2004). (Refer, also, to pages 46–47 in Chapter 2 for Piaget's description of a schema.) Schemata help students determine the meaning of what they read. The value of using the right schema is illustrated in the paragraph below. Read it and try to figure out what it is about:

> With hocked gems financing him, our hero bravely defied all scornful laughter that tried to prevent his scheme. "Your eyes deceive" he had said, "an egg not a table correctly typifies this unexplored planet." Now three sturdy sisters sought proof, forging along sometimes through calm vastness, yet more often over turbulent peaks and valleys. Days became weeks as many doubters spread fearful rumors about the edge. At last from nowhere welcome-winged creatures appeared signifying momentous success. (Dooling & Lachman, 1971, p. 217)

Now that you have read it, cover it up and try to remember what it said and what it meant. Did it sound to you like it was about "Star Wars"? In fact, it was not, but in your effort to make sense out of it, you had to search for the right schema that would enable you to decode and then encode the content. The real title of the

long-term memory
where information that must be remembered for longer periods of time is stored

semantic memory
memory of facts, concepts, and principles

episodic memory
memory of life experiences

explicit memory
memories of which we are aware

implicit memories
memories of which we are not consciously aware but can influence our actions

semantic encoding
process of long-term memory storage

semantic networks
transforming information into meaningfully and purposefully connected verbal chunks

propositions
knowledge about facts

productions
knowledge about operations or how to do something

conditional knowledge
knowing when and why to use declarative and procedural knowledge

schema
a mental image or code that can be used to organize or structure information and control its encoding, storage, and retrieval

List 3

kitchen

house

door

attic

wall

stair

room

window

roof

garage

bath

floor

Summarize and contrast the factors that affect memorization: meaningfulness, serial position, practice, organization, transfer and interference, and mnemonics.

paragraph is "Christopher Columbus Discovering America." Does it make more sense when you have the right schema to process it? Can you remember it better? Most people answer yes to both questions (Dooling & Lachman, 1971).

Some theorists (for example, Paivio, 1971, 1986) contend that information is stored in long-term memory as *both* a semantic network (verbally) and a schema (images). This is called the **dual-coding theory**. The advantage of a dual code is that, if one form is lost or forgotten, the other will still remain. In other words, two memories are better than one.

Factors Affecting Memorizing

Several factors affect memorizing, all of which can be brought to bear in your classroom with your students. This section is a toolbox to draw from in your teaching, as you and your students need and require.

Meaningfulness

The more meaningful information is, the easier it is to memorize and retain. In addition, the more meaningful information can be made to be, the easier it will be to memorize and retain. In *The Memory Experiment*, this point is best illustrated by a comparison of your results on Lists 1 and 2. List 1 is made up of nonsense syllables (consonant—vowel—consonant nonwords). Nonsense syllables are meaningless. List 2 is made up of real words; words have meaning. Therefore, List 2 should be easier to remember than List 1, and you should have correctly recalled more words from List 2 than from List 1. Also, the "Christopher Columbus" story should be more easily remembered after you have figured out or discovered the right schema, because the right schema helps give the paragraph meaning.

The memorability of information, such as a list of words, can be increased if you substitute more familiar, concrete words for unfamiliar, abstract words (Wittrock, Marks, & Doctorow, 1975). When you have new material to learn that involves new terminology or vocabulary, try to link the new terms to older, more familiar ones to make them easier to remember. Pictorial illustrations can also help students improve their learning from text (Carney & Levin, 2002).

Serial Position

Serial position effects result from the location of an item in a list, whether at the beginning, the middle, or the end. (These might also be called *sequence* effects.) Those items that come first tend to be remembered best (called the **primacy effect**), as do those that come last (the **recency effect**), while those in the middle are least remembered (Storandt, Kaskie, & Von Dras, 1998). When you are introduced to a group of people you do not know, you tend to "catch" the names of only the first few and last few people, while "losing" those in the middle. There is definitely a memory advantage for items having nothing before them (like those that come at the beginning) or nothing after them (like those at the end) over items surrounded

dual-coding theory

theory that information is stored in long-term memory as both a semantic network and a schema

primacy effect

items that come first tend to be remembered best

recency effect

items that come last tend to be remembered best

by other items (like those coming in the middle). There may well be less interference at the two ends of a list than in the middle.

Go back to your results in *The Memory Experiment*. Chances are you always got the first two words on each list right, as the result of primacy. See if you also got the last two words on each list right. Chances are you did not. Sometimes more time is spent studying the beginning of a list at the expense of the words at the end, thereby giving the first few words the benefits of both primacy and recency. Remember, whatever is focused on last has the benefit of recency. If you practiced the list one and a half times, for example, the words in the middle would have been practiced most recently. Whatever word you had reached when you stopped would have the benefit of recency.

Practice

Practice may not necessarily make perfect but, in general, the more people practice the more they remember (Willingham, 2004). Ericsson (1996) has shown, for example, that the more deliberate practice one engages in (including teachers), the better one gets, regardless of initial level of ability, and that initial differences between people decrease over time as a function of practice. In the case of *The Memory Experiment*, if you were given 20 seconds to practice the words rather than 10 seconds, you would have remembered more words—although not necessarily twice as many. The corollary to this rule would be that the more you study, or the more times you read the assignment, the more you will remember.

However, there are two types of practice: **massed practice**, which is continuous, nonstop practice, and **distributed practice**, or practice spread over time with rest periods interspersed. When you study all night before an exam, you are engaging in massed practice. When you study two hours each night during the week before the exam, you are engaging in distributed practice.

Distributed practice has been shown to be more efficient than massed practice (Ashcraft, 1994; Mumford, Costanza, Baughman, Threlfall, & Fleischman, 1994), perhaps because it allows for the dissipation of fatigue, but also because it allows you to make associations or connections to more than one context (Glenberg, 1976). The implication is that "cramming" is a poor way to study because it represents massed practice. Frequent but short practice sessions with breaks in between will likely lead to better memorization of information. In *The Memory Experiment*, the instructions were intended to keep the amount and the type of practice constant.

Mika/Comet/Corbis

Practice contributes to memory. Going over or rehearsing key information before a test will make it easier to remember later. But practice should be spread out or distributed over time, not all crammed into the night before the test.

Think It Over

as a LEARNER	Think about your own study habits. Do you tend to use massed practice or distributed practice? Describe an experience you had when you actually used one or the other. Why did you choose to do it that way?
as a TEACHER	What would be a good way to get your students to use distributed, rather than massed, practice?

massed practice
continuous, nonstop practice

distributed practice
practice spread over time with rest periods interspersed

List 4
Charles
first
cousin
was
once
town
mayor
after
winning
the
close
election

Organization

Remember from an earlier discussion that short-term memory was reported to have a capacity limited to about seven units of information. However, if several pieces of information can be organized into a single unit by means of a technique such as chunking, then more pieces of information can be remembered.

Consider Lists 3 and 4 in *The Memory Experiment*. The words in List 3 all relate to the same topic, the house, so they possess some degree of topical organization or **semantic organization** by virtue of their common meaning. The words in List 4 have an even greater degree of organization. They form a sentence that provides **structural organization** so that each word can be directly connected to the words immediately before and after it. List 4 can be considered a single chunk, so it should be the easiest of all four lists to remember.

Your own performance on the four lists, therefore, should have become progressively better from List 1 to List 4 because the lists increase progressively in both meaningfulness and organization. These are two of the important factors that affect learning by memorizing.

Taylor and Samuels (1983) have shown that children who are aware that reading material has been structured into main idea plus supporting detail can remember it better than children who are not aware of the text structure. For another example of the effect of organization on the ability to remember, see Box 7.2 (on page 282).

Transfer and Interference

Transfer is the effect of prior learning on new learning. New information is easier to learn when other information has already been learned that has much in common with the new information. The atomic weights of elements in chemistry will be easier for students to learn once they have learned the atomic numbers, because the two sets of information have some commonalities. This is called **positive transfer**. However, sometimes prior learning makes new learning more difficult, as in learning to read Greek after learning English. Because some Greek letters look like the English letters to which they correspond (*A* and *Alpha,* for example), there will be positive transfer. But some Greek letters look like English letters to which they do not correspond (*Rho*, the Greek letter *R*, looks like a *P*), so there will also be significant **negative transfer**. Another example of negative transfer would be changing from driving a car with an automatic transmission to one with a manual shift, and forgetting to push down on the clutch before changing gears.

While transfer has to do with the effect of prior experience on learning something new, **interference** has to do with forgetting something as a result of receiving new information. Interference, as the name implies, does not have a positive side and a negative side, only a negative one. New information forces old information out of short-term memory, making the older information harder to remember. Hence, what is being learned may interfere with the ability to remember what has already been learned (although it may transfer positively—that is, help what will be learned next).

To prove this to yourself, take out a piece of paper and write down as many words as you can remember from List 2 of *The Memory Experiment*. If you are like

semantic organization

items are related by virtue of their common meaning

structural organization

each word can be directly connected to the words immediately before and after it

positive transfer

new information is easier to learn when other information has already been learned that has much in common with the new information

negative transfer

new information is harder to learn when other information has already been learned that conflicts with the new information

interference

forgetting something as a result of receiving new information

most people, you will remember fewer words than you did originally because what you have learned since then has interfered with your memory of List 2.

Let's say you are trying to remember a list of numbers, such as a telephone number, and a friend teases you by repeating random numbers aloud. The new numbers tend to interfere with the old ones, and may make you forget the phone number you are trying to remember or cause you to insert new, incorrect numbers so that you remember it incorrectly. When interference works backward like this, it is called **retroactive interference**. If, on the other hand, you are trying to remember a phone number and then you hear a second phone number and try to remember it as well, the first number may interfere with the second. This interference, working forward, would be called proactive. **Proactive interference** can also be considered negative transfer.

Because memorizing depends so greatly on short-term memory, transfer effects will likely be negative and interference effects will likely be frequent. In massed practice situations, such as cramming for a test, last chapter's notes will negatively transfer to memorizing this chapter's notes (which is proactive), and memorizing this chapter's notes will interfere with remembering last chapter's notes (which is retroactive). In trying to minimize negative transfer and interference effects, it is helpful to (1) space out or distribute practice, (2) focus on meaningful learning (the subject of the next section of this book) rather than memorizing, and (3) use mnemonic devices—the topic we will cover next.

Mnemonic Devices

Mnemonic devices are techniques or "tricks" for aiding memory by associating less meaningful material with more meaningful or more memorable images, words, or sayings. Think about how you were taught to remember the musical notes that appear on the *lines* of the staff in treble clef. It may have been by being taught using the **first-letter method** (Boltwood & Blick, 1978) via the mnemonic *Every Good Boy Does Fine*, whose first letters correspond to the notes: EGBDF. Chances are, you will remember this for the rest of your life because of the ease of learning and remembering the mnemonic phrase.

One of the most popular mnemonic techniques is the **peg method**, a useful way to remember numbered items in a list. Create the image of a rhyming word for each number and then form an image that combines the rhyming-word image with the word to be remembered. This technique is illustrated in Box 7.3. The rhyming words serve as the "pegs" or "hooks" on which the numbered words to be remembered are "hung." To use this technique you need to create and commit to memory a set of peg words and images that you are sure you can remember.

A popular and powerful mnemonic technique for remembering vocabulary words or words in a foreign language is the **keyword method** (Carney & Levin, 2000). In this method, students are given a keyword that sounds like the word to be learned, and an interacting image to combine the keyword and the definition of the word to be learned. In a study by Levin, McCormick, Miller, Berry, and Pressley (1982), fourth-grade students were given pictures with dialogue that showed, for example, a woman trying to talk a friend into or *persuade* (the vocabulary word) her to buy a *purse* (the keyword). These students were considerably more likely

retroactive interference

new information interferes with old information, causing the old information to be remembered incorrectly

proactive interference

old information interferes with new information, causing the new information to be remembered incorrectly

first-letter method

using the first letters of words to create a mnemonic phrase that helps you remember something

peg method

creating the image of a rhyming word for each of the numbered items in a list and then forming an image that combines the rhyming-word image with the word to be remembered

keyword method

giving a keyword that sounds like the word to be learned, and an interesting image to combine the keyword and the definition of the word to be learned, in order to remember it

The Chess Masters Study

DeGroot (1965) conducted a classic study using a group of people who were among the best chess players in the world. These people had qualified as chess masters by earning victory points in national and international competitions. In this study, they played not against other chess masters but against amateurs, except they played against a number of amateurs at the same time. (You may have heard of such demonstrations, where one master plays a number of chess matches simultaneously against local chess enthusiasts. The master walks up and down along a row of tables with an active chess game going on at each table. The idea is for the master to try to win every game.)

In the experiment, the masters were taken out of the room in the middle of the games and asked to correctly recall the location of the chess pieces on every board. The masters were remarkably accurate in their recall, much more so than the amateurs.

Then, on another trial of the experiment, the chess pieces were placed on the board randomly rather than in the positions they would take as the result of actual moves. Suddenly, the masters had lost their advantage. Their recall of the random boards was no better than that of the amateurs.

Why could the masters remember the real boards so much better than the random ones? Obviously, it could not be a function of how good their memories were or they would have remembered both equally; rather, it seemed to depend on how they used their memories. It appeared that the masters "had recognized the structure of pieces on the board, coded it in memory in terms of the pattern, and used the coded pattern as the recall cue" (Taylor & Samuels, 1983, p. 518). In other words, the masters used their vast knowledge of the game to *chunk* the many pieces into a smaller, more memorable, number of units.

Jim Commentucci/Syracuse Newspapers/The Image Works

These kids aren't chess masters yet, but the more experience they have playing the game, the better they will get at remembering the location of the pieces on the board, by remembering patterns or "chunks."

BOX 7.3

TAKE IT TO THE CLASSROOM

A Mnemonic System for Remembering Numbers (Middle School/High School)

1. WAND picture of wand
2. TOOL picture of hammer
3. TREE picture of tree
4. FORE! picture of golfer saying 'fore'
5. FIFE picture of fife
6. SICK picture of sick boy
7. CHEVRON picture of gas station emblem
8. APE picture of ape
9. NEON SIGN picture of neon 'motel' sign
10. TIN (CAN) picture of can of peas w/lid open

If you need to remember, for example, that the fourth item in a list is the word "can" (see List 2 on page 276 in The Memory Experiment), visualize a golfer hitting a soda can (instead of a golf ball) and shouting "Fore!" Images of action that connect the above "number pictures" with "pictures" of the words or ideas to be remembered make the connections easer to code into long-term memory.

- How can you, as a student, utilize this mnemonic system as a tool for studying?

- As a teacher, how would you illustrate to your students how this system can be used?

to remember the definitions than other fourth graders who were given only the definitions.

Research, like that, has shown that mnemonic techniques that rely on images to connect old words to new words make those new words easier to remember than they would be without the mnemonic images (McDaniel & Pressley, 1984; Pressley & Woloshyn, 1995). This reflects the dual-coding theory (coding both by words and images) previously described. See Table 7.1 for a *Concept Review* of factors affecting memorizing.

C O N C E P T   R E V I E W   T A B L E   7 . 1
Factors Affecting Memorizing

FACTOR	HOW IT WORKS	APPLICATION
Meaningfulness	The more meaningful information is, the easier it is to remember.	Substitute more familiar, concrete words for less familiar, abstract ones.
Serial Position	Words coming first and last are most remembered; those in-between are least remembered.	Spend the same amount of time studying each word on the list, regardless of location.
Practice	The more you practice, the better you remember and perform.	Distribute your practice over time; do not do it all at once.
Organization	Organizing information into blocks enables you to remember more.	Use chunking: combine individual units of information into blocks.
Transfer and Interference	Transfer is the effect of prior learning on new learning. Interference is the effect of new learning on prior learning.	Transfer can be positive or negative, so try to use prior learning in a positive way. Interference is always negative so try to write information down.

(Continued)

CONCEPT REVIEW TABLE 7.1
Factors Affecting Memorizing

FACTOR	HOW IT WORKS	APPLICATION
Mnemonic Devices	These are "tricks" for aiding memory through association.	3 methods: first-letter, e.g., "**E**very **G**ood **B**oy **D**oes **F**ine"; peg (rhyming words for numbers; Box 7.3); keyword (fitting words with images and definitions).

Cognitive Strategies Affecting Meaningful Learning

Learning Objective 5

Explain the cognitive strategies that affect meaningful learning: abstracting, elaborating, schematizing, organizing, questioning, and notetaking.

Mrs. Patel is an English teacher in a rural junior high school. During the course of a school year, her eighth-grade students read a number of books, including *Huckleberry Finn* by Mark Twain and *Little Women* by Louisa May Alcott. Over half of her students tend to have trouble understanding the storylines of these books and the underlying meaning of much of what happens. They are particularly challenged by the essay tests they have to take on what they have read, in part because they have not learned how to separate out the main points from the details, or to take good notes on what they have read, or how to get information into long-term memory and then recall it. These are important strategies for learning and understanding what you have read. Mrs. Patel spends a good deal of time trying to impart these skills to her students and has found that when she is successful, it has opened a new world of opportunity for them. Think about books you have read in school that you felt you truly understood, and how, as a teacher, you could better help students understand what they read.

Meaningful learning, what Mrs. Patel was trying to foster, is less automatic than memorization. It requires that learners employ systematic processes or strategies for coding and storing information in long-term memory and for retrieving it, including strategies for selecting relevant information, and organizing and integrating it (Mayer, 2001). These strategies represent ways that learners can acquire thoughts rather than the thoughts themselves. Using these cognitive strategies alone, or in combination with metacognitive strategies (described later in this chapter) has been shown to facilitate student learning (Berthold, Nuckles, & Renkl, 2007). As you study the strategies described below, think about what

meaningful learning

requires that learners employ systematic processes or strategies for coding and storing information in long-term memory and for retrieving it, and organizing and integrating it

you might do to help your students with mental tasks like sorting main points from details.

Abstracting

Abstracting represents the technique of extracting the main point or gist of a passage or section of text, and we do it by skimming the passage for an overview and then writing down the phrase or sentence that best describes what the passage is about. The purpose of abstracting is to reduce the written material or text to an amount that can be understood and retained. Hence, the first principle for learning information from a book or article is to *reduce the information to a manageable amount by picking out the most essential elements*. The key ideas here are (1) to make more into less and (2) to have the "less" capture the essential meaning of the "more."

The product of abstracting is a **summary** of main points (hence, abstracting may also be called **summarizing**) that may be organized into an outline. This summary can sometimes be abstracted to form a shorter, more concise summary. The idea is to continually reduce information by making each summary "richer" in essential information than the one that preceded it. Creating a final product short enough to be contained within short-term memory would be a desirable result.

The idea of abstracting is somewhat analogous to creating a juice concentrate or freeze-dried coffee. Each represents the essence of what it started out as, but in considerably reduced form. However, importantly, the reduction has not been at the expense of essential ingredients; these have been retained. When the original substance is desired, water is added to the concentrate and, presto, the original is restored. With textbook information, for example, the essential parts can be abstracted to form a "knowledge" concentrate. Later, these bits of information can be expanded to reproduce a more detailed account of what has been read.

Elaborating

The **elaboration** strategy helps students understand and remember what they read (Willoughby et al., 1999). It is somewhat the opposite of abstracting in that it produces more information rather than less. However, the additional information produced is different from the original in that, by virtue of having been produced by the learner, it is clearer to him or her than the original. Moreover, the new version of the original idea or concept typically is more concrete, realistic, and familiar than the old, and often connects the material to ideas the student has already learned (Ayaduray & Jacobs, 1997). The elaboration can be an *example, illustration, drawing, analogy, metaphor,* or *rewriting* of the idea in the learner's own words. Weinstein and Mayer (1985) describe elaborating as making connections between new material and more familiar material.

A good example of elaborating appears in the preceding subsection under abstracting. In order to facilitate understanding of the idea or concept of abstracting, the metaphor of preparing food concentrates such as frozen juice or freeze-dried coffee was used. The idea of abstracting or *reducing* ideas to their essence was elaborated on in a different form in that it was likened to the idea of *reducing* food

abstracting

the technique of extracting the main point or gist of a passage or section of text, and we do it by skimming the passage for an overview and then writing down the phrase or sentence that best describes what the passage is about

summary

a brief description of main points that have been taken out or abstracted from text to form an outline

summarizing

the process of creating a summary

elaboration

the learner produces additional, original information about a topic to help understand what he/she learned

Students can draw a picture to help them understand something they are learning about. The process of adding information from your own head to help you learn about something new is called "elaboration."

Michael Newman/PhotoEdit

substances like juice or coffee to their *essences*. Presumably, the elaboration in the form of a metaphor or an analogy helped make the description of abstracting more understandable.

When text material is read, it must be understood if it is to be learned, expounded on, and used. Moreover, since there is invariably too much information to be memorized verbatim, it must be understood if it is ever to be reduced or abstracted into its essential points. For this reason, elaborating on each new point and relating new information to what is already in memory, called **elaborative encoding**, helps to ensure that it is understood and can be recalled later (Craik & Brown, 2000). This point is further supported by Weinstein (1982), who found that students trained in elaboration (including rewriting the author's explanations in their own words) did better on tests than students who were not given this training.

How would you elaborate on the concept of "elaborating"? Does it seem to you like stuffing a pillowcase to make a pillow, or is it more like the cuckoo bird that springs out of the clock so that you can hear the time in addition to seeing it? Is it the string you tie around your finger to help you remember something, or a pink elephant that can't be lost or hidden? Finding a way to help see a point increases the chances of both understanding it and remembering it. Maybe it is more like a bedtime story used to help children understand why they are punished. Or it might be like the electric bulb that goes off in someone's head when something difficult has finally been brought to "light." Note the many "boxes" in this book that are labeled "An Aid to Understanding." These boxes are there to help you apply the cognitive process of elaboration to your own learning of the material.

Make believe you are reading a story and you come to the following two sentences:
TIM WANTED A NEW MODEL AIRPLANE.
HE SAW THE CHANGE LYING ON HIS FATHER'S DRESSER.

elaborative encoding
elaborating on each new point and relating new information to what is already in memory

As you read these sentences, think of how you might elaborate on them. Write three or four more sentences that come into your head that help make these two sentences into a story. Then look below to see the elaborations that a researcher came up with.

Reder (1976, p. 394) came up with the following elaborations: "Tim is about 8 to 12, has a crew cut; the father's dresser is just at Tim's eye level; the model airplane is silver with chevron decals; the father is the absentminded type who would not notice the change missing but who would be furious if he found out his son took it."

Schematizing

As you will recall from earlier in the chapter (and in Chapter 2), schema is a framework or code for structuring information so that it can be both understood and stored in long-term memory. Mayer (2003) refers to a schema as a *general knowledge structure* that helps learners select and organize information into a meaningful framework. If information is schematized or coded, then when it is ready to be used, it can be found. Schemata, therefore, are a critical component of the cognitive process used in learning meaningful material. In fact, in abstracting, it is schemata that help to diagnose what the main points of the passage to be summarized are, and what information can be disregarded. Moreover, the purpose of elaborating is to try to find or uncover the proper schema to use in making sense out of or decoding the text. Schemata are like mental forms or templates or blueprints that are used to help us understand and retain what is learned.

Researchers like Anderson (1984) have discovered the importance of schemata. Most directly, schemata help learners to (1) understand what they read and (2) focus on the most important parts. Less obviously, schemata also help learners to (3) figure out what is implied but not directly said (in other words, read between the lines); (4) search through memory for what other information they must know in order to understand what is being read; (5) pick out the main points for long-term storage (which, as has already been said, is abstracting); and (6) fill in the gaps in memory when the main points are recalled later (a form of elaborating). Schemata, therefore, are important learning and thinking tools.

Some very important general schemata are used over and over to process information effectively. Sometimes these are referred to as **structures** because they help the reader to structure or interpret what has been read. Other times they are referred to as **levels of processing** because they help the reader go beneath the surface of the text to extract its true meaning (Bruning et al., 2004)

Meyer (1975; Meyer, Brandt & Bluth; 1980) has identified the following set of five structures (called *top-level structures*) that can be used for processing or schematizing text in order to extract the main point or meaning:

structures

schemata that help the reader to structure or interpret what has been read

levels of processing

schemata that help the reader go beneath the surface of the text to extract its true meaning

antecedent/consequent—structure that shows a cause-and-effect relationship between topics (for example, drinking before driving causes accidents);

comparison—points out similarities and differences between topics (for example, the effects of drinking and taking drugs on driving are similar);

collection—brings together and lists the components of a topic (for example, alcohol, marijuana, and cocaine are all mind-altering substances);

description—gives a general statement, along with supporting details or explanations (for example, the effect of drinking and driving is illustrated by the number of traffic fatalities in drunk driving cases); and

response—presents a problem and solution or question and answer (for example, government can solve the problem of drunk driving by making the penalties for it more severe).

To see how these five structures actually work, read the material in Box 7.4 and try to use each one of the five structures to describe the passage or some aspect of it. Then check your answers against those given at the end of Box 7.4.

The value of using the structures (or schemata) to process information is that it makes it possible to abstract the main point more easily and to code, store, and retrieve it in memory (Meyer, Brandt, & Bluth, 1980). Learning and remembering seem to work much better when there is a focus on exactly what is to be learned and

---

BOX 7.4

Did You Know? **The Supertanker Passage (High School)**

A problem of vital concern is the prevention of oil spills from supertankers. A typical supertanker carries a half-million tons of oil and is the size of five football fields. A wrecked supertanker spills oil in the ocean; this oil kills animals, birds, and microscopic plant life. For example, when a tanker crashed off the coast of England, more than 200,000 dead seabirds washed ashore. Oil spills also kill microscopic plant life that provides food for sea life and produces 70 percent of the world's oxygen supply. Most wrecks result from the lack of power and steering equipment to handle emergency situations, such as storms. Supertankers have only one boiler to provide power and one propeller to drive the ship.

The solution to the problem is not to immediately halt the use of tankers on the ocean, because about 80 percent of the world's oil supply is carried by supertankers. Instead, the solution lies in the training of officers of supertankers, better building of tankers, and installing ground control stations to guide tankers near shore. First, officers of supertankers must get top training in how to run and maneuver their ships. Second, tankers should be built with several propellers for extra control and backup boilers for emergency power. Third, ground control stations should be installed at places where supertankers come close to shore. These stations would act like airplane control towers, guiding tankers along busy shipping lanes and through dangerous channels.

- How would you use each of the five structures on pages 288–289 to describe some aspect of this passage? (Some sample answers appear below.)

Source: Meyer, B.J.F.; Brandt, D.M., & Bluth, G.J. (1980). Use of top-level structure in text: Key for reading comprehension of ninth-grade students. *Reading Research Quarterly*, 16, 72–103.

Structures illustrated for the Supertanker passage (Box 7.4):

antecedent/consequent: "Lack of power and steering in supertankers" *leads to* "oil spills?"

comparison: "Ground control stations for supertankers" *are similar to* "control towers for aircraft."

collection: *Three ways to improve supertankers safety are* "training officers," "building safer ships," *and* "installing ground control stations."

description: *The fact that* "oil spills kill wildlife" *is supported by the example* "that 200,000 seabirds died."

response: *The problem is* "that supertankers spill oil," *and the solution is* "to improve their safety."

Taken together, the five structures provide a reasonably complete account of the passage sections.

remembered, and when there is a mechanism, such as a structure or schema, that can be used to provide that focus.

Organizing

Organizing involves the learner imposing a structure on the material rather than trying to discover the "structures" within it. To organize the material in the form of a traditional **outline**, the reader subdivides it into sections and subsections. An additional feature of this imposed organization is that the parts, sections, or headings have a *hierarchical relationship*: Smaller parts fit into, or, when taken together, make up larger parts. For example, you should note how this book has been "organized!" The major headings are parts, which in turn are made up of chapters and then subtopic headings. Major chapter topic sections then have been further divided into subsections. You can get a "picture" of the organization of this or any book by looking at its table of contents.

In Chapter 12, you will be introduced to Gagné's learning hierarchies. These represent organizational structures that are derived from an analysis of a final or terminal learning task. The type of organization referred to here is a less formal one, in which the idea is simply to separate information into subsets that relate to a common point or idea. However, both Gagné's analytical approach to organization and the one here based on commonality of ideas are intended to make learning easier and more complete.

When information is organized, it is put into subsets, which enhances or adds to the capacity of working memory to store it. Glynn and DiVesta (1977) gave some college students the following outline before reading a passage on minerals:

I. Metals
    A. Rare metals
        1. Silver
        2. Gold
    B. Alloys
        1. Steel
        2. Brass

II. Stones
    A. Gemstones
        1. Diamonds
        2. Ruby

organizing

imposing a structure on the material rather than trying to discover the "structures" within it

outline

subdividing material into sections and subsections

B. Masonry stones
1. Granite
2. Marble

Other students read the passage without the outline. Afterward, both groups tried to recall what they had read. Both groups recalled general ideas equally well, but the group with the outline recalled specific details better than the group without it.

Sometimes the material to be learned is already well organized, in which case it will be easier to learn (Thorndyke, 1977). However, when it is not organized well enough to be clear, organizing or reorganizing it yourself will make it easier to understand and remember. Organizing or reorganizing textbook material is a way of chunking it and schematizing it to make it easier to process. Consider, for example, the Supertanker passage in Box 7.4. One way of organizing it is shown in Table 7.2.

In the next section of this chapter, we explore further the effects of organizing and organization as specific instructional aids in the construction of text.

Questioning

Rather than listening or reading passively, without active engagement with the material, a student can play an active role in extracting meaning from what is heard or read by **questioning**, that is, generating and answering relevant questions about the material. Often, students do this on their own as a way of providing themselves with **self-explanations** of what they read (Chi, Bassok, Lewis, Reimann & Glaser, 1989; Chi, 2000). Eighth-grade students who were prompted

questioning
generating and answering relevant questions about material

self-explanations
students providing themselves with explanations of what they read

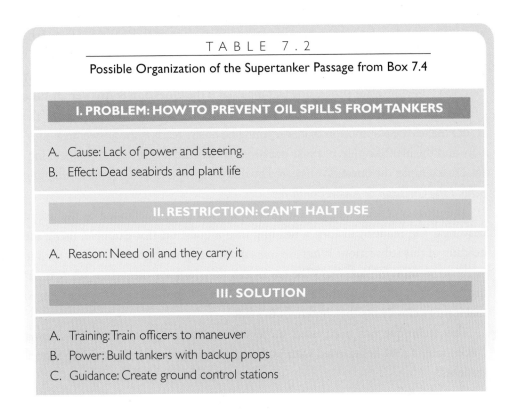

TABLE 7.2

Possible Organization of the Supertanker Passage from Box 7.4

I. PROBLEM: HOW TO PREVENT OIL SPILLS FROM TANKERS

A. Cause: Lack of power and steering.
B. Effect: Dead seabirds and plant life

II. RESTRICTION: CAN'T HALT USE

A. Reason: Need oil and they carry it

III. SOLUTION

A. Training: Train officers to maneuver
B. Power: Build tankers with backup props
C. Guidance: Create ground control stations

to use the technique of providing self-explanations to provide meaning for what they read developed a more accurate mental model of it than students who merely repeated each sentence after reading it (Chi, de Leeuw, Chiu, and LaVancher (1994).

Teaching self-questioning techniques to students has proved a good way to improve comprehension. In a review of 26 intervention studies, Rosenshine, Meister, and Chapman (1996) concluded that teaching students the cognitive strategy of generating questions as a means of improving their comprehension of material they had read led to greater gains in test performance than not teaching them this technique.

King (1992) taught college students how to use 13 general questions to process lecture content (notetaking with questions). The questions, using notetaking as the topic for illustrative purposes were: **Explain why** you should take notes. **Explain how** you should take notes. **What is the main idea of the** material you are taking notes about? **How would you use** notes to help you study for a test? **What is a new example of** the effect of taking notes? **What do you think would happen if** you didn't take notes? **What is the difference between** taking notes **and** just listening? **How are** notetaking and highlighting **similar? What conclusions can you draw about** notetaking? **How does** notetaking **affect** how you do on tests? **What are the strengths and weaknesses of** notetaking? **What is the best way** to take notes and **why? How is** notetaking **related to** questioning **that we studied earlier?** She then compared their performance to students who did notetaking with only a review of the same lecture material and found that the self-questioning group produced lecture notes with considerably more important ideas than the review group; they also did better on a comprehension test of the ideas contained in the lecture. She followed this up with a similar study using eighth graders taught a science lesson and again found better comprehension test performance by those trained to use the self-questioning technique.

A way of combining the questioning strategy with the organizing strategy described previously for processing text material is the **Question & Answer Outline** (Tuckman, 2003a, 2003b; Tuckman, Abry & Smith, 2008). In this approach, the reader makes the assumption that everything he or she reads is the answer to a question, and the identification of those questions makes the text information meaningful. For example, the question answered by this paragraph is: *What is the assumption behind the Question & Answer Outline?*

The process of identifying the appropriate questions is facilitated by the use of headings. The reader can turn a heading into a question (for example, using the heading of this subsection: *What are some questioning strategies that can be used to facilitate meaningful learning?*) The reader can then look for the answer while reading the section, and highlight it when found. Or if not found, revise the question so that it more closely fits the content of the text.

This technique has been used successfully with college students (Tuckman, 2003a) and is now being tried with high school students and even middle school students.

Think It Over

as a LEARNER	How do you go about studying the material you are supposed to learn? How do you study for a test? Which of the strategies described so far do you use, and how do you use them?
as a TEACHER	How would you teach your students to study or prepare for a test?

Notetaking

Notetaking is a technique for outlining or abstracting main ideas presented in a lecture or in written text (Mayer, 1984). It also includes the subcategories of highlighting and making notes in the margins, neither of which provides the same level of processing as notetaking, but both of which are more effective than passive reading. What advice can be given about notetaking? Armbruster and Brown (1984) suggest six rules for taking notes from written text that you might teach your students:

1. delete trivial material;
2. delete redundant material;
3. substitute a superordinate (that is, more inclusive) term for a list of subordinate items when possible;
4. substitute a superordinate event for a list of subordinate actions when possible;
5. select a topic sentence if the author has provided one; and
6. write your own topic sentence if necessary.

For example, rather than writing out in detail the three ways to solve the oil spill problem in the Supertanker passage (Box 7.4), you could list two superordinate (that is, more inclusive) terms to cover the three detailed statements. These would be *power* and *guidance*. Remembering these terms should then cue you to remember more of the detailed information in the passage.

When students take notes based on materials they read, is it better to copy statements from the book verbatim or to summarize the main ideas in their own words? Mayer (2003) reasoned that because summary notes require organizing and integrating the material, you would expect this approach to help students use the information to answer essay questions better than using verbatim notes. Indeed, summary notes were found to produce better answers to transfer questions than verbatim notes (Slotte and Lonka, 1999).

Another question is: How should students go about taking lecture notes? Carrier and Titus (1981) recommend they do the following:

1. distinguish between superordinate and subordinate information,
2. abbreviate words,
3. paraphrase in their own words, and
4. use an outline format.

notetaking

a technique for outlining or abstracting main ideas presented in a lecture or in written text

Taking notes on what the teacher says is one way students can assist in their own learning. It helps them organize and remember verbally presented information.

It is much more efficient to focus on capturing main ideas and distinguishing between major headings (superordinate information) and minor ones or details (subordinate information) than to try to take down verbatim everything the lecturer says (Kiewra, 1985; Keiwra and DuBois, 1998). It is also helpful to look and listen for schemata and structures, such as were presented on pages 288–289, to use in processing information. Another set of structures, described by Cook and Mayer (1988), can be very helpful in reading science texts. These structures are:

1. generalization (look for a main idea followed by an explanation, a clarification, or an extension of that idea);
2. enumeration (look for facts listed one after the other);
3. sequence (look for a connected series of events or steps in a process);
4. classification (look for material grouped into categories); and
5. comparison/contrast (look for the relationship between two or more things).

These structures can be used to organize the notes taken from course reading. They can also be used to organize lecture notes.

In regard to notetaking from either lecture or text, but particularly from lecture, it is highly advisable to go over notes as soon as possible after taking them and organize them so that they represent accurate, processed information rather than just raw input. Notes are not intended to be a "soundtrack." They should be information that has been processed in the ways described in this chapter. Tuckman, et al. (2008) recommend viewing items in notes as "answers" to "questions" that the lecturer had posed to him- or herself, and writing down alongside each item, the question for which it had been an answer. So, for example, if the note said "the issue of slavery was a major source of controversy leading up to the civil war," the question would be: "What was a major cause of the civil war?"

See Table 7.3 for a *Concept Review* of cognitive strategies affecting meaningful learning.

Explain three instructional techniques that enhance the meaningfulness of text: advance organizers, signals, and adjunct questions.

Instructional Techniques to Enhance the Meaningfulness of Text

According to Ausubel, "the most important factor influencing the meaningful learning of any new idea is the state of the individuals existing cognitive structure at the time of learning" (Ausubel & Robinson, 1969, p. 143). In other words, content presented in an organized, learnable form will be easiest for students to learn because it

CONCEPT REVIEW TABLE 7.3

Cognitive Strategies Affecting Meaningful Learning

FACTOR	HOW IT WORKS	APPLICATION
Abstracting	You can only understand and retain a limited amount of what you read.	Pick out the most essential information and summarize it.
Elaborating	When you add information to an idea, you can better understand and remember it.	Make up examples, analogies, or illustrations to help you understand new concepts.
Schematizing	A schema is like a file you use to store important information you want to remember.	Look for cause/effect relationships, comparisons, lists of items, descriptions, and solutions to problems to help you understand what you read.
Organizing	When information is organized, it is put into subsets, which enhances or adds to the capacity of working memory to store it.	Organize material into an outline to help you see the relationships between the parts.
Questioning	Teaching self-questioning techniques to students has proved a good way to improve comprehension.	Ask yourself questions about the material you are reading to increase your understanding.
Notetaking	This is a technique for outlining or abstracting main ideas presented in lecture or in written text.	Take notes based on materials you read and hear, and then summarize the main ideas in your own words.

will help provide them with the cognitive structure they need to satisfactorily process it. In this section, we will consider what some of the techniques might be for cognitively structuring text material to ensure that it will be meaningfully received and learned by students.

Advance Organizers

Advance organizers are previews or summaries provided at the beginning of the text (Ausubel, 1968) that characterize the purpose of the text and the approach taken to fulfill that purpose. Advance organizers relate to what students have already learned to help them look for the salient points in the new material. Advance organizers alert students to the cognitive structures or schemata that will be needed to process the new text information, and they do so in familiar terms (Derry, 1984). The organizational outline of the Supertanker passage shown in Table 7.1 would be a useful advance organizer for the passage itself because it not only summarizes the passage but provides an organizational structure for representing the meaning of the passage as well. Instructional objectives and concept maps that appear at the beginning of chapters also serve as effective advance organizers (Chmielewski & Dansereau, 1998).

Ausubel (1968) reported that advance organizers are especially valuable when the material to be learned is poorly organized and the students have limited ability, that is, they will have trouble organizing it themselves. In such cases, the material is more likely to go unorganized and hence unlearned without the assistance of advance organizers.

What makes the *best* organizers? According to Mayer (2003a), these include:

- concrete models (such as illustrations);
- analogies;
- examples (concrete ones work better than abstract ones; Corkhill, 1992);
- sets of general, higher-order rules; and
- discussions of main themes in familiar terms.

What makes the *worst* organizers? Mayer (2003a) says these include:

- specific factual pre-questions;
- outlines;
- summaries; and
- directions to pay attention to specific key facts or terms.

Signals

Signals are noncontent words placed within a passage to emphasize or call attention to either the organization or the meaning of a passage. If recognized, signals can cue the student to the most important points in the passage and their relationship to one another. Signals also represent what Skinner called (in Chapter 6) discriminative stimuli. Knowing the signals means knowing "when" to look and "what" to look for (Mautone & Mayer, 2001). According to Mayer (2003), the four major types of signals are:

1. cues to the structure of ideas in the passage and how they relate to one another ("the problem is" "the solution is" "first" "second" "third");
2. advance, abstracted statements of key information to follow ("the main ideas to be discussed in the chapter are");

---

advance organizers

previews or summaries provided at the beginning of the text that characterize the purpose of the text and the approach taken to fulfill that purpose

signals

noncontent words placed within a passage to emphasize or call attention to either the organization or the meaning of a passage

3. summary statements at the end of a passage, section, or chapter summarizing the main points ("the main points were"); and

4. pointer words that emphasize important information ("more importantly," "also," "for example").

Lorch (1989) extended this list to include *typographical cues* (underlining, boldface, italicizing, coloring, centering); *enumeration devices* (numbering or bulleting items in a list); and *headings* and *subheadings* (such as those used in the *Question & Answer Outline* discussed earlier in this chapter as a basis for identifying questions).

Reread the Supertanker passage in Box 7.4 and try to find the signals. Underline them. Note that the passage begins with "A problem of vital concern" and then states the solution. The second paragraph begins with "The solution to the problem" and then states what the solution "is not." It follows this with "Instead, the solution lies" and then states the solution. The details of the solution in the second paragraph are signaled by the words *first, second,* and *third.* In the first paragraph, details are signaled by the point words *for example* and *also.* If you can locate these eight signals, you can form an organized outline of the passage that contains its meaning.

Adjunct Questions

Adjunct questions are questions about the text material that are inserted into the text at the beginning of a section or chapter to serve the *forward* function of informing the reader in advance of what to pay attention to. These can also appear at the end of a section or chapter to serve the *backward* function of requiring the reader to go back and review what was already read. Hence, adjunct questions are intended to direct and increase the reader's attention, and to help him or her build internal connections such as between the main points and external connections such as applications (Mayer, 2003).

Adjunct questions can be test questions or question-based activities for the student to complete. It has been clearly shown that answering these questions or completing these activities helps students learn and remember what they have read (Reynolds & Anderson, 1982).

A major issue is the placement of adjunct questions in the text, whether at the beginning of the passage (i.e., **pre-questions**) or the end (i.e., **post-questions**). In a classic study, Rothkopf (1966) found that *intentional learning* (i.e., learning on purpose) was improved by questions in either location, while *incidental learning* (i.e., unintended learning) was improved only by questions at the end. Compared to those at the beginning, questions at the end of a segment or section are less likely to narrow the reader's focus and are more likely to enable them to encode the material in their own words (Sagaria & DiVesta, 1978).

Pre-questions, as we have already discussed, can serve as advance organizers; as such, they should be as general as possible and focus on the main points of the material. Their purpose is to prepare students for the information to follow by providing structures and schemata to process it. The questions at the end

Tom & Dee Ann McCarthy/Encyclopedia/CORBIS

When you read a textbook, you may find questions to answer at the beginning of a chapter or the end of a chapter. These "adjunct questions" are placed in the textbook to help students pay attention to certain ideas or remember what they have read.

adjunct questions

questions about the text material that are inserted into the text at the beginning or end of a section or chapter to serve the forward function of informing the reader in advance of what to pay attention to serve a different purpose. They are most valuable when they direct attention to points typically misunderstood, that is, to so-called student misconceptions (McConkie, 1977).

Answering questions at the end of an instructional unit can help the student to (1) recall information explicitly stated in the text, (2) make appropriate inferences that go beyond but are based on information stated, and (3) activate schemata to draw conclusions about related issues that are neither included nor implied in the text (Wixson, 1984). This activity is most successful when text designers try to provide questions that will serve all three of these purposes. Of course, no purpose is served if students make no effort to answer these adjunct questions.

Students can also be helped to become more involved with and aware of text information by constructing their own test items to measure their learning (Tuckman & Sexton, 1990; also, refer to a previous section on questioning). A homework assignment of constructing test questions that cover text material can help students process text content and concepts.

Providing students with questions to answer about text material is an effective form of instruction. Asking them to provide answers to "why" questions, in particular, has been found to lead to greater retention of text material than giving them the "answers" as part of the text (Wood, Pressley, & Winne, 1990), owing to the fact that they cause the learner to engage in elaboration of text, and hence add meaning to it. (For further discussion, refer back to the section on elaboration on pages 286–288.) Asking "why" questions has been referred to as **elaborative interrogation** (Bruning et al., 2004). An example would be to ask: *Why is elaborative interrogation a good technique?* rather than: *What is elaborative interrogation?*

Combining Organizers

Using the behavioral approach described in the preceding chapter (and again in Chapter 11), instruction involves the systematic presentation of what is to be learned, an opportunity for the student to respond, and a reinforcement contingent on the student's correct response. We can now modify this approach or change it dramatically by using instructional design principles based on the cognitive view of instruction described above. The cognitive approach combines three organizers: advance organizers, signals, and adjunct questions, resulting in the old teaching adage: "Tell them what you are going to tell them; then tell them; then tell them what you told them." More specifically, this means doing the following:

1. begin instruction with advance organizers such as previews, outlines, questions, behavioral objectives, or concepts maps;
2. make sure new concepts and terms are defined and illustrated;
3. organize and sequence new material, using headings and signals so it can be followed;
4. keep the student as active as possible during instruction by means of questions and activities;
5. end instruction with a review of main points; and
6. follow up instruction with questions or other assignments that require students to process and use the information they have just learned.

elaborative interrogation

asking "why" questions

Think It Over

as a LEARNER   What instructional techniques for enhancing meaning, described in the previous section, are used in this textbook? How do they help you better understand what you are reading?

as a TEACHER   What instructional techniques would you employ with your students to help enhance the meaning of materials they were required to read?

DISCOURSE ON DIVERSITY

Computational Mathematical Abilities of African American Girls (Elementary/Middle School)

BOX 7.5

Mathematics requires its own set of cognitive skills just as reading does, although the cognitive skills are not necessarily the same. A study of mathematics performance and cognitive skills by Park and Bauer (1999) in the *Journal of Black Studies* attempted to answer the following three questions: (1) Are there racial differences in mathematics performance among the highest performing group of elementary school students? (2) If there are racial differences, in which cognitive skill area—computation or concepts and applications—do the differences show up? (3) If a pattern of racial differences is found, is it consistent across boys and girls?

The study was restricted to fourth- and sixth-grade African American and Caucasian students who scored at or above the 95th percentile on the California Achievement Test mathematics total battery, that is, the brightest students in mathematics. The test of cognitive skills in mathematics included 44 items for mathematics computation skills and 50 items for mathematics concept and application skills.

For research question 1, the results showed significant racial differences and significant gender differences on overall mathematics performance for both grades 4 and 6. For research question 2, the results showed that African Americans outperformed Caucasians on computational skills (that is, understanding of computations) while Caucasians outperformed African Americans on conceptual and application skills (that is, understanding of concepts and their application), and this occurred at both grade levels. For research question 3, the results showed that African American girls were the lowest-performing group in conceptual and application skills at both grade levels, while they were the highest-performing group in computational skills at both grade levels.

The authors concluded that African Americans, especially girls, showed superiority in understanding and performing mathematical computations, representing a "pure" mathematical ability area, while Caucasians performed better in the "applied mathematical area," which they conjectured could be related to "the use of verbal strategies in solving mathematical problems," suggesting that "language differences" may have influenced this cognitive skill area. The authors did say, however, that identifying the causes of the racial gaps in their study would be "pure speculation."

Learning Objective 7

Outline and illustrate the metacognitive strategies of planning, monitoring, affecting, and evaluating.

Metacognitive Strategies

Metacognition is the internal master control of thinking behavior designed to make sure that learning takes place. It represents "thinking about thinking." It includes processes that help people learn and processes that help people know whether or not they are learning. If learning is not taking place, metacognition triggers other processes that will correct the situation. It includes both the knowledge of cognition and the regulation of cognition (Bruning et al., 2004; Pintrich, Wolters, & Baxter, 2000; Schraw, 1998). Metacognitive knowledge involves knowing *when, why* and *how* to use all of the cognitive strategies that have been described in this chapter, namely: abstracting, elaborating, schematizing, organizing, questioning, and notetaking. Metacognitive regulation includes the following four strategic activities that can be carried out by students to help themselves learn and understand what they are reading or being taught, or by teachers to help them design and carry out effective instruction.

Goal Setting/Planning

The first step in metacognition is twofold: (1) goal setting or establishing goals, that is, deciding for oneself, "What level of performance do I want to achieve?" (for example, if the goal is an A grade, then the answer to the question may be different than if the goal is a grade of C); and (2) planning how to go about reaching these goals. One can have an academic goal such as achieving high grades or a social goal such as gaining the teacher's approval. One goal could lead to the other with the high grades leading to teacher approval or teacher approval leading to high grades (Wentzel, 2000). Middle school students with learning disabilities who were given a goal of including more reasons for supporting a paper's premise wrote better essays than students not given a goal (Page-Voth & Graham, 1999). Furthermore, college students who lacked confidence in their own academic performance did better on tests when they engaged in goal setting than when they did not (Tuckman, 1990).

Planning can also help students gain direction, for example, writing out a list of school assignments to complete for the upcoming week (Tuckman et al., 2008). Working without a plan is like driving in an unfamiliar area without a roadmap. Planning is particularly important for teachers who spend a lot of time preparing lesson plans, without which their classroom activities may very well lack direction.

Monitoring

Monitoring, or self-observation, is the process of paying attention to one's own behavior by continually keeping track of whether or not learning is taking place (Mace, Belfiore, & Hutchinson; 2001). To a certain extent, the teacher does the monitoring, but this may turn out to be too little and too late. It is far better for students to do their own monitoring on a regular basis, that is, continuously, whenever they are in a learning situation. This has been referred to as **comprehension monitoring** (Bruning et al., 2004), a process shown to

metacognition

the internal master control of thinking behavior designed to make sure that learning takes place

monitoring

the process of paying attention to one's own behavior by continually keeping track of whether or not learning is taking place

comprehension monitoring

continuous monitoring of one's own progress in a learning situation

Masterfile

Having a plan can help students reach their goals. It helps them to write down what they're expected to do in the coming week.

be enhanced during reading by applying effort and concentration to the task (Linderholm & Zhao, 2008).

Monitoring includes activities such as the following (Schunk & Zimmerman, 2003; Tuckman et al., 2008):

1. Self-questioning: asking yourself, "Do I understand this? Can I make sense out of it? Am I ready to take an exam on it? Do I need help? Do I need to study more?"
2. *Self-testing:* giving yourself a test to find out as accurately as possible how much has been learned and how much has not been learned.
3. *Searching the environment:* looking at materials and listening to other students and teachers to help determine whether or not one understands something well enough to meet the goals established above. Something may seem well understood until someone else is consulted.

Affecting

Once students find out where they stand, they need to do something about it. If they want to meet their goals, they need to use all the cognitive processes at their disposal. This is called **affecting**, or using what they have learned to produce a change in their metacognitive strategies. This should include such activities as the following (Tuckman et al., 2008):

- going to class
- paying attention in class
- taking notes in class
- reading assignments before class
- reading assignments after class
- taking notes on the reading
- doing homework
- correcting test mistakes
- answering questions in the textbook
- studying for exams
- keeping up-to-date on all assignments
- managing time
- asking for help when needed
- joining a study group
- choosing studious persons as friends

Evaluating

Evaluating means looking closely at the results of one's academic performance, which means *using feedback* such as test results, homework assignments, and in-class activities to help determine what a student understands and what he or she does not understand. Going over the mistakes on a test as soon as it is given back is a good way to determine exactly what is not understood (Tuckman et al., 2008). Of particular importance is evaluating the effectiveness of the strategies or approaches a student uses in terms of the outcomes attained, and then altering or eliminating ineffective strategies and replacing them with more effective ones. For example, if you are using the strategy of listening but not notetaking during classroom lectures and find yourself doing poorly on tests, then that self-evaluation should incline you to adopt the notetaking strategy.

Jones (1994) studied disadvantaged college students who, unlike many of their peers who came from similarly difficult circumstances, were earning grades of A in college courses and were on the Dean's List at their respective colleges. He asked these "overachieving" students about their secrets of success. Their answers were all the same: "When you don't understand something, ask questions. Stay after class if necessary, and talk to the instructor or go to his or her office. Use all the resources at your disposal, such as libraries and study groups. Hang out with other 'A' students, not with people who are always in some sort of trouble. Keep up with your work; don't fall behind and end up always playing catch up." These are sound strategies and are consistent with what has been said in this chapter.

See Table 7.4 below for a *Concept Review* of metacognitive strategies.

affecting

using what has been learned

evaluating

looking closely at the results of one's academic performance

Tetra images/Getty Images

Evaluating your performance by going over your mistakes on a test is a good way to check and improve your own understanding. It's called "using feedback."

CONCEPT REVIEW TABLE 7.4
Metacognitive Strategies

FACTOR	HOW IT WORKS	APPLICATION
Goal Setting/Planning	Decide what level of performance you want to achieve and how you will go about doing it.	Setting goals and constructing plans will help you do better in school.
Monitoring	Keep track of how well you are doing and whether you understand what you are being taught.	Testing yourself, asking yourself questions, and trying to find answers can help you determine what works and what doesn't.
Affecting	Go to class, pay attention, take notes, read assignments, do your homework, study for exams, ask for help when you need it.	Doing all of the activities associated with being a good student will lead you to success.
Evaluating	Examine your performance to see if it is acceptable, and use feedback to learn from your mistakes.	You will know if your learning and motivation strategies are effective if you understand what you are learning and earn high grades.

Study Skills

What has been described in this chapter? The answer is: *How people learn*. Students are people, so what has been described in this chapter is, *How students learn*. If you apply all that you have read in this chapter to yourself as a student, then you will have developed **study skills**. If you teach all that you have read in this chapter to your students, then they will develop study skills. Here are some points to remember:

Learning Objective 8

Describe combinations of the above that constitute study skills.

study skills

techniques and approaches to use for studying that will enable a student to be a successful learner

- Practice what you want to remember, but space out the practice rather than "cram."
- If you don't understand something you've read, *make* up an example or analogy or some other elaboration to help you understand.
- Use structures and schemata to help make sense out of and organize what you read.
- Take notes on each chapter as you read it.
- Identify and write down the main points, and organize them in terms of superordinates and subordinates.
- Answer the questions at the end of chapters.
- Be aware of what you don't understand.
- If you don't understand something, don't ignore it. Ask for clarification.
- Look for signals to help you find the main points in a textbook or lecture.

A good learning strategy is to look outside of class for information that will help you better understand something you learned in class. Using all the available resources is the mark of a good student.

Studying requires more than passive exposure to information and more than memory. It requires cognitive processing of the information to encode it into long-term memory and to be able to decode it back into short-term memory when needed. To learn, therefore, students need to do the kinds of cognitive processing described in this chapter, and manage these cognitive processes using the metacognitive processes described in this chapter.

Monkey Business Images | Dreamstime.com

T e a c h S o u r c e
V i d e o   C a s e

Metacognition: Helping Students Become Strategic Learners

In this video segment, you'll see how a middle school teacher, Julie Craven, shows how developing students' metacognitive skills can help them understand the meaning of difficult text material, in this case a newspaper article about Chinese culture.

After viewing the video case, consider what you have just watched about classroom management and answer the questions below:

1. The middle school teacher in this video encourages students to mark up the text as a form of metacognitive strategy. How would you incorporate this strategy into your own teaching?
2. As you saw in the video, the teacher showed students how to figure out the meaning of unfamiliar words (e.g., liberation). How could you help students develop metacognition to figure out the meaning of words they don't know?
3. How did the video illustrate "thinking about thinking?"

You can view the video case at the Education CourseMate. Go to:
CengageBrain.com

SUMMING IT UP

Distinguish between behaviorism and cognitivism.

Learning Objective 1

The **behavioral approach** focuses on teaching behaviors on the basis of the situation in which they will be performed and the consequences that follow (for example, to raise one's hand in class to gain the teacher's attention). In contrast, the **cognitive approach** is typically used to teach students the thinking, remembering, and self-monitoring skills that enable them to reason and solve problems

Key Concepts:

behaviorism, cognitivism (p. 272); behavioral approach, cognitive approach (p. 272).

Outline and illustrate a three-stage information-processing model including sensory register, short-term memory, and long-term memory.

Learning Objective 2

Incoming information enters first the **sensory register** and then the **short-term** (or working) **memory**, which has a very limited capacity. To be stored more permanently and then retrieved when necessary, incoming information must be semantically encoded into **long-term memory**.

Key Concepts:

semantic encoding, modal model, sensory register, perception, pattern recognition, assignment of meaning, short-term memory (p. 274); rehearsal, chunking, working memory (p. 275); long-term memory, semantic memory, episodic memory, explicit memory, implicit memories (p. 277).

Learning Objective 3

Key Concepts:

semantic networks, propositions, declarative knowledge, productions, procedural knowledge, conditional knowledge schema (p. 277); dual-coding theory (p. 278).

Define and differentiate types of semantic networks that are made up of units of declarative and procedural knowledge, and schemata.

New information maybe chunked into **semantic networks**, which are interconnected units of **declarative knowledge** called **propositions** and interconnected units of **procedural knowledge** called **productions**. **Conditional knowledge** is knowing when and why to use declarative and procedural knowledge. According to the **dual-code theory**, information may also be stored in the form of mental images, or codes, called **schemata**.

Learning Objective 4

Key Concepts:

primacy effect, recency effect (p. 278); massed practice, distributed practice (p. 278); semantic organization, structural organization, positive transfer, negative transfer, interference (p. 280); retroactive interference, proactive interference, first-letter method, peg method, keyword method (p. 281).

Summarize and contrast the factors that affect memorization: meaningfulness, serial position, practice, organization, transfer and interference, and mnemonics.

Material is best memorized—and most likely to be remembered—if it is (a) **meaningful**; (b) located at the beginning or end of the list to be learned; (c) **practiced** a lot, but practice is distributed over time; (d) **organized** into chunks; (e) **similar** to material already learned; (f) **tested immediately**, before anything else is learned; and (g) learned using a **mnemonic** device.

Learning Objective 5

Key Concepts:

meaningful learning, cognitive strategies (p. 285); abstracting, elaboration (p. 286); elaborative encoding (p. 287); structures, levels of processing (p. 288); organizing, outline (p. 290); questioning, self-explanations (p. 291), question and answer outline (p. 292); notetaking (p. 293).

Explain the cognitive strategies that affect meaningful learning: abstracting, elaborating, schematizing, organizing, questioning, and notetaking.

Information learned by processing or encoding into long-term memory so that it can be stored and subsequently retrieved is called meaningful learning. It can be facilitated by the following cognitive processes: (a) **abstracting** the material to be learned by forming a summary of the main points; (b) **elaborating** it by creating examples, diagrams, images, analogies, metaphors, and stories that will help in understanding what the material means; (c) **schematizing,** or structuring it, by connecting it to specific schemata, such as cause–and-effect or problem and solution, that help give it meaning ; (d) **organizing** it by using a system of headings and subheadings (as in a table of contents); (e) **generating questions** about it intended to help reveal its meaning, and then answering them; and (f) **notetaking** to capture the main points, particularly of material presented orally.

Explain three instructional techniques that enhance the meaningfulness of text: advance organizers, signals, and adjunct questions.

Instructional techniques to enhance the meaning of text, thereby assisting students in remembering and understanding what they read or hear, include (a) **advanced organizers** (previews, summaries, or objectives that appear prior to the students' reading of the material that alert them to the schemata that will be needed to process the new text information); (b) **signals,** or key words and phrases, words in italics, boldface, or underlined, and summaries, such as the one you are now reading, that call attention to the meaning or main points of a passage; and (c) **adjunct questions**, such as might appear at the beginning or end of a chapter, informing the reader in advance of what to pay attention to, or requiring the reader to go back and review what was already read.

> **Learning Objective 6**
>
> **Key Concepts:**
>
> advance organizers, signals (p. 296); adjunct questions (p. 297); pre-questions, post-questions (p. 297); elaborative interrogation (p. 298).

Outline and illustrate the metacognitive strategies of planning, monitoring, affecting, and evaluating.

Students can use **metacognitive strategies** to help themselves learn. They can set directions for themselves by **goal setting/planning**. They can activate their master control processes by **monitoring** or keeping track of what they are and are not learning by self-questioning, self-testing, and searching the environment for and using feedback. They can also use the **affecting** strategy to facilitate their own learning by going to class, paying attention, asking questions, keeping up-to-date, and studying for exams. Finally, they can determine how well all these processes are working by **evaluating** the results and making the necessary adjustments.

> **Learning Objective 7**
>
> **Key Concepts:**
>
> metacognitive strategies, metacognition, goal setting, planning, monitoring, comprehension, affecting (p. 300); evaluation (p.302).

Describe combinations of the above that constitute study skills.

Following the techniques for memorizing and meaningful learning, taking advantage of the techniques provided by the authors for learning, and consistently employing the metacognitive strategies of goal setting/planning, monitoring, affecting, and evaluating represent the sum total of what is meant by **study skills**.

> **Learning Objective 8**
>
> **Key Concepts:**
>
> study skills (p. 303).

Visit the Education CourseMate for *Educational Psychology* to access study tools and resources including the Virtual Psychology Labs, TeachSource Video Cases, chapter web links, tutorial quizzes, glossary flashcards, and more. Go to CengageBrain.com to register using your access code.

8 | Constructivism, Problem Solving, and Creativity

After reading this chapter, you should be able to meet the following learning objectives:	Chapter Contents
LEARNING OBJECTIVE 1 Outline the types and general characteristics and ingredients of constructivism, and explain and illustrate six specific models of constructivist teaching.	Constructivism and Constructivist-based Teaching and Learning • Types and Essential Ingredients • Constructivist Teaching Models and Environments
LEARNING OBJECTIVE 2 Describe the dilemmas of constructivism.	The Dilemmas of Constructivism
LEARNING OBJECTIVE 3 Differentiate general problem-solving strategies in terms of the heuristics or approaches used for attacking the problem and generating solutions, and describe the (a) differences in the ways experts and novices solve problems, particularly in terms of the role of domain-specific knowledge and (b) combination of general strategies and expert knowledge, especially as it affects the transfer of solution strategies.	Problem Solving • General Problem-Solving Strategies • Experts Versus Novices: Specific Problem-Solving Strategies • Combining General Strategies and Expert Knowledge
LEARNING OBJECTIVE 4 Apply metacognitive models for teaching problem-solving skills in the domains of reading, social studies, and mathematics, as well as one general model.	Applying Metacognitive Strategies to Teaching Problem-solving Skills • Reading • Social Studies • Mathematics • General Problem Solving
LEARNING OBJECTIVE 5 Explain what creativity is, how it is determined, and procedures for increasing it, including reframing and brainstorming.	Creativity • What Is Creativity and Its Sources and Properties? • How Can Creativity Be Measured? • Is Creativity Necessarily a Valued Capability? • Increasing Creative Performance

Students Constructing Knowledge by Constructing Models

Children in a middle school math class have just finished watching a video that showed them some of the things that architects do to help communities, for example, designing safe playgrounds for children. At the end of the video, the members of the class are challenged to design a neighborhood playground as a way of bringing real-world problems into their classroom. Students then help two young architects design sandboxes, swingsets, slides, and other playground equipment, and help them build a model of what the playground will look like. Working on the problem requires them to get involved with subjects such as measurement, mathematics (arithmetic and geometry), and other subjects. They are confronted by questions such as "How do you measure angles, draw to scale, or determine how much gravel you need?" As a result of the project, students have come to understand geometry concepts better and communicate their ideas to real audiences. (Cognition and Technology Group at Vanderbilt, 1997.)

- What are some other projects that students could engage in that would help them to build understanding through experience?

Lessons We Can Learn from the Story In the previous chapter, you learned about the information-processing approach to learning, an approach that applies particularly to learning from text, that is, acquiring information by reading. However, alternative learning models exist, such as the one described in the story, that are based primarily on learner participation or active involvement with learning materials you may want to use in your teaching. While stimulating, this type of learning may pose more of a challenge to you, its effect on your students may be more meaningful and long lasting as a result. In this chapter, we will begin by introducing you to constructivism, an overall philosophical approach to learning by active participation, including some concrete examples, and follow with problem solving and creativity, two complex, thinking-based cognitive models for you, as a prospective teacher, to consider.

Learning Objective 1

Outline the types and general characteristics and ingredients of constructivism, and explain and illustrate six specific models of constructivist teaching.

Constructivism and Constructivist-based Teaching and Learning

Constructivism is an explanation about the nature of learning that has implications for teaching and learning in school. The basic nature of the explanation is that "learners actively *construct* their own knowledge rather than receive preformed information transmitted by others" (Green & Gredler, 2002, p. 54). What this means is that information cannot merely be deposited into learners' heads. According to constructivism, information must be discovered through some activity on the learner's part, in order to have meaning for him or her. It is also believed by constructivists that current curricular emphases and classroom interaction and dynamics do not lend themselves to the process of knowledge construction, and would need to be changed in order for meaningful learning to occur.

Types of Constructivism and Essential Ingredients

Constructivist approaches to teaching and learning may follow a number of different perspectives. Bruning et al. (2004) distinguish between the following three:

- **Exogenous**—in which the acquisition of knowledge reflects the reality of the external world, that is, via teaching and experiences, the external world strongly influences knowledge construction; hence the accuracy of knowledge is based on its match to reality (the cognitive approach to learning, basically schema theory, described in the previous chapter reflects this perspective).
- **Endogenous**—in which new knowledge develops out of earlier knowledge through a process of cognitive development of the structures into which knowledge is organized (essentially the model proposed by Piaget and described in detail in Chapter 2).
- **Dialectical**—in which knowledge comes from the interactions between learners and the environment, as well as interactions with one another and with teachers (Vygotsky's approach, also described in Chapter 2, fits this model as do all the models described in this chapter).

It is important to reemphasize that all of the above perspectives share the common assumption that knowledge must be constructed to be meaningful and can only be achieved through active involvement of the learner.

The Vygotsky approach (described in Chapter 2) is referred to as **social constructivism**, the idea that social interaction facilitates learning, that is, students working together to construct understanding is more effective than them working apart (Gauvain, 2001). Sutinen (2008) argues that education is the medium in which the creative and constructive actions of individuals come together in a social environment. In other words, social interaction can be used by teachers to helps students construct understanding (Fleming & Alexander, 2001), and is an essential teacher role (Meter & Stevens, 2000). It can also be used by parents to help their children make sense of mutually-shared experiences (Crowley & Jacobs, 2002).

A fundamental belief of constructivism is that learning and thinking occur in a context or situation, not in a vacuum. Meaningful learning occurs within real-world tasks, that is, constructivism as a learning theory can guide the process of learning and teaching in real classroom settings (Yilmaz, 2008). This contextualization of learning is referred to as **situated cognition**. This concept plays an important role in teaching. Many concepts can be better taught by situating them in naturally occurring, so-called *authentic*, settings (van Merriënboer, Kirschner, & Kester, 2003). For example, Schunk (2004) describes a third-grade teacher who uses pumpkins as the basis for teaching an integrated unit on social studies,

constructivism

"learners actively *construct* their own knowledge rather than receive preformed information transmitted by others"

exogenous

in which the acquisition of knowledge reflects the reality of the external world

endogenous

in which new knowledge develops out of earlier knowledge through a process of cognitive development of the structures into which knowledge is organized

dialectical

in which knowledge comes from the interactions between learners and the environment, as well as interactions with one another and with teachers

social constructivism

the idea that social interaction facilitates learning

situated cognition

a learning theory can guide the process of learning and teaching in real classroom settings

mathematics, art, and language arts that includes a field trip, calculating, cooking, sculpting, and storywriting. (Refer back to Chapter 1 where the differences between situated or real-world learning and school learning is discussed.) Another example of situated cognition is the use of apprenticeships, as described later in this chapter.

The essential ingredients of constructivist instruction and of participative learning in general are (1) the active involvement of the learner and (2) challenging, thought-provoking experiences. Examples include small group learning and peer collaboration as described in Chapter 9, and experiments such as those used by Piaget as described in Chapter 2. In fact, the five instructional practices derived from Piaget's constructivist approach and described in Chapter 2—learning by exploration, learning centers, use of themes (an example of which appears in the chapter-opening story), learner-centered orientation, and focus on the development of schemata—all reflect the application of constructivist principles to instruction. Vygotsky's concept of scaffolding for providing students with assistance in their discovery of meaning, also described in Chapter 2, is another major component of the constructivist approach.

Driscoll (2008) suggests the following six conditions for learning, using the knowledge construction approach:

- embed learning in relevant, realistic learning environments;
- make shared responsibility among students a part of learning;
- support the use of multiple perspectives;
- use multiple representations of content;
- help students understand that knowledge is constructed; and
- encourage students to take ownership in learning.

Motivationally, the most constructivist approach—one that focuses on learner autonomy—is called self-determination theory, and is described in Chapter 10. Additional features of constructivist-based instruction include the use of manipulatives, choice of activities, opportunities to make observations and collect data, guided discussions, problem solving (described later in this chapter), and apprenticeships.

Alesandrini & Larson (2002) offer the following **tenets of constructivism**:

- Learning results from exploration and discovery, that is, actively exploring new information and constructing meaning from it by linking it to previous knowledge and experience.
- Learning is a community activity facilitated by shared inquiry; it requires learners to reflect on and share their insights with the group.
- Learners play an ongoing, active, and critical role in assessment; it is through the self-assessment activities of reflection and verbalization that learners realize the meaning of what they have experienced.
- Learning results from participation in authentic activities, that is, it should be based on activities and problems that students might encounter in the real world.

tenets of constructivism

learning results from exploration, shared inquiry, self-assessment, and participation in authentic activities

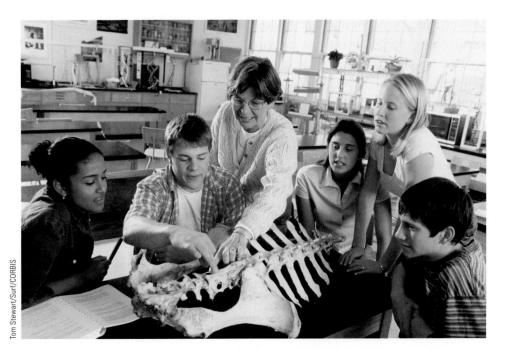

Constructivism is a form of learning that involves active exploration, shared inquiry, and critical assessment, where teachers function as facilitators to help students increase their understanding.

- Learners create knowledge from new information in light of their previous experiences.
- Teachers should function as facilitators who coach learners as they create their own paths toward personally meaningful goals.

Constructivist Teaching Models and Environments

Constructivist-based learning environments have been characterized as ones that (1) provide opportunities to manipulate and experiment; (2) employ meaningful problems that link concepts to everyday experience; (3) center around higher order concepts and multiple perspectives; (4) allow learners to evaluate their own needs, and test and revise their knowledge; (5) connect cognition to context; and (6) emphasize the value of overcoming flawed beliefs as the basis for understanding (Hannafin, Land, & Oliver, 1999).

There are numerous constructivist teaching models and environments that incorporate constructivist-based learning environments, six of which will be described.

Teaching for Understanding

This model, developed by Perkins & Unger (1999) focuses on (1) choosing generative topics to teach, (2) setting goals of understanding, (3) having learners engage in performances that contribute to understanding, and (4) providing ongoing assessment that yields informative feedback and refinement of performance. *Generative topics* are:

- central to a domain or discipline,
- accessible and interesting to students,
- interesting to the teacher, and
- connectable to diverse themes.

In short, they are important topics that stimulate engagement by both students and teachers, for example, political actions that affect our everyday lives.

Understanding goals are explicit, public (clearly made known to both teachers and students), nested (situated within or part of larger learning units), and central to the discipline. An example would be: How do different political actions affect aspects of our own personal lives such as privacy, security, and economic well-being? *Understanding performances* (i.e., performances to enhance understanding) should relate to specific goals, be advanced by practice activities that deepen understanding, allow for different styles of learning and forms of expression, promote reflective engagement, and provide visible evidence of understanding. Finally, *ongoing assessment* should be based on relevant, explicit, and public criteria provided frequently by multiple sources that serve to gauge progress and inform planning by both student and teacher.

Collaborative Problem Solving

This alternative constructivist teaching model (Nelson, 1999) is based on the following fundamental values or precepts of constructivist teaching and learning built on the natural collaborative processes of learners:

- create collaborative learning environments that are situated and learner-centered;
- honor the importance of authenticity, ownership and relevance;
- allow students to learn by doing;
- foster critical thinking and problem solving;
- encourage exploration and analysis from multiple perspectives;
- include rich social contexts for learning;
- cultivate supportive, respectful relationships; and
- develop lifelong learning interests and skills.

Its collaborative processes, extending over time, include activities that enable group members to build readiness (developing an authentic problem or project), form and norm groups (encouraging the establishment of operational guidelines), determine a preliminary problem definition, define and assign roles, engage in problem solving activities, finalize the solution, synthesize and reflect on their experiences, assess products and processes, and provide closure.

Fostering a Community of Learners

A third constructivist model is Fostering a Community of Learners (FCL; Brown & Campione, 1994, 1996; Brown, 1992, 1997) that puts an emphasis on philosophy and principles. In this model, originally designed for grades 1–8, but applicable in higher grades as well, students collaborate by (a) carrying out *research* on topics in small groups where each student specializes in a particular subtopic area; (b) *sharing* what they learn with other students in their group and in other groups; and (c) preparing for, participating in, and *performing* a larger, more consequential task where students combine their individual learning so that they all come to better understand the topic. This is called the "research, share, perform cycle."

In the FCL model, students approach the task with the goal of developing and sharing expertise on a particular topic in order to create solutions to real-world problems. Teachers approach the task as an opportunity to teach students how to enhance their intellectual skills, such as providing evidence and making sound arguments, and social skills, such as learning from others and participating in cooperative groups.

An example of one topic is food chains, with subtopics including photosynthesis, energy exchange, producers and consumers, food webs, ecosystems, and so on. Each student in a group would focus on one of these topics, research it, and then share what they learned with the others. They would also have the opportunity to consult with subject matter experts outside the classroom.

The consequential task, chosen by the teacher and students together, could be a bulletin board display, a presentation to a larger group, or some other concrete representation of what they have learned. The purpose of this learning process is to cause students to think deeply about complex content, share knowledge across groups, and take advantage of opportunities for exhibition and reflection.

A similar approach, called Philosophy for Children (Lipman, 2003), also features a community of inquiry that involves the formulation and exploration of questions and a collaborative dialogue among students to determine what the answers to those questions might be.

Apprenticeships in Thinking

This fourth constructivist model was developed by Rogoff (1990, 1998). In this model, novice learners work with teachers and more experienced peers in collaborative problem-solving activities to acquire skills they are not able to acquire on their own. In this view, cognitive development is seen as inherently social in nature with adults such as parents and teachers (1) stimulating children's interest in cognitive tasks, (2) simplifying the tasks so that children can accomplish them, (3) providing direction and stimulating motivation, (4) offering feedback, (5) minimizing frustration and risk, and (6) modeling versions of the acts to be performed.

Rogoff (1995) refers to the process that adults engage in with children to provide a social context and gradually transfer to them the responsibility for problem solving as *guided participation*. This enriches the mental processes of children and leads to purposeful actions (what Rogoff calls "accomplishing something"). Adult acts of guided participation often are undertaken without children's explicit awareness that they are experiencing instructional acts. For example, a parent or teacher may help a child draw a picture without either one perceiving it as teaching.

Rogoff's apprenticeships in thinking help children construct or form new thoughts or cognitions, and thereby move to new cognitive levels, as a result of guided participation provided by parents and teachers functioning as expert partners. These activities support children's attempts to acquire new knowledge. In schools, teachers can direct their guidance to help students acquire effective "tools" for thinking and problem solving in the different subject matter areas through collaboration.

The problem-solving process plays an important role in constructivist learning. Natural learning environments are a good context for instruction and discovery.

Bill Bachman/Alamy

Problem-based Learning

A fifth constructivist model, Problem Based Learning (PBL), involves experiential learning organized around the investigation, explanation, and resolution of meaningful problems (Torp & Sage, 2002). Hmelo-Silver (2004) describes this approach as student-directed learning focusing on solving complex problems that do not have a single correct answer. Students work in collaborative groups to acquire new knowledge and then use it to solve real-world problems. The teacher's role is to facilitate the learning process rather than to provide knowledge.

Students follow a cycle called the problem-based learning cycle or PBL tutorial process that follows this sequence: (1) presentation of the problem scenario; (2) identifying the relevant facts associated with the scenario; (3) generating hypotheses as to possible solutions; (4) identifying knowledge deficiencies or learning issues, that is, self-directed learning necessary for solving the problem; (5) applying the new knowledge to test the hypotheses generated in the third step; and (6) reflecting on the abstract knowledge gained (Hmelo-Silver, 2004).

According to Barrows and Kelson (1995), PBL is designed to help students:

- construct an extensive and flexible knowledge base;
- develop effective problem-solving skills;
- develop self-directed, lifelong learning skills;
- become effective collaborators; and
- become intrinsically motivated to learn.

An example of a PBL tutorial session is asking middle school children to build artificial lungs, which they did by first performing experiments to determine how much air the lungs had to displace (Hmelo-Silver, Holton, & Kolodner, 2000). To solve the problem, the children had to go through the steps in the PBL tutorial process, that is, they had to generate questions, hypothesize solutions, identify learning issues, independently research the learning issues they generated and then regroup to share what they had learned, reconsider or generate new hypotheses, and then reflect on what they had come up with and the self-directed process they had used.

According to Hmelo-Silver (2004), "evidence suggests that PBL is an instructional approach that offers the potential to help students to develop flexible understanding and lifelong learning skills" (p. 235), with the teacher functioning as facilitator, guide, or coach. Teaching using PBL provides students with opportunities to develop their critical-thinking skills while practicing important team-building behaviors (Vernon, 1995). Moreover, research results have shown that problem-based learning leads to better outcomes than lecture-based learning among engineering students (Hsieh & Knight, 2008).

The Jasper Woodbury Problem Solving Series

An excellent example of constructivist learning environments is the Jasper Woodbury Problem Solving Series (Cognition and Technology Group at Vanderbilt, 1992, 1997). This series consists of 12 video-disk adventure stories that provide opportunities for mathematical problem finding and problem solving. The adventures are designed like good detective novels where all the data necessary to solve the adventure are embedded in the story. The adventures are unique in that they present a believable, challenging story that has interesting characters, and applications to a variety of curricular areas. Designed to be used in typical classroom situations, they provide many of the advantages of natural learning environments, such as a common context for instruction, an authentic task, and a chance to see that school knowledge can be used to solve real problems.

To illustrate, one of the stories involves a wounded eagle that Jasper discovers while fishing in an area about 65 miles away from the nearest veterinarian. Given that time is of the essence, Jasper's plan is to have his friend Emily fly to where he is in an ultralight plane belonging to one of his friends, and then fly the bird from there to the vet. The problem to be solved is: How long will that take? Students, working together, must use all the information contained in the story as clues to allow them to calculate the answer to the problem.

Problems such as the one above, unlike most typical textbook problems, are engaging for most students to solve, a feature considered by Jonassen (1999, 2003) to be the key to meaningful learning. There are many possible solutions and criteria for evaluating them, while at the same time, no clearly prescribed rules or principles that have to be used. The result is that students must make and defend judgments about solution routes, giving them a sense of ownership in the problem and its result. It is the prompting of this "ownership" that Jonassen regards essential to the design of constructive learning environments, according to the theory.

The six constructivist teaching models are summarized in the *Concept Review* in Table 8.1.

How Teachers Can Encourage Meaningful Learning

Here are some suggestions for teachers offered by Mark Windschitl (2002; p. 137):

1. Ask students to present their experiences and ideas about the topic of study, then create learning situations that help them elaborate on and restructure their knowledge of the topic.
2. Give students frequent opportunities to engage in meaningful, problem-solving activities.
3. Provide students with information resources and the conceptual and technological tools to process and apply that information.
4. Have students work on a task in collaborative groups and give them support for their efforts to engage in task-oriented discussions.
5. Make one's own thinking process explicit and encourage one's students to do the same through discussions, writings, or other representations.
6. Ask students to apply knowledge in a variety of "authentic" contexts and to explain and interpret texts and ideas, predict phenomena, and construct arguments based on evidence rather than place all their focus on acquiring predetermined "right answers."
7. Encourage reflective and autonomous thinking.
8. Employ a variety of assessment strategies to understand the evolution of students' ideas and to provide them with feedback on the processes and products of their thinking.

CONCEPT REVIEW TABLE 8.1

Six Constructivist Teaching Models

MODELS AND ENVIRONMENT	DEVELOPER	KEY FEATURES AND FOCI
Teaching for Understanding	Perkins & Unger	• Choosing generative topics • Setting explicit goals of understanding • Doing performances that aid understanding • Providing ongoing assessment
Collaborative Problem Solving	Nelson	• Creating collaborative environments • Honoring importance of authenticity • Learning by doing • Encouraging exploration • Including social contexts • Cultivating relationships • Developing lifelong learning
Fostering a Community of Learners	Brown & Campione	• Collaborating in small groups where each student has a subtopic area • Sharing learning among students • Participating in more consequential tasks
Apprenticeships in Thinking	Rogoff	• Stimulating children's interest in cognitive tasks • Simplifying tasks to foster accomplishment • Providing direction and stimulating motivation • Offering feedback • Minimizing frustration & risk • Modeling acts to be performed
Problem-based Learning	Barrows & Kelson	• Presenting problem scenarios • Identifying relevant facts • Generating hypotheses • Identifying learning issues • Applying new knowledge to test hypotheses • Reflecting on knowledge gained

MODELS AND ENVIRONMENT	DEVELOPER	KEY FEATURES AND FOCI
Jasper Woodbury Problem-Solving Series	Cognition & Technology Group at Vanderbilt	• Presenting believable, challenging video-disk adventure stories • Providing opportunities for problem solving • Designed like detective novels • Applying to a variety of curricular areas • Generating many possible solutions

Think It Over

as a LEARNER   Can you describe a classroom learning experience in which you utilized the constructivist approach to instruction? What were your thoughts about it and your evaluation of it?

as a TEACHER   How might you go about teaching students to construct the meaning of an idea? For example, how might you teach students to construct the meaning of the idea of *freedom* or the idea of *gravity* or the idea of a *fraction*?

D I S C O U R S E   O N   D I V E R S I T Y

Addressing the Needs of Students with Learning Difficulties (Elementary/Middle School)   BOX 8.1

Green & Gredler (2002) identify the following ways in which low-ability, low socioeconomic, and diverse learners from minority cultures may present special challenges in constructivist classrooms:

1. Many constructivist teaching models place great importance on learners constructing meaning for themselves in natural settings in order to truly understand what they are learning, and make connections that allow them to generalize beyond the specific context where the learning has taken place. Because low-ability learners tend to focus on details and do not make the connections that would enable them to elaborate on what they have learned in a personally meaningful way, they tend to have difficulty managing their own learning.

2. Many constructivist teaching models also place great importance on individual exploration. Students in such classrooms read books they themselves choose and write on topics in which they have a personal interest. Students with learning difficulties typically find the level of skill and self-regulation required of such work to be a great challenge for them and may find explicit instruction more suited to their cognitive skill level than implicit instruction.

3. Students with learning difficulties may also be challenged by the participation structure in social constructivist classrooms, particularly in regard to constructing meaning through dialogue. This may impede them from full participation in their classroom community. Diverse students (e.g., those with low SES or from minority cultures) may lack the knowledge and skills for full participation and thereby be deprived of the opportunity.

4. Students with learning difficulties may also require more targeted instruction, focused practice, and incentives to achieve the literacy skills for higher-level thinking and understanding.

5. Students with learning difficulties may be disadvantaged by having to struggle with content while given less attention by their teachers, leading to more referrals for special education.

Green and Gredler (2002) recommend the following for helping students with learning difficulties in constructivist classrooms. These include (1) flexible grouping and student collaboration, (2) teacher modeling followed by practice, and (3) input and assistance from school psychologists in the form of consultation and designing interventions.

T e a c h S o u r c e
V i d e o   C a s e

Constructivist Teaching in Action:
A High School Classroom Debate

In this video segment, you'll see how constructivism comes into play in a high school history classroom in which students prepare for a debate. You'll see how the teacher sets the stage for students to apply their expertise and best express opposing ideas.

After viewing the video case, consider what you have just watched about constructivist teaching and answer the questions below:

1. In what ways is the teacher's approach to the debate as an instructional tool consistent with constructivist teaching philosophy?

2. One of the students discusses the benefits of participating in classroom debates, including that it offers a good way to connect ideas and think about implications. How is this consistent with the constructivist learning approach?

3. What do you see as the benefit of doing a debate evaluation? Is this consistent with constructivism?

You can view the video case at the Education CourseMate. Go to:
CengageBrain.com

While Polya's approach was focused on mathematics, it clearly could be applied to problems of all sorts.

Bruning et al. (2004) propose a stage sequence for attacking a problem featuring the following stages:

1. *Identifying the problem*—determining what you are being asked to do;
2. *Representing the problem*—understanding what information the problem requires and what is given (sometimes referred to as the **problem space**; Hayes, 1988; Bruning et al., 2004);
3. *Selecting an appropriate strategy*—devising a plan, step by step, for connecting the given information to the unknown (using the four heuristics listed above or those described below);
4. *Implementing the strategy*—carrying out the plan, one step at a time; and
5. *Evaluating solutions*—looking back at the solution and making sure it actually solves the given problem while fitting in all of the given information.

After succeeding, the problem solver should make a record of exactly how she went about solving the problem, because she may have invented a useful heuristic for herself.

A common general problem-solving strategy or heuristic is called **means-end analysis** (Bruning et al., 2004). Given the input of a *beginning state,* (the chess pieces on a board), an end or *goal state* (checkmating the opponent's king), and all allowable operations for changing one state into another, the problem solver pursues a chain of operations for transforming the beginning state into the goal state. He or she does this by seeking an operation or means that would make the beginning state more like the goal state. After carrying out that operation, the problem solver seeks another operation to reduce the difference still further, and keeps doing this until no difference exists at all. If a dead end is reached, the problem solver backs up and tries another path.

Often, it is not possible to pursue all possible solution paths by performing all possible operations (called the **algorithmic solution**), because there are too many. Instead, the operations that the problem solver performs typically represent heuristics or general-solution strategies (Korf, 1999), such as always moving the important pieces toward the center of the board, always keeping pieces around the king, or never giving up a piece if it can be avoided.

Experts versus Novices: Specific Problem-Solving Strategies

Remember the chess masters, and how they chunked information so that they could remember so many more real chessboards than ones with randomly placed pieces (see Box 7.2) These results showed that chess masters knew something not only very powerful but also very specific to chess. Otherwise, they would have done well on the random layouts, too. In fact, Chase and Simon (1973) figured out that chess masters knew approximately 50,000 chess-specific configurations or schemata.

means-end analysis

given the input of a beginning state, an end or goal state, and all allowable operations for changing one state into another, the problem solver pursues a chain of operations for transforming the beginning state into the goal state

algorithmic solution

pursuing all possible solution paths by performing all possible operations

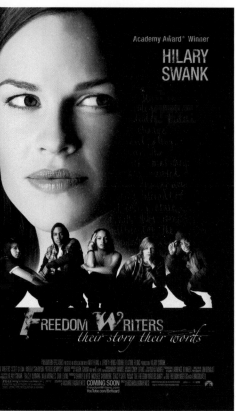

The 2007 movie *Freedom Writers* shows the process of how Erin Gruwell develops from novice to expert teacher.

In other words, chess masters were experts, and being experts meant they had a lot of very organized, **domain-specific**, or **expert knowledge** (Alexander, 1992)—in this case, knowledge of chess. Perhaps it was not their general problem-solving ability but their chess expertise that made them such good chess players. Rabinowitz and Glaser (1985) studied the performance of experts in other fields and discovered that their performance was characterized by such things as (1) a large knowledge base of domain-specific patterns, (2) rapid recognition of situations in which these patterns apply, and (3) reasoning that moves from such recognition directly toward a solution (called forward reasoning). Indeed, years of research strongly suggest that domain specific or expert knowledge is the factor most closely related to effective problem solving (Taconis et al., 2001).

By comparison, novices tended not to see the relevant patterns, because they did not know them or did not know them well enough to rapidly recognize them. Novices based their reasoning on superficial problem content. And novices worked backward, rather than forward, by focusing on working from the unknowns to the givens. Novices used working backward while experts used forward reasoning, and this was true in fields as diverse as figure skating (Deakin & Allard, 1991) and medicine (Patel & Groen, 1986).

In other words, experts depend not on general strategies but on a rich database and on an elaborate structure into which those data are organized for rapid retrieval. Their major heuristic for problem solving is **working forward**, or examining a current situation and performing operations to change it. Those operations, however, are not necessarily constrained or limited by the goal (as in means-end analysis). The working-forward technique works for experts but not for novices because experts have the data or knowledge (based in large measure on experience) to recognize which operation is likely to work in a given situation. Novices do not. A *Concept Review* of the many differences between experts and novices in solving problems appears in Table 8.2. Finally, if expertise and specific problem-solving strategies are not needed to solve problems but general strategies or heuristics will suffice, then, to go back to the original example, the fictitious chess master ought to be as good a political or military tactician as he is a chess player. However, just as it was long ago discovered that learning Latin does not improve your mind's faculty (Thorndike, 1923), some research has shown that teaching children to use general strategies has no clear benefits outside the specific domains in which they are taught (Detterman, 1993).

Hence, the fictitious chess master will not necessarily give his leader the right advice to outwit the enemy if the contest between them is not carried out with chess pieces on a chessboard.

However, it has also been shown that problem-solving skills may transfer to other domains *provided that people are trained to use these skills in a variety of settings* (Mayer & Wittrock, 1996; Beyer, 2008), such as by presenting them with examples that contribute to discovery of problem solutions (Bernardo, 2001). Therefore, chess masters—perhaps with the necessary training in military strategy—might indeed turn out to be effective generals!

domain-specific or **expert knowledge**

knowledge about a particular subject

working forward

examining a current situation and performing operations to change it

PARAMOUNT/THE KOBAL COLLECTION/Picture Desk

CONCEPT REVIEW TABLE 8.2

Differences in Problem Solving Between Novices and Experts

NOVICE	EXPERT
Relies on raw memory	Uses chunking and schemata to remember relationships and groups
Classifies problems according to concrete (surface) similarities	Classifies problems according to underlying structural features
Focuses on specific features of a problem and tries to link them to a memorized formula	Focuses on the big picture and looks for relevant principles
Relies on disorganized, general knowledge	Relies on hierarchically (concrete to abstract) domain-specific knowledge
Considers a large number of alternatives and works through all logical possibilities	Cuts problem down to size by quickly identifying relevant schemata and then uses them (for example, analyze, categorize, solve)
Works backward (from goal to beginning state)	Works forward: Uses shortcuts, estimates ballpark answers, converts unfamiliar problems to familiar ones
Focuses on problem–solution rather than problem–problem-solving process.	Focuses on problem formulation and solving process and knows solution will come
Has little self-awareness of the strategies used	Has great self-awareness and a plan for the strategies used

Think It Over

as a LEARNER Is there some area in which you see yourself as expert? If so, how did you become one? If not, do you know anyone who is an expert in some area? If so, how did they become one?

as a TEACHER If you were a teacher who wanted to be considered an expert teacher, what would be the things you would do that would lead your students to consider you an expert teacher?

Combining General Strategies and Expert Knowledge

Even though experts usually are good problem solvers only in their own domains where they have the necessary knowledge base, most of the work on expertise has dealt with experts solving only standard or common problems in their own domain. What might happen if an expert were given an atypical or unusual problem in his or her domain (for example, a physician diagnosing an illness that has never been diagnosed before)? Clement (1989) has found that physicists fall back on more general strategies when attacking the unfamiliar. For example, (1) they use analogies to connect the unfamiliar problem to systems or related areas that they understand better, (2) they search for the areas or aspects in which the analogy does not fit, (3) they try to create visual images or pictures to help them understand how the given system might work if it were pushed to its limits, and (4) they construct a simpler problem of the same sort.

These approaches discovered by Clement represent heuristics or general strategies, and even the experts seem unable to solve some problems without them. However, these heuristics do not substitute for domain knowledge. Instead, they seem to provide a basis for gaining access to and using domain knowledge. But will these heuristics or general strategies transfer from one area to another? Or, to return to our original question, will the chess master be a master of politics and military tactics as well?

That depends—according to Brown and Kane (1988), who studied the transfer of problem-solving strategies among three-and four-year-olds—on the following:

1. whether learners are shown how problems resemble each other;
2. whether learners' attention is drawn to the underlying structure of comparable problems;
3. whether learners are familiar with the problem domains or areas;
4. whether examples are accompanied by rules, particularly when those rules are formulated by the learners themselves; and
5. whether learning takes place in a social context (where students work together) and the interaction produces explanations, justifications, and principles that are then discussed and defended.

In other words, if the goal is for students to use general problem-solving strategies, supported by the necessary knowledge base or expertise, and to transfer those strategies to a variety of problem domains, they must be taught by teachers to do that. They must be taught to apply the principles stated above to facilitate the transfer of problem-solving strategies. To accomplish this, teachers must first look at the ways people can be taught to use or transfer problem-solving strategies. If we rely on just teaching people the knowledge base or expertise that these strategies are built on, they will not learn to be good general problem solvers (Mayer, 2003).

So after all is said and done, it looks like our fictitious chess master would need to be taught something about politics and military tactics as well as something about how to transfer his chess strategies to these new domains. Unfortunately, by the time he has had all this training, it might be too late. His country's enemy may have already successfully made its move. (To see if you can transfer your problem-solving skills, try the problems in Box 8.3.)

Lehman, Lampert, and Nisbett (1988) found that students who did graduate study in psychology or in medicine were able to transfer the strategies they learned in courses on statistics and research methodology and in actually doing research to solving everyday problems that required similar kinds of reasoning. Samples of those problems appear in Box 8.3. Even though you have not done graduate study in psychology or medicine, you may want to "test" your reasoning skills against those who have.

AN EXAMPLE TO AID UNDERSTANDING   Box 8.3

Test Your Problem-Solving Skills* (High School/College) Statistical Reasoning—Everyday Life

After the first two weeks of the major league baseball season, newspapers begin to print the top ten batting averages. Typically, after two weeks, the leading batter has an average of about .450. Yet no batter in major league history has ever averaged .450 at the end of a season. Why do you think this is?

(a) A player's high average at the beginning of the season may be just a lucky fluke.

(b) A batter who has such a hot streak at the beginning of the season is under a lot of stress to maintain his performance record. Such stress adversely affects his playing.

(c) Pitchers tend to get better over the course of the season, as they get more in shape. As pitchers improve, they are more likely to strike out batters, so batters' averages go down.

(d) When a batter is known to be hitting a high average, pitchers bear down more when they pitch to him.

(e) When a batter is known to be hitting a high average, he stops getting good pitches to hit. Instead, pitchers "play the corners" of the plate because they don't mind walking him.

Methodological Reasoning—Everyday Life

The city of Middleopolis has had an unpopular police chief for a year and a half. He is a political appointee who is a crony of the mayor, and he had little previous experience in police administration when he was appointed. The mayor has recently defended the chief in public, announcing that in the time since he took office, crime rates decreased by 12%. Which of the following pieces of evidence would most deflate the mayor's claim that his chief is competent?

(a) The crime rates of the two cities closest to Middleopolis in location and size have decreased by 18% in the same period.

(b) An independent survey of the citizens of Middleopolis shows that 40% more crime is reported by respondents in the survey than is reported in police records.

(c) Common sense indicates that there is little a police chief can do to lower crime rates. These are for the most part due to social and economic conditions beyond the control of officials.

(d) The police chief has been discovered to have business contacts with people who are known to be involved in organized crime.

Conditional Reasoning—Permission Schema

You are a public health official at the international airport in Manila, capital of the Philippines. Part of your duty is to check that every arriving passenger who wishes to enter the country (rather than just change planes at the airport) has had an inoculation against cholera. Every passenger carries a health form. One side of the form indicates whether the passenger is entering or in transit, and the other side of the form lists the inoculations he or she has had in the past six months. Which of the following forms would you need to turn over to check? Indicate only those forms you would have to check to be sure.

Form 1	Form 2	Form 3	Form 4
Transit	Entering	Inoculated against: cholera hepatitis	Inoculated against: typhoid

(a)   Forms 2 & 3
(b)   Form 2 only
(c)   Forms 2, 3, & 4
(d)   Forms 2 & 4
(e)   Form 3 only

Verbal Reasoning

The new miracle drug Amotril has caused unforeseen side effects of a devastating nature; therefore, no new drugs should be released for public consumption without a thorough study of their effects. Which of the following arguments most closely resembles the argument above?

(a)   Because exposure to several hours of television a day has been shown to undermine children's interest in reading, children should be prevented from watching television.

(b)   Because it is difficult to predict whether the results of pure research will be of practical benefit to human beings, the amount of money spent on such research should be sharply curtailed.

(c)   The 1977 model of this compact station wagon has been shown to have a faulty exhaust system; therefore it is urgent that this model be recalled immediately.

(d)   Some of the worst highway accidents have been caused by teenagers between the ages of 16 and 18; therefore, only carefully screened members of this age group should be granted driver's licenses.

(e)   Rising medical costs have put many routine medical procedures out of the reach of low- and middle-income families; therefore, doctors should prescribe only the most essential laboratory tests.

Source: Lehman, D.R., Lampert, R.O., and Nisbett, R.E. (1988). The effects of graduate training on reasoning: Formal discipline and thinking about everyday-life problems. *American Psychologist, 43,* 431–442.

*Answers: a, a, d, d

Applying Metacognitive Strategies to Teaching Problem-Solving Skills

There are a number of ways to teach problem-solving skills. These ways differ according to how problem solving is viewed. One issue is whether problem solving is a single skill or a set of component skills. Most teachers agree on the latter, that problem solving requires a set of component skills. A second issue is whether the focus in problem solving should be on process or product, that is, on the thought processes used versus merely getting the right answer. The predominant approach is to focus on the problem-solving process. The third issue is whether to teach problem solving as a general course by itself or to integrate it into existing subject matter domains. The tendency has been to teach it as part of the approach to an existing subject matter, which is what will be considered first.

In Chapter 6, instructional techniques built primarily on behavioral theories were described. In Chapter 7, the concepts of metacognitive processes and metacognitive strategies were introduced. These are processes and strategies teachers and learners use to ensure that learning takes place. They include abstracting, elaborating, schematizing, organizing, monitoring, and affecting. These and similar techniques can also be used to ensure that problem solving takes place. The techniques for teaching these metacognitive strategies, as applied to problem solving in specific subject matter contexts as well as generally, are described below.

Recall also that in Chapter 7 two techniques were presented for "schematizing" a textbook's content in order to understand its meaning, both representing *structure strategies* (Mayer, 2003). The first, *top-level structures*, was related to the analysis of the Supertanker passage (Box 7.4); the second, called *text structures* training by Cook & Mayer (1988), was related to reading and outlining science textbooks. Both can be considered problem-solving procedures related to solving the problem of interpreting textbook content. Other approaches are described below.

Reading

Four approaches to teaching problem solving as a way to improve **reading comprehension** are worth noting. Meichenbaum and Asarnow (1979) describe three strategies for teaching reading comprehension skills to seventh and eighth graders with reading problems. They are (1) breaking the text into manageable chunks, (2) determining the skills needed for each chunk, and (3) translating these skills into rehearsable self-statements. For each chunk of a story, students are taught to ask themselves the following three questions:

1. What is the story about (what is its main idea)?
2. What are the important details (such as the order or sequence of the main events)?
3. How do the characters feel and why?

Students are also taught to take pauses, to think of what they are doing, and to listen to (monitor) what they say to themselves to make sure they are saying the right things. They are also taught not to worry about mistakes, but when they make them, to try again, and to be calm and relaxed while they read. And when they succeed, they are taught to be proud of themselves.

A note to teachers: Reading comprehension strategies, like those described above, are more likely to be learned and used when they are taught explicitly rather than implicitly (Dole, 2000; Pressley, 2002).

A second model, **reciprocal teaching**, has been developed by Palincsar and Brown (1984; Brown & Palincsar, 1989) for use with the same group. Initially, the

reading comprehension

a student's level of understanding readings

reciprocal teaching

teacher models strategies; students take turns playing teacher's role, sometimes prompted by teacher; students given feedback and praise

When one student helps another solve a problem, it represents a type of *reciprocal teaching*. Playing the role of the teacher is a good way to learn.

classroom teacher demonstrated or modeled four strategies: *summarizing* (what was the passage about?), *questioning* (who did what?), *clarifying* (what does it mean?), and *predicting* (what is likely to happen next?), always in that order. The students were taught to take turns at playing the teacher's role and asking the other students the four questions. When they faltered, they were prompted by the teacher; they were also given feedback and praise by the teacher when appropriate. This approach produced noteworthy and stable gains in reading comprehension that generalized and transferred both to other tests and to other tasks, indicating that teaching problem-solving strategies is a good way to teach reading.

A third, highly operational model, aimed at producing a **coherent**, **accurate representation** of what has been read, identifies the following seven steps as ones that expert student readers follow when they read (Goldman & Rakestraw, 2000; Tuckman et al., 2008):

1. SKIM the chapter before you read it, to see what it's about.
2. FOCUS on MEANING and MAIN POINTS when you read it through.
3. TAKE NOTES on main points while you are reading.
4. MONITOR YOUR COMPREHENSION as you read. If you don't understand something, REREAD IT.
5. CHECK and REVIEW what you've learned relative to your purpose for learning it.
6. LOOK UP words and ideas you don't understand in other reference sources or ask for help.
7. GET RIGHT BACK TO WORK if you're interrupted.

dialogic reading
involves multiple readings in small group settings, with teachers questioning and responding to children during the readings

Finally, a fourth approach, called **dialogic reading** (Bramwell & Doyle, 2008), particularly effective for preschool and early elementary school children, involves multiple readings in small group settings, with teachers questioning and responding to children during the readings. A critical component of dialogic reading is the interactive behavior between teachers and students, with the child becoming the teller and the teacher becoming the listener, questioner, and audience. Using stories with social-emotional content provides models for problem solving, decision making, and interacting with others, thus giving children the opportunity to develop their individual reading skills while participating in activities that enhance their social competence.

The steps in the dialogic reading technique are (1) *prompting* the child to say something about the book (e.g., What seems to be bothering the child in this story?), (2) *evaluating* the child's response (e.g., Don't you think there may be something bothering him more?), (3) *expanding* the child's response by rephrasing and adding information to it, (e.g., What about what his brother did; taking his favorite toy and breaking it?) and (4) *repeating* the prompt to make sure the child has learned from the expansion (e.g., Wouldn't you be upset if someone broke your favorite toy?).

Social Studies

Armbruster and Anderson (1984) recommend teaching a particular problem-solving strategy or schema called a **goal frame** to help students comprehend what they read in history textbooks. The goal frame has four slots, or components—goal, plan, action, and outcome—that represent the four steps or stages in explaining a historical event such as a war or passage of a law. The **goal** is what the principal persons or groups want to happen (such as independence or expansion); the **plan** is the strategy for attaining the goal (such as attacking or trading); the **action** is the actual behavior taken to implement the plan; and the **outcome** is the consequence of the action, which may or may not result in the goal being met.

For example, when the Pilgrims set off for the New World, their goal was to attain religious freedom, their plan was to establish a colony in the New World, their action was to set sail in the Mayflower, and the outcome was the establishment of the Plymouth Colony. Using the goal frame this way—to study history as a series of problems to be solved—is expected to make the subject easier for students to understand.

Beyer (2008) recommends three techniques that teachers can use for "scaffolding" or supporting practice to facilitate students' development of problem solving and thinking skills in social studies. Recall that "scaffolding" is a step-by-step approach developed by Vygotsky (1978), and described in Chapter 2, for providing students with structure and guidance to enable them to apply a new skill or problem-solving procedure. The three techniques teachers can use, in order of use, are as follows:

- Step 1: Have students construct a **procedural checklist** to describe the steps in carrying out a specific skill or problem-solving procedure (e.g., state problem, state goal, identify possible approaches, predict possible consequences of each, evaluate consequences, select best alternative).
- Step 2: Pose **process-structured questions** for students to answer (e.g., what do you want to use the skill or problem-solving procedure to accomplish, what

goal frame
a schema or problem solving strategy involving four components: goal, plan, action, and outcome

goal
what the principal persons or groups want to happen

plan
the strategy for attaining the goal

action
the actual behavior taken to implement the plan

outcome
the consequence of the action

procedural checklist
describes the steps in carrying out a specific skill or problem-solving procedure

process-structured questions
questions related to the problem-solving procedure

alternatives do you have, what are the possible consequences of each and which are good and which are bad, what is the best choice?).

- Step 3. Have students develop **graphic organizers** (problem-solving diagrams or charts that present the sequence of steps in the problem-solving procedure that they can fill in as they carry out the procedure).

Once the students become more skilled in problem solving, the scaffolding can be altered or removed.

Mathematics

Remember that heuristics are general strategies for solving problems of a particular kind. Schoenfeld (1985, 1992) tried to teach students to think the way real mathematicians do in solving real problems. He taught them the kind of heuristics mathematicians use. For example:

1. drawing a diagram to represent the problem;
2. considering a similar problem with fewer variables;
3. trying to establish subgoals;
4. looking for an inductive argument, a general explanation for all the facts;
5. arguing the contrapositive: instead of trying to prove that if x is true, then y is true, trying to prove that if y is false, then x must be false;
6. arguing by contradiction: assuming that the statement they are trying to prove is false, and then trying to prove that one of the given conditions in the problem is false, or that something they know to be true is false, or that what they wish to prove is true (and if they can do any of these, then they will have proved what they want).

Teaching students to use these heuristics or general strategies to solve sample mathematics problems more than tripled their success in solving similar mathematics problems. Lampert (1986) devised methods for teaching mathematics to fourth-grade students based on their understanding of the world beyond the classroom. She starts teaching multiplication, for example, by using simple coin problems, such as "How can you make 82 cents using only nickels and pennies?" This builds on the students' implicit knowledge of how to solve multiplication problems based on their everyday experiences with coins.

In the second phase of teaching multiplication through problem solving, Lampert has her students create stories for multiplication problems. Through the stories, the students perform a series of decompositions or breakdowns of the problem and discover that it has no one "right" representation, just more and less useful representations depending on the context. Finally, in the third phase, students are introduced to the standard multiplication tables.

Using this technique, Lampert's students ended up with four kinds of knowledge: (1) **intuitive**—knowing the shortcuts or heuristics for solving problems, (2) **computational**—knowing how to do the computations, (3) **concrete**—knowing how to solve real problems, and (4) **principled**—knowing the mathematical principles involved. Most noteworthy is that this approach treats the learning of mathematics as

graphic organizers

problem-solving diagrams or charts that present the sequence of steps in the problem solving procedure that students can fill in as they carry out the procedure

intuitive

knowing the shortcuts or heuristics for solving problems

computational

knowing how to do the computations

concrete

knowing how to solve real problems

principled

knowing the mathematical principles involved

Purestock (RF)/Jupiter Images

Students do better at math when they use some of the strategies or *heuristics* that mathematicians use. One such strategy is drawing a diagram to represent the problem.

problem solving. It shows the students the real-world importance and value of what they have already learned. It also teaches them that mathematical problems often can be solved by more than one heuristic or strategy and helps them realize that they can create their own solution paths by behaving as a real mathematician would.

Classifying arithmetic problems into types can help students determine the appropriate procedure to solve them. Baroody & Standifer (1993; Bruning et al., 2004) have classified addition and subtraction problems into five types, the first two of which, **change-add-to** and **change-take-from** begin with a single collection and add to it or subtract from it to arrive at a larger or smaller one. An example of change-add-to: Tim had nine toy cars and then was given two more for his birthday. How many toy cars does he have now? An example of change-take-from: Tim has nine toy cars and gave two of them to his best friend. How many toy cars does Tim have now? In the first instance, addition would be the correct operation, in the second subtraction.

The remaining three problem types, part-part-whole, equalize, and compare each begin with two quantities that are either added or subtracted to find either the new whole amount or one of the parts. An example of **part-part-whole**: Tim has nine toy cars and two toy soldiers. How many toys does Tim have? An example of **equalize**: Tim has nine toy cars and his best friend has two. How many more toy cars does his best friend need to buy to have as many toy cars as Tim? An example of **compare**: Tim has nine toy cars and his best friend has two. How many more toy cars does Tim have than his best friend? In the first instance, addition would be the correct operation, while in the second and third it would be subtraction.

Problem classification is carried out differently by experts and novices (see Table 8.2). This is certainly true in mathematical areas such as statistics. Quilici & Mayer (1996) asked students to sort statistics word problems into categories by grouping together problems that could be solved in the same way. College students

change-add-to

problems begin with a single collection and add to it to arrive at a larger one

change-take-from

problems begin with a single collection and subtract from it to arrive at a smaller one

part-part-whole

begin with two quantities that are either added or subtracted to find the new whole amount

equalize

begin with two unequal quantities and determine what has to be done to make them equal

compare

begin with two unequal quantities and identify the correct operation for determining the difference

with no experience in statistics, hence novices, grouped the problems by surface features (e.g., the objects described in the problem—typists). Students with extensive experience in statistics, hence experts, grouped the problems by structural features (e.g., number of groups involved, nature of the data, type of statistical test to be used). Appropriate problem classification increases the likelihood of using the correct procedures to achieve the solution.

General Problem Solving

Perhaps the best known and proven program for teaching thinking and problem-solving skills is the **Productive Thinking Program** (Covington, Crutchfield, Davies, & Olton, 1974), which uses detective stories as the vehicle for helping fifth and sixth graders improve their problem-solving skills. Each story presents clues and then asks students to generate ideas to explain and ultimately solve the mystery. Two of the characters in the stories are Jim and Lila, who try to solve the mystery as well as serve as models for students to emulate.

Because of the success of this program in improving the problem-solving capabilities of youngsters in areas other than the Jim-and-Lila mysteries (Mansfield, Busse, & Krepelka, 1978), it is worthwhile to consider the problem-solving skills the program teaches. These appear below.

1. Decide early what the problem is that you are trying to solve before you begin working on it.
2. Get all of the facts first.
3. Follow a plan for working on the problem.
4. Don't jump to conclusions about the answer. Keep an open mind.
5. Think of as many ideas as you can, especially unusual ones. Don't stop with one idea.

Productive Thinking Program

uses detective stories as the vehicle for helping fifth and sixth graders improve their problem-solving skills

The *Productive Thinking Program* uses detective stories to help students improve their problem-solving skills. They are provided with clues to help them solve a problem.

David Grossman/Photo Researchers, Inc.

6. To get ideas, think carefully about all the important persons and objects in the problem.

7. Think first of general solutions and then figure out more specific ideas for each one.

8. When you're trying to think of ideas, let your mind roam. Good ideas can come from anywhere.

9. Check each idea against the facts to make sure it fits.

10. If you get stuck, keep trying.

11. When you run out of ideas, try looking at the problem differently.

12. Review all the facts to make sure you haven't missed anything.

13. Make up an unlikely answer and see how it works.

14. Keep an eye out for odd or puzzling facts. Explaining them may lead you to the solution.

15. If there are a number of puzzling facts, try to find a single explanation that connects them all.

Creativity

Learning Objective 5

Explain what creativity is, how it is determined, and procedures for increasing it, including reframing and brainstorming.

Mary McKeon was a very creative teacher. She taught American History I to high school sophomores. It covered the American Revolution era and the Civil War era. What made her approach creative was that it focused on reliving history rather than just reporting it. This is how it worked. At the beginning of the term, she presented the students with a list of the major figures in the era of the American Revolution and asked each student to pick one. Obviously, everybody wanted to be George Washington, but there could only be one. Some of the historical figures were larger than life (e.g., Benjamin Franklin, Alexander Hamilton), and they were picked pretty fast. Students who took too long to decide ended up with less well-known figures (e.g., Thomas Pinckney).

Everybody then had to try to learn as much about their chosen figure as they could in the following month so they would be ready for the reenactment. She started out with the Boston Tea Party and the Battle of Lexington, which provided the Samuel Adams character with a lot of on-stage time as the class battled its way through the American Revolution. The same procedure was used for the Civil War era, but those who managed to pick early the first time around had to wait until later the second time around.

It turned out to be a very fun way to learn, and the students carried their knowledge of American history around in their heads for a long time after they graduated from high school.

In previous chapters, we have described classical conditioning of simple reflexes and progressed through more complex conditioning, learning from memorization, meaningful learning, and problem solving. We have now reached what some consider the pinnacle, or zenith, of the thinking process: creativity.

This final section of the chapter introduces a third approach to learning and thinking, creativity. Creativity is a mode of cognitive activity that causes unique ideas to come into being, such as when a "light bulb" seemingly goes off in our head and leads us to a novel idea or a practical solution to a problem. We turn to that now.

What Is Creativity and Its Sources and Properties?

Creativity, in a technical sense, refers to the ability to generate many unique yet appropriate solutions to a problem for which there is no one right answer, that is, something not only original, but also appropriate and useful (Runco, 2000; Berk, 2005). Guilford (1967) calls creativity an example of **divergent thinking**, generating more than one acceptable solution to a problem, in contrast to **convergent thinking,** or generating the one correct solution. Creativity is different from intelligence, which is a measure of verbal knowledge and intellectual skills (see Chapter 4). It is also different from wisdom (Sternberg, 2001), practical intelligence (Sternberg & Wagner, 1986), and tacit knowledge (Wagner, 1987), each of which represents a combination of knowledge and thinking applied to finding correct answers for problems in the real world. In other words, creativity is unique among the mental processes insofar as the others require going from the facts to the one solution. Creativity requires going from the facts to the many solutions.

It has been argued that it is difficult to separate "creativity" from the "construction of meaning" because the constructivist approach to learning (described in the first part of this chapter) is similar to creativity. It is claimed that both approaches involve the generation of unique yet appropriate solutions to problems (Moran, 2008). It has also been proposed that social engagement is a primary site for creative activity, labeled **creative collaboration** (see Box 8.4 on "brainstorming"), in which the teacher plays a significant role (Craft et al., 2007).

Capossela (2000) describes a theory of the development of creativity proposed by Vygotsky (whose work was described in Chapter 2). According to the theory, the **expressive play** of children (e.g., acting out and vocalizing as they play) leads to the development of the mental processes of creativity as does an internal maturation process that proceeds gradually as the child matures. Furthermore, the theory proposes that children's creative processes begin with the practice of **object substitution**, that is, using a variety of objects interchangeably during play, propelled by a combination of imagination and intelligence, which suggests that parents and teachers should contribute to this pattern.

Studies of the factors associated with creativity suggest that a person's needs for uniqueness and understanding are important predictors of creativity (Dollinger, 2003), as are **extraversion** (interest in interacting with other people), but not intelligence (Furnham & Bachtiar; 2008), **tolerance for ambiguity** (i.e., uncertainty) and parents' level of creativity (Zenasni, Besancon, & Lubart, 2008). Factors that negatively affect creativity are perfectionism (Gallucci, Kline, & Middleston, 2000) and over-emphasis on testing (Holliday, 2008). Finally, research shows that creativity is **domain-general**, meaning it is not limited to a single domain such as mathematical creativity, but can occur in a variety of domains (Chen, Himsel, & Kasof, 2006).

---

creativity

refers to the ability to generate many unique yet appropriate solutions to a problem for which there is no one right answer

divergent thinking

generating more than one acceptable solution to a problem

convergent thinking

generating the one correct solution to a problem

creative collaboration

uses social engagement as a primary site for creative activity

expressive play

children acting out and vocalizing as they play

object substitution

using a variety of objects interchangeably during play

extraversion

interest in interacting with other people

tolerance for ambiguity

can handle uncertainty

domain-general

not limited to a single domain

Expressive play of children involves acting out and vocalizing in order to develop their mental processes of creativity.

7h6135, Lawrence Migdale/Photoresearchers

How Can Creativity Be Measured?

Psychologists such as Guilford (1967) and Torrance (1984), who have studied creativity extensively, detect it in one of three ways. One way is to give someone the name of a familiar object, such as a shoe, and ask him to generate as many uses for that object as he can. Take a minute to see how many different uses for a shoe you can think of. The only ones that count toward creativity are the ones that are unusual yet appropriate. If you said a shoe could be used for walking, then you would not score a point because that answer is too obvious. But if you said a shoe could be used as a paperweight, a bug killer, or a flowerpot, you would get one point for each answer.

The second way to find out how creative people are is to give them an unusual situation and ask them to generate as many consequences of that situation as they can. Try this one: The earth's surface, except for the highest mountain peaks, will be entirely covered by water within three months. Write as many consequences as you can. Again, if you said that everyone will go out and buy a boat or move to the mountain peaks, you would not get any points because these are obvious consequences. But if you came up with some remote yet possible consequences, such as an increase in swimming lessons or a sudden shift to hydroponics (underwater farming) or a good time to go into the business of selling scuba gear, you would be demonstrating your creativity. And the more of these you came up with, the more creative you would be.

The third way to discover creativity is to look at people's drawings. For example, draw some triangles on a piece of paper and then make as many unique drawings from them as you can. Do not merely scribble or doodle. That is not creative. The drawings must be recognizable or representative in the eyes of the judges. Now compare your drawings to the ones in Figure 8.1. This is called

FIGURE 8 . 1

Making Creative Pictures from Incomplete Figures and Triangles.

For practice, see if you can make an object or picture of each of the two line patterns above. Then see how many pictures or figures you can make from the triangles below, just as you did with the line patterns above. Work for 3 minutes. Don't forget to add a label or title to each triangle picture.

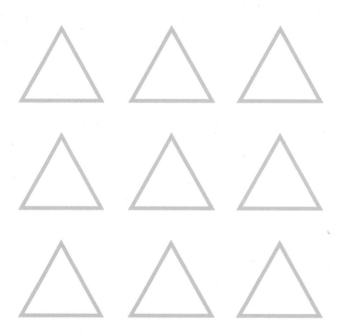

Reprinted by Permission of The Creative Education Foundation, Amherst, MA.

---

figural creativity, in contrast to the **verbal creativity** measured by how many uses or consequences you can generate using words.

Is Creativity Necessarily a Valued Capability?

Although people tend to express admiration and high regard for creativity and for those who exhibit it, this expression usually is either in the abstract or after the fact. Children who exhibit creativity in the classroom often are regarded as nonconformists by their teachers. Wallach and Kogan (1965) found that highly creative girls who were not equally high in measured intelligence had difficulty coping with the achievement demands of their teachers and carrying out the classroom

figural creativity

creativity measured by how many consequences you can generate using figures

verbal creativity

creativity measured by how many uses or consequences you can generate using words

SUMMING IT UP

Outline the types and general characteristics and ingredients of constructivism, and explain and illustrate six specific models of constructivist teaching.

The basic premises of **constructivism** are that learners actively *construct* their own knowledge rather than receive preformed information transmitted by others; to have meaning, information must be discovered through some activity on the learner's part; learning and thinking are contextualized, that is, occur in a context or situation, not in a vacuum, referred to as **situated cognition.** Three types of constructivism are: **exogenous**—in which the acquisition of knowledge reflects the reality of the external world, **endogenous**—in which new knowledge develops out of earlier knowledge through a process of cognitive development, and **dialectical**—in which knowledge comes from the interactions between learners, the environment, and others in it. Six models or environments of constructivist teaching are **Teaching for Understanding, Collaborative Problem Solving, Fostering a Community of Learners, Apprenticeships in Thinking, Problem-Based Learning,** and the **Jasper Woodbury Problem-Solving Series,** described in Concept Review: Table 8.1.

Learning Objective 1

Key Concepts:

constructivism, exogenous constructivism, endogenous constructivism, dialectical constructivism, social constructivism, situated cognition (p. 311); tenets of constructivism (p. 312); Teaching for Understanding, Collaborative Problem Solving (p. 313); Fostering a Community of Learners (p. 314); Apprenticeships in Thinking (p. 315); Problem-Based Learning, Jasper Woodbury Problem–Solving Series (p. 316); meaningful learning (p. 317).

Describe the dilemmas of constructivism.

Classroom teachers are finding the implementation of constructivist instruction far more difficult than the reform community acknowledges. To employ constructivist teaching methods, teachers must "make personal sense of constructivism as a basis for instruction, reorient the cultures of classrooms to be consonant with the constructivist philosophy, and deal with the pervasive educational conservatism that works against efforts to teach for understanding.

Learning Objective 2

Key Concepts:

dilemmas of constructivism (p. 321).

Differentiate general problem-solving strategies in terms of the heuristics or approaches used for attacking the problem and generating solutions, and describe the (a) differences in the ways experts and novices solve problems, particularly in terms of the role of domain-specific knowledge and (b) combination of general strategies and expert knowledge, especially as it affects the transfer of solution strategies.

Problem-solving strategies can be subdivided into **general** ones that can be used in many situations and **context-specific** ones that fit only one specific problem or class of problems.

Learning Objective 3

Key Concepts:

problem solving, ill-defined problems, well-defined problems (p. 323); general problem-solving strategies, heuristics, problem space (p. 324); means-end analysis, algorithmic, specific problem-solving strategies

General strategies for attacking a problem are called **heuristics** and include such activities as breaking a problem into subproblems, solving simpler problems that reflect aspects of the main problem, using diagrams to represent problems, and examining special cases to get a feel for the problem. One common problem-solving strategy is **means-end analysis**, a technique for transforming a beginning state into an end state, one step at a time. This strategy also represents a heuristic, in contrast to the alternative approach of trying all possible combinations or solution routes (called an **algorithm**). **Experts** used chunking, schemata, and underlying principles to classify problems and cut them down to size. They used highly organized, **domain-specific knowledge** to develop shortcuts and plan their strategies. They knew enough about the problem to **work forward** in solving it, without constantly referring to the desired goal or end state. **Novices**, by comparison, considered many alternatives and relied on *working backward* from the desired end state to decide what the solution was. In order for students to function as true experts, they must be taught not only appropriate general strategies but also how to transfer these strategies or use them to solve a variety of problems.

Apply metacognitive models for teaching problem-solving skills in the domains of reading, social studies, and mathematics, as well as one general model.

Problem-solving skills, or **metacognitive strategies**, are best taught as a *set of component skills* with an emphasis on process or how to proceed (rather than on product or solution), in the context of a *specific subject-matter domain*. When **reading comprehension** is treated as problem solving, strategies such as *summarizing, questioning, clarifying*, and *predicting* help students determine what a story is about, what its important details are, and what the characters feel and why. In social studies, the **goal frame** helps students treat history reading as problem solving in that they look for the **goal, plan, action,** and **outcome** of each historical event. In mathematics, students as problem solvers are encouraged to use *diagrams*, to *scale* problems down, to establish *subgoals*, to look for *general explanations*, to argue the *contrapositive*, to argue by, and to create stories to break the problem into more solvable parts. Finally, *representation training* can be used to teach students how to represent mathematical word problems using the number line so that they can tell when to add and when to subtract. There is also a general approach to teaching problem-solving skills, the **Productive Thinking Program**, that uses detective stories as the teaching vehicle. Students are given a series of 15 rules to use in order to function as good detectives and solve the given problems.

Explain what creativity is, how it is determined, and procedures for increasing it, including reframing and brainstorming.

Learning Objective 5

Key Concepts:

creativity, divergent thinking, convergent thinking, creative collaboration, expressive play, object substitution, extraversion, tolerance for ambiguity, domain-general (p. 338);
figural creativity, verbal creativity (p. 340);
creative performance (p. 341);
reframing, brainstorming (p. 342).

Creativity requires a different kind of problem solving: using **divergent thinking**—finding many solutions—in contrast to **convergent thinking,** or finding the right solution. It is measured in such ways as giving someone a familiar object and asking for *unusual* or *alternative uses*, giving a situation and asking for unusual or *remote consequences*, and giving lines or triangles and asking for a variety of *drawings*. To increase creativity, people should ask why (and not just follow suit), be open to new ideas, use visualization, think out loud with others, not pressure themselves, try a lot of answers, put themselves in others' shoes, write down their ideas, not be self-critical, and use their sense of humor. Two particular techniques are **reframing,** which can help a person change perspective, and **brainstorming,** which can help produce new ideas.

Visit the Education CourseMate for *Educational Psychology* to access study tools and resources including the Virtual Psychology Labs, TeachSource Video Cases, chapter web links, tutorial quizzes, glossary flashcards, and more. Go to CengageBrain.com to register using your access code.

9 | Group Processes in Instruction

After reading this chapter, you should be able to meet the following learning objectives	Chapter Contents
LEARNING OBJECTIVE 1 Outline a model of group dynamics to explain group processes in the classroom.	A Model of Group Dynamics
LEARNING OBJECTIVE 2 Summarize the influence of teacher expectations on student expectations—the self-fulfilling prophecy—and discuss how these expectations are communicated.	Expectations—An Influence on the Behavior of Teachers and Students • Self-Fulfilling Prophecy • Communicating Expectations
LEARNING OBJECTIVE 3 Define group norms and explain how they influence behavior; define normative goal structures and cooperative learning and explain how they effect student performance.	Norms—The Rules Followed by Groups • The Influence of Norms • Normative Goal Structures • Cooperative Learning
LEARNING OBJECTIVE 4 Distinguish between the different bases of leadership, and explain how to use various leadership styles and techniques for effective classroom management.	Leadership—The Teacher as Leader • Bases of Leadership • Leadership for Classroom Management • Leadership Styles
LEARNING OBJECTIVE 5 Explain the effects that the communicator, the content of the communication, audience predisposition, and audience response, have on the influence of the communication, and give examples of effective and congruent communication skills.	Communication Between Teachers and Students • Credibility of the Communicator • Content of the Communication • Audience Predisposition • Audience Response
LEARNING OBJECTIVE 6 Point out factors that make groups attractive to their members and outcomes or benefits that result from association with an attractive group, and categorize the components of effective classroom climate.	Friendship, Liking, and Classroom Climate • What Makes a Group Attractive? • Liking Patterns Among Students • Classroom Climate

Mr. Sachs Forms Classroom Groups

"Okay class, when I say the word, I want you to divide up into small groups of four and sit yourselves down at one of the six tables. First, we'll go around the room and count off from one to four to see what group you'll be in. After you count off, be sure to remember your number so you know what group you're in. Okay, let's count off....Very well done. I've put a number on each of the tables, so what I want you all to do right now is go to the table that has your number. Please pay attention to what you're doing; we won't continue until everybody is sitting quietly at his or her table.....Very good!

Now you're going to work as discussion groups for our discussion of the video about the making of ethanol that we've just seen. I've written six questions on the chalkboard, numbered 1 to 6, and I want each table to discuss and answer the question that is the same as their table number. I will give you 15 minutes for your discussion.... No! No! Don't start yet; I haven't given you all your instructions. I want one person at each table to be the discussion leader and another person to be the note taker. The discussion leader will have the job of keeping the group focused on its task, and the note taker will have the job of taking notes on what was said and then reporting the group's ideas to all the other groups after we're all done with discussion. Please make sure to spend your 15 minutes, all of it, talking about the question for your group. I will tell you when your 15 minutes are up. Does everybody understand what to do? Any questions? Good! Let's begin!"

- How does this sound to you as a way to form classroom groups?
- What are your thoughts about learning and teaching in groups?

Lessons We Can Learn from the Story Students, especially young ones, may not be accustomed to learning in small groups and taking responsibility for their outcomes. They need to learn about effective group functioning and group dynamics and a good teacher will make sure they do.

Learning Objective 1

Outline a model of group dynamics to explain group processes in the classroom.

A Model of Group Dynamics

A classroom is a social setting and a class is a social group insofar as the members of the class interact. Sometimes students in a class work interdependently: in pairs or small groups. Even when functioning as a single group, class members may interact with one another through discussions or various kinds of informal behavior (for example, passing notes). And, of course, they often interact with the teacher.

Classmates also share some common goals, such as learning (or perhaps just surviving), as well as developing their own sense of self and having a satisfying—and we hope enjoyable—time. The interplay or interaction between the characteristics of the members of a group (such as expectations) and the characteristics of the group as a whole (such as norms or rules of conduct) produces various group processes (for example, development, communication, leadership, and conflict). These processes, in turn, produce various group outcomes (say, friendship, influence, and climate; Jewell & Reitz, 1981). This arrangement of interdependent parts, shown in Figure 9.1, represents a model of group dynamics.

For example, if class members have highly positive expectations about the experiences they will have in a class, and the norms or rules of the class are ones that permit a lot of freedom and interaction between class members, then the process of communication in the class is likely to be facilitated. This will tend to produce considerable friendship between class members and a positive classroom climate.

Of course, in a classroom, all of the participants are not equally influential. The teacher's role is more central than that of any individual student. Adams and Biddle (1970) concluded that teachers are the principal communicators 84 percent of the time. They also make the rules. That is why, in applying the group dynamics model to the classroom, we will give particular attention to the teacher's role and influence on the interaction process.

FIGURE 9.1

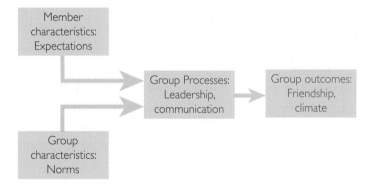

A Group Dynamics Model of the Classroom

Expectations—An Influence on the Behavior of Teachers and Students

Expectations are beliefs people hold about how they and others will behave in various situations and what the result of those behaviors will be. People hold many beliefs, but the beliefs they hold about themselves are particularly influential, and so will be a major topic of the next chapter. In this chapter, the beliefs or expectations that teachers have for their students are examined, as well as how these beliefs can affect teachers' own behavior and what impact that behavior has on their students. These effects are discussed within the context of the classroom as a social community.

Learning Objective 2

Summarize the influence of teacher expectations on student expectations—the self-fulfilling prophecy—and discuss how these expectations are communicated.

Self-Fulfilling Prophecy

The strong influence of one's expectations on one's own subsequent behavior as well as on the behavior of others is reflected in the concept of the self-fulfilling prophecy, first coined by Merton (1949). The **self-fulfilling prophecy** says that what someone expects (or prophesies) to happen will indeed come to pass. People's expectations will be fulfilled merely because they believe that they will. If you believe you are smart, you will act smart, and others will perceive you, based on how you have acted, to be smart. If you believe someone else is smart, you will probably, though unconsciously, treat him as if he were smart; he, in turn, will unconsciously "read the message you are sending him"—that he is smart—and will probably behave as if he were smart. Hence, your belief will provoke his behavior, which will reinforce your belief. This circular process is the self-fulfilling prophecy.

An example of the self-fulfilling prophesy is provided by a research study in which women were given a mathematics test, but were told before taking it that the test was a measure of whether men or women were better at mathematics. The resulting outcome was that women performed more poorly on the test than men. However, when the test was given to another group of women who were not told this, they performed as well as men (Spencer, Steele, & Quinn, 1999). The explanation was that what the first group of women were told lowered their performance expectations, leading them to expect men to do better on the test, thus fulfilling their own prophesy.

Rosenthal and Fode (1963) established that the self-fulfilling prophecy can apply to animals (see Box 1.3). In 1968, Rosenthal and a colleague set out to prove that it can apply to schoolchildren (Rosenthal & Jacobson, 1968). Their study, *Pygmalion in the Classroom*, made reference to a story by George Bernard Shaw in which a plain girl from the slums of London is made into a "fair lady" by a doting professor. In the original Greek myth, Galatea, a beautiful statue, is transformed into a living woman through the belief of her adoring creator, Pygmalion.

If a professor can turn a slum girl into a fair lady and a sculptor can turn a statue into a live woman just by believing in them, then, thought Rosenthal and Jacobson, a teacher may be able to turn an ordinary student into a "bloomer." To test this hypothesis, they selected a group of students at random in a San Francisco school and told their teachers that these students were expected to bloom based on a test that had been administered at the start of the year. At the end of the year, these students had, in fact, "bloomed" by exceeding normal expectations in tested reading, intelligence, and teachers' ratings of social and personal adjustment.

Tuckman and Bierman (1971), working within a small city high school—arbitrarily, and without the knowledge of either students or teachers, but with the concurrence of the school's administration—reassigned a certain percentage of students from the middle and lowest tracks to the next highest track. Some of the higher C track students were moved up to the B track, and some of the higher B track students were moved up to the A track. By the end of the year, more than half of the students arbitrarily moved up in track were recommended by their teachers

expectations

beliefs that people hold about how they and others will behave in various situations and what the result of those behaviors will be

self-fulfilling prophecy

says that what someone expects to happen will indeed come to pass

Russell Burden/Index Stock Imagery/PhotoLibrary

Telling a teacher that her students were expected to improve their academic performance resulted in her students actually demonstrating the expected improvement. This illustrates the power of expectations on behavior.

to remain in the new, higher track. More than half had proven that they could do better if their school and their teachers believed in them enough. Even their scores on independent, standardized tests were beginning to reflect their new ability to perform. Shouldn't Pygmalion be at work in more schools?

It has been generally concluded by Good and Brophy (2003) and others that the expectations of teachers influence the self-expectations of students and, hence, their performance in school. Schmuck and Schmuck (2001) refer to this effect as a **circular interpersonal process** and represent it as shown in Figure 9.2. It shows that your feelings and expectations about yourself and others influence your behavior, which, in turn, affects how others see themselves and you, and then affects how they behave toward you. Others' behavior toward you then affects your feelings and expectations about yourself and others, making a big and never-ending circle.

For example, suppose a new student feels fearful and insecure in the classroom because of her past school experiences with teachers who have threatened and embarrassed her. In her new classroom, she will expect the same thing to happen and it will make her defensive. As a result, she will withdraw from interactive situations or will behave in a hostile fashion. This behavior will cause teacher and classmates alike to begin to expect her to behave in an unfriendly manner, which will cause them to feel threatened by her and to form negative feelings toward her. These negative feelings will lead the teacher and many classmates to respond to her with hostility of their own. When she perceives their hostility, it will only intensify her original feelings of fear and insecurity and cause the whole cycle to continue, until and unless something can be changed. If the teacher does not perceive the student's withdrawn or hostile acts in a negative light, and so does not react to them negatively, it may be possible to alter the cycle.

circular interpersonal process

when the expectations of teachers influence the self-expectations of students and, hence, their performance in school

FIGURE 9.2

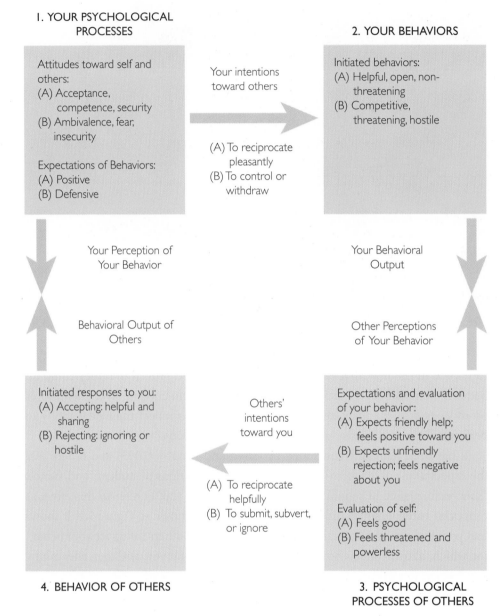

The Circular Interpersonal Process

Adapted from Schmuck and Schmuck, 2001, pp. 34-35.

Communicating Expectations

How do teachers communicate their expectations to students? Good and Brophy (2003) report that students whom teachers perceived to have high ability received (1) more praise, (2) more help and coaching, and (3) more time in answering questions than those students believed to be of low ability. Teachers were more critical of those students believed to be of low ability, gave them little time to answer a question (because they believed they did not know the answer), and accepted poor-quality answers from them. Instead of waiting longer for the poorer students to answer questions, they waited longer for the better students to answer questions—reflecting greater patience and higher expectations. Similar findings were obtained by others.

Rosenthal (1974) described four ways teachers can communicate positive expectations for student performance:

1. Climate: create warmth; provide attention and emotional support.
2. Feedback: provide encouraging feedback and praise.
3. Input: give hints, rephrased questions, additional information.
4. Output: give opportunities to respond and wait for answer to be given.

Babad (1998) grouped Rosenthal's four factors into two, calling them *emotional support* (the first factor above) and *learning support* (a combination of factors 3 and 4).

Cooper (1979) believed that teachers are concerned with the *performance* of high-expectation students but not of low-expectation students. With the latter group, they are concerned primarily with being able to *control* their behavior. Therefore, teachers praise and encourage high-expectation students, which enhances those students' performance and strengthens teachers' belief in their high expectations. Low-expectation students do not feel as personally in control of situations (which they are not, because teachers are trying to control them), so they do not perform as well, thereby strengthening their teachers' belief in the correctness of their low expectations. Hence, the circular interpersonal process is in operation again.

How can teachers break this negative circular interpersonal process in the classroom group? Some suggestions are given in Box 9.1.

BOX 9.1

TAKE IT TO THE CLASSROOM

Breaking the Cycle of Negative Expectations in the Classroom Group (Middle/High School)

When Carrying Out Discussion or Recitation Lessons

1. Purposely call on the students you believe are less able.

2. Give them more time to answer than other students.

3. Demand the same from them as from other students.

4. Give them as much help, praise, and encouragement as possible.

In Performance Situations

1. Have students estimate the performance expectations they have of themselves and of one another.

2. Have them compare actual performance to expected performance.

3. Talk to students about their self-image and performance expectations.

4. Give accurate and supportive performance feedback to all students.

In Classroom Interaction

1. Be friendly and warm to students, regardless of your expectations for their academic performance.

2. Avoid criticism, rejection, and avoidance of students from whom you expect less.

In General

1. Be aware of your feelings toward and expectations of each of your students.

2. Be aware of the messages you are sending out to individual students.

• Can you describe a personal experience where you had to overcome negative expectations? How did you deal with it?

Think It Over

as a LEARNER Can you describe an experience you have had where a teacher acted toward you in a way that suggested he or she had negative expectations about your ability to perform or behave, and the influence, if any, this experience had on your self-beliefs?

as a TEACHER What would you do to ensure that you would not communicate negative expectations to individual students in your class?

Norms—The Rules Followed by Groups

Norms are agreed-upon or shared beliefs by members of a group on such matters as (1) how to view the world around them, (2) what to think, (3) what to like or dislike, and (4) how to behave. Norms may be *formal* or *informal*, depending on whether or not they are carefully stated. In either case, they are adhered to by the group. They can be *static* or unchanging or alternatively, *dynamic*. Some examples of the four types of classroom norms are given in Figure 9.3.

Learning Objective 3

Define group norms and explain how they influence behavior; define normative goal structures and cooperative learning and explain how they effect student performance.

FIGURE 9.3

	FORMAL	INFORMAL
STATIC	Rules followed with little prompting: 1. No cheating 2. Asking permission to leave the room 3. Addressing teacher when seeking permission to change something in the room	Procedures and routines: 1. How students enter the room 2. Who talks to whom for how long 3. Saying "Good Morning," "Thank you," etc., to the teacher
DYNAMIC	Rules in need of at least occasional enforcement: 1. No talking during story time or individual study time 2. Turning work in on time 3. Using correct grammar in talking and writing	Interpersonal actions that involve active monitoring: 1. Addressing the teacher in a nasty fashion 2. Wearing hair in a style extremely different from that of other students 3. Acting abusively toward others

Examples of Classroom Norms Schmuck and Schmuck, 2001, p. 197.

The Influence of Norms

The fact that norms can affect how we see things is illustrated in a classic experiment by Asch (1952). Group members were asked to tell which of three lines was the same length as a given test line. The judgment was not difficult to make, but all

norms

a group's agreed-upon or shared beliefs about how to view the world around them, what to think, what to like or dislike, and how to behave

of the members of each group except for one were working for the experimenter, and they all intentionally gave the same wrong answer. About one-third of the real subjects yielded to the group judgment even though they did not see it as representing the right answer. They yielded because they either questioned their own judgment ("I must need glasses; all these people can't be wrong") or did not want to stand out and be different ("I know they're wrong, but I don't want to seem the oddball"). In other words, the informal norm was to go along with the group, to acquiesce to the group judgment or action.

The fact that behavior can be influenced by norms is further illustrated in a famous study by Milgram (1963) on obedience. Subjects watched a confederate of the experimenter whom they believed to be another subject like themselves deliver an electric shock to someone. Actually, no real shock was being delivered, but they did not know that. When they were asked to deliver a painful and perhaps even harmful shock to someone, many of them complied. The norm to obey commands or even requests from someone in authority is for many people both powerful and compelling. Teachers must remember that they have this power, particularly when children are in early stages of moral development and tend to react in an absolute fashion to adult authority.

Factors That Affect the Influence of Norms

When the group is (1) a highly close-knit one like a club or team, (2) a source of gratification for its members, (3) one in which members share group goals or aims, and (4) one in which norms are highly relevant to group functioning, then norms will be very influential and will affect the feelings and behaviors of the members (Nowack, A., Szamrej, J., & Latane, B., 1990). In most cases, classroom communities do not have these characteristics, so their norms will be less influential than those of other groups or communities of which students are members. However, teachers can make classroom norms more influential by providing evidence that everyone is following them and experts recommend them (Cialdini, 2001).

Jackson (1960) has shown that when the *range of tolerable behavior* approved of by a group is narrowly defined, then both the probability of transgression and its ensuing punishment are increased. Teachers who demand a narrow range of tolerable behavior, for example, sitting entirely still in their seats and not talking for a whole class period, therefore, are more likely to spend time disciplining students than teachers whose range of tolerable behavior is broader.

Norms also differ in *intensity* depending on how important they are to persons of a given age. Among teenagers, for example, norms that govern dress and dating are very important and therefore intense, while among nursery school or kindergarten children, the more intense norms are those that govern sharing of toys.

Particularly strong are norms agreed on by virtually all members of a group, called *highly crystallized* norms by Jackson (1960). However, norms that are highly crystallized for each subgroup in a classroom community but that differ, or are in disagreement, are considered *ambiguous* norms and may lead to conflict. If the more serious students want to pay attention but the less serious students want to talk, the result may be some unpleasant interaction between the two subgroups.

Sometimes, norms are not well *integrated*, in which case they can easily lead to confusion. If the teacher tries to establish a norm for working independently and a norm for attending to his or her every word, then there may be confusion when the teacher tries to interrupt individual work sessions to give out general instructions.

Finally, people are all members of many groups, each of which has its own norms. When a norm is shared by all groups, such as being quiet when someone else is talking, then that norm has *congruence*. Congruent norms are easier to follow than incongruent ones. If one teacher expects students to raise their hands and be recognized before they may speak, while another teacher permits students to speak out spontaneously, students may forget when they are supposed to raise their hands and when they need not.

Normative Goal Structures

Normative goal structures are shared expectations about the best or proper way to attain desired goals, such as achieving knowledge or developing skills in a classroom. Johnson and Johnson (2003) identify and describe three normative goal structures for instruction particularly relevant for teachers: cooperative, competitive, and individualistic.

When working within a **cooperative goal structure**, each member seeks an outcome that will be beneficial to all members. In other words, the members share the same goal and can attain it only interdependently and to the same degree. On a baseball team, for example, a victory is a victory for all and a loss is a loss for all, even though some players may have gotten more hits than others or made more errors. Hits and errors are individual outcomes. The cooperative goal is winning. In a classroom, the use of the cooperative goal structure, referred to as cooperative learning, has enjoyed growing popularity. Research findings indicate that this is the most effective goal structure in promoting achievement (Johnson, Maruyama, Johnson, Nelson, & Skon, 1981).

In the **competitive goal structure**, by comparison, students seek not only to succeed but also to make other students fail—what economists call a *zero-sum* situation. In order for there to be a winner, there must be a loser. When a teacher gives only a fixed percentage of A's to a class, the goal structure becomes competitive because for someone to get an A, others must get B's, C's, etc. (The baseball example above, while cooperative within a team, is obviously competitive between teams, where there will be a winner and a loser; however, it is considered to be primarily cooperative.)

Finally, an **individualistic goal structure** is one in which the goals of individuals are independent of one another. Thus, whether or not one person attains his or her goal has nothing to do with the success or failure of anyone else. Typically, classrooms are structured in this way—each student is out for him- or herself and does not affect the goal attainment of others.

ABStudio/ Workbook Stock/ Jupiter Images

When people cooperate on a task, they are likely to have a positive outcome.

normative goal structure

shared expectations about the best and proper way to attain desired goals

cooperative goal structure

each member seeks an outcome that will be beneficial to all members

competitive goal structure

students seek not only to succeed but to make others fail

individualistic goal structure

the goals of individuals are independent of one another

To restate, the possibilities are as follows:

- cooperation: If I win, you win; if I lose, you lose.
- competition: If I win, you lose; if I lose, you win.
- individualism: My winning or losing has nothing to do with you; your winning or losing has nothing to do with me.

Cooperative Learning

Cooperative learning is interdependent (or collaborative) learning, an accepted—and often preferred—instructional method at all levels of education (Johnson, Johnson, & Smith, 2007). Championing the increased use of cooperative learning in the classroom, in contrast to either competitive or individualistic learning, has been a central aim of Johnson and Johnson (2003) and Slavin (1995). Slavin's approach to *student team learning*, called Student-Teams and Academic Divisions, or STAD, involves grouping students into four-member heterogeneous learning teams to study material initially presented by the teacher. Students then take a test on the material individually but are rewarded based on the average test performance of the four team members. The idea is to provide incentives for students to encourage and help one another to master academic materials. Slavin (1995) has found that the student team learning model produces consistently more positive effects on student achievement, across all students, than the traditional or individualistic approach, and that these effects are primarily due to the idea of team incentives rather than individual ones.

Yamarik (2007) found that students taught by cooperative learning achieved greater academic performance than students taught by the traditional lecture format, while Bramwell and Doyle (2008) report that multiple readings in small group settings, with questioning and responding is a critical factor necessary for children's reading comprehension. Results from a study by Johnson, Johnson, and Stanne (1986) showed that cooperative group students did best on worksheets, tests, bonus points, and all other achievement measures. Competitive group students did the next best and individualistic students did the worst. A *Concept Review* of the Johnson and Johnson approach (2003) to cooperative learning in comparison to the other types is given in Table 9.1.

But what could be the reason for the success of so-called cooperative groups? If we presume that within such groups, the less able students are likely to solicit help from the more able students and, in turn, the more able students are likely to give help to these less able students when they solicit it, then help would account for the greater achievement in such groups (Webb, 1982; Webb & Palincsar, 1996). Cooperative groups work best when the rewards are given out on a group basis, thus motivating less able group members to seek help and more able group members to provide it (Webb, 1982). In competitive and individualistic situations, there will be little motivation for students to help one another. Based on Webb's findings, teachers are encouraged to (1) have students work in groups when possible, (2) compose each group of students of all levels of ability rather than the more typical approach of segregating the "highs" from the "lows," and (3) provide rewards and recognition on a group basis to stimulate students who need help to seek it and receive it from their more able group mates. See Box 9.2 (on page 365) for an example.

cooperative learning

an interdependent, or collaborative, instructional method

CONCEPT REVIEW TABLE 9.1

Comparing Cooperative, Competitive, and Individualistic Learning Methods, Johnson & Johnson Style

	COOPERATIVE	COMPETITIVE	INDIVIDUALISTIC
Basis for a Student's Grade on Worksheets and Final Test	Average performance of group members	Relative position in group	Individual performance compared to preset criteria
Basis for a Students' Bonus Points	Each student gets 10% of what total class earns	Given only to students first in class standing	Based on individual work
Basis for Daily Feedback	Group performance	Individual performance relative to group and class	One's own performance only
Interaction Pattern	Group members assigned specific roles; roles rotated daily	Everybody works alone	No interaction permitted
How Daily Worksheets Are Completed	Individually	Individually	Individually
How Final Tests Are Taken	Individually	Individually	Individually
Resulting Achievement	The best	The next best	The worst

In his handbook for using cooperative learning procedures, Sharan (1994) describes five steps for students to follow in planning and carrying out a group project:

1. The topic is selected and students are grouped into teams of six to research it.
2. The topic is divided into subtopics; pairs of individuals within groups select subtopics for study and decide what to study, how to study, and the purpose of the study.
3. The investigation is carried out by pairs first; later the group integrates everyone's contributions into a single outline.
4. A final report is presented to the whole class, including activities and total class discussion.
5. An evaluation is made of the final reports and of the work done to construct the reports. Achievement tests can be given, but it is equally important to carry out a cooperative evaluation, involving both students and teacher, that includes peer reactions and may lead to revisions in subsequent group procedures.

Interactive learning and teaching offers teachers a variety of ways to proceed. Sharan (1980) has grouped these alternatives into two categories: peer tutoring and group investigation. The rules for setting up both types are listed and compared in Table 9.2.

TABLE 9.2

Critical Differences Between Peer Tutoring and Group Investigation
Methods of Cooperative Learning in Teams

Peer Tutoring	Group Investigation
SOURCE AND VARIETY OF INFORMATION AND THE NATURE OF THE LEARNING TASK	
1. Information is transmitted by the teacher or a text.	1. Information is gathered by pupils.
2. Learning sources are limited to cards, a worksheet, or a lecture.	2. Learning sources are varied in number and kind.
3. Tasks emphasize information and/or skill acquisition.	3. Tasks stress problem-solving, interaction, synthesis, and application of information.
INTERPERSONAL RELATIONS AND COMMUNICATION	
4. Peer communication in teams is primarily unilateral or bilateral (in pairs).	4. Communication in teams is primarily bilateral and multilateral (discussion).
5. Peer communication is for rehearsal of teacher taught materials	5. Peer communication is for interpretation and exchange of ideas.
6. Peer interactions frequently imply status distinctions ("I teach, you listen.")	6. Interactions are primarily based on mutual exchange.
7. Pupils interact sporadically or in pairs	7. Group members coordinate activities on a group-wide basis.
ACADEMIC PRODUCT, EVALUATION, AND REWARDS	
8. Academic product is independent (that there is cooperation in means in but not in goals)	8. Academic product is interdependent (that is, there is cooperation in means and in goals).
9. Evaluation is primarily individual (individual tests, scores).	9. Evaluation is both individual and group (group report or project as collective product).
10. Rewards are extrinsic (reinforcement in the form of personal praise).	10. Rewards are primarily intrinsic (self-directed in topic).
CLASSROOM ORGANIZATION	
11. The class functions as an aggregate of teams that are uncoordinated or are engaged in a uniform task.	11. The class functions as a "group-of-groups" with between-group coordination and division of labor and tasks

Source: Sharan, S. (1980). Cooperative learning in small groups: Recent methods and effects on achievement, attitudes, and ethnic relations. *Review of Educational Research, 50,* 241–272.

In peer tutoring, benefits to helpers are emphasized as much as benefits to those helped, and social and emotional gains are treated as equal in importance to cognitive gains (Topping, 2005).

The Jigsaw Model of Cooperative Learning

The **jigsaw model** is one example of a cooperative learning strategy that can be particularly effective for students in the middle elementary grades. In this model, students are divided into working groups and then each member of each group is sent to a separate group to become an expert in a different aspect of the content of a lesson, after which each rejoins his or her original groups to share what each has learned with his or her groupmates (Aronson & Patnoe, 1997).

For example, if the topic was the culture of the American Indian, then different aspects of the topic might be the role of chief, the tribal council, shaman, acquiring food, and shelter. One member of each group would be responsible for providing his or her group with information about one of the topics by becoming an "expert" on that topic (usually accomplished by coming together with counterparts in other groups and being provided with information on that topic). The experts then return to their original groups and take turns sharing their information. The idea is to maximize individual participation in a cooperative group by having each member know something that none of the other group members knows, that is, having information that he or she can share.

S. Kuttig/plainpicture/Corbis

In peer-tutoring, helpers are likely to benefit as much as the students they are helping, because when one teaches, one learns, and the benefits of getting to know another person can be as great as the amount one learns.

jigsaw model

a cooperative learning strategy in which students work in groups, are separated to join another group, and brought back to their original group to share newly acquired knowledge

Think It Over

as a LEARNER   In what ways does the jigsaw model represent cooperative learning and incorporate the process of cooperation in contrast to competition and individualism, and how is it different in its approach from merely having students working on an assignment in groups?

as a TEACHER   What do you see as your role in facilitating the use of the cooperative learning groups in general and the jigsaw model in particular, and in what ways would your role be instrumental in the effectiveness of this approach to learning?

TeachSource Video Case

Multimedia Literacy: Integrating Technology into the Middle School Curriculum

In this video segment, you'll see how Gretchen Brion-Meisels at The Fletcher-Maynard Academy in Massachusetts uses a group approach to teaching in order to help her students learn about the weather patterns, biodiversity, and social structure of Costa Rica. In this video, you will see how she incorporates the use of the Jigsaw teaching strategy, a group-centered approach where students play different roles in the learning environment.

After viewing the video case, consider what you have just watched about integrating technology in the middle school curriculum and what you have read about constructivism and answer the questions below:

1. What teaching strategies demonstrated are typical of a classroom using small group learning methodology?
2. How did the use of technology contribute to the ability of the group to work on a project together?
3. In your experience, how can critiquing a fellow group member's work improve your group project?

You can view the video case at the Education CourseMate. Go to:
CengageBrain.com

Learning Objective 4

Distinguish between the different bases of leadership, and explain how to use various leadership styles and techniques for effective classroom management.

functional leadership

leadership is viewed as a transactional exchange between the person exerting influence and those being influenced

Leadership—The Teacher as Leader

Leadership has typically been thought about and described in two ways: (1) as a set of psychological characteristics of the person exerting influence and (2) as a set of behaviors that exert interpersonal influence on other people. The latter approach, **functional leadership**, has been more productive (Bass, 1990, 1997) and is more appropriate for describing the leadership of a teacher in the classroom. This is so because it views leadership as a *transactional* exchange or interpersonal event between the person exerting influence, the teacher, and those being influenced, the students. Leadership can then be described as a set of behaviors that helps a group of students move toward a particular objective. In part, the effect of those behaviors will depend on such factors as the prestige and authority of the teacher and the relationship between the teacher and the students.

Alternatively, **transformational leadership** focuses on creating new goals, based on the vision of the leader and his or her inspiration, stimulation, creativity, and

Using Groups to Help Students from Different Backgrounds Work Together (Elementary/Middle/High School)

BOX 9.2

How do you create a group of diverse individuals with different backgrounds and cultures that pulls all of its members together and enables them to function cohesively, that is, with *positive interdependence*? The answer to this question, according to Johnson & Johnson (2003) is to operate the group so that "group members perceive that they can reach their goals if and only if the other members also do so" (p. 473). The secret is to convince diverse group members that they will sink or swim together in their efforts to achieve mutual goals if they work together, which means sharing not only the labor, but the rewards as well. How can they do this? It's simple: work in cooperative groups rather than in competitive groups or individualistically. In other words, run your classroom as a set of cooperative groups.

The fact that culturally or ethnically diverse students experience proximity to one another by being in the same classroom together day after day does not guarantee effective interaction and positive results. Face-to-face interaction can often result in discrimination and discord if class members act on the basis of prejudice and stereotyping. To avoid that from happening, Johnson & Johnson (2003) emphasize the identification of mutual goals that require trust, openness, and cooperation to achieve and cite much evidence to support their contention (Johnson & Johnson, 1989). Moreover, all students must be afforded equal status and social norms must promote the formation of friendships.

Have your classroom groups, assembled to maximize diversity, work on assignments and tasks with the clear knowledge that individual outcomes will depend on group outcomes so that working together increases the likelihood that each individual group member will benefit. In other words, helping other group members is a way of helping oneself, because individual outcomes depend on group outcomes. To help ensure that every group member can make a positive contribution to the group outcome, it is often helpful to assign members different roles. This works especially well in the Jigsaw Model, where each member's role is to become expert in a different area or aspect of the overall task and then share his or her expertise with the other group members (Aronson & Patnoe, 1997). Having members with diverse backgrounds and experiences provides an opportunity for different perspectives on a topic.

In one high school sociology class, for example, cooperative learning groups were working on the topic of the welfare system in the United States and examining its strengths and weaknesses. There were a number of students in the class who had or currently were directly experiencing the welfare system in their own lives and were able to provide information to their groupmates about how the system functioned in helping them and their families meet their needs. Having this kind of information enabled the cooperative learning groups to answer the series of questions posed to them by their teacher and earned them high grades as a result.

personal attention (Bass & Avolio, 1993). Transformational leadership, when effective, may lead to group members being willing to expend more effort and generally have more positive effects on their organizations (Fiol, Harris, & House, 1999). In highly effective schools, transformational leadership is not uncommon.

Bases of Leadership

French and Raven (1960) identified five bases for influence. In terms of teacher/student relationships, they can be illustrated in the following ways:

1. *Expert power*—Students perceive the teacher as having much knowledge and skill; as a consequence, they believe they can learn from such an individual.
2. *Referent power*—Students perceive the teacher as someone they like and with whom they can identify; as a consequence, they attempt to imitate or be like that individual.
3. *Legitimate power*—Students perceive the teacher as the boss; as a consequence, they believe the teacher is entitled to tell them what to do.
4. *Reward power*—Students perceive the teacher as one who is empowered to hand out rewards; as a consequence, they do what the teacher wants in order to get rewarded.
5. *Coercive power*—Students perceive the teacher as one who is empowered to hand out punishments; as a consequence, they do what the teacher wants in order to stay out of trouble.

The position of teacher automatically carries with it three of the five bases for influence: legitimate power, reward power, and coercive power. In the classroom, the teacher is the legitimate leader, with the power to reward and punish. But the teacher's power will be even greater if he is liked and respected by his students. Kounin (1970) and others have shown that the most successful teachers develop expert and/or referent bases for power. To develop expert power and referent power, teachers should create conditions in the classroom that facilitate academic work and a positive learning environment. This means taking steps to encourage independence, stimulate open communication, and make oneself liked by students. Being the absolute ruler in the classroom leads either to student dependency and apathy, or to resistance and friction. Teachers who rely too heavily on coercive power to deal with individual students, particularly ones who are seen as having high power themselves, create what Kounin and Gump (1958) called the "ripple effect," or a spread of tension and disaffection among the entire class. Coercion may yield short-term compliance but may reduce long-term student interest and respect.

transformational leadership
the leader's vision is used to create new goals based on his or her inspiration, stimulation, creativity, and personal attention

The teacher's capacity to help students learn is increased when the teacher is liked and respected by their students.

Jose Luis Pelaez, Inc./Surf/Corbis

Think It Over

as a LEARNER	Can you describe a teacher you have had that you regard as having referent power? What was it about the teacher that would lead you to make this judgment?
as a TEACHER	When you teach, which of the different types of power would you be inclined to use, and why?

Leadership for Classroom Management

Research has shown that the key to classroom management lies not in merely disciplining students who are misbehaving (Kounin, 1970), but in maintaining student involvement in work activities and resolving minor disruptions. Good classroom management serves to *prevent* major problems.

The keys to effective leadership for classroom management, according to Good and Brophy (2003) are these:

1. Make sure students clearly understand and accept classroom rules.
2. Try to maximize classroom work time rather than stressing control of misbehavior.
3. Get students to develop inner self-control rather than trying to control them by coercive power.
4. Gear classwork to students' interests and aptitudes.

To accomplish or implement these keys to classroom management, say Good and Brophy (2003), the teacher must place great stress on planning and organizing lessons and classroom activities and having them go on without delay or disruption. Clear rules should be established and students should have the responsibility for carrying them out. Work assignments should also be clear, and positive language should be used to reinforce appropriate behavior. In other words, students should be told what to do rather than what not to do.

Good and Brophy (2003) also emphasize the pacing of lessons as a key to maintaining students' attention and thereby avoiding disruptions. Teachers should gain attention at the start of a lesson, stimulate and monitor it throughout the lesson, and terminate a lesson when student attention can no longer be held.

When a problem does occur, Good and Brophy (2003) recommend eliminating it as quickly as possible and with as little distraction of other students as possible. Specific techniques they suggest using to cause the disruptive student to behave are (1) eye contact, (2) touch and gesture, (3) physical closeness to the offender, (4) asking the offender a lesson-related question, and (5) praising the desirable behavior of a student sitting near the offender.

Leadership Styles

Do all leaders perform the same way? Are all types of leadership appropriate in every situation? The answer to both questions is "no," especially for teachers. Two contrasting styles of leadership have been named **task leadership** and **social-emotional leadership**. Task leaders focus on successful performance of the activity a group is dealing with. Task leaders present and elicit information, opinions, and suggestions (Bales, 1970). As teachers, they teach content, present lectures, give tests, and concentrate on helping students acquire information. Social-emotional leaders focus on encouragement, harmony, compromise, and morale building. As teachers, they manage, control, discipline, and motivate. Obviously, teachers have to be part task leader and part social-emotional leader.

Virtual Psychology Lab
Do all leaders perform the same way? Are all types of leadership appropriate in every situation? The answer to both questions is "no." Go to the *Judging Leadership Virtual Psychology Lab*, you will see teachers as presenters of content, lecturers, test administrators, and helpers of students, using task leadership. You will also see teachers managing, motivating and encouraging as do social-emotional leaders. Go to CengageBrain.com to access this Virtual Psychology Lab in the Education CourseMate.

task leadership
leadership that focuses on successful performance of the activity the group is dealing with

social-emotional leadership
leadership that focuses on encouragement, harmony, compromise, and morale building

autocratic leadership

the teacher serves as the sole authority and makes all rules and decisions

democratic leadership

everyone is given a fair chance to participate in rule making and decision making

laissez-faire

the teacher is not involved at all in the process of making rules or decisions

model of teaching

the way a teacher chooses to run their classroom at any given moment

information-processing style

presenting information in the way that is easiest to understand when the principle purpose is to transmit information to students

social interaction style

using small group or other interactive techniques to help students learn to get along with and help one another

focus-on-the-individual-person style

using discussions and personal contact to help students develop a sense of identity

behavior modification model

using rewards and shaping to control behavior and maintain discipline

organized demeanor

style where the teacher uses organization as her primary management tool, through use of objectives, planning, and evaluation

dynamism

style where the teacher uses enthusiasm and charisma to stimulate student attention

Leadership styles can vary, and include (1) **autocratic**—the teacher serves as the sole authority and makes all the rules and decisions; (2) **democratic**—the teacher gives everyone a fair chance to participate in rule making and decision making; and (3) **laissez-faire**—the teacher is not involved at all in the process of making rules or decisions. Lewin, Lippitt, and White (1939) discovered in their classic experiment that while autocratic leadership might be more productive in the short term, its long-term effects were quite deleterious. Group members learned very little self-control in autocratically led groups and did very little useful work in those led by laissez-faire leaders. For a teacher, the best course appears to be the more moderate one of being a democratic leader and involving students in some classroom rule and decision making.

Because the teacher is the legitimate leader in the classroom, the way he or she chooses to run that classroom at any given moment constitutes both a leadership style and a **model of teaching**. Some teachers establish a routine style or model by always informing, involving, and controlling students in the exact same way. But does that make sense? Might it not make better sense for teachers to adapt their leadership style to the situation at hand?

Joyce and Weil (2008) describe four basically different leadership or teaching styles that teachers can choose from depending on what it is they are trying to accomplish. When their principal purpose is to transmit information to students, they should adopt an **information-processing style** or model. They should function like a TV documentary or newspaper and present information in the way that is easiest for their students to understand. When their purpose is to help students learn to get along with and help one another, they should adopt a **social interaction style** using small-group and other interactive techniques. When their purpose is to help students develop a sense of identity, they should adopt a **focus-on-the-individual-person style** and use discussions and personal contact. Finally, when their purpose is to control behavior and maintain discipline, they should adopt a **behavior modification model** (see Chapter 6) and use rewards and shaping to achieve acceptable classroom behavior.

Tuckman (1995) presents an alternative model of styles teachers may adopt to lead their classrooms, each reflecting a different classroom management approach. In the first, **organized demeanor**, the teacher uses organization as her primary management tool, through the use of objectives, planning, and evaluation. In the second, **dynamism**, the teacher uses enthusiasm and charisma to stimulate student attention. The third, **warmth and acceptance**, features the establishment of relationships and the providing of support as the primary mechanisms of leadership. Finally, the fourth relies on **creativity** in creating a learning environment that provides a basis for learning by discovery. Tuckman suggests that while many teachers rely exclusively on one of these approaches, others progress through all four, starting with organization and ending up with creativity.

Mosston and Ashworth (1994) describe a *spectrum* or continuum of teaching styles that have been applied to the teaching of physical education. Each style represents a possible option in the relationship between teacher and students. At one end of the spectrum, the teacher makes all of the decisions about what and how to teach, and attempts to totally control the classroom environment and all the students in it. At the opposite end of the spectrum, many of the decisions and much of the control are in the hands of students. Each style, starting at the teacher-control end, is described briefly below.

- **Command Style:** The teacher chooses the lesson goals and the exact procedures for meeting them. In other words, the teacher makes all the decisions, in the traditional manner. An example would be having students complete a worksheet or perform some other prescribed task.
- **Task or Practice Style:** Students are allowed to choose where and at what pace they will complete each task, as they typically do in a laboratory, gymnasium, art studio, or music studio. Practicing a piece on the piano would be an example.
- **Reciprocal Style:** This involves using the small-group method or tutor method, in which students take turns functioning as teachers of other students under the supervision of the teacher. (See peer tutoring in Table 9.2 for an example.)
- **Inclusion Style:** This involves using the small-group method that maximizes social involvement and enables students to help one another to succeed. (See group investigation in Table 9.2 for an example.)
- **Guided-Discovery Style:** The teacher creates a learning environment in which students find the information or explanations they need, rather than being told to them by the teacher. The teacher may ask the questions, but the students must find the answers. This style closely fits the Piagetian approach covered in Chapter 2.
- **Learner-Initiated or Problem-Solving Style:** Students choose what to study while the teacher functions as an adviser. Students are encouraged to invent multiple solutions to their problems. This is like independent study, such as completing a research project.

There also exists the possibility of teachers picking the style that best fits or matches the way the majority of their students learn (Hunt & Sullivan, 1974). Some students like structure and control. They like being given information and told what to do. They should be taught using a **teacher-directed** (or structured) **style** with methods such as lecture and seatwork-recitation. Other students prefer controlling their own learning and are mature enough to do so. They should be taught by a more **self-directed** (or unstructured) **style** in which the teacher functions more as guide and adviser and meets with students individually or in small groups. (See the different instructional models described in Chapter 12.)

Clearly, as a teacher you do not always have to use the same approach or style to lead your classroom. You can pick the style that best fits the situation and the students, provided you have learned to use more than one style and have enough self-awareness and self-control to change from one style to another.

warmth and acceptance

style that features the establishment of relationships and the providing of support as the primary mechanisms of leadership

creativity

style that relies on creativity to create a learning environment that provides a basis for learning by discovery

teacher-directed style

style where the teacher gives information and instructions to students

self-directed style

style where the teacher functions more as a guide and adviser and meets with students individually or in small groups

Learning Objective 5

Explain the effects that the communicator, the content of the communication, audience predisposition, and audience response, have on the influence of the communication, and give examples of effective and congruent communication skills.

Communication Between Teachers and Students

Ms. Slater wanted to increase the involvement of her students in classroom activities and teach them how to work as groups. She believed that giving her students the opportunity to participate as a group in classroom decision making was a good way to do that. She had her whole class meet as a group twice a week for 30 minutes each time. She prepared an agenda for each meeting, using student input, with items such as a discussion of classroom rules, homework, disruptive behavior, use of classroom material, or any classroom problem or issue that currently concerned either she or her students, and that related to the quality of life and work in her classroom. She also appointed a student steering committee to help set the agenda for each meeting and to help conduct each meeting. Her steering committee members were rotated monthly to give everybody a chance.

In conducting the meeting (which was carried out with everybody sitting in a circle), the first step was to identify problems. The steering committee provided a short list of problems, but group members were allowed to add others to it. Then each problem was described by those who had identified it. The next step was for the group to generate solutions to each problem by brainstorming (see Box 8.4), and then evaluate these solutions by combining their individual judgments or voting to try to achieve a consensus. During the meetings, emphasis was placed on (1) giving everyone a chance to participate and to candidly express his or her opinion; (2) listening to what others say (and repeating it, if necessary), keeping an open mind, and looking for merit in others' ideas; (3) giving feedback to one another and credit where due; (4) not engaging in personal attacks (criticizing ideas but not people); and (5) maintaining a climate of friendship and cooperation but resolving conflict when it does arise. This means that her students had to become skillful communicators.

The effectiveness or influence of a communication is based on a number of factors, each of which will be considered in turn. Taken together, they deal with who says what to whom and with what effect.

Credibility of the Communicator

Teachers are communicators. How effective or opinion-changing their communications are depends on their **credibility** or how believable their audience—the students—perceives them to be (Johnson & Johnson, 2003). Hovland (1963) reports that the more similar the communicator's position on an issue is to one's own, the more credible one is likely to perceive the communicator to be and the more fair one is likely to perceive the message. In other words, people interpret a communication in light of their own position on the issue.

In addition, the more the communicator is respected, the more the communication is likely to change the audience's opinion (Hovland, 1963; Petty, Wegener, & Fabrigar, 1997). That is why advertisements and commercials use people who are trusted and believed in to deliver the intended message. Therefore, the words of a

credibility

how believable an audience perceives a communicator to be

Mira/Alamy

Getting students involved in classroom activities and helping them learn how to work in groups can be facilitated by having them participate in decision making. It can also improve the communication between teachers and their students.

respected teacher will carry more weight with students than the words of a lightly regarded teacher, unless the message deviates too much from the students' current views. Sports heroes may be more effective than law enforcement officials in convincing students of the dangers of drugs—but only if the students are *not* already totally committed to drug use.

Content of the Communication

A communication's effectiveness or influence in changing opinions also depends on *what* it says. Developing communication skills means knowing how to prepare effective communications. But what should be contained in an effective communication? Should it arouse the emotions of the audience? Can you frighten people into changing their opinion, as, for instance, in telling people about how they may lose their teeth if they don't brush them or about how they may lose their lives if they take drugs? Not according to research findings. Liberman & Chaiken (1992) found that people tend not to believe pronouncements of "gloom and doom" or tend not to take them as seriously as they do more factual, less emotional messages, and so are not much influenced by them. (Witness, for example, the fact that nations often do not take seriously the threats of overpopulation or global warming.) Sometimes, in fact, highly emotional messages cause the audience to "tune out" or even become hostile toward the communicator. It is better to just communicate the facts.

But, of course, there often are facts that support the position and facts that refute it. Should both be presented? Crowley & Hoyer (1994) report relevant findings. If the audience is on your side to begin with, then just presenting your side is better than presenting both sides—unless someone else is likely to come along later and present the other side. Then, presenting both sides is better. Because teachers do not know whether their students agree with them, or who will be trying to convince their students next, it is better for teachers to present both sides of an issue. However, the side of the issue presented first is likely to be more influential than the side presented second, unless some time passes before hearing the other side, and one does not decide until then. In that case, the position presented second is more influential (Haugtvedt & Wegener, 1994).

In reality, teachers do not always have the last word, nor are they perhaps always the most credible on matters of attitude in the eyes of their students. Peers and influential adults on the "street" may hold more sway in some instances.

What should be done if the purpose of the message is simply to inform rather than to influence? Schmuck and Schmuck (2001) offer the suggestions below for persons such as teachers sending and receiving a message:

Sending a Message

- MAKE CLEAR STATEMENTS and make them short (three or four sentences). The receiver should be able to successfully paraphrase them.
- DESCRIBE ONE'S OWN BEHAVIOR both as an illustration and to communicate empathy.
- DESCRIBE FEELINGS directly in order to establish trust (for example, "I feel pleased," "I like your sense of humor").
- AIM STATEMENTS at the audience's level of experience, expertise, and understanding.

Receiving a Message

- PARAPHRASE IDEAS that you hear the other person say to show that you are listening (for example, "Did I hear you say...?").
- DESCRIBE OTHERS' BEHAVIOR rather than trying to describe their character or motivation, neither of which you can see (for example, "That's the fourth time you've interrupted" rather than "You're a rude little boy").
- CHECK IMPRESSIONS to determine whether you are accurately perceiving the feelings of the message-sender toward you, rather than just assuming what those feelings are or condemning them (for example, "I gather from the look on your face that you're angry. Is that right?" rather than "What right do you have to be angry?").

Box 9.3 also contains some concrete suggestions for functioning as a skillful communicator.

AN EXAMPLE TO AID UNDERSTANDING   Box 9.3

Congruent Communication (Elementary/Middle/High School)

Ginott (1993) calls communication that is harmonious and authentic, and where words fit feelings, congruent. Congruent communicators substitute a language of ACCEPTANCE for a language of rejection. Congruent communication acknowledges a child's situation; incongruent communication derogates and degrades a child's character and personality.

Congruent

1. I see the paint spilled. We need a rag to clean it up.
2. I am concerned about your work in English. It needs improvement.
3. I am appalled at your behavior.
4. I get angry when I see food on the floor. This room needs to be cleaned.
5. The noise is annoying.
6. I would like to finish my statement.
7. You seem upset about the homework. It does seem like a lot.
8. You forgot your book. Here it is.
9. Get right to the point. Start with your facts.
10. We have a problem. What's the solution?
11. You've raised an important question.

Incongruent

1. Why are you so clumsy and careless?
2. You're smart enough to do better. Isn't it time to buckle down?
3. You are so stupid.
4. You boys are slobs. You belong in a pigsty. Clean it up now.
5. Stop the noise.
6. You are rude.
7. It's your own fault for being lazy and not finishing it in class.
8. Scatterbrain! You'd forget your head if it weren't attached to your shoulders.
9. You write as though you had verbal diarrhea.
10. Why are you never ready to take a test?
11. How would I know? That's beside the point.
   - Can you create some of your own examples of congruent and incongruent communications in the classroom?

Audience Predisposition

The next factor affecting the influence of a communication is the audience (i.e., the students), the people to whom the message is sent. It has already been said that if the audience is made up of people who think like the speaker, they will pay much more attention to what the speaker is saying. Of equal importance are the norms of the groups of which these people are members. The more the members of the audience value the groups they belong to and hence accept their norms, the less likely they are to be influenced by the message if it goes against those norms (Hovland, 1963). Telling youngsters who are members of gangs about the dangers of violence has little effect because they have already accepted the gang's norms that pronounce violence to be acceptable. In order to change the members' beliefs and attitudes about violence, efforts must be made through the gangs and their leaders to change the norms of the gangs.

Finally, teenagers, impressionable as they are, are much more susceptible to attitude change than adults (Krosnick & Alwin, 1989). Attempts to influence the attitudes of students in middle and high school in a positive way have the potential to be effective.

Hovland (1963) also reports on the effects that a particular personality characteristic may have on the ease with which a person can be persuaded. That personality characteristic is self-esteem. Persons with low self-esteem are more easily influenced than those with high self-esteem. (This can be related to the concept of self-efficacy described in the next chapter.)

Audience predisposition is also influenced by seating arrangements, particularly by how much access to communication each person has by virtue of his or her physical relationship to the other participants. People like to have more access to information; even though giving it to them may not maximize efficiency, it will maximize satisfaction. When every participant has equal access to information being passed in the form of notes, as they do in a circle pattern, or almost equal access, as they do in a line pattern, they tend to like what they are doing more than when one person has more access than all the others, as in an X or Y configuration (Leavitt, 1951).

Teachers need to ensure that all of their students are in the flow of communication, even though doing so may occasionally require that specific communications be repeated.

Creatas/PhotoLibrary

Congruent communication uses the language of acceptance rather than the language of rejection. It never "puts down" a student's character.

Audience Response

An active audience is much more likely to be influenced than a passive one. King and Janis (1956) had students not merely listen to a communication but play a role that required them to deliver a persuasive communication to others. The role players changed their opinions more than those who just listened to the same communication. Perhaps the desire to be consistent in one's thoughts and actions is what causes a change in action to result in a change in thought (Festinger, 1957).

It is, therefore, very important for students to participate in the communication process. They can do this by answering or asking questions of the teacher, paraphrasing the content of the message, checking their perception of the sender's feelings, interacting with other students in discussion groups, or participating in other forms of small-group instruction, such as cooperative learning (Johnson, 2000). Over time, students may forget the source of a message, but they are much less likely to forget its content, particularly if they paid close attention to it (Hovland, 1963).

Friendship, Liking and Classroom Climate

Learning Objective 6

Point out factors that make groups attractive to their members and outcomes or benefits that result from association with an attractive group, and categorize the components of effective classroom climate.

An important group outcome is friendship or the liking that individuals have for one another. In a group setting, friendship and liking between members manifests itself as **cohesiveness**—the attraction and attachment group members feel toward their group. Members of cohesive groups (1) share a common group identity (they think of themselves as members of the group); (2) share a common sense of purpose; (3) communicate differently with one another than with nonmembers; (4) share and follow common norms of acceptable behavior; (5) accept specific roles, including that of leader; and (6) establish a status system or a hierarchy of worth (that is, a chain of command, a pecking order) for the group. These characteristics are much less true of groups that lack cohesiveness.

The groups a person likes the most and identifies with the most come to be that person's **reference groups**. These are the groups whose influence and judgment that person is most willing to accept. People compare and judge themselves relative to the other members of their reference groups, and they conform to the norms of these groups. Clubs, gangs, fraternities, organizations, and even particular classes can become the reference groups that young people choose to identify with and follow. When they do, they will adhere to the norms of these groups.

What Makes a Group Attractive?

The better able a group is to fulfill someone's needs, the more attractive the group will be to that person (Wright & Duncan, 1986). In other words, if someone stands to gain a lot from belonging to a particular group, membership in that group will be most valued and appealing. Consequently, the norms of that appealing group will be most influential on that person's behavior and opinions.

One factor that affects a group's ability to fulfill someone's needs is its *prestige*. The more important a group is, the greater the satisfaction of its members (Meir, Keinan, & Segal, 1986; Napier & Gershenfeld, 2004). Being in a highly regarded social club, sorority, or fraternity or in an honors class or honor society will make a student feel important and, hence, will increase the appeal that group has for him or her. Successful groups or teams are much more appealing to their members than unsuccessful ones.

cohesiveness

the attraction and attachment group members feel toward their group

reference groups

the groups a person likes the most and identifies with the most, whose influence and judgment the person is most willing to accept

The *climate* of a group also influences its attractiveness. Interestingly, group members find cooperative groups more appealing than competitive groups (Worchel, Andreoli, & Folger, 1977; Napier and Gershenfeld, 2004). This is particularly true in racially integrated or cross-ethnic groups (Johnson & Johnson, 2003). In part, the climate of these racially mixed groups, and consequently their attractiveness, was increased because students *interacted* more within them than within competitive groups. Also, groups whose members perceive one another as being committed to the group and compatible with one another are regarded as more attractive than those lacking these qualities (Spears, Lea, and Lee, 1990). (See the section on classroom climate, later in this chapter.)

Size is another factor that influences a group's appeal (Napier & Gershenfeld, 2004). Smaller groups tend to be more appealing than large ones because it is easier to get to know the other members and because there is more chance to participate (Lindeman and Koskela, 1994; Wicker, 1969). Smaller classes have this appealing quality as well, except perhaps for students who would prefer the protection of anonymity afforded by a larger class. Another factor that makes a group appealing is its *protectiveness* (Napier & Gershenfeld, 2004). Often the attraction of gangs is their ability to protect their members against aggression by other gangs.

The primary *activity* or task the group is engaged in is another factor that influences its appeal. Stamp collectors like stamp clubs, athletes like sports teams, and good students like highly motivated academic groups. It will take effort to make school groups attractive to students who do not like academic work. However, a class will become more attractive to students when the class activity is more game-like and thus more likable. (Review the illustration on page 14 of Chapter 1 on how to make classroom activities more appealing.)

The *social structure* of a group or class also affects its appeal. *Centrally structured* groups that have powerful and controlling leadership and narrow and defined friendship patterns are less attractive to the majority of their members than *diffusely structured* groups, such as classroom groups, that have a wide range of support and less focus on interpersonal acceptance and rejection (Marshall, 1978).

Another important feature of social structure is the *opportunity for interaction* among members (Napier and Gershenfeld, 2004). In classrooms and schools where students have more opportunity to interact with one another—for example, in the so-called "open" classrooms (described in Chapter 2) in contrast to the traditional ones, or in the cooperative learning model (described earlier)—there are more friendship choices (Epstein, 1983). *Self-reliance*, too, seems to be an influential factor: Where there is more self-reliance built into the classroom structure, there is more opportunity for friendships to form (Epstein, 1983).

Finally, an important determinant of the attractiveness of a classroom group is the *behavior of the teacher*. Students who are satisfied with their teachers usually feel good about school, learning, and themselves. Pepitone (1964) proposed that persons are attracted to those who assign them a position of high status or who help them feel secure. They tend to feel hostile toward those who demean them in their own eyes or in the eyes of others. Students who are valued by their teachers, therefore, tend to find their classroom experiences satisfying, while students who are devalued by their teachers tend to find their classroom experiences unsatisfying (Stensaasen, 1970).

What Happens in Attractive Groups?

Attractive groups tend to improve the **self-esteem** of their members by making them feel more important. They also produce a sense of trust and **openness** among their members that leads not only to more communication, but to more open communication. Luft (1969) proposed the framework shown in Figure 9.4 known as the **Johari Window** (named by combining the first names of Joe Luft and Harry Ingram). In attractive groups, in the first quadrant the area of sharing and openness expands while the other three areas—blindness, avoided information, and unconscious activity—contract. Teachers can use the Johari Window concept to help students reveal more about themselves from quadrants 2 and 3, which will result in the development of greater emotional closeness and lead to yet more openness and spontaneity.

Attractive groups are also productive groups, if the norms of the groups support productivity (Kafer, 1976; Napier and Gershenfeld, 2004). When friends as a group endorse academic performance as a mutual goal, then the academic performance of each member will be enhanced. Teachers would do well to encourage their students to work together (as in cooperative learning) on academic tasks in order to help them develop group norms conducive to productivity. Teachers can develop a sense of camaraderie and group cohesion within their own classrooms by involving students as a group in decision making.

self-esteem

the importance that individuals feel about themselves

openness

a sense of trust that leads to more open communication between members of a group

Johari Window

a framework made of quadrants that can be used to help students reveal more about themselves to achieve greater emotional openness

FIGURE 9.4

	KNOWN TO SELF	NOT KNOWN TO SELF
KNOWN TO OTHERS	1. **Open.** Area of sharing and openness.	2. **Blind.** Area of blindness.
NOT KNOWN TO OTHERS	3. **Hidden.** Area of avoided information.	4. **Unknown.** Area of unconscious activity.

The Johari Window of Awareness in Interpersonal Awareness (from Luft, 1969)

joefoxphoto/Alamy

In attractive groups, ones that students like to be in, they experience a sense of trust and openness. This contributes to their self-esteem.

Think It Over

as a LEARNER	Can you describe a group or class of which you are or were a member that you find or found very attractive, and a group or class of which you are or were a member that you find or found very unattractive? What are or were the characteristics of these two groups that made one attractive and the other unattractive?
as a TEACHER	What would you do to make a class that you were teaching into an attractive group for its members?

Liking Patterns among Students

It can be helpful to determine liking patterns among students in order to provide unpopular students with social support or special assistance, or to solicit the cooperation of popular and influential students. In setting up work groups or teams, knowledge of individual student popularity and friendship choices can help the teacher create new combinations (1) to foster new friendships or (2) to help less popular children interact with more popular ones (Berg, 2001). It can also help teachers detect any biases, say, racial or gender, that exist in the classroom and may be deterring smooth interaction. Measuring student popularity makes it possible to identify selected, rejected, and neglected students (Burn, 2004).

One way to proceed in determining liking patterns is to ask each student to choose or *nominate*, in writing and in private, the three students he or she likes

---

FIGURE 9.5

A Sample Sociogram of Seating Choices among 15 Students

Eight girls (numbers 1–8 or circles) and seven boys (numbers 9–15 or squares); solid lines represent positive choices and dashed lines represent negative choices. (Adapted from Schmuck and Schmuck, 2001, p. 171.)

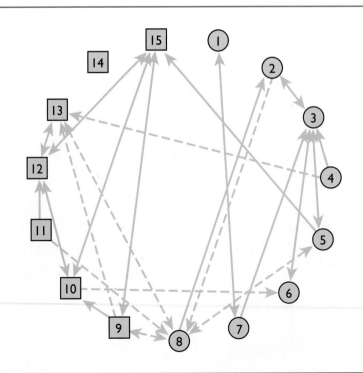

most. (The nomination procedure often includes asking each student to name the three he or she likes least, though this question may be avoided to avoid hurt feelings.) Another approach is to ask class members to write down the names of the person or persons they would most like to sit next to and those they would least like to sit next to (again, with caution exercised in using the second question). No prespecified number is requested and no names need to be given for least favorite(s) if none apply. Schmuck and Schmuck (1988) provide a sample diagram of the resulting patterns of choice among a class of 15, shown in Figure 9.5.

This diagram of liking patterns is called a sociogram. The **sociogram** in Figure 9.5 shows that all the boys (numbers 9 through 15) chose to sit next to boys and all the girls (numbers 1 through 8) except one (number 5) chose to sit next to girls. Among the girls, number 3 was the most popular while number 8 was specifically rejected by five classmates. Moreover, the girl she chose rejected her. Girl number 8 may be a candidate for the teacher's help, as may boy number 13, who also received three negative choices. Both are probably experiencing rejection. Boy number 14 is an isolate who neither chose anyone nor was chosen by anyone. He will also need teacher assistance to be integrated into the class social structure. "Stars" like girl number 3 and boy number 15 who are chosen by many classmates should be called on to help overcome the rejection and isolation of other students.

sociogram

a diagram of liking patterns

When students are rejected by their classmates, it often causes them to stop interacting with their classmates and stay away from school.

Toby Maudsley/The Image Bank /Getty Images

It is important that teachers deal with relationship issues between students, especially at the elementary school level. Early peer rejection has been shown to be associated with declining classroom participation and increasing school avoidance, which leads to decrements in children's achievement (Buhs, Ladd, & Herald, 2006).

Classroom Climate

Those students on the bench and the plastic crates pull up cardboard boxes to use as makeshift desks. The students who are standing balance their notebooks with one hand and write with the other. The students are serious, intent, and the only sounds are the occasional whispers: "Who was the preacher in The Scarlet Letter?" or "What was the name of the narrator in The Great Gatsby?"

In many inner-city high schools, teachers are confronted with rows of bored, insolent students, but [Miss] Little teaches at Crenshaw High School's program for gifted students. The students, who are from throughout South Central Los Angeles, have been given a special opportunity to succeed. And the vast majority go on to college. They are used to a more rigorous and disciplined academic environment, so as they write their first essay, the class has a decidedly different ambience than the rest of the school. Outside the classroom, students walk the halls and scrawl graffiti on the walls, and in a few nearby classrooms, students shout and pound their feet while teachers frantically try to establish order. In Little's classroom, however, the students hunch over their papers and scribble furiously until the bell rings. (From Corwin, M. (2001). *And Still We Rise* (p. 23). NY: HarperCollins.)

What is **classroom climate**? As illustrated in the above story, it is the product of all the factors that affect groups and that have been described in this chapter: expectations, norms, leadership, communication, and friendship. Taken together, these social and interpersonal dimensions produce an overall point of view or *ideology* in

classroom climate

the overall point of view or ideology in a classroom or school

Students are more interested in class activities when engaged in shared learning.

a classroom or school, along with a consistent *organizational structure*, which gives rise to a set of *instructional practices*.

Climates have been described as open and closed (Halpin, 1966) or *effective* and *ineffective* (Brookover et al., 1982). In an open or effective climate, teachers believe and expect that

- all students are worthwhile and can learn and reach high standards of achievement based on their own ability and on the commitment and efforts of teachers.

In an open or effective climate, the organizational structure and norms provide

- recognition and rewards for high achievement;
- opportunities for students to express themselves and be treated with fairness and dignity;
- cooperative and supportive interaction between students and between teachers and students; and
- nondiscrimination, that is, equal interactional and instructional opportunities for all students regardless of gender, race, or ethnicity.

A good example of a technique that contributes to effective classroom climate is the approach to interactive decision making described on page 370 of this chapter.

This does not mean that in an effective climate the teacher will always teach and behave the same way. Sometimes the teacher will provide more structure, sometimes less. Sometimes the teacher will use direct instruction, sometimes small-group or cooperative instruction; sometimes the teacher will lead with a firm hand, sometimes with less control and discipline (see the different teaching styles described earlier in this chapter). At all times, the teacher's goal will be to maximize the gains a class can make, both as individuals and as a group, in knowledge and in feelings or attitudes. (The fact that how this is done will have to vary as the classroom group develops is illustrated in Box 9.4.)

BOX 9.4

Did You Know?

Like People, Groups Grow (Elementary/Middle/High School)

Groups deal with two areas or domains at the same time: (1) their task, or what they are there to accomplish, such as learning; and (2) the interpersonal or social relationships among their members. Tuckman and Jensen (1977) described groups as going through five stages of development as they deal with both their job and their social sphere. They called these stages

forming, storming, norming, performing, and *adjourning,* and knowing about them can help a teacher produce an effective classroom climate.

In the beginning, groups *form.* They come together for the first time. They seek structure, guidance, and direction. They are dependent on their leader to tell them what to do. A teacher should provide some direction and guidance, but it should be neither total nor absolute, or else students will not be motivated to take some responsibility for their own learning and social development.

When group members discover what the rules are, or when they discover that part of the responsibility for making the rules is theirs, they may become hostile and dissatisfied. They may even rebel. That is to say, they *storm*. An effective leader or teacher, rather than becoming threatened and trying to stamp it out, permits this expression of feelings and helps students understand it. More freedom, rather than less freedom, often is the key to further development. The group members are now ready to establish both rules and a sense of trust. It is at this time that they *norm*. A pattern of relationships and interpersonal rules begins to develop that will enable the group to be an effective learning and teaching medium.

If the teacher has given the class the freedom and opportunity to grow through the first three stages, they will now begin to *perform*. A few months of the school year may have to pass before this last stage develops, but if it does develop, the teacher's patience will be rewarded. Students will finally work together productively and harmoniously to learn the subject matter and to enjoy the chance of being together as a classroom group.

When the term or school year ends, the work of the classroom group is over, and it ceases to function as a group, or *adjourns*.

- How do you think you could use this information if you were the teacher of the class?

Another way to categorize the climate or academic environment of a classroom or school is the degree to which it reflects **academic optimism** (Hoy, Tarter, & Woolfolk Hoy, 2006). Academic optimism requires teachers and staff *as a group* to have (a) a belief or expectation that they can have positive effects on students, (b) a feeling that they can put their trust in parents and students, and (c) a behavior pattern that reflects a drive or quest for academic excellence. Academic optimism has been found to help shape school norms and expectations in a way that leads to an improvement in students' academic achievement (Hoy et al., 2006).

In sum, there are climates that are positive and desirable, that students enjoy being in, and that they learn in. Maximizing all the group processes described in this chapter—which include being open, positive, and accepting in (1) expectations, (2) classroom norms or rules, (3) style of leadership, and (4) communication style—will lead to group cohesiveness as well as to a sense of satisfaction and greater academic accomplishment among students. Students will want to come to school and will feel that they can have some direct influence on what goes on there. They will feel accepted and respected by their teachers and their classmates. Their schools will engender positive classroom climates and a high degree of academic optimism.

academic optimism

a belief that teachers can have positive effects on students and that they can put their trust in parents and students in order to achieve academic excellence

SUMMING IT UP

Outline a model of group dynamics to explain group processes in the classroom.

Class members interact as a group, subject to the principles of **group dynamics**. The teacher, as **classroom leader**, is influenced by **member characteristics** such as **expectations** and by **group characteristics** such as **norms,** which also influence other **group processes** such as **communication** and, in turn, affect **group outcomes** such as **attraction** to the group and **classroom climate**.

Summarize the influence of teacher expectations on student expectations—the self-fulfilling prophecy—and how these expectations are communicated.

Expectations are beliefs people hold about themselves and others. When they act on these beliefs, they influence their own behavior and the behavior of others in ways that cause the beliefs to come true. This is called the **self-fulfilling prophecy**. Teachers communicate their expectations to students by praising the ones they believe to have high ability and controlling the ones they believe to have low ability. The **circular interpersonal process** works like this: your expectations influence your behavior, affecting how others see and behave toward you, affecting your expectations of yourself (a never-ending circle).

Define group norms and explain how they influence behavior; define normative goal structures and cooperative learning and explain how they affect student performance.

Norms are shared agreements by group members on world views, beliefs, likes and dislikes, and standards of behavior. They can be formal or informal, static or dynamic. Group influence can be strong enough to cause people to see things differently than they really are, or at least to say they do. Norms describe the range of behavior tolerable to the group. They vary across groups in their levels of intensity or importance, crystallization or degree of endorsement, ambiguity or clarity, degree of integration or confusion, and congruence or consistency. **Normative goal structures** are shared expectations about the best way to attain goals. When each member seeks an outcome that is beneficial to all, it is called a **cooperative goal structure**, in contrast to a **competitive goal structure**, in which each member seeks a goal that will cause all others to fail, and an **individualistic goal structure** when members' goal attainments are independent. **Cooperative learning** is interdependent or collaborative learning.

Distinguish between the different bases of leadership, and explain how to use different leadership styles and techniques for effective classroom management.

Functional leadership is a set of influential behaviors rather than a set of personal traits. The basis of functional leadership can be **expertise** or the leader's possession of knowledge, **reference** or the degree to which the leader is identified with, **legitimacy** or a part of the leadership job, or the leader's power to **reward** or punish (or **coerce**). Teachers automatically have the last three, but must earn the first two. To be an effective classroom manager, a teacher must be able to plan, organize, and pace lessons to gain student attention and should use positive language. The teacher can control or avoid disruptiveness through eye contact and physical closeness. Leadership can be focused on the task or **work goal** of the group or on the **social-emotional climate**. Leaders can use a **democratic**, **autocratic**, or **laissez-faire** style. Effective teachers can use more than one style or model of teaching, ranging from **teacher-directed** to **student-directed**, depending on the task and the circumstances.

Explain the effects that the communicator, the content of the communication, audience predisposition, and audience response have on the influence of the communication and give examples of effective and congruent communication skills.

The effectiveness of classroom communication intended to persuade depends on who says what to whom and with what effect. **Credible communicators** are more influential than noncredible communicators. Highly emotional messages are not as influential as less emotionally charged ones. **Two-sided messages** are more effective for general audiences than **one-sided** ones. Messages that conflict with group norms are not very effective and set patterns that isolate individuals from information. When the audience participates in the communication process, such as by role-playing, the influence of the communication is greatest. **Congruent communication** is harmonious and authentic, and words fit feelings. Congruent communicators substitute a language of acceptance for a language of rejection. Congruent communication acknowledges a child's situation; **incongruent communication** derogates and degrades a child's character and personality.

Point out factors that make groups attractive to their members and outcomes or benefits that result from association with an attractive group, and categorize the components of effective classroom climate.

Important group outcomes are **friendship** and **liking**. Groups whose members share these feelings are **cohesive**, which makes them **attractive**. Such groups often serve as **reference groups** in that their influence and judgment are accepted. The

After reading this chapter, you should be able to meet the following learning objectives	Chapter Contents
LEARNING OBJECTIVE 1 Describe and apply the social cognitive approach to motivating students.	The Social Cognitive Approach to Motivation • Reciprocal Determinism • Self-Reflective Capability • Self-Regulatory Capability
LEARNING OBJECTIVE 2 Discuss the concept of self-efficacy and the impact of school and teachers on a student's self-efficacy.	Self-Efficacy—The Belief in Oneself • Sources of Efficacy Information • Self-Efficacy and School
LEARNING OBJECTIVE 3 Describe the concept of self-regulation and its relation to self-efficacy; and detail ways students can become self-regulators.	Self-Regulation—The Control of Oneself • Becoming a Self-Regulator • Helping Students Enhance Self-Regulation
LEARNING OBJECTIVE 4 Explain attribution as a basis for motivation, and identify its key features. Document the teacher's role in using attribution to motivate students.	Attribution as a Basis for Motivation • How Students Make Attributions • Reasons for Students' Judgments of Success and Failure • Judging Responsibility and Intentionality • Learned Helplessness • The Teacher's Role in Motivating Students
LEARNING OBJECTIVE 5 Describe needs and goals as motivators of learner achievement.	Needs and Goals as Motivators • Maslow's Hierarchy of Needs • Needs and Strategies for Helping Students Achieve • Learner Goal Orientation
LEARNING OBJECTIVE 6 Illustrate various incentives and values as motivators of learner achievement.	Incentives and Values as Motivators • Learner's Incentive Values
LEARNING OBJECTIVE 7 Describe self-determination as an approach to motivation, distinguishing between intrinsic and extrinsic motivation.	The Self-Determination Approach to Motivation • Intrinsic and Extrinsic Motivation • Enhancing the Intrinsic Motivation of Students

Marathon Man or Marathon Moose

"This is a true story! It's about believing in yourself. I used to be a marathon runner; you know that foot race that's 26 and a quarter miles long. I ran 36 marathons until my body rebelled and turned me into an exercise walker, but that's beside the point. The point of the story is about one particular marathon I ran, the Skylon Marathon, that started out in Buffalo, NY and ended up in Canada at Niagara Falls.

It was a terrible day to run a marathon, but I had traveled all the way to Buffalo, and was determined to run it. By the time we got to the 8 mile mark, the temperature was 37 degrees and little pellets of ice were falling from the sky. The wind was blowing at 20 miles an hour and gusting at 45. To add insult to injury, I had underestimated the weather and was wearing only a singlet, shorts, a pullover cap, and a pair of gloves that I had borrowed that went almost up to my elbows (thank goodness for the gloves!). When I got to the 8 mile mark, I looked over and saw two runners who were wearing three layers of clothes and realized that I had better start running faster than I was.

Because of the wind, people were running in clusters so that they could use the runners in front of them to break the wind. It's called drafting. I got myself into the cluster in front of me and started running at their pace. Suddenly, I started to believe that I was a moose. Is that crazy or what! Maybe it was my gloves turning into hooves and my cap turning into antlers, but I couldn't get it out of my mind that I was a moose. And so I started picking up the pace from person-pace to moose-pace and telling myself that that I could outrun any human person. Soon I had passed the cluster I was in and charging toward the next cluster in front of me. It was cold, but I was feeling no pain. The moose was on the move!

Because my gloves covered my watch and it was too cold to take them off, I had no idea how long I had run. Because the distance markers were on the metric system, I had no idea how far I had run. But no matter; those would just be distractions. I was the moose and I just kept passing one cluster after another until I passed all the clusters and fell in behind a handful of runners running in single file. Before I knew it, I came up to a big sign that said "2 more miles to go" and I came back down to earth. The moose had decided that it had had enough and I was on my own. Fortunately, the last two miles were downhill and I crossed the finished line in 3 hours and 7 minutes, despite the persistent headwind.

Thanks to my mind and my moose, I believed that I could run as fast as I wanted, and it enabled me to run the fastest marathon I ever ran!

●   If you were a teacher, how could you use this story in your classroom?

> *Lessons We Can Learn from the Story* One of the most important concepts or ideas that can be applied to motivation is **self-efficacy**, the belief in oneself and one's capability to perform successfully (Bandura, 1997). People who believe they can do an activity well will be inclined or motivated to perform that activity and perform it well, while others, who believe that performing the activity is beyond their capability, will be fearful and will avoid undertaking it. This is particularly true of activities that people can choose to do or not do. In the story, the storyteller believed he could run as fast as a moose, and it helped him to run faster.

To successfully perform an act, a person must have the pertinent skill, knowledge, or competencies. But these are not enough; they are *necessary,* but not *sufficient.* The person must also be inclined to invest the energy the act requires and direct or focus that energy on performing that act. In other words, the person must be motivated to perform the act. **Motivation** refers to what *propels* and *directs* people to act. A particularly important and relevant area of motivated behavior, particularly in the case of students, is **self-regulation**, the ability to exercise influence over what you do (Bandura, 1997). A student may know what and how to study, for example, and may realize that studying is important, yet she may not study because the motivation or drive to self-regulate is lacking. Martinez-Pons (2002) recommends that teachers integrate the teaching of self-regulation into regular classroom lessons.

Another factor influencing motivation is the belief that you are responsible (or not) for the results of your behavior, based on what you attribute as its cause (Weiner, 1995, 2004). The **attribution approach** deals with the possible causes of one's outcomes and the characteristics of those causes. People are more likely to apply effort if they believe it to be the cause of the outcomes they desire.

One key feature of the motivation to achieve is having achievement as a **goal** or **need**. Being motivated to achieve means wanting to attain that goal or fulfill that need, and using the kinds of strategies that will facilitate that outcome. In addition, the goal of achievement may be based on different orientations, such as developing mastery or being able to outperform others.

Another factor that may influence motivation is the **incentive** or **value** associated with the outcome. Students often are more motivated to perform or approach an academic task such as studying if they perceive the result as being worth it to them

Finally, the source of motivation may be based on a desire for autonomy or **self-determination**, deciding for oneself what to do or not do, and as a result one's **intrinsic interest** in a task may be the determining factor in whether to do it or not.

In this chapter, some different notions or models of what motivates people to act will be described, some of which focus on what people believe about themselves, and others on the outcome or result of their behavior. Recommendations for

self-efficacy
the belief in oneself and one's capability to perform successfully

motivation
what propels and directs people to act

self-regulation
the ability to exercise influence over what you do

attribution approach
deals with the possible causes of one's outcomes and the characteristics of those causes

goal
what someone is motivated to achieve

need
what someone would like to achieve

incentive
the benefit or payoff associated with an outcome

value
the importance to oneself of achieving a particular outcome

self-determination
motivation based on a desire for autonomy

intrinsic interest
the determining factor in deciding whether or not to do something

how teachers can apply each motivational approach will be provided along with the description of each approach.

The Social Cognitive Approach to Motivation

Bandura (1977, 1997) proposed the **social cognitive approach** to motivation. This approach emphasizes cognitive and social strategies and beliefs that influence the motivation of learners. The social cognitive approach includes the three basic principles described below.

Reciprocal Determinism

One basic principle of the social cognitive approach is that *behavior*, *personal factors*, and *environmental events* all operate together as interactive determinants or causes of each other in what Bandura (1997) calls the *self-system*. This interlocking system, shown in Figure 10.1, represents the three factors—P or personal ones, E or environmental ones, and B or behavior—as points of a triangle. The double arrows between each factor indicate that each may affect or determine each of the others in a reciprocal way, hence **reciprocal determinism**.

Imagine how this would work. You are a person (P) with expectations and values as well as a personal style or personality. You like intellectual challenges and social interaction. Consequently, you like going to school, and when you get there your behavior (B) is positive and gregarious. Your friends know your personality (P), and they react with environmental events (E) or friendliness. They also react (E) to your behavior (B). If you do something strange or unexpected, they will react to it. Their reactions (E), in turn, influence your behavior (B) as well as affecting your personality (P). If they stop being nice to you (E), you may become

social cognitive approach

emphasizes cognitive and social strategies and beliefs that influence motivation

reciprocal determinism

the interlocking system of behavior, personal factors, and environmental events

People react to your personality and your behavior. You, in turn, are affected by how they react to you. This is called *reciprocal determinism*, and it makes you feel good about yourself when someone likes you.

Brand X Pictures/Jupiter Images

FIGURE 10.1

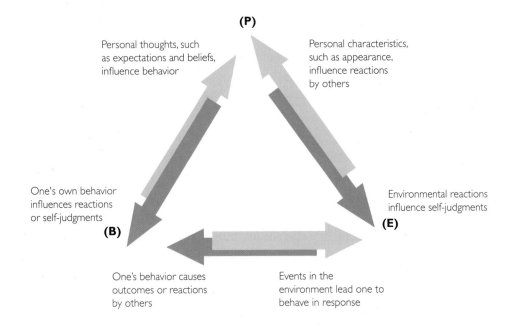

(P)

Personal thoughts, such as expectations and beliefs, influence behavior

Personal characteristics, such as appearance, influence reactions by others

One's own behavior influences reactions or self-judgments

Environmental reactions influence self-judgments

(B)

(E)

One's behavior causes outcomes or reactions by others

Events in the environment lead one to behave in response

Reciprocal Determinism: The Three-Way Relationship Between Personal Factors (P), Behavior (B), and Environmental Events (E)

Adapted from Bandura, 1997, p.6.

moody (P). The self is a system and the factors in it—personal, behavioral, and environmental—affect one another.

Self-Reflective Capability

Perhaps of greatest importance, Bandura (1997) proposed that students often *think about* or *reflect upon themselves* (**self-reflection**). Individuals monitor their ideas and judge the adequacy of their thoughts, and thus of themselves, by the results of their acts. Of all the judgments people make of themselves, the most important, according to Bandura (1977), is how competent or capable they think they are to perform a task successfully. He calls this judgment **self-efficacy**, and it affects choice of activity, amount of effort invested in an activity, length of perseverance in the face of difficulty, and likelihood of approaching a task with anxiety and apprehension versus self-assurance (Bandura, 1982). This important concept is described below.

Self-Regulatory Capability

A third basic principle of this approach is that students have the *ability to control their own behavior*. How hard people work, how many hours they sleep, what they eat, whether they use alcohol or drugs, whether they gamble, how they deport themselves in public, how much they talk, whether they do their homework, and on and on, are behaviors that they control. These behaviors do not *have* to be done, necessarily, to suit others. People do them based on their own internal standards and their own motivation (Bandura, 1982). Of course, people will be influenced by the way others react to them, but the principle responsibility will be their own.

self-efficacy

judgment of one's capability to deal with a prospective difficult situation

Learning Objective 2

Discuss the concept of self-efficacy and the impact of school and teachers on a student's self-efficacy.

Self-Efficacy—The Belief in Oneself

Milton White had a very positive student teaching experience. He was at a great high school with a very supportive supervising teacher who brought out the best in him. Whenever he ran into even small problems, his supervising teacher sat him down and helped him realize how to deal with the problem at hand. Of course, it helped that he had motivated students who were planning to go to college. When his student teaching was over, he walked away a very confident young man, secure in the belief that he was a very effective teacher. When Milton graduated and got his teaching certificate, he discovered that jobs for history teachers were few and far between. Eventually, he managed to get a job in a high school in the poorest part of town and discovered right away that the class size was considerably greater than what he experienced while student teaching and that the students were very different from the ones he student taught. He began to think that maybe he wasn't cut out for teaching and that perhaps he should begin looking for another kind of job. He needed to find something he felt good at.

Self-efficacy is Bandura's major concept in terms of its projected influence on motivation and behavior. Technically called *perceived self-efficacy*, it is defined as *"people's judgments of their capabilities to organize and execute courses of action required to attain designated types of performances"* (Bandura, 1986, p. 391). In other words, it is a personal belief about how successfully one can deal with a prospective difficult situation, such as a test, an interview, a contest, teaching a class, or a gathering of family members. Self-efficacy is *not* a function of a person's skills but of the *judgments* a person makes of what he or she can do with those skills. Self-efficacy is a self-belief in the capability to cope or excel in different situations. (Obviously, Milton White, in the above example, was suffering from a loss of self-efficacy.)

Role of Self-Efficacy in Behavior

Bandura (1997) distinguishes between **self-efficacy expectations**, or *the conviction that one can successfully execute a behavior*, and **outcome expectations,** or the *estimate that a behavior will lead to certain outcomes*. Their relationship is shown in Figure 10.2. As the figure shows, performing the behavior depends on the *belief* that the behavior can be performed successfully, not on the estimated likelihood

self-efficacy expectations

the conviction that one can successfully execute a behavior

outcome expectations

the estimate that a behavior will lead to certain outcomes

FIGURE 10.2

The Difference Between Efficacy Expectations and Outcome Expectations as They Affect Behaviors and Outcomes

Adapted from Bandura, 1997, p. 22.

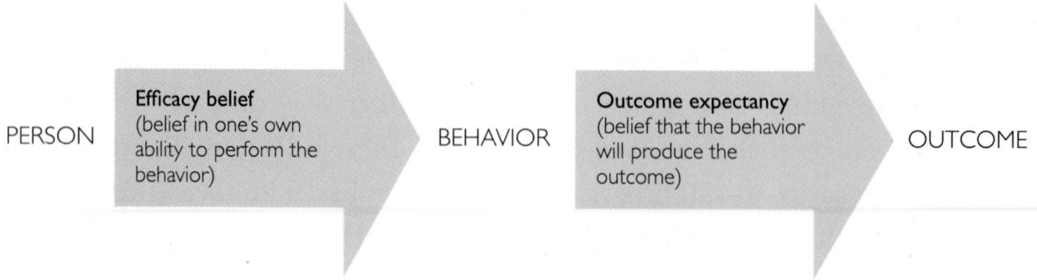

PERSON → **Efficacy belief** (belief in one's own ability to perform the behavior) → BEHAVIOR → **Outcome expectancy** (belief that the behavior will produce the outcome) → OUTCOME

that performing the behavior will produce a particular outcome. It is not the value of the outcome or its likelihood that motivates behavior, according to Bandura; it is the belief that the behavior can be performed successfully. (Of course, having the skill necessary to perform it successfully is also a requirement.)

Effects of Self-Efficacy

Self-efficacy theory predicts that people will (1) avoid situations they believe exceed their coping skills, but (2) get involved in situations they believe themselves capable of handling. In other words, self-efficacy beliefs will affect the *choice* of whether or not to attempt a behavior or task (Bandura, 1997). Judgments of efficacy will also affect the amount of energy or *effort* someone chooses to expend, and the degree of *persistence* in expending that effort, in the face of obstacles or over extended periods of time. A strong sense of self-efficacy helps someone withstand failure in challenging situations. However, sometimes students have a tendency to overestimate their skills (for example, students with learning disabilities; Klasson, 2002), which may result in unrealistically high self-efficacy beliefs and a resulting sense of failure in performance situations. Students can be taught through practice and experience to have more realistic self-efficacy beliefs (Zimmerman, 1990, 2002).

Bandura (1997) also proposed that self-efficacy beliefs produce feelings or emotions in anticipation of performing. In other words, thinking that you are likely to succeed or cope gives rise to good feelings, such as pleasure, while expecting failure produces bad feelings, such as anxiety. These feelings then affect the performance itself. Thus, thoughts are the source of feelings. To change or eliminate certain negative feelings like anger, fear, or depression, you must first change your thoughts, particularly thoughts about being able to cope with difficult situations. For an illustration, see Box 10.1: Squeezing an Orange.

Sources of Efficacy Information

How do people develop self-efficacy or the beliefs they hold about their own capabilities? Bandura (1997) proposes four sources of information that cause perceptions of self-efficacy to develop and change. These are described below and shown in Figure 10.3.

Mastery Experience

The most influential source of information about performance capabilities is actual *performance accomplishments,* or *personal mastery experiences.* What more convincing way to learn that something can be done than to actually try to do it and succeed. Success teaches people that they can succeed, and repeated early successes provide a cushion against occasional later failures. Moreover, when the basis for the sense of self-efficacy is someone's own actions and attainments, it tends to generalize to a range of similar activities.

How can a teacher help or induce a student to perform a task, and consequently enable that student to experience the sense of self-efficacy that comes from success? One technique is called **participant modeling**: The student is helped (or prompted) to carry out or model one small step of the task at a time, or to complete the task starting with the easiest version and graduating to

participant modeling
doing a task oneself with all the help needed, and then having that help gradually withdrawn

BOX 10.1

Did You Know?   Squeezing an Orange

Wayne Dyer, the noted psychologist, often asks his audiences: "What would you get if you squeezed an orange?" "Orange juice" is the usual reply. "But what if you squeezed it at night?" is his next question. Again, the reply is "Orange juice." "And if your mother squeezed it?" "Orange juice." "If you squeezed with two hands or one?" Same answer: "Orange juice."

The next question to be asked is "Why do you always get orange juice when you squeeze an orange?" Think about that for a moment and see what you would say. The answer the audience gives is "Because that's what's inside."

Now ask yourself this next question: "What do you get when you get squeezed? What comes out?" Not orange juice, silly, because that's not what's inside you. What you get is whatever's inside you.

And that is where self-efficacy theory comes into the picture.

It looks like this: When you're "squeezed" by mom or by your teacher or by your students, what comes out of you will be what is inside you, based on your thoughts about whether you can deal with the situation and how those thoughts make you feel. Do you want "sweetness" to come out of you the next time you're "squeezed"? Then you'd better start thinking positive thoughts about yourself and your ability to cope.

● Can you describe a situation where you were stressed and something other than sweetness came out of you? How did you deal with it? How should you have dealt with it?

FIGURE 10.3

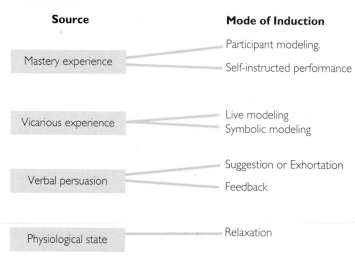

EFFICACY EXPECTATIONS

Major Sources of Efficacy Information and Ways of Providing This Information

Adapted from Bandura, 1977, p. 195.

progressively harder versions (as in shaping). Another way is to have the student complete the task jointly with another, more capable student or even with the teacher as a partner. As the student progresses, supplementary aids are gradually withdrawn (or faded) so that the student can eventually perform successfully unassisted. Participant modeling, therefore, means doing it oneself with all the needed help, and then having that help gradually withdrawn.

Also, performance can be aided through the use of **self-instructions**, such as in thinking about the performance of a task beforehand or viewing one's prior performance on video and telling oneself exactly what to do differently to improve. This process can be stimulated by having students verbalize aloud their thought processes during mastery experiences (Bandura, 1983). Seeing or otherwise being aware of one's successful performances strengthens self-beliefs in the capability to perform.

Personal accomplishment—the experience of success—or what Bandura calls mastery experience, is the best way for both students and teachers to learn to believe in themselves. With success, they will have their sense of self-efficacy enhanced.

Jose Luis Pelaez, Inc./Blend Images/Corbis

Personal accomplishment—the experience of success—or what Bandura calls *mastery experience*, is the best way for someone to learn to believe in herself. With success like this, this young woman will have her sense of self-efficacy enhanced.

Think It Over

as a LEARNER	When was the last time you had a mastery experience? Describe it. How did it make you feel about yourself? When was the last time you had a failure experience? Describe it. How did it make you feel about yourself?
as a TEACHER	How could you increase the likelihood of the students you teach having mastery experiences and decrease the likelihood of them having failure experiences?

Vicarious Experience

People do not rely on personal experience as the *sole* source of information about their level of self-efficacy. If they did, they would have to try everything themselves. *Seeing others who are similar perform activities successfully* can raise perceptions of one's own level of self-efficacy (Bandura, 1986; Schunk & Miller, 2002). In other words, people say to themselves: "If they can do it, I can do it too." By the same token, seeing others who are similar fail at a given task causes judgments of one's own capabilities to be lowered (Brown & Inouye, 1978). (Recall that social or observational learning was described in Chapter 6.) The reliance on others' experiences for one's own judgments of self-efficacy is especially great when *uncertainty* exists about one's own capability to perform a given task.

self-instructions

telling yourself how to successfully complete a task

To whom do students compare themselves? They compare themselves to **live models**, or people actually there, and to **symbolic models**, or people seen on television, in movies, or in magazines. Because the teacher may be viewed as a model, how should he or she model performances to enhance the self-efficacy of students? First, the teacher should always engage in a difficult activity in ways that exemplify what that activity is like so that students can learn to *predict* the capabilities that will be required to perform that activity. In doing a math problem, for example, a teacher should not use shortcuts and thus cause students to think that the problem is easier to do than it will actually turn out to be. Second, the teacher should demonstrate highly effective techniques for handling the threatening aspects of the activity, so that students can learn to *control* their fears in that situation and cope with it in a capable fashion (Miller, 1981). For example, if there are ways for students to check their work as they try to complete a difficult math problem, the teacher should show them what these are.

Verbal Persuasion

This is an attempt to *talk people into believing* that they have the capabilities they need to achieve what they seek. Often, what is accomplished through verbal persuasion is to convince people that they have the capability to do the job *if* they put in enough effort. However, it is easier to undermine self-efficacy by persuasion than to enhance it (Bandura, 1997).

The effectiveness of verbal persuasion depends on the perceived credibility and expertness of the persuader; just as the effect of any communication depends on these qualities in the communicator (see Chapter 9). The more the persuader is believed, the more likely the recipient is to change his or her self-perception of capability. However, if someone is persuaded to believe that he can do something, and then tries it and fails, his regard for the opinion of the persuader is likely to go down.

Most persuaders rely on **suggestion**, a more casual form of persuasion (e.g., as used in television commercials—"Be all you can be"), or on **exhortation**, a more intense form of persuasion (e.g., as used by athletic coaches—"You can do it.") There is also **feedback**, the kind that tells someone that she is doing a good job (or, perhaps, a poor job) at some task, as a reflection of her capability. Encouraging feedback that leads to higher self-efficacy leads students to work harder and to accomplish more (Schunk, 1983; Tuckman, 1992).

In using persuasion, teachers are encouraged to (1) link it to self-efficacy, and (2) provide it in the form of specific task feedback, for example, "Your performance on this task shows me that you know what you are doing and that you're capable of doing it well."

Physiological State

People rely partly on their *emotional state* or *state of arousal* to judge whether or not they are capable of doing something successfully. People are much more likely to expect success on a task when they are not nervous about doing it than when they are

live models

people actually there

symbolic models

people seen on television, in movies, or in magazines

suggestion

a more casual form of persuasion

exhortation

a more intense form of persuasion

feedback

information about how well or poorly one has done on a task

nervous. Fear and anxiety create the anticipation of stress in an upcoming task and thus reduce the sense of self-efficacy. Techniques that eliminate this anticipatory fear increase self-efficacy and lead to improvements in performance (Barrios, 1983).

The combined sources of efficacy information are illustrated by the anecdote, *The Lost Boys,* in Box 10.2 (on page 398).

Self-Efficacy and School

In school, children's knowledge and thinking skills continually are tested and evaluated, and children often are compared to one another. Good students quickly develop a strong sense of self-efficacy. Poorer students find their self-efficacy judgments undermined, leading to a continuing downward spiral of performance. This is particularly true when (1) classroom instructional practices are lockstep, requiring that everyone be taught the same thing at the same time; (2) students are grouped by ability, thereby diminishing the self-efficacy judgments of those cast into the lower ranks; or (3) performance is competitive, dooming many to fail in order to provide success for a relative few (Bandura, 1986).

Teachers who endure frustrations due to the repeated failures of their low-achieving students also experience a loss of what has been called **teacher efficacy** (Dembo & Gibson, 1985), as evidenced in the story of Milton White, with which we began. Woolfolk Hoy & Burke-Spero (2005) report that this is not uncommon among new teachers who miss the support they received as student teachers. Thus, teachers also suffer losses in self-efficacy when they perceive themselves as unable to cope with the stresses and demands of teaching. Teachers must be sensitive to the needs of their students, but they also need success experiences themselves in order to feel good as teachers.

Is there a solution? Because self-perceptions of cognitive ability are based in large part on social comparison or comparisons between students, teachers are encouraged to

- have students engage in diversified activities;
- tailor instruction to individual student skills;
- use a cooperative rather than a competitive approach; and
- avoid making comparative evaluations.

The above techniques stimulate students to compare their progress to personal standards and, hence, to expand their competencies, rather than facing demoralizing social comparison (Rosenholtz & Rosenholtz, 1981). A more personalized classroom structure produces higher perceived efficacy and decreases students' dependence on the opinions of teachers and classmates. Students' success in such a personalized and accepting classroom environment enhances teachers' sense of success or teaching efficacy.

Some specific techniques teachers can use to enhance student self-efficacy and performance are offered in the "Take it to the Classroom" example (see Box 10.3 on pages 399–400).

teacher efficacy
a teacher's self-judgment of how well or poorly he or she has done teaching

The Lost Boys (Middle School)

At the end of the boardwalk was an old, abandoned railroad bridge that looked like the one in the movie *The Lost Boys*. It stood on huge concrete "feet" and spanned a narrow channel of water about 30 feet below it. A boy of about 10 or 11 stood on the inside edge of the platform, at the edge of the rusty tracks, holding onto a pillar and looking down. Wearing a bathing suit, he was shivering and obviously trying to decide whether or not to jump the 30 feet into the water below to join his two friends who were already there. A group of onlookers gathered around him, waiting to see what he would do. Landing in the water meant jumping clear out over the base of one of the cement feet, a challenging act no doubt, and one that gave the boy great pause, as his shivering body revealed.

He was obviously asking himself: "Can I make it?" (or, in terms of the concepts of this chapter, "Do I have the self-efficacy?") His body, his physiological state, was answering him NO, as evidenced by the fear in his face and the goosebumps on his skin. As a result, he held firmly to the pillar. But his friends below were looking to change his level of self-efficacy through verbal persuasion—exhortation, to be exact. "You can do it." "It's easy." "We did it." "Don't be afraid." "Come on." "You'll make it," were the shouts coming up from below, but to no avail. The boy held fast.

So the other two boys decided to try a better method of enhancing self-efficacy: vicarious experience. They would serve as live models. They climbed out of the water and ran to the middle of the bridge where the boy and the onlookers were congregated. "Look, we'll show you how easy it is." And they both popped off the bridge like buttons on a shirt and landed safely in the water 30 feet below.

But even modeling didn't work, because the boy still held fast to the pillar and refused to jump. Only enactive mastery experience, actually jumping and living to tell of it, would convince him that he could do it, but his fear blocked him from trying. So the two friends came back again to the middle of the bridge and each took a hand of the lost boy. "Close your eyes and imagine jumping and landing in the water," they told him. "Now give us each a hand, and jump out as far as you can, but don't look down."

And so the frightened boy closed his eyes and tried to see himself capable enough to complete the leap successfully, in order to be willing to try it. But would having his friends on either side offer enough reassurance? The onlookers waited in great anticipation. And then, "Frankie!" It was his mother's angry voice calling him. "Frankie, you come here this instant." Little Frankie no longer had thoughts about fear of the jump in his head. They were replaced by thoughts of fear of his mother. For a brief instant, he thought: "I can do it." And poof, he was gone—30 feet down into the water below.

Think It Over

as a LEARNER Have you had a teacher in high school or college who did things that enhanced your self-efficacy? If so, what were those things? Have you had a teacher in high school or college who did things that reduced your self-efficacy? If so, what were those things?

as a TEACHER How would you recognize and facilitate each of the four sources of efficacy information illustrated in Box 10.2?

Self-Regulation—The Control of Oneself

Learning Objective 3

Describe the concept of self-regulation and its relation to self-efficacy; and detail ways students can become self-regulators.

LaTisha had convinced herself she was no good at math. No matter how much she tried, she just couldn't understand math. That was all there was to it! But she still had every intention of getting her degree, despite her self-proclaimed "learning disability" in math. When she was forced to take a required statistics course and realized how tough it was, she decided to go out and get herself a tutor. The tutor gave her "homework" assignments and then checked her work. When she did not understand something, which was often at first, her tutor went over it with her until she understood it. When she got a test back, her tutor went over her mistakes with her until she could explain them herself. LaTisha, who could barely pass any math classes she had ever taken, earned a grade of B in that tough statistics course and had a huge boost in self-confidence.

Self-regulation, or *the exercise of influence over one's own behavior,* is a fact of human existence. If actions were determined solely by external circumstances, people would be like "weathervanes" (Bandura, 1986, p. 335), shifting direction at a moment's notice to conform to whatever outside influence was impinging on them. Self-regulation, however, is not achieved solely by willpower. "People do possess *self-directive capabilities* that enable them to exercise some control over their thoughts, feelings, and actions by the consequences that they produce for themselves" (Bandura, 1986, p. 335). However, people who are skeptical of their ability to exercise control over their behavior tend to undermine their own efforts to deal effectively with situations that tax or challenge their capabilities. Fortunately for LaTisha (in the story above), she recognized she needed help and decided to exercise control over her behavior by getting the help she needed.

Steve Skjold/Alamy

Many students have trouble with a particular subject, like math, and then try to avoid having to deal with it. They need to engage in self-regulation, that is, to motivate themselves to study the challenging subject, and one way to do that is to work with a tutor who functions like a *personal trainer.*

Becoming a Self-Regulator

The ability to control oneself—to choose, persist, persevere, and succeed in attempting to study, to diet, to exercise, to be in a good mood, to get up in the morning,

BOX 10.3

TAKE IT TO THE CLASSROOM

What Can Teachers Do to Enhance Students' Self-Efficacy and Self-Regulated Performance? (Middle/High School)

Tuckman (1990) reports that the following teacher behaviors help students—particularly those low in self-efficacy—increase their self-efficacy and, as a result, perform more consistently.

1. Keep the tasks small. Require that more assignments be done but keep the length of each assignment as small and manageable as possible. This encourages short-term goal setting and task completion.

2. Use preset criteria for evaluating student task performance, and inform the students of the criteria prior to their undertaking the task (so they know exactly what they have to accomplish).

3. Provide specific numerical feedback to students after each assignment and test, to help them know exactly where they stand relative to the performance criteria.

4. Provide encouragement in response to student performance, by telling students what they have done well rather than what they have done poorly.

5. Have students participate in formal, written goal setting prior to undertaking specific tasks and tests, and urge them to set attainable goals.

6. Have students plan, in writing, when, where, and how they will complete assignments and what they will do to overcome obstacles that may arise.

7. Provide incentives for performance, beyond the normal grades, such as bonus points that can be accumulated to elevate a grade.

8. Use a cooperative learning approach to instruction (as described in Chapter 9), but have students submit their work individually for evaluation.

9. *Get students into the performance "habit" by using the above guidelines.*

- *Can you relate an experience you've had where your teacher did any one of the behaviors described above? How did it help you improve your performance?*

to go to work, or to carry out any behavior that is taxing or challenging—depends, in part, on the belief in one's capability to do it. In short, self-regulation depends on self-efficacy, hence self-regulatory efficacy. Barrios and Niehaus (1985) have shown that efficacy and, consequently, self-control to resist the use of drugs is undermined by inability to cope with negative emotions, social pressure to use drugs, and interpersonal conflict. People who have the necessary sense of self-efficacy to cope are able to produce the effort needed to succeed in high-risk situations. Success, in turn, further strengthens self-regulatory efficacy, while slip-ups, even when only occasional, may create a disbelief in one's coping efficacy and a tendency to relapse. Once a person sees him- or herself as powerless, further coping efforts are abandoned, resulting in a total loss of self-control (Bandura, 1997).

Necessary coping skills and the belief in one's ability or efficacy to self-regulate are built, in large measure, through enactive mastery experiences and can be enhanced by training (Cleary & Zimmerman, 2004). Persons with high self-regulatory efficacy were more likely to resist the urge to smoke following treatment, even after an occasional relapse, than persons with low self-regulatory efficacy (Condiotte & Lichtenstein, 1981).

College students with high self-efficacy were more inclined to participate in a voluntary homework program, and so gain the potential bonuses offered, than were those with low self-efficacy (Tuckman & Sexton, 1991). Recovering heart attack victims who saw themselves as high in physical efficacy expended more effort in exercising than did those who saw themselves as low (Ewart, Taylor, Reese, & DeBusk, 1983). Self-regulation is clearly important in maintaining health and wellness (Bandura, 2005).

Thus, it would be fair to conclude that "believing is seeing" (rather than the other way around). If you *believe* in your ability to control yourself, then you are likely to behave in a manner that enables you to *see* the results that you expect. If you *believe* you cannot do something, the result you *see* will be consistent with that belief: You will fail. (This is illustrated in the Story to Learn From: "Marathon Man or Marathon Moose" at the beginning of the chapter.) The key to self-regulation is believing in your capability to control yourself in difficult, risky, or challenging situations, and that includes knowing when to seek help, as LaTisha did (in the earlier example).

Think It Over

as a LEARNER	Overall, are you a self-regulated person? How does your behavior reflect that? In what area of behavior would you like to be more self-regulated
as a TEACHER	How would you go about teaching your students to be more self-regulated?

Helping Students Enhance Self-Regulation

The three elements or components of self-regulation (Zimmerman, 1998, 2000; Zimmerman & Schunk, 2004) are the following:

1. **Self-monitoring**—knowing what you are doing; being aware; perceiving things accurately, not simply acting out of habit. This provides you with the information you need to set realistic performance standards and to evaluate ongoing changes in behavior.

2. **Self-evaluation**—deciding whether a given performance should be regarded favorably or unfavorably based on internal standards and comparisons with others. This provides you with the information you need to react to your own behavior.

3. **Self-reaction**—creating incentives for your own behavior; acknowledging and verifying your competencies and capabilities; feeling satisfied with yourself; increasing your interest in continuing. (The weaker the external demands for performance, the heavier the reliance on self-reaction.)

Two procedures described below—goal setting and commitment—are recommended to make these three components contribute positively and maximally to self-regulation.

Goal Setting

According to Bandura (1997, p. 128), "goals operate largely through self-reactive influences. Personal self-efficacy is one of the important self-influences..." When people commit themselves to an explicit goal, they are likely to do what they need to do to meet that goal. When they fall short of it, the resulting dissatisfaction usually serves as an incentive to make them work harder. Both knowledge of performance (what they have done) and a standard of comparison (what they could do) are needed to produce motivational effects (Bandura & Cervone, 1983; Locke & Latham, 2002), and goals provide such a standard of comparison. Goals not only help people judge how well they are doing, they also provide them with a basis for judging their capabilities. Hence, they contribute to self-efficacy. They also have a strong influence on academic attainment (Zimmerman, Bandura, & Martinez-Pons, 1992).

What does Bandura (1997) recommend about the goals that are to be set? He says that goals should be

1. *specific* (rather than vague), so that you can hold yourself to them;
2. *challenging, yet attainable* (rather than too easy or too difficult), so that they will make you work hard but not be discouraged if you don't reach them;
3. *short-term,* or in the here-and-now (rather than distant or in the future), so that you can do something about them now;
4. *self-determined,* or chosen by you (rather than somebody else), so that you will hold yourself responsible for progress toward the goal; and
5. *incremental,* or made up of small, stepwise subgoals (rather than a single, over-all, stable entity), so that the attainment of each can be satisfying and instrumental in your achieving subsequent ones, and also so that occasional failure can be taken in stride. Subgoals do two things: They provide a *guide* and an *inducement* for present action.

Subgoal attainments also do two things: They produce *efficacy information* and *self-satisfactions* that help sustain effort along the way. "Persistence that leads to eventual mastery of an activity is thus ensured through a progression of subgoals, each with a high probability of success" (Bandura, 1986, p. 475).

Commitment

Once you set your goals, you must make a commitment to them. It is your commitment that ensures that you will

- consider them important,
- pledge yourself to attain them,
- feel constrained to work toward them,
- not put off or postpone your effort,
- judge yourself unfavorably for failing to try, and
- feel responsible for the outcome.

The stronger the commitment to a goal, the stronger the attempt to attain it. Bandura (1986) suggests making a public commitment to a goal—telling others—because that will likely make you work even harder in order to avoid any negative social consequences such as embarrassment.

One of the greatest "enemies" of self-regulation is **procrastination**. As teachers, we can teach our students and ourselves to do the things listed below (Tuckman, 1989):

- Pick out subgoals that can be realistically achieved, for example, study for 30 minutes at a time.
- Write down both the positive and the negative consequences of doing what should be done and of doing what should not be done. This means thinking rationally. What turns out to make better sense: doing what ought to be done or what ought not be done?
- Make up a daily to-do checklist: list the day's tasks in order of priority; no tasks should take more than one hour; and all should be written to describe exactly what activities have to be done.
- Provide an immediate positive consequence (reward) for effort, for example, take a break to listen to music or a snack after a study time goal is met.
- Provide social support for working. (Work in study groups.)

procrastination

the practice of avoiding or delaying doing an activity or task and making excuses for your behavior

Think It Over

as a LEARNER   How do you or should you keep yourself from putting off completing your school assignments or test preparation?

as a TEACHER   What can you do to help your students avoid procrastination?

Attribution as a Basis for Motivation

DeJuan had just moved and transferred to a new high school in the suburbs. He was taking an English course that involved reading a variety of materials and writing papers. DeJuan had grown up in a large city. He had never spent any time away from his community and his family. Now, he was in a school setting that was very different from what he was used to, and almost all of the material he was reading had very little to do with his life, his culture, and his experience. The teacher was a young white guy who seemed very smart but very snooty. For example, he talked about things like snorkeling, gourmet cooking, and the stock market. DeJuan knew little to nothing about these things, and cared less. He began to feel like he didn't have a chance in this class. No matter what he did, he was going to get ripped. At least that's what he believed. His head began to fill with bad thoughts about the teacher, the subject matter, and the school. He became discouraged and felt there was no way he could be motivated to work hard in this course. As a result, he didn't spend much time going over the readings and writing the papers. When he got a failing grade, he felt it was the instructor's fault.

Attribution theory, proposed by Weiner (1986, 1992, 2004), explains motivation on the basis of the perceived *causes* a person might use to explain success or failure in a particular performance. Because every behavior has its consequences, the person who is acting to succeed experiences not only the act itself, but its outcomes as well. And according to attribution theory, he or she will *attribute* those outcomes to certain causal agents, seeking answers to such questions as, What made me succeed? What made me fail? To what cause do I attribute my success or my failure? Because the cause cannot be observed, it must be decided by inference. Hence, attribution theory is a theory about the causal inferences people make to explain their successes and failures, that is, the **causal attributes** they choose to account for their outcomes.

Weiner (1986, 2004) proposed that people use the following causal attributes to explain their successes and failures: *ability, effort, task difficulty, luck,* and *help from others.* Outcomes depend on (1) how much ability or skill one has, (2) how much effort one puts in, (3) how difficult the task is, (4) how lucky one is, and (5) how much help one receives.

causal attributes

inferences or judgments people make to explain to themselves what causes

How Students Make Attributions

Weiner incorporated his ideas and beliefs about how students make attributions to explain their successes and failures into the model specified below and shown in Figure 10.4.

Step 1. Determine the relative success or failure of some activity that has been undertaken (e.g., *I just got a bad grade on another test or I just got a good grade.*)

Step 2. Determine the emotional consequences of the outcome (e.g., *Getting bad grades makes me mad or getting good grades makes me happy.*)

Step 3. Look back or think about past experiences to explain this outcome (e.g., *Tests are often unfairly difficult or they are not that difficult if you study for them.*)

Step 4. Identify the causal attribute that explains the current success or failure (e.g., *This course is just too tough for a student to survive or with a little help I can handle it; i.e., task difficulty.*)

Step 5. Evaluate the causal attribute chosen as the explanation for the current outcome in terms of its properties (described below) to see what can be done about it (e.g., *Nothing I do will make this course any easier or if I join a study group this course won't be that hard.*)

Step 6. Decide exactly how to feel: proud, ashamed, angry, guilty about what happened (e.g., *This predicament I'm in sure makes me angry about this school or I feel proud of myself for doing well.*)

Step 7. Form expectations for the future in the form of beliefs about what is likely to happen next (e.g., *There's no way I can pass this course or I'm going to get a high grade.*)

Step 8. Choose a subsequent behavior and carry it out (e.g., *I think I'll drop this course or I'll recommend it to my friends.*)

⌐ F I G U R E   1 0 . 4 ⌐

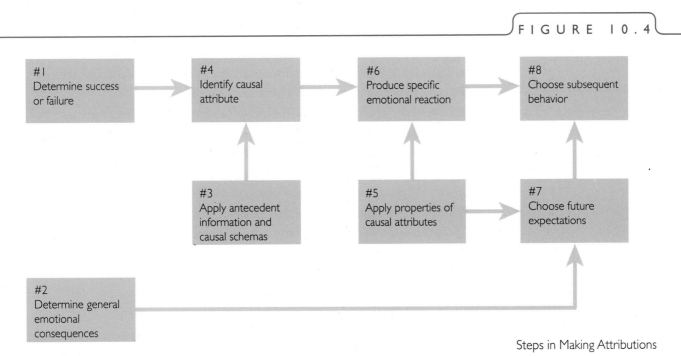

Steps in Making Attributions

Then return to Step 1 and carry out all the steps again.

Thus, the general pattern looks like this (Weiner, 1992):

The belief in or inference about causal attribution gives rise to both an emotional reaction and an explanation, which together influence subsequent behavior. Will a person try again or not? That depends on what that person believes the cause of his prior outcomes has been, as elaborated below.

Reasons for Students' Judgments of Success and Failure

How do students decide what is causing their successes and failures? How do they know whether it is effort or ability, luck or task difficulty, that has caused them to succeed or fail on a specific task? Here are some sources of information that help students decide why things have come out as they have, or the reasons for their successes and failures.

- *Past success history.* A consistent record of prior successes leads students to conclude that high ability is the cause of their successful outcome. Similarly, a consistent record of failure leads to the inference that low ability is the cause.
- *Performance success of others.* When many others also succeed or fail at a task, the inferred cause may be task easiness or difficulty rather than ability. For example, if you are a student who typically succeeds, as on classroom tests, and you get a higher score than most others on a given test, your explanation of success will be high ability. If you get a lower score than you usually do, and everyone else does too, then task difficulty will be your likely explanation.
- *Time-on-task*, which translates into how much effort has been put into task preparation and completion. If a student spends a lot of time preparing for a test and then gets a high grade, the attribution will probably be high effort. But if a student gets a low grade, the likely perceived cause would be task difficulty.
- *How much help was received.* If a student copied someone else's paper and then got an A, the copier would not conclude that either ability or effort was the key to success.
- *Randomness of outcome.* If students have no personal control over an outcome, as, for example, in the roll of the dice, then the likely conclusion will be that any outcome achieved is based on luck.

Properties and Their Functions

Once the reason or causal attribute for success or failure at a particular task has been decided, the next step is to determine the consequences of that decision. Will people be affected differently if they infer ability as cause for success in contrast to

White/PhotoLibrary

According to *attribution theory*, students try to determine the causes for their successes and failures. After taking a test, students often compare their judgments of its difficulty to use as an explanation for their level of performance.

effort, or effort in contrast to task difficulty, and so on? The answer is *yes*. Weiner (1986, 1992) identified three dimensions of causal attributes—locus of causality, stability, and controllability—that lead people to react differently to the various causal attributes. (See Table 10.1 for a *Concept Review* of the properties of each causal attribute on each dimension.)

Locus of Causality

This refers to the location or *origin* of the perceived reason for the outcome. *Internal causes* come from within while *external causes* come from outside. Internal causes include ability, effort, mood, personality, and physical health. External causes include task difficulty, luck, and help. When success is perceived to be caused by internal attributes, it contributes to self-esteem; alternatively, causes perceived to be external have no such effect (Weiner, 1992). If someone does well in a course because of ability or how hard she worked, she will feel good about herself. If someone does well because the teacher made it easy for him, he cannot give himself very much credit for his success. If he fails, though, he will feel better blaming that failure on the teacher than blaming it on his own lack of ability or effort. DeJuan, whose story appears at the beginning of this section, blamed his failure on an external cause (the way his teacher taught) in order to avoid having to blame himself.

CONCEPT REVIEW TABLE 10.1
Properties of Various Causal Attributes on Each of the Three Dimensions

CAUSAL ATTRIBUTE	LOCUS OF CAUSALITY		STABILITY		CONTROLLABILITY	
	INTERNAL	EXTERNAL	STABLE	UNSTABLE	CONTROL-LABLE	UNCONTROL-LABLE
Ability	X		X			X
Effort	X			X	X	
Task Difficulty		X	X			X
Luck		X		X		X
Help		X		X		X
Illness	X			X		X
Mood	X			X		X
Strategy	X			X	X	

Stability

This refers to the constancy or unchanging nature of a causal attribute. When a prior outcome is believed to be caused by a stable attribute (such as ability or task difficulty), then subsequent outcomes will be readily predicted to be the same. If someone lost a game of tennis today because she had little ability to play the game, she would expect to lose the game tomorrow as well because her ability would not likely change in such a short time.

Outcomes based on unstable causes (effort, luck, mood, or help) would not necessarily guarantee subsequent outcomes, as those based on stable causes (Weiner, 1992). If a person lost a game of doubles because his partner had a bad day, he would not necessarily expect to lose again. People react with greater emotion to outcomes based on stable causes than to outcomes from unstable causes because they expect that such outcomes will continue. Hence, stability affects emotional reactions and expectations for future outcomes.

Controllability

Controllability refers to the extent to which a causal attribute is within a person's control and can be intentionally altered by choice, as opposed to being relatively unalterable. Among Weiner's dimensions, only effort is controllable. Effort is the only thing you can alter in order to change failure to success. Tuckman et al. (2008), however, have proposed *strategy*, or the way something is done, as a second controllable causal attribute.

Dweck (1999, 2002) proposed two ways to think about ability as a causal attribute: (1) using an *entity theory* that views ability as stable and uncontrollable, or (2) using an *incremental theory* that views ability as unstable and controllable. In the latter case, the application of effort, through practice for example, leads to an improvement in one's knowledge and skills; hence, it is unstable and controllable. The difference between Weiner's view of ability and Dweck's can be resolved by reverting to the term aptitude (Heider, 1958), rather than ability, to describe the unstable and uncontrollable aspects of a person's intellectual endowment or capacity.

Some functions of the causal properties are listed below.

- They affect future goal expectancies and subsequent behavior; for example, failure attributed to a *stable* cause is expected to recur, and may cause one to avoid the failure situation.
- They generate particular emotional reactions: Failure attributed to *controllable* effort produces guilt or shame, while failure attributed to an *uncontrollable* lack of help, to poor luck, or to a difficult task produces anger (as was the case with DeJuan).
- They contribute to self-image: Success based on *internal* ability or effort produces pride and a positive self-image, while success based on *external* causes produces no emotional consequences.

In one research project, Weiner (1980) exposed some people to a person falling down in the subway as a function of being drunk, a *controllable* circumstance (because people choose to drink). Others were exposed to a person falling down in the subway as the result of an *uncontrollable* infirmity or physical disability. The emotional reaction to the drunk person was disgust and the subsequent behavior was avoidance; the reaction to the disabled person was sympathy and the subsequent behavior was to offer help. People react not just to the occurrence of an event itself but to what they perceive or judge to be the cause of the event. They are more likely to pronounce blame on themselves and others when the cause is controllable than when it is uncontrollable, but they are also more likely to help another student with a problem when they see the cause of the problem as uncontrollable (e.g., ability) than controllable (e.g., effort) (Ahles, P. & Contento, J., 2006).

Overall, effort emerges as a particularly important cause because it comes from within, is changeable, and is under one's control. It is hard to alter ability and impossible to do anything about luck. People can ask for help but are not guaranteed getting it, and they can seek out easier tasks but are never assured that the tasks will turn out to be that way. If you want to succeed, therefore, your best option is to choose to apply effort.

Some of the causal explanations sound like rationalizations, and indeed they are. They serve as a protective device against admitting to one's own lack of ability or unwillingness to apply effort. They allow students to dissociate themselves from the true causes. Teachers should focus students' attention on *effort* as a controllable cause that can lead to success.

Cross-cultural research (Hong, Morris, Chiu, & Benet-Martinez, 2000) suggests that different cultures may classify specific attributions along different dimensions. For example, persons in more interdependent cultures such as in Japan or China may place much more emphasis on external attributions than internal ones, viewing external attributions as representing their family, community, or society and thus implicitly including themselves.

The Role of Emotions

Remember that the attribution model looks like this:

PERCEIVED CAUSE → EMOTIONAL REACTION → FUTURE EXPECTATION → SUBSEQUENT BEHAVIOR

Our emotional reactions and the emotional reactions of others influence what to expect and what to do. Similarly, our emotional reactions to others tell us how to feel, what to expect, and how to behave. (This is similar to reciprocal determinism, described in the previous section.) For example, when people feel apathetic or resigned, what do they do? They usually stop trying, or they try something else, because they feel it would be useless to continue on their present course. Feelings of gratitude or relief make people behave in a thankful manner or cause them not to proceed without help. Feelings of pride make them confident and lead them to take on or continue a task.

What about the feelings a person *receives*? What information do they convey? A teacher pitying or feeling sorry for a student may tell him that he is not very able or smart. A teacher's expression of anger toward a student and her work may tell the student that she has not put forth enough effort. Even teachers' expressions of sympathy may not make students feel good about themselves; they may instead suggest that the students are not able to do something on their own (Weiner, Russell, & Lerman, 1979).

Judging Responsibility and Intentionality

When a student perceives a negative or unsuccessful behavior to be based on a controllable cause such as effort, then he or she feels a sense of **responsibility**. Failing a test because of inadequate preparation would be an example. If you chose not to study, that would reflect **intentionality**. You can control effort, so it is your responsibility to do so if you want a good result. However, when the cause is perceived as uncontrollable such as task difficulty or ability, he or she does not feel responsible. Failing a test because it did not cover what was taught in class and hence was unreasonably difficult would be an example. You cannot control what is on the test, so doing poorly is not your fault. The same judgments would be made by someone else, such as the teacher, observing your behavior. If you got sick and

responsibility

the expectation or judgment that an outcome depends on you

intentionality

doing something on purpose

had a doctor's note to prove it, your teacher would not hold you responsible for your absence, but if you stayed home to watch TV, then you would be held responsible. If you, along with almost everyone else, failed the test the teacher would be less likely to hold you responsible than if he knew you did not study.

Weiner (1995) cites evidence showing that our judgments of our own irresponsibility has the potential to produce guilt and thus lead us to change our behavior in order to perform better, while judgments by others of our irresponsibility provoke anger and typically lead to punishment. After seeing yourself as failing the test because of not studying enough, you are likely to become personally motivated to study more next time, but your parent or teacher is inclined to punish you. Indeed, a failing grade is itself a punishment that may have a lasting effect on your grade point average.

Typically, the two causal explanations contrasted are effort and ability; both are internal, but the first is controllable and the other is not. Ability can be used to represent any internal characteristic a person has that is beyond that person's control. Consider *hyperactivity* and *shyness*. Hyperactive children often tend to provoke anger and neglect by peers and teachers because they are perceived as responsible for their behavior, while shy children elicit sympathy and support because shyness typically is perceived to be part of their "nature" (Juvonen, 1991, 1992). Rejection is commonly based on perceptions of others' responsibility for their actions. Similar judgments are made of conditions like poverty, alcoholism, obesity and AIDS. When persons with these conditions are viewed as responsible for them, they are more likely to provoke negative reactions and nonsupport than when they are viewed as not responsible for them (Weiner, 1995).

Some insight into the relationship between perceptions of attribution and judgments of responsibility and intentionality is provided by the "Discourse on Diversity" in Box 10.4.

Creatas Images (RF)/Jupiter Images

When students are seen as being responsible for a negative action such as bullying other students, teachers and administrators are more likely to punish them than when they are not seen as being responsible.

D I S C O U R S E   O N   D I V E R S I T Y

Attributions of Hostile Intent by African American Eighth-Grade Boys and Their Mothers (Middle/High School)

BOX 10.4

Sandra Graham, an educational psychologist with a focus on motivation, began her career teaching African American children from inner-city Boston. She reports that "these students, although showing great potential, were doing very poorly as a group, and many were in constant trouble for behavior problems" (Graham, 1997, p. 21). She felt then, as now, that "far too many minority children perform poorly in school, not because they lack basic intellectual competencies or even specific learning skills, but because they feel hopeless, have low expectations, deny the importance of effort, or give up in the face of failure" (Graham, 1997, p.21), all achievement motivation concerns. Many also do poorly in school because "they have few friends, adhere to an oppositional peer culture, or evoke anger from their teachers and classmates" (Graham, 1997, p. 21), all social motivation concerns. To understand achievement and social motivation in the context of attribution theory among African American children, Dr. Graham has done a number of research studies such as the two described below.

Perceptions of **intentionality**, according to attribution theory, are linked with judgments of responsibility. If a person is seen as doing something intentionally, then that person is judged to be responsible for the result. Graham (1997) reports on studies of aggression among African Americans. In one study, eighth-grade African American boys were classified as aggressive or not aggressive based on judgments of peers and teachers. They were then given the following scenario:

Imagine that you are on your way to school one morning. You look down and notice that your shoelace is untied. You put the notebook that you are carrying down on the ground to tie your shoelace. An important homework paper that you worked on for a long time falls out of your notebook. Just then, another kid walks by and steps on the paper, leaving a muddy footprint right across the middle. (Graham, 1997, p. 24)

Some of the eighth graders were then told something to suggest that the peer provocateur's intention was **hostile** (he *starting laughing as he stepped on the homework paper*), and some **ambiguous** (he *looked down at your homework paper and then up at you*). The students were then asked whether the kid did it on purpose, how much anger they would feel, and how they would react (from "do something nice for this kid" to "have it out right then and there"). Responses of the eighth graders classified as aggressive were compared to those classified as nonaggressive. In the ambiguous scenario, the aggressive students were much more likely to view the hypothetical peer's action as reflecting hostile intent, to report feeling more angry, and to prefer to respond aggressively than the nonaggressive students. The findings show that "aggressive children are biased toward perceiving peer provocation as intentional, especially in situations of attributional ambiguity" (Graham, 1997, p. 25). In other words, they believe the kid who stepped on the paper was responsible for doing it (i.e., did it on purpose).

In a follow-up study to gain insight into what might have led these aggressive students to perceive malicious intent, the mothers of aggressive and nonaggressive sons were given a different scenario of ambiguous peer provocation, and then asked to judge the "provocateur's responsibility, their own anger, and their likelihood of retaliating."

The results showed that "when they reasoned about their own situations of ambiguous provocation, mothers of aggressive sons were also more likely than mothers of nonaggressive ones to infer that their adult peers acted with hostile intent; they were more angry, blameful, less sympathetic, and more endorsing of hostile behavior" (Graham, 1997, p. 28). In other words, the mothers responded to an ambiguous peer provocation scenario very much the same way as the eighth-grade boys in the study previously described did to theirs, suggesting a possible way in which judgments of intentionality and responsibility are learned.

Think It Over

as a LEARNER   Can you remember a situation in which you had to make a judgment of the intentionality of a person who performed a seemingly hostile act toward you? What was the situation? Did you judge the act to be intentional or not, and on what basis did you make the judgment?

as a TEACHER   How might you help your students make judgments of intentionality, and how to subsequently behave toward persons who they perceive as acting intentionally?

Learned Helplessness

Compare the student who succeeds on a consistent basis with the one who fails with equal regularity. What is the succeeder likely to infer as the cause for his or her success? The choice is usually ability—a stable, internal cause. And what about an occasional, and unexpected, failure? Here the choice will be an unstable or external cause such as luck or task difficulty (Weiner, 1992). In this way, self-esteem will be maintained and confidence will not be undermined. The result will be, more often than not, continued success. Moreover, when the tasks get harder, the succeeder will be inclined to exert more effort (a controllable cause) based on the expectation that effort expenditure and likelihood of success are related.

But what of those students characterized by persistent failure? No matter what some students do, they still seem to fail, academically or socially. They soon develop low self-esteem and the expectation to fail. Moreover, they come to believe that their outcomes are independent of their actions. In other words, they believe that no matter what they do, they still will fail. They see all causes as uncontrollable, stable, and external—and themselves as thus doomed to failure. Seligman (1990) has termed this state **learned helplessness**. Some children come to believe they are helpless when they discover they cannot seem to help themselves.

How do children with learned helplessness behave? According to Dweck (1975), *first, they give up easily*, especially in the face of failure, however minimal. They are quickly convinced that they are not capable of determining their own outcomes and so tend to regard any adverse circumstance as insurmountable. *Second, they avoid taking personal responsibility for their failure* for as long as possible by not perceiving a relationship between their own behavior and their failure. As long as they can believe the cause of failure is external and uncontrollable, it is out of their hands. *Third*, when they must acknowledge that their failure is their fault, *they blame failure on a lack of ability* rather than a lack of effort. *And fourth, their failures are followed by a consistent deterioration in performance.* They go from bad to worse to worse yet.

These are the unmotivated students, the ones who are not inclined to put forth the effort because they believe it will be to no avail. What are teachers to do?

The Teacher's Role in Motivating Students

Being a motivated student means expending effort, and expending effort requires a belief that effort is a necessary prerequisite (or causal attribute) for success. Being motivated also means believing you can help yourself succeed and being confident that you will succeed. Finally, being motivated requires you to believe that you have the ability to succeed.

Teachers Convey Attributional Information

The task facing teachers is not only to *help students succeed but also to help students believe that it is their own ability and effort that is the cause of that success.* Figure 10.5 (on page 414) shows the three important ways that teachers influence students' beliefs about what has caused their successes and failures (Graham & Weiner, 1983). These are (1) specific performance feedback, or what the teacher tells the student about the correctness of his or her work; (2) the teacher's nonverbal affective reaction to the student (e.g., sympathy, anger, resignation, surprise); and (3) the subsequent behavior of the teacher toward the student (e.g., giving help or extra work). Teachers need to be aware of the causal information they are conveying to students, particularly low-achieving students, by their words and manner, because students use this information to make inferences about their ability.

How Teachers Treat Low Achievers

According to Good & Brophy (2002), teachers treat low achievers differently from high achievers. Specifically, teachers are less demanding of, pay less attention to, and yet may give more unsolicited help to low achievers. These teacher behaviors, combined with a feeling of pity, convey to students the causal inference that their low achievement is caused by a lack of ability. Because ability is seen as an internal, stable, and uncontrollable cause of behavior, and hence something about which students can do little, they are likely to lapse into a pattern of learned helplessness. No one wants to believe that a lack of ability is the reason for their poor performance, so students react to such a message by assuming a helpless, uncontrollable stance.

learned helplessness
the perception that there is no relation between one's behavior and one's outcomes, which leads to the feeling of being helpless

FIGURE 10.5

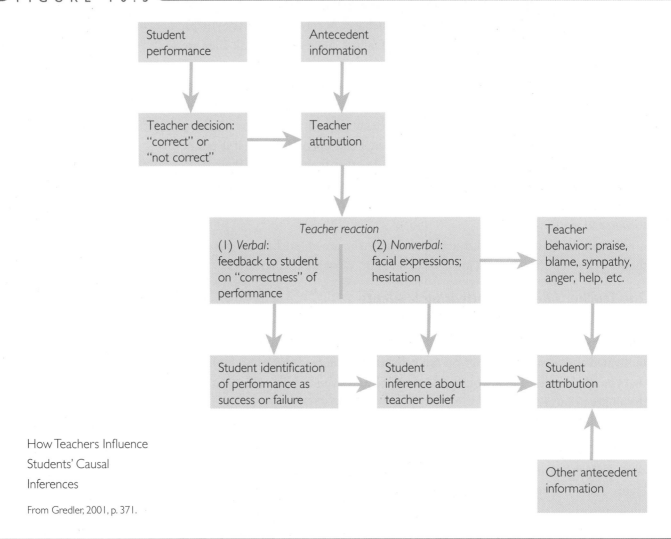

How Teachers Influence Students' Causal Inferences

From Gredler, 2001, p. 371.

Of particular concern is the use of praise and blame. When a teacher perceives a student of low ability and responds to this student's performance with excessive criticism, then it is clear to the student how negative the teacher feels. To avoid this critical behavior, many teachers adopt a different approach (described in the following) but one that sends out the same message equally strongly (Good & Brophy, 2002): When a teacher gives a student *a noticeably easy task and then praises the student excessively for completing it successfully* (in an honest effort to provide praise for success), the student cannot help but perceive that the teacher believes he or she has low ability. Teacher overreactions to student performance often indicate to low-achieving students their lack of ability. "Oh how wonderful you are for being able to complete this terribly easy task" tells students that their teacher expects very little from them.

What Can a Teacher Do?

First, a teacher can *emphasize learning* or the process of acquiring skills and knowledge *rather than achievement* or the product or result of that acquisition. Teachers should react to students' efforts rather than to just the results of their work. Giving

> ### *Think It Over*
>
> **as a LEARNER** Have you ever seen a teacher conveying attributional information to a student, possibly yourself? How was the attributional information conveyed (i.e., what did the teacher do or not do)? How did the student seem to feel (or how would you have felt)? How did the student react?
>
> **as a TEACHER** How would you deliver attributional messages to students?

specific feedback to students on the correctness or incorrectness of their responses rather than merely grading their performance, reacting specifically to their performance rather than to their personality and upbringing, reacting to their performance without reference to the performance of other students—all help students focus on learning.

Second, a teacher can improve the motivation or effort of students by *reducing the competitiveness* among them. The cooperative learning approach (as described in Chapter 9) and the mastery learning approach (as described in Chapter 12) are ways to help students avoid making negative causal inferences about their behavior as a result of contrasting it to that of other students. Cooperative learning and mastery learning are much more likely than the conventional classroom approach to yield successful experiences for students who need them.

Third, a teacher needs to help students evaluate their outcomes on the basis of *causal attributes other than ability*. This is important because judgments of ability are tied to self-esteem and self-confidence, and negative judgments have the most harmful effect on a student's willingness to try to perform. As already mentioned, one way to do this is to reinforce *effort* rather than results, so that students will see effort, not ability, as the cause of success. Another way is to introduce a new causal attribute, *strategy*, as proposed by Tuckman et al. (2008). Strategy refers to the way you go about doing something. If a student does poorly on a test, it may not be due to ability or lack of effort in preparation. Instead, the problem may lie in poor study and test-taking strategies. By helping students view strategies as causes of failure, and by helping them improve their strategies and praising their efforts to do so, teachers may be able to turn failure into success for many students.

Fourth, a teacher should emphasize *realistic goal setting* (as discussed earlier in this chapter) in order to increase the likelihood of success and improve the student's personal appraisal of his or her own ability.

Fifth, teachers should monitor the attributional messages they send students and modify their verbal feedback statements. Audiotaping and videotaping can be most helpful in this regard. Teachers must become aware of if and how they convey to students the message that they regard them as inept, and must try to change these expressions and the manner in which they use them (see Box 9.3 on congruent communications).

Sixth, teachers need to avoid falling into their own pattern of learned helplessness as a result of their perceived failures and frustrations in the classroom.

Attribution theory applies to teachers as well as students, and teachers make causal inferences about their own outcomes, particularly their successes and failures in helping students learn. Perceptions of excessive failure can lead teachers to judgments of low teaching ability or to a dissociation between their own actions and their teaching outcomes. Extreme cynicism and a progressive deterioration of performance can be the results. Teachers can also come to see themselves as the target of undesirable student behavior and believe themselves to be the victim (a symptom of learned helplessness), rather than realizing that students really victimize themselves by their unconstructive behavior.

Seventh, teachers need to *use encouragement* to help students view themselves more positively so they will become motivated or feel a desire to achieve. Some suggestions about what constitutes encouragement are listed below.

1. Encouragement is based on a positive belief in your own ability and the ability of others; on accepting students as they are, not as they could be.
2. Encouragement is intended to help students believe in themselves and their own ability.
3. Encouragement helps students risk imperfection by helping them realize that mistakes are not failures. Mistakes can promote learning.
4. Encouragement is different from praise. The student does not have to earn it by being first. It can be given for any positive movement. It means treating the student with acceptance and respect.
5. Encouragement focuses on effort. It does not place a value judgment on the student like praise does.
6. Encouragement begins by finding students' assets: their talents, positive attitudes, and goals, not their faults. Every student has strengths.
7. Encouragement is the opposite of discouragement. *Do not* discourage students by providing

    - negative comments and expectations ("put-downs"),
    - unreasonably high and double standards, or
    - competition and overambition.

8. Encouragement affirms that the student is trying and that trying is worthwhile.

Learning Objective 5

Describe needs and goals as motivators of learner achievement.

Needs and Goals as Motivators

Need and goal approaches focus on explaining the motivation of students to achieve, as reflected in the tasks they choose and the energy they invest in doing them, on the basis of the needs satisfied and goals met by this behavior (Wigfield & Eccles, 2002). (The beliefs that also underlie the motivation to achieve have already been dealt with earlier in this chapter under the social cognitive theory and attribution approaches.) Needs and goals are powerful motivators, influencing both the target of behavior and the driving force behind it.

Maslow's Hierarchy of Needs

Ana and her family migrated to Columbus, Ohio, from Peru. She and her two brothers were enrolled in the public schools while her mother and father found restaurant jobs that paid a low hourly wage. Ana, who like the rest of her family spoke little English, was in third grade. Eligible for free meals, she was able to get her breakfast and lunch in school and her parents often brought leftover food home from the restaurant for dinners. But the apartment they rented had little insulation and in the cold winter little Ana was always painfully cold. Her meager wardrobe provided little protection from the chill, making it difficult for her to concentrate on her school lessons.

Maslow (1970) distinguishes between the motivation to realize and actualize one's inherent potential and others' view of needs, this way:

Healthy growth is a neverending series of free-choice situations, facing each person throughout life, in which each must regularly choose between growth and safety. To choose growth, the person must find it more attractive and less dangerous than its alternative, safety. If growth is either too unattractive or too dangerous, a person will retreat to safety.

Maslow proposed that we have, inherent within us, a hierarchy of needs (arranged in order of priority), as shown in Figure 10.6. The lower, more fundamental needs are called **deficiency needs** because they involve overcoming deficiencies that can threaten survival. The higher needs are called **growth needs** because they contribute to the improvement of quality of life.

People begin by satisfying the lowest deficiency needs, ensuring that they can eat, sleep, and be free from danger. For most people, these needs are easily satisfied;

deficiency needs
lower, more fundamental needs

growth needs
higher needs, contribute to the improvement of quality of life

FIGURE 10.6

Growth Needs	Self-Actualization Need
	Aesthetic Needs
	Need to Know and Understand
Deficiency Needs	Esteem Needs
	Belongingness and Love Needs
	Safety Needs
	Physiological Needs

Maslow's Hierarchy of Needs

Teachers who believe that all students can learn, who create an open and friendly climate, and who allow students to participate freely, without fear of judgment, are acting to enhance the *self-actualization* of their students.

Ariel Skelley/Blend Images/Jupiter Images

for some, they are not. When safety is more attractive and less dangerous than growth, especially when total effort is required to maintain safety, people will not proceed beyond this level of the hierarchy. They will not be motivated to grow. Once they feel safe, people will reach out for acceptance from others and will then attempt to satisfy the growth needs for self-esteem, mastery, and aesthetics through their own actions and performances. When they have experienced success, they will finally proceed to the challenge of the pinnacle of growth: **self-actualization**. Motivation, according to Maslow, is striving to satisfy all the needs in the hierarchy, culminating with self-actualization. The goal is to *become* a self-actualized person.

The implication for teachers and schools of Maslow's hierarchy of needs is that students will not be motivated to pursue the growth needs—esteem, knowledge, aesthetic experiences, or self-actualization—if they come to school hungry, sleep-deprived, anxious, frightened, or feeling a total lack of emotional support. Like little Ana in the above story, their motivational focus will be on satisfying these fundamental deficiency needs. Providing them with free and reduced-cost meals, adequate clothing and shelter, a sense of personal security, and a feeling of acceptance and affection are the prerequisites to students willing and able to take the next steps toward satisfying their needs for intellectual and personal growth.

Needs and Strategies for Helping Students Achieve

McClelland (1985; McClelland, Atkinson, Clark, & Lowell, 1953; Atkinson, 1964) proposed that some individuals develop a motive for success that affects their drive for accomplishments. He designated it as the **need for Achievement** or more simply, *nAch*. And though it is one of many possible motives (Murray, 1938, had

self-actualization

the ultimate process of personal growth

need for achievement

a motive for success that affects one's drive for accomplishment originally proposed 20), it is especially important to success in educational and business settings.

In contrast to this need for achievement, McClelland believed that some people possess a need to avoid failure. While those with a high need for achievement tend to choose tasks of moderate difficulty, people with a need to avoid failure choose either exceptionally easy tasks, for which success virtually is guaranteed or exceptionally hard tasks, for which failure is expected and, therefore, not a matter of personal responsibility (Atkinson, 1964). Failure stimulates need achievers to try harder, while high failure avoiders prefer the safety of sure success.

Stipek (2002) studied elementary school children and concluded that the competitiveness of the later grades encourages students to shift from a task focus to an outcomes focus and to become more concerned with avoiding failure. As elementary school children progress through the grades, the performance they expect from themselves is increasingly influenced by the performance feedback they receive from teachers (Eshel & Klein, 1981). Excessively harsh feedback and poor grades can quickly turn a high-need achiever into a high-failure avoider.

Over time, need for achievement was reconceptualized as **mastery motivation**, the inherent need to feel competent and deal effectively with the environment (Harter, 1981). Applied to specific areas of achievement rather than viewed globally as McClelland did, it was referred to as perceived competence, which Harter & Connell (1984) regarded as including the following five aspects:

- preference for challenging, rather than easy, work;
- inclined to work to satisfy one's own interest rather than to please the teacher or get good grades;
- attempting to achieve independent mastery, rather than depending on the teacher;
- relying on one's own independent judgments, rather than the teacher's; and
- using one's own criteria for success and failure.

This is also referred to as intrinsic motivation.

Enhancing Achievement Motivation: Strategies for Achievement

When Ivana got to college, she soon realized she was in over her head. High school had been easy for her; she never really had to study and she somehow managed to avoid the really hard courses. She was so pleasant that her teachers never seemed to put much pressure on her, and her parents were always there to help her with stuff she didn't understand. Now she was on her own, and the assignments were hard and the amount of reading was excessive. How in the world, she wondered, was she to survive?

McClelland (1965, 1985) proposed a technique for increasing people's motivation to seek achievement, which was used to train business leaders in various countries. Tuckman (2003; Tuckman et al., 2008) expanded on this approach, with a particular focus on training students to achieve academic success. Called **strategies for achievement**, this technique centers on the four strategies described below.

The first strategy is *take reasonable risk*. This strategy guides and directs students' choices, and leads them to avoid both the sure success and the sure failure and seek

mastery motivation
the inherent need to feel competent and deal effectively with the environment

strategies for achievement
McClelland's four-strategy technique for increasing people's motivation to seek achievement

Students can use computer-mediated instruction to learn and apply "*strategies for achievement.*"

instead the middle road. The middle road is both challenging and attainable, and following it will lead to steady, progressive growth. Investigations by Meyer, Folkes, & Weiner (1976) demonstrated the informational value of choosing tasks of intermediate difficulty. The substrategies that allow one to adjust risk are *goal setting* (described earlier in this chapter) and *breaking tasks down* into small manageable steps, or subgoals.

Employing the following conditions will help teachers implement this strategy:

- provide students with tasks of varying difficulty levels;
- demonstrate to students how to subdivide a large task into smaller ones;
- teach and encourage students to set goals; and
- allow students to use failure as a learning experience.

If all students are given the same tasks with the same difficulty levels, as is often the case in school, then individual students cannot be exposed to the level of challenge that represents reasonable risk for them at a particular time. Teachers can adjust risk levels for students by using books and other materials such as mathematics problems of differing difficulty levels, depending on the student's current level of mastery. Differentiated instruction and ability grouping, described in Chapter 4, are ways of adjusting difficulty levels to meet students' needs. If failure causes pain or embarrassment, children will always be motivated to choose the easiest tasks they can. Teachers need to create learning situations involving choice while at the same time minimizing personal consequences, so that students can learn to pursue the motivating choice of challenging themselves. To succeed at this, students should be taught to set goals and break tasks down into small steps.

The second strategy is *take responsibility for your outcomes*. (The concept of responsibility was described earlier in this chapter.) This means that, rather than attributing either failure or success in achievement situations to factors for which they themselves cannot be held responsible, such as teachers, the more desirable state is for students to assume self-responsibility for their outcomes (Graham, 1997). The substrategies that assist one in taking responsibility are *focusing on effort* (described in attribution theory) and *planning*.

Employing the following conditions will help teachers implement this strategy:

- acknowledge and reward students' effort and self-reliance, and
- teach and encourage student planning (especially in regard to time management).

Students will be more likely to expend effort if teachers recognize and value it. Their effort, moreover, is less likely to be misplaced if they plan for its expenditure (particularly in terms of studying and staying on task).

The third strategy is *search the environment for information;* the fourth is to *use feedback*. Both place great emphasis on getting and using information. Searching the environment directs students to try to find out everything they can about the task and about the resources, including human ones, available to accomplish it, and involves the substrategies of *asking questions* and *using visualization*. Rosenshine, Meister, and Chapman (1996) reported a meta-analysis showing that teaching students to generate questions resulted in gains in comprehension, and Mayer (1984, 1989) has shown the value of conceptual models for visualizing ways of solving problems. Using feedback tells students to pay particular attention to the results of their actions in deciding what to do next, and involves the substrategies of *monitoring one's actions* and *giving oneself instructions* (referred to as *self-monitoring* and *self-instructing* by Zimmerman, 1998).

Employing the following conditions will help teachers implement these strategies:

- provide an information-rich environment that students are taught to use, and within which they can move freely;
- teach students to use the questioning approach to learning (see *questioning* in Chapter 7);
- give students informative and detailed performance feedback, going beyond just evaluation; and
- show students how to incorporate feedback into their subsequent performance.

Students trained in the use of the four strategies earned higher grades than comparable students who did not receive this training (Tuckman, 2003). Fortunately for Ivana, in the earlier story, her college offered a course that taught the four strategies, and she was able to use them to get herself on track.

Learner Goal Orientation

Mr. Gomez was a ninth grade biology teacher whose goal was to have his students really understand and appreciate biology rather than single-mindedly focus on just getting good grades. To this end, he spent a lot of his own personal time creating lessons that students could actually experience. He helped his students design and carry out projects to help them explore concepts like photosynthesis, cell growth, heredity, and digestion. For example, he showed them how to obtain samples of single-celled organisms and make slides, and use microscopes to reveal a whole new world of existence. Taking his class was a real learning experience!

Recently, there has been a growing interest in the different types of goals students choose to pursue, rather than the needs that may underlie them. Ames (1992), among others, proposed two alternative **goal orientations**, or ways of approaching, engaging in, and responding to achievement situations (Pintrich, 2003): **mastery** and **performance**. **Mastery goals** (sometimes called learning goals or task goals) are focused on learning for its own sake, like trying to accomplish something challenging or developing new competencies, while **performance goals** reflect a desire for specific positive outcomes, such as getting high grades or being the best in the group. Pintrich (2000a) points out that goal orientation is indicative of one's standards for defining one's own competence, that is, the degree to which one has succeeded or failed in reaching a goal, with the mastery-oriented person defining competence as improving at something and the performance-oriented person as outperforming others. For those students motivated to avoid academic work altogether, the term **work-avoidance goals** has been coined (Nicholls et al., 1990), or **mastery-avoidance goals** by Elliott and McGregor (2001).

A mastery goal orientation has been described in more positive terms than a performance goal orientation. Dweck & Leggett (1988) associate the mastery goal orientation with having an incremental view of intelligence, that is, that intelligence can be improved through effort, while the performance goal orientation they link with an entity view of intelligence, that it is fixed and unchangeable. Maehr & Midgley (1996) see success for the mastery goal-oriented learner to be improvement, compared to high grades, winning, and recognition for the performance goal-oriented learner. They also see mastery-oriented learners evaluating themselves based on their own internal standards compared to the norms and social comparisons used by performance-oriented learners. Ryan, Pintrich, & Midgley (2001) found that mastery goals were related to self-regulation among college students. Students who adopted a personal mastery goal were more likely to engage in adaptive help-seeking than those adopting a performance goal. And, furthermore, setting mastery goals for achievement helped students in shaping information seeking and learning, stimulated their interest in what they were being taught (Butler, 2000; Harackiewicz, Barron, Tauer, Carter, & Elliot, 2000), and achieving better in school (Sins, vanJoolingen, Savelsbergh, & van Hout-Wolters, 2008).

Unfortunately, though, this two-category model of goal orientations has not proven entirely adequate to classify the possible goals students set. Mastery goals, for example, appear less related to school achievement than performance goals, suggesting that the simple dichotomy of "good" mastery goals versus "bad" performance goals is inadequate (Harackiewicz, Barron & Elliott, 1998). The recognition that performance goals may be more adaptive for certain outcomes than mastery goals has led some to further subdivide performance goals into *performance approach* (trying to outperform others) and *performance avoidance* (trying

---

goal orientations

ways of approaching, engaging in, and responding to achievement situations

mastery

how much expert skill or knowledge one has

performance

how well one does in completing a task

mastery goals

goals focused on learning for its own sake

performance goals

goals that reflect a desire for specific positive outcomes

work-avoidance goals

motivation to avoid work

mastery-avoidance goals

motivation to avoid academic work

not to look stupid or incompetent relative to others, with the former more adaptive than the latter (Harackiewicz, Barron & Elliott, 1998). Indeed, the performance approach goal orientation may be a close fit to McClelland's original concept of need for achievement, and the combination of mastery and performance goals have been shown to be associated with the effective use of cognitive strategies (Pintrich, 2000b).

What can teachers do to help students adopt mastery goals? Pintrich & Schunk (2002) recommend the following:

- use a variety of relevant and "authentic" learning activities that are novel, diverse, and interesting (as Mr. Gomez, the biology teacher, did in the above story);
- offer students a range of tasks that are reasonable in terms of their capabilities, allow them some choice and control over these, and adjust time available to complete them for students having trouble (this also fits "taking reasonable risk" from the preceding theory);
- focus on and acknowledge individual improvement, progress and mastery, and insofar as possible, make evaluation a private (not public) process;
- recognize student effort and react to student mistakes as opportunities for learning; and
- use cooperative learning (Chapter 9) with heterogeneous groups.

Incentives and Values as Motivators

Learning Objective 6

Illustrate various incentives and values as motivators of learner achievement.

Marybeth was a confirmed procrastinator. She would never start writing a paper or studying for a test until the night before. Her father couldn't understand how she could stand the pressure of waiting until the last minute, but Marybeth insisted she worked better under pressure, when in reality she worked *only* under pressure. Everything seemed to go her way until she took trigonometry. Trigonometry was really tough for her, but she couldn't seem to break her habit of putting her studying off until the last minute. What was she to do?

Incentives, or goal objects that individuals desire to obtain or avoid, have figured prominently in a number of approaches to motivation (e.g., Atkinson, 1964; Rotter, Chance & Phares, 1972; Vroom, 1964).

In these approaches, the degree to which the object is desired is referred to as its **incentive value** (or reward value). The incentive approach to motivation suggests that people will perform an act when its performance is likely to result in some outcome they desire. That desire may be based on an internal incentive, such as interest or personal value, or an external incentive, such as a reward. Behavior that is motivated or prompted by the desire to attain or avoid an incentive can be said to be the result of **incentive motivation** (Petri, 1996). It may represent either intrinsic or extrinsic motivation.

Overmier & Lawry (1979) theorized that incentive motivation can be regarded as a process that goes or mediates between the characteristics of a situation containing

incentive value

the degree to which the object is desired

incentive motivation

prompted by the desire to attain or avoid an incentive

An incentive for working hard in school is to be able to graduate. Graduation requires *incentive motivation,* the desire to be able to achieve an important goal.

frequent testing

giving students weekly tests to motivate them to study on a regular basis

inventive value

the reciprocal of the probability of success; the easier or less challenging a task is, the less incentive there is to undertake it

achievement task value

a more recent label for incentive value

a goal object (i.e., the stimulus) and the responses directed toward that object. For example, in anticipation of a situation in which a student is required to perform, that student may spend considerable effort in preparation because of the mediation provided by the desire to achieve success or avoid failure. That desire would be said to provide incentive motivation for the student to expend the effort, particularly for a student who, in the absence of an incentive, is unlikely to expend the effort by, for example, procrastinating.

Tuckman (1996, 1997) reasoned that a test as a stimulus situation would be likely to motivate students to study because of the mediation of the desire to achieve success or avoid failure on that test. If so, **frequent testing could** be expected to improve the performance of students who performed poorly, and students who tended to procrastinate—who indeed may well be the same students. To test this hypothesis, he conducted two studies, both of which compared the performance on major course examinations of equivalent classes, one of which was given short weekly tests, the other of which completed weekly homework assignments outlining chapters. In the first study, he also separated students for analysis purposes into high, middle, and low GPA groups, and in the second study separated them into high, middle, and low procrastination-tendency groups. As predicted, the low GPA group, in the first study, and the high-procrastination group, in the second, demonstrated dramatically better performance in the frequent testing condition than in the homework condition. The other two groups in both studies performed reasonably similarly in both conditions. The results for different procrastination groups are shown in Figure 10.7. (Marybeth, in the earlier story, was really lucky that Ms. Jermaine, her trigonometry instructor, gave a test every Friday, so she couldn't procrastinate more than four days. That meant she only had to learn a week's worth of trig in time for the test!)

Learner's Incentive Values

Atkinson (1964) defined **incentive value** for the success-seeking learner as the reciprocal of the probability of success, meaning that the easier or less challenging a task was for them, the less incentive there would be for them to undertake it. For failure avoiders on the other hand, it would be just the opposite; the easier the task, the greater the incentive value. Wigfield and Eccles (1992, 2000) referred to incentive value as **achievement task value**, and distinguished between the following six aspects:

FIGURE 10.7

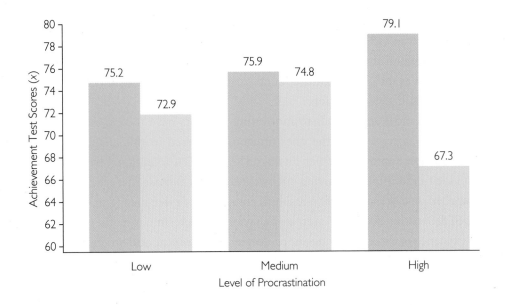

Mean Scores on the Final Exam by High, Medium, and Low Procrastinators in the Frequent Testing (Blue Bars) and Homework Condition (Green Bars) (Tuckman, 2000)

- attainment value ("how important is it for you to get a high grade in this course?")
- task value ("how important is it for you to learn what is taught in this course?")
- ego value ("how important is it for you to do better in this course than other students?")
- intrinsic interest ("how interested are you in the content of this course?")
- utility value ("how much will you be able to use what you learn in this course?")
- perceived cost ("is what it would take to do well in this course worth the effort?")

They found that while students' expectancy for course success was a better predictor of actual achievement than achievement task values, values were a better predictor of what courses students actually chose to take.

The Self-Determination Approach to Motivation

Conrad, a seventh grader, was a funny kind of kid. When it came to science projects or writing stories, he would work endlessly and tirelessly and do wonderful things. His science projects were far and away the best in the class. He would just come up with an idea and go to work on it until he had completed it. Motivation was never a problem. But the other stuff, math worksheets, book essays, preparing for tests, just didn't seem to turn Conrad on. He would do them if he had to, but not with same gusto and brilliance that he showed on the things that really interested him. Although he had the intelligence, he would never be a straight A student because of that.

Virtual Psychology Lab

What is self-determination? It is deciding for yourself how to act in your environment in order to achieve optimal learning and adjustment. To energize behavior, self-determination theory proposes three needs: competence, relatedness, and autonomy. In order to stimulate self-determination, teachers are encouraged to employ autonomy-support approaches to teaching, rather than focusing on control. As shown in the *Self Description Virtual Psychology Lab*, intrinsic motivation stimulates students to engage in behaviors for the pleasure and satisfaction they provide. They perform an activity, not because they have to, but because they want to. Go to CengageBrain.com to access this Virtual Psychology Lab in the Education CourseMate.

Learning Objective 7

Describe self-determination as an approach to motivation, distinguishing between intrinsic and extrinsic motivation.

Deci (1980, p. 26) defines **self-determination** as "the process of utilizing one's will," that is, deciding for yourself how to act in your environment in order to achieve optimal learning and adjustment. Deci & Ryan (1985) and Deci, Vallerand, Pelletier & Ryan (1991) regard conceptual understanding, flexible use of knowledge, feeling good about oneself, acting volitionally, and being attuned to the social environment as the central features of optimal learning and adjustment, and hence the result of self-determination.

Whereas most approaches to motivating students have the concept of intention at their core, such as the ones previously covered in this chapter, the self-determination approach further distinguishes between intentional behaviors that are (1) self-determined or carried out by choice, and (2) those that are controlled or compelled by external forces to result in compliance or defiance (Deci et al., 1991; Orbell & Sheeran, 2000). To energize behavior, self-determination theory proposes the existence of three innate needs: *competence*, *relatedness*, and *autonomy* (or self-determination), which, when satisfied, allow people to maximize their motivation, performance, and development (Ryan & Deci, 2000).

Intrinsic and Extrinsic Motivation

Based on the above premises, this approach places central importance on the distinction between **intrinsic motivation**—engaging in behaviors for the pleasure and satisfaction they provide versus **extrinsic motivation**—engaging in behaviors believed to be instrumental to some consequence. Reading a book, for example, because you are interested in its content, would reflect intrinsic motivation; reading it because it was assigned would reflect extrinsic motivation. Clearly, Conrad, in the above story, does his best work on activities for which he has intrinsic motivation and tends to do minimal work on activities that require extrinsic motivation.

Within extrinsic motivation, a distinction is made between four types that vary along a continuum of degree of internalization or autonomy, that is, going

self-determination

deciding for yourself how to act in your environment in order to achieve optimal learning and adjustment

intrinsic motivation

engaging in behaviors for the pleasure and satisfaction they provide

extrinsic motivation

engaging in behaviors believed to be instrumental to some consequence

Engaging in a behavior for the pleasure and satisfaction it provides represents *intrinsic motivation*. Students often are motivated to perform an activity, not because they have to, but because they want to.

Corbis/Jupiter Images

progressively from external causes to internal causes, and ending at intrinsic motivation (Deci et al.,1991; Ryan & Deci, 2000). This progressive movement from extrinsic to intrinsic motivation is motivated, according to self-determination theory, by the three basic needs. The four regulatory styles on the autonomy or **internalization** continuum are described below.

- *External regulation* is motivation by external forces, for example, the offer of reward or threat of punishment (e.g., coming to class on time because you will be punished by the teacher if you are late). This is the least self-determined.
- *Introjected regulation* is motivation based on external forces that have been internalized enough to cause one to pressure oneself to comply (e.g., you come to class on time so you will not feel like a bad person if you are late).
- *Identified regulation* is motivation based on coming to value the behavior, and which reflects one's identification with and acceptance of the regulatory process (e.g., you come to class on time because you feel it is important to succeeding in the class).
- *Integrated regulation* is motivation based on one's sense of self (e.g., you come to class on time because that is the kind of person you are). This is the most self-determined.

Stimulating Self-Determination

Deci et al. (1991) encourage teachers to employ autonomy-support approaches to teaching rather than focusing on control, based on some evidence that this approach is related to students' positive learning outcomes. Gottfried (1990), for example, reports a positive correlation between students' intrinsic motivation for particular subjects and their achievement on standardized tests of those subjects. To support self-determination, Deci et al. (1991) recommend that teachers do the following:

- minimize the influence of external events—such as rewards, punishments, performance evaluations, and deadlines—intended to control student behavior;
- instead of the above, give students choices, and when they must do an uninteresting or routine task, acknowledge their negative feelings;
- adopt a noncontrolling style of presentation (e.g., use nonpressuring language rather than *should* and *must*) that recognizes rather than undermines students' sense of independence; and
- focus on creating an overall classroom climate that students perceive to be autonomy supportive rather than controlling.

Different Types of Rewards

Regarding rewards, Deci (1975) contends that all rewards have two aspects, a *controlling aspect* and an *informational aspect*, the latter providing recipients with information about their competence and self-determination. If the controlling aspect is dominant, it will be perceived as external; if the informational aspect is dominant, it will engender feelings of competence and self-determination. Rewards that are contingent on a student's accomplishing a task or performing at a certain level (e.g., if you finish all your school work, you can go outside) are aimed at controlling behavior, and cause students to attribute their actions to an outside force—the person offering the reward. According to Deci, Koestner, &

internalization

the progressive movement from extrinsic to intrinsic motivation

Ryan (1999), continued interest will become dependent on the availability of the reward. Rewards that convey information about one's competence by following an actual successful performance (e.g., praise after solving a problem you couldn't solve previously) result in the recipient feeling competent, and placing the cause within him- or herself, allowing for interest to be maintained. (Bandura referred to such rewards as task-contingent and competence-contingent.) In the above set of teacher recommendations, it is rewards emphasizing the controlling aspect that are to be avoided.

Enhancing the Intrinsic Motivation of Students

What about students who demonstrate little intrinsic motivation toward learning? How may a teacher instill intrinsic motivation in them? Lepper & Hodell (1989) suggest four sources: challenge, curiosity, control, and fantasy. We have already encountered *challenge* in this chapter. Bandura suggested that students be encouraged to set goals that were "challenging yet attainable," and Tuckman (2003) listed the first strategy for achievement as "take reasonable risk" which also recommended goals that were challenging yet attainable. Challenges met are overcome more readily when students exhibit **hope**, a concept of *positive psychology* (Snyder, Rand, & Sigmon, 2002). Teachers who help students develop a sense of self-determination when challenged will cause them to feel hopeful, and subsequently make them more likely to do well in school (Snyder, Shorey, Cheavens, Pulvers, Adams, & Wiklund, 2002).

Curiosity, say Lepper & Hodell, is instigated by information that is discrepant, incongruous, or surprising, relative to what one knows. It can be fostered by information one encounters in exploring the environment, an approach advocated by Piaget (Chapter 2). It can also be stimulated by a home environment that is supportive and encourages exploration (Gottfied, Fleming, & Gottfried, 1998; Meece, 2002). *Control* means students having control over their academic outcomes. Giving students choices of activities and a say in classroom decision making engenders feelings of control. Finally, *fantasy* through make-believe, simulations, and games often can change boredom into interest. Teachers are encouraged to blend their own creativity with elements of students' existing interests to create techniques for turning lessons into adventures.

Think It Over

as a LEARNER	What do you see as the desirable features of intrinsic and extrinsic motivation? What do you see as the limitations of each, and in what situations would you be inclined to use each one?
as a TEACHER	How would you go about increasing the intrinsic motivation of your students?

hope
the feeling that what is wanted can be had or that events will turn out well

CONCEPT REVIEW TABLE 10.2

Comparing the Five Approaches for Motivating Students

APPROACH	IMPORTANT CONCEPTS	WHAT THEY MEAN	HOW TEACHERS CAN HELP
Social-Cognitive (Self-Efficacy, Self-Regulation)	• Reciprocal determinism • Self-efficacy • Self-regulation	• Behavior, person and environment operate together • Judgments of one's own competence • Ability to influence one's own behavior	• Tailor instruction to individual needs • Facilitate mastery experiences • Teach students to self-monitor, set goals
Attribution	• Causal attributes • Causal properties • Responsibility • Learned helplessness	• Causes of success and failure (effort, ability, luck) • Locus, stability, and controllability • Attributing outcomes to controllable causes • Losing one's sense of controllability due to persistent failure	• Treat all students the same • Emphasize learning, not achievement • Monitor attributional messages • Don't offer unsolicited help
Needs and Goals	• Hierarchy of needs • Need and strategies for achievement • Goal orientation	• Food, safety, love, esteem, self-actualization • Wanting to achieve and using techniques for success • Mastery (learning) goals versus performance goals	• Start with first need and move up • Teach students strategies for success • Encourage mastery goals
Incentives and Values	• Incentive motivation • Achievement task value	• Goal objects that students want to obtain or avoid • Importance of doing well	• Use frequent testing • Let students select their own tasks
Self-Determination	• Intrinsic motivation • Extrinsic motivation • Internalization	• Performance by choice • Performance compelled • Changing extrinsic motives to intrinsic	• Provide activities that provide and stimulate challenge, curiosity, control, and fantasy

TeachSource video case

Motivating Adolescent Learners: Curriculum Based on Real Life

In this video segment, you'll see how Kelly Franklin, a sixth-grade teacher, motivates her students to learn math by getting them to participate in a real-world project: a student-operated school store. The experience of working in the store teaches them to apply concepts like fractions and decimals, thus increasing their enthusiasm for learning math.

After viewing the video case, consider what you have just watched about motivating students and answer the questions below:

1. What aspects of the student-operated school store were the strongest motivators for the students to learn math concepts?

2. What led the teacher to perceive that participating in the store increased students' sense of responsibility?

3. How could the motivational approaches described in the chapter be used to explain the motivating effects of participating in the school store?

You can view the video case at the Education CourseMate. Go to:
CengageBrain.com

SUMMING IT UP

Learning Objective 1

Key Concepts:

self-efficacy, motivation, self-regulation, attribution approach (p. 389); goal, need, incentive, value, self-determination, intrinsic interest, social cognitive approach (pp. 389-390); reciprocal determinism (pp. 390-391); self-reflection, self-regulatory capability (p. 391).

Describe and apply the social cognitive approach to motivating students.

Bandura proposed **social cognitive theory**, with its three major principles: **reciprocal determinism**, the idea that behavior, personal factors, and environmental events operate together as interactive determinants or causes of each other; **self-regulatory capability**, that is, people have the ability to control their own behavior based on their own internal standards and motivation; **self-reflective capability**, or the ability to think about oneself.

Discuss the concept of self-efficacy and the impact of school and teachers on a student's self-efficacy.

Learning Objective 2

A person's most important self-thought is his judgment of his own competence or capability to perform a task successfully, called **self-efficacy expectations**. This is contrasted with **outcome expectations**, or the estimate that a behavior will lead to a certain outcome. Based on the concept of self-efficacy, people are expected to *choose, persist in,* and *expend effort on* tasks they believe themselves capable of handling and *avoid* situations they believe exceed their coping skills. There are four sources of information on which self-efficacy judgments are based. Enactive **mastery experiences**, or actual performance accomplishments, are the most influential source of information. **Vicarious experience,** or the outcomes for others similar to oneself, can be used to judge whether or not one also can do something. **Verbal persuasion**—ranging from the weaker **suggestion** to the stronger **exhortation**—can also be used to affect self-efficacy. Finally, **physiological state** helps tell people whether they should expect to succeed or fail at an oncoming task. To enhance student self-efficacy, teachers are encouraged to diversify classroom activities, tailor instruction to individual needs, use cooperative approaches, and avoid comparative evaluations.

Key Concepts:

self-efficacy expectations, outcome expectations (pp. 392-393); mastery experience, participant modeling (pp. 393-395); self-instructions (p. 395); vicarious experience, live models, symbolic models, verbal persuasion (pp. 395-396); suggestion, exhortation, feedback, physiological state (pp. 396-397); teacher efficacy (p. 397).

Describe the concept of self-regulation and its relation to self-efficacy; and detail ways that students can become self-regulators.

Learning Objective 3

Self-regulation, or the exercise of influence over one's own behavior, which requires **self-monitoring**, **self-evaluation**, and **self-reaction**, is greatly affected by self-efficacy, or the belief that one can control oneself. Belief in oneself leads to self-control and hence to seeing improvements in one's life. To make these processes contribute to self-regulation by enhancing self-efficacy, **goal setting**, particularly of goals that are specific, challenging, proximal (in the here-and-now), self-determined, and incremental and **commitment** to ensure effort and perseverance are recommended.

Key Concepts:

self-regulation (p. 399); self-monitoring, self-evaluation, self-reaction (p. 402); goal setting, commitment (pp. 402-403).

Explain attribution as a basis for motivation, and identify its key features. Document the teacher's role in using attribution to motivate students.

Learning Objective 4

The *attribution* approach, developed by Weiner, focuses on the five causes or **causal attributes** to which students attribute their successes and failures—*ability, effort, task difficulty, luck,* and *help from others*—that can be used to explain behavior based on information obtained from prior experiences. Judgments of cause are based on *specific informational* cues such as past successes (an indication of ability), the performance of others (an indication of task difficulty), time-on-task (an indication of effort), randomness of outcome (an indication of luck), and amount of help received; they have three properties: **locus of causality**, or whether the cause is *internal* to the

Key Concepts:

causal attribute (p. 404); locus of causality (p. 407); stability, controllability (p. 408); responsibility, intentionality (p. 410); learned helplessness (pp. 412-413).

person (like ability and effort) or *external* (like task difficulty, luck, or help); **stability**, or resistance to change, with ability and task difficulty being relatively *stable* and the others more changeable or *unstable*; and **controllability**, or being within a person's control, with only effort being controllable. The causal properties affect future goal expectations, emotional reactions to outcomes, self-image, and subsequent behavior. One feels **responsibility** when outcomes are based on controllable causes (e.g., effort), producing feelings of guilt and the motivation to do better; whereas, when someone else's behavior is perceived as controllable, he is judged *irresponsible*, yielding anger and punishment. Doing something on purpose reflects **intentionality**. For uncontrollable causes (e.g., ability), the judgments are just the opposite. *Persistent success* yields self-esteem and pride, while *persistent failure* leads to a syndrome called **learned helplessness**. Teachers convey *perceived causes* to their students via performance feedback, nonverbal reactions, and subsequent behavior. They often treat high-achieving and low-achieving students differently, leading the latter to believe they are of low ability and lapse into learned helplessness. They are encouraged to emphasize learning rather than achievement, effort or strategy rather than ability, and realistic goal setting; to monitor the attributional messages they send students, teachers should reduce classroom competitiveness and use encouragement.

Learning Objective 5 **Key Concepts:** Maslow's hierarchy of needs (p. 417); deficiency needs, growth needs (p. 417); self-actualization (p. 418); need for achievement (pp. 418-419); mastery motivation (p. 419); Strategies for Achievement (pp. 419-421); goal orientation, mastery goal, performance goal (pp. 421-422).	*Describe needs and goals as motivators of learner achievement.* Maslow proposes a need theory that offers a **growth** rather than a **deficiency** approach by positing an inherent motivation to grow and develop to a point of *realizing one's potential*. This is manifested in his proposed **hierarchy of needs**, starting with physiological gratification, and advancing through safety, love, and esteem to **self-actualization**. Another need-based approach to motivation is to look at the individual predispositions to succeed and avoid failure—called **need for achievement** and *need to avoid failure* by McClelland. To encourage need for achievement to develop, teachers should teach students the **Strategies for Achievement**: *take reasonable risk, take responsibility for your outcomes, search the environment for information,* and *use feedback*. The **goal orientation** approach proposes two alternatives: **mastery goals**, focused on learning for their own sake, and **performance goals** or specific positive outcomes (e.g., high grades). Performance goals have been divided into *approach* and *avoidance* categories.
Learning Objective 6 **Key Concepts:** incentive value, incentive motivation (pp. 423-424); frequent testing (p. 424); achievement task value (pp. 424-425).	*Illustrate various incentives and values as motivators of learner achievement.* **Incentive value**, or the value of goal objects that individuals desire to obtain or avoid, either because of external consequences or one's internal values, form the basis for **incentive motivation**. *Frequent testing*, for example has been shown to lead students to perform better based on the incentive or **achievement task value** of achieving success or avoiding failure.

Describe self-determination as an approach to motivation, distinguishing between intrinsic and extrinsic motivation.

Self-determination *theory* distinguishes between behaviors students perform by choice (self-determined ones) based on satisfying a need for autonomy and those they are compelled to perform. Chosen behaviors reflect **intrinsic motivation**, while those instrumental to some consequence represent **extrinsic motivation**. Extrinsic motives can be transformed into intrinsic ones through the process of **internalization,** based on teachers giving students choices, teaching in a noncontrolling manner, and, when rewards are used, making them *informational* rather than *controlling*. Activities that present *challenge*, provoke *curiosity*, engender feelings of *control*, and allow students to engage in *fantasy* are recommended as are those that provoke **hope**.

Learning Objective 7

Key Concepts:
self-determination (p. 426);
intrinsic motivation, extrinsic motivation, internalization
(pp. 426-427);
hope (p. 428).

Visit the Education CourseMate for *Educational Psychology* to access study tools and resources including the Virtual Psychology Labs, TeachSource Video Cases, chapter web links, tutorial quizzes, glossary flashcards, and more. Go to CengageBrain.com to register using your access code.

11 | Effective Learning Communities

After reading this chapter, you should be able to meet the following learning objectives:	Chapter Contents
LEARNING OBJECTIVE 1 Describe the importance of creating a learning community in your classroom and detail Kohn's three prerequisites and four strategies for increasing its effectiveness.	Creating a Learning Community • Prerequisites for Community • Effectiveness and the Learning Community
LEARNING OBJECTIVE 2 Discuss procedures involved in maintaining an effective learning community that include: (1) using time effectively, (2) creating an engaging curriculum, (3) discussing the connection between different learning activities and the physical arrangement of the classroom, and (4) detailing general principles in developing coherent classroom rules that involve students in their creation.	Maintaining an Effective Learning Community • Using Time Appropriately • Engaging Curriculum • Designing and Organizing the Physical Space • Creating Classroom Rules
LEARNING OBJECTIVE 3 Articulate how to respond to misbehavior by having concern and respect for students and families, modeling appropriate behaviors, and intervening with nonverbal and I-messages.	Responding to Misbehavior in a Classroom Community • Concern and Perspective Taking • Home Cultures and Family Connections • An Intervention Continuum
LEARNING OBJECTIVE 4 Discuss the importance of preventing bullying and cyberbullying for the well-being of all members of the learning community.	Bullying in School • Teachers' Beliefs about Bullying • The Prevention Process • Cyberbullying
LEARNING OBJECTIVE 5 Outline the five components of culturally responsive classroom management and demonstrate how a classroom could be transformed into this type of environment.	Culturally Responsive Classroom Management • Recognition of Ethnocentrism • Knowledge of Students' Culture • Understanding the Broader Context • Use of Appropriate Management Strategies • Commitment to Caring Classrooms
LEARNING OBJECTIVE 6 Detail the Kounin method for maximizing engagement in the learning environment and describe Assertive Discipline approaches to classroom management. Create examples of discipline plans appropriate for elementary and secondary classrooms.	Other Classroom Management Paradigms • The Kounin Approach • The Assertive Discipline Approach

Caring Classrooms

When Barack Obama, the 44th President of the United States, was asked on national television to name his favorite teacher, he named Mrs. Mabel Hefty, his fifth-grade teacher at Punahou School in Hawaii, because she made "every single child feel special." Below are some thoughts published in the *Honolulu Star Bulletin* about the classroom climate that Mrs. Hefty created, given by some of her former students:

- "She knew how to combine the right amount of enthusiasm, love, high expectations, and discipline to get the most out of each and every student."
- "You knew that she cared about you so much."
- "She expected a lot out of you and she was tough, but she loved you as if you were her own."
- "She brought out your self-confidence."
- "She was the person who really showed me the way."
- "She called it like she saw it."
- "I thrived in her class because I could trust her."
- "She was there for me all the way."
- "You can get into an environment where you start to get afraid of learning because you are afraid of failing. In her culture of education, you never felt that at all."
- "She had us thinking about issues that were broader than you were used to thinking about."
- "She affected her students somehow to make them want to learn."
- "She tried to have an impact on students. If you're a good teacher, and she was, you're going to teach students about life as much as anything."
- "She was probably the first teacher who opened my eyes to the outside world."
- "Her legacy reached far beyond the knowledge imparted in the classroom."

Mrs. Hefty invited family members of her students to participate in the classroom. Mrs. Hefty invited Barack's father to address the class. President Obama, in his autobiography *Dreams From My Father*, wrote that his father talked about "Kenya's struggle to be free." Tani (2009) wrote, "That message of common aspiration uniting people across racial lines was one that would be powerfully evoked by the son three decades later. Years after returning to Kenya, yet before his son could see him again, Barack Obama's father dies in a car crash."

- Have you been in a classroom environment similar to the one that President Obama experienced?
- How could you help the students in your class feel as if you have very high standards for their learning while at the same time exhibiting care and concern for their well-being?

Sources:

- Punahou School Web site http://www.punahou.edu/page.cfm?p=1715
- Article entitled "A teacher's Hefty influence" from July 29, 2007 issue of *Honolulu Star Bulletin*

Lessons We Can Learn from the Story Teachers have incredible ability to influence students. This influence can be encouraging and productive like Mrs. Hefty, or it can be discouraging and negative. By sharing your interest in students and your belief in their potential for success, you have the ability to create a classroom environment that the students would choose to be a part of instead of an environment where they are required to attend.

This chapter focuses on the development of an effective learning environment. What will your future students say about the learning environment you create? Understanding how to involve a diverse range of students and their families into a classroom takes a combination of knowledge and experience. Research shows that emphasizing shared goals and giving students appropriate amounts of autonomy can lead to effective classroom communities (Schaps, 2003). One way to start thinking about what power you might be able to give students and their caregivers is by knowing what elements contribute to a sense of community. We begin this chapter with an examination of the importance of unity in the classroom.

Creating a Learning Community

Learning Objective 1

Describe the importance of creating a learning community in your classroom and detail Kohn's three prerequisites and four strategies for increasing its effectiveness.

How you resolve the questions and issues posed in this chapter will be important because in a very real sense those reflections and resolutions will guide how you set about to create your own classroom. However, our goal is for you to recognize that you have the potential to create something much grander than just a classroom; with careful thought and planning, you have the potential to create a learning community. While a classroom is just a physical space where students and teachers (and occasionally parents/caregivers) meet, a **learning community** is a group of individuals focused on increasing the academic, personal, and social development of the community members. That is to say, a learning community is a place where students feel supported and safe enough to ask difficult questions, make mistakes, and work toward developing the knowledge, skills, and understandings that will help them become productive and thoughtful adults. Research conducted by Thompson, Gregg, and Niska (2004) reported that teachers and principals who organized their classrooms and schools as learning communities witnessed a flourishing of student learning. Phillips (2003) studied the impact of learning communities on urban students' academic achievement and found that, over a five-year period, teachers in the learning community spent increased time developing and modifying innovative curricula that resulted in increased academic achievement of their students.

Prerequisites for Community

According to Kohn (1996), developing a learning community that fosters responsibility and caring in children requires the satisfaction of the three very important prerequisites described below.

1. *Time.* Teachers, students, and caregivers cannot be expected to enter a classroom and immediately become a community. Developing the trust and respect that effective learning communities are built on requires spending time together. (See Box 9.4: Like People, Groups Grow.)

learning community

a group of individuals focused on increasing the academic, personal, and social development of the community members

Learning communities emphasize that students can learn from one another.

Seiya Kawamoto/Lifesize/Getty Images

2. *Small number of members.* As the size of the group increases, the opportunity for the quality and quantity of interactions between members of the community is decreased. In most smoothly functioning organizations, the size of groups is carefully considered.

3. *Committed teacher.* A learning community needs to have a committed teacher who is a part of a learning community within a school whose mission is school improvement. The resulting learning communities open up communication between educators about how best to serve students in their classrooms and school buildings by discovering innovative solutions to the challenges they face within a supportive context.

Effectiveness and the Learning Community

If the prerequisites are met, the teacher has an opportunity to work with students to create an effective learning environment. According to Kohn (1996), there are several strategies that will increase the effectiveness of learning communities. The first is to *strengthen the connection between teacher and students.* Traditionally, the teacher's role has been defined as a stoic leader who is considered weak when he or she displays typical human emotion. This role is, of course, a creation that inhibits authenticity and discourages students from developing relationships with the teacher. The learning environment is improved when students have a teacher who is genuine and caring.

The second strategy to increase the functioning of a learning community is to *strengthen the connection between students* in the class. In an effectively functioning learning community, students learn about and from one another. The learning community values not only what each student brings to the classroom, but what they are able to create collectively.

The third strategy to improve a learning community is to *offer classwide and schoolwide learning opportunities*. In most American classrooms, students tend to engage in learning activities independently. Students each complete their own homework assignments, book reports, take their own tests, and create their own portfolios. However, this emphasis on individual achievement is somewhat different from how most professional organizations function. Most companies and employers have individuals work toward some kind of group goal and capitalize on the various strengths of the individuals who make up the group. A learning community can be improved by offering classroom groups opportunities to work toward a shared goal.

The final strategy to increase the functioning of a learning community is to *emphasize academic instruction*. This strategy is based on the premise that academic issues should be freely discussed by the learning community just as any other issues (e.g., social, behavioral) would be discussed within the community. Relevant to building an effective learning community are the affective elements that students feel when they are in their classroom.

Think It Over

as a Learner	Think about the courses you are currently taking in college. Do you notice any differences in the learning environments of the various courses? What is the nature of those differences, that is, are any of them learning communities?
as a Teacher	How could you create a learning community in your classroom?

Maintaining an Effective Learning Community

The National Education Association released a classroom management brief report in 2006 that described some of the issues involved in maintaining an effective learning community. The report championed the notion that modern classrooms need to be learning centered. **Learning-centered classroom management** involves changing the nature of discipline from control to encouraging student self-regulation and community responsibility. There are numerous decisions a teacher makes that will influence the success of the class, including how they use their classroom time, the quality of their curriculum, designing and organizing the physical space, and creating classroom rules. We will discuss each of these topics in turn.

Using Time Appropriately

One of the most important resources a teacher has at his or her disposal is time. Given that the amount of instructional time is fixed and because students learn at different rates, how the teacher utilizes that time is critical to increasing the achievement of each student. Regarding the management of time, an integral task of the effective teacher is to increase the amount of time students spend pursuing

Learning Objective 2

Discuss procedures involved in maintaining an effective learning community that include: (1) using time effectively, (2) creating an engaging curriculum, (3) discussing the connection between different learning activities and the physical arrangement of the classroom, and (4) detailing general principles in developing coherent classroom rules that involve students in their creation.

learning-centered classroom management

changing the nature of discipline from control to encouraging student self-regulation and community responsibility

productive academic and personal development goals and minimize the amount of time utilized for nonproductive purposes.

Despite the fact that research from the National Education Commission on Time and Learning (1994) was critical of the traditional organization of schools that focused on calendar time instead of learning, a majority of schools still maintain fairly conventional school schedules. As one might predict, in its biennial report, The Council of Chief State School Officers found that American students typically spend 180 days in school each year. The U.S. Department of Education's National Center for Education Statistics (2002) conducted a thorough analysis of the number of days American children spend in school and found that not only are the number of days fairly standard, but the organization of the school day is also customary. According to the National Center for Education Statistics, schools traditionally maintain six school periods and average approximately 5.6 hours of instructional time each day.

One of the most obvious things a teacher must recognize is the actual amount of time he or she is allotted to work with students. **Allocated time** represents the total amount of time students spend in school each year. However, effective teachers need to concentrate more on how the time is used as opposed to how much time they are given. **Engaged time** is the amount of allocated time that the students spend actively pursuing learning goals. Teachers should help students maximize the amount of engaged time by helping them understand goals and allocating and using their time appropriately (National Educational Association, 2006).

Engaging Curriculum

Proper use of the allocated time educators have with children is important in maintaining an effective learning environment, but the simple act of filling up all of the classroom time will not create the type of learning environment that will actually facilitate children's learning. Sometimes teachers, parents, and other caregivers incorrectly assume that as long as students are busy, they are productive. This thinking could lead new teachers toward overdependence on activities that put emphasis on being busy over learning. One of the most important things a teacher can do to maintain the effectiveness of their learning environment is to have an interesting and well-planned curriculum. The most important outcome of such a curriculum is an increase in student learning, however, this type of curriculum will also have an impact in regards to the prevention of inattention and misbehavior. Techniques for creating a well-planned curriculum that will help foster student learning are described in Chapter 12.

Designing and Organizing the Physical Space

The environment of the classroom, referred to as *classroom climate* in Chapter 9, is important to the learning and motivation of the students in your care. This is influenced by a number of factors, one of which is the arrangement of the classroom. The organization of the physical environment is very important and suggests to students the commitment the teacher has toward creating a culturally responsive classroom (Weinstein, Curran, & Tomlinson-Clarke, 2003). Six principles have been proposed to help elementary and secondary education teachers arrange their classrooms (Marzano & Marzano, 2003; Evertson, Emmer, & Worsham, 2002):

allocated time
the total amount of time students spend in school each year

engaged time
the amount of allocated time that the students spend actively pursuing learning goals

Effective teachers think of creative ways to design their classrooms, like allowing students to use stability balls instead of traditional chairs.

DAVE RACZKOWSKI/Grand Rapids Press/Landov

- Arrange the classroom so you can easily see all students. This will help you to be responsive to their needs; for example, facial expressions might help you to determine whether they want help or feedback. This will also help you to assess the pacing of your instruction and activities.
- Organize the physical environment so all students can easily see and participate in presentations and demonstrations. Teachers should be sure their dry erase board or chalkboard, overhead screen, and computer display are easily visible by all students.
- Organize your classroom so community resources are easily accessible. Office supplies like pencil sharpener, paper, pencils, pens, markers, scissors, stapler, and project in- and out-box should be in a reserved area.
- Arrange the seating areas and working surfaces so there are clear and wide pathways that allow easy movement through the classroom. Small aisles create bottlenecks and make student feel cramped and can cause unnecessary bumping and crowding.
- Have the classroom arranged so the students can easily work in small groups. This is important so that instructional time is not lost rearranging the entire classroom during activity or project times.
- Try to create a space that does not cause or emphasize unnecessary distractions. Decorations and resources are integral to the classroom environment although there is a fine line between creativity and clutter. Cluttered and overly full spaces seem confusing and make it difficult for some students to work.

One way to think about the classroom space is to try and match the physical arrangement of the class with the learning activities of the classroom. In Box 11.1 we explore some of the possible arrangements and try to align them with potential learning activities.

AN EXAMPLE TO AID UNDERSTANDING   Box 11.1

When the class is engaging in direct instruction, teacher-lead activites, question-and-answer sessions, or displaying educational video, the physical arrangement might be in a manner similar to the chevron row and column below.

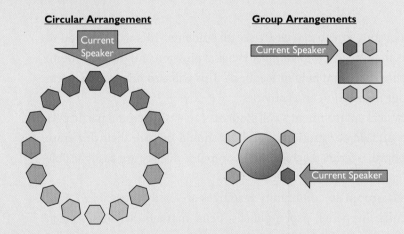

Chevron Arrangement

Front of Classroom

Row & Column Arrangement

Front of Classroom

When the class is engaging in class discussion, cooperative learning activities, or peer question-and answer opportunities, the physical arrangement might be in a circle or small group as illustrated below:

Circular Arrangement

Current Speaker

Group Arrangements

Current Speaker

Current Speaker

• What other ways could you organize the physical space of your classroom?

• What type of impact do you think the organization would have on the interaction and learning of the students?

Creating Classroom Rules

Another important way in which we communicate our expectations for the classroom learning community to students is through the manner by which we create, teach, and maintain classroom rules. Rules are important in educational systems as they allow for the maximization of personal freedoms while counterbalanced by the necessity of not infringing on others rights. In Box 11.2, this chapter's Discourse on Diversity feature, new research on the discipline gap is described when classroom rules are not applied equally to all ethnic groups. The problems with such inequities are discussed, and three potential solutions are presented.

D I S C O U R S E   O N   D I V E R S I T Y

Understanding the Discipline Gap through a Cultural Lens: Implications for the Education of African American Students

BOX 11.2

Monroe (2005) studied how African American students are disciplined in America's public schools. Through her review of the research, she found that African American students are overrepresented in school discipline. This finding typically is referred to as the "discipline gap," and the term essentially means there are racial/ethnicity differences with regard to the frequency of school discipline. The author indicates three appropriate methods to address the disparity:

Method #1: Culturally Responsive Discipline

Culturally-responsive discipline seeks to address behavioral issues and concerns in the classroom instead of sending students to school principals. This might help limit the amount of school suspensions. Culturally-responsive discipline also attempts to help teachers recognize certain student actions that are not intended to be disruptive while at the same time suggesting management strategies that respect students' culture.

Method #2: Teacher Recruitment

One way to minimize the discipline gap is to help match the culture of students with that of the teachers so some similarity exists between the proportion of African American students and African American educators. Increased emphasis should be placed on the recruitment of students of color to participate in teacher education programs.

Community Immersion Experiences

Community immersion involves going out into the areas where students live so that a preservice or inservice teacher can understand some of the students' experiences. These immersions can take various forms, such as visiting homes, speaking with representatives from the community, and spending time in community centers. Monroe (2005) writes, "For educators committed to democratic aims, the exploration of African American students' experiences offers the greatest promise of eradicating disparities, as Blacks are the group most likely to be overrepresented on institutional measures such as suspension and expulsion" (p. 318).

● What are steps you could take in your classroom to minimize the "discipline gap"?

An excellent way for a new teacher to start thinking about classroom rules is to locate a copy of the overall school rules. It is important that coherence exists between the broader school community's expectations and those of the individual classroom (Weinstein, 1996). For example, teachers and students are able to operate under less stress and confusion when they are not worried that certain behaviors are acceptable in one setting in the school, but not in another.

After you familiarize yourself with the procedures of the school community, you can turn your attention to your classroom rules. Expert teachers often look for substantial student input in developing classroom rules. In fact, all students have a

TeachSource Video Case

Cardinal Rules for Classroom Management: Perspectives from an Urban Elementary School

In this video segment, you'll see how Benvinda Timas models her method of creating and communicating classroom rules in an urban elementary school setting. In this video, you will see how she works with her students to create and post classroom rules and how she builds rapport with her class.

After viewing the video case, consider what you have just watched about classroom management and answer the questions below:

1. What teaching strategies demonstrated by Mrs. Timas would help you begin the school year effectively?

2. Mrs. Timas taught the children to use their "inside voice"? Do you think this was a valuable skill to teach? If so, how might you try to teach and model the skill to your class?

You can view the video case at the Education CourseMate. Go to:
CengageBrain.com

CLASSROOM RULES

1. Be Prepared
   ★ Come ready to learn
   ★ Have materials

2. Be Respectful
   ★ Show respect to others and their property
   ★ Respect YOURSELF!

3. Be Safe
   ★ DO NOT verbally or physically abuse or hurt anyone!
   ★ Think before you do !!!

4. Raise Your Hand
   ★ DO NOT speak when others are speaking... Classmates, teacher

5. Do Your Best !!!
   ★ Always try
   ★ Give 100%
   ★ Have pride in all you do

Richard Mittleman/Alamy

One way to create an effective learning community is to prominently display rules that all community members agree to follow.

need for some degree of autonomy, competence, belonging, relatedness, self-esteem, involvement, and enjoyment (Raffini, 1996). By soliciting student input in the formulation of classroom rules, students and teachers are able to critically examine the expectations of the classroom to help make it a predictable and fair learning environment.

Students of all ages need opportunities to participate in creating classroom rules; this helps to create a democratic learning environment (DeVries & Zan, 2003). However, this is not to say that a teacher should not have given the classroom rules considerable thought and consideration before the learners enter the classroom. While expert teachers allow students to participate in the establishment of rules, they also bring ideas of their own about the kinds of classroom rules that help to protect all students and give them the greatest opportunity to learn. Let's take a look at some important general principles for developing classroom rules (Miller, 2004; Rademacher, Callahan, & Pederson-Seelye, 1998).

Rules should be:

● *Rational.* Rules should focus on important matters that are created to help students learn, not simply to control their behavior. Reasons behind classroom rules need to be clear to teachers, students, and their parents.

- *Clearly Articulated and Positively Communicated.* Students do not respond well to situations lacking in structure regarding acceptable and unacceptable behaviors. While it is not possible to eliminate all ambiguity, expert teachers strive to use rules that are clear to all students both in terms of acceptable behavior and the consequences for unacceptable behavior. The expert teacher also communicates these rules in positive ways so that students do not feel overly controlled. Moreover, the teacher models appropriate behavior by following the same classroom rules that the students follow.

- *Be Positively Worded.* It is not useful to create rule lists that are simply "Thou Shall Not's". Instead teachers should work with students to create rules that emphasize what they should do instead of always focusing on what they shouldn't do.

- *Equitable.* It is critical that students have equal protection and treatment under the classroom rules. Students should not be differentially treated or punished under the rules and consequences of the school and classroom. Students will quickly notice and become distressed when there has been an inequitable resolution to a behavioral incident.

- *Few in Number.* This principle relates to the standard that rules should be rational. Essentially, there should only be necessary rules, that is, rules about issues that are essential to creating an environment conducive to students learning and safe interaction. Extra rules often cause misunderstanding, frustration, and confusion and make students feel like they are being micromanaged.

- *Specifically Taught.* Like important academic concepts and skills, learning rules that are important to an effectively functioning classroom should not be left to chance. Classroom rules that ensure everyone's safety and success need to be deliberately taught.

- *Prominently Displayed.* Important information should be displayed in the learning environment. What teachers choose to display in the learning environment is one way they have of communicating what they think is valuable. This is one of the reasons why effective teachers display student work in the classroom. Displaying the rules helps emphasize their value to the community while also providing a concrete reminder of what they are.

- *Consistently Employed.* Students respond with confusion and frustration when rules are inconsistently applied. It causes them to struggle with predicting what behaviors are unacceptable in various situations and upsets the sense of order within the community.

While there is not a cookie cutter set of rules that will work in every classroom, or even in the same classroom from year to year, the general principles described above will help you to create an environment that is equitable, fair, and focused on learning. Table 11.1 provides examples of classroom rules developed for the primary, elementary, and secondary levels. If you look at the sample rules carefully, you will notice a progressive modification of a rule as the developmental level of the child changes.

Lastly, when collaborating with students to create rules for a learning community at the beginning of the school year, it is possible that the group included rules

TABLE 11.1
Examples of Appropriate Classroom Rules (Larrivee, 1999).

PRIMARY SCHOOL (GRADES PREK–2)	1. Help each other. 2. Take turns and share materials. 3. Walk in the classroom. 4. Raise your hand before you talk.
UPPER-ELEMENTARY SCHOOL (GRADES 3–5)	1. Give your best effort. 2. Be kind to classmates. 3. Follow directions and ask for help if they are not clear. 4. One person talks at a time.
SECONDARY SCHOOL (GRADES 6–12)	1. Be punctual. 2. Be prepared by coming to class with needed materials. 3. Show your classmates consideration and courtesy. 4. Return borrowed items.

that were unimportant, need to be changed, or forgot one or more rules that would improve the functioning of the community. For this reason, it is important to discuss with the students a procedure for how the community might modify, add, or delete rules as necessary. Remind students that sometimes rules need to be revisited and revised (Miller, 2004).

Think It Over

as a Learner | Of the factors discussed in the chapter, which do you think is most important in maintaining an effective learning community? Why do you think that?

as a Teacher | How might you arrange your classroom for the first day of school? How might different classroom layouts influence the student's behavior?

Learning Objective 3

Articulate how to respond to misbehavior by having concern and respect for students and families, modeling appropriate behaviors, and intervening with nonverbal and I-messages.

Responding to Misbehavior in a Classroom Community

The previous section asked you to consider strategies you can use to create and maintain an effective learning community. These strategies included planning a curriculum that the students find meaningful, demonstrating to the students how the time that you have with them is valuable, considering how the classroom space is arranged, and creating community rules in a way that keeps the classroom climate

Frank Siteman/PhotoEdit

Effective learning communities frequently meet as a group to discuss issues important to the class.

respectful and productive. In addition to improving the learning of your students, these types of considerations will also help prevent a lot of behavior that interferes with the class. However, it is highly likely that disruptions to the classroom environment will still exist, and how a teacher interprets those disruptions and what actions he or she takes to react to them will influence the class' future success.

Misbehavior is an inappropriate action that hurts another individual or interferes with learning. Misbehavior is not a new phenomenon; it has existed and will continue to exist in environments where students have needs and motivations that are not met. When classroom misbehavior occurs, teachers must make many decisions about it. Do we intervene immediately, ignore the behavior, or intervene at a later time? What should the nature of our intervention be? How we interpret the cause of the misbehavior might influence how we answer these questions. If a teacher personalizes student misbehavior, they could inadvertently escalate a problem. We also must remember that a teacher's beliefs, background, misconceptions, and stereotypes can impact what he or she views as misbehavior. There is a classic riddle that presents the following scenario:

"A father and son go on an afternoon drive and are involved in an automobile accident. The father is killed immediately; the son is rushed to the hospital for

misbehavior

an inappropriate action that hurts another individual or interferes with learning

emergency surgery. The doctor walks into the room, looks down at the boy, and says 'I can't operate on this boy. He's my son.' Who is the doctor?"

If you are having trouble answering this riddle, it might be related to your pre-conceptions about the gender of doctors. The answer to the riddle is that the doctor is the boy's mother. Because our prior beliefs and attitudes can unconsciously affect our interpretations of student behavior, teachers must think critically about what behaviors in their classroom reflect misbehavior and develop fair and culturally sensitive strategies to help students participate in a more prosocial way.

Bond (2007) has found that misbehavior typically occurs when students are not motivated by the lesson or if the teacher does not teach and demonstrate appropriate behavior in a learning activity. Tileston (2004) details many possible reasons for student misbehavior, such as students needing more attention, more autonomy/power, or are feeling inadequate in the classroom. Would you react differently to a student's misbehavior if you knew that they desired more attention from you or their peers instead of if you thought they were trying to be rude to you and/or the class? If a student disrupted a class activity because they were bored, how might you react? One possible reaction is to think of a way to redirect the student toward an activity or experience that he or she would be motivated to participate in. **Redirection** is helping a student move their attention from problematic behavior to an on-task behavior (Rothstein-Fisch & Trumbull, 2008). While there is not a script a teacher can follow that will redirect or eliminate misbehavior in all situations, certain beliefs and actions can help you think about classroom management in a way that minimizes your need to try and maintain the learning community with coercion and control (Belvel & Jordan, 2003).

Concern and Perspective Taking

Your relationship with the student could impact the frequency of misbehavior and how they respond to intervention. In a comprehensive analysis of over 100 studies, it was found that teachers who had good relationships with students had about a third less misbehavior (Marzano, Marzano, & Pickering, 2003). Brown (2004) indicates that one of the most important factors in determining how successful a teacher will be with helping students from urban environments is the degree to which they are able to show the students that he or she cares about them. Mendes (2003) indicates that when he worked to establish a relationship with a student based on mutual respect and concern, he always saw improvements in his and the student's achievement and behavior. Students who you have a good rapport with are more likely to participate fully in the community and less likely to interfere with the learning of the class.

One innovative strategy to help demonstrate that each student has value is a morning meeting (Kriete, 2003). This methodology involves a half an hour commitment at the beginning of the school day for students in the K–8th grade environment to welcome one another, share things going on in their lives, and practice socializing. To be effective with students we need to know more about their lives, deepen our trust in them, allow them more choices and control in their learning and behavior, and find ways to honor their diverse strengths (Hoffman & Levak,

redirection

moving a student toward an activity or experience that he or she would be motivated to participate in

2003). Teachers working at the secondary level can build rapport and a sense of community in their classrooms by making meaningful use of the cooperative learning methods discussed in Chapter 9. Building these types of relationships can occur by knowing about students' interests and finding ways to involve those interests in the classroom, being sensitive to your students' wants, and listening to what your students share with you (Mendes, 2003).

A teacher also must consider what he or she knows about a student before administering an intervention. Students respond differently to various types of intervention. **Perspective taking** is the process of considering another person's feelings and imagining another's point of view. Try to put yourself in the student's situation and consider how you would react to the intervention you are administering to address the misbehavior. Where possible, make an effort to intervene in ways that you would respond appropriately and positively to.

Home Cultures and Family Connections

A way of helping a student learn to respect others is by modeling and consistently demonstrating it. Students watch their teachers and pay careful attention to the way they interact with other adults and other students. Are we setting a positive example for our students? Instead of simply applying punishment for misbehavior, we need to use misbehavior as an opportunity to teach students how to make good decisions regarding how they treat others and how they can effectively participate in the classroom (Curwin & Mendler, 1997). Often, students who interfere with the learning community do not know why a teacher expects a particular behavior in a situation (Appelbaum, 2002). Thus, it is as important for us to teach why certain behaviors are important as it is to share with students what behaviors members of the community should exhibit.

It is difficult for students to be respectful of a teacher when he or she says or does things that marginalize students or when the teacher lets one member of the community marginalize another without intervening. One way to fully include students in the classroom is to have regard for and value the culture that your students come from (Delpit, 2006). Valuing students' cultural and familial background will minimize classroom misbehavior, but more importantly, it will increase student learning. When teachers incorporate intellectual contributions from various cultures into the curriculum they teach, they help students be involved who might otherwise be on the periphery of the standard curriculum. For all students to achieve, schools need to have organized and long-term partnerships with families (Epstein & Salinas, 2004). It is also important for a teacher to stay current with trends in their field and be able to adjust their practice based on the needs of their learners. An example of how teachers keep current in best practices in education is described in Box 11.3.

An Intervention Continuum

Deciding on the timing and nature of intervention is an important teacher skill. Each student, classroom, and situation is unique and trying a one-size-fits-all approach to delivering interventions will result in frustration. It is not only important when

perspective taking
the process of considering another person's feelings and imagining another's point of view

BOX 11.3

Did You Know?

Professional Development and Classroom Management

Teachers periodically receive training in order to improve their knowledge and skills in targeted areas. This process is referred to as *professional development*. Classroom management is the most commonly requested area for professional development by teachers. One very popular and innovative classroom management professional development program is called Classroom Organization and Management Program (COMP) developed by Dr. Carolyn M. Evertson of Peabody College at Vanderbilt University.

COMP is a researched-based classroom management system based on four principles: (1) the program focuses on preventing problems, (2) class-

room management and instructional design and methods are connected, (3) students should be active in the classroom environment and, (4) teachers need to communicate with one another in order to improve their practice (Evertson & Harris, 1999). The U.S. Department of Education has validated the COMP program and certified that students of COMP-trained teachers had better achievement and less disruptive behavior. If you would like to find out more about COMP training, information is available at: http://www.comp.org/.

● Why would a teacher need or want professional development training?

and what your intervention is, but how it is delivered. What a teacher does and says has great power in the classroom and can easily hurt students' feelings, therefore it is important that interventions are administered without anger and sarcasm (Pedota, 2007).

It is recommended that minor misbehavior be addressed initially through nonverbal means such as making eye contact or moving closer to the student who is off task (Evertson & Harris, 1992). It is important to consider using nonverbal interventions first in responding to minor misbehavior because it will probably disrupt the learning environment less than other approaches and will help the student avoid any potential embarrassment. If the teacher determines verbal intervention is appropriate, Weinstein and Mignano (2007) recommend using nondirective verbal interventions and *I-messages*. Nondirective verbal approaches permit the teacher to help the student refocus without calling direct attention to their off-task behavior (Weinstein and Mignano, 2007). For example, you could ask a student who is off task to help you with something, answer a question, or help a peer. When misbehavior occurs, another approach is stating in a straightforward manner the rule and the consequence for not following it (Curwin & Mendler, 1988).

Another verbal strategy is called an I-message. **I-messages** are teacher statements that describe a misbehavior in a nonaccusatory fashion and suggest how the

I-messages

teacher statements that describe a misbehavior in a nonaccusatory fashion and suggest how the misbehavior impacts the learning environment

misbehavior impacts the learning environment. For example, if a student laughs at another student's mistake, the teacher might intervene by saying something like, "if you laugh at me when I make a mistake writing on the dry erase board, then I feel bad" (Weinstein and Mignano, 2007). This type of response is very different than a U-message, like saying, "you are being rude to your classmate." Weinstein and Mignano (2007) argue that I-messages are more effective than U-messages because they do not tend to make a misbehaving student respond stubbornly; in fact, instead of changing their misbehavior because they are told to, they have the autonomy to choose to change their behavior. Refer back to Box 9.3 for some further examples.

Whatever manner in which you respond to misbehavior, the important concept to remember is to make every attempt to preserve the dignity of the student and try to show him or her how they could act more appropriately and why those actions might be desirable. When administering interventions and consequences, be consistent with how you respond and avoid hostility (Curwin & Mendler, 1988). Also be sure to address students when they are behaving appropriately, not just when they are misbehaving. A general rule of thumb in elementary classrooms is to positively recognize a student every 15–20 minutes; and in a secondary classroom, about 2–3 times per class period (Curwin & Mendler, 1988).

CONCEPT REVIEW TABLE 11.2
Strategies to Address Misbehavior

Redirect a student's attention from problematic behavior to an on-task behavior (Rothstein-Fisch & Trumbull, 2008).

Have concern and respect for students (Brown, 2004).

Have concern and respect for students' families and culture (Delpit, 2006; Epstein & Salinas, 2004).

Teach and model appropriate behaviors (Curwin & Mendler, 1997).

Deliver interventions without anger and sarcasm (Pedota, 2007).

Try a nonverbal approach such as making eye contact or moving closer to the student who is off task (Evertson & Harris, 1992).

Use nondirective verbal interventions and I-messages to refocus students and minimize student embarrassment (Weinstein & Mignano, 2007).

Give attention to appropriate behavior more often than misbehavior (Curwin & Mendler, 1988).

Learning Objective 4

Discuss the importance of preventing bullying and cyberbullying for the well-being of all members of the learning community.

Bullying in School

When Michael Phelps was growing up in Baltimore, Maryland, he sometimes had difficulty in school. As a child, he was sometimes bullied over the way he looked and his difficulty with learning. Eventually, Michael Phelps grew into the ears that once appeared overly large, and he went from long-limbed and gangly to arguably the most successful Olympian in history. The pinnacle of his achievements came at the 2008 Summer Olympics in Beijing, China, where he held the attention of the world with the unprecedented winning of eight gold medals. Despite being one of the world's most successful and recognizable athletes, he and his mother, Deborah Phelps, still talk about the distress of being bullied.

Bullying is the repeated hurting of another person by either physical or emotional means. Bullying takes many forms; it can be repeated pushing or hitting, or the use of constant cruel words, or it could be more subtle, like starting rumors about another student or trying to isolate a classmate by excluding him or her from a party, lunch table, or study group. While both boys and girls participate in bullying, boys tend to engage in more physical bullying whereas girls tend to use indirect methods like leaving a certain child out of an activity (Bullock, 2002). Bullies often are similarly aged and in the same class as the person(s) they are bullying (Beaty & Alexeyev, 2008). Research indicates that about one in 10 students is the victim of bullying (Perry, Kusel, & Perry, 1988). However, even if a student is not a victim of bullying, he or she might still be impacted by perpetrating or witnessing bullying.

Teachers' Beliefs about Bullying

Some well-meaning teachers hold beliefs about bullies that might make it harder to end bullying in their classrooms. Hence, a first step for teachers to prevent and minimize bullying might start with reflecting over their beliefs about bullying.

bullying

repeated hurting of another person by either physical or emotional means

It may surprise you to know that Olympian Michael Phelps was bullied in school. What are strategies that teachers can use to eliminate bullying?

AP Photo/David J. Phillip

Teachers often believe that bullies and other aggressive students suffer from low self-esteem and thus think they need to try to increase the bully's view of his or her own value and worth. Research, however, indicates that aggressive individuals tend to have an incredibly high self-esteem and sense of entitlement to begin with (Baumeister, 2001). Therefore, instead of helping bullies feel better about themselves, teachers need to help bullies develop empathy for others in order to reduce their bullying behavior.

Teachers and counselors also need to help bullies learn more socially acceptable ways to interact with others (McAdams & Schmidt, 2007). In fact, teasing has become such an entrenched part of popular culture in the United States that hit movies, such as 2004's *Mean Girls*, focuses on this type of callous behavior among students. While teachers certainly do not like bullying, research shows that teachers might view repeated teasing and aggression as a typical part of childhood and therefore not immediately get involved (Bullock, 2002).

The Prevention Process

Preventative steps can be effective in minimizing and eliminating bullying in the classroom environment. Beyond modifying one's own beliefs about bullying, another important step is to create a clear policy against bullying. Cooper and Snell (2003) indicate that the school should formally state a commitment to be safe and secure, give clear examples of bullying behavior, and have clear steps for dealing with bullying behavior. In addition, there should be (1) scheduled classroom meetings to discuss the prevention of bullying, (2) private meetings with students who bully and students who are bullied, (3) meetings with the parents of students who are either bullies or bullied, and (4) a prevention plan that the bully, his or her parents, and the teacher create (Olweus, 2003).

A teacher might ask his or her students to anonymously write down what scares them in class or makes them feel unsafe, and then use that information to begin class meetings (Bullock, 2002). Another strategy involves working directly with students who are being bullied to help them generate specific statements they can say to the bully in order to stop the bullying behavior (Piotrowski & Hoot, 2008). For example, McKinley (2004) recommends that when a bully says something hurtful to a victim, they could counter with a self-assured statement like "leave me alone" or a more dispassionate statement like "Thanks for telling me that." A teacher might also ask victims to role play with him or her, their parent/caregiver, and a school counselor about how to react when another student tries to bully them (Beaty & Alexeyev, 2008).

It is a teacher's responsibility to ensure that the classroom environment is safe and focused on learning. Bullying detracts from that kind of prosocial environment, and if bullying is present among members of the class, then the teacher and the class need to take steps to eliminate the problem. Students in a class should have confidence that they can report bullying to their teacher, and that the teacher will respond by taking steps to eliminate the bullying. Based on the studies cited above, it is recommended that you, as a teacher: (1) provide your class with a clear definition and specific examples of what bullying is, (2) survey your class in an anonymous way to learn about the climate of the class and any problems of which you might be unaware, (3) intervene by holding meetings with students who are involved with bullying and their families, (4) privately practice with a student specific things he or she could say when another student initiates bullying, and (5) role play with a student about effective ways to address bullying.

Cyberbullying

Technology has become an integral part of students' lives. Just over a decade ago, the Internet opened incredible opportunities to today's students that were unthinkable to previous generations of students. Students used these opportunities to significantly expand their social interactions through email, social networking sites, online gaming communities, and blogs. Mobile devices now seem to be the next wave in technology, with cell phones permitting even more immediate access to students through text, photo, and video messaging and with smart phones providing wireless Internet access and software similar to what can be found on home computers and laptops. While this mobile technology has incredible potential to support learning and redefine what literacy is in the coming century, it also opens students up to the possibility of a new form of psychological distress referred to as cyberbullying.

Cyberbullying is using technology like text messaging or social networking Web sites to make statements or post images that hurt, threaten, or demean another student. Students who are cyberbullied often are the very same students who are bullied at school in the more traditional sense (Feinberg & Robey, 2008). Cyberbullying has the potential to be just as hurtful and distressing as traditional bullying, and might be even more damaging because more individuals might be exposed to the statements and/or images, and the bully might be somewhat harder to identify. Like old-fashioned bullying, cyberbullying is also very common. A cross-cultural analysis of students revealed that one in four Canadian students and one in three Chinese students indicated that they had been cyberbullied (Li, 2008).

One example of the dire potential of cyberbullying is the 2006 Lori Drew case, which received headlines through most major news outlets. Lori Drew, her daughter Sarah, and one of Lori Drew's employees used a social networking site to cyberbully Megan Meier, a student at Sarah's school in Missouri. This cyberbullying led to the suicide of Megan Meier on October 17, 2006. This case underscores how cyberbullying a child can have a tragic ending. It also demonstrates how parents/caregivers and educators need to be especially vigilant with cyberbullying, because cyberbullies may in fact be adults, as was the case with Lori Drew.

It is important for educators to take a proactive stance toward cyberbullying, because a high percentage of student victims do not inform an adult about the cyberbullying (Juvonen & Gross, 2008). Beale and Hall (2007) recommend numerous strategies to address cyberbullying, the most important of which are to make sure that as a teacher you incorporate lessons on bullying and cyberbullying into your curriculum, provide parents/caregivers with information about bullying and cyberbullying and encourage them to have discussions with their students about the negative consequences that can result from cyberbullying, and advocate that the school create associations with law enforcement personnel who would come to the school to discuss the issue and its consequences.

cyberbullying

using technology like text messaging or social networking Web sites to make statements or post images that hurt, threaten, or demean another student

Think It Over

as a Learner	What memories do you have of bullying from your own school experiences?
as a Teacher	How might a teacher create a classroom environment that is incongruent with bullying?

Culturally Responsive Classroom Management

Learning Objective 5

Outline the five components of culturally responsive classroom management and demonstrate how a classroom could be transformed into this type of environment.

Beliefs about which behaviors are appropriate or not in a school environment are culturally related. When a difference exists between the students and teacher with regard to culture, a potential for conflict exists in the classroom (Weinstein, Tomlinson-Clarke, & Curran, 2004). Recently, an emphasis has been placed on how the curriculum and pedagogy is influenced through culture (Gay, 2000), however teachers need to consider that numerous factors beyond curriculum influence student achievement (Weinstein, Tomlinson-Clarke, & Curran, 2004). For example, Wang, Haertel, and Walberg (1993/1994) indicated that classroom management has a powerful influence on student achievement.

Culturally responsive classroom management (CRCM) is an approach to classroom management that fosters a supportive classroom environment that values the culture of the students and teacher and uses those cultures in the selection of management strategies. As Weinstein, Tomlinson-Clarke, and Curran (2004) wrote, "We need to ask whether diversity requires different approaches to classroom management, to examine the kinds of cultural conflicts that are likely to arise in ethnically diverse classrooms, and to consider the best ways to help preservice teachers become multi-culturally competent" (p. 27). To address these questions, Weinstein, Tomlinson-Clarke, and Curran (2004) discuss five components critical to teachers using CRCM methods in their classrooms: recognition of one's own ethnocentrism; knowledge of students' cultural backgrounds; understanding the broader social, economic, and political context; ability and willingness to use culturally appropriate management strategies; and commitment to building caring classrooms. We will discuss each of these components in turn.

Recognition of Ethnocentrism

To be a teacher who possesses multicultural competence, one must first recognize oneself as having a culture. **Ethnocentrism** is the recognition and valuing of one's culture. Data show that teacher education programs are overwhelmingly Caucasian, with 86 percent of the preservice teachers Caucasian, 7 percent African American, and 3 percent Latino (Ladson-Billings, 2001). However, when asked about their culture, teacher education students often consider themselves normal and neutral (Weinstein, Tomlinson-Clarke, & Curran, 2004), as if they do not possess a culture.

culturally responsive classroom management

an approach to classroom management that fosters a supportive classroom environment that values the culture of the students and teacher and uses those cultures in the selection of management strategies

ethnocentrism

the recognition and valuing of one's culture

Collectivist cultures tend to value group harmony.

Christian Kober/Robert Harding World Imagery/Getty Images

individualistic cultures

cultures that focus on the self and value personal goals, independence, and achievement

collectivist cultures

cultures that give priority to the wants of the group over the self and tend to value group harmony

Tomlinson-Clarke and Ota Wang (1999) suggest three activities to help students interested in working in the field of education to recognize their ethnocentrism. One of the activities involves asking students to read texts that focus on personal belief systems and values, a second activity involves having the students examine how being part of a particular group moderates how we interact with other individuals and groups, and the final activity involves practicing dealing with culturally responsive classroom management through role play and student teaching activities. Self-awareness of ethnocentrism is also important because we often look at other individuals and cultures through the perspective and value systems of our own culture.

Knowledge of Students' Culture

Once teachers begin to think of themselves as cultural beings, a door is opened to think about their students as possessing a culture that influences their thoughts, beliefs, and values. Just as mathematics content knowledge is required to competently teach mathematics, cultural content knowledge is useful to effectively teach students. However, Villegas and Lucas (2007) argue that given the large number of cultures and ethnicities attending public schools, and the small amount of time they have to train preservice teachers, teacher education programs cannot teach the students all of the cultural content knowledge they will need to be successful in the schools. Therefore, decisions have to be made about what should be taught in the teacher training programs.

Weinstein, Tomlinson-Clarke, and Curran (2004) mention the importance of recognizing that some cultures tend to be oriented toward the individual, whereas others tend to focus more on the group. **Individualistic cultures** focus on the self and value personal goals, independence, and achievement. **Collectivist cultures** give priority to the wants of the group over the self and tend to value group harmony. While teacher education students need to understand and respect differences within and between cultures, it is also critical to see the similarities. Weinstein, Tomlinson-Clarke, and Curran (2004) write, "core cultural characteristics are not exhibited by all group members and certainly not in the same way or to the same extent. The display of cultural characteristics is influenced by variables such as gender, education, social class, and degrees of cultural affiliation" (p. 30). The key idea regarding knowledge about students' culture is being aware of norms and values without stereotyping the students.

Understanding the Broader Context

When a student's culture differs from the dominant culture of the society, there is potential that the student's attitudes, beliefs, and behaviors will also be different from the norms for the larger society. Teachers need to recognize that the organization and practices of public schools have been heavily influenced by the dominant culture of the larger society, placing students from outside that dominant culture in settings that could disenable them. Weinstein, Tomlinson-Clarke, and Curran (2004) write, "we need to reexamine the ways that current practices and policies may reinforce institutional discrimination. If we look at which children are being disciplined most often (namely, African American boys), we can determine if there are patterns of racial or gender profiling" (p. 31).

Use of Culturally Appropriate Management Strategies

It is important to thoughtfully consider how you intend to set up your classroom environment and how you will address classroom management procedures and practices. One of the major points of CRCM is that when you are planning and making classroom management decisions, you consider insights about your own culture and the culture of your students when you reflect about types of questions you might ask yourself, and ultimately the classroom decisions you make. Example questions you might ask and discuss with mentors are: How will you respond to misbehavior? Will you use nonverbal approaches such as proximity or eye contact? Or might you try verbal approaches such as voice volume? In what situations might you use both or neither approach? What type of consequences will you administer and how will those consequences be enforced? One thought-provoking strategy suggested by Weinstein, Tomlinson-Clarke, and Curran (2004) was asking students to "articulate their own cultural assumptions and values and to compare them with the assumptions and values of the school and the dominant culture" (p. 33).

Commitment to Caring Classrooms

Classroom environments effectively incorporate CRCM principles when both the teacher and the students value one another and are willing to cooperate with one another. Weinstein, Tomlinson-Clarke, and Curran (2004) write that students are in a position to, "resist or cooperate, ignore or acquiesce—and the key factor determining which option they choose is often their perception of the teacher's caring" (p. 33). Consider your own educational experiences; who were the teachers you remember as most effective? What factor(s) make you think they were effective? We are willing to bet that very high up on the list was the teacher's ability to demonstrate concern and care for you. However, success with your students will probably involve caring in a way different than you might expect. Research indicates that the type of caring most effective with CRCM is, "strong yet compassionate, authoritative yet loving, firm yet respectful. In contrast, White teachers tend to be less comfortable with the image of teacher-as-authority figure" (Weinstein, Tomlinson-Clarke, & Curran, 2004, p. 34).

Other Classroom Management Paradigms

The maintenance of a learning-centered classroom requires that the teacher give serious consideration to how he or she fundamentally thinks about classroom management. We provide a summary of three different paradigms that may inform your thinking about classroom management. We will discuss the Kounin approach, the behavior modification approach, and the assertive discipline approach.

The Kounin Approach

Kounin (1970) studied the different practices of teachers who were able to increase the engagement of learners versus those who struggled to gain and maintain student attention and subsequently were less able to increase student achievement in their classrooms. Kounin was an early proponent of the notion that effective learning environments are planned for in advance and that being proactive is more important than being reactive. One of the key understandings that should be gleaned from Kounin's work is the notion that how teachers behave and design their learning environments influence how children act. Kounin developed four behaviors to help teachers be effective practitioners: (1) withitness, (2) overlapping, (3) maintaining smoothness and momentum, and (4) maintaining group focus. Kounin's four techniques are summarized in Box 11.4.

BOX 11.4

TAKE IT TO THE CLASSROOM

Techniques from Effective Classroom Managers

To be effective classroom managers, teachers need to master the proven techniques of withitness, overlapping, group focus, and movement management (Kounin, 1970; Emmer & Evertson, 1981). Let's look at how you might take these concepts and implement them in the classroom.

Withitness Strategies

1. Be aware of what is happening in the classroom.

2. Don't become preoccupied with a few students to the exclusion of all of the students you are responsible for.

3. When there is a disruption that requires intervention, don't make a target error by blaming the wrong student or a timing error by waiting too long before doing something.

4. Don't waste your time on minor actions while ignoring or being unaware of major ones. When there is an issue that needs intervention, try to do so clearly and assertively, but in a friendly, nonhostile way.

Overlapping Stategies

1. Keep track of and supervise more than one activity at the same time.

2. Deal with individual and small-group work simultaneously. For example, if a student requires one-on-one assistance, make sure the other groups have been assigned their learning activities so that you can give the individual student attention.

Group Focus Strategies

1. Keep as many students as you can (all, if possible) involved in class activities at the same time. Don't concentrate on or involve just a few students while the rest are left to their own devices.

2. Set a series of activities in motion at the same time so that everyone has something productive to think about and work on.

3. Don't have some students work and others watch.

Movement Management Strategies

1. Create a sense of movement and pace or tempo in the classroom by creating smooth transitions from activity to activity.

2. Don't take too much time to start a new activity.

3. Don't start a new activity in the middle of something else or when you don't have the attention of all the students.

4. Bad timing tends to create confusion about the learning objectives of your classroom activities.

• Can you remember a situation where you did the majority of the work in a group project? Which of the four techniques described would have more equally divided the opportunity for learning?

Withitness

Withitness refers to the teacher being keenly aware at all times of what is occurring in the classroom. Withitness as a teacher skill often is characterized as knowing where misbehavior is occurring in the classroom and knowing who is at fault for the misbehavior (commonly referred to as "having eyes in the back of your head"). However, this is a far too narrow interpretation of withitness. Teacher withitness is probably best utilized when it is used to help increase student learning; in addition, it can be a means to respond to student misbehavior. An example of using withitness to improve the achievement of a learner is when a teacher recognizes that even though she or he is currently answering a student's question, other students in other areas of the classroom might be finished with their activity and need an enrichment experience. Accordingly, the teacher answers the first student's question, redirects other students toward a new challenge, and then returns to scanning the learning environment. To effectively demonstrate withitness, teachers should:

● circulate around the room;
● try to be in areas of the room that permit viewing and/or hearing all of the members of the class; and
● routinely interact with students during independent work time and cooperative learning time.

withitness

refers to the teacher being keenly aware at all times of what is occurring in the classroom

overlapping

an important teaching practice in which the teacher monitors and even supervises two or more activities at one time

Overlapping

Overlapping is an important teaching practice in which the teacher monitors and even supervises two or more activities at one time. For example, if one student is asking the teacher a question at the same time that another student is trying to hand in her work, the teacher would demonstrate overlapping behavior by collecting the paper with a quick smile without losing focus on the other student's question.

There are two occasions when overlapping skill is particularly relevant. First, during group learning the teacher will have to effectively overlap and help meet the needs of several groups of individuals. Second, during whole group instruction, when the teacher is presenting or demonstrating for the entire class, she may need to use overlapping to respond to misbehavior without losing the focus of the activity and the attention of the students.

Maintaining Smoothness and Momentum

Teaching as a profession in many ways resembles a middle-level management position in the business world. One of the most overlooked aspects of the teaching position is that the teacher is a leader who is typically responsible for 20–30 individuals, depending on the grade level and setting. As a leader, a teacher is responsible for coordinating the movement of those individuals and to help them to start, continue, and stop various activities.

Kounin described two general ways in which students are expected to make transitions between activities. One type of transition is a **physical** one in which a student moves from one part of the classroom to another or moves from one area of the school to another area. This might occur when an elementary school teacher transitions students from the classroom to the lunchroom. The second type of transition is a **psychological** one. Psychological transitions involve changes in the content area about which students are learning. For example, a teacher might direct the students to transition from a poetry lesson to an individual journal writing activity. Thus, the psychological transition is a modification of what the students are thinking about, and the physical transition is a change of the student's location. Regardless of transition type, physical or psychological, we learn from Kounin's research that the teacher must conduct changes with smoothness and momentum.

As a teaching practice, **smoothness** means that the teacher transitions students between activities or locations without sudden and jarring breaks and manages those transitions in a harmonious manner. Kounin indicated that the opposite of transition smoothness was something he referred to as "jerkiness," a teaching behavior that causes sudden and unpredictable stops and starts to activities. There are several behaviors that teachers should avoid because they interfere with a lesson's smoothness: stimulus-boundedness, thrusts, dangles, and truncations.

Stimulus-boundedness means that a teacher has trouble maintaining the focus of an activity. A stimulus-bound teacher responds to every event or stimulus presented to the point where a new stimulus takes over whatever they were currently working on. These teachers are like boats without paddles, shifted in any direction the current takes them. In essence, these teachers can be characterized as directed instead of directing the classroom learning environment. A stimulus-bound teacher might be discussing the parts of an atom when he overhears a student talking about a play coming to town the upcoming week. Responding to the stimulus, he alters his discussion from the proton, neutron, and electron to what he remembered about the plot of the play. A key idea to recognize about stimulus-boundedness is that time is taken away from important learning goals in order to pay attention to a stimulus irrelevant to the current focus of instruction.

physical transitions

students moving from one part of the classroom to another or from one area of the school to another

psychological transitions

transitions that involve changes in the content area about which students are learning

smoothness

the teacher transitions students between activities or locations without sudden and jarring breaks and manages those transitions in a harmonious manner

stimulus-boundedness

the teacher responds to every event or stimulus, causing a new stimulus to take over whatever the teacher was working on

A **thrust** is a "sudden bursting in" on a child's activity with a question, direction, request, or statement without preparing the child for the interruption. Perhaps you have worked with someone who will walk into someone else's office without knocking, regardless of the fact that he was on the phone or meeting with another. This behavior is characterized as a thrust. A classroom example would be a student working on several arithmetic problems on a worksheet, and the teacher walking by and interjecting that the student had done one of the problems incorrectly without the student having an opportunity to go back and review the problems first.

A **dangle** is when a teacher is involved in one activity, stops it for a brief time to work on another activity, and then returns to the initial activity. An example of a dangle would be a history teacher discussing some content on the classroom board, breaking off in the middle to check whether a DVD she wanted to show in another class was in the DVD player, and then coming back to the original lesson. A **truncation** is very similar to a dangle, except the teacher never returns to the original activity after breaking off abruptly to deal with something else. For example, a teacher may be answering a student's question, and halfway through the response get involved with looking at another student's paper and then never return to finish the answer.

Momentum refers to the teaching practice of maintaining an appropriate pace during learning activities. When teachers fail to maintain momentum during learning activities, they often fail to maintain students' attention. Kounin indicated that a preventable but common type of slowdown in learning activities is called overdwelling.

Overdwelling is a negative teacher practice in which the teacher focuses on an action or issue for a period of time beyond what is necessary. Overdwelling is commonly referred to as "beating a dead horse" and can be seen when the teacher perseverates beyond the point of productivity, resulting in student inattention. One common way a teacher overdwells is by giving directions for activities at a level of detail beyond what is necessary for the vast majority of students.

Overdwelling also occurs when teachers spend too much time dealing with the materials of an activity as opposed to the actual activity. For example, a teacher who wants to show some Web sites to illustrate the points of his lesson, but discovers that the school's Internet connection is temporarily down, spends the remainder of the class time trying to log back onto the Internet rather than continuing the lesson without it. Teachers can also overdwell by nagging student(s) about previous behavior. All of these examples illustrate that overdwelling slows down the pace of the classroom and thus minimizes students' attention.

Maintaining Group Focus

The professional teacher is responsible for the learning of approximately 20–30 children at a time. Therefore, the teacher's skill in maintaining the learning focus of a large group of individuals is important. Kounin's work suggests two key ways that teachers can increase the group focus of a learning environment: group alerting and accountability.

thrust

a "sudden bursting in" on a child's activity with a question, direction, request, or statement without preparing the child for the interruption

dangle

when a teacher is involved in one activity, stops it for a brief time to work on another activity, and then returns to the initial activity

truncation

the teacher never returns to the original activity after breaking off abruptly to deal with something else

momentum

the teaching practice of maintaining an appropriate pace during learning activities

overdwelling

a negative teacher practice in which the teacher focuses on an action or issue for a period of time beyond what is necessary

Various cultures have different rules about nonverbal behavior. Your students may be more or less likely to make direct eye contact with you depending on their cultural background.

Group alerting often is described as a technique where the teacher asks a question of the whole class, then calls on a student at random to answer the question. While this may effectively keep the attention of the group, Kounin characterized the concept of group alerting as a broader technique to help maintain group focus, namely any practice used by the teacher to keep the entire group focused or "alerted" to the learning focus of the class. Kounin described five practical ways a teacher could increase group alerting and three practices that reduce group alerting and therefore should be avoided. These are shown in the following *Concept Review*.

CONCEPT REVIEW TABLE 11.3
Increasing and Decreasing Group Alerting

PRACTICES THAT INCREASE GROUP ALERTING	PRACTICES THAT DECREASE GROUP ALERTING
Creating "suspense" before asking a question (e.g., "This question will really show me who has been thinking.")	Becoming completely focused on one learner's response without drawing input from other students
Not letting children know who might be given a chance to share their understandings (i.e., called upon) next	Prepicking a student to respond to a statement before the statement has even been made

(Continued)

group alerting

a technique where the teacher asks a question of the whole class, then calls on a student at random to answer the question

CONCEPT REVIEW TABLE 11.3

Increasing and Decreasing Group Alerting (Continued)

PRACTICES THAT INCREASE GROUP ALERTING	PRACTICES THAT DECREASE GROUP ALERTING
Ensuring that all of the children participate instead of just a select few who always seem to have the "right" answer	Having learners respond to statements or answer questions in a highly predictable and pre-established order
After initially asking a child to add her input to a discussion, asking additional children to elaborate on the initial child's statement	
Adding a novel or interesting demonstration, content, or story	

Accountability is another teaching practice that contributes to group focus in a learning environment. **Accountability** is expecting that all learners be able to explain their ideas. By being responsible to explain the logic underlying their answer, not just giving a correct answer, accountability fosters heightened attention. Kounin's four methods of increasing learner accountability are detailed in the following *Concept Review*.

The Assertive Discipline Approach

Canter and Canter (2001) developed an approach to classroom management called **assertive discipline** Underpinning assertive discipline is the notion that students have "a right to learn" and a right to have a classroom free from behavior disruptive to their learning. Evidence suggests that this program can be effective in

accountability

expecting that all learners be able to explain their ideas

assertive discipline

the notion that students have a "right to learn" and a right to have a classroom free from behavior disruptive to their learning

choral response

asking learners to respond to a question in unison

CONCEPT REVIEW TABLE 11.4

Methods of Increasing Learner Accountability

Asking learners to demonstrate their knowledge or skill and explain their thinking

Asking learners to respond to a question in unison, also known as **choral response**

Circulating through the room, observing the independent or group work of learners

Asking for volunteers who are prepared to display their work or voice and defend a position or understanding

promoting positive learning environments, particularly at the elementary school level (Mandlebaum, Russell, Krouse, & Gonter, 1983). According to the assertive discipline approach, teachers must possess the following four basic competencies:

- to clarify, through observable classroom rules, the behaviors that are vital for student success;
- to respond consistently to appropriate behavior, (remember the saying, "love me, hate me, but please don't ignore me")—essentially, this helps remind teachers to make sure students are getting noticed and affirmed for behavior that will help them succeed;
- to respond systematically and without bias when students disrupt their own learning or the learning of the other students in the learning environment; and
- to be able to gain the support of caregivers, families, and administrators and request their help and expertise when needed.

Furthermore, the assertive discipline approach maintains that teachers have one of three response styles that set the tone for the learning environment. A major component of the assertive discipline model is helping teachers identify the response style they tend to utilize and emphasize components of their response style that are effective and minimize or eliminate elements that are not effective.

The first, the **nonassertive response style** is a passive approach where the teacher is seldom clear about expectations and is inconsistent in responding. Students who work with teachers with nonassertive response styles often are confused about the norms and expectations in the classroom and experience a learning environment where the consequences of their behavior often are unpredictable.

The second, the **hostile response style** is an approach to classroom management where the teacher is more interested in controlling students and their behavior than in helping students learn strategies to self-regulate and manage their own behavior according to a reasonable and consistent set of criteria. Teachers with hostile response styles tend to view the classroom as a war zone where they are pitted against the students. Teacher's behavior often is typified as authoritarian and inflexible.

The third, the **assertive response style** is an approach where the teacher creates a learning environment that enables students to be aware of and clearly articulate the teacher's expectations for their behavior. In this type of environment, students recognize what consequences will occur depending on how they contribute to or detract from the learning environment. Teacher's using this response style are viewed by students and others as secure and fair.

nonassertive response style

a passive approach where the teacher is seldom clear about expectations and is inconsistent in responding

hostile response style

an approach to classroom management where the teacher is more interested in controlling students and their behavior than in helping students learn strategies to self-regulate and manage their own behavior according to a reasonable and consistent set of criteria

assertive response style

an approach where the teacher creates a learning environment that enables students to clearly articulate teacher expectations for their behavior

Think It Over

as a Learner | How might students react to teachers who display the three response styles?

as a Teacher | Which type of response style do you think you will employ in your classroom? Why?

Effective teachers create activities that students want to participate in and learn from.

Big Cheese Photo/Jupiter Images

Another key element of creating an effective learning environment according to assertive discipline is developing a **classroom discipline plan**, one that clearly indicates to the students what is necessary to create a positive learning environment. The plan spells out three components: rules, positive recognition, and consequences, and are critical to the success of assertive discipline because they help ensure that all students are treated equally and fairly. The most important aspect of the plan is its focus on **positive recognition**, that is, students' ability to gain the teacher's attention by behaving appropriately. Ferguson & Houghton (1992) studied one aspect of positive recognition, teacher praise, to determine how it would affect children's on-task behavior. They found that in almost all cases, positive recognition in the form of praise increased children's performance. However, they also found that when they returned to the classrooms for a follow-up visit, the teachers had reverted to their original levels of praise. This suggests that teachers need to be vigilant about the implementation of their classroom discipline plans by making frequent use of positive recognition (Canter & Canter, 2001). Tables 11.5 and 11.6 provide illustrations of discipline plans appropriate for elementary-aged students and secondary students, respectively.

classroom discipline plan

indicating to students what is necessary to create a positive learning environment

positive recognition

students' ability to gain the teacher's attention by behaving appropriately

TABLE 11.5
Sample Discipline Plan for Elementary Students (Canter & Canter, 2001)
CLASSROOM RULES
• Follow directions
• Keep hands, feet, and objects to yourself
• No teasing or name calling

TABLE 11.5

Sample Discipline Plan for Elementary Students (Canter & Canter, 2001)

SUPPORTIVE FEEDBACK

- Verbal recognition
- Individual rewards such as:
     Positive notes sent home to parents
     Positive phone calls to parents
     Classroom privileges
- Classwide rewards

CORRECTIVE ACTIONS

First time student breaks a rule	Reminder
Second time	5 minutes away from group, near teacher
Third time	10 minutes away from group
Fourth time	Teacher calls parents with student; student completes behavior journal
Fifth time	Send to principal
Severe Clause	Send to principal

CONCEPT REVIEW TABLE 11.6

Sample Discipline Plan for Secondary Students (Canter & Canter, 2001)

CLASSROOM RULES

- Follow directions
- Be in the classroom and seated when the bell rings
- Use appropriate language; no put-downs or teasing

SUPPORTIVE FEEDBACK

- Verbal recognition
- Individual rewards such as:
     Positive notes sent home to parents
     Privilege pass
- Classwide rewards

(Continued)

CONCEPT REVIEW TABLE 11.6

Sample Discipline Plan for Secondary Students (Canter & Canter, 2001)

CORRECTIVE ACTIONS	
First time student breaks a rule	Reminder
Second time	Stay in class 1 minute after bell, or change seat for remainder of period
Third time	Stay in class 2 minutes after bell
Fourth time	Call parents
Fifth time	Send to administrator
Severe Clause	Send to administrator

SUMMING IT UP

Describe the importance of creating a learning community in your classroom, and detail Kohn's three prerequisites and four strategies for increasing its effectiveness.

The type of classroom environment you create will impact the academic, social, and personal development of the students you teach. One recommended type of classroom environment is a **learning community**—a group of individuals focused on increasing the academic, personal, and social development of the community members. Developing a learning community that fosters responsibility and caring in children requires the satisfaction of the three very important prerequisites: time, small number of members, and having a committed teacher. To increase the effectiveness of a learning community you should attempt to: strengthen the connection between teacher and students, strengthen the connection between students, offer classwide and schoolwide learning opportunities, and emphasize academic instruction.

Discuss procedures involved in maintaining an effective learning community that include: (1) using time effectively, (2) creating an engaging curriculum, (3) discussing the connection between different learning activities and the physical arrangement of the classroom, and (4) detailing general principles in developing coherent classroom rules that involve students in their creation.

Once you have created a learning community, efforts must be made to maintain it. Current research suggests that classrooms need to be learning centered. **Learning-centered classroom management** involves changing the nature of discipline from control to encouraging student self-regulation and community responsibility. There are numerous decisions a teacher makes that will influence the success of the class such as how they use their classroom time, the quality of their curriculum, designing and organizing the physical space, and creating classroom rules.

Articulate how to respond to misbehavior by having concern and respect for students and families, modeling appropriate behaviors, and intervening with nonverbal and I-messages.

Learning Objective 3

Key Concepts:

misbehavior (p. 447);
redirection (p. 448);
perspective taking (p. 449);
I-messages (p. 450).

Misbehavior occurs for various reasons, but one of the most preventable reasons is when misbehavior occurs because students are not engaged or motivated by what they are learning and do not see the application of the learning to their lives. To be an effective teacher, it is important to work on positive, respectful, and caring professional relationships with the students. When you make a decision to intervene, be sure to do so in a clear way without embarrassing the student or using sarcasm. Model the behaviors and values you would like to see in your students; show value and respect for both your students and the cultures and values of their parents.

Discuss the importance of preventing bullying and cyberbullying for the well being of all members of the learning community.

Learning Objective 4

Key Concepts:

bullying (p. 452);
cyberbullying (p. 454).

Teachers must ensure that the learning community is safe and focused on the learning of all of the members. **Bullying** and **cyberbullying** take away from the safety and security of the students and create an environment that individuals do not want to be a part of. Students need to have a clear picture of bullying and cyberbullying and must understand the learning community's clear policy against it. Teachers need to meet individually and privately with individuals involved with bullying to work on solutions. Appropriate ways to respond to bullies include helping students and parents see the value in empathizing with others and valuing their perspectives and contributions and with victims, helping them by rehearsing statements and then role playing.

Outline the five components of culturally responsive classroom management and demonstrate how a classroom could be transformed into this type of environment.

Learning Objective 5

Key Concepts:

culturally responsive
classroom management,
ethnocentrism (p. 455);
individualistic cultures,
collectivist cultures
(p. 456).

Culturally responsive classroom management (CRCM) is an approach to **classroom management** that fosters a supportive classroom environment that values the culture of the students and teacher and uses those cultures in the selection of management strategies. Weinstein, Tomlinson-Clarke, and Curran (2004) discuss five components critical to teachers using CRCM methods in their classrooms: recognition of one's own **ethnocentrism**; knowledge of students' cultural backgrounds; understanding the broader social, economic, and political context; ability and willingness to use culturally appropriate management strategies; and commitment to building caring classrooms.

Detail the Kounin method for maximizing engagement in the learning environment and describe Assertive Discipline approaches to classroom management and create examples of discipline plans appropriate for elementary and secondary classrooms.

Kounin (1970) studied the different practices of teachers who were able to increase the engagement of learners versus those who struggled to gain and maintain student attention and subsequently were less able to increase student achievement in their classrooms. Kounin was an early proponent of the notion that effective learning environments are planned for in advance and that being proactive is more important than reactive. Kounin developed four behaviors to help teachers be effective practitioners: (1) **withitness**, (2) **overlapping**, (3) maintaining **smoothness** and **momentum**, and (4) maintaining group focus. Canter and Canter (2001) developed an approach to classroom management called **Assertive Discipline**. Underpinning assertive discipline is the notion that students have "a right to learn" and a right to have a classroom free from behavior that is disruptive to their learning. According to the Assertive Discipline approach, teachers must possess the following four basic competencies: to clarify, through observable classroom rules, the behaviors that are vital for student success; to respond consistently to appropriate behavior; to respond systematically and without bias when students disrupt their own learning or the learning of the other students in the learning environment; and to be able to gain the support of caregivers, families, and administrators and request their help and expertise when needed.

Visit the Education CourseMate for *Educational Psychology* to access study tools and resources including the Virtual Psychology Labs, TeachSource Video Cases, chapter web links, tutorial quizzes, glossary flashcards, and more. Go to CengageBrain.com to register using your access code.

- How does the manner in which the skill of dribbling a soccer ball is taught help students learn how to do it?
- Can you describe an instance of when you were taught a specific skill in a similar manner?

Lessons We Can Learn from the Story Teachers provide instruction to help students learn. Instruction can take many forms, one of which is illustrated in the above story. In this chapter, you will be introduced to several prominent approaches or models that will help you, as a teacher, design your instruction.

The first half of this chapter will focus on an approach to learning from instruction developed by Robert M. Gagné (1985; Gagné & Driscoll, 1988; Gagné & Medsker, 1996; Driscoll, 2008; Gredler, 2005). This approach describes learning as a sequence of processes or phases, each of which requires that different conditions be met for learning to take place. Because this approach can be applied to both lesson planning and the delivery of instruction, it might more accurately be called a model of instruction. How might the introductory story about soccer instruction be viewed as an example of **Gagné's model** of instruction? By the end of the Gagné's model sections of the chapter, you will be able to review instructional situations and analyze them based on Gagné's approach.

The remainder of the chapter examines several commonly used instructional and learning models, among them mastery, direct instruction, and discovery learning. Note that the constructivism approach, similar to discovery learning, was introduced in Chapter 8.

By the end of the chapter, you can expect to gain a sense of the approaches you might use to plan and deliver lessons. You might picture using different approaches for different subjects or different learning goals or with different students, as individuals or groups.

Gagné's Conditions of Learning and Instruction

Learning Objective 1

Describe and differentiate the eight phases or processes that help define Gagné's conditions of learning, and explain the specific learning conditions embodied in each of the steps or events of the instructional sequence.

Gagné's approach focuses on (1) the phases or **processes** that learners go through while learning meaningful material, and on the **conditions** that facilitate each phase, as a way of understanding the learning process; (2) the various **outcomes** of learning, that is, the specific competencies to be acquired as a result of learning; and (3) the **events** that must occur in order for learning to proceed successfully. By incorporating into his or her instruction the events and their required conditions, the teacher can facilitate the various learning outcomes. Hence, Gagné's model provides us with a framework for determining the conditions most conducive to learning and that should therefore be provided through instruction. The following subsections will pace you through the foundation concepts of Gagné's approach.

The Processes of Learning from Instruction

Gagné's learning model is divided into three parts: conditions before learning, conditions during learning, and outcomes after learning. The relationship of the parts of Gagné's model to one another is shown in Table 12.1.

Gagné's model

a system of learning and instruction developed by R.M. Gagné that focuses on processes, events, and outcomes

processes

the phases that learners go through while learning meaningful material

TABLE 12.1

Component Parts of the Gagné Model

BEFORE LEARNING	DURING LEARNING	AFTER LEARNING
Learner with entering capabilities	Learning phases (internal conditions)	Learning outcomes: verbal information, intellectual skills, cognitive strategies, attitudes, motor skills
Learning analysis (to identify competencies)	Instructional events (external conditions)	

As you can see from Table 12.1, the conditions during learning, the most critical part, is made up of the eight phases or processes of learning that describe the internal conditions required for the learner to acquire new skills and the nine instructional events that describe the external conditions or environmental events required to support the learning process.

The learning processes and instructional events are described in more detail in Figure 12.1, with the processes of learning from instruction appearing in sequence in the left column of Figure 12.1 and the events in the center column. Together they represent an attempt to explain the entire process, beginning with the reception of a stimulus and ending with the results of an action. For example, a traffic light turns red, your receptors (five senses) perceive this and send a message via your sensory register, or sensory memory, to your short-term memory to be recorded. Long-term memory tells you that red means stop, and so your response generator (in this case, your foot) hits the brakes. While this example is a common event in everyday living, later in this chapter we will see how the same processes may be applied to the necessary events of classroom instruction.

Attention

For learning to begin, a stimulus must be received, and such reception requires that the learner attend to or focus on the stimulus. If the learner does not pay attention to instruction, it will not be received and little learning will take place. Students who are off task while the teacher is instructing are not attending to instruction and so will often not receive its message.

The teacher could gain students' attention by changing the intensity of her voice or waving her arms, as in hailing a taxi. But most characteristically she will gain it by giving students verbal directions, such as "Look carefully at what I've written on the board" or, even more directly, "This is important; pay close attention." College students often become quite adept at knowing what they really need to pay attention to—such as anything the professor says twice or writes on the board and then underlines. For younger students, constant efforts to gain or maintain attention *may* be required.

conditions

the necessary requirements for learning to take place

outcomes

specific competencies to be acquired as a result of learning

events

what must occur in order for learning to proceed successfully

FIGURE 12.1

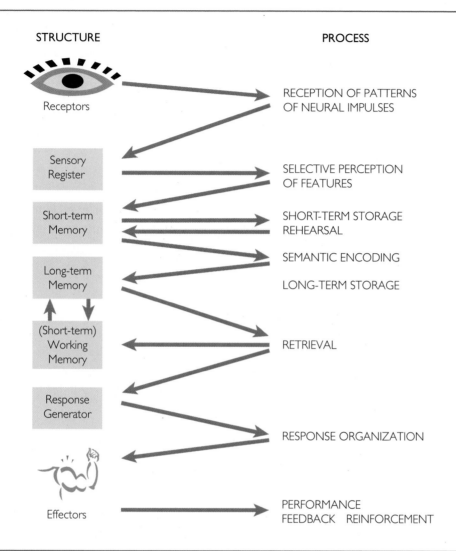

STRUCTURE PROCESS

Receptors

RECEPTION OF PATTERNS
OF NEURAL IMPULSES

Sensory
Register

SELECTIVE PERCEPTION
OF FEATURES

Short-term
Memory

SHORT-TERM STORAGE
REHEARSAL

Long-term
Memory

SEMANTIC ENCODING

LONG-TERM STORAGE

(Short-term)
Working
Memory

RETRIEVAL

Response
Generator

RESPONSE ORGANIZATION

Effectors

PERFORMANCE
FEEDBACK   REINFORCEMENT

Relation of Learner
Structures and Processes
in an Act of Learning
and Remembering
From R.M. Gagné
and K.L. Medsker (1996)

Motivation

An early learning process is motivation, specifically incentive motivation (see Chapter 10), in which the learner strives to reach some goal and then receives something for the result. Most individuals are believed to have the urge or desire to achieve or perform in a competent manner (White, 1959); if they are to be engaged in the learning process, this desire must be activated.

In order to establish motivation based on the incentive to achieve a particular goal, Gagné advocates establishing in learners an *expectancy* of what they will gain as a result of engaging in learning or participating in instruction. The teacher establishes this expectancy by telling learners what they will be able to do at the completion of learning (Gagné & Driscoll, 1988; Driscoll, 2008). Motivation, therefore, is established by creation of an expectancy of learning, which, in turn, is based on the anticipation of being able to know or do something new at the completion of instruction. "When I'm done teaching this unit, you'll be able to solve problems involving fractions" is a statement of expectancy designed to motivate learners. Motivation does not ensure learning, but it does prepare someone to learn from subsequent instruction.

The Discourse on Diversity box extends these concepts of motivation to multicultural classrooms. Again, this chapter of your text focuses on the topic of instructional design and how teachers can design curricula to maximize the learning, attention, and motivation of learners. One of the key ideas of the chapter is that for learning to occur from instruction, students must be motivated. Therefore, if students perceive that the instructional choices the teacher makes are sensitive to the cultural, ethnic, and racial diversity in their world, they are more likely to be engaged in learning of that curriculum.

Selective Perception of Features

What students must attend to in order to learn is more than a mere impression of the information presented. Students must focus on the pattern of new information. This focus or perception is selectively based on the goal or expectancy that has motivated it. As Gagné and Driscoll (1988; Driscoll, 2008) illustrate, in written

DISCOURSE ON DIVERSITY

Multiculturalism: Beyond Food, Festival, Folklore, and Fashion

BOX 12.1

Calvin F. Meyer of Marshall University and Elizabeth Kelley Rhoades of West Texas A&M University are interested in connecting the concept of multicultural education with the process of instructional design. They report that "simply recognizing diversity is not enough. Understanding and respecting different cultural values and ethnicity are essential if a teacher is going to actualize these ideals in the classroom. The ultimate goal of all educators is to improve the quality of life of the individuals. For that to happen, a teacher must be realistic about his or her own conceptualization, values, and internalized emotions regarding cultural diversity" (Meyer & Rhoades, 2006, p. 85).

The authors of this article were careful to point out some of the interpretations that have been implemented as multicultural curricula have the potential to be too simplistic. They wrote that "grasping a realistic meaning of 'multiculturalism' can be difficult. Often, interpretations of the concept result in a mix of classroom activities emphasizing Black History Month, illustrating how different cultures celebrate Christmas, and tasting food from different countries. At best, educators recognize the lack of true multicultural understanding; and at worst, they stereotype various cultures in terms of language, ethnicity, and traits" (Meyer & Rhoades, 2006, p. 83).

What are some of the ways educators can infuse multicultural considerations into their instructional design? They need to recognize that "discussions of ethnicity, race, racism, and cultural values are not 'safe' topics, and interpersonal change requires the individual to examine assumptions that never before may have been challenged" (Meyer & Rhoades, 2006, p. 85). They can explore this when they "challenge their own values and beliefs through examining the life stories of others. Reading biographical stories, corresponding with a culturally different pen pal, or interviewing an individual whose experiences have been different from one's own can enlarge a student's worldview, provided these activities focus on the deeper meanings of values, beliefs, and feelings rather than on superficial differences" (Meyer & Rhoades, 2006, p. 85). Thus, the concept of multiculturalism can be used to deepen your thinking about instructional design and to increase the attention, motivation, and learning of your students.

material such as this textbook, the reader focuses on the words and their meaning, not on the size, shape, darkness, and texture of the printed type. The reader selectively perceives some aspects of what he is presented with, as opposed to others, because the perceived aspects are relevant to the purpose of the reading.

Furthermore, selective perception of the features of a stimulus situation requires the learner to discriminate or distinguish between the various features, the appearances, the letters, the words, the meanings. You, as a learner, must distinguish between the main points and the less important or supportive material so you can selectively perceive or pay more attention to the former. When you go through a textbook and highlight the key points, you are selectively perceiving the features relevant to your learning goal. Note that this is one of many techniques your students will be learning from you.

Once students have selectively perceived the key features, they must store this information in **short-term memory**. For material to be stored, it must be transformed into a form that is most storable and subsequently recognizable. One difficulty is that short-term memory has a limited capacity, limited in terms of both (1) the amount of time something can remain in it—approximately 20 seconds according to Anderson (1995); and (2) the number of items that can be stored simultaneously—seven, plus or minus two, according to Miller (1956). To overcome the time limitation, students can repeat the stored material over and over to themselves (called **rehearsal**) as you would a phone number. To overcome the number-of-items limitation, students can combine units into groups or clusters (called **chunking**), and then remember the groups, as you might the members of a baseball team or the cast of a movie. (Rehearsal and chunking were encountered in Chapter 7 covering cognitive approaches to learning.)

Semantic Encoding

New information must be transformed again if it is to enter into long-term memory. The process of organizing new information meaningfully to make it more memorable—and hence lasting—is called semantic encoding. Semantic encoding can be accomplished in many ways (most of which were covered in Chapter 7 on thinking and memory). Some examples are connecting words into sentences (Bruning et al., 2004) or providing pictures along with words (Sadoski, Goetz, & Rodriguez, 2000). Often, learners will learn or develop their own ways of accomplishing the semantic encoding process, especially when they are given little guidance in the instructional process.

Storage in Long-Term Memory

The new information that has just been semantically encoded now enters into long-term memory. It may be remembered for a while and then fade, or information entered after it may interfere with its being remembered. Review and practice are activities that help maintain information in long-term storage.

Search and Retrieval

When a person needs to use a piece of information that has been stored in long-term memory, that information must be searched for among all the stored information and, once found, must be retrieved or recalled. **Cues** can be used to jog someone's memory, that is, to help him or her recall something previously learned. Even though learners should be taught responsiblity for their own recall, designers

short-term memory
memory of limited capacity

rehearsal
repeating stored material over and over

chunking
combining units into groups or clusters

cues
used to recall something previously learned

of instruction would be well advised to provide cues to stimulate or activate the retrieval process.

Performance

In order to (1) verify that learning has taken place and (2) provide an opportunity for feedback, Gagné proposes that the next process in the learning sequence be performance. The actual nature of the performance represents a learning outcome (described in a later section). To be sure learning has occurred, it is usual for the teacher to require more than a single performance.

It is often important that the performance situation not be exactly the same as the learning situation, in order to ensure that learning can be applied in a variety of contexts. Being able to perform in a variety of situations is called **transfer** and is typically an important goal of learning.

Feedback

It is also important that learners discover whether or not their performance has satisfied the requirements of a given situation or met a given goal, so that they can confirm or discontinue the expectancy they established in the first phase. Feedback represents the knowledge of the adequacy or inadequacy of the given performance. It also represents what Skinner (in Chapter 6) refers to as reinforcement. In Gagné's model, however, reinforcement simply confirms an expectancy and hence closes the learning loop—rather than strengthen the tendency to respond in a given way to a given situation, as in Skinner's model. Thus, feedback or reinforcement is seen by Gagné as primarily having informational value rather than functioning as an automatic strengthener. With feedback, a student can tell whether he or she has done the task right, either by seeing the obvious results, as in trying to hit a target with a dart, or by being told, as in getting a test back and seeing the grade and the teacher's comments.

The Events of Instruction

The most concrete aspect of Gagné's approach is the events of instruction: the nine experiences or sets of conditions that must occur in an instructional sequence or lesson to ensure the desired learning takes place. If you apply the eight processes of learning already described to the five learning outcomes, you come out with the nine events. The events incorporate each of the necessary processes into a lesson so that each type of learning outcome may be mastered. Knowing the events of instruction provides a solid basis for designing instruction or constructing a lesson plan. Knowing the processes of how students learn provides a basis for deciding how to teach them; that is, for identifying the appropriate instructional events. Each of the nine events will be described in turn.

Event 1. Gaining Attention

According to Gagné, the first thing to be done in teaching a lesson is to get the students' attention. Often, this is done by means of a verbal instruction: "This is important." "I want you to pay particular attention to this." However, teachers should also think of other attention-getting devices, such as a demonstration or the use of some strong stimulus (e.g., engaging instructional materials, or sound).

transfer
being able to perform in a variety of situations

Event 2. Informing the Learner of the Objective

The second condition of learning is an expectancy for the end state of learning. Telling students the aim or **objective** of instruction helps establish such an expectancy: "This is what you will be able to do when this unit is completed." It may be to recite the state capitals, measure the volume of a gas, or analyze a poem; whatever the objective is, students are more likely to achieve it, according to Gagné, if they are told in advance what it is.

It may also be motivating to a student to try to master an objective if the *relevance* of that objective to the student's subsequent learning or performance is made clear (Keller, 1987). Finally, students cannot tell when they have accomplished a learning task and experience the satisfaction of that accomplishment unless they know what final performance is expected of them. It is the objective that tells students what final performance is expected. (We will encounter objectives again later in this chapter.)

Event 3. Stimulating Recall of Prior Learning

The third condition of learning is that the learner has already mastered the essential skills on which the new material builds. New learning invariably builds on prior learning. Therefore, the success of the new learning will depend on whether (1) the necessary prior learning has already taken place, (2) the student knows what prior learning to try to remember and apply, and (3) the student can remember the necessary prior learning. To accomplish this learning event, the teacher must first determine what prior learning is relevant to the new learning and then must either point it out ("Remember that you have already learned how to convert a mixed number to an improper fraction") or restate it ("You need to remember how to convert a mixed number to an improper fraction, so I want us to go over that again quickly"). The teacher may then reteach the old material or have the students try to perform the previously taught task themselves.

Tasks that must be learned before new ones can be learned are called **prerequisites**. Without both learning and remembering prerequisites, new learning cannot occur. Therefore, many subjects must be taught in sequence and the teacher must ensure that previously learned prerequisite tasks are retrieved from memory by students before presenting new tasks that depend on these prerequisites. According to Gagné, the teacher should not depend on the learner to determine which previously learned tasks are relevant. The teacher should point them out.

Event 4. Presenting the Stimulus

The fourth condition of learning is that what is to be learned must be presented to the learner in some fashion. Learning requires the presentation of new information. It is the old information and the new information combined that enables an attentive, expectant student to achieve mastery of a task. Providing new information means providing students with a new stimulus. This may take the form of pointing out to students the **distinctive features** of the stimulus. ("These fractions have the same denominator so they can be added or subtracted!") The stimulus may take the form of a definition or a rule. It may be a proposition (a piece of declarative knowledge) or a production (instructions about how to do something). In any event, it will be a stimulus, it will be new, and the teacher's task is to present its distinctive features so that it can enter the students' short-term memory. The teacher must determine (1) what new stimulus information is required by an objective and (2) how to present that new stimulus information so that students can perceive and retain it.

objective
the aim of instruction

prerequisites
tasks that must be learned before new ones can be learned

distinctive features
new stimulus information that is required by an objective and that students can perceive and retain

Event 5. Providing Learning Guidance

The fifth condition of learning is that all the components of the task to be learned be combined in the necessary way. To properly combine old and new information and to make it possible for the result to be entered into long-term memory, students must be given help or guidance. This help should focus on ways that the combined information can be semantically encoded. Gagné (1985; Driscoll, 2008; Gagné & Medsker, 1996) has referred to this as **integrating instructions** that supply the learner with the rule or model for using all the relevant information to perform the task properly. Examples, demonstrations, diagrams, and step-by-step instructions (such as recipes) all serve to help the learner combine, store, and retrieve all the information in a way that will be suitable or appropriate for performing the objective.

Teachers need to plan what techniques they will use to guide the learners in a given task and how they will present these techniques. Sometimes it is best to let students try to discover how to use the information they have been taught to perform the task. At other times, prompting or cuing may be required, and occasionally only explicit step-by-step instructions will do the job. Teachers may want to plan to try more than one approach.

Event 6. Eliciting Performance

The sixth condition of learning is that the combined components of the learning task actually be carried out by the learner. The preceding steps ensure that learning has taken place, that new information or skills have been encoded into long-term memory. The sixth step serves as an opportunity for learners to demonstrate (to themselves and their teachers) that the new learning has, in fact, occurred. Now is the time for learners to actually complete the task they have been just taught to do.

Performance is elicited when students complete a worksheet, do homework, answer questions in class, complete an experiment, or take on any other form of practice that gives them the chance to try out what they have learned.

Event 7. Providing Feedback

The seventh condition of learning is the opportunity to find out how successful or accurate the performance has been. Hence, the follow-up to practice is feedback—information about the student's performance that tells him or her how good it is or how it could be improved. Successful performance yields positive feedback, which serves as a reinforcement for performance of the task. Students now know that they have developed the capability set forth in the original objective. Those whose performance needs improvement and who realize, from the feedback, what improvements to make should be allowed to practice some more and should again be provided with feedback. Eventually, they will experience success and be reinforced for their efforts.

Event 8. Assessing Performance

The eighth condition is that learning be evaluated so that decisions about subsequent learning can be made. Now that the performance has been practiced and reinforced, it is time to test it. This time students have to demonstrate their learning

integrating instructions
semantically encoding combined new and old information

Jaume Gual/age fotostock/PhotoLibrary

Performance is a key process in learning. It helps the student show what she has learned from instruction and provides the teacher with a chance to give her feedback.

to the satisfaction of the teacher before they can be deemed ready to continue on to new work. Moreover, the test situation will confront the students with circumstances and details that are not precisely the same as those previously tried, to ensure that understanding, rather than mere memorization, has taken place.

Event 9. Enhancing Retention and Transfer

The ninth and last condition of learning is that experiences occur that will enable new learning to generalize to situations and be used again. Hence, the last step features review and application. Reviewing the material helps ensure that it will be remembered. Applying it in a variety of contexts and situations helps ensure that it will transfer and be useful beyond the specific situation in which it was originally learned. Adding fractions and mixed numbers may have been learned in the abstract, for example, but it would be useful to have knowledge transfer or apply to real situations, such as measuring pieces of lumber to build a doghouse or dollhouse. To facilitate such transfer, the teacher must show students how and when to apply their newly learned skills.

Thus, we have the teaching/learning sequence according to Gagné. It forms a highly useful model of instructional design. Its application to the design of an actual lesson is shown in Box 12.2 (on page 485). Additionally, the *Concept Review* in Table 12.2 will help you connect the learning processes and instructional events. The relationship between the processes, in the left column, and the events, in the center column, is shown with examples of each in the right column.

The Conditions of Learning: A Cognitive-Behavioral Perspective

R.M. Gagné's model of the conditions of learning from instruction is partially a behavioral approach because of its emphasis on external influences, but it includes an important cognitive component: semantic encoding. Because it focuses on

CONCEPT REVIEW TABLE 12.2

The Relationship Between the Learning Processes and the Instructional Events

PROCESS	EVENT	EXAMPLE
Attention	Gaining learner's attention	"You know how important it is to get a job. Listen up because we're going to learn something that helps you get one."
Motivation	Informing learner of objective	"Now you're going to learn how to write a job application letter in business format!'
Selective perception of features	Stimulating recall of prior learning	"You've already learned how to write a business letter."
	Presenting the stimulus	"A job application letter is a business letter that describes your background, interests, qualifications, and job desires."
Semantic encoding Storage in long-term memory	Providing learning guidance	"Here's an example of a job application letter. Let's go over it together and identify and describe each of its parts."
Search and retrieval Performance	Eliciting performance	"Now I want you to write your own job application letter."
Feedback	Providing feedback	"I have read each of your letters and written my comments on them."
	Assessing performance	"Now I am going to test you on your ability to write this kind of letter."
	Enhancing retention and transfer	"Here is a case of an actual student. I want you to write a letter for that student."

behavioral objectives, predetermined prerequisite skills, repetition, practice, and feedback, the model has many of the features of the behavioral approach, but it is considerably more complex than Skinner's reinforcement model or any of the early behavioral approaches. And it goes beyond simple associations as the explanation

Box 12.2

TAKE IT TO THE CLASSROOM

Teaching First Graders to Read the Calendar

Instructional Event	Classroom Activity
1. Gain attention	Ask students to raise their hand if they know their birthday.
2. Inform learner of the objective	Explain that they are going to learn how to read a calendar.
3. Stimulate recall of prior learning	Ask students if they remember the names of the days of the week. Ask students if they remember the 12 months of the year. Ask students to count to 31 by ones.
4. Present distinctive stimulus	Show students a large calendar. Discuss how it is made. Talk about the number in the first square and the number in the last one. Then count out all the numbers on the calendar.
5. Provide learning guidance	Show the name of the current month as well as the names of the other months. In addition, ask students to name the dates of their birthdays. Also, ask students the dates of any holidays they might know. Then discuss marking the days with appropriate symbols. For example, a

birthday cake could symbolize a child's birthday. Ask the children to look at the calendar each day and determine which child's birthday or holiday is next.

6. Elicit performance

Ask each student to make his own copy of the large calendar. Ask him to mark his calendar each day using the appropriate symbols. Give him worksheets and ask him to answer various questions about his calendar orally.

7. Provide feedback

Check the calendar the student has made and make any necessary corrections. Tell her if the answers she gives to the worksheet exercise are correct.

8. Assess performance

Give the students a new calendar and ask them to answer questions to see if they can read it correctly.

9. Enhance retention and transfer

Ask the students to help make a classroom calendar. Dates can be marked for important events such as visitors, field trips, and special school occasions.

• How would you use this approach to teach first graders to tell time?

Think It Over

as a LEARNER | What is it about the Gagné model of instruction that you, as a student, find most appealing and helpful? Why?

as a TEACHER | What is it about the Gagné model of instruction that you, as a teacher, would be likely to find most appealing and helpful? Why?

for learning. Gagné embraces and includes aspects of what goes on inside the learner's head, albeit in less detail than the cognitivists who were covered in Chapters 2, 7, and 8.

Gagné has attempted to blend behaviorism and cognitivism within the instructional design framework. His model lends itself well to systematic instructional design, as will be seen in the next section of this chapter.

Gagné's Outcomes of Learning

Learning Objective 2

Distinguish between Gagné's five outcomes of learning.

Gagné has identified five categories of learning outcomes that represent ways of classifying performance. The five categories of learning outcomes are verbal information, intellectual skills, cognitive strategies, attitudes, and motor skills. The value of the classification process is that it enables us to group together performances that have common features and thereby enables us to focus on those common features or conditions that must be met to facilitate instruction. In other words, learning how to ride a bike is more similar to learning how to sew than it is to learning the capitals of the states, in that riding a bike and sewing both represent actions, while the capitals of the states represents knowledge. Isolating the common features or necessary conditions of the learning performances or outcomes described below helps teachers determine what they must do to ensure that such outcomes are mastered.

Verbal Information

Verbal information represents knowledge. It is made up of facts that have been learned and remembered and that can be recalled later. Verbal information includes such facts as telephone numbers, lines of a poem, football rules, names of the planets, and the multiplication tables. When students are asked to *name, list,* or *state* something, they are usually being asked to provide verbal information.

Declarative knowledge is a unit of verbal information. It may be considered to be a fact or, alternatively, an idea, which is a connection between facts. E D. Gagné, C.W. Yekovich, & F.R. Yekovich (1993) refer to ideas as **propositions** and use the

verbal information

made up of facts that have been learned and remembered and that can be recalled later

declarative knowledge

a unit of verbal information such as a fact, an idea, or a connection between facts

propositions

ideas that represent knowledge

proposition to represent what they call declarative knowledge, or knowledge that "something is the case." A proposition contains a noun, called the argument, and a verb, called the relation *(R)*. Arguments are further divided into subject *(S)*, objects *(0)*, and recipients *(r)*. In the proposition "Tony gave Herb a ride," *Tony* would be the subject, *Herb* the recipient, and *a ride* the object. The relation would be *gave*.

Propositions can be connected to form networks to help researchers understand how people may be able to remember as many ideas as they do. With propositional networks, related bits of information can be stored closer to each other than unrelated bits in order to increase the storage capacity of working memory. An example of a propositional network is given in Figure 7.1 on page 276.

Knowledge serves a number of functions for students. It may serve as a *prerequisite for further learning,* in the sense that learning is made up of building blocks of ideas. It may be of *practical importance in providing labels for everyday communication.* Some people carry a wealth of information in their heads and use it for a variety of purposes, including "making small talk." Finally, knowledge provides *"food" for thought,* that is, it provides the elements for thinking and for problem solving.

Intellectual Skills

Intellectual skills represent knowing *how* to do something, whereas declarative knowledge means knowing *that* something is the case. Intellectual skills are also called **procedural knowledge** (by E.D. Gagné et.al. 1993). They enable the learner to transform information from one form to another, that is, from a problem, such as how to find something, to a solution: finding it. Procedural knowledge is represented by productions, or condition–action statements. The condition is represented by an IF clause, and the action by a THEN clause. For example, "IF the goal is to find out what kind of geometric shape something is, THEN count the number of sides."

Intellectual skills are important because if we had to learn everything as knowledge, there would be far too much to remember. Instead, we learn to use symbols to represent entire classes or categories of objects or events. These skills or productions then become the mechanism for transforming facts into acts. R.M. Gagné (1985; Driscoll, 2008; Gagné & Medsker, 1996) identifies five kinds of intellectual skills, arranged (and described below) in order of complexity from simplest to most complicated.

Discriminations represent the ability to distinguish one feature of an object or symbol from another, that is, the performance made possible by discrimination learning is the ability *to tell the difference among stimuli.* This does not necessarily mean being able to use or even name these stimuli, only being able to recognize that they are different. Discrimination is the mechanism involved in the process of learning what was previously described as the selective perception of features: separating what is important to you at the moment from what is not.

intellectual skills
represent knowing how to do something

procedural knowledge
enables the learner to convert problems into solutions

discriminations
represent the ability to distinguish one feature of an object or symbol from another

Consider these two symbols:

One is smaller than the other, and they are shaped differently. You may or may not know what they mean, but at least you know they are different. You can discriminate between them. Below are pictures of two objects. Even if you do not know their names, you can see that they are different. They look different; hence, you can discriminate between them.

Concrete concepts go beyond the ability to tell that objects or events are different. It is the ability to identify, name, or label them. Above are a football and a soccer ball. We learn to recognize objects such as these by sight. The manufacturer or even the material from which they are made may vary, but their identity and hence their recognizability remain the same. They represent some of the many concrete

concrete concepts
the ability to identify, name, or label objects and events

The teaching of *intellectual skills* begins in the early grades.

concepts we learn to identify, usually as children. We also learn to recognize and name object qualities, such as smooth versus scratchy or round versus pointed. Relational concepts such as near and far, above and below, higher and lower are also learned.

According to Gagné and Driscoll (1988, p. 50), the performance indicative of concrete concept learning is "the ability to identify a class of objects, object qualities, or relations by pointing out one or more instances of the class!" The learner must know the name or label for the concrete concept (for example, those in the middle, the squares, the largest, the whales) and must be able to identify the class by means of its particular instances. Thus, upon seeing a picture of one whale, the student can either identify the class of whales as the name for both the instance and the entire class or can fit the label "whale" when provided by the teacher, to the appropriate picture.

Defined concepts (per R.M. Gagné 1985 and Gagné & Medsker, 1996) provide definitions for objects, object qualities, and relations between objects, initially in order to be able to identify them. Examples are "state capital" or "supermarket" or "chemical element." A principal activity of school learning is to acquire an understanding of these complex concepts. Learners demonstrate the acquisition of a defined concept by classifying instances of the concept. Given an array of food merchandising establishments, students will point out the supermarkets; given a list of chemical substances, students will check those that are elements.

The distinction between a concrete concept and a defined concept is that to use the latter, you must know what it means or what its essential features are. You cannot simply rely on being able to recognize every possible instance. To recognize the essential features of a class of objects, you must know what they are: You must know the definition.

Rules represent the ability to do something rather than simply describe how it is done. Rules, in E.D. Gagné, et al.'s terms, embody procedural knowledge, or knowing how to do something. Rules are represented by "if–then" statements or productions telling students what to do under particular conditions. Rules link actions to conditions.

Many rules are at work in reading and computing. Reading represents decoding of printed symbols, and we employ rules to pronounce words and determine their meaning. Carrying out operations on numbers also requires the extensive use of rules. Solving the equation $4x + 3 = 19$ for x requires a student to know the rule for transposing a number from one side of an equation to another and the rule for dividing both sides of an equation by the same number.

According to Gagné and Driscoll (1988; Driscoll, 2008), rules make it possible to connect a class of objects, events, or instructions with a class of performances. You do not need to learn a separate response to every equation you might be called on to solve and carry them all around in your memory. Once you learn the rules for solving equations you can generate a solution to any equation that

defined concepts
provide definitions for objects, object qualities, and relations between objects

rules
represent the ability to do something rather than simply describe how it is done

fits those rules, even equations you have never seen before. Thus, rules extend our mental capabilities enormously without requiring an equivalent extension of our memories.

Higher-order rules, according to R.M. Gagné, are complex rules made up of combinations of simple rules. When a teacher draws up a lesson plan for a class, he or she employs higher-order rules that tell him or her how to choose the material to be covered, how to prepare objectives, how to plan to present the material, and how to determine whether students have learned it.

Cognitive Strategies

Whereas verbal information and intellectual skills refer to *what* is learned, cognitive strategies refer to the *way* something is learned. Such strategies, including self-guidance and self-monitoring, may be called **executive control** processes. When a student skims a chapter in a textbook, or outlines it, or makes notes in the margin, he or she is utilizing cognitive strategies. In other words, cognitive strategies are ways to manage the learning process a person chooses to employ.

R.M. Gagné does not provide much detail about cognitive strategies, but we have encountered them before, in considerably more detail, in Chapter 7 on cognitive approaches to learning.

Attitudes and Motor Skills

Attitudes represent *preferences* or *likes* and *dislikes*. Like all of the outcomes previously described, attitudes are learned: Teachers try to influence or teach children to like school, to like learning, to like the subjects they are taught. Attitudes fall into what is called the **affective domain** (Krathwohl, Bloom, & Masia, 1964), or the area of feelings. In contrast, all of the preceding learning outcomes fall into the **cognitive domain** (Bloom, 1956), or the area of ideas. (Bloom's cognitive taxonomy will be described in the next part of this chapter.)

General attitudes or feelings about things or people are referred to as *values*. Our values and our attitudes about ourselves constitute self-esteem and can be expected to have a great influence on school behavior and performance. Attitudes play a much greater role in social learning approaches like those of Bandura and Weiner (encountered in Chapter 10) than they do in Gagné's approach.

Motor skills are precise, accurate movements involving our muscles that enable us to accomplish some task. Sports activities, such as shooting a basket, hitting a baseball, or getting a bulls-eye, require motor skills, as do various work activities, such as typing or driving a bus. Each of these activities may involve intellectual skills and attitudes as well, but the primary requirement to learn to carry out the performance smoothly and automatically is in the motor area.

4x5 Coll-Anton Vengo/Superstock/PhotoLibrary

To do mathematics problems, students must be given the guidance they need to learn the *procedural rules*.

higher-order rules
complex rules made up of combinations of simple rules

executive control
cognitive strategies used to manage the learning process

attitudes
represent preferences

affective domain
the area of feelings

cognitive domain
the area of ideas

motor skills
precise, accurate movements involving our muscles that enable us to accomplish some task

Think It Over

as a LEARNER   What might be a topic to which Gagné's categorization of learning outcomes would apply?

as a TEACHER   How might you use Gagné's categorization of learning outcomes to help you teach a lesson on the topic you selected?

Learning Objective 3

Categorize the steps in the instructional planning model for teachers (based on Gagné's theory), including how to (1) classify goals using Bloom's taxonomy, (2) prepare instructional objectives, (c) develop instructional activities, and (d) choose media.

An Instructional Planning Model for Teachers

An **instructional planning model** for teachers derived from Gagné's model of learning, described above, has been proposed by Reiser and Dick (1996). This model is shown in Figure 12.2 and has the following distinctive features, each of which will be described below:

1. Instruction is based on clearly stated objectives.
2. Tests are based on the same objectives as is instruction.
3. Instructional media are used as part of the instructional delivery system.
4. Instruction is evaluated based on student performance and is revised as needed prior to reuse.

Identifying Instructional Goals

The goals of instruction usually are provided to teachers in the form of a curriculum. These goals have been established over time on the basis of experience and by consideration of statewide and national instructional goals as embodied in textbooks and testing programs. These goals can be divided into the different types of learning outcomes proposed by Gagné (see the previous section of this chapter).

instructional planning model

classifying goals, preparing instructional objectives, developing instructional activities and choosing media

FIGURE 12.2

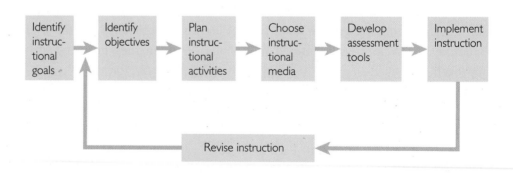

A Model for Developing Effective Instruction
Source: Reiser, R.A. and Dick, W. (1996). *Instructional planning* (2nd ed., p.5). Boston: Allyn and Bacon.

Goals can also be divided on the basis of another, more commonly used classification system, **Bloom's taxonomy** (Bloom et al., 1956), shown in Figure 12.3. (This taxonomy applies only to the cognitive domain. Taxonomies for the affective and psychomotor domains are not shown here.) The taxonomy includes six major categories of increasing complexity: knowledge, comprehension, application, analysis, synthesis, and evaluation. Bloom (1956) suggests that taxonomies such as his will help teachers (1) define ambiguous terms like *understand* so that they can communicate curricular and evaluative information among themselves, (2) identify goals that they may want to include in their own curricula, (3) identify directions in which they may want to extend their instructional activities, (4) plan learning experiences, and (5) prepare measuring devices. It might also be added that taxonomies such as Bloom's may help teachers put instructional goals in their proper sequence because of their *hierarchical* nature, that is, the fact that taxonomies are organized into levels or ranks.

Bloom's taxonomy

a classification system of the categories of the cognitive domain, organized into levels

---

F I G U R E   1 2 . 3

1.00 KNOWLEDGE
  1.10 of specifics
    1.11 of terminology
    1.12 of specific facts

  1.20 of Ways and Means of Dealing with Specifics
    1.21 of conventions
    1.22 of trends and sequences
    1.23 of classifications and categories
    1.24 of criteria
    1.25 of methodology

  1.30 of the Universals and Abstractions in a Field
    1.31 of principles and generalizations
    1.32 of theories and structures

2.00 COMPREHENSION
  2.10 Translation
  2.20 Interpretation
  2.30 Extrapolation

3.00 APPLICATION

4.00 ANALYSIS
  4.10 of Elements
  4.20 of Relationships
  4.30 of Organizational Principles

5.00 SYNTHESIS
  5.10 Production of a Unique Communication
  5.20 Production of a Plan, or Proposed Set of Operations
  5.30 Derivation of a Set of Abstract Relations

6.00 EVALUATION
  6.10 Judgments in Terms of Internal Evidence
  6.20 Judgments in Terms of External Criteria

Taxonomy of the Cognitive Domain (From Bloom et al., 1956)

Consider a middle-school or high-school social studies teacher who is interested in having students attain the goal of "knowing where to go to get information about a topic." In the taxonomy, this would be categorized as "1.00: Knowledge"; more exactly, "1.20: Knowledge of Ways and Means of Dealing with Specifics"; and within that, "1.25: Knowledge of Methodology." In other words, the teacher wants students not to learn about a topic (that would be "1.10: Knowledge of Specifics"), but to learn ways and means of finding out about a variety of topics. This might take the form of interviewing or doing library or Internet research or making observations. Classifying the goal this way may make it easier to formulate specific learning objectives (see below), to determine when in the sequence to teach this unit (after, for example, teaching knowledge of specifics), and to decide about some possible instructional activities.

A revised version of Bloom's Taxonomy, called "A Taxonomy for Learning, Teaching and Assessing," was developed by Anderson and Krathwohl (2001). The original six categories were renamed as (1) Remember, (2) Understand, (3) Apply, (4) Analyze, (5) Evaluate, and (6) Create.

Keep in mind that taxonomies such as Bloom's are made by people, not by nature. While they often help to organize thoughts and observations, they are not guaranteed to include all possible learning goals or to ensure that all users will classify every goal the same way.

Think It Over

| as a LEARNER | How could you use Bloom's taxonomy to help you write a paper for a class? |
| as a TEACHER | What is a specific way that you could use Bloom's taxonomy in teaching a lesson? |

Identifying Objectives

A **learning objective** is a clear-cut statement of exactly what it is the teacher wants the student to be able to do as a result of instruction. It must be written in such a way that its attainment, or lack thereof, can be observed and measured. In other words, an objective is *not* a statement describing what the teacher will do to provide a learning experience; rather, it describes what the *student* will be able to do after completing a learning experience. Moreover, an objective does *not* specify what a student will know, think, or understand, because we cannot determine these outcomes directly. An objective does specify only *actions* that can be seen by the teacher, who can then validate that the objective has been attained.

Most objectives are written as *brief action statements* using an *action verb* (for example, the objectives at the beginning of each chapter). In more detailed form, objectives include two other parts: a statement of the *conditions* or *givens* under which the action is to be performed, and the *criteria* by which the action is to be

learning objective
a clear-cut statement of exactly what it is the teacher wants the student to be able to do as a result of instruction

judged. The objective or action statement, either by itself or in combination with the conditions and criteria, is a *descriptive statement of intended student performance using an action verb*. A list of possible action verbs to use in writing objectives based on the taxonomy of the cognitive domain is shown in Table 12.3. A much shorter list appears below. (These types of items are described in more detail in the next chapter.)

Identify—Given a list of possible answers to a question (as in a multiple-choice item), circle the correct one.

State— Given a *specific* question calling for a specific fact (as in a completion item), provide that fact.

TABLE 12.3

Action Verbs for Writing Objectives Based on the Taxonomy of the Cognitive Domain

CATEGORY	ALTERNATIVE ACTION VERBS
knowledge	define, describe, identify, label, list, match, name, outline, select, state
comprehension	convert, defend, distinguish, estimate, explain, extend, generalize, give examples, infer, paraphrase, predict, rewrite, summarize
application	change, compute, demonstrate, discover, manipulate, modify, operate, predict, prepare, produce, relate, show, solve, use
analysis	break down, diagram, differentiate, discriminate, distinguish, identify, illustrate, infer, outline, point out, relate, select, separate, subdivide
synthesis	categorize, combine, compile, compose, create, design, devise, rewrite, summarize, tell, write
evaluation	appraise, compare, conclude, contrast, criticize, describe, discriminate, explain, justify, interpret, relate, summarize, support

Describe—Given a topic or an object (as in an essay item), write about it.

Demonstrate—Given a problem (as in a problem-solving item), show how to solve it.

Construct—Given materials and a task (as in a performance item), use the materials to complete the task.

If, for example, one goal in a high school chemistry class were to teach the students Boyle's Law, a first glance might lead the teacher to say that the objective was to have the students understand Boyle's Law. But *understand* is not an action verb. What could the students do to show that they understood Boyle's Law? Suppose the teacher gave them the volume and temperature of a gas and asked them to find the pressure of the gas. If they could do this—if they could *demonstrate a procedure for finding the pressure of a gas given its volume and its temperature*—then the teacher could conclude that the students "understood" Boyle's Law.

Let us try another example, this one from third-grade language arts. The goal deals with teaching students words that rhyme. The teacher wants them to "know" when words rhyme and when they do not rhyme. His objective, therefore, is this:

● Given a single word and a list of words, identify the word on the list that rhymes with the single word.

In seventh-grade English, a teacher wants her students to be able to tell about the characters in a story. So:

● Given a story, describe the characters in the story by writing descriptions that include physical characteristics, personality, and how they behaved in the story.

Note that in this last example, it was necessary to include in the objective a detailed criterion—what the descriptions of the story's characters were to include—because otherwise someone judging the students' performance would not be able to distinguish success from failure. In each of the first two examples, there was only one right answer, which could be specified in advance, while in the third example the determination of an answer's "rightness" required a judgment and hence a specific criterion.

Often, for convenience's sake, we write our objectives in their short form, or the action that the student should succeed in learning to do. When we are preparing test items, however, or evaluating them (see Chapter 13), we include all three parts—action statement, conditions, criteria—in our objectives.

The instruction to be designed, according to this model, depends on two things: the objectives to be learned and the characteristics of the students to whom those objectives will be taught. The characteristics important in a particular instance are those that serve as **prerequisite skills** for the objectives to be taught. Prerequisite skills represent *what the students must already have learned and must be able to use in order to be able to master the objective given the appropriate instruction*. Because much learning is sequential, many units of instruction teach the prerequisite skills required for beginning subsequent units. All a teacher need do, then, is proceed in sequence from unit to unit.

However, we cannot always assume that all prerequisite skills have been mastered by all students. When there is any doubt, it is better to check. But in order

prerequisite skills

represent what students must already have learned and must be able to use in order to be able to master an objective given the appropriate instruction to check, the teacher must be able to specify what the prerequisite skills are. Once the prerequisite skills have been identified, the teacher can assess them with a **diagnostic test**, a test given before instruction to detect the presence or absence of prerequisite skills.

Planning Instructional Activities

The instructional plan, according to Reiser and Dick (1996), should include six activities based on, and therefore reflecting, Gagné's instructional events that were summarized in Table 12.2. The Reiser and Dick elements are (1) motivation, (2) objectives, (3) prerequisites, (4) information and examples, (5) practice and feedback, and (6) summary. An example of an instructional plan covering these six areas appears in Box 12.3.

diagnostic test

a test given before instruction to detect the presence or absence of prerequisite skills

---

AN EXAMPLE TO AID UNDERSTANDING	**Box 12.3**

An Example of Instructional Planning

Objective: The student will correctly solve written word problems involving rate, time, and distance by using the formula $D = R \times T$.

Type of Instructional activity	Description
1. Motivation	a) Show videotape reminding students of increase in state speed limits.
	b) Ask students: How can we figure out how long it will take to get to various places?
2. Objective	a) Tell students they will solve word problems involving how far, fast, and long it takes to travel.
3. Prerequisites	a) Remind students that travel takes time.
	b) Remind students how to use an algebraic equation (e.g., $A = L \times W$).
4. Information and examples	a) Explain concepts of rate, time, and distance.
	b) Explain formula $D = R \times T$.
	c) Give examples of using each part of the formula as the unknown; use "real world" contexts (plane, train, etc.).
5. Practice and feedback	a) Group students to work on a set of 10 written problems.
	b) Review answers to problems with class.
6. Additional examples	a) If needed, provide additional examples.
7. Additional practice and feedback	a) If needed, give students additional problems to work on individually.
	b) Review answers to problems with class.
8. Summary	a) Remind students: we have learned how to solve word problems involving rate, time, and distance.
	b) Ask students to state the formula for each type of problem covered.

Source: Reiser, R.A., Dick, W. (1996). *Instructional planning*, (2nd ed.; p. 60). Boston: Allyn & Bacon.

Choosing Instructional Media

Reiser and Dick (1996) present three questions for choosing an **instructional medium:**

1. Is it practical, that is, is it available or obtainable?
2. Is it appropriate for the students?
3. Is it well suited to present a particular instructional activity?

The medium should fit into and be suitable for one of the above six instructional activities that constitute the plan. An example of how this might be done is also shown for activity 1a in Box 12.3 (on page 497).

"Media" does not necessarily mean just TV, films, or computers. Many media—worksheets, other handouts, overhead transparencies—can be prepared and produced by the teacher. Textbooks also represent a medium for instruction. Moreover, when the teacher delivers instruction, he or she is the medium; when the students present information, through prepared reports and discussion, they are the medium.

In the case of textbooks and other printed material, teachers should review them to determine the following (Reiser & Dick, 1996):

1. whether the content is accurate, up-to-date, understandable, and unbiased toward any particular group;
2. whether the format represents good writing at the proper grade level with main themes and sufficient illustrations;
3. whether the instructional design reflects components that match the teacher's objectives and will facilitate learning by the inclusion of summaries, practice activities, and motivational activities (other aspects of this feature were described in Chapter 7 on cognitive approaches to learning); and
4. whether data are available that indicate how effective the material has been, whether activities are included that can be carried out in the classroom, and whether supplementary materials are available.

instructional medium
material used to facilitate instruction (e.g., films, worksheets)

Students can acquire information from instructional media that are well-suited for this purpose. Teachers can include media presentations in their lesson plans.

Ableimages/Getty Images

Implementing and Revising Instruction

Any of the instructional design models described on the following pages of this chapter can be used for implementing instruction. Teaching teachers how to actually deliver instruction represents the content of education "methods" courses rather than educational psychology. However, educational psychology has produced some relatively unique implementation models, which will be described later in this chapter. This instructional design model can be applied most clearly to the design and evaluation of the lesson to be taught, rather than to the specific methods teachers use to teach that lesson. In addition, the next step in the model is actually *Developing Assessments,* but it is covered in more detail in Chapter 13 and will not be repeated here.

Key to the instructional planning model are the notions that (1) instruction should be revised, that is, it should not just be developed and then always remain the same; and (2) the basis for this revision should be the results of using the instruction with students and determining what works and what does not. Often, the tendency is to design a lesson and then teach it that way thereafter. However, good instructional designers evaluate their materials, not only by observing how students react to them, but also by seeing how well students do on the assessments that accompany them. This is called **formative evaluation.** If all or nearly all students fail to master one or more of the lesson's objectives, as reflected in the assessment results, then the teacher as formative evaluator not only notes this but changes the instructional plan and materials to minimize the likelihood that this will happen again. The teacher also develops new activities to reteach the content and skills the students did not succeed on. Formative evaluation, then, becomes an ongoing process until the result meets with the teacher's and learner's satisfaction.

The Mastery Learning Model

The **mastery learning model,** a variation on the general theme of individualized instruction, is based on an approach to school learning proposed by Bloom (1976). The key to the mastery model is to provide as much instructional time and as much instruction as are necessary for each student to achieve mastery on each learning task before moving on to the next one. It is possible, therefore, to virtually guarantee mastery by each and every student on each and every learning task *if some students can be given different instruction than other students at the same time.* This section will acquaint you with the concepts and techniques of Bloom's model.

School Learning Theory

The model of Bloom's approach is shown in Figure 12.4 (on page 500). It posits that on a learning task the three learning outcomes—(1) level and type of achievement, (2) rate of learning, and (3) affective outcomes (principally attitudes)—are a function of three variables: (a) cognitive entry behaviors of students (what they know when they start), (b) affective entry characteristics of students (how they feel when

Learning Objective 4

Explain Bloom's mastery teaching/learning model based on his theory of school learning, including its characteristics and effectiveness.

formative evaluation

using an instructional approach with students and determining what works and what doesn't

mastery learning model

providing as much instructional time and instruction necessary for each student to achieve mastery on each learning task, before moving on to the next

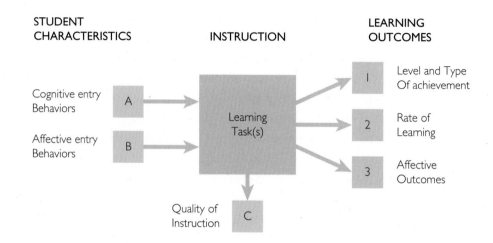

Major Variables in Bloom's
Approach to School
Learning

From Bloom, 1976

they start), and (c) quality of instruction. In other words, school learning is proposed to be a joint function of the *learner's history* (what has already been learned and what feelings already exist) and the *quality of instruction*. Its proponents believe that *both can be modified.*

Bloom's approach to school learning is based in large measure on a theory originally proposed by John B. Carroll in 1963 (and updated in 1985) that hypothesized that the amount of student learning would depend on two factors: (1) how much time and instruction the student needed in order to learn and (2) whether the opportunity to learn and the quality of instruction were sufficient to meet those needs. In other words, if the time allotted for instruction and the quality of instruction given during that time are equal to what the student needs to learn, then learning will take place.

Both Bloom's and Carroll's approaches lead to the inevitable and perhaps controversial conclusion that virtually *any student can be taught to complete any learning task successfully, given sufficient instruction.* First, the student would have to be taught the prerequisites in order to attain the necessary entry characteristics. Then the necessary instruction, necessary in terms of both amount and quality, would have to be provided. The result should be learning success, or **mastery** as termed by Bloom (1976).

In much of instruction, learning is sequential: Mastery of the first task is a prerequisite for the learning of the second task, mastery of the second task is a prerequisite for the learning of the third task, and so on. Hence, the most critical tasks are the ones early in the sequence, because if they are not mastered, the student will have difficulty with all tasks that follow. If students are allowed to progress through the sequence without regard to whether or not they master each task, the result will be a greater incidence of differences in level and rate of achievement as more and more students fail at an increasing number of tasks. Alternatively, if students are not permitted to move from one task to the next unless and until they master the one they are on, the result will be a decreasing variation in level or rate of achievement because all students should succeed at each successive task.

mastery

being able to complete a task
successfully, given sufficient
instruction

Mastery Teaching

Translated in a practical manner, this is the model of mastery learning (or, perhaps, more accurately, the model of **mastery teaching**), as shown in Figure 12.5 (on page 502). In it, the teacher provides sufficient instruction so that students will master each task, and should not allow them to proceed to the next task until they have mastered the one they are on. What varies from student to student, as accurately predicted by Carroll in 1963, will be the amount of *instructional time* each student requires. Some will require extra instruction to ensure mastery; others will not. Instruction should be individualized if the mastery model is to be applied. It can be expected to require a good deal of individual or small-group instruction.

In other words, after providing all students with instruction on Unit 1, the teacher must test them to see if they have mastered all the objectives of Unit 1. Those students who have failed one or more Unit 1 objectives must be given additional instruction and then retested. If they fail again, the sequence must be repeated until they pass. As a result, all students should learn all units and, theoretically, they should not differ in final achievement. However, *different students will require different amounts of instructional time.* To operate this instructional model, therefore, teachers must be able to vary the amount of instructional time per unit from student to student.

In 1976, Bloom reported on a number of studies comparing the effect of mastery and nonmastery teaching. In each case, two initially equivalent groups of students were taught the same subject matter by the same teacher. In the mastery class, students were given feedback and corrective help, if necessary, after taking a test on task objectives. In the nonmastery class, students were provided with neither feedback nor corrective help after testing.

The expectation was for the two classes to be about even after taking the test on Task 1, but for the mastery class to get further ahead on each successive task test because all of those students would have mastered the criterion entry behaviors for each task before they were allowed to start the next one. The graph in Figure 12.6 shows how well this expectation was borne out by the data. Note how the performance gap between mastery and nonmastery groups widened from the first to the fourth learning task.

Current mastery teaching approaches focus on developing a mastery-oriented classroom environment. Three key approaches to accomplishing this are: (1) promoting learning as an active process, (2) demonstrating enthusiasm for learning, and (3) developing positive teacher–student relationships (Anderman, Patrick, & Ryan, 2004). Research has shown that the use of a mastery teaching approach is more effective than the use of a traditional lecture approach (Ironsmith & Eppler, 2007) and has a positive effect on the transfer of knowledge from the classroom to a work-related task (Lee & Kahnweiler, 2000). It results in high expectations among teachers and students for academic success (Zimmerman & Dibenedetto, 2008). When trained in the use of the mastery approach, in-service teachers indicated

Lisa F. Young, 2009/Used under license from Shutterstock.com

In *mastery teaching,* extra instruction is given to those students who need it before they can move on to the next unit.

mastery teaching

teacher provides sufficient instruction so that students can master each task, or not be allowed to proceed to the next

FIGURE 12.5

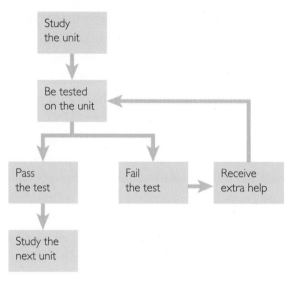

Bloom's Mastery Teaching
Model

positive attitudes toward its use and a willingness to incorporate it into their own teaching (Verdinelli & Gentile, 2003).

It has been suggested that the use of computers has contributed significantly to the recent success of the mastery learning/teaching approach (Motamedi & Sumrall, 2000). In a study of the effects of a learning strategies course on students' mastery of the subject matter, as measured by subsequent academic achievement, the use of computer-mediated class activities resulted in significantly better results than teaching the class in a traditional way (Tuckman, 2002). Focusing on student mastery as an outcome and utilizing a variety of techniques for achieving it provides teachers with a powerful approach for helping students learn.

FIGURE 12.6

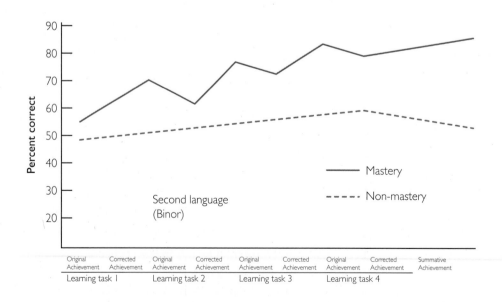

Comparing the Effects of
Mastery and Nonmastery
Teaching

Source: Bloom, B.S. (1976). *Human characteristics and school learning* (p. 59). New York: McGraw-Hill.

Think It Over

as a LEARNER   What would be the advantages and disadvantages of using the mastery learning model in comparison to other models such as the Gagné model or the Reiser and Dick model?

as a TEACHER   How do you see yourself using the mastery learning model?

The Direct Instruction Model

Learning Objective 5

Summarize the direct instruction model based on the process–product approach, including its recommended teaching behaviors.

Traditional group or whole-class instruction necessitates teaching all students the same content at the same time and thus does not lend itself easily to the mastery teaching model. This next model is more amenable to the limitations of the typical classroom.

This approach, named **the direct instruction model** by Rosenshine (1979), utilizes teacher-directed activities (such as seatwork) and features clearly stated goals, an emphasis on the coverage of content, virtually all classroom time spent on-task, performance monitoring, and immediate feedback. The choice of instructional activities, materials, and tempo or pacing is made by the teacher.

Process–Product Research

Where does the direct instruction model come from? It comes from research studies in which effective teachers were first identified based on their ability to affect an increase in student achievement as measured by nationwide achievement testing programs. Those teachers whose classes made clear gains on these tests, over and above their starting levels, were observed and their teaching behaviors recorded (Tikunoff, Berliner, & Rist, 1975). Similarly observed were teachers whose classes made no such gains. The purpose of observation was to identify those teaching behaviors carried out by the teachers whose classes gained in the tested achievement. The conclusion was that if other teachers were to carry out the same teaching *process* as the successful teachers, then they too would achieve a successful *product*.

Good and Grouws (1979) carried the process a step further with fourth-grade mathematics. After they identified the teaching behaviors that separated achievement-producing and nonachievement-producing teachers, they taught those presumed achievement-producing behaviors to a third group of teachers. This third group then used those behaviors in their subsequent teaching of mathematics and, lo and behold, the mathematics achievement of their students went up.

In summarizing teacher-effects research, Good & Brophy (2003) report the following characteristics of teachers whose classes exhibit large achievement test gains: (1) they believe their students are capable of learning and they themselves are capable of teaching; (2) they spend the bulk of their classroom time on instruction, so that their students can spend more time on academic tasks; (3) they organize their classrooms effectively and maximize student learning time; (4) they use

the direct instruction model
teacher utilizing directed activities, clearly stated goals, coverage of content, classroom time spent on task, performance monitoring, and immediate feedback

Active participation by students is a key element of *direct instruction*. Asking questions is a good way to get students to participate in instruction rather than letting them just sit and listen.

Kurt Gordon/istockphoto.com

rapid curriculum pacing based on taking small steps; (5) they apply active teaching (described below); and (6) they teach students to mastery (as described above under mastery teaching). These characteristics form the basis for the direct instructional behaviors described below.

Direct Instructional Behaviors

The key behaviors identified through process–product research (Good, Grouws, & Ebermeier, 1983) are shown in the *Concept Review* in Table 12.4 (on page 505). Clearly, a very heavy emphasis is placed on review, presentation or lesson development, and active participation by learners through seatwork and homework. Instruction is presented to the whole class at the same time, while seatwork and homework are individual activities. Emphasis on subject matter has been found to be one of the keys to increasing achievement.

Whole class instruction involves **recitation** as its major feature, with three primary teacher processes: structuring, soliciting, and reacting, contributing to effectiveness. All have been shown to relate to achievement (Anderson, 1995; Gage & Berliner, 1998; Hirsch, 1996). **Structuring** represents the way the teacher manages the recitation, by giving signals, for example, to indicate transitions between different parts of a lesson, highlighting the importance of an idea, or calling for attention. **Soliciting** represents seeking student responses or contributions by asking questions, particularly ones that are at the appropriate cognitive level for

recitation

teacher providing structure, soliciting student input, and reacting to student input to increase effectiveness of instruction

structuring

teacher managing recitation by indicating transitions between lesson parts, highlighting important ideas, and calling for attention

soliciting

teacher seeking student responses by asking questions

CONCEPT REVIEW TABLE 12.4

Summary of Key Direct Instructional Behaviors

TASK	BEHAVIORS
Daily Review (First 8 minutes Except Mondays)	1. Review the concepts and skills associated with the homework 2. Collect and deal with homework assignments 3. Ask several mental computation exercises

Development (About 20 minutes)	1. Briefly focus on prerequisite skills and concepts
	2. Focus on meaning and on promoting student understanding by using lively explanations, demonstrations, process explanations, illustrations, and so on
	3. Assess student comprehension by
	   a. Using process–product questions (active interaction)
	   b. Using controlled practice
	4. Repeat and elaborate on the meaning portion as necessary

Seatwork (About 15 minutes)	1. Provide uninterrupted successful practice 2. Momentum—keep the ball rolling—get everyone involved, then sustain involvement 3. Alerting—let students know their work will be checked at the end of the period 4. Accountability—check the students' work
Homework Assignment	1. Assign on a regular basis at the end of each math class except Fridays 2. Should involve about 15 minutes of work to be done at home 3. Should involve one or two review problems

Special Reviews	1. Weekly Review/Maintenance
	   a. Conduct during the first 20 minutes each Monday
	   b. Focus on skills and concepts covered during the previous week
	2. Monthly Review/Maintenance
	   a. Conduct every fourth Monday
	   b. Focus on skills and concepts covered since last monthly review

Source: Good, T.L., Grouws, D., & Ebermeir, H. (1983). *Active mathematics teaching.* New York: Longman.

the students, giving them sufficient time to answer, and redirecting and probing where necessary. **Reacting** represents responding to student responses by evaluating, clarifying, expanding, or synthesizing in either a positive (e.g., with praise or acceptance) or negative (e.g., with criticism) fashion. (Acceptance tends to be the most effective.)

It is important to point out an aspect of this instructional model that differentiates it from most of the others described in this chapter. Unlike the other models,

reacting

teacher responding to student responses by evaluating, clarifying, and praising or criticizing

the process–product approach is not a theoretical approach. It is based instead on observation. In other words, there is no explanation for why this model works, only evidence that it does work. A limiting factor is that most of the evidence that the model does work comes primarily from the elementary grades in the area of basic skills (reading and mathematics), areas for which nationwide achievement testing is routinely done. The model may not apply equally well to other subject matter areas.

It is also important to recognize that the criterion for successful teaching on which the process–product model is based is limited to tested achievement, primarily of acquired skill and knowledge. There is no guarantee that this model will contribute equally well to the development of thinking skills or to the enhancement of motives and attitudes; however, within its limits, direct instruction has proven quite effective. It seems to guarantee that young learners will get maximum exposure to and practice in the performance of basic skills.

Direct Instruction in Thinking Skills

Beyer (2008) describes essential features of direct instruction in thinking skills that includes providing detailed explanations, modeling strategies, procedures and rules, instructing when they can be applied, providing systematic, structured practice, and coaching. He cites numerous studies (e.g., Bryson & Scardamalia, 1991) that demonstrate that such direct instruction helps improve student proficiency in performing cognitive operations.

Furthermore, he offers a framework for direct instruction that includes an introduction, including modeling, guided practice, including scaffolding, and transfer. Some of the specific techniques he recommends are previewing (naming the skills, giving examples of their use), making the skills explicit (modeling, metacognitive reflection, thinking aloud), offering guided and supportive practice (scaffolding, cuing, rehearsal, coaching, providing feedback), and facilitating transfer (reintroducing the skill in a different context, follow-up practice).

It is recommended that direct instruction in thinking skills be taught in academic subject matter courses in order to improve the quality of student thinking (Pressley & Harris, 1990). Students score higher in subject matter learning in courses that include direct instruction in thinking skills than those in the same courses that do not include such instruction (Rosenshine, 1997, 2002). Moreover, in a study of third and fourth graders, direct instruction in the method of experimental design during the initial phase of learning and during the processes of transfer and application led to broader, richer scientific judgments than requiring students to discover the method on their own (Klahr & Nigam, 2004).

Learning Objective 6

Demonstrate the application of discovery learning to the design of instruction.

Discovery Learning

Discovery learning, a term used by Jerome Bruner (1960; 1961), is often referred to as "inquiry learning." It provides problem situations that stimulate and encourage students to discover or figure out the structure of the subject matter for themselves. In other words, it is a form of problem solving, not simply letting students do what they want (Klahr & Simon, 1999). While discovery sometimes happens by chance, the discoverer often creates the circumstances for it to happen. "Structure" refers to the ideas, relationships, and patterns of the subject matter, not to the facts and details. By arranging the learning environment and by introducing specific materials and tasks, what Bruner (1961) called the *hypothetical mode*, teachers could increase the likelihood, but not necessarily guarantee, that such discovery will take place. Hence, the approaches of discovery learning and direct instruction are reasonably opposite to one another. Direct instruction, what Bruner (1961) called the *expository mode*, tells students what they need to know, as does mastery learning—these being primarily behavioral approaches; the discovery approach creates the situations necessary for students potentially to figure out for themselves what they are expected to learn. Hence, discovery learning is a more cognitive approach.

Mayer (2003, p. 288) defined three basic levels of guidance in instruction:

- **pure discovery**: the student receives problems to solve with minimal teacher guidance;
- **guided discovery**: the student receives problems to solve, but the teachers provides hints about how to solve the problems; and
- **expository**: the final answer is presented to the student.

Teaching for Discovery

The discovery approach, according to Bruner, should produce learning on an *inductive* basis, that is, going from the specific to the general or from facts and observations to more general principles and theories. In effect, discovery learning

discovery learning
teacher providing problem situations that stimulate and encourage students to figure out the structure of the subject matter for themselves

pure discovery
student receives problems to solve with minimal teacher guidance

guided discovery
teacher provides hints to students about how to solve problems

expository
teacher provides the student with the final answers to problems

Bob Daemmrich/The Image Works

Discovery learning occurs when students are put in a situation in which they have to figure out something for themselves. A laboratory is the kind of place where students like these are likely to make discoveries.

should make the student behave like a theorist. Learning can be more meaningful for students if they are given the opportunity to explore the areas and environments of study rather than simply listening to explanations from teachers.

Bicknell-Holmes & Hoffman (2000) identify five learning "architectures" that make up discovery learning: (1) case-based learning, (2) incidental learning, (3) learning by exploring, (4) learning by reflection, and (5) simulation-based learning, the use of which enhance the application of skills and concepts. They recommend the gradual application of discovery learning activities to instruction. Borthick & Jones (2000) describe the steps in discovery learning as recognizing a problem, describing what a solution would look like, searching for relevant information, developing a solution strategy, and carrying out the chosen strategy. Gijlers & de Jong (2005) found that prior knowledge influenced the discovery learning process, that is, students with greater prior knowledge could more accurately interpret the results of a discovery learning activity than students with lesser prior knowledge.

To facilitate discovery learning, teachers need to provide examples of or access to phenomena from which students can make conclusions and generalizations. Specific facts, therefore, would come from observations that students themselves make of the phenomenon under study as they might in a laboratory, for example, and from which they induce the general principles that apply. An example of this for you to try yourself is given in Box 12.4 (on page 509).

Teachers may want to consider the advantages of guided discovery over pure discovery, as advocated by Kirschner, Sweller, and Clark (2006) and Mayer (2004). Instructional guidance and a curricular focus may work better until students reach a level of prior knowledge to provide their own internal guidance. Teachers can provide possible questions to answer and suggestions on how to proceed (Schunk,

Students' discoveries can be made in settings outside of the classroom. Field trips often stimulate students to use their intuition.

Keith Brofsky/Photolibrary

BOX 12.4

Discovery Learning and the Prisoner's Dilemma

Here is a game called The Prisoner's Dilemma. It is played by two people, PRISONER ONE and PRISONER TWO. Each player may make either one of two possible moves, playing RED or playing BLUE, but neither player knows what move the other has made until after he or she has made his or her own move. Moreover, the players may never communicate with one another.

The *payoff matrix* below tells what the result will be for each player for each of the four possible combinations of moves sufficient to meet those needs. In other words, if the time allotted for instruction and the quality of instruction given during that time are equal to what the student needs to learn, then learning will take place.

The purpose of the game is to learn what the defined concepts of *competition* and *cooperation* mean in operational terms. In the classroom, students are paired off and actually play the game with (or against) one another. The teacher changes the payoff matrix a few times during the activity. The object is to win as much money as you can.

Think about the following questions and try to answer them by imagining yourself playing the game (or by actually playing it) with a friend.

- Which response is competitive and how can you tell?
- Which response is cooperative and how can you tell?
- How would you change the payoff matrix to increase the likelihood of cooperation?
- How would you change the payoff matrix to increase the likelihood of competition?
- How does this apply to the real world? (In other words, what have you learned?)

Answers to these questions appear at the bottom of page 510 in footnote 3.

Prisoner ONE plays

		RED	**BLUE**
Prisoner TWO plays	**RED**	Both win 5¢	Prisoner One wins 10¢ Prisoner Two loses 5¢
	BLUE	Prisoner Two wins 10¢ Prisoner One loses 5¢	Both lose 5¢

2004). However, it is often helpful for students to have some prior experience and background information regarding the material being covered, or to be provided with some worked-examples in order to reduce cognitive load (Tuovinen & Sweller, 1999).

Another way to enhance the discovery learning process is to have students work collaboratively rather than alone, because communication can be an essential ingredient of discovery (Saab, van Joolingen, & Hout-Wolters, 2005). Discoveries can go beyond the classroom. They can be fostered by field trips and other experiences outside of school where students can engage in problem solving and use their intuition.

Think It Over

as a LEARNER   How would you compare the direct instruction and discovery learning models? What are the situations or circumstances in which you think you would learn better from one than the other?

as a TEACHER   What are the situations or circumstances where you think the students you teach would learn better from one than the other?

T e a c h S o u r c e   V i d e o   C a s e

Elementary School Language Arts: Inquiry Learning

In this video segment, you'll see how the inquiry/discovery approach can be adapted for a lesson on writing poetry. You'll see how the teacher, Jenerra Williams, constructs a lesson for children to write "sensory poems" by reaching inside paper bags containing a variety of objects and writing about them.

After viewing the video case, consider what you have just watched about inquiry/discovery learning and answer the questions below:

1. What do you think of the way the teacher applies the philosophy of inquiry learning (called "discovery learning" in the chapter)?
2. What questions has this video raised about your own position on how to provide instruction in writing?
3. What are some types of writing, other than sensory poetry taught in the video, that lend themselves to the inquiry/discovery approach?

You can view the video case at the Education CourseMate. Go to:
CengageBrain.com

[3]Answers to questions in Box 12.4:

1. Blue, because you win and the other player loses and the difference between you is 15¢.
2. Red, because you both win and the amount you both win is the same.
3. By increasing the payoff for each player playing red, increasing the mutual loss for both playing blue, and making the red/blue combination more costly for the player who plays blue.
4. By increasing the difference in payoff for a blue/red combination in favor of blue and against red, and reducing the joint cost of the blue/blue combination.
5. People will cooperate when it is sufficiently to their mutual gain and when not cooperating is sufficiently costly. Therefore, if we want cooperation we must increase mutual payoffs for cooperative behavior.

Contrast the discovery learning approach to the previously described instructional approaches that focus on mastery of basics, employ well-defined learning objectives, emphasize practice, and vary external conditions to activate internal conditions of learning.

Discovering Your Own Instructional Preferences

Imagine you have just purchased a new, advanced software package for your computer and have taken it home. Which of the five ways described below would you most prefer for learning how to use it, and why?

1. Insert a disk containing a tutorial about the software that takes you through instructional units and unit tests, and you can then go back over units you haven't mastered, in much the same way as the mastery learning model works.
2. Read and follow a well-constructed instructional manual that has been produced by instructional designers using the Reiser and Dick model.
3. Watch a videotape of an instructor giving direct instruction, followed by practice "homework" activities.
4. Install the software and experiment with discovering how to use it, and each time you get confused, search the HELP menu or ask a friend for help.

By carrying out the above activity, what have you learned about yourself relative to the four instructional models described in this chapter?

SUMMING IT UP

Describe and differentiate the eight phases or processes that help define Gagné's conditions of learning, and explain the specific learning conditions embodied in each of the steps or events of the instructional sequence.

Gagné's model provides a framework for identifying the conditions under which learning takes place. It can thus serve as a theory of instruction, because clearly teachers would want to teach in the way that students learn. The learning process is described as having eight phases: **attention, motivation, selective perception of features, semantic encoding, storage in long-term memory, search and retrieval, performance,** and **feedback.** Applying the learning phases to the learning outcomes produces Gagné's nine instructional events: **gaining attention, informing the learner of the objective, stimulating recall of prior learning, presenting the stimulus, providing learning guidance, eliciting performance, providing feedback, assessing performance,** and **enhancing retention and transfer.** These are the steps the teacher must carry out to provide the conditions that will ensure that learning takes place.

Learning Objective 1

Key Concepts:

Gagné's model, learning processes (p. 474); attention, motivation (p. 477); selective perception of features (p. 477); semantic encoding, storage in long-term memory (p. 479); search and retrieval, performance, transfer, feedback (p. 480); learning events (p. 480); learning objective (p. 480); prerequisites, distinctive features (p. 481); integrating instructions (p. 482).

Learning Objective 2

Key Concepts:

learning outcomes, verbal information, declarative knowledge, propositions (p. 487); intellectual skills, procedural knowledge, discriminations (p. 488); concrete concepts (p. 489); defined concepts, rules (p. 490); higher-order rules, cognitive strategies, attitudes, affective domain, cognitive domain, motor skills (p. 491).

Distinguish between Gagné's five outcomes of learning.

Gagné classifies learning outcomes into five categories. The facts or declarative knowledge taught constitute **verbal information** or knowing "that," while **intellectual skills** or procedural knowledge represent knowing "how." **Intellectual skills,** a major target of school teaching, are further subdivided into **discriminations** (telling things apart), **concrete concepts** (identifying things based on their appearance), **defined concepts** (classifying things based on their definitions), **rules** (applying information to solve problems), and **higher-order rules** (generating new rules by combining old ones). Next come **cognitive strategies,** which represent ways of learning, followed by **attitudes** (choices based on preference), and **motor skills** (actual physical movements).

Learning Objective 3

Key Concepts

instructional planning model, instructional goals (p. 492); Bloom's taxonomy (p. 493); learning objective (p. 492); instructional medium (p. 498); formative evaluation (p. 499).

Categorize the steps in the instructional planning model for teachers (based on Gagné's theory), including how to (1) classify goals using Bloom's taxonomy, (2) prepare instructional objectives, (3) develop instructional activities, and (4) choose media.

The first step in the **instructional planning model** for teachers is to identify instructional **goals,** which can be classified, according to Bloom's (1956) taxonomy of the cognitive domain, as knowledge, comprehension, application, analysis, synthesis, or evaluation. The second step is to identify **objectives,** clear-cut statements of exactly what observable behaviors the teacher wants the student to do as a result of instruction. Objectives include a statement of the *conditions* under which the action will be performed and the *criteria* by which the action will be evaluated. Third is to plan **instructional activities** in the form of an instructional plan. Fourth is to choose instructional **media** based on considerations of practicality, appropriateness for students, and suitability for the chosen instructional activity. **Implementing instruction** is fifth, followed by **revision** of instruction based on **formative evaluation.**

Learning Objective 4

Key Concepts:

mastery learning model (p. 499); mastery (p. 500); mastery teaching (p. 501).

Explain Bloom's mastery teaching/learning approach based on his model of school learning, including its characteristics and effectiveness.

The **mastery learning/teaching model** proposes that learning outcomes are a function of students' **cognitive** and **affective entry behaviors** (i.e., what they know and how they feel at the start) and the **quality of instruction.** Because both entry behavior and quality of instruction can be modified, students can be taught to complete or master any learning task successfully, given sufficient instruction. To achieve mastery, students are not permitted to proceed to a new unit until they pass a test on the current unit. Those who demonstrate mastery move on; those who fail receive additional instruction and are retested. This cycle is repeated as necessary until all students reach mastery. While students will not differ in achievement if the mastery model is used, they will differ in the amount of instructional time they require, necessitating that the teacher be able to provide different amounts of instruction to different groups of students.

Summarize the direct instruction model based on the process–product approach, including its recommended teaching behaviors.

Learning Objective 5

Key Concepts:

direct instruction (p. 503); process–product research (p. 503); recitation, structuring, soliciting (p. 504). reacting (p. 505).

The **direct instruction model** utilizes behaviors identified through **process–product research** rather than from theories. Achievement-producing teachers are compared to nonachievement-producing teachers to see how they differ, and those teaching behaviors that were shown to contribute to achievement then become the model. The model is called direct instruction because it emphasizes teacher-directed, -controlled, and -paced activities with a definite content orientation, such as review, lesson development and presentation, and student participation through seatwork and homework. Instruction is also group-based rather than individualized, and it works best for teaching basic skills as well as thinking skills to learners.

Demonstrate the application of discovery learning to the design of instruction.

Learning Objective 6

Key Concepts:

discovery learning (p. 507).

Bruner's (1960) **discovery learning** utilizes the presentation of problem situations that stimulate and encourage students to figure out for themselves the structure or meaning of the subject matter (**pure discovery**), or having the teacher provide hints (**guided discovery**), rather than having the teacher explain the solutions to them (**expository**). Learning can be more meaningful for students if they are given the opportunity to explore the areas and environments of study rather than simply listening to explanations from teachers. Teaching for discovery means that students are taught to learn from their own observations.

Visit the Education CourseMate for *Educational Psychology* to access study tools and resources including the Virtual Psychology Labs, TeachSource Video Cases, chapter web links, tutorial quizzes, glossary flashcards, and more. Go to CengageBrain.com to register using your access code.

13 | Classroom Assessment of Student Learning

After reading this chapter, you should be able to meet the following learning objectives	Chapter Contents
LEARNING OBJECTIVE 1 Describe the procedures involved in making a content outline and preparing instructional objectives, and discuss how these tools help teachers create assessments that increase student learning.	The Steps in the Classroom Assessment Process • Making Content Outlines • Preparing Instructional Objectives • Selecting the Type of Assessment
LEARNING OBJECTIVE 2 Demonstrate how the higher cognitive processes of application, analysis, synthesis, and evaluation can be utilized to create high-quality essay items.	Constructing Essay Items • Items That Measure Application • Items That Measure Analysis • Items That Measure Synthesis • Items That Measure Evaluation
LEARNING OBJECTIVE 3 Distinguish between criterion point scoring and holistic methods of scoring essay items and attach importance to the practice of scoring blind.	Scoring Essay Items • Criteria for Scoring Essay Items • Improving the Reliability of Essay Scoring
LEARNING OBJECTIVE 4 Identify advantages and disadvantages of and techniques for writing quality constructed-response and selection-response items.	Constructing Short-Answer Items • Completion Items • Multiple-Choice Items • Other Choice-Type Items • Matching Items
LEARNING OBJECTIVE 5 Identify the characteristics of a performance assessment and apply that knowledge by detailing the steps involved in the creation of a performance assessment relevant to the students.	Performance Assessments • Constructing a Performance Assessment • Scoring Performance Assessments • Portfolio Assessment
LEARNING OBJECTIVE 6 Demonstrate procedures for evaluating the content validity of a test and discuss factors that make tests valid and those that make them invalid.	Evaluating the Validity of Classroom Assessments • How Can a Test's Validity Be Determined? • What Makes Tests Invalid?
LEARNING OBJECTIVE 7 Explain procedures for improving the reliability of test scoring.	Evaluating the Reliability of Classroom Assessments • What Makes Tests Unreliable? • Building More Reliable Tests

Hole in the Earth

John Dewey (1859–1952) was a progressive educator who argued that experiences could be judged to be valuable for students if they led to intellectual and moral growth; if there was a benefit to the community; and if the process of education helped develop curiosity, initiative, and a sense of purpose.

It is noteworthy that Dewey saw traditional education as overly structured and inherently undemocratic, and argued that in order to promote the development of a thoughtful and active citizenry, students in schools needed to participate democratically in all aspects of the school program.

Benjamin Bloom (1956) told the following story about the famous educational philosopher and creator of progressive education, John Dewey.

John Dewey gave the class a little test, he asked: *"What would you find if you dug a hole in the earth?" Getting no response, he repeated the question; again he obtained nothing but silence. The teacher chided Dr. Dewey, "You're asking the wrong question" Turning to the class, she asked, "What is the state of the center of the earth?" The class replied in unison, "Igneous fusion." (p. 29)*

- What, exactly, is the point of the story? What does it illustrate about teaching and learning?
- How do you see this true story fitting into a chapter on "classroom assessment?"

Lessons We Can Learn from the Story This story about John Dewey illustrates the distinction between rote knowledge, which is memorized ("The state of the center of the earth is igneous fusion") and comprehension, which means understanding ("If you dug a hole in the earth, eventually you would come to molten rock"). Both statements are similar, but one comes out of memory while the other reflects an understanding of what is in memory. For teachers to encourage students to think in sophisticated ways beyond simply memorizing and restating information, they must create and utilize high-quality classroom assessments. Classroom assessments help to focus learners on important knowledge and skills about a content area and are one of the most important learning experiences a teacher arranges. We do not want students to only be able to share their understandings if a question is asked in a certain way, like in the Dewey story. Instead, we want to be able to teach and assess in ways that helps students use their knowledge and skills in a variety of situations and contexts.

There are many different types of classroom assessments. Like other kinds of tools, you as a teacher must select an assessment well suited to the instructional needs of the situation. An **assessment** is a diagnostic tool that helps you determine what students have learned. To be effective in the classroom, you need to master not only instructional skills but also the skills to create high-quality classroom assessments that encourage student thinking and learning. Effective classroom assessment typically involves sharing learning goals with students, demonstrating those expectations by showing high-quality models and examples, and then providing frequent assessment information to students in manageable amounts (Stiggins, 2007). In this chapter, we turn our attention to understanding the importance and reflection necessary to create and use high-quality classroom assessments. We will proceed by examining classroom-proven concepts and techniques for your selection in building your own toolbag of assessment tools.

The Steps in the Classroom Assessment Process

Learning Objective 1

Describe the procedures involved in making a content outline and preparing instructional objectives, and discuss how these tools help teachers create assessments that increase student learning.

In general, there are four steps you should follow to create a high-quality classroom assessment. The first step is the creation of a content outline. The second step is the creation of instructional objectives that identify precisely what concepts or skills you would like students to learn and how you will know if they learned them. Assessments at each grade level should make a direct connection to instructional goals (Niemi, Baker, & Sylvester, 2007). The third step in the process is deciding the type of assessment most appropriate to address the goals of instruction and the particular learning needs of the students. The last step in the test creation process is the evaluation of the assessment you have created to ensure it has acceptable validity and reliability and is not biased toward any particular set of students. This chapter is organized around these four steps and each step will be described in turn.

Creating high-quality classroom assessments is one of the most important responsibilities for a teacher. Excellent teaching requires that teachers have reliable and valid information about their students' performance. This high quality information helps teachers provide students with feedback that helps them increase their knowledge and skills.

Think It Over

as a LEARNER Can you describe the experience of taking a test that you did not believe was a valid indicator of your learning?

as a TEACHER Why is it important that teachers be able to create high-quality classroom assessments?

assessment
a diagnostic tool that helps teachers and students determine what has been learned

DISCOURSE ON DIVERSITY

Using Student-Involved Classroom Assessment to Close Achievement Gaps between Majority and Minority Groups

BOX 13.1

Rick Stiggins and Jan Chappuis at the Assessment Training Institute in Portland, Oregon, are interested in using effective classroom assessment practices to help reduce the achievement gap between different student groups. They propose that "low performers have judged themselves to be incapable of succeeding" (Stiggins & Chappuis, 2006, p. 18). To help these students be more successful in the classroom and to reduce the achievement gap, four classroom assessment conditions need to be met.

Condition #1: Assessment Develop ment Must Always Be Driven by a Clearly Articulated Purpose. This chapter focuses on the topic of classroom assessment and how teachers can envision and utilize quality assessments that will increase student learning. One of the key ideas of the chapter is that assessments should be created based on the learning needs of the class and designed based on credible content outlines. Thus, "students need to know what the intended learning or expected standard of quality is. They need to know how to judge and monitor their own progress" (Stiggins & Chappuis, 2006, p. 15).

Condition #2: Assessments Must Arise from and Accurately Reflect Clearly Specified and Appropriate Achievement Expectations. One of the key ideas of this chapter is that instructional objectives should be created to clearly help learners recognize what they will learn during instruction and how that learning will be measured. "To meet any standard, students must master subject matter content, meaning to know and understand. Some standards demand that they learn to use knowledge and reason and solve problems, whereas others require mastery of specific performance skills, where it's the doing that is important, or the ability to create products that satisfy certain criteria of quality. Student success hinges on the clarity of these expectations in the minds of teachers and then of their students" (Stiggins & Chappuis, 2006, p. 15).

Condition #3: Assessment Methods Used Must Be Capable of Accurately Reflecting the Intended Targets and Are Used as Teaching Tools Along the Way to Proficiency. "Accurate assessment conclusions are dependent on the selection or development of proper assessment tools" (Stiggins & Chappuis, 2006, p. 16). Thus, a major focus of this chapter is to help preservice teachers develop techniques for writing high-quality constructed-response items and selection-response items.

Condition #4: Communication Systems Must Deliver Assessment Results into the Hands of Their Intended Users in a Timely, Understandable, and Helpful Manner. Thus, "in assessments FOR learning, the assessment purpose is to provide teachers and students with information they need along the way, during the learning process, to make decisions that will bring about more learning. In this room of the assessment house, an effective communication system provides regular diagnostic information to the teacher and frequent descriptive feedback to the learner" (Stiggins & Chappuis, 2006, p. 17). A main idea of this chapter is that a table of specifications should be provided to learners to help them determine during instruction and before assessment where they need to focus their efforts.

● Why is it important that students understand the purposes of an assessment that we administer?

Making Content Outlines

Assessment construction begins with instructional planning. For many teachers, this means making a content outline of the unit to be taught. A **content outline** is a list of the concepts, ideas, and skills to be covered in the instructional unit that the assessment will measure. A content outline normally is developed as a prerequisite to building a lesson plan. The existence of the content outline facilitates building a test because it also serves as a plan for what the test should measure. It is important to remember that a teacher should include content that requires higher levels

content outline

a list of the concepts, ideas, and skills to be covered in the instructional unit that the assessment will measure

of thought in addition to the basic skill material traditionally taught (Wiggins & McTighe, 2008).

Thus, the teacher's first decision is determining the segment of instruction—a lesson, a unit, a group of units—to be covered by the assessment. The second decision is identifying the content of the segment because that content is what will be covered in the test. The content should be outlined as briefly as possible because it is intended only as a guide to the material that must be covered on the test. The creation of the content outline is critical to increasing the quality of assessments and will be utilized to create a table of specifications. We will describe tables of specifications and how to create them later in the chapter.

Two sample content outlines, one for a group of units in reading and one for a group of units in mathematics, are shown in Table 13.1.

TABLE 13.1

Sample Content Outlines

READING CONTENT OUTLINE	MATHEMATICS CONTENT OUTLINE
Final consonant digraphs	Place value (1's, 10's, 100's)
Initial consonant blends	Addition without carrying
Final consonant blends	Associative principle
Vowels modified by "r" in words	Subtraction without borrowing
Vowel diphthongs in words	Distributive principle
Singular and possessive nouns	Common fractions
Adjective endings	Improper fractions
Irregular verbs and verb endings, present tense	Place value (1,000's, 10,000's)
Compound words	Decimal fraction values
Contractions	Decimals
Synonyms and antonyms	Decimals to fractions

(Continued)

TABLE 13.1 (continued)
Sample Content Outlines

READING CONTENT OUTLINE	MATHEMATICS CONTENT OUTLINE
Personal pronouns	Fractions to decimals
Context and configuration clues	Adding with regrouping
Sequences of details	Multiplication facts
Main ideas	Multiplication of two-digit numbers

Preparing Instructional Objectives

Instructional objectives provide specific information about how a concept, an idea, or a skill that has been taught can be measured. They also help the teacher in selecting test-item type, constructing items, and scoring. A brief review of what objectives are and how they are written is provided below.

What Is an Objective?

An **instructional objective** is an intended outcome or learner capability resulting from instruction, stated in an observable and measurable way. The measurability of an objective is what makes it a useful guide for test construction.

The second step in test construction (after a content outline is prepared) is to precede each entry in the content outline with the appropriate *action verb,* to produce a list of *shorthand objectives* describing intended learner behaviors. Doing this enables the teacher to specify in measurable or observable form the concepts, ideas, and skills covered in the lesson or unit. Here are some examples of abbreviated objectives made from the entries in the sample content outlines shown in Table 13.1, the action verbs that were added are in italics.

- *Recognizing* the sound of final consonant blends
- *Identifying* vowel diphthongs in words
- *Classifying* adjective endings
- *Stating* the main idea
- *Identifying* common fractions
- *Converting* decimals to fractions
- *Stating* multiplication facts

Starting with a content outline makes it easy to prepare a list of shorthand objectives by attaching the appropriate action verb to each entry in the outline; however, a

instructional objective
an intended outcome or learner capability resulting from instruction, stated in an observable and measurable way

decision must be made about which action verb to use. The verb chosen should be one that describes the exact behavior the students will be expected to perform. Will the students point to the correct answer? Then the verb should be *identify*. Will they put things in categories? If so, they will be *classifying*. The verb must describe the action the student is taking in using the concept, idea or skill listed in the content outline.

Instructional objectives also contain (1) a statement of the *conditions* (or givens) necessary for performing the intended behavior and (2) a statement of the *degree* of correctness required for evaluating acceptability of the intended behavior. These two components of an objective are combined with the action statement in the process of test construction (Mager, 1984).

Think It Over

as a LEARNER	What is the difference between the *conditions* and the *degree* components of instructional objectives?
as a TEACHER	How do instructional objectives help teachers create valid classroom assessments?

Selecting the Type of Assessment

The third step in the process of classroom assessment is deciding on the type of assessment most appropriate for the intended learning outcomes. Box 13.2 elaborates on these ideas. At times, a traditional paper-and-pencil assessment will be appropriate; in other instances, a performance assessment will better match the needs of the class. We will first turn our attention to the creation and scoring of traditional assessments and then look at the creation and scoring of performance assessments. **Traditional assessment** is a paper-and-pencil measurement, like a test, that students have typically taken to assess learning in public schools.

Traditional Assessments

If a teacher decides to use a traditional assessment, it is necessary to decide which types of items to write and how many of each to include. Test items generally are organized into two broad categories: (1) **constructed-response items**, or those for which the test taker must *generate* an answer; and (2) **selected-response items**, or those for which the test taker must *choose* an answer. There are three types of constructed-response items (short answer, essay, and completion) and four types of selected-response items (multiple choice, true/false, two choice, and matching). The bases for constructing each of the specific item types from these two categories will be discussed in turn.

There is no automatic way to decide how many items a test should contain; it will depend on the number and type of objectives to be measured, the type of items used, the amount of time available for testing, and the age of the students. While there should be at least two items per objective, the more items there are to

traditional assessment

a paper-and-pencil measurement, like a test, that students have typically taken to assess learning in public schools

constructed-response items

test items that require the test taker generate an answer

selected-response items

test items in which the test taker must choose an answer

Jim West/Alamy

Assessment can occur both in and out of the classroom. The type of assessment the teacher chooses should match his or her goals.

BOX 13.2

Did You Know?

Educators use numerous types of assessments in their classrooms to assess student learning. The type of assessments utilized has a significant influence on the classroom learning environment. According to James Popham, there are generally three types of classroom tests that teachers can use:

What Are the Purposes for Your Classroom Assessments?

Instructionally Insensitive Tests

- Intended to compare student scores to one another
- Scores on these assessments highly related to the achievement that the students started with

– Scores on these assessments tend to be correlated with socioeconomic status

Instructionally Sensitive Tests

– These assessments focus on a reasonable number of instructional objectives
– The focus of these assessments is increasing student mastery
– The results of these assessments are used to make instructional changes

Instructionally Informative Tests

– Built upon task analyses (or learning progressions) that show what subskills a student is mastering or failing to master
– Focused on not only whether teaching is succeeding or not, but why the student is learning
– Emphasizes diagnostic properties of the assessment

● What is the difference between an "insensitive" and an "informative" test?

Used by permission of Dr. James Popham

Assessment expert Dr. James Popham advocates teachers using classroom assessments to help a student determine what concepts he or she has mastered.

Source: Popham, W.J. (2006). Those [fill-in-the-blank] tests! *Educational Leadership, 63*(8), 85–86.

measure an objective, the greater the accuracy. Therefore, teachers should have as many items as possible per objective.

All objectives, however, are not necessarily equal in importance. More instructional time is spent on more important objectives. Therefore, the more important objectives should have more items on the test to measure them than the less important objectives. The importance of each objective should be weighed against the importance of other objectives, and items for each objective should be allocated in reference to this weighting.

Selection of types of items is perhaps easier because it is based on the action verb used in each objective. Verbs such as *name, list,* and *state* require that a person provide or generate a short answer, as in a completion item; verbs such as *identify, distinguish,* and *recognize* require that a person choose a correct answer from among choices, as in item types such as multiple choice and matching. The verb *classify* requires putting things into categories, which generally means the two-choice item format.

Longer answers that are descriptive, analytic, or interpretive require essay items for their measurement. While identification choices (as in a multiple-choice item) are made up by the test builder, in an essay item the test builder indicates what is to be described or explained and the test taker generates the description or explanation.

Some verbs, such as *demonstrate* and *construct,* call for an actual performance. Many objectives in mathematics, science, or the arts, for example, call for students to demonstrate a procedure. Objectives of this type would call for a test item that requires students to carry out a computational or physical performance. These types of tests are called performance assessments and are described later in this chapter.

Thus, test objectives contain the information needed to decide which kinds of items to use. A summary of action verbs and the kinds of items to measure them appears in Box 13.3. If the item type chosen reflects the action verb in the objective but not the type of performance the teacher desires, then the objective should be rewritten to contain the action verb that would measure the desired performance.

AN EXAMPLE TO AID UNDERSTANDING   **Box 13.3**

Item Types Associated with Different Evidence of Learning

Item Type	Evidence of Learning a Student Can Present
Completion	Name
	State
	List
Multiple Choice, Matching	Identify
	Distinguish
	Recognize
Two Choice	Classify
Essay	Describe
	Analyze
	Interpret
Performance	Demonstrate
	Construct

• How would the type of evidence of learning a teacher wants the students to demonstrate influence the type of assessment a teacher uses?

Both the test objectives and the items to measure them must correspond very closely in action, conditions, and scoring criteria.

Think It Over

What is the difference between constructed-response and selection-response items?

Can you name some examples of test items from each category that you could place on an exam you create for your students?

Constructing Essay Items

Learning Objective 2

Demonstrate how the higher cognitive processes of application, analysis, synthesis, and evaluation can be utilized to create high-quality essay items.

Short answer and essay items can be used to measure the higher cognitive processes represented in Bloom's Taxonomy (Bloom, Englehart, Furst, Hill, & Krathwohl, 1956). In other words, if the purpose is to measure knowledge or comprehension, selected-response items work better; if the purpose is to measure application, analysis, synthesis, or evaluation, essay items would be the better choice. **Essay items** are test questions whose answers range from a written paragraph to several pages. Techniques for writing essay items for each of the higher levels of Bloom's Taxonomy are described below.

Items That Measure Application

Application involves taking general rules or patterns that have been learned and applying them to new situations or contexts. The general objective for an application item is:

> Given an appropriate problem situation in which no mode of solution is specified, demonstrate the use of a concept or rule by solving the problem correctly.

Here is an example of an essay item to measure application:

- You are in charge of planning meals and ordering food at a summer camp for 100 teenage boys and a staff of 15 adults. Taking into consideration cost and nutritional value, create menus for five days of meals (breakfasts, lunches, and dinners) and explain your choices based on cost and nutritional value.

To successfully complete application-based essay assessments, often it is helpful for students to follow a systematic process in explaining their logic. For example, a teacher might help the student to:

1. search for familiar elements in the problem;
2. restructure the problem in a familiar context;

essay items

test questions whose answers range from a written paragraph to several pages

application

taking general rules or patterns that have been learned and applying them to new situations or contexts

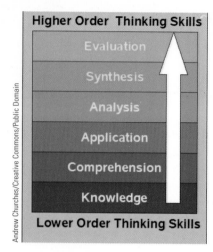

Bloom's Taxonomy is a tool that teachers can use to reflect over the types of thinking his or her students are demonstrating.

3. classify the type of problem;
4. select the suitable concept or rule; or
5. use the concept or rule to solve the problem.

To write the item, select a concrete situation that contains a problem to be solved, or think of a problem and then identify the situation in which it occurs. The problem must be one that the test takers have not seen before in its exact form, but its solution must rely on knowledge and abstractions that the test takers have already been taught. The concrete situation can be either an entirely new one or an old one with new elements.

How can you determine a concrete situation in order to write an application item? Try one of the following:

1. a fictional situation,
2. a situation that will come up later in instruction but has not been encountered yet, or
3. an old situation with a new slant (like the camp illustration).

It is usually easiest to come up with a new slant for an old situation.

In addition to the *situation* and *problem,* essay items often contain specific *response instructions,* covering things such as:

1. minimum or maximum number of words or pages to write;
2. specific points to be covered;
3. requirements for explanations and/or details;
4. number of solutions required;
5. special criteria for evaluating performance (e.g., neatness, clarity); and
6. number of points the item is worth or amount of time to spend on it.

Such response instructions may be provided for any essay item to help structure the student's response. In addition, it is recommended that at the time an essay question is written, teachers compose an answer key or a model answer in order to ensure that the question is written appropriately to elicit what is deemed the correct response.

Items That Measure Analysis

Analysis involves breaking down material into its constituent parts: (1) *elements* (such as assumptions, facts, hypotheses, beliefs, conclusions, or supportive statements); (2) *relationships* (such as cause and effect, sequence, assumptions and conclusions, or details and main idea), or (3) *organizational principles* (such as form, pattern, materials and their connection to point of view, meaning, purpose, or bias). Here is an example of an essay item to measure analysis:

- State four reasons why Hamlet did not kill King Claudius until the end of the play, despite his commitment to do so at the beginning. Describe how you determined what these reasons were.

analysis

breaking material down into its constituent parts

In writing an analysis item, determine the information or experience to be analyzed, compared, or contrasted and the aspects or components of that information or experience. The information or experience usually is read, observed, or listened to (e.g., a story, painting, piece of music, or other kind of direct experience), and the student is asked to analyze what he or she has seen or heard or learned in terms of elements, relationships, or organizational principles. Presumably, the student has already learned how to conduct an analysis and has already acquired the information or had the experience, but has never had to conduct an analysis of the specific information or experience given in the item. Carrying out that analysis demonstrates the use of a higher cognitive process.

Like application items, analysis items may include response instructions such as asking students to supply details, explanations, or reasons for their answers. This enables the teacher to see and evaluate the mechanics of the analysis process used by the student. Without these response instructions, students may produce "short answers" (as they would in completion items) rather than demonstrate the process of analysis as the teacher or test builder intends.

Items That Measure Synthesis

Synthesis is the combining of elements to form a unique whole. The product of synthesis may be

1. a unique communication intended to inform, describe, persuade, impress, or entertain (like a story or poem);
2. a plan or proposed set of operations (like a lesson plan or problem-solving plan); or
3. a set of abstract relations (like a theory of learning).

An example of a synthesis item is as follows:

- Suppose you have been put in charge of developing a day-care program for your school. Plan and describe how you would go about this task and what your intended result would be. Do not omit the details.

Synthesis is a creative and inventive process. As such, it has some unique testing requirements. In testing for synthesis, you might try to:

1. provide conditions suitable for creative work, including no time pressure, few controls, and minimal restrictions (e.g., in a take-home, open-book, or untimed test);
2. require more than one performance sample (because the synthesis skill may vary from problem to problem);
3. break the typical pattern of test administration with its limits on time, place, and resources, rather than choosing not to measure creative performance and resorting instead to short-answer items; or
4. use competent judges for the evaluation of products.

Synthesis is an important cognitive skill. Despite the difficulty in measuring it, you, as the teacher, are encouraged to try. To do so, you must pose problems outside the range of the familiar so that students will be required to generate novel

synthesis
the combining of elements to form a unique whole

solutions. In particular, asking students to write a creative piece, formulate a theory, design a novel piece of equipment, or propose a new procedure gives them an opportunity to synthesize. Make sure, however, that the problem is one for which students have not seen the solution before, or else they will rely on memory rather than synthesizing skill to solve it.

Items That Measure Evaluation

Evaluation involves *making judgments about the value of ideas, works, solutions, methods, or materials for some particular purpose.* These judgments may be either *quantitative* (i.e., numerical) or *qualitative* (i.e., in terms of quality). Evaluations are typically characterized as formative or summative. **Formative evaluations** are evaluations that take place during units of instruction. A teacher typically uses information gathered from these evaluations to decide how to adjust his or her teaching. It is also important that students be given this information so that they can focus their effort in what they consider the most important place (Stiggins & Chappuis, 2008). **Summative evaluations** are evaluations that take place at the end of units of instruction and summarize performance. In addition, the evaluative judgments are made using *criteria* and *standards* that are either determined by the students themselves or provided to them. These criteria and standards are used to appraise or evaluate the extent to which the work, idea, or particular solution is *accurate, effective, economical,* or *satisfying,* using two kinds of judgment:

1. in terms of *internal* evidence such as logic, exactness, consistency, documentation, and clarity;
2. in terms of *external* evidence such as comparison with other works or ends to be satisfied, application of given rules or standards, and consistency with known facts.

evaluation

making judgments about the value of ideas, works, solutions, methods, or materials for some particular purpose

formative evaluations

evaluations that take place during units of instruction

summative evaluations

evaluations that take place at the end of units of instruction and summarize performance

Just like the judges on the hit television show *Dancing with the Stars,* it is important for students to be able to effectively and honestly evaluate their work.

Kelsey McNeal/ABC/Retna Ltd./Corbis Entertainment/Corbis

Here is an example of an essay item to measure evaluation:

- You just received a third-grade reading textbook in the mail from a publisher. Describe how you would go about evaluating whether or not the textbook you received is good enough to recommend to others.

Give at least four different ways that you might evaluate the textbook. In writing an evaluation essay item, choose something about which students can be expected to have extensive knowledge and understanding. Students must know the criteria used in judging the idea or object, and they must have skill in the application of these criteria. The evaluation item is intended to measure whether or not students know and can use the appropriate evaluative criteria.

To write the item, select a work or an idea to which specific internal or external (or both) evaluative criteria can be applied and then ask the students to evaluate it as a member of a given class or category, in comparison with another given work or idea.

Think It Over

as a LEARNER	How does Bloom's taxonomy (as described in Chapter 12) impact the type and nature of a test item?
as a TEACHER	Why do teachers want to create classroom assessments that require students to utilize the higher levels of Bloom's Taxonomy? What are some ways the classroom teacher can create assessments that address several different levels of the taxonomy?

Scoring Essay Items

Learning Objective 3

Distinguish between criterion point scoring and holistic methods of scoring essay items and attach importance to the practice of scoring blind.

Essays cannot be scored unless scorers predetermine what they are looking for in scoring them. Lists of criteria or model answers enable scorers to judge whether or not (or to what degree) the predetermined requirements are present in the answer by giving them something to which each answer can be compared.

For example, in items that measure analysis, students are expected to determine the components or elements of an object or experience and their relationship, and to explain how these were determined or what they mean. The scorer must specify, in advance, what elements should be found in the response, what kind of reasoning should have been used to identify an element, how elements relate to one another, and how these relationships relate to the solution.

Imagine that students were presented with a piece of abstract art or poster art and asked (1) what they thought the artist was "trying to say" and (2) what elements of the art led them to that conclusion. Before scoring their answers, you the teacher should first decide what answers would be acceptable for the first part and what elements must be cited as satisfactory explanations in the second part. In other words, to score an essay test reliably, you must decide in advance not only what answers are acceptable but also what justifications or explanations are required in support of those answers.

Criteria for Scoring Essay Items

This section examines accepted practices for scoring essays and for improving your own reliability in that scoring. There are three kinds of criteria for scoring an essay item response: (1) content criteria, (2) process criteria, and (3) organization criteria. *Content criteria* refer to *the information, knowledge, or facts that must be present in order for the student to answer the question adequately*. Although essay items are not written primarily to measure knowledge, they usually require that some be presented. The scorer should specify, before scoring essay responses, exactly what content must be present in the response for the response to be adequate. The scorer may want to identify both necessary knowledge and optional knowledge, the latter depending on the particular direction the essay writer has taken.

Process criteria are used to evaluate the solution or recommendation presented in the response in terms of (1) *its accuracy or workability*, (2) *the reasons given to support it*, and (3) *the logic or rationale used to arrive at it*. For example, suppose the test scorer defines the appropriate problem-solving process to include the following six steps:

1. defining the problem,
2. generating alternative solutions,
3. weighing the alternative solutions against criteria,
4. choosing what seems to be the best solution,
5. applying the solution to the problem, and
6. evaluating the extent to which the solution fits the problem.

Using the above list, you can score students' essay responses by judging whether or not (or to what degree) each of the six problem-solving steps are reflected in the response. In other words, essay responses would be judged in terms of (a) the correctness of the given solution and (b) whether the process of finding that solution was accomplished using the above problem-solving steps.

The third type of criteria are *organization criteria*. As the name implies, these criteria refer to the manner in which an essay response is organized or structured. Does the essay follow a logical pattern? Does it have an introduction, arguments, and a conclusion or does it ramble along in a disorganized fashion?

Essay responses are far easier to score when they have a coherent structure. Students should be encouraged to prepare an outline before writing an essay response. To foster this, response instructions can indicate that the organization of the response will be taken into account when the essay is scored. To score classroom assessments fairly and appropriately, specific protocols should be followed so that each student is evaluated based on the same criteria (Marzano, 2002).

Essay scorers may also want to take into account *originality* and *creativity* in scoring essay responses. To do so, they should include judgments of these qualities in the scoring procedure.

Improving the Reliability of Essay Scoring

For essay tests, reliability is based not on the items, as it is in multiple-choice tests, but on the scoring. In other words, the error or inaccuracy in essay testing is not in the writing of items, as it is for selected-response items, but in the judging of answers. Therefore, essay test scoring must be done systematically and consistently, as described below.

On essay tests, the teacher reads the responses and makes judgments about students' competency or proficiency. What would happen if you, as the teacher, were to read that essay a second time? Would the same judgments of performance be made? If the second-round judgments are different from the first, who is to say which is more accurate? Maybe some of the essays were read late at night when you were tired, and the remainder were read in the morning when you were more alert. Or perhaps you read the names of the students before reading their responses and, because of the difficulty in making the judgments that essay-response scoring requires, were influenced by expectations based on the students' past performances and abilities. When unconscious biases or expectations affect scoring consistency, reliability suffers.

To assure the reliability of scoring, responses should be rescored (Tuckman, 1988). That is, responses to every essay item, or some proportion of them, should be read twice. The minimum number of essays to read twice to establish reliability is one out of five. Teachers should try to read one out of every five essay responses twice to see how closely the judgment determinations agree. If scoring criteria are established or model answers are prespecified, scoring can be done much more quickly. Knowing exactly what to look for and how much the different criteria will be weighed can help you score and rescore all the essays efficiently.

Here are some suggestions about how to improve your reliability as a scorer. First, cover the students' names before scoring in order to avoid being influenced by expectations based on prior performance. This process is called **scoring blind**. Second, structure your response key in terms of the ideal answer and the number of points given for organization, content, creativity, problem solution, and rationale. The more scoring specifications, the more likely the scoring will be consistent, time after time, student after student. Communicating these criteria to students also helps them write better, easier-to-score essay responses.

scoring blind
scoring student work anonymously so that you minimize bias

Think It Over

as a LEARNER	What is the "scoring blind" procedure?
as a TEACHER	What potential problems can you foresee if a teacher does not cover up student names before she or he evaluates the assessment?

Learning Objective 4

Identify advantages and disadvantages of and techniques for writing quality constructed-response and selection-response items.

Constructing Short-Answer Items

Now that we have covered essay items, we turn to short-answer items. The following four types will be described: completion items, multiple-choice items, other choice-type items, and matching items. Each type has an optimal circumstance, such as using short answers to assess factual knowledge. You can expect to use all of these types, sometimes in combination, on a frequent basis.

Completion Items

Completion items are single-sentence questions for which a test taker must produce a free-choice short answer (usually a word or a phrase). Sometimes a word or phrase is left out of a sentence and the test taker must supply it. Answer choices are *never* given in this type of item. Answers are generated by the test taker.

Advantages and Disadvantages

Completion items generally are easy to construct but occasionally hard to score. They work best when they are written to measure recall of specific, discrete facts one or two words long. If a teacher tries to make a completion item too tricky or too clever, it will become ambiguous and produce many possible answers, more than one of which may be correct. This will make scoring difficult and highly subjective.

Writing the Item

Listed below are rules for writing effective completion-type items.

1. Keep the item clear, unambiguous, and narrow in scope so there will be only one correct answer.
2. Do not provide so much information in the item that the correct answer becomes obvious.
3. Make sure the correct answer is short and does not include extraneous words.
4. Do not let the grammar of the sentence serve as a clue to the correct answer.
5. Make sure that the missing part is exactly what the test taker should be expected to remember.
6. Place the blank at or near the end of the statement.

Consider the following alternative items that, presumably, all measure the same point:

completion items

single-sentence questions for which a test taker must produce a free-choice short answer

- The assumption that organisms will behave to gain _____ is the basis of the behavioristic theory of _____.
- The assumption that organisms will behave to gain reinforcement is the basis of the behavioristic theory of _____.
- The behavioristic theory of Skinner is based on the assumption that organisms will behave to gain _____.
- The _____ theory of Skinner is based on the assumption that organisms will behave to gain reinforcement.

In this example, which piece of information should the test taker be able to remember? Should the test taker be able to name Skinner as the theorist of reinforcement, or reinforcement as the theory of Skinner, or behaviorism as the kind of theory that Skinner's reinforcement theory is? Asking the test taker to name more than one fact in the same item invites ambiguity. In this case, Pavlov or Thorndike might be paired with their appropriate theory (which would not be "correct" on the test if the purpose of the item was to measure knowledge of Skinner). The best version of the item is the third, in which the essential feature to be remembered is the principle of *reinforcement,* on which Skinner's behaviorism is based.

A good way to construct a completion item is to write an entire statement first, without leaving anything out. Then, refer to the objective the item is intended to measure and block out the one word or phrase that represents the essence of what the test taker will be expected to produce. This procedure should create a clear, meaningful, and easily scored item, and it can also be applied to writing completion items that measure information in textbooks.

Look at the first sentence in the above paragraph. It could be used directly to produce the following completion item:

> Writing an entire statement without leaving anything out at first is a good way to write a (an) _____ item.

The word *an* has been added to keep the grammar of the sentence from providing a clue to the answer. The item measures whether a test taker can name the kind of item represented by a statement from which something has been left out.

Multiple-Choice Items

The most widely used choice-type item is the multiple-choice item. There are many examples of multiple-choice items in the Appendix of this book. **Multiple-choice items** are like completion items except that, instead of a blank, they have a set of usually four potential answer choices. The actual question is commonly referred to as a **stem** and instead of having to recall or remember the right answer, in a multiple-choice item the test taker must identify or recognize the right answer by distinguishing it from the wrong answers or **distractors**. The distinction between the right answer and the distractors should be based on the instructional objective. If the objective, for example, were to identify the basic principle of Skinner's theory, reinforcement, then a possible item might be:

multiple-choice items
a type of test question where students select the best answer from a list of choices

stem
the question in a multiple-choice item

distractors
the incorrect options in multiple-choice items

© Mike Baldwin / Cornered

BALDWIN

Mike Baldwin/Cartoonstock.com

Multiple-choice items are a very common item format. How can you create multiple-choice items that are more meaningful than the one suggested in this comic?

According to Skinner, behavior increases when it is immediately followed by:

a.   *a stimulus.*

b.   *a drive.*

c.   *a reinforcer.*

d.   *another response.*

Advantages and Disadvantages

The major advantages of a multiple-choice item are the ease of scoring it, the ease of analyzing its results, and its potential use for measuring comprehension (described later in this chapter). A final advantage is its capability for testing whether students can distinguish between the correct answer and common misconceptions or erroneous lines of thought. By constructing particular answer choices, the test builder can set up the requirement to distinguish between the right answer and frequent wrong answers. Multiple-choice items also have their disadvantages. These include the following:

1. they are difficult to write because they require not only the right answer, but three or four plausible distractors;
2. if the distractors are not truly wrong, there will be more than one right answer;
3. if the distractors are obviously wrong, everyone will be able to figure out the right answer (by process of elimination); and
4. even if the item is good, some students will select the right answer by guessing.

Overcoming these disadvantages requires not only developing some skill at writing multiple-choice items, but also testing out the items and rewriting them, if necessary, on the basis of the results.

Writing the Item

A useful technique for writing a multiple-choice item is to start out by writing a statement of fact or knowledge based on an objective, just as was suggested for writing a completion item. If, for example, the objective says,

GIVEN THREE FRACTIONS, IDENTIFY THEIR LEAST COMMON DENOMINATOR

then a possible statement of knowledge would be:

THE LEAST COMMON DENOMINATOR OF ½, ¼, AND ⅙ IS 12.

The next step would be to convert this statement of knowledge into a multiple-choice test item. The item or *stem* would be:

THE LEAST COMMON DENOMINATOR OF ½, ¼, AND ⅙ IS _____

and the right answer choice is 12. All that remains is to write three or four distractors. The third rule for how not to write multiple-choice items in Box 13.4 (on page 537) says: "Don't choose distractors that are unrelated to the kinds of mistakes test takers are likely to make," which means the test builder should determine the kinds of mistakes students are likely to make and use them as a basis for constructing distractors. In calculating the least common denominator, one type of mistake students might make is to calculate a common denominator other than the least or lowest one. To test this, 24 would be a good distractor. Another common mistake might be to compute a denominator common to two of the fractions but not to the third, so 8 would be a good distractor. A third common mistake might be to assume that the largest denominator of the three given fractions will work as a common denominator, so that 6 might be a good distractor.

Try another example. If the objective were to:

IDENTIFY THE FUNCTIONS OF DIFFERENT COURTS IN THE AMERICAN SYSTEM OF JUSTICE,

one statement of fact would be:

AN APPELLATE COURT REVIEWS THE DECISIONS OF OTHER COURTS.

The item stem could then be:

WHEN A COURT IS CALLED AN APPELLATE COURT, THAT MEANS THAT IT

and the correct answer is:

REVIEWS THE DECISIONS OF OTHER COURTS.

Think of what misconceptions students might have so that they can be used to write the distractors. Students might confuse appellate courts with lower courts, which MUST HAVE A JURY and CAN CONDUCT THE ORIGINAL TRIAL, or they might confuse them with supreme courts, which CAN DECLARE LAWS UNCONSTITUTIONAL. Thus, there are three possible distractors, all of which resemble the correct answer in length and grammar and are not only plausible, but are likely mistakes. Yet all three choices are clearly wrong.

Another point about answer choices for this item must be made. It would have been equally correct to say that appellate courts HEAR APPEALS OF THE DECISIONS OF OTHER COURTS, but the word *appeals* is a clue for the "appellate" function (one word is derived from the other). The word *appeals*, therefore, is best avoided to eliminate the possibility of an extra clue.

As a final example, consider the objective below:

IDENTIFY THE FORM OF THE VERB "TO BE" THAT CORRECTLY FITS THE PRONOUN AND TENSE OF THE SENTENCE.

One statement of fact would be:

FOR THE PAST TENSE, USE "WAS" OR "HAVE BEEN" WITH "I."

Now the item can be:

WHICH SENTENCE IS CORRECT?

A right answer choice will be I WAS LATE. I HAVE BEEN LATE cannot be used as a distractor because it is also grammatically correct. But there are many common mistakes in forming the past tense of the verb "to be" that will form good distractors. For example:

I BEEN LATE.
I BE LATE.
I WERE LATE.
I IS LATE.

Being around children and knowing the speaking mistakes they make will help you construct distractors for this kind of grammar item.

When writing multiple-choice items, you should remember to:

1. start with the objective,
2. write statements of fact that fit the objective,
3. write distractors that reflect common mistakes, and
4. avoid the 13 "don'ts" listed in Box 13.4.

Other Choice-Type Items

There are three other types of choice items: *true/false* items, *other two-choice* or *classification* items, and *matching* items. The construction of each will be described briefly.

True/False Items

True/false items are statements that the test taker must judge to be either true or false. Here are some examples:

The capitol of Florida is Orlando.	TRUE	FALSE
The plural of ox is oxes.	TRUE	FALSE
The branch of government charged with making the laws is the executive.	TRUE	FALSE
Colorado produces more copper ore than any other state.	TRUE	FALSE
ACTH is a hormone secreted by the pineal gland.	TRUE	FALSE

true/false items

statements that the test taker must judge to be either true or false

Box 13.4

TAKE IT TO THE CLASSROOM

The Do's and Don'ts of Writing Multiple-Choice Items

Do's	Don'ts
Write distractors that are plausible.	Don't write distractors that are totally implausible or obviously wrong.
Write distractors that are wrong.	Don't write distractors that are actually correct.
Write distractors that represent likely mistakes.	Don't write distractors that are unrelated to the kinds of mistakes test takers are likely to make.
Make all answer choices comparable in appearance and structure.	Don't write distractors that are different from the correct answer in length or grammar.
Make all answer choices independent.	Don't write distractors that overlap one another or that overlap the correct answer.
Use common words.	Don't use words that test takers won't understand.
Use statements with only one meaning.	Don't use statements that have more than one meaning.
Write clear items that only have one correct answer to the knowledgeable student.	Don't use absolute terms such as **always**, **never**, and **all**.

Do's	Don'ts
Write short answer choices.	Don't write long answer choices.
Use words in answer choices that are as different as possible from words used in the item statement.	Don't build clues into the item statement or answer choices.
Test only one point at a time.	Don't test more than one point at a time.
Make items independent and nonoverlapping.	Don't let one item give a clue to the answer to another.
Randomize the letter of the correct choice from item to item.	Don't always assign the correct choice to the same letter.

- Based on the list above, which incorrect practice do you think teachers most likely follow when they create multiple-choice questions? Why do you think that?

All of the above items are false, but on an actual test it would be preferable to mix true items and false items together. As in writing other types of test items, begin with an objective, derive from it statements of fact, and then, in the case of true/false items, change some of the statements of fact to make them false.

True/false items usually are easy to write, at least for the measurement of recognition of facts, a use for which they are best suited. The difficulty in writing these items lies in generating plausible false statements, particularly in deciding which aspect of the fact to make false. In deciding this, just as in choosing distractors for multiple-choice items, consider the misconceptions and likely mistakes of students and embody them in the false statement. Think of a false item as a distractor.

If the statement of fact, for example, were:

FRANKLIN DELANO ROOSEVELT, IN HIS FIRST INAUGURAL SPEECH, SAID: "WE HAVE NOTHING TO FEAR BUT FEAR ITSELF."

a teacher would have to decide what the important mistake would be. Would it be (1) attributing the quote to someone else; (2) attributing someone else's quote ("blood, sweat, and tears," for example) to FDR; or (3) realizing that FDR made the fear comment but thinking he said it in his second, third, or fourth inaugural speech rather than his first? Once the important mistake has been decided, a false statement can be written, such as:

> *WINSTON CHURCHILL, AT THE START OF WORLD WAR II, SAID: "WE HAVE NOTHING TO FEAR BUT FEAR ITSELF."*

The biggest problem with true/false items, apart from their possible ambiguity, is that because there are only two answer choices the probability of guessing the correct answer is 50 percent. This probability is twice as large as for a multiple-choice item with four answer choices; moreover, a multiple-choice item tests three or four misconceptions rather than one. But multiple-choice tests also require the test builder to write three or four distractors for each item, compared to only one for a true/false item.

Other Two-Choice Items

These items are like multiple-choice items in a series but they have only two choices: a correct one and a distractor. However, in any item there may be many correct answers and many distractors. Some examples:

- Use *a* or *an* before each word: _____ cat, _____ elf, _____ arm
- Circle all the *even* numbers: 12 6 19 11 1 10 7 21 34
- Check all the cities below that are state capitols.

Pierre	St. Louis
San Francisco	Santa Fe
Milwaukee	Olympia

- Circle all the words below that are used in Skinner's theory of learning.

emotion	cognition	discrimination
reinforcement	efficacy	assimilation
extinction	contingency	generalization

This type of item, described as being in a classification format, is useful for measuring whether a student can distinguish items that fit a category (or exemplars) from items that do not fit a category (or nonexemplars). The above illustrations have (1) nouns that begin with vowels versus those that begin with consonants, (2) even numbers versus odd numbers, (3) capitols versus big cities, and (4) Skinnerian terms versus non-Skinnerian terms. Whenever the task is to determine whether students can distinguish between exemplars and nonexemplars of a given category, other two-choice items can be constructed.

Like most of the various short-answer item types, other two-choice items work best for assessing factual knowledge, but are susceptible to guessing and are often ambiguous. It is important to include in other two-choice items only terms that very clearly either fit or do not fit the classification category. In other words, (1) the classification category itself must be clear and distinct from other potentially confusable categories, and (2) the terms to be classified must be clear examples or nonexamples of that category. As in writing the other types of short-answer items, begin with the objective, such as:

GIVEN A LIST OF ORGANISMS THAT LIVE IN WATER, DISTINGUISH BETWEEN MAMMALS AND NONMAMMALS (FISH, AMPHIBIANS, AND REPTILES).

Then, produce a statement of fact, such as:

SOME MAMMALS THAT LIVE IN WATER ARE WHALES, DOLPHINS, OTTERS, AND SEALS.

Distractors, or nonmammals that live in water and that may be confused with mammals, must then be identified. They may include tuna, sharks, frogs, eels, and water moccasins. From this list of mammals and nonmammals that live in water, a two-choice item can easily be written:

Circle the Mammals Below:

OTTERS	DOLPHINS	TUNA
SHARKS	EELS	FROGS
WHALES	WATER MOCCASINS	SEALS

Remember: choices for categories and for nonexemplars should be based on the distinctions made in the objectives of the lesson. If, in the above example, the objective is to teach students to distinguish between mammals and fish only, then the nonexemplars would be limited to fish.

Matching Items

Matching items present two lists of information and have the student connect one list with the other. These often are the most difficult selection type items to construct. They are multiple stems with multiple choices, and each choice is a distractor for the other choices. Their biggest shortcoming, beyond their difficulty to write, is that as a test taker gets closer to completing the item, the number of distractors is steadily reduced, which increases the success rate of guessing. It is also difficult to write an item as complex as a matching item without giving any extra clues. Here is an example of a matching item: In items 1 through 5, match each of the following statements to a particular person:

STATEMENT	PERSONS
1. The only president to resign.	a. Hubert Humphrey
	b. John Kennedy
2. The last Republican president.	c. Jimmy Carter
	d. George Bush
3. This president was never elected.	e. Gerald Ford
	f. Ronald Reagan
4. He served two full terms as president.	g. Richard Nixon
	h. Herbert Hoover
5. He was never president.	

matching items

type of assessment that presents two lists of information and has the students connect one list with the other

The characteristics described in the item are some of the ones that are appropriate for distinguishing between these presidents. (Note: To add rigor, the teacher in this example gave three more persons than were necessary to match each statement.)

In writing a matching item, the test builder must ensure that each component deals with common elements of a *single* category (such as all presidents' characteristics). If categories are mixed, it becomes impossible to decide which choices go together. In addition, each choice must *uniquely* fit each stem, or else there will be more than one correct answer. Suppose, in the previous example, that one of the stems was "A Republican president." Because five of the choices were Republican presidents, any of them would be a correct choice. Consequently, a student could not choose *the* correct answer.

It is important, therefore, that the response choices be (1) nonoverlapping, (2) uniquely fitted to one of the stems, (3) plausible distractors to one another in terms of their connection to the other stems, (4) focused on the critical characteristics set forth in the objective, and (5) greater in number than the descriptions.

Performance Assessments

Learning Objective 5

Identify the characteristics of a performance assessment and apply that knowledge by detailing the steps involved in the creation of a performance assessment relevant to the students.

In **performance assessment,** students construct a product or demonstrate a procedure such as writing a letter, repairing an automobile engine, bisecting an angle, doing a swan dive, making a bookcase, or drawing a flag. Performance assessments can sometimes be done with paper and pencil (such as in writing a letter) but more often require different kinds of tools (such as laboratory tools in preparing a slide of a tissue specimen in a biology lab, or carpentry tools in building a bookcase). Performance testing is sometimes done by itself and sometimes done in conjunction with essay or short-answer item testing. Sometimes students are performance-tested individually and sometimes they are assessed in groups. Performance assessments are useful to teachers because they enable them to measure very complex skills. They also help increase students' interest in the skills and concepts measured by the performance assessment, because the skills and concepts are measured in ways very similar to real tasks that students perform in their lives outside of school. Most performance assessments have the following features:

1. a hands-on exercise or problem to solve (the student must actually be asked to do something, such as a construction or demonstration);
2. a material outcome or product at the end of the process (the student creates an actual product);
3. a focus on the process (the teacher must observe not only the end result or product but also how that result or product was arrived at);
4. students use specific cognitive and psychomotor skills in the performance;
5. students can self-evaluate their performance; and
6. criteria in the form of a rubric are utilized to provide feedback about the performance.

performance assessment

a type of assessment where students demonstrate learning by producing or presenting a product

Performance assessments, like building a robot, have students directly demonstrate what they know.

AP Photo/Nam Y. Huh

This section will guide your skill development in constructing and scoring performance assessments and in guiding your students to construct their own work portfolios.

Constructing a Performance Assessment

In constructing a performance assessment, the first step is to *specify the desired performance outcome*. This means writing an objective requiring an actual performance, such as a construction or demonstration. Below are some examples:

- Construct a collage that expresses how you feel about the environment.
- Demonstrate a procedure for baking a lemon meringue pie.
- Construct a picture of a pueblo that was used by the Hopi Indians.
- Demonstrate a procedure for tuning a piano.

All of the above examples require hands-on performance, yield a product (a collage, a pie, a picture, a tuned piano), and make use of a process (finding, selecting, cutting, arranging, and gluing, in the case of the collage).

The second step is to *specify the conditions*, which is the set of givens, or situations, under which the student will attempt to produce the desired performance. Here are the test situations, or givens, for the above examples:

- Collage: given a group of specific magazines, a large piece of fiber paper, scissors, glue
- Pie: given all necessary ingredients (e.g., flour, fruit, sugar), measuring implements, cookware, oven
- Drawing: given paper, ruler, and crayons

Virtual Psychology Lab

Are you concerned about the fairness and accuracy of the grades you will assign to your students? When you go to the *Personality Test Virtual Psychology Lab,* you will have an opportunity to participate in a classic experiment in psychology where you can see how easy our assessment of a concept can be influenced. Go to CengageBrain.com to access this Virtual Psychology Lab in the Education CourseMate.

- Piano tuning: given an out-of-tune piano and a set of tuning forks

The third step is to *specify the response instructions,* such as the following:

- Show all your work.
- Don't leave anything out.
- The finished pie should be tasty.
- You will get 10 points for creativeness and 10 points for technical accuracy.
- The display should be able to be mounted on the wall.
- You have 30 minutes to complete the task.

If there are any particular performance requirements, they should be specified as part of the response instructions.

The fourth step is to *specify process and product criteria* in the form of a *performance rubric.* The rubric will be used to score the performance assessment by providing a basis for judging both the performance and the product.

These steps are summarized for you in the *Concept Review* in Table 13.2. The next subsection will explain more about rubrics.

Scoring Performance Assessments

An aid to scoring a performance assessment reliably is the rubric. When scoring a performance using a rubric, you should be aware of potential errors that can occur

CONCEPT REVIEW Table 13.2
How Do Teachers Create Performance Assessments?

STEPS	TEACHER ACTION	CLASSROOM EXAMPLE
1st	Specify the desired performance outcome	Students will create a science project that demonstrates the impact of using an inclined plane, lever, pulley, and wheel on work
2nd	Specify the conditions	Science project: will be presented on tri-fold poster
3rd	Specify the response instructions	Students will stand by their tri-fold poster and answer questions about their results
4th	Specify process and product criteria	The science project will be scored on the quality of the scientific hypothesis/prediction; how clearly organized the data are; the degree to which the conclusions are interpreted given the data collected; the quality of the future research questions recommended; and the clarity of the verbal explanation of the project and results

(Meier, Rich, & Cady, 2006). Again, the last step in constructing a performance assessment is specifying process and product criteria. Operationally, these criteria are set forth in a **rubric,** a list of every feature or characteristic of the performance process or resulting product that must be observed in order to certify the quality of the performance. The rubric emphasizes for the teacher what to look for and how many points to award if it occurs. Breaking down the scoring process this way tends to make it more reliable. Detailed scoring criteria are specified in advance, and points are awarded based on the extent to which each individual criterion is met.

In other words, a rubric is a list of prespecified behaviors for evaluating the process of performing a given task successfully. To construct a rubric, you, as the teacher, must first separate the correct performance into its component behaviors and then list them. Then you mark all the checklist behaviors that you observe and use them as the basis for scoring the performance.

Imagine a performance for fourth graders was, after they completed a unit on trees, to create a poster that contained (1) pictures of local trees and their leaves, (2) information about trees in terms of their contributions to ecology and quality of life, and (3) recommendations to help protect trees. An example rubric for this poster is provided in Figure 13.1.

rubric

a list of every feature or characteristic of the performance process or resulting product that must be observed in order to certify the quality of the performance

FIGURE 13.1

Criterion	Points Possible	Points Earned
At least three different types of trees are drawn and labeled	10	
Each type of tree is described	10	
Value of trees is described.	5	
Ways to protect trees are described	5	
Neatness	5	
Total Points Possible = 35		
Total Points Obtained =		
Percent Score = Obtained / Possible × 100 =		
Comments:		

Rubric for Poster on Trees

Think It Over

as a LEARNER | What is a performance assessment? How are performance assessments scored?

as a TEACHER | Can you think of a hypothetical example of a situation in your future classroom where performance assessments might be a more useful source of evidence than traditional assessment?

portfolio assessment

the evaluation of a collection of student's work over a period of time

artifact

any work produced by a student

Effective teachers creatively use instructional technology, like helping students create electronic portfolios.

You would use the rubric to evaluate each student's poster by checking whether or not each of the criteria was met. Hence, a performance rubric is a technique for specifying, in detail, the criteria by which a performance is to be evaluated. In Figure 13.1, criteria are scored on either a 10-point scale or a 5-point scale and partial credit may be given.

Portfolio Assessment

Portfolio assessment is the evaluation of a collection of student's work over a period of time. A portfolio often includes a variety of artifacts that are evidence of how a student has mastered learning objectives. An **artifact** is any work produced by a student. Artifacts placed in a portfolio can include things like student essays, projects, science lab analyses, drawings, pictures, and recordings.

It is important to recognize that a portfolio is not just meant to warehouse a student's work. It is intended to demonstrate a student's learning. There are numerous ways a portfolio can be managed and stored. For example, a kindergarten teacher may keep all of the student portfolios in one place in his or her classroom. Electronic portfolios might also be created. These can be accessed by parents and caregivers through the Internet (Fahey, Lawrence, & Paratore, 2007). Regardless of the format, all portfolios should be part of systematic assessment program that has clear instructional goals (Niguidula, 2005).

Portfolios typically accomplish one of two classroom assessment purposes: They either accentuate a student's best work relative to a learning objective, or they show how a student has developed relative to a learning objective (Nitko & Brookhart, 2007). For teachers and students to use portfolios effectively, they should be sure to designate the purpose of the portfolio and establish standards for selecting and evaluating entries into the portfolio (Linn, Miller, & Gronlund, 2005).

Creatas Images/Creatas/Jupiter Images

Determining what to include and what to exclude from a portfolio will take careful consideration by you and the student. It is important to give the student an opportunity to reflect over what he or she has learned from creating the artifact and ways that the artifact could be changed. Some researchers recommend having a cover sheet for each artifact in the portfolio containing (1) the student's reasons for choosing to include it, (2) a description of the artifact, (3) a description of what was done well, and (4) a description of what could be improved (Linn, Miller, & Gronlund, 2005).

T e a c h S o u r c e V i d e o C a s e

Portfolio Assessment: Elementary Classroom

In this video segment, you'll see how Mr. Frederick Won Park helps his students create a writing reflection that they will place in their portfolio. In this video, you will see how he works with his students to create artifacts and then how he gets his students to reflect about what they learned from creating the artifact and why the artifact was meaningful. He then helps the students create new learning goals, and the class begins to work on new artifacts.

After viewing the video case, consider what you have just watched about portfolio assessment and answer the questions below.

1. What do you think would be most challenging about using portfolio assessment in your class?
2. In the video case, Mr. Park taught the children to use self-reflection. Do you think this was a valuable skill to teach? If so, how might you try to teach and model the skill for your class?

You can view the video case at the Education CourseMate. Go to:
CengageBrain.com

Learning Objective 6

Demonstrate procedures for evaluating the content validity of a test and discuss factors that make tests valid and those that make them invalid.

Evaluating the Validity of Classroom Assessments

Classroom assessments are used to make important judgments about students and their performance. Results are used to determine what skills and content students have mastered, to recommend or require additional assignments, and to assign grades. Teachers should not want to make such important decisions on the basis of faulty results. They should build the best assessments they can, and they should also examine the results on those assessments as a way of improving them. Teachers need to use their assessment results not only to evaluate their students but to evaluate their assessments as well.

No measurement is perfect; each one contains errors. If a test is too hard, you may erroneously conclude from its results that students have learned little, and as a result give them low grades. Conversely, a test that is too easy may result in grade inflation. Because item-writing is a task that requires skill and practice, items may be written that have nothing to do with the lesson, that are ambiguous, that have more than one right answer, or that have an obvious right answer. Bad items introduce error into a test and cause you to make mistaken judgments. The two main criteria you should use to evaluate a test are validity and reliability. In this section, we offer you guidelines for constructing valid assessment tools.

How Can a Test's Validity Be Determined?

The first criterion of a quality assessment is *validity*. **Validity** is based on *whether the assessment measures what it is supposed to measure* or whether data from the assessment can be used to draw conclusions based on the test's intended purpose. So it is not whether a test is valid or not, but whether the conclusion we draw from the results of the test is appropriate (Popham, 2006b). How can the judgment of what an assessment is supposed to measure be made so that its validity can be determined? The answer is based on an examination of the *objectives* for the lessons that have been taught and for which students are being assessed. There should be considerable alignment between objectives, instruction, and testing. This alignment is represented in Figure 13.2.

An assessment should fit or match the instructional objectives (just as the instruction should fit or match those same objectives) because that is what the assessment is *supposed* to measure (Sireci, 1998).

The measure of a test's validity is the degree to which its test items fit or match the objectives of the lessons they are testing. By laying test items alongside objectives, the teacher can determine whether there are (1) test items to measure each objective (so that no objective goes unmeasured) and (2) objectives to match each test item (so that no test item measures something other than what was supposed to have been taught).

validity

the degree to which an assessment measures what it is intended to measure

F I G U R E   1 3 . 2

The Alignment Between Objectives, Instruction, and Assessment

In doing this matching, teachers must take specific considerations into account. These considerations are described below.

1. *Do items that measure a particular objective actually require students to carry out the action specified by that action verb in that objective?*

    If, for example, an objective uses the verb *identify*, test items measuring that objective should require the student to select the right answer, as in a multiple-choice item. If an objective uses *state* or *name* or *list*, test items should call for this behavior, as in a completion item. The verb *describe* would require a free response as on an essay item, and *demonstrate* or *construct* would require actual performances, as in a performance assessment. Valid items require the same kind of performance specified in the objectives as they measure. Items that require performances that differ from those called for in the objectives they measure are invalid.

2. *Do items that measure a particular objective cover the same content called for in the objective?*

    To be valid, test items must correspond in content to the objective they measure. The fact, concept, skill, or rule named in the objective must be the one measured by the test item. The correspondence must be as exact as possible. If, for example, the objective says "identify mammals," then the items must measure the identification of mammals, not the identification of fish or the distinction between potentially confusable mammals and fish.

3. *Do items that measure a particular objective provide the same conditions and require the same scoring criteria as those called for in that objective?*

    Objectives written in long form contain conditions and degree. The *conditions* indicate what materials and information the students must be given to perform the objective. The *degree* indicates how that performance will be evaluated. Valid test items provide students with the "givens" called for in the objective they measure, and they are scored according to the criteria called for in the objective they measure. If the objective says, "Given a list containing the names of fish and fishlike mammals" that list must appear in the item in order for it to be valid. If the objective indicates that "students' descriptive responses will include mention of the differences in breathing and in bone structure," then the scoring key for that item must include that description in order for the item to be valid.

4. *Does the number of items that measure a particular objective accurately reflect the relative importance of that objective?*

    All objectives are not equally important. An objective's importance is reflected in the amount of instructional time devoted to teaching it. You might spend two or three class periods on an important objective but only a single class period on a less important objective. A valid test should contain a minimum of two items per objective for the least important objectives and more than two items as a function of the importance of the objective. An objective three times as important, for example, would have six items testing it, in contrast to two for the objectives of lesser importance.

With these four considerations in mind, you can set out to create a table of specifications. A **table of specifications** shows which concepts and skills you have included on a test and how many items will measure each concept and skill. In a classroom focused on student learning, giving students tables of specifications for classroom assessments can help learners determine during instruction and before assessment where they need to focus their efforts.

Imagine you just finished teaching a social studies unit on the deserts of Africa. You started with a list of seven objectives and taught all of them to your students. You and the class learned about (1) the location of the deserts, (2) their names, (3) the plants that grow there, (4) the animals that live there, (5) how the people there satisfy their basic needs, (6) what it is like to grow up there, and (7) the culture of the people who live there.

You constructed a test for measuring the unit objectives on African deserts. Then you matched up the test items to the list of objectives to see where there was and was not correspondence. Figure 13.3 shows this for two examples, as it might be done for two tests covering the seven objectives. The example at the top of Figure 13.3 shows that the test in question has high validity. It has met all validity criteria in that (1) the content of all objectives has been measured, (2) all items measure objectives, (3) all items fit the action, conditions, and criteria called for by the objective they measure, and (4) the number of items per objective fits the relative importance of that objective. The test measured in the top half of Figure 13.3 fits its objectives. By contrast, the example table of specifications at the bottom of Figure 13.3 shows a lack of correspondence between objectives and test items. One objective (#2) has not been measured at all. Moreover, one item fits the content of an objective (#4) but not the action of that objective. Finally, the correspondence between the number of items per objective and the importance of each objective is not exact. Objective 3 has been overmeasured by one item and objectives 5 and 6 undermeasured by one item each. The test measured in the bottom of Figure 13.3 lacks validity and the teacher should revise it to improve the correspondence to its objectives.

What Makes Tests Invalid?

Three factors that can make tests invalid are described below. You should avoid these pitfalls when creating your checklists.

Testing What Was Never Taught

At the two extremes of achievement testing are "teaching for the test" and "testing what was never taught." A valid achievement test is one that tests what was taught, with both instructional content and test items a function of the same set of objectives. However, although based on the same objectives, a test must in some respects be independent of what was taught. On a test, students must demonstrate their ability to transfer or apply what was learned to unfamiliar material. Learning must have taken place prior to testing, but the test items on which that learning is to be demonstrated must be new. Those test items must not have been seen or practiced during instruction.

Teachers may occasionally feel a mischievous urge to spring some surprises in a test, but too many surprises will result in a test that has little to do with what was

table of specifications
a table that shows the concepts and skills on a test and the number of items that measure each concept and skill

FIGURE 13.3

High Validity

Objectives for Unit on Deserts of Africa Given a map of North Africa, students can		Units of Importance*					
		1	2	3	4	5	6
1	Mark in the location of three major deserts	◉	◉				
2	Recall and write in the names of these deserts	◉	◉				
3	Identify indigenous plant life	◉	◉				
4	Identify indigenous animal life	◉	◉				
5	Describe how humans satisfy their basic needs there	◉	◉	◉			
6	Describe what it is like to grow up there	◉	◉	◉	◉		
7	Describe the culture (that is, the rules of getting along together)	◉	◉	◉			

Low Validity

Objectives for Unit on Deserts of Africa Given a map of North Africa, students can		Units of Importance*					
		1	2	3	4	5	6
1	Mark in the location of three major deserts	◉	◉				
2	Recall and write in the names of these deserts	X	X				
3	Identify indigenous plant life	◉	◉	◉			
4	Identify indigenous animal life	◉	●				
5	Describe how humans satisfy their basic needs there	◉	◉	X			
6	Describe what it is like to grow up there	◉	◉	◉	X		
7	Describe the culture (that is, the rules of getting along together)	◉	◉	◉			

* Based on class time spent on each.

◉ Single test item or point of credit on a test item that measures a given objective.

○ Test item that does not measure a given objective.

X Given objective for which test item is missing.

● Given objective for which test item measures wrong action.

Two Examples of Tables of Specifications

taught. A test need not be mundane or ordinary; it can be creative; and students must not be shown the test items in advance. But students' instructional experiences should bear directly on the material and skills to be covered on the test or it cannot be considered a content-valid measure of what students have learned.

Failing to Test What Was Taught

Testing what was never taught is testing performance on objectives that are new and different from those on which the lesson was based. The reciprocal of this testing what was never taught is failing to test what was taught. It does not matter what the objectives of testing are if they are not even measured. If a test is given at the completion of instruction, and the items test in whole or in part what was never taught (or new objectives), then there will be less room to test the instructional objectives that were actually taught. The solution is to use the instructional objectives to build the test so that no instructional objective goes unmeasured.

Bias

Sometimes, test items that appear to measure performance on instructional objectives actually do not. They may measure how well students read; how familiar they are with white, middle-class culture; or how closely their outside interests correspond to the context of the test items. If test items are written with a context that goes beyond the specifics of the objective they are measuring, performance on them may be the result of bias. **Bias** represents a relative advantage or disadvantage of test takers based on some lasting characteristic they have that is unrelated and irrelevant to the purpose of the test and the test's objectives. For example:

- A test item that uses stocks and bonds as a context may be biased against children from less privileged families. A test item that uses city streets may be biased against rural dwellers.
- A test item that uses unnecessarily "big" words or irrelevant technical terms may be biased against readers with smaller vocabularies. A test item that uses unrelated facts or abstractions may be biased against test takers possessing less general knowledge.

Teachers must make every effort to avoid introducing any unnecessary bias. The context should be made general enough and the wording simple enough for all students to understand. In this way, the item will measure only what it is intended

bias

represents a relative advantage or disadvantage based on a characteristic that is unrelated and irrelevant to the purpose of the assessment

Think It Over

| as a LEARNER | What is test validity? |
| as a TEACHER | How can classroom teachers help to ensure that their tests are valid? |

CONCEPT REVIEW TABLE 13.3

How Do Teachers Evaluate the Validity of Assessments?

- Classroom assessments should be used to evaluate students' learning and to evaluate the quality of the assessments.

- Recognize that no classroom assessment is perfect, each contains error.

- Assessments should be linked to the instructional goals of the lesson.

- Assessments should be fair representations of what was taught.

- Classroom assessments should not be biased.

to measure, or its objective. The concept review in Table 13.3 summarizes main ideas for you to remember about evaluating the validity of assessment tools.

Learning Objective 7

Explain procedures for improving the reliability of test scoring.

Evaluating the Reliability of Classroom Assessments

If an assessment does not provide a reliable picture of what students have learned, then those students who have come to every class, paid attention, completed the assignments, and prepared for the assessment may not earn higher scores than students who have done none of these things. Failure of an assessment to distinguish between constructive learning behavior and its absence casts a great shadow on the educational process.

Thus, in addition to validity, another criterion of a good assessment is *reliability*. **Reliability** is based on *whether an assessment measures something accurately or consistently* (Tuckman, 1988). Regardless of what quality an assessment measures, it must measure it in a way that reflects as closely as possible the degree to which it is present in the learner. In other words, the evaluation of student performance must correspond as closely as possible to the *true* or actual amount.

Technically, an assessment's reliability is based on the correspondence of the scores it measures to true or actual scores, but this correspondence is hard to

reliability

the consistency of assessment results

determine directly because it is not possible to know the true scores. One way to overcome this problem would be to give the same assessment over and over to the same students and actually see how much their scores varied from setting to setting, but this is obviously impractical. While no assessment can be perfect, meaning that no assessment can measure every true score with exact precision, as a teacher you can be familiar with the factors that make your classroom tests and assessments more reliable. Then you can use those ideas to try to construct and score assessments more effectively.

What Makes Tests Unreliable?

In order to create more reliable tests, the test builder must identify the factors that affect test reliability. These are described below.

Number of Test Items

The more items, the greater the sample of student performance and thereby the greater the reliability of the assessment. Evaluation of performance to determine knowledge of an objective would be much less accurate on a single item than on 10 items. Of course, there is a limit to the number of test items students can complete in a given period, but within limits, the teacher can increase a test's reliability by adding items.

Item Difficulty

Poorly written items may turn out to be too easy or too hard. When students can determine the answer to an item from the item itself, then virtually all of them will get the item right. A whole test made up of such items will be very

Assessments should be challenging to students, not too easy or too difficult.

unreliable. The teacher cannot gain an accurate picture of what students know if they can all figure out the right answers from the items themselves. The same can be said of items that are too hard. For example, when items have more than one acceptable answer, students will have to guess at which answer is right, thereby making the test result an inaccurate picture of what students know. By writing high-quality items of moderate difficulty and not including too many items that are excessively easy or difficult, teachers can improve the reliability of their tests.

Conditions of Assessment

If the room in which the assessment is given is hot or noisy or poorly lighted, the accuracy of the assessment as a measure of individual performance may suffer. Assessment conditions should be kept as constant and comfortable as possible across all administrations.

Conditions of Scoring

On tests that require scoring judgments, such as essay tests, there are many factors that may affect the accuracy of the results. Inconsistencies in the scorer or judge brought on by fatigue, biases for and against particular students, and changes in the scoring criteria will all have an adverse affect on reliability. Scoring criteria and model answers should be developed in advance, and multiple judges or multiple scorings should be used to overcome this problem.

Building More Reliable Tests

To build more reliable tests, you should strive to:

- include enough test items (to combat the effects of individual item inaccuracy and guessing);
- write high-quality items that follow the rules of item writing covered in this chapter;
- write items of intermediate difficulty, avoiding writing items that seem too hard or too easy;
- administer tests consistently and under comfortable conditions; and
- when scoring requires judgment, use preset scoring criteria, score all tests twice, and score without seeing the student's name.

Think It Over

as a LEARNER	What is reliability?
as a TEACHER	What are some methods teachers could utilize to increase the reliability of their classroom assessments?

SUMMING IT UP

Describe the procedures involved in making a content outline and preparing instructional objectives, and discuss how these tools helps teachers create assessments that increase student learning.

The first step in constructing a test is to make a **content outline** or list of concepts, ideas, and skills covered in the instructional segment or unit that the test is intended to measure. Teachers normally do this prior to teaching the unit. The second step is to prepare instructional objectives, or statements of intended student outcomes in measurable or observable form. (The key element of the objective is the action verb, which helps provide the basis for the selection of the proper test-item form.) Teachers often prepare these prior to instruction as well.

Learning Objective 1

Key Concepts:

assessment (p. 517);
content outline (p. 518);
instructional objective (p. 520);
traditional assessment, constructed-response items, selected-response items (p. 521).

Demonstrate how the higher cognitive processes of application, analysis, synthesis, and evaluation can be utilized to create high-quality essay items.

Essay items are used to measure **application**, or the ability to solve an unfamiliar problem correctly by applying or using the correct abstraction (abstractions may be ideas, methods, rules, principles, and so on). Writing the item means identifying or creating a real world situation and then making up a problem within that situation to be solved. Essay items also measure **analysis**, or the ability to break down materials into constituent elements, relationships, or organizational principles. In writing these items, teachers must determine the material or experience they want analyzed and present it to the students along with any special response instructions. Essay items can be used to measure **synthesis**, or the putting together of elements to form a unique whole. Synthesis is a creative and inventive process and, as such, has some unique testing requirements. It should be measured without either time or information-source constraints. Essay items can also measure **evaluation**, the ability to make judgments about the value (accuracy, effectiveness, or satisfaction) of some work or method using either internal (e.g., logic) or external (e.g., comparison with other work) standards.

Learning Objective 2

Key Concepts:

essay items, application (p. 525);
analysis (p. 526);
synthesis (p. 527);
evaluation, formative evaluations, summative evaluations (p. 528).

Distinguish between criterion point scoring and holistic methods of scoring essay items and attach importance to the practice of scoring blind.

Essay-test responses may actually be scored one of two ways. In criterion point scoring, specific scoring criteria are listed on a scoring sheet, the essay response is evaluated on each criterion, and points are awarded for each evaluation. The

Learning Objective 1

Key Concepts:

scoring blind (p. 531).

points are then added up to arrive at the total score for the essay. In holistic scoring, sample responses for each scoring grade—A, B, C, D, F—are created or identified and then each essay response is compared to each model to yield a grade.

<table>
<tr><td>

Learning Objective 4

Key Concepts:

completion items (p. 532);
multiple-choice items,
stem, distractors (p. 533);
true/false items (p. 536);
matching items (p. 540).

</td><td>

Identify advantages and disadvantages of and techniques for writing quality constructed-response and selection-response items.

Next, the test builder must decide the type and number of items to write. There should be at least two items per objective, and, at most, as many as can reasonably be answered in the allotted time. **Completion** items are single-sentence questions or fill-ins for which a free-choice word or phrase answer must be supplied. No answer choices are given; test-takers must *recall* the correct answer. **Multiple-choice** items are stems with a set of four or five answer choices, one of which is correct. The other, wrong answer choices are called distractors. Test takers must **recognize** the correct answer. **True/false** items are statements or misstatements of fact that the test taker judges to be true or false. These items are easy to write but also easy to answer by guessing, because the test taker has a 50–50 chance of being right. **Other two-choice items** help a teacher determine if a student can determine if a concept fits a particular category or not. **Matching items** present two lists of information and have the student connect one list with the other.

</td></tr>
<tr><td>

Learning Objective 5

Key Concepts:

performance assessment
(p. 541);
rubric (p. 544);
portfolio assessment,
artifact (p. 545).

</td><td>

Identify the characteristics of a performance assessment and apply that knowledge by detailing the steps involved in the creation of a performance assessment relevant to the students.

A **performance assessment** is one in which students actually have to construct a product or demonstrate a procedure, rather than just write about it. These classroom assessments require a hands-on problem to solve, a material outcome or product, a solution process the teacher can access, the use of specific skills, and the application of both knowledge and comprehension. In constructing a performance assessment, teachers must specify (1) the desired performance outcome, (2) the test situation, (3) the response instructions, and (4) the process and product criteria. Performance assessments can be reliably scored if the teacher first prepares a **rubric** that lists each criterion by which the performance of a particular task is judged. The rubric lists necessary behaviors or necessary features of the appropriate performance, and the teacher checks all that are observed in each student's performance to produce a performance score. **Portfolio assessment** is the evaluation of a collection of student's work over a period of time. A portfolio often includes a variety of **artifacts** that are evidence of how a student has mastered learning objectives.

</td></tr>
</table>

Demonstrate procedures for evaluating the content validity of a test and discuss factors that make tests valid and those that make them invalid.

Tests can be evaluated in terms of their validity—the extent to which they measure what they are intended to measure. A test's validity may be determined relative to its objectives, if that is what the test is intended to measure. If objectives are used to guide both what is taught and what is tested, then the resulting test is likely to be valid in that it will differentiate between students who have learned the lessons and those who have not.

Learning Objective 6

Key Concepts:

validity (p. 547);
table of specifications (p. 549);
bias (p. 551).

Explain procedures for improving the reliability of test scoring.

Another basis for evaluating a test is its **reliability** or its accuracy or consistency across items. Technically, reliability means the extent to which measured scores on a test are consistent. The factors that tend to affect a test's reliability are (1) its length, or number of items; (2) the difficulty level of its items; (3) the conditions of test administration; and (4) the conditions of scoring. Writing a large enough number of high-quality test items that are consistent with one another and of intermediate difficulty is likely to result in a reliable test.

Learning Objective 7

Key Concepts:

reliability (p. 552).

Visit the Education CourseMate for *Educational Psychology* to access study tools and resources including the Virtual Psychology Labs, TeachSource Video Cases, chapter web links, tutorial quizzes, glossary flashcards, and more. Go to CengageBrain.com to register using your access code.

The Iowa Tests of Basic Skills (ITBS) published by The Riverside Company is a widely used standardized achievement test for Kindergarten through 8th grade students.

Volvo Effect

says that because standardized test scores are so highly correlated with parents' wealth, you might easily look at what car parents drive to determine how likely a given student would be to do well on a standardized tests

standardized tests

published tests that teachers administer and interpret in a customary and established way

achievement tests

tests intended to measure what students have learned in school as a result of instruction

Before we delve into examples of interpreting and converting test scores and techniques commonly used with standardized test results, it is helpful to understand what standardized tests are and to identify their principal characteristics.

Achievement and Aptitude Tests

Standardized tests are most commonly achievement tests. **Achievement tests** are tests intended to measure what students have learned in school as a result of instruction. They are designed to measure achievement based on what students are expected to learn. Teachers have the responsibility of properly administering and interpreting standardized achievement tests. There are other types of standardized assessments teachers need to be familiar with; intelligence tests are most common and are called aptitude tests. An **aptitude test** is an examination of an individual's mental ability and is intended to predict how a person might perform in an educational setting.

The content of standardized achievement tests may not perfectly fit the curriculum taught at each and every school. Since standardized tests are given across many school districts, nationwide, their content cannot in every instance fit the curriculum as closely as do the teachers' own tests. Standardized tests must be designed to fit a fictitious or ideal national curriculum (often based on textbooks) and so will overlap individual curricula somewhat but not perfectly (Freeman, Kuhs, Porter, Floden, Schmidt, & Schwille, 1983). However, efforts are being made to improve the alignment between standardized assessments and state learning objectives. One approach to improve the standardized assessment process is through the use of an innovative technology called **computer adaptive assessment**. These tests are administered by a computer instead of the more common paper-and-pencil-approach. As a student answers a question on a computer adaptive assessment, the test automatically adjusts to his of her responses to provide questions that more closely match the student's current understanding. One excellent example of this is the Measures of Academic Progress (MAP) tests created by the Northwest Evaluation Association. The results of MAP tests can be compared to previous scores students earn to determine the academic growth a student has made.

The items on standardized achievement tests have been tested and refined. Created by professional test-item writers, the questions on standardized tests have been tried out (field-tested), reviewed for possible bias, and revised when necessary. As a result of this process, these tests have higher reliability than teacher-built tests. In fact, the reliabilities of these tests are almost always between 0.90 and 0.97 (out of a possible 1.00). Hence, these tests yield highly consistent results.

The instructions for administration of these tests are formalized. The way these tests are administered is as standardized as the tests themselves (another reason they are called "standardized" tests.) To help standardize the administration of these assessments, instructions for administration are written out in detail.

Many are accompanied by national norms for score interpretation. The norming process is described in detail later in this chapter, however, it is important to know that before commercially available, standardized tests typically are administered to a large, national sample of students—broadly representative of the population—who serve as a **norming group**. The test builders convert the raw scores to norm-referenced scores by using these norming groups for comparison purposes. (Local norms are also often provided for comparison purposes). These tests typically are scored by the testing companies and the results are provided on forms or printouts (an example is available later in this chapter). Manuals are also available from the testing companies that containing norms tables that can be used for purposes of score conversion and interpretation, based on the results of the norming group.

Test Takers' Rights

If teachers are going to use the results of standardized assessments to improve the academic achievement of their students, they must (1) ethically prepare students to take the assessments, (2) administer the tests in an appropriate manner, and (3) correctly interpret the tests results so that students and caregivers can meaningfully utilize the information. One of the most important ways that you as a teaching professional can participate in the standardized testing process is to ensure that these three processes are guided by the use of professional ethics and guidelines. The American Psychological Association (1999) developed a list of rights that test takers have. As a professional, you have an obligation to make sure that test takers receive these rights. A brief summary of the rights appears in Table 14.1.

aptitude test

an examination of an individual's mental ability intended to predict how a person might perform in an educational setting

computer adaptive assessment

tests administered by a computer instead of the more common paper-and pencil-approach

norming group

a large, random, nationally representative collection of scores on a norm referenced test; the norming group is the benchmark that student scores are compared to on the test

CONCEPT REVIEW TABLE 14.1
The American Psychological Association (1999) List of Rights

1. Test takers have the right to be informed of their rights and responsibilities as test takers, it is normally the responsibility of the individual who administers a test (or the organization that prepared the test) to inform test takers of these rights and responsibilities.

2. Test takers have the right to be treated with courtesy, respect, and impartiality, regardless of their age, disability, ethnicity, gender, national origin, race, religion, sexual orientation, or other personal characteristics.

3. Test takers have the right to be tested with measures that meet professional standards that are appropriate for the test use and the test taker.

(Continued)

CONCEPT REVIEW TABLE 14.1
(continued)

The American Psychological Association (1999) List of Rights

4. Test takers have the right to be informed, prior to testing, about the test's purposes, the nature of the test, whether test results will be reported to the test takers, and the planned use of the results (when not in conflict with the testing purposes).

5. Test takers have a right to be informed in advance when the test will be administered, if and when test results will be available, and if there is a fee for testing services that the test takers are expected to pay.

6. Test takers have the right to have their tests administered and interpreted by appropriately trained individuals.

7. Test takers have the right to be informed about why they are asked to take particular tests, if a test is optional, and what the consequences are should they choose not to complete the test.

8. Test takers have a right to receive a written or oral explanation of their test results within a reasonable amount of time after testing and in commonly understood terms.

9. Test takers have the right to have the results of tests kept confidential to the extent allowed by law.

10. Test takers have the right to present concerns about the testing process and to receive information about procedures that will be used to address such concerns.

Cautions with Standardized Testing

In a short amount of time, you will begin your teaching career. You will probably have the responsibility of administering one or more standardized tests each academic year and then help students and parents understand the results. Some teachers and parents feel that America's preoccupation with testing and test preparation results in students being overtested. However, despite warnings from concerned educators, the American public has reported that it supports the use of standardized tests in schools (Phelps, 2006).

Reflecting a different point of view, a survey conducted in North Carolina found teachers saying that the classroom learning environment could be improved through less standardized assessment (Dagenhart, O'Connor, Petty, & Day, 2005). Moreover, the Association for Childhood Education International (ACEI) is opposed to the use

of standardized assessment in the primary grades (Solley, 2007). Other researchers like Wolf (2007) argue that frequent testing of students serves to improve their learning and long-term life outcomes, and Cankoy and Tut (2005) found that the students who put the most time into learning test preparation scored higher on assessments. (Again, essential controversies about standardized tests are summarized in Box 14.1.)

Regardless of your feelings about standardized testing, administering and interpreting them is an important job and needs to be taken seriously because of the potential impact the results can have on your students. While tests can provide information that can help you diagnose a student's academic strengths and deficits, you should also recognize some implications and issues with standardized assessment.

Standardized assessment has the potential to narrow the curriculum a teacher concentrates on. This can happen when a teacher only covers objectives assessed on the test, while ignoring or minimizing other important academic objectives. Some researchers also argue that standardized tests cause educators to focus on academic goals while putting less emphasis on the emotional and social development of students (Barrier-Ferreira, 2008). Narrowing can also occur on a school-wide basis because standardized tests tend to focus on only certain subjects, like English and mathematics, while ignoring other areas like history and art.

Testing can also impact how content is taught in a class. One analysis of the assessment practices in England, Turkey, Germany, Singapore, Japan, and China and another

CONCEPT REVIEW TABLE 14.3
Potential Issues with Standardized Tests

- Standardized tests can narrow the curriculum a teacher focuses on and impact how the content is taught.

- Standardized tests have the potential to be biased against students from different cultures and against students whose first language is not English.

- Standardized tests are sometimes inappropriately used as the single source of data to make critical decisions about students.

- Standardized tests have the potential to be politicized and may be used inappropriately to alter decision-making power at a school or label some neighborhoods as more desirable to live in than others.

- Standardized teacher tests might limit the number of minority teachers.

administrators, teachers, and other school stakeholders and makes it easier to manage and control them. Whether there are political intentions with the wide use of standardized tests or not, it does seem that standardized assessment removes control from local school systems and places it in the hands of state and national government (Hursh, 2005). The publishing of standardized assessment also has other implications. Realtors, for example, have used the published scores to illustrate the desirability of various neighborhoods (Simmons, 2004).

Standardized tests are also used by some states as part of the teacher certification process, despite the minimal amount of data that supports a direct connection between teachers' standardized test scores and the quality of classroom performance (Guisbond & Neill, 2004). The PRAXIS I assessment is the most commonly used basic skills assessment for preservice teachers, with more than 100,000 taking it in the 2004–2005 academic year at an approximate cost of $18 million (Wakefield, 2007). Because of a connection between minority students' passing the PRAXIS I assessment and their SAT scores (Bennett, McWhorter, & Kuykendall, 2006), standardized teacher tests might limit the number of minority teachers. Table 14.3 presents a *Concept Review* of issues to be aware of in using standardized tests with your students.

Learning Objective 2

Explain criterion-referenced and norm-referenced test interpretation, mean, median, mode, range, and standard deviation as tools to interpret and understand student data.

Why Do Test Scores Require Interpretation?

A test score is just a number or a set of numbers. Test scores tell us little about a student's academic performance unless some basis is used for determining the test scores' meaning. Test interpretation is the process that helps educators understand the information a test score conveys. Test scores must be accurately interpreted to determine what they indicate about the characteristics or capabilities of the test takers.

The score a student or test taker receives on a test is called a **raw score**. The raw score represents the number of items answered correctly on the test. Questions on standardized tests often are referred to by test publishers as **items**. But, what do these raw scores actually mean? Suppose a student received 60 raw score points on a standardized algebra test. How would a mathematics teacher interpret that result? Is it high? Is it low? Does it reflect competence or mastery? Is it average? Is it acceptable? If this standardized test is an end-of-course exam, should the student pass the course or receive extra help from the teacher and peers? Without a basis for interpreting the test score, the results are difficult to use for any educationally useful purpose.

As a teacher, you need to relate the test scores to reference points or benchmarks that can be used to give the test scores meaning, or to which the test scores can be compared for interpretation. There are two such referencing systems available. One is called criterion-referencing and the other norm-referencing. Criterion-referencing evaluates raw scores based on pre-established criteria and norm-referencing compares a test taker's performance on an assessment to the performance of a group of individuals who previously took the assessment. Criterion-referencing, the simpler of the two approaches, will be described first in the next section.

Criterion-Referenced Test Interpretation

As the name implies, **criterion-referenced** test interpretation means test scores are interpreted in terms of what proportion of the pre-established criteria or content have been correctly answered by the test taker. Criterion-referenced tests indicate how well students are performing relative to a specific group of educational goals included in the local or state curriculum (Bond, 1996). The results of these assessments give teachers information regarding how well students are learning the curriculum and what areas of the curriculum teachers and students might need to review.

Think It Over

as a LEARNER — Have you ever had the experience of looking at standardized assessment reports and not knowing how to interpret them? If so, describe it.

as a TEACHER — What are the possible benefits for the classroom teacher for properly interpreting standardized test scores?

Most classroom assessments are criterion-referenced. One popular technique used by teachers to make criterion-referenced interpretations of their classroom assessments is the **percent-correct score**. To convert a raw score into a percent-correct score, the teacher must know the maximum possible score on the test. The teacher must also know the student's raw score. The raw score typically is the number of items the student got correct on the assessment. On a 50-point test, for example, a raw score of 40 would represent 80 percent correct. On a 20-point test, a raw score of 16 would also represent 80 percent correct. The two scores, 40 and 16, are the same in terms of percent-correct since one was obtained on a 50-point test and the other on a 20-point test.

raw score
the number of items answered correctly on a test

items
questions on standardized tests

criterion-referenced
interpreting test scores in terms of what proportion of the pre-established criteria or content have been correctly answered by the test taker

percent-correct score
the percent of questions the student got correct on the assessment

as a LEARNER How would you explain to a parent the difference between measures of central tendency and variability?

as a TEACHER What other ways could you apply these concepts in your classroom other than for interpreting standardized test results?

> **Learning Objective 3**
>
> Explain the elements of the normal curve and specify proportions of individuals that can be found in different areas of the curve.

The Normal Curve

Up to this point, we have defined standardized tests and emphasized the rights of test takers. You have also read about how criterion-referenced standardized tests are interpreted. The following section will provide the information necessary to correctly interpret and utilize information from norm-referenced standardized tests. To interpret norm-referenced tests, you need to be familiar with the normal distribution, which represents an expected but ideal (or theoretical) distribution of a set of test scores on any independent and random measure. Measurements of height, weight, intelligence, self-esteem, or many other variables for a group of people can result in the "normal" or bell-shaped distribution.

The Shape of the Distribution

The normal curve follows a predictable pattern as is shown in Figure 14.1. It is perfectly symmetrical; the mean raw score for the norming group can be found by locating the vertical line directly in the center of the curve. **Symmetry** means that both halves of the curve appear identical.

The Mean and Standard Deviation

As discussed previously in this chapter, the mean for the normal curve is at the center. Recall also the concept of standard deviation. You learned that standard deviation is a statistic that gives you a sense of how spread out scores are. In the normal distribution, because it is symmetric, there are three standard deviations to the right and three standard deviations to the left of the mean. Figure 14.1 shows these along the bottom axis of the curve.

From the mean to one standard deviation to the right of the mean contains approximately 34 percent of individuals. What proportion of individuals do you think will fall between the mean and one standard deviation to the left of the mean? We know it is also about 34 percent of individuals because the normal distribution is symmetrical. Therefore, approximately two-thirds of the test takers (68 percent) are clustered toward the center of the distribution. In other words, it is "normal" for the majority of test takers to be in the average range on the variable tested, regardless of what that variable is so long as it is independent and random. It is also normal for fewer individuals to be at either extreme. Therefore, most people are average on most measures; fewer people are at the extremes.

symmetry
both halves of the normal curve appear identical

FIGURE 14.1

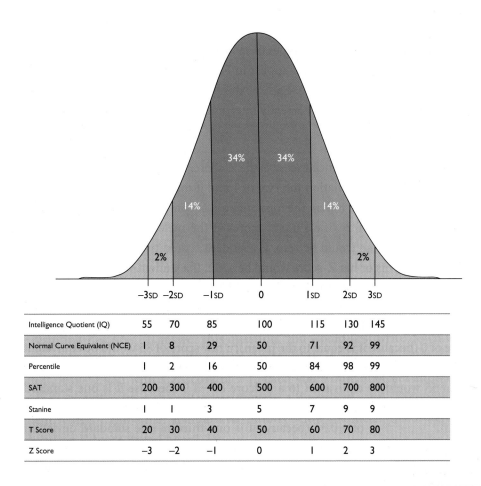

	−3SD	−2SD	−1SD	0	1SD	2SD	3SD
Intelligence Quotient (IQ)	55	70	85	100	115	130	145
Normal Curve Equivalent (NCE)	1	8	29	50	71	92	99
Percentile	1	2	16	50	84	98	99
SAT	200	300	400	500	600	700	800
Stanine	1	1	3	5	7	9	9
T Score	20	30	40	50	60	70	80
Z Score	−3	−2	−1	0	1	2	3

Normal Curve with
Standard Scores

From one standard deviation to the right of the mean to two standard deviations to the right of the mean one can find an additional 14 percent of individuals. Likewise, from one standard deviation to the left of the mean to two standard deviations to the left of the mean one can find an additional 14 percent of individuals. As you might predict, the percentage of individuals that fall between two standard deviations away from the mean and three standard deviations from the mean is even smaller. In fact, only 2 percent of individuals fall between two standard deviations to the right of the mean and three standard deviations to the right of the mean. Thus, due to symmetry, the same percentage of individuals will fall to the left of the normal distribution.

Think It Over

as a LEARNER What percentage of norm-referenced test takers are typically below average? Why is this?

as a TEACHER If you have a student in your class that is one standard deviation below the mean on a norm-referenced mathematics test, how is that child doing with respect to the norm group he is compared to?

Stanine Score

A **stanine score** is a single-digit standard score with a fixed mean of 5 and a fixed standard deviation of 2. Stanine scores get their name by combining the words "standard" and "nine." Stanines range from a low score of 1 to a high score of 9 (see Figure 14.1). On most published tests, stanine scores are reported because of their ease of interpretation. The fact that there are only nine possible scores, spread out equally across the normal curve, gives the stanine score its easy interpretability. It has one other important advantage with regard to interpretation. Often, new teachers do not realize that, any time data are collected on student performance, there is always error. For example, if you administer a standardized reading test to students, the scores the students receive is an estimate of their reading performance. While tests results like these often are very helpful to the teacher as he or she plans curriculum, they are certainly not exact. Thus, with a score from 1 to 9 teachers, students, parents, or caregivers are not likely to conclude that they have an exact measurement of the student's performance. They might think this if they were given a score like 74.35 percent, and they are more likely to understand that a test result represents a sample of student performance.

Students scoring at the average level respective of the norm groups' performance are assigned a stanine score of 5, while those one standard deviation above the mean are assigned a stanine score of 7, and one standard deviation below the mean a stanine score of 3. Two standard deviations above the mean are assigned a stanine score a 9, and two standard deviations below the mean are assigned a 1. Remember, the range that stanine scores occur is fixed from a low score of 1 to a high score of 9. Therefore, if a student is 3 standard deviations above the mean, she is assigned a stanine score of 9—exactly the same score as it would have been had she been only two standard deviations above the mean.

NCE Score

NCE score stands for Normal Curve Equivalent score. **NCE scores** have a fixed mean of 50 and a fixed standard deviation of 21. The NCE can range from a low score of 1 to a high score of 99. Therefore, if students are one standard deviation above the mean, they have a NCE score of 71; if they are two standard deviations above the mean, they have a NCE score of 92; and if they are three standard deviations above the mean, they have a NCE score of 99. Likewise, if students are one standard deviation below the mean, they have a NCE score of 29; if they are two standard deviations below the mean, they have a NCE score of 8; and if they are three standard deviations below the mean, they have a NCE score of 1.

SAT Score

The **Scholastic Assessment Test (SAT)** is used by many colleges and universities for entrance purposes. For each half of the test, the verbal portion and the quantitative portion, the preset mean is 500 and the preset standard deviation is 100. Considering the total score, or both halves of the test together, then the overall mean is 1000 and the overall standard deviation is 200.

stanine score

a standard score used in norm-referenced tests with a mean of 5 and a standard deviation of 2

NCE scores

a Normal Curve Equivalent score is a standard score that has a mean of 50 and standard deviation of 21

Scholastic Assessment Test (SAT)

a college entrance exam that is administered by the Educational Testing Service (ETS)

So, if a student gets a total SAT score of 1000, that student is average compared to other students who take the SAT, and 50 percent of the test takers in the norming group fall below that student's score. To be in the top 84 percent requires a Z-score of 1, which means an SAT score of 1200. Imagine a student who gets a combined or total SAT score of 800. Suppose that is 400 on each half, which is the minimum entrance requirement at many colleges. This 800 score will have below it only 16 percent of the test takers in the norming group. If another student gets a combined or total SAT score of 700, the percentage of test takers in the norming group who are below this student will be about 9 percent.

Percentile Rank

The **percentile**—often represented as "%ile"—is the percentage of persons in the norming or comparison group scoring lower than or equal to a given test taker. For example, if you had a child in your class who earned a 75%ile score, you would interpret that as the child has scored higher on the test then 75 percent of the norm group. Essentially, the student did better then about three out of every four students in the norm group. On some norm-referenced assessments, teachers are given a percentile score based on a comparison with the national norm group; they are also given a percentile score based on a comparison with local norms. Therefore, a student might have two different percentile scores on the test results sheet. For example, you may have a student in your class with an 82%ile national score and an 86%ile local score.

It is critical to remember that the %ile and % correct are very different types of scores, even though they appear so similar. The %ile indicates relative standing in comparison to other students' performance. The % correct reflects absolute test performance in relation to the maximum possible test score. Thus, the %ile is a norm-referenced type of interpretation (an interpretation based on comparison with others), and the % correct is a criterion-referenced interpretation (an interpretation based on comparison with a preset standard).

Grade-Equivalent Score

Grade-equivalent score, sometimes labeled GES, are scores that compare a test taker's performance to that of the norming group that is composed of individuals from a given grade. GES is reported in school years and months, with the school year divided into 10 months. Hence, a GES of 6.5 would represent a test score equal to the average sixth grader after he or she has completed five months of school (or half of the sixth grade).

(The GE score was not included on Figure 14.1 because the first number in the GE score represents the school year. Including this score would have required one line beneath the normal curve figure for each grade, making the figure much harder to visualize and understand.)

Grade-equivalent scores were invented to aid teachers and parents in interpreting published test scores, but they may produce misinterpretation because they cannot always be taken literally. Students who score very high or very low on the test (plus or minus two or more standard deviations) may not have any counterparts

percentile
the percentage of persons in the norming or comparison group scoring lower than or equal to a given test taker

grade-equivalent score
scores that compare a test taker's performance to that of the norming group that is composed of individuals from a given grade

in the norming group who scored as high (or as low), so a literal grade-equivalent score cannot be computed. In these cases, the testing companies extrapolate a score by going farther up or down on the grade scale to compute a GES. Hence, a third grader could conceivably be given a GES of 6.5 on mathematics or a sixth grader a GES of 9.2 on language arts. This does not necessarily mean that the third grader can do sixth-grade work in mathematics or that the sixth grader can do ninth-grade work in language arts, because (1) neither level of work was included on the test they took and (2) few, if any, students at those higher grade levels took the same test they did.

Therefore, as a teacher you should be very cautious when interpreting GES. Essentially, the score tells you how a given child is performing compared to a comparison group of children from the same grade. For example, if a child takes a test in the fifth grade first month and scores as well as half of the norm group, he or she would be assigned a GES of 5.1. Remember, if you have a child who scores a very high or very low GES, that should not be interpreted in a literal fashion to conclude that the child should be in that higher or lower grade or that the child should be doing the work typically assigned at that higher or lower grade. The test the student took likely only had content and skills germane to their grade level and not specific to a higher or lower grade. If you want to know how a fifth grader would perform on ninth-grade content, the child would need to be assessed using a ninth-grade test.

Think It Over

as a LEARNER   Why do you think there are so many different types of test scores?

as a TEACHER   How would you go about explaining to students and parents a strength and weakness of each of the different score types?

Learning Objective 5

Demonstrate procedures for interpreting and evaluating test score results from standardized tests provided in score reports.

Converting Test Scores

Now that you know about the common scores reported on the test results that you will interpret for parents and students, it is important to recognize how you will be able—with some practice and study—to quickly convert from one score type to another.

Explaining Test Scores to Others

Imagine you are in a parent-teacher conference with the mother of one of your students. She scheduled this appointment with you because she has received the results from a norm-referenced test her daughter took. The parent is having trouble understanding the results because there are so many score types on the report and it seems overwhelming. In order to help this parent, you must have mastered the concepts presented in this chapter.

For example, let's say this norm-referenced test is attempting to measure the student's reading comprehension, and you see on the report that the child has a Z-score of 1 on the test. Based on that information and without looking at the rest of the test results, you know that the T-score will be a 60, and the stanine score will be a 7, and the NCE score will be a 71. Essentially, these scores are different ways of representing that the student is doing very well in reading comprehension when compared to a national sample of students. In fact, she is doing one standard deviation better then average and scored at the 84th percentile. The percentile score means she has outperformed 84 percent of the national norm group on this standardized test.

Your ability to explain test results to students and parents and convert from one test score to another are directly based on whether you understand the properties of the normal distribution and can remember the fixed means and standard deviations of the different score types. Box 14.2 provides additional examples of how you could convert from one type of test score to another.

Score Reports

Standardized or published test results are provided to students, parents, and teachers in the form of **individual score reports**. These reports provide information about how a student performed on a standardized test relative to a norm group or a pre-established standard. They contain the kinds of scores that have already been described with little or no conversion required by the teacher. It will be useful to see examples of these reports and to examine the information they contain and the interpretations that can be made from this information.

A sample individual score report is presented in Figure 14.2 (on page 584). This report provides percentile ranks, stanine, and percentile scores for each subtest in

individual score reports

a score report for an individual student that details how the student performed on the test

---

A N   E X A M P L E   T O   A I D   U N D E R S T A N D I N G   **Box 14.2**

Converting Three Students' Test Scores

You have the following three students' test data. What would the scores be that have a question mark? The answers are given below.

Student #1: The following scores were reported for her sixth-grade norm-referenced mathematics achievement test.

NCE Score	T-Score	Stanine	Z-Score
50	?	5	0

Student #2: The following scores were reported for his third-grade norm-referenced language achievement test.

NCE Score	T-Score	Stanine	Z-Score
29	40	?	-1

Student #3: The following scores were reported for her fifth-grade norm-referenced science achievement test.

NCE Score	T-Score	Stanine	Z-Score
71	60	7	?

Answers: Student #1 = T-score of 50 ; Student #2 = stanine score of 3; Student #3 = Z-score of 1.

FIGURE 14.2

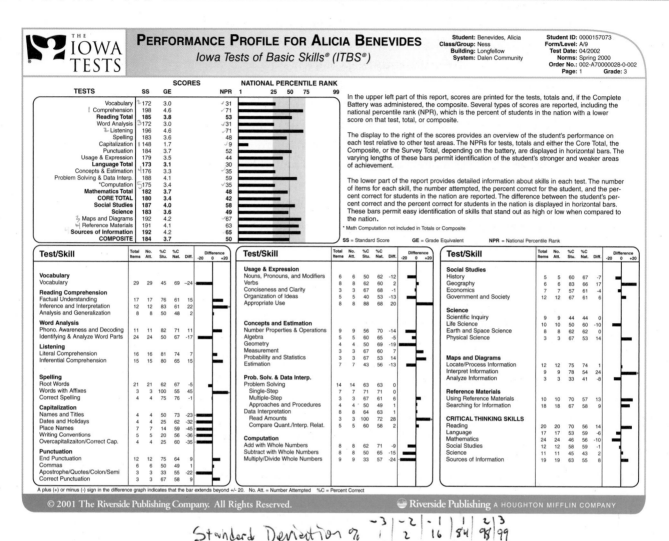

ITBS Individual Score Report

the test battery. In addition, this report includes national percentile bands that indicate the range within which each test score falls. Such bands are appropriate since, as discussed previously, test scores are not exact. Hence, individual test scores may be more properly considered to fall within a band of possible scores. This is already true for the stanine score, which is itself a band.

An examination of the percentile scores detailed in the upper portion of the individual score report in Figure 14.2 for a fictitious student, Alicia Benevides, a third grader, reveals that her relative areas of strength are (1) reading comprehension, (2) listening, and (3) maps and diagrams. However, notice several scores are very close to the same magnitude as these three relative strengths. For example, look at the (4) reference materials and the (5) problem-solving results.

The lower portion of Figure 14.2 provides more detailed information about the specific skills within each test. This is important information for the teacher because it can help her or him determine specific types of educational interventions that may improve this student's academic performance.

This information conveyed in the bottom half of the form in Figure 14.2 provides teachers with information they can use for diagnostic and prescriptive purposes. Not just a set of numbers, this kind of report gives teachers the information necessary to decide what additional help, if any, each individual student may need. This lower portion is a combination of a criterion-referenced report (because it reveals the total number of items covering a specific skill and the number of those items a given student answered correctly) and a norm-referenced report (because it compares that performance to a national norm group of similarly aged students) for each specific skill measured in the achievement test battery. From these results, Alicia's teacher can see exactly what skills this student needs help to master. For example, her teacher may want to help her work in the areas of (1) vocabulary, (2) identifying and analyzing word parts, and (3) geometry.

Meaningful Grading

Learning Objective 6

Evaluate the different approaches to grading, and choose an approach that results in fairness for students.

Grading is the process of making a decision about a student's performance (Tomlinson, 2005). Grades represent one form of feedback to students, caregivers, teachers, and schools. Grading practices tend to differ by level; for example, grading tends to be more demanding in the middle grades than the elementary grades (Randall & Engelhard, 2009). There are many ways for a teacher to assign grades to their students' work which will be described below.

To be successful, teachers should create a clear and fair grading system that informs students and their families of their learning. To accomplish this, teachers need to help students and their families see a clear connection between the learning goals for the class and the grades a student earns. Students and their families should be provided with this information at the beginning of the school year and reminded periodically through class meetings, parent teacher nights, letters, and calls home. They should have full access to their grades. Some school districts have systems that allow parents to access their children's grades through a school Web site. Many students and parents appreciate this service, however, you still need to consider that not all parents will have home Internet access. You do not want to emphasize socioeconomic differences between students in your class, so you might provide every family in your class with a listing of places where parents can access the Internet for free, like the local public library.

We must be cautious not to grade everything that a student does in a classroom. By not grading every learning activity, students are given an opportunity to learn, and possibly fail, without it severely impacting their final grade. Some learning activities should be ungraded to determine if a student has learned the necessary concepts and skills and to help the teacher determine how to adjust his or her teaching (Tomlinson, 2005). While grades sometimes function as student motivators, we must be cautious about using them in that way (Winger, 2005).

the Web space your school dedicates to your class. It is also important to be clear as to how the student's grade is generated; in addition, the system should allow the student and his or her family to monitor his or her own progress in the class.

Think It Over

as a LEARNER	In which of the courses you currently take do you put more effort into getting a good grade than you do on learning the content?
as a TEACHER	When you begin your teaching career, how will you create your grading system? How will you share this system with students and their families?

Fairness and Confidentiality in Grading

When teachers make errors dealing with student artifacts and grades, they usually take the form of either not fairly and consistently applying standards or not working to protect the confidentiality of their students. To increase fairness in grading, it is important to remember the moral dimensions of grading that a teacher must consider such as truthfulness and trust (Zoeckler, 2007).

It is very important that you not grade in a way that reflects bias against any of your students. One strategy for minimizing bias is using "blind" grading practices (Malouff, 2008). Malouff (2008) suggests that teachers can protect student anonymity during grading by covering their names with Post-it Notes. Students and their families are typically satisfied with a teacher when he or she sets appropriate learning goals and when the grading procedures are clearly defined and consistently followed.

It is important to remember that teachers might not be the only members of the learning community who are grading student work. Students are also sometimes asked to grade one another's work in a process called **peer-grading**. One benefit of the practice of peer-grading is that it potentially minimizes teacher workload, which would allow a teacher to spend additional time planning for instruction. Another benefit is that student's have an opportunity to see how other student's view concepts that the class is learning and learn about different ways of understanding and see potential errors. The most obvious negative is that a student could potentially be embarrassed through this process. In fact, the practice of peer-grading was challenged in the U.S. Supreme Court case *Owasso Independent School District v. Falvo*. This 2002 case found that Oklahoma's Owasso district and other school districts could legally utilize the peer-grading practice. While peer-grading is a legal practice, the ethical implications of potentially embarrassing a child in front of his or her peers might cause you to consider other grading approaches that might achieve some of the benefits of peer-grading without all of the difficulties. For example, you might instead use a practice called **self-grading**. In this practice, student score their own papers and then instead of calling for the grade aloud, the teacher solicits the grade information from the students in a more private way (like walking around the room with his or her gradebook recording scores). Another major benefit of self-grading is that students can directly see

peer-grading
students grade one another's work

self-grading
students score their own papers, and the teacher solicits the grade information from the students in a more private way

where they made errors and potentially ask immediate questions that clarify their thinking and problem solving.

Teachers sometimes engage in practices that, although not biased, can make students more likely to diminish their efforts in class. One example of a practice that discourages students is when teachers take an entire letter grade off an assignment for each day it is late (Wormeli, 2006). Instead, Wormeli (2006) recommends taking a few points off of the project for each day it is late. Another example of how grades can discourage students is when teachers assign a grade of zero when a student does not turn in an assignment. Table 14.7 shows the impact of a zero on a student's grade.

By assigning a zero, the student's grade is reduced by two letter grades and the mathematics of the zero make it very difficult for a student to achieve a passing grade. One approach commonly used to address this is to assign an incomplete as opposed to a zero. This puts the onus on the student to complete the work necessary for them to learn, as opposed to just deciding not to do it and taking a zero. Teachers concerned that this is not fair to other students may choose to subtract a nominal amount of points for lateness, but still permit the student to complete the learning activity.

Another common mistake that new teachers make is sharing student grades by posting them publicly or sharing them with a party that should not have access to them. This is not only inappropriate, but also violates the Buckley Amendment (which you will learn about later in this chapter). Teachers also need to be cautious when they present student work in the community, at workshops, or at conferences, by getting permission to display the work from students and their families. Teachers sometimes also incorrectly place photos of students on Web sites without permission. If you need to show student work to another teacher, counselor, or administrator to get their professional opinion on it, it is suggested that you

CONCEPT REVIEW TABLE 14.7

Grade Comparison With and Without a Zero

GRADES WITH A ZERO	GRADES WITHOUT A ZERO
72%	72%
67%	67%
0%	65%
79%	79%
77%	77%
Current Average: 59%	Current Average: 72%
Current Grade: F	Current Grade: C

CONCEPT REVIEW TABLE 14.8
Ideas Teachers Can Use to Inform Their Grading Practices

- Be cautious not to grade everything a student does (Tomlinson, 2005).

- Remember to not use grades as the only approach to increasing student motivation (Winger, 2005).

- Regardless of what grading system you or your school decide to use, make sure it is clear and that you have adequately explained and shared it with students and their families.

- Realize that grading on a curve creates unnecessary competition between students and may encourage some of them to disengage from the class.

- Be clear about how the student's grade is generated, and ensure that the student can monitor his or her progress in the class.

- Minimizing bias by using blind grading practices (Malouff, 2008).

- Do not inappropriately share student grades.

obscure the name and the grade until such time that the student's identity becomes relevant or appropriate to share. The *Concept Review* in Table 14.8 provides a summary of guidelines for your grading practices.

National Trends in Standardized Assessment

Learning Objective 7

Identify and discuss implications of national aspects of standardized testing in schools.

It is important for teachers to be aware of some of the laws and court cases that might impact how school systems select, administer, and interpret standardized tests. The results of standardized tests are used to make very important decisions about students and therefore teachers need to approach the administration and interpretation of standardized tests with the utmost care and seriousness. Educators need to understand and value the obligation they have to protect the information of test takers. We will begin by looking at two pieces of important legislation: the Family Educational Rights and Privacy Act and the No Child Left Behind Act, and then we will turn our attention to the National Assessment of Education Progress.

FERPA: Family Educational Rights and Privacy Act

The Family Educational Rights and Privacy Act (FERPA) was enacted August 21, 1974, and is known as the Buckley Amendment after one of its key supporters, New York senator James Buckley. **FERPA** legislation protects the privacy of student data, places restrictions on who and how these data can be accessed, and allows for student data to be corrected or amended when appropriate. The Buckley Amendment is a critical piece of legislation because it prevents individuals from sharing student's grades, test results, and other personal information and it also prevents student data from being inappropriately placed in the public domain; for example, listing student scores on an office door or putting papers with grades on a classroom bulletin board are prohibited.

NCLB: Public Law 107-110

In the spring of 2002, then President George W. Bush signed the No Child Left Behind Act (NCLB), which substantially increased the accountability for schools on students' academic performance. Under the Act, each state is required to test students from third grade to eighth grade in reading and mathematics. Starting in the year 2007, states were also required to test those students in science.

The focus of the Act is on improving test results, and school districts must publish a report card on each school in their district. The report card is required by the federal government and must contain six items: (1) test results of the students in the school (with the scores also broken down by subgroup), (2) proportion of students who are performing at the *basic*, *proficient*, and *advanced* levels on the assessments, (3) proportion of student who drop out of school, (4) name and number of schools within the district identified as needing improvement, (5) a description of the teaching credentials of the teachers, and (6) the proportion of students who did not take the standardized tests.

The schools' report cards are analyzed to determine if they are making adequate yearly progress. The U.S. Department of Education defines adequate yearly progress as a 12-year process where, by the end of the period, all students will have mastery over basic reading and math skills. If a school fails to meet the state-defined adequate yearly progress for two consecutive school years, school officials will receive assistance in developing a turn-around plan, and students and parents are given options for transferring to another, better performing, public school.

Box 14.3 provides results on closing minority reading and mathematics achievement gaps since the passage of NCLB.

FERPA
legislation which protects the privacy of student data, places restrictions on who and how that data can be accessed, and allows for student data to be corrected or amended when appropriate

DISCOURSE ON DIVERSITY

Narrowing the Achievement Gap

BOX 14.3

A report by the Center on Education Policy in June 2007 revealed that student achievement in reading and math has increased since the enactment of the NCLB Act in 2002. The number of states where the gaps have narrowed exceeds the number in which the gap has widened.

In 14 of the 38 states that provided appropriate data, the gap in reading for African American students narrowed, while in no state did it widen. In mathematics, 12 states narrowed the gap for African Americans, while it widened only in one state. For Hispanics, the gap in reading was narrowed in 13 of the 40 states providing appropriate data and widened in none, while for mathematics, the gap was narrowed in 11 of the 41 states reporting and widened in none. For low-income students, the reading gap was narrowed in 15 of the 31 states with appropriate data, while the gap in mathematics was narrowed in 13 of the 29 states reporting.

The largest gains were in elementary school mathematics in 37 of 41 states, while more states showed declines in reading and mathematics achievement at the high school level than either the elementary or middle school level. Nevertheless, states reporting high school gains outnumbered those showing declines.

"The weight of evidence indicates that state test scores in reading and mathematics have increased overall since No Child Left Behind was enacted. However, there should be no rush to judgment as there may be many factors contributing to the increased achievement," said the President of the Center for Education Policy. The report states possible reasons for the results may include "increased learning, teaching to the test, more lenient tests, scoring and data analyses, and changes in the populations tested."

● Why do you think there is an achievement gap between students from different groups?
● What are some steps you can take to minimize the achievement gap in your classroom?

NAEP: The National Assessment of Education Progress

The NAEP program is run by the National Center for Educational Statistics and is intended to evaluate academic progress.

The NAEP was started in 1969 and is coordinated by the National Center for Education Statistics, housed under the U.S. Department of Education. The NAEP is an assessment process with the purpose of determining what America's students know and are able to demonstrate in a number of key areas such as mathematics,

NewsFlash Staff Contact Site Index Help KIDS ZONE

| Publications & Products | Surveys & Programs | Data Tools | Tables & Figures | Fast Facts | School, College, & Library Search | Annual Reports | What's New | About Us |

Permission to Link to NCES or Replicate Information

LINKING to NCES: All information on our site is in the public domain. If you feel that a link to our website from yours is beneficial, please feel free to create a link.

REPLICATION: Unless specifically stated otherwise, all information on the U.S. Department of Education's NCES website at http://nces.ed.gov is in the public domain, and may be reproduced, published or otherwise used without NCES' permission. This statement does not pertain to information at websites other than http://nces.ed.gov, whether funded by or linked to, from NCES or not.

Please use the following citation when referencing NCES products and publications:
National Center for Education Statistics, U.S. Department of Education.

Return to Contact NCES

NCES Headlines

▪ Teacher Strategies to Help 4thGraders Having Difficulty in Reading
▪ TIMSS 2007 U.S. Technical Report and User Guide
▪ High School Dropout and Completion Rates in the United States
▪ Projections of Education Statistics to 2018

Pubs/Products | Surveys/Programs | DataTools | Tables/Figures | FastFacts | School/LibrarySearch | Annuals | What's New | Kids Zone
EDgov | Institute of Education Sciences | NCER | NCEE | NCSER

1990 K Street, NW
Washington, DC 20006, USA
Phone: (202) 502-7300 (map)

NewsFlash | Staff | Contact | Site Index | Help | RSS | Privacy Policy

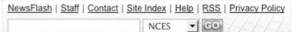

Statistical Standards | FedStats.gov

nces.ed.gov

reading, and science. This assessment does not yield individual scores for students. Instead, NAEP is meant to gauge the performance of America's schools. NAEP results focus on students in grades 4, 8, and 12. NAEP assessments are administered in a standardized way with students at each level all having the same test booklets. This permits a common metric that the U.S. Department of Education can use to evaluate America's schools over a period of time.

Preparing Students for Standardized Tests

Most students feel some degree of anxiety before and during an exam. This stress often motivates preparation and study for the exam. When stress is not harmful to a student, but instead serves to help him or her complete an activity or project, the stress is termed **eustress**. Unfortunately, not all stress is adaptive and helpful; sometimes anxiety becomes so extreme that it interferes with test performance. This negative type of stress is known as **distress**. The Video Case for this chapter demonstrates some strategies for preparing your students and their families for standardized assessments. In this section, you will also read about ways you can help your students minimize test anxiety.

Learning Objective 8

Discuss ways teachers can help prepare students for standardized tests and help reduce test anxiety.

eustress

stress that is not harmful to a student, but instead serves to help him or her complete an activity or project

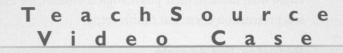

T e a c h S o u r c e
V i d e o   C a s e

Preparing Students for Standardized Tests: Strategies for Success

In this video segment, you'll see how Maria Fenwick prepares her students for standardized tests. You will see how the students learn to react to an open-response question about the biography of a famous African American explorer named Matthew Henson who explored the North Pole. This type of activity is very typical of what might be required on a standardized assessment of reading and writing.

After viewing the video case, consider what you have just watched about classroom management and answer the questions below:

1. How did Mrs. Fenwick teach her students to find quality evidence and use that evidence to support a written argument?
2. Why did Mrs. Fenwick bring her students up to the round table?
3. How did Mrs. Fensick involve parents in the standardized test preparation process?

You can view the video case at the Education CourseMate. Go to:
CengageBrain.com

- *Beyond what was suggested by the researchers, what are some additional things you can do with your students and their families to prepare them for standardized tests they might have to take?*

Source: Calkins, L., Montgomery, K., & Santman, D. (1999). Helping children master the tricks and avoid the traps of standardized tests. Practical Assessment, Research & Evaluation, 6(8). Retrieved November 17, 2008 from http://PAREonline.net/getvn.asp?v=6&n=8.

As the occurrence of standardized testing in K–12 increases, it is likely that we will see an increased incidence of anxiety symptoms in the classroom. However, there are some techniques Drummond (2004) recommends that educators follow when administering standardized tests in order to help minimize test anxiety:

1. Make sure examinees understand test directions by checking with them and asking if they comprehend the directions.
2. Make sure the environment is as relaxed and free of stress as possible. Check to make sure that each student has enough space, good lighting, and appropriate temperature. When administering standardized tests, be positive and friendly to students, but be sure to follow the test's standardized administration procedures.
3. To reduce some of the pressure, conduct class sessions on how to take a test, give opportunities to take practice tests, and provide students with a list of potential guidebooks and resources.

Think It Over

as a LEARNER	Is all anxiety and stress bad? What is the basis for your answer?
as a TEACHER	What advice can you offer your students about how they prepare and take standardized tests that might minimize their distress?

SUMMING IT UP

Examine the importance of test takers' rights and analyze the cautions that educators should have regarding standardized assessment.

Standardized tests are published, nationally administered tests with formalized administration instructions. Their content does not necessarily fit the curriculum of each individual classroom, school, or school district perfectly, so the validity of these tests must be substantiated for each use of the test. Because they are tested and refined, though, they often are very high in test reliability. **Achievement tests** are intended to measure what students have learned in schools and **aptitude tests** are designed to predict how well a student might do in an educational program or setting. It is imperative that teachers inform test takers of their rights and responsibilities. They must also ethically prepare students to take assessments, administer the tests appropriately, and correctly interpret the results. It is also critical that educators approach the administration and interpretation of standardized tests with appropriate caution.

Learning Objective 1

Key Concepts:

Volvo effect (p. 562);
standardized tests (p. 562);
achievement tests (p. 562);
aptitude test (p. 562);
computer adaptive
assessment (p. 562);
norming group (p. 563);
high stakes assessment
(p. 566).

Explain criterion-referenced and norm-referenced test interpretation, mean, median, mode, range, and standard deviation as tools to interpret and understand student data.

Test scores are interpreted to determine what they mean. Actual or **raw scores** on a test cannot be interpreted without benchmarks or reference points that tell how high or low test scores are. Benchmarks or criteria for test interpretation can be preset on an absolute basis. This is called **criterion-referencing** and its principle score is the percent-correct score. The **percent-correct score** is the raw score divided by the maximum possible score times 100. Standardized tests can also be interpreted by comparing a test taker's performance to that of a representative group of prior test takers. This method of interpretation is called **norm-referencing**. **Descriptive statistics** help teachers to interpret data. **Measures of central tendency** help teachers to describe the middle of a data set and the **standard deviation** helps them to know how spread out the data set is.

Learning Objective 2

Key Concepts:

raw score (p. 568);
items (p. 568);
criterion-referenced (p. 569);
percent-correct score
(p. 569);
cut score (p. 569);
norm referencing (p. 570);
norms (p. 570);
descriptive statistics (p. 572);
measures of central
tendency (p. 572);
mean (p. 572);
median (p. 573);
mode (p. 574);
range (p. 575);
standard deviation (p. 575).

Explain the elements of the normal curve and specify proportions of individuals that can be found in different areas of the curve.

The normal distribution is a symmetrical curve with the majority of scores in the middle and a decreasing number toward either end. The mean for the norming group can be found by locating the vertical line directly in the center of the curve.

Learning Objective 3

Key Concepts:

symmetry (p. 576).

598

References

A teacher's hefty influence. (2007, July 29). Honolulu Star Bulletin available online at: http://archives.starbulletin.com/2007/07/29/news/story04.html

Adams, R. & Biddle, B. (1970). *Realities of teaching: Explorations with video tape.* New York: Holt.

Ahles, P. & Contento, J. (2006). Explaining helping behavior in a cooperative learning classroom setting using attribution theory. *Community College Journal of Research & Practice, 30*(8), 609–626.

Alberto, P. A. & Troutman, A. C. (2006). *Applied behavioral analysis for teachers* (7th ed.). Upper Saddle River, NJ: Pearson/Merrill/Prentice Hall.

Alesandrini, K, & Larson, L. (2002). Teachers bridge to constructivism. *Clearing House, 75*(3), 118–121.

Alexander, P. A. (1992). Domain knowledge: Evolving themes and emerging concerns. *Educational Psychologist, 27*(1), 33–51.

Alibali, M. W. & Don, L. S. (2001). Children's gestures are meant to be seen. *Gesture, 1,* 113–127.

Allday, R. A., & Pakurar, K. (2007). Effects of teacher greetings on student on-task behavior. *Journal of Applied Behavior Analysis, 40,* 317–320.

Alloway, N. & Gilbert, P. (1997). Boys and literacy: Lessons from Australia. *Gender & Education, 9,* 49–58.

Altermatt, E. R., Jovanovic, J. & Perry, M. (1998). Bias or responsivity? Sex and achievement level effects on teachers' classroom questioning practices. *Journal of Educational Psychology, 90*(3), 516–527.

American Association on Mental Retardation. (1992). *Mental retardation: Definition, classification, and systems or supports* (9th ed., p. 26). Washington, DC: Author.

American College Testing (2004). Crisis at the core: Preparing all students for college and work. Iowa City, IA.

American Psychiatric Association. (2000). *Diagnostic and statistical manual of mental disorders, text revision: DSM-IV-TR.* (4th ed.). Washington, DC: Author.

American Psychological Association. (1999). *Standards for educational and psychological testing.* Washington, DC: American Psychological Association.

American Speech-Language-Hearing Association. (1993). Definitions of communication disorders and variations. *ASHA, 35* (Suppl.10), 40–41.

Ames, C. (1992). Classrooms: Goals, structures, and student motivation. *Journal of Educational Psychology, 84,* 261–271.

Ames, D. L., Jenkins, A. C., Banaji, M. R., & Mitchell, J. P. (2008). Taking another person's perspective increases self-referential neural processing. *Psychological Science, 19*(7), 642–644.

Anastasi, A., & Urbina, S. (1997). *Psychological testing* (7th Ed.). Upper Saddle River NJ: Prentice-Hall.

Ancheta, A. N. (2006). Civil rights, education research, and the courts. *Educational Researcher, 35*(1), 26–29.

Anderman, L. H., Patrick, H., & Ryan, A. M. (2004). Creative adaptive motivational environments in the middle grades. *Middle School Journal, 35*(5), 33–39.

Anderson, J. R. (1995). *Cognitive psychology and its implications* (4th ed.). New York: Freeman.

Anderson, J. R. (2000). *Cognitive psychology and its implications* (5th ed.). NY: Worth.

Anderson, L. W. & Krathwohl, D. R. (Eds.) (2001). *A taxonomy for learning, teaching, and assessing: A revision of Bloom's taxonomy of educational objectives.* New York: Addison Wesley Longman.

Anderson, R. (1984). Role of the reader's schema in comprehension, learning, and memory. In R. Anderson, J. Osborne, & R. Tierney (Eds.), *Learning to read in American schools: Basal readers and content texts.* Hillsdale, NJ: Lawrence Erlbaum.

Anglin, J. M. (1993). Vocabulary development: A morphological analysis. *Monographs for the Society of Research in Child Development, 58*(Serial No. 238).

Antes, R. L. & Norton, M. L. (1994). Another view of school reform: Values & ethics restored. *Counseling and Values, 38,* 215–222.

Appelbaum, P. (2002). *Multicultural and diversity education.* Santa Barbara, CA: ABC-CLIO, Inc.

Armbruster, B. B. & Anderson, T. H. (1984). Mapping: Representing informative text diagrammatically. In C.D. Holley & D.F. Dansereau (Eds.), *Spatial learning strategies.* Orlando, FL: Academic Press.

Armbruster, B. B. & Brown, A. (1984). Learning from reading: The role of metacognition. In R. Anderson, J. Osborn, & R. Tierney (Eds.), *Learning to read in American schools: Basal readers and content texts.* Hillsdale, NJ: Lawrence Erlbaum.

Arnett, J. J. (2000). The case for emerging adulthood in Europe. *Journal of Youth Studies.*

Arnett, J. J. (2007). *Adolescence and emerging adulthood* (3rd ed.). Upper Saddle River, NJ: Pearson Prentice Hall.

Arnold, M. L. (2000). Stage, sequence, and sequels: Changing conceptions of morality post-Kohlberg. *Educational Psychology Review, 12*(4), 365–383.

Aronson, E. & Patnoe, S. (1997). *Cooperation in the classroom: The jigsaw method.* New York: Longman.

Arredondo, P., Santiago-Rivera, A., & Gallardo Cooper, M. (2007). *Culturally-responsive situational counseling with Latinos.* Alexandria, VA: American Counseling Association Press.

Asch, S. E. (1952). *Social psychology.* Englewood Cliffs, NJ: Prentice-Hall.

Ashby, C. (2007). *No Child Left Behind Act: Education assistance could help states better measure progress of students with limited English proficiency (GAO-07-646T).* Washington, DC: U.S. Government Accountability Office.

Ashcraft, M. H. (1994). *Human memory and cognition* (2nd Ed.). New York: HarperCollins.

Atkins, R., Hart, D., & Donnelly, T. M. (2004). Moral identity development and school attachment. In Lapsley, D. & Narvaez, D. (Eds.), *Moral development, self, and identity.* Mahwah, NJ: Lawrence Erlbaum.

Atkinson, J. W. (1964). *An introduction to motivation.* Princeton, NJ: Van Nostrand.

Ausubel, D. P. (1968). *Educational psychology: A cognitive view.* New York: Holt, Rinehart & Winston.

Ausubel, D. P. & Robinson, F. (1969). *School learning: An introduction to educational psychology*. New York: Holt, Rinehart & Winston.

Autism Society of America (2000). *Advocate, 33*(1), 3.

Ayaduray, J. & Jacobs, G. M. (1997). Can learner strategy instruction succeed? The case of higher order questions and elaborate responses. *System, 25*(4), 561–570.

Azrin, N. H., & Holz, W. C. (1966). Punishment. In W. K. Honig (Ed.), *Operant behavior: Areas of research and application* (pp. 380–447). New York: Appleton-Century-Crofts.

Babad, E. (1998). Preferential affect: The crux of the teacher expectancy issue. In J. Brophy (Ed.), *Advances in research on teaching: Expectations in the classroom* (Vol. 7, pp. 183–214). Greenwich, CT: JAI Press.

Baddeley, A. (2001). Is working memory still working? *American Psychologist, 56*, 851–864.

Baillargeon, R. (2004). Infants' physical worlds. *Current Directions in Psychological Science, 13*, 89–94.

Baldwin, J. D., & Baldwin, J. I. (1998). Sexual behavior. In H. S. Friedman (Ed.), *Encyclopedia of Mental Health*. San Diego, CA.

Bales, R. F. (1970). *Personality and interpersonal behavior*. New York: Holt, Rinehart & Winston.

Bandura, A. (1969). Social-learning theory of identificatory processes. In D. A. Goslin (Ed.), *Handbook of socialization theory and research* (pp. 213–262). Chicago: Rand-McNally.

Bandura, A. (1977). Self-efficacy: Toward a unifying theory of behavioral change. *Psychological Review, 84*, 191–215.

Bandura, A. (1982). Self-efficacy mechanism in human agency. *American Psychologist, 37*, 122–147.

Bandura, A. (1983). Self-efficacy determinants of anticipated fears and calamities. *Journal of Personality and Social Psychology, 45*, 464–469.

Bandura, A. (1986). *Social foundations of thought and action*. Englewood Cliffs, NJ: Prentice-Hall.

Bandura, A. (1997). *Self-efficacy: The exercise of control*. New York: W. H. Freeman.

Bandura, A. (2005). The primacy of self-regulation in health promotion. *Applied Psychology: An International Review, 54*, 245–254.

Bandura, A. & Cervone, D. (1983). Self-evaluative and self-efficacy mechanism governing the motivational effects of goal systems. *Journal of Personality and Social Psychology, 45*, 1017–1028.

Bandura, A., & Jeffry, R. W. (1973). Role of symbolic coding and rehearsal processes in observational learning. *Journal of Personality and Social Psychology, 26*, 122–130.

Bandura, A., Ross, D., and Ross, S. A. (1961). *Journal of Abnormal and Social Psychology, 63*, 575–582.

Banks, J. A. (1995). Multicultural education: Historical development, dimensions, and practice. In J. A. Banks & C. A. M. Banks (Eds.), *Handbook on Research on Multicultural Education* (pp. 2–24). New York: Macmillan.

Barbetta, P. M. (2002). GOALS: A group-oriented adapted levels system for children with behavior disorders. *Academy Therapy, 25*, 645–656.

Barkley, R. A. (1998). *Attention-deficit/hyperactivity disorder: A handbook for diagnosis and treatment*. (2nd ed.). New York: Guilford.

Barnhill, G. P., Hagiwara, T., Myles, B. S., Simpson, R. L., Brick, M. L., & Griswold, D. E. (2000). Parent, teacher, and self-report of problems and adaptive behaviors in children and adolescents with Asperger syndrome. *Diagnostique, 25*(2), 147–167.

Baroody, A. J., & Standifer, D. J. (1993). Addition and subtraction in the primary grades. In L. A. Penner (Ed.), *Research Ideas for the Classroom. Early Childhood Mathematics*. (pp. 72–102). New York: Macmillian.

Barrier-Ferreira, J. (2008). Producing commodities or educating children? Nurturing the personal growth of students in the face of standardized testing. *Clearing House: A Journal of Educational Strategies, Issues and Ideas, 81*(3), 138–140.

Barrios, B. A. (1983). The role of cognitive mediators in heterosocial anxiety: A test of self-efficacy theory. *Cognitive Therapy and Research, 7*, 543–554.

Barrios, F. X. & Niehaus, J. C. (1985). The influence of smoker status, smoking history, sex, and situational variables on smokers' self-efficacy. *Addictive Behaviors, 24*, 13–19.

Barrows, H. S. & Kelson, A. C. (1995). *Problem-based learning in secondary education and the problem-based learning institute* (Monograph 1). Springfield, IL: Problem-Based Learning Institute.

Bass, B. M. (1990). *Bass and Stogdill's handbook of leadership*. New York: The Free Press.

Bass, B. M. (1997). Does the transactional-transformational paradigm transcend organizational and national boundaries? *American Psychologist, 52*, 130–139.

Bass, B. M. & Avolio, B. J. (1993). Transformational leadership: A response to critics. In M.M. Chemers & R. Ayman (Eds.), *Leadership theory and research; Perspectives and directions*. San Diego, CA: Academic Press.

Bateman, B. D. & Linden, M. L. (1998). *Better IEP's: How to develop legally correct and educationally useful programs*. Longmont, CO: Sopris West.

Batshaw, M. L. (Ed.). (1997). *Children with disabilities* (4th ed.). Baltimore: Brookes.

Bauer-Sanders, K. (2000). Voices from a native American classroom in Nebraska. In A. A. Glatthorn & J. Fontana (Eds.), Coping with standards, tests, and accountability: Voices from the classroom (pp. 37–50). Annapolis Junction, MD: National Education Association Teaching and Learning Division.

Baumeister, R. F. (2001). Violent pride. *Scientific American, 284*(4), 96–102.

Baumrind, D. (1991). Effective parenting during the early adolescent transition. In P. A. Cowen & E. M. Hetherington (Eds.), *Advances in family research* (Vol. 2, pp. 111–163). Hillsdale, NJ: Erlbaum

Beale, A. V., & Hall, K. R. (2007). Cyberbullying: What school administrators (and parents) can do. *Clearing House: A Journal of Educational Strategies, Issues and Ideas, 81*(1), 8–12.

Beaty, L. A., & Alexeyev, E. B. (2008). The problem of school bullies: What the research tells us. *Adolescence, 43*(169), 1–11.

Beck, J., Broers, J., Hogue, E., Shipstead, J., & Knowlton, E. (1994). Strategies for functional community-based instruction and inclusion for children with mental retardation. *Teaching Exceptional Children, 26*(2), 44–48.

Becker, W. C., Engelmann, S., & Thomas, D. R. (1975). *Teaching 1: Classroom management*. Chicago: Science Research Associates.

Bee, H. L. & Boyd, D. R. (2003). *Lifespan development.* Boston: Pearson.

Beilin, H. (1977). *Inducing conservation through training.* In G. Steiner (Ed.), *Psychology of the 20th century: Vol. 7, Piaget and beyond.* Zurich: Kindler.

Belfiore, P. J., & Hornyak, R. S. (1998). Operant theory and application to self-monitoring in adolescents. In D. H. Schunk & B. J Zimmerman, (Eds.) Self-regulated learning: From teaching to self-reflective practice (pp.184–202). New York: The Guilford Press.

Bell, J. H. & Bromnick, D. (2003). The social reality of the imaginary audience: A grounded theory approach. *Adolescence, 38,* 205–219.

Belvel, P. S., & Jordan, M. M. (2003). *Rethinking classroom management: Strategies for prevention, intervention, and problem solving.* Thousand Oaks, CA: Corwin Press, Inc.

Bennett, C. I., McWhorter, L. M., & Kuykendall, J. A. (2006). Will I ever teach: Latino and African American students' perspectives on PRAXIS I. *American Educational Research Journal, 43*(3), 531–574.

Berg, B. L. (2001). *Qualitative research methods for the social sciences* (4th ed.). Boston: Allyn & Bacon.

Berk, L. E. (2005). *Infants, children and adolescents* (5th ed.). Boston: Allyn and Bacon.

Berk, L. E. (2006). *Child development* (7th ed.). Boston: Allyn & Bacon.

Bernardo, A. B. I. (2001). Principle explanation and strategic schema abstraction in problem solving. *Memory and cognition, 29,* 627–633.

Berndt, T. J. (2004). Children's friendships: Shifts over a half century in perspectives on their development and their effects. *Merrill-Palmer Quarterly, 50,* 206–223.

Berninger, V. W. & Richards, T. L. (2002). *Brain literacy for educators and psychologists.* San Diego, CA: Academic Press.

Berthold, K., Nuckles, M., & Renkl, A. (2007). Do learning protocols support learning strategies and outcomes? The role of cognitive and metacognitive prompts. *Learning and Instruction, 17,* 564–577.

Berzonsky, M. D., & Adams, G. R. (1999). Reevaluating the identity status paradigm: still useful after 35 years. *Developmental Review, 19,* 557–590.

Beyer, B. (2008). How to teach thinking skills in social studies and history. *The Social Studies, 99*(5), 196–201.

Beyer, B. K. (2008). What research tells us about teaching thinking skills. *The Social Studies, September/October,* 223–232.

Bicard, D. F. & Neef, N. A. (2004). History effects of strategic versus tactical rules on adaptations to changing contingencies in children with ADHD. *Journal of Applied Behavior Analysis, 35,* 375–390.

Bicknell-Holmes, T. & Hoffman, P. S. (2000). Elicit, engage, experience, explore: Discovery learning in library instruction. *Reference Services Review, 28*(4), 313–322.

Binet, A. (1916). *The development of intelligence in children* (E.S. Kite, Trans.). Baltimore: Warwick & York.

Binet, A., & Simon, T. (1908). Le developpment de l'intelligence chez les infants. *L'Année Psychologique, 14,* 1–94.

Blake, C., Wang, W., Cartledge, G., & Gardner, R. (2000). Middle school students with serious emotional disturbances serve as social skills trainers and reinforcers for peers with SED. *Behavioral Disorders, 25,* 280–298.

Bloom, B. S. (1956). *Taxonomy of educational objectives. Handbook I: Cognitive domain.* New York: David McKay.

Bloom, B. S. (1976). *Human characteristics and school learning.* New York: McGraw-Hill.

Bloom, B. S. (Ed.), Engelhart, M. D., Furst, E. J., Hill, W. H., and Krathwohl, D. R. (1956). *Taxonomy of educational objectives. Handbook I: Cognitive domain.* New York: David McKay.

Bloom, B. S. Englehart, M. B., Furst, E. J., Hill, W. H., & Krathwohl, O. R. (1956). *Taxonomy of educational objectives: The classification of education goals.* New York, NY: Longman.

Bloom, S. G. (September, 2005). Lesson of a lifetime. Smithsonian magazine, available at http://www.smithsonianmag.com/history-archaeology/lesson_lifetime.html.

Boekaerts, M., Pintrich, P. R., & Zeidner, M. (eds.). (2000). *Handbood of self-regulation.* San Diego: Academic Press.

Bogdan, R. C. & Biklen, S. K. (2003). *Qualitative research for education* (4th ed.). Boston: Allyn and Bacon.

Boltwood, C. R., & Blick, K. A. (1978). The delineation and application of three mnemonic techniques. *Psychonomic Science, 20,* 339–341.

Bond, L. A. (1996). Norm-and criterion-referenced testing. *Practical Assessment, Research, & Evaluation, 5*(2). Retrieved December 28, 2003 from http://PAREonline.net/getvn.asp?v=5&n=2.

Bond, N. (2007). 12 questioning strategies that minimize classroom management problems. *Kappa Delta Pi Record, 44*(1), 18–21.

Borthick, A. & Jones, D. (2000). The motivation for collaborative discovery learning online and its application in an information systems assurance course. *Issues in Accounting Education, 15*(2), 181–210.

Bouchard, T. J., Jr. (1997). IQ Similarity in twins reared apart: Findings and responses to critics. In R. J. Sternbergy & E. Grigorenko (Ed.), *Intelligence, Heredity, and Environment* (pp. 126–162). New York: Cambridge University Press.

Boyd, H. (September 27–October 3, 2007). Little Rock nine paved the way. The New York Amsterdam News, Page 28.

Boyer, E. (1991). *Ready to learn: A mandate for the nation.* Princeton, NJ: Carnegie Foundation for the Advancement of Teaching.

Bracey, G. W. (1999). The demise of the Asian math gene. *Phi Delta Kappan, 80*(8), 619–620.

Bracey, G. W. (2008). Cut scores, NAEP achievement levels and their discontents. *School Administrator, 65*(6), 20–23.

Bradshaw, J. L. & Nettleton, N. C. (1981). The nature of hemispheric specialization in man. *The Behavioral and Brain Sciences, 4,* 51–91.

Bramwell, W. & Doyle, B. G. (2008). *Power of repeated reading in small group instruction.* New York: Scholastic.

Branch, M. N. (2000). Encyclopedia of psychology, Vol. 6. Kazdin, Alan E. (Ed); pp. 482–484. Washington, DC, US: American Psychological Association; New York, NY, US: Oxford University Press.

Bransford, J. D., Brown, A. L., & Cocking, R. R. (2000). *How people learn: Brain, mind, experience and school.* Washington, D.C.: National Academy Press.

Bransford, J. D., Zech, L., Schwartz, D., Barron, B., Vye, N., & the Cognition and Technology Group at Vanderbilt. (1996). Fostering mathematical thinking in middle school students: Lessons from research. In R. J. Sternberg & T. Ben-Zeev (Eds.), *The nature of mathematical thinking* (pp. 203–250). Mahwah, NJ: Erlbaum.

Brookover, W., Beamer, L., Efthim, H., Hathaway, D., Lezotte, L., Miller, S., Passalacqua, J., & Tournatzky, L. (1982). *Creating effective schools.* Holmes Beach, FL: Learning Publications.

Browder, D. M. & Snell, M. E. (2000). Functional academics. In M. E. Snell & F. Brown (Eds.), *Instruction of students with severe disabilities* (5th ed.) (pp. 493–542). Upper Saddle River, NJ: Merrill/Prentice Hall.

Brown v. Board of Education of Topeka, 347 U.S. 483 (1954).

Brown, A. L. (1992). Design Experiments: Theoretical and methodological challenges in creating complex interventions. *Journal of the Learning Sciences, 2,* 141–178.

Brown, A. L. (1997). Transforming schools into communities of thinking and learning about serious matters. *American Psychologist, 52,* 4, 399–413.

Brown, A. L. & Campione, J. C. (1996). Psychological theory and the design of innovative learning environments: On procedures, principles, and systems. In L. Schauble & R. Glaser (Eds.), *Innovation in learning* (pp. 289–326). Hillsdale, NJ: Erlbaum.

Brown, A. L. & Kane, M. J. (1988). *Cognitive flexibility in young children: The case for transfer.* Paper presented at the Annual Meeting of the American Educational Research Association, New Orleans.

Brown, A. L. & Palincsar, A. S. (1989). Guided cooperative learning and individual knowledge acquisition. In L. B. Resnick (Ed.), *Knowing, learning, and instruction: Essays in honor of Robert Glaser* (pp. 393–452). Hillsdale, NJ: Erlbaum.

Brown, A. L., & Campione, J. C. (1994). Guided discovery in a community of learners. In K. McGilly (Ed.), *Classroom lessons: Integrating cognitive theory and classroom practice* (pp. 229–270). Cambridge, MA: MIT Press.

Brown, B. B. (2004). Adolescent relationships with peers. In R. Lerner & L. Steinberg (Eds.), *Handbook of adolescent psychology.* New York: Wiley.

Brown, D, F. (2004). Urban teachers' professed classroom management strategies. *Urban Education,* 266–289.

Brown, H. H. & Klute, C. (2003). Friends, cliques, and crowds. In G.R. Adams & M.D. Berzonsky (Eds.), *Blackwell handbook of adolescence* (pp. 330–348), Maldea, MA: Blackwell.

Brown, I., Jr. & Inouye, D. K. (1978). Learned helplessness through modeling: The role of perceived similarity in competence. *Journal of Personality and Social Psychology, 36,* 900–908.

Brown, L. (1971). *Television: The business behind the box.* San Diego: Harcourt Brace Jovanovich.

Brown, L., Tappan, M., & Gilligan, C. (1995). Listening to different voices. In W. Kurtines & J. Gewirtz (Eds.), *Moral development: An introduction.* Needham Heights, MA: Allyn & Bacon.

Bruer, J. T. (1999). *The myth of the first three years: A new understanding of early brain development and lifelong learning.* New York: Free Press.

Bruner, J. S. (1960). *The process of education.* New York: Vintage.

Bruner, J. S. (1964). The course of cognitive growth. *American Psychologist, 19,* 1–15.

Bruner, J.S. (1961). The act of discovery. *Harvard Educational Review, 31,* 21–32.

Bruning, R. H., Schraw, G. J., Norby, M. M., & Ronning, R. R. (2004). *Cognitive psychology and instruction* (4th ed.). Upper Saddle River, NJ: Pearson Education.

Bryson. M. & Scardamalia, M. (1991). Teaching writing to students at risk for academic failure. In B. Means, C. Chelemer, & M.S. Knapp (Eds.), *Teaching advanced skills to at-risk students* (pp. 141–167). San Francisco: Jossey-Bass.

Buhs, E. S., Ladd, G. W., & Herald, S. L. (2006). Peer exclusion and victimization: Processes that mediate the relation between peer group rejection and children's classroom engagement and achievement. *Journal of Educational Psychology, 98*(1), 1–13.

Bullock, J. R. (2002). Bullying among children. *Childhood Education, 78(3),* 130–133.

Burchard, J. D., & Barrera, F. (1972). An analysis of time out and response cost in a programmed environment. *Journal of Applied Behavior Analysis, 5,* 271–282.

Burn, S. M. (2004). *Groups: Theory and practice.* Belmont, CA: Wadsworth/Thomson Learning.

Butler, R. (2000). What learners want to know: The role of achievement goals in shaping information seeking, learning, and interest. In C. Sansone & J. M. Harackiewicz (Eds.), *Intrinsic and extrinsic motivation: The search for optimal motivation and performance* (pp. 161–194). San Diego: Academic Press.

Buunk, B. P. & Mussweiler, T. (2001). New directions in social comparison research. *European Journal of Social Psychology, 31,* 467–475.

Byrnes, J. P. (2001). *Minds, brains, and learning: Understanding the psychological and educational relevance of neuroscientific research.* New York: Guilford Press.

Byrnes, J. P. (2003). Factors predictive of mathematics achievement in White, Black, & Hispanic 12th graders. *Journal of Educational Psychology, 95*(2), 316–326.

Cabrera, N. L., & Cabrera, G. A. (2008). Counterbalance assessment: The chorizo test. *Phi Delta Kappan, 89*(9), 677–678.

Caine, R. & Caine, G. (1994). Making connections: Teaching and the human brain. Boston: Addison-Wesley.

Calero, M. D., Garcia-Martin, M. B., Jimenez, M. I., Kazen, M., & Araque, A. (2007). Self-regulation advantage for high IQ children: Findings from a research study. *Learning and Individual Differences, 17,* 328–343.

Calkins, L., Montgomery, K., & Santman, D. (1999). Helping children master the tricks and avoid the traps of standardized tests. *Practical Assessment, Research & Evaluation, 6*(8). Retrieved November 17, 2008 from http://PAREonline.net/getvn.asp?v=6&n=8.

Calsoyas, K. (2005). Considerations in the educational process relative to Native Americans. *Cambridge Journal of Education, 35*(3), 301–310.

Cameron, S. (1994). *What is an inclusion specialist? A preliminary investigation.* Specialized Training Program, University of Oregon.

Cammilleri, A. P., Tiger, J. H., & Hanley, G. P. (2008). Developing stimulus control of young children's requests to teachers: Classwide applications of multiple schedules. *Journal of Applied Behavior Analysis, 41,* 299–303.

Cankoy, O., & Tut, M. A. (2005). High-stakes testing and mathematics performance of fourth graders in North Cyprus. *Journal of Educational Research, 98*(4), 234–243.

Canter, L., & Canter, M. (2001). *Assertive discipline: Positive behavior management for today's classroom.* Santa Monica, CA: Lee Canter and Associates.

Capossela, A. (2000). Are children really more creative than adults? An examination of Lev Vygotsky's theory. *Yearbook (Claremont Reading Conference), 2000,* 48–57.

Carney, R. H & Levin, J. R. (2002). Pictorial illustrations still improve students' learning from text. *Educational Psychology Review, 14*(1), 5–26.

Carney, R. H., & Levin, J. R. (2000). Mnemonic instruction, with a focus on transfer. *Journal of Educational Psychology, 92,* 783–790.

Carolan, J., & Guinn, A. (2007). Differentiation: Lessons from master teachers. *Educational Leadership, 64*(5), 44–47.

Carrier, C. A. & Titus, A. (1981). Effects of notetaking, pretraining, and test-made expectations on learning from lecture. *American Educational Research Journal, 18,* 385–397.

Carroll, J. B. (1963). A model of school learning. *Teachers College Record, 64,* 723–733.

Carroll, J. B. (1985). The "model of school learning", Progress of an idea. In C. Fisher & D. C. Berliner (Eds.), *Perspectives on instructional time* (pp. 29–58). New York: Longman.

Case, R. (1985). *Intellectual development: A systematic reinterpretation.* New York: Academic Press.

Case, R. (1992). The role of the frontal lobes in the regulation of cognitive development. *Brain and Cognition, 20,* 51–73.

Case, R. & Griffin, S. (1990). Child cognitive development: The role of central conceptual structures in the development of scientific and social thought. In C.A. Hauert (Ed.), *Developmental psychology: Cognitive, perceptuo-motor, and neuropsychological perspectives.* Amsterdam: North Holland.

Center for Positive Behavioral Interventions & Supports (2001). *School-wide behavioral support.* http://www.pbis.org/

Center on Education Policy. (2007, June). Answering the question that matters most. Has student achievement increased since No Child Left Behind? Washington, DC: Author.

Chall, J. S. (1983). Literacy: Trends and explanations. *Educational Researcher, 12,* 3–8.

Chase, W. G. (1987). Visual information processing. In K. R. Boff, L. Kaufman, & J. P. Thomas (Eds.), *Handbook of perception and human performance: Vol. 2. Information Processing* (pp. 28–60). New York: Wiley.

Chase, W. G. & Simon, H. A. (1973). Perception in chess. *Cognitive Psychology, 4,* 55–81.

Chavous, T., Bernat, D., Schmeelk-Cone, K.,Caldwell, C., Kohn-Wood, L., & Zimmerman, M. (2003). Racial identity and academic attainment among African American adolescents. *Child Development, 74,* 1076–1090.

Chen, C., Himsel, A., & Kasof, J. (2006). Boundless creativity: Evidence for the domain generality of individual differences in creativity. *The Journal of Creative Behavior, 40*(3), 179–199.

Chi, M. T. H. (2000). Self-explaining: The dual processes of generating inference and repairing mental models. In R. Glaser (Ed.), *Advances in instructional psychology: Volume 5, Educational design and cognitive science* (pp. 161–238). Mahwaw, NJ: Erlbaum.

Chi, M. T. H., & Bassok, M. (1989). Learning from examples via self-explanations. In L. B. Resnick (Ed.), *Knowing learning, and instruction* (pp. 251–282). Hillsdale, NJ: Erlbaum.

Chi, M. T. H., Bassok, M., Lewis, M. W., Reimann, P., & Glaser, R. (1989). Self-explanations: How students study and use examples in learning to solve problems. *Cognitive Science, 13,* 145–182.

Chi, M. T. H., de Leeuw, N., Chiu, M-H., & LaVancher, C. (1994). Eliciting self-explanations improves understanding. *Cognitive Science, 18,* 439–477.

Chmielewski, T. L., & Dansereau, D. F. (1998). Enhancing the recall of text: Knowledge mapping training promote implicit transfer. *Journal of Educational Psychology, 90,* 407–413.

Chomsky, N. (1972). *Language and mind.* New York: Harcourt Brace Jovanovich.

Cialdini, R. B. (2001). *Influence: Science and practice* (4th ed.). Boston: Allyn & Bacon.

Clark, K. (1989). *Prejudice and your child* (3rd ed.). Middletown, CT: Wesleyan University Press.

Clark, S. G. (2000). The IEP process as a tool for collaboration. *Teaching Exceptional Children, 33*(2), 56–66.

Classroom management (2006, July). The National Education Association Best Practices Brief available online at: http://www.nea.org/assets/docs/mf_cmbrief.pdf

Cleary, T. J. & Zimmerman, B. J. (2004). Self-regulation empowerment program: A school-based program to enhance self-regulated and self-motivated cycles of student learning. *Psychology in the Schools, 41*(5), 537–550.

Clement, J. (1989). Nonformal reasoning in physics: The use of analogies and extreme cases. In J. Voss, D. N. Perkins, & J. Segal (Eds.), *Informal reasoning.* Hillsdale, NJ: Erlbaum.

Cochran-Smith, M. & Lytle, S. L. (1990). Research on teaching and teacher research: The issues that divide. *Educational Researcher, 19* (2), 2–11.

Cognition and Technology Group at Vanderbilt (1992). The Jasper series as an example of anchored instruction: Theory, program description, and assessment data. *Educational Psychologist, 27*(3), 291–315.

Cognition and Technology Group at Vanderbilt (1997). *The Jasper projects: Lessons in curriculum, instruction, assessment, and professional development.* Mahwah, NJ: Erlbaum.

Cohen, L. B. & Cashon, C. H. (2006). Infant cognition. In D. Kuhn & R. Siegler (Eds.), *Handbook of child psychology: Vol. 1. Cognition, perception, and language* (6th ed.).

Cole, E. & Stewart, A. (1996). Meanings of political participation among Black and white women; Political identity and social responsibility. *Journal of Personality and Social Psychology, 71,* 130–140.

Condiotte, M. M. & Lichtenstein, E. (1981). Self-efficacy and relapse in smoking cessation programs. *Journal of Consulting and Clinical Psychology, 49,* 648–658.

Cook, J. L. & Cook, G. (2005). *Child development: Principles and perspectives.* Boston: Allyn and Bacon.

Cook, L. K., & Mayer, R. E. (1988). Teaching readers about the structure of scientific text. *Journal of Educational Psychology, 80,* 448–456.

Cook, L. S., Smagorinsky, P., Fry, P. G., Konopak, B., & Moore, C. (2002). *The Elementary School Journal, 102*(5), 389–413.

Coolahan, K., Fantuzzo, J., Mendez, J., & McDermott, P. (2000). Preschool peer interactions and readiness to learn: Relationship between classroom peer play and learning behaviors and conduct. *Journal of Educational Psychology, 92*(3), 458–465.

Cooper, D., & Snell, J. L. (2003). Bullying—Not just a kid thing. *Educational Leadership, 60*(6), 22–25.

Cooper, H. M. (1979). Pygmalion grows up: A mode for teacher expectation communication and performance influence. *Review of Educational Research, 49*, 389–410.

Coplan, R. J., Arbeau, K. A., & Closson, L. M. (2007). Gender differences in the behavioral associates of loneliness and social dissatisfaction in kindergarten. *The Journal of Child Psychology and Psychiatry and Allied Disciplines, 48*(10), 988–995.

Corkill, A. J. (1992). Advance organizers: Facilitators of recall. *Educational Psychology Review, 4*, 33–68.

Corwin, M. (2001). *And still we rise*. New York: HarperCollins Publishers.

Cossairt, A., Hall, R. V., & Hopkins, B. L. (1973). The effects of experimenter's instructions, feedback, and praise on teacher praise and student attending behavior. *Journal of Applied Behavior Analysis, 6*, 89–100.

Cote, C. A., Thompson, R. H., Hanley, G., & McKerchar, P. M. (2007). Teacher report and direct assessment of preferences for identifying reinforcers for young children. *Journal of Applied Behavior Analysis, 40*, 157–166.

Covington, M. V., Crutchfield, R. S., Davies, L. B., & Olton, R. M. (1974). *The Productive Thinking Program*. Columbus, OH: Merrill.

Craft, A., Cremin, T., Bernard, P., & Chappell, K. (2007). Teacher stance in creative learning: A study of progression. *Thinking Skills & Creativity*, Vol. 2, Issue 2, Autumn 2007, pp. 136–147.

Craft, M. A., Alber, S. R., & Heward, W. L. (1998). Teaching elementary students with developmental disabilities to recruit teacher attention in a general education classroom. *Journal of Applied Behavior Analysis, 31*, 399–415.

Craig, D. (2003). Brain-compatible learning: Principles and applications in athletic training. *Journal of Athletic Training, 38*(4), 342–350.

Craik, F. I. M. & Brown, S. C. (2000). Memory: Coding processes. In A. E. Kazdin (Ed.), *Encyclopedia of psychology* (Vol. 5, pp. 162–166). Washington, DC: American Psychological Association.

Cronbach, L. J. (1984). *Essentials of psychological testing* (4th ed.). New York: Longman.

Cronbach, L. J., & Snow, R. L. (1977). *Aptitudes and instructional methods*. New York: Irvington.

Cronin, M. S. & Patton, J. R. (1993). *Life skills instruction for all students with special needs: A practical guide for integrating real life content into the curriculum*. Austin, TX: PRO-ED.

Cross, W. (1998). Black psychological functioning and the legacy of slavery. In Y. Danieli (Ed.), *International handbook of multigenerational legacies of trauma* (pp. 387–400). New York: Plenum Press.

Crowley, A. E. & Hoyer, W. D. (1994). An integrative framework for understanding two-sided persuasion. *Journal of Consumer Research, 20*, 561–574.

Crowley, K. & Jacobs, M. (2002). Building islands of expertise in everyday family activity. In G. Leinhardt, K. Crowley, & K. Knutsen (Eds.), *Learning conversations in museums* (pp. 333–356). Mahwah, NJ: Erlbaum.

Cummins, J. (2004). Bilingual education. In J. Brewer (Ed.), *Introduction to early childhood education: Preschool through primary grades*. (5th edition). (pp. 294–295). Boston: Allyn & Bacon.

Curwin, R. L., & Mendler, A. N. (1988). *Discipline with dignity*. Association for Supervision and Curriculum Development.

Curwin, R. L., & Mendler, A. N. (1997). Discipline with dignity: Beyond Obedience. *The Education Digest, 63*(4), 11–14.

Dagenhart, D. B., O'Connor, K. A., Petty, T. M., & Day, B. D. (2005). Giving teachers a voice. *Kappa Delta Pi Record, 41*(3), 108–111.

Danielson, C. (1996). *Enhancing professional practice: A framework for teaching*. Alexandria, VA: Association for Supervision and Curriculum Development.

Davis, B. & Sumara, D. (2003). Why aren't they getting this? Working through the regressive myths of constructivist pedagogy. *Teaching Education, 14*(2), 123–140.

De Maio, L. J. (2000). *Parent-child communication program*. Morehead, MN: Minnesota State University.

Deakin, J. M., & Allard, F. (1991). Skilled memory in expert figure skaters. *Memory Cognition, 19*, 79–86.

Deci, E. L. (1975). *Intrinsic motivation*. New York: Plenum.

Deci, E. L. (1980). *The psychology of self-determination*. Lexington, MA: D. C. Health.

Deci, E. L., & Ryan, R. M. (1985). *Intrinsic motivation and self-determination in human behavior*. New York: Plenum.

Deci, E. L., Koestner, R., & Ryan, R. M. (1999). A meta-analytic review of experiments examining the effects of extrinsic rewards on intrinsic motivation. *Psychological Bulletin, 125*, 627–668.

Deci, E. L., Vallerand, R. J., Pelletier, L. G., & Ryan, R. M. (1991). Motivation and education: The self-determination perspective. *Educational Psychologist, 26*, 325–346.

DeGroot, A. D. (1965). *Thought and choice in chess*. The Hague: Mouton.

Deitz, S. M., & Hummel, J. H. (1978). *Discipline in the schools: A guide to reducing misbehavior*. Englewood Cliffs, NJ: Educational Technology Publications.

DelGuidice, M. (2008). Is your school stuck in a testing rut? Use your library media center to make learning fun again! *School Library Media Activities Monthly, 25*(4), 30–32.

Delpit, L. (2006). Lessons from teachers. *Journal of Teacher Education, 57*(3), 220–231.

Dembo, M. H. & Gibson, S. (1985). Teachers' sense of efficacy: An important factor in school improvement. *Elementary School Journal, 63*, 210–219.

Demmert, W. G. (2005). The influences of culture on learning and assessment among Native American students. *Learning Disabilities Research and Practice, 20*(1), 16–23.

Dempster, F. N., & Corkill, A. (1999). Interference and inhibition in cognition and behavior: Unifying themes for educational psychology. Educational *Psychology Review, 11*(1).

Derry, S. J. (1984). Effects of an organizer on memory for prose. *Journal of Educational Psychology, 76*, 98–107.

Detterman, D. K. (1993). Giftedness and intelligence: One and the same?. In G. R. Bock and K. Ackrill (Eds.), *The origins and development of high ability, Ciba foundation symposium* (Vol. 178, pp. 22–43). West Sussex, UK: John Wiley and Sons.

DeVries, R., & Zan, B. (2003). When children make rules. *Educational Leadership, 61(1)*, 64–68.

Diamond, L. (2008). *Sexual fluidity: Understanding women's love and desire.* Cambridge, MA: Harvard University Press.

Dingfelder, S. (2005). Closing the gap for Latino patients. *Monitor on Psychology, 36*(1), 58–59.

Dole, J. (2000). Explicit and implicit instruction in comprehension. In B. M. Taylor, M. F. Graves, & L. van den Broek (Eds.), *Reading for meaning: Fostering comprehension in the middle grades* (pp. 52–69). New York: Teachers College Press.

Dollinger, S. J. (2003). Need for uniqueness, need for cognition, and creativity. *The Journal of Creative Behavior, 37*(2), 99–116.

Dooling, D. & Lachman, R. (1971). Effects of comprehension on retention of prose. *Journal of Experimental Psychology, 88*, 216–222.

Doyle, W. (1986). Classroom organization and management. In M. Wittrock (Ed.), *Handbook of research on teaching* (3rd ed.; pp. 392–431). New York: Macmillan..

Driscoll, M. (2009). *Psychology of learning for instruction* (4th ed.). Columbus, OH: Pearson Merrill.

Driscoll, M.P. (2008). *Psychology of learning for instruction* (4th ed.). Boston: Allyn and Bacon.

Drummond, R. J. (2004). *Appraisal procedures for counselors and helping professionals* (5th ed.). Upper Saddle River, NJ: Pearson.

Dubois, W. (1903). *Souls of Black folk.* Chicago: A.C. McClurg.

Dweck, C. S. (1975). The role of expectations and attributions in the alleviation of learned helplessness. *Journal of Personality and Social Psychology, 31*, 674–685.

Dweck, C. S. (1999). *Self-theories: Their role in motivation, personality, and development.* Philadelphia, PA: Psychology Press.

Dweck, C. S. (2002). The development of ability conceptions. In A. Wigfied & J. Eccles (Eds.), *The development of achievement motivation.* San Diego, CA: Academic Press.

Dweck, C. S., & Leggett, E. (1988). A social-cognitive approach to motivation and personality. *Psychological Review, 95*, 256–273.

Dwyer, C., & Johnson, L. (1997). Grades, accomplishment, & correlates. In W. Willingham & N. Cole (Eds.), *Gender & fair assessment* (pp.127–156). Mahwah, New Jersey: Erlbaum.

Eberly, J. L., Rand, M. K., & O'Connor, T. (2007). Analyzing teachers' dispositions towards diversity: Using adult development theory. *Multicultural Education, 14*(4), 31–36.

Ediger, M. (2006). Present day philosophies of education. *Journal of Instructional Psychology, 33*(3), 179–182.

Eisenberg, N., Martin, C. L., & Fabes, R. A. (1996). Gender development and gender effects. In D. C. Berliner & R. C. Calfee (Eds.), *Handbook of educational psychology* (pp. 358–396). New York: Prentice-Hall.

Eisenberg, N., Zhou, Q., & Koller, S. (2001). Brazilian adolescents' prosocial moral judgment and behavior: Relations to sympathy, perspective taking, gender-role orientation, and demographic characteristics. *Child Development, 72*, 518–534.

Eisman, J. W. (1981). What criteria should public school moral education programs meet? *The Review of Education, 7*, 213–230.

Elkind, D. (1985). Egocentrism redux. *Developmental Review, 5*, 218–226.

Elliott, A. J., & McGregor, H. (2001). A 2 x 2 achievement goal framework. *Journal of personality and social psychology, 80*, 501–519.

Emmer, E. T., & Evertson, C. M. (1981). Synthesis of research on classroom management. *Educational Leadership, 38(4)*, 342–343, 345–347.

Emmer, E. T., Evertson, C. M., & Worsham M. E. (2002). *Classroom management for secondary teachers (6th ed.).* Boston, MA: Allyn and Bacon.

Engelmann, S. (1977). Sequencing cognitive and academic tasks. In R. D. Kneedler & S. G. Tarver (Eds.), *Changing perspectives in special education.* (pp 46–61). Upper Saddle River, NJ: Merrill/Prentice Hall.

Epstein, J. (1983). Selection of friends in differently organized schools and classrooms. In J. Epstein & N. Karweit (Eds.), *Friends in school.* New York: Academic Press.

Epstein, J. L., & Salinas, K. C. (2004, May). Partnering with families and communities. *Educational Leadership, 61*, 12–18.

Ericsson, K. A. (1996). The acquisition of expert performance. In K. A. Ericsson (Ed.), *The road to excellence: The acquisition of expert performance in the arts, sciences, sports, and games* (pp. 1–50). Mahwah, NJ: Erlbaum.

Erikson, E. H. (1963). *Childhood and society* (2nd ed.). New York: Norton.

Erikson, E. H. (1968). *Identity: Youth and crisis.* New York: Norton.

Eshel, Y. & Klein, Z. (1981). Development of academic self-concept of low-class and middle-class primary school children. *Journal of Educational Psychology, 73*, 287–293.

Evans, B. (2007). *Barbara Evans's Weblog: Facilitating language development.* http://www.glnd.k12.va.us/weblog/bevans/Spee chLanguage/?permalink=FacilitatingLang

Everest, C. (2003, February 18). Differentiation, the new monster in education. *The Education Guardian.*

Evertson, C. M., & Harris, A. H. (1992). What we know about managing classrooms. *Educational Leadership, 49(7)*, 74–78.

Evertson, C. M., & Neal, K. W. (2006, July). Looking into learning-centered classrooms implications for classroom management. *Best Practices NEA Research Working Paper, 1–6.* Available online at: http://www. eric.ed.gov/ERICDocs/data/ericdocs2sql/content_ storage_01/0000019b/80/28/05/0d.pdf.

Ewart, C. K., Taylor, C. B., Reese, L. B., & DeBusk, R. F. (1983). Effects of early lost-myocardial infarction exercise testing on self-perception and subsequent physical activity. *American Journal of Cardiology, 51*, 1076–1080.

Fahey, K., Lawrence, J., & Paratore, J. (2007). Using electronic portfolios to make learning public. *Journal of Adolescent & Adult Literacy, 50*(6), 460–471.

Fecho, B. (1998). Teacher as researcher: Taking an inquiry stance on the classroom. Paper presented at a meeting of the State of South Australia Department of Education, Training and Employment, Adelaide, Australia.

Federal Register, February 10, 1993, p. 7938.

Feinberg, T., & Robey, N. (2008). Cyberbullying. *Principal Leadership, 9(1)*, 10–15.

Ferguson, E. & Houghton, S. (1992). The effects of contingent teacher praise, as specified by Canter's assertive discipline programme, on children's on-task behaviour. *Educational Studies, 18(1)*, 83–93.

Ferkany, M. (2008). The educational importance of self-esteem. *Journal of Philosophy of Education, 42*(1), 119–132.

Ferster, C. B., & Skinner, B. F. (1957). *Schedules of reinforcement.* New York: Appleton-Century-Crofts.

Festinger, L. (1954). A theory of social comparison processes. *Human Relations, 7*, 117–140.

Festinger, L. (1957). *A theory of cognitive dissonance.* Stanford, CA: Stanford University Press.

Feuerstein, A. (2000). School characteristics and parent involvement: Influences on participation in children's schools. *Journal of Educational Research, 94*(1), 29–41.

Feuerstein, R., Rand, Y., Hoffman, M., & Miller, R. (1980). *Instrumental enrichment: An intervention program for cognitive modifiability.* Baltimore: University Park Press.

Finn, J. D., Gerber, S. B. & Boyd-Zaharias, J. (2005). Small classes in the early grades, academic achievement , and graduating from high school. *Journal of Educational Psychology, 97*, 214–223.

Fiol, C. M., Harris, D., & House, R. J. (1999). Charismatic leadership: Strategies for effecting social change. *Leadership Quarterly, 10*, 449–482.

Flavell, J. H. (1963). *The developmental psychology of Jean Piaget.* Princeton, NJ: Van Nostrand.

Fleming, V. & Alexander, J. (2001). The benefits of peer collaboration: A replication with a delayed posttest. *Contemporary Educational Psychology, 26*, 588–601.

Fleming, W. C. (2006). Myths and stereotypes about Native Americans. *Phi Delta Kappan, 88*(3), 213–217.

Flick, G. L. (2000). *How to reach and teach teenagers with ADHD.* West Nyack, NY: Center for Applied Research in Education.

Fombone, E. (1999). The epidemiology of autism: A review. *Psychological Medicine, 29*, 769–786.

Fordham, S. & Ogbu, J. (1986). Black students' school success: Coping with the burden of acting white. *Urban Review, 18*, 176–206.

Foubert, J. D. & Granger, L.U. (2006). The effects of involvement in clubs and organizations on the psychosocial development of first-year and senior college students. *NASPA Journal, 43*, 166–182.

Fraenkel, J. R. & Wallen, N.E. (2006). *How to design and evaluate research in education* (6th ed.). New York: McGraw Hill.

Fraga, E. D., Atkinson, D. R., & Wampold, B. E. (2004). Ethnic group preferences for multicultural counseling competencies. *Cultural Diversity and Ethnic Minority Psychology, 10*, 53–65.

Frame, M. J. (2000). The relationship between visual impairment and gestures. *Journal of Visual Impairments and Blindness, 94*, 155–171.

Freeman, D., Kuhs, T., Porter, A., Floden, R., Schmidt, W., & Schwille, J. (1983). Do textbooks and tests define a national curriculum in elementary school mathematics? *Elementary School Journal, 83*, 501–513.

Freeman, F. & Alkin, M. (2000). Academic and social attainments of children with mental retardation in general education and special education settings. *Remedial and Special Education, 21*, 3–18.

Freire, P. (2000). Pedagogy of the Oppressed: 30th anniversary edition. Continuum International Publishing Group, New York, NY.

French, J. R. P., Jr., & Raven, B. (1960). The bases of social power. In D. Cartwright & A. Zander (Eds.), *Group dynamics* (2nd ed.) (pp. 607–623). Evanston, IL: Row, Peterson.

Fry, R. (2007). The changing racial and ethnic composition of U.S. public schools. Pew Hispanic Center, Washington, DC.

Fry, R. (2008). The role of schools in the English language learner achievement gap. Pew Hispanic Center, Washington, DC.

Fujimora, N. (2001). Facilitating children's proportional reasoning: A model of reasoning processes and effects of interventions on strategy change. *Journal of Educational Psychology, 93*, 589–603.

Furnham, A. & Bachtiar, V. (2008). Personality and intelligence as predictors of creativity. *Personality and Individual Differences, 45*(7), 613–617.

Futrell, M. H., & Gomez, J. (2008). How tracking creates a poverty of learning. Educational leadership, 65(8), 74–78.

Gage, N. L. & Berliner, D. C. (1998). *Educational psychology* (6th ed.). New York: Houghton Mifflin.

Gagné, E. D., Yekovich, C. W., & Yekovich, F. R. (1993). *The cognitive psychology of school learning* (2nd ed.). New York: HarperCollins.

Gagné, R. M. (1985). *The conditions of learning* (4th ed.). New York: Holt, Rinehart & Winston.

Gagné, R. M. & Driscoll, M. P. (1988). *Essentials of learning for instruction* (2nd ed.). Englewood Cliffs, NJ: Prentice-Hall.

Gagne, R. M. & Medsker, K. L. (1996). *The conditions of learning: Training applications.* Fort Worth, TX: Harcourt Brace.

Gallucci, N. T., Kline, A., & Middleton, G. (2000). Perfectionism and creative strivings. *The Journal of Creative Behavior, 34*(2), 135–141.

Garcia, E., & Jensen, B. (2007). Helping young Hispanic learners. *Educational Leadership, 64*(6), 34–39.

Gardner, H. (1993). *Creating minds.* New York: Basic Books.

Gardner, H. (1999). *Intelligence reframed: Multiple intelligences for the 21st century.* NY: Baric Books.

Gauvain, M. (2001). *The social context of cognitive development.* New York: Guilford Press.

Gay, G. (2000). *Culturally responsive teaching: Theory, research, and practice. Multicultural education series.* New York, NY: Teachers College Press.

Ge, X. & Land, M. (2004). A conceptual framework for scaffolding ill-structured problem-solving processes using question prompts and peer interactions. *Educational Technology Research and Development, 52*(2), 5–22.

Geary, D. C. (1998). What is the function of mind and brain? *Educational Psychology Review, 10*, 377–387.

Geen, R. G. (1980). Test anxiety and cue utilization. In I. G. Sarason (Ed.), *Test anxiety: Theory, research, and applications.* Hillsdale, NJ: L. Erlbaum Associates.

Geiger, K. & Turiel, E. (1983). Disruptive school behavior and concepts of social convention in early adolescence. *Journal of Educational Psychology, 75*, 677–685.

Gelman, R. (1990). First principles organize attention to and learning about relevant data: Number and the animate-inanimate distinction. *Cognitive Science, 14,* 79–106.

Gelman, R. & Gallistel, C. R. (1978). *The child's understanding of number.* Cambridge, MA: Harvard University Press.

Gersten, R. (1998). Recent advances in instructional research for students with learning disabilities: An overview. *Learning Disabilities Research and Practice, 13,* 162–170.

Giangreco, M. F. (1992). Curriculum in inclusion-oriented schools: Trends, issues, challenges, and potential solutions. In S. Stainback & W. Stainback (Eds.), *Curriculum considerations in inclusive classrooms; Facilitating learning for all students* (pp. 239–263). Baltimore: Brookes.

Giangreco, M. F., Cloninger, C. J., Dennis, R. E., & Edelman, S. W. (2000). Problem solving methods to facilitate inclusive education. In R. A. Villa & J. S. Thousand (Eds.), *Restructuring for caring and effective education: Piecing the puzzle together* (2nd ed.), (pp 293–327). Baltimore: Brookes.

Gibbons, F. X., Lane, D. J., Gerrard, M., Reis-Bergan, M., Lautrup, C. L., Pexa, N. A., & Blanton, H. (2002). Comparison-level preferences after performance: Is downward comparison theory still useful? *Journal of Personality and Social Psychology, 83,* 865–880.

Gijlers, H. & de Jong, T. (2005). The relation between prior knowledge and students' collaborative discovery learning processes. *Journal of Research in Science Teaching, 42*(3), 264–282.

Gilliard, J. L., & Moore, R. A. (2007). An investigation of how culture shapes curriculum in early care and education programs on a Native American Indian reservation. *Early Childhood Education Journal, 34*(4), 251–258.

Gilligan, C. (1982). *In a different voice: Psychological theory and women's development.* Cambridge, MA: Harvard University Press.

Gilligan, C., Hamner, T., & Lyons, N. (1990). *Making connections.* Cambridge, MA: Harvard University Press.

Ginott, H. G. (1993). *Teacher and child.* New York: Collier Books.

Giroux, H. A. (1994). Doing cultural studies: Youth and the challenge of pedagogy. *Harvard Educational Review, 64*(3), 278–308.

Glassman, M. (2001). Dewey and Vygotsky: Society, experience, and inquiry in educational practice. *Educational Researcher, 30*(4), 3–14.

Glenberg, A. (1976). Monotonic and non-monotonic lag effects in paired-association and recognition memory paradigms. *Journal of Verbal Learning and Verbal Behavior, 15,* 1–16.

Glenzer, H. (2005). Living learning theory through My Fair Lady. *British Journal of Educational Technology, 36*(1), 101–105.

Glynn, S. M. & DiVesta, F. J. (1977). Outline and hierarchical organization as aids for study and retrieval. *Journal of Educational Psychology, 69,* 89–95.

Goldberg, M. L., Passow, A. H., & Justman, J. (1966). *The effects of ability grouping.* New York: Teachers College Press.

Goldman S. & Rakestraw, J. (2000). Structural aspects of constructing meaning from text. In M. Kamil, P. Mosenthal, P. D. Pearson, R. Barr (Eds.), *Handbook of Reading Research,* (Vol. 3 pp. 311–335). NJ: Lawrence Erlbaum Associates.

Gonzales, P., Guzman, J. C., Partelow, L., Pahlke, E., Jocelyn, L., Kastberg, D., et al. (2004). Highlights from the Trends in International Mathematics and Science Study (TIMSS) 2003. Washington, DC: National Center for Educational Statistics.

Good, T. L. & Brophy, J. E. (2003). *Looking in classrooms* (9th ed.). Boston: Allyn & Bacon.

Good, T. L. & Grouws, D. (1979). The Missouri Mathematics Effectiveness Project; An experimental study in fourth-grade classrooms. *Journal of Educational Psychology, 71,* 355–362.

Good, T. L., & Brophy, J. E. (2002). *Looking in classrooms* (9th Ed.). Boston: Allyn & Bacon.

Good, T. L., Grouws, D., & Ebermeier, H. (1983). *Active mathematics teaching.* New York: Longman.

Gorski, P. (2008). The myth of the "culture of poverty". Educational Leadership, 65(7), 32–36.

Gottfried, A. E. (1990). Academic intrinsic motivation in elementary and junior high school students. *Journal of Educational Psychology, 77,* 631–645.

Gottfried, A. E., Fleming, J. S., & Gottfried (1998). Role of cognitively stimulating home environment in children's intrinsic academic motivation. *Child Development, 69,* 1448–1460.

Gottleib, G. (2000). Environmental and behavioral influences on gene activity. Current *Directions in Psychological Science, 9,* 93–97.

Gould, R. L. (1978). *Transformations: Growth and change in adult life.* New York: Simon & Schuster.

Graham, C., & Neu, D. (2004). Standardized testing and the construction of governable persons. *Journal of Curriculum Studies, 36*(3), 295–319.

Graham, S. (1997). Using attribution theory to understand social and academic motivation in African American youth. *Educational Psychologist, 32,* 21–34.

Graham, S. & Weiner, B. (1983). Some educational implications of sympathy and anger from an attributional perspective. In R. Shaw & M. Farr (Eds.), *Cognition, affect and instruction.* Hillsdale, NJ: Lawrence Erlbaum.

Gredler, M. E. (2001). *Learning and instruction: Theory into practice* (4th ed.). Upper Saddle River, NJ: Merrill Prentice Hall

Gredler, M. E. (2005). *Learning and instruction: Theory into practice* (5th ed.). Upper Saddle River, NJ: Merrill/Prentice Hall.

Green, S. K. & Gredler, M. E. (2002). A review and analysis of constructivism for school-based practice. *School Psychology Review, 31*(1), 53–70.

Greenfield, P. M. & Smith, J. (1976). *The structure of communication in early language development.* New York: Academic Press.

Greenwood, G. E. & Fillmer, H. T. (1999). *Educational psychology cases for teacher decision-making.* Upper Saddle River, NJ: Merrill.

Grigorenko, E. L. (2000). Heritability and intelligence. In R. J. Sternberg (Ed.), *Handbook of intelligence* (pp. 53–91). New York: Cambridge University Press.

Grossman, H. (Ed.). (1983). *Classification in mental retardation.* Washington, DC: American Association on Mental Deficiency.

Gu, W. (2008). New horizons and challenges in China's public schools for parent involvement. *Education, 128*(4), 570–578.

Guilford, J. P. (1967). *The nature of human intelligence.* New York: McGraw-Hill.

Guisbond, L., & Neill, M. (2004). Failing our children: No child left behind undermines quality and equality in education. *Clearing House, 78*(1), 12–16.

Hadley, P. A., Simmerman, A., Long, M., & Luna, M. (2000). Facilitating language development for inner-city children: Experimental evaluation of a collaborative, classroom-based intervention. *Language, Speech, and Hearing Services in the Schools, 31,* 280–295.

Halford, G. S. & Andrews, G. (2006). Reasoning and problem solving. In D. Kuhn & R. Siegler (Eds.), *Handbook of child psychology: Vol. 2. Cognition, perception, and language* (6th ed.). New York: Wiley.

Halpin, A. W. (1966). *Theory and research in administration.* New York: Macmillan.

Halvorson, H., Crooks, J., LaHart, D. A., & Farrell, K. P. (2008). An outbreak of itching in an elementary school—A case of mass psychogenic response. *Journal of School Health, 78*(5), 294–297.

Hamilton, K. (2006). Bilingual or immersion? *Diverse: Issues in Higher Education, 23*(5), 23–36.

Hammerman, E. (2005). Linking classroom instruction and assessment to standardized testing. *Science Scope, 28*(4), 26–32.

Hannafin, M., Land, S., & Oliver, K. (1999). Open learning environments: Foundations, methods and models. In C. M. Reigeluth (Ed.), *Instructional-design theories and models* (Vol. 2; pp. 115–140). Mahwah, NJ: Erlbaum.

Harackiewicz, J. M., Barron, K. E., Tauer, J. M., Carter, S. M., & Elliot, A. J. (2000). Short-term and long-term consequences of achievement goals in college: Predicting continued interest and performance over time. *Journal of Educational Psychology, 92,* 316–330.

Harackiewicz, J., Barron, K., & Elliot, A. (1998). Rethinking achievement goals: When are they adaptive for college students and why? *Educational Psychologist, 33,* 1–21.

Hardman, M. L., Drew, C. J., & Egan, M. W. (2005). Human exceptionality: Society, school, and family (8th ed.). Boston: Allyn and Bacon.

Harper, B. & Tuckman, B. W. (2007). Racial identity beliefs and academic achievement: Does being black hold students back? *Social Psychology of Education, 9,* 381–403.

Hart, B. & Risley, T. R. (1995). *Meaningful differences in the everyday experience of young children.* Baltimore: Brookes.

Harter, S. (1981). A model of mastery motivation in children: Individual differences and developmental change. In W. A. Collins (Ed.), *Aspects on the development of competence: The Minnesota symposia on child psychology* (Vol. 14, pp. 215–255). Hillsdale, NJ: Erlbaum.

Harter, S. (1998). The development of self-representations. In W. Damon (Series Ed.) & N. Eisenberg (Vol. Ed.), *Handbook of child psychology* (5th ed., Vol. 3, pp. 553–618). New York: Wiley.

Harter, S. (1999). *The construction of the self: A developmental perspective.* New York, Guilford.

Harter, S. (2003). The development of self-representations during childhood and adolescence. In M. R. Leary & J. P. Tagney (Eds.), *Handbook of self-identity* (pp. 610–642). New York: Guilford Press.

Harter, S. & Connell, J. P. (1984). A comparasin of children's achievement and related self-perceptions of competence, control, and motivational orientation. In J. G. Nicholls (Ed.), *Advances in motivation and achievement: The development of achievement motivation* (Vol. 3, pp. 219–250). Greenwich, CT: JAI Press.

Haugtvedt, C. P. & Wegener, D. T. (1994). Message order effects in persuasion: An attitude strength perspective. *Journal of Consumer Research, 21,* 205–219.

Hawkins, H. L. & Presson, J. C. (1987). Auditory information processing. In K. R. Boff, L. Kaufman & J. P. Thomas (Eds.), *Handbook of perception and human performance: Vol. 2. Information processing* (pp. 26–1 to 26–48). New York: Wiley.

Hayes, B., Hindle, S., & Withington, P. (2007). Strategies for developing positive behavior management. Teacher behavior outcomes and attitudes to the change process. *Educational Psychology in Practice, 23*(2), 161–175.

Hayes, J. K. (1988). *The complete problem solver* (2nd. Ed.). Manwah, NJ: Erlbaum.

Haynes, W. & Pindzola, R. (1998). *Diagnosis and evaluation in speech pathology.* (5th ed.). Needham Heights, MA: Allyn and Bacon.

Healy, A. F. & McNamara, D. S. (1996). Verbal learning and memory: Does the modal model still work? *Annual Review of Psychology, 47,* 143–172.

Heider, F. (1958). *The psychology of interpersonal relations.* New York: John Wiley.

Helms, J. (1990). Applying the interaction model to social dyads. In J. Helms (Ed.), *Black and white racial identity: Theory, research and practice* (pp. 177–186). Westport, CT: Praegar.

Helweg-Larsen, M. & Shepperd, A. (2001). Do moderators of the optimistic bias affect personal or target risk estimates? A review of the literature. *Personality & Social Psychology Review, 5*(1), 74–95.

Henderlong, J., & Lepper, M. R. (2002). The effects of praise on children's intrinsic motivation: A review and synthesis. *Psychological Bulletin, 128,* 774–795.

Hendrickson, P. (Jan 25, 1993). Orval Faubus and the shadow of history. The Washington Post, Page B1.

Hernstein, R. J., & Murray, C. (1994). *The bell curve: Intelligence and class structure in American Life.* New York: The Free Press.

Herrell, A. L., & Jordan, M. (2008). *50 strategies for teaching English language learners.* Upper Saddle River, NJ: Pearson.

Hess, R. (1970). Class and ethnic influences upon socialization. In P. Mussen (Ed.), *Carmichael's Manual of Child Psychology* (3rd ed., Vol. 2). New York: Wiley.

Heward, W. L. (2003). *Exceptional children: An introduction to special education.* Upper Saddle River, NJ: Merrill/Prentice Hall.

Hickman, C. W., Greenwood, G. E., & Miller, M. D. (1995). High school parent involvement: Relationship with achievement, grade level, SES, and gender. *Journal of Research & Development in Education, 28*(3), 125–134.

Hill-Jackson, V., Sewell, K. L., & Waters, C. (2007). Having our say about multicultural education. *Kappa Delta Pi Record, 43*(4), 174–181.

Hirsch, E. D., Jr. (1996). *The schools we need: Why we don't have them.* New York: Doubleday.

Hmelo-Silver, C. E. (2004). Problem-based learning: What and how do students learn? *Educational Psychology Review, 16(3)*, 235–266.

Hmelo-Silver, C. E., Holton, D., & Kolodner, J. L. (2000). Designing to learn about complex systems. *Journal of Learning Science, 9*, 247–298.

Hoffman, D., & Levak, B. A. (2003, September). Personalizing Schools. *Educational Leadership, 61(1)*, 30–34.

Holliday, T. K. (2008). My inner conflict between logic and creativity. *School Administrator, 65(2)*, 48–51.

Hong, Y., Morris, M., Chiu, C., & Benet-Martinez, V. (2000). Multicultural minds: A dynamic constructivist approach to culture and cognition. *American Psychologist, 55*, 709–720.

Horner, R. H., & Crone, D. A. (2005). Functional Behavioral Assessment Interview available online at: www.pbis.org/common/pbisresources/tools/F_BSP_protocol.doc

Horse, P. G. (2001). Reflections on American Indian idenity. In C. L. Wijeyesinghe and. W. Jackson III (eds.), New Perspectives on Racial Identity Development: A theoretical and Practical Anthology. New York: New York University Press, 2001.

Horse, P. G. (2005). Native American identity. *New Directions for Student Services, 109*, 61–68.

Hovland, C. I. (1963). Yale studies of communication and persuasion. In W. W. Charters & N. L. Gage (Eds.), *Readings in the social psychology of education* (pp. 239–253). Boston: Allyn & Bacon.

Hoy, W. K., Tartar, C. J., & Woolfolk Hoy, A. (2006). Academic optimism of schools: A force for student achievement. *American Educational Research Journal, 43*, 425–446.

Hsieh, C. & Knight, L. (2008). Problem-based learning for engineering students: An evidence based comparative study. *The Journal of Academic Librarianship, 34(1)*, 25–30.

Hughes, E., & Forbes, S. (2005). Keeping Alaskan tradition alive: Building relationships in the curriculum. *Childhood Education, 81(3)*, 145–151.

Huitt, W. (2003). A transactional model of the teaching/learning process. *Educational Psychology Interactive*. Valdosta, GA: Valdosta State University.

Hunt, D. E. & Sullivan, E. V. (1974). *Between psychology and education*. Hinsdale, IL: Dryden Press.

Hursh, D. (2005). The growth of high-stakes testing in the USA: Accountability, markets and the decline of educational equality. *British Educational Research Journal, 31(5)*, 605–622.

Hyslop-Margison, E. & Strobel, J. (2008). Constructivism and education: Misunderstandings and pedagogical implications. *Teacher Educator, 43(1)*, 72–86.

Iacovou, M. (2002). Regional differences in the transition to adulthood. *Annals of the American Academy of Political Science Studies, 580*, 40–69.

Inhelder, B. & Piaget, J. (1958). *The growth of logical thinking*. New York: Basic Books.

Ironsmith, M. & Eppler, A. (2007). Mastery learning benefits low-aptitude students. *Teaching of Psychology, 34(1)*, 28–31.

Jackson, J. M. (1960). Structural characteristics of norms. In N. Henry (Ed.), *The dynamics of instructional groups* (59th yearbook, part 2). Chicago: National Society for the Study of Education.

Jensen, P. S. (2000). Pediatric psychopharmacology in the United States: Issues and challenges in the diagnosis and treatment of attention–deficit/hyperactivity disorder. In L. L. Greenhill & B. B. Osman (Eds.), *Ritalin: Theory and practice* (2nd ed.). Larchmont, NY: Mary Ann Liebert Inc.

Jewell, L. N. & Reitz, H. J. (1981). *Group effectiveness in organizations*. Glenview, IL: Scott, Foresman.

Johnson, D. W. (2000). *Reaching out: Interpersonal effectiveness and self-actualization* (7th ed.). Boston: Allyn & Bacon.

Johnson, D. W. & Johnson, F. P. (2003). *Joining together: Group theory and group skills* (8th ed.). Boston: Allyn & Bacon.

Johnson, D. W., Johnson, R. T., & Smith, K. (2007). The state of cooperative learning in postsecondary and professional settings. *Educational Psychology Review, 19(1)*, 15–29.

Johnson, D. W., Maruyama, G., Johnson, R. T., Nelson, D., & Skon, L. (1981). The effects of cooperative, competitive, and individualistic goal structures on achievement: A meta-analysis. *Psychological Bulletin, 89*, 47–62.

Johnson, P., Buboltz, W. C., & Seemann, E., (2003). Ego identity status: A step in the differentiation process. *Journal of Counseling & Development, 81(2)*, 191–195.

Johnson, R. T., Johnson, D. W., & Stanne, M. B. (1986). Comparison of computer-assisted cooperative, competitive, and individualistic learning. *American Educational Research Journal, 23*, 382–392.

Johnson, S. & Johnson, D. W. (1989). *Cooperation and competition: Theory and research*. Edina, MN: Interaction Book Company.

Joiner, L. L. (2007). Nine lives: The nation celebrates the 50th anniversary of the integration of Central High School. *Crisis, 114(5)*, 30–33.

Jonassen, D. H. (1999). Designing constructivist learning environments. In C. M. Reigeluth (Ed.), *Instructional-design theories and models* (Vol. 2; pp. 215–240. Mahwah, NJ: Erlbaum.

Jonassen, D. H. (2003). Designing research-based instruction for story problems. *Educational Psychology Review, 15*, 267–296.

Jones, K. (1994). Success factors among inner-city college students. Paper presented at the Annual Meeting of the American Educational Research Association, New Orleans.

Joyce, B. & Weill, M. (2008). *Models of teaching* (8th ed.). Boston: Allyn & Bacon.

Juvonen, J. (1991). Deviance, perceived responsibility, and negative peer reactions. *Developmental Psychology, 27*, 672–681.

Juvonen, J. (1992). Negative peer reactions from the perspective of the reactor. *Journal of Educational Psychology, 84*, 314–321.

Juvonen, J., & Gross, E. F. (2008). Extending the school grounds?-Bullying experiences in cyberspace. *Journal of School Health, 78(9)*, 496–505.

Kafer, N. (1976). Friendship choice and performance in classroom groups. *The Australian Journal of Education, 20*, 278–284.

Kamii, C. & DeVries, R. (1978). *Physical knowledge in preschool education*. Englewood Cliffs, NJ: Prentice-Hall.

Kanner, L. (1985). Autistic disturbance of autistic contact. In A. M. Donnellan (Ed.), *Classic readings in autism* (pp. 11–53). New York: Teachers College Press.

Kaufman, J. M., Conroy, M., Gardner, R., III. & Oswald, D. (2008). Cultural sensitivity in the application of behavior principles to education. *Education and Treatment of Children, 31*(2), 239–262.

Keller, J. M. (1987). The systematic process of motivational design. *Performance & Instruction, 26*, 1–8.

Kelley, J. E. (2008). Harmony, empathy, loyalty, and patience in Japanese children's literature. *Social Studies, 99*(2), 61–70.

Kelly, K. M., Adams, J. M., & Jones, W. H. (2002). Using the imaginary audience scale as a measure of social anxiety in young adults. *Educational and Psychological Measurement, 62*(5), 896–914.

Kember, D. (2000). Misconceptions about the learning approaches, motivation, and study practices of Asian students. *Higher Education, 40*, 99–121.

Kennedy, C. H. & Fisher, D. (2001). *Inclusive middle schools.* Baltimore: Brookes.

Kent, R. D. & Miulo, G. (1995). Phonetic abilities in the first year of life. In P. Fletcher & B. MacWhinney (Eds.), *The handbook of child language.* Cambridge, MA: Blackwell.

Kerka, S. (2003). Possible selves: Envisioning the future. *Trends and Issues Alert, ERIC Clearinghouse on Adult, Career, and Vocational Education,* Columbus, OH.

Kiewra, K. A. (1985). Providing the instructor's notes: An effective addition to student notetaking. *Educational Psychologist, 20*, 33–39.

Kiewra, K. A. & DuBois, N. F. (1998). *Learning to learn: Making the transition from student to lifelong learner.* Needham Heights, MA: Allyn and Bacon.

Kincheloe, J. L. (2008). Critical pedagogy and the knowledge wars of the twenty-first century. *International Journal of Critical Pedagogy, 1*(1), 1–22.

King, A. (1992). Comparison of self questioning, summarizing, and note taking-review as strategies for learning from lectures. *American Educational Research Journal, 29*, 303–323.

King, A., Staffieri, A., & Adelgais, A. (1998). Mutual peer tutoring: Effects of structuring tutorial interaction to scaffold peer learning. *Journal of Educational Psychology, 90*, 134–152.

King, B. T. & Janis, I. L. (1956). Comparison of the effectiveness of improvised versus non-improvised role playing in producing opinion changes. *Human Relations, 9*, 177–186.

King, N. J., Ollendick, T. H., & Prins, P. J. (2000). Test-anxious children and adolescents: Psychopathology, cognition, and psychophysiological reactivity. *Behavior Change, 17*(3), 134–142.

Kirschner, P., Sweller, J., & Clark, R. (2006). Why minimal guidance during instruction does not work: An analysis of the failure of constructivist discovery, problem-based, experiential, and inquiry-based teaching. *Educational Psychologist, 41*(2), 75–86.

Klahr, D. & Nigam, M. (2004). The equivalence of learning paths in early science instruction: Effects of direct instruction and discovery learning. *Psychological Science, 15*(10), 661–667.

Klahr, D. & Simon, H. A. (1999). Studies of scientific discovery: Complimentary approaches and convergent findings. *Psychological Bulletin, 125*, 524–543.

Klassen, R. (2002). A question of calibration: A review of the self-efficacy beliefs of students with learning disabilities. *Learning Disability Quarterly, 25*, 88–102.

Kline, E. M., Silver, M. B., & Russell, S. C. (2001). *The educator's guide to medical issues in the classroom.* Baltimore: Brookes.

Kohlberg, L. (1969). State and sequence: The cognitive-developmental approach to socialization. In D. Goslin (Ed.), *Handbook of socialization theory and research.* Chicago: Rand-McNally.

Kohlberg, L. (1975). The cognitive-developmental approach to moral education. *Phi Delta Kappan, 56*, 670–677.

Kohlberg, L. (1981). *The philosophy of moral development.* New York: Harper & Row.

Kohn, A. (1993). *Punished by rewards: The trouble with gold stars, incentive plans, A's, praise, and other bribes.* Boston: Houghton Mifflin.

Kohn, A. (1994). Grading: The issue is not how but why. *Educational Leadership, 52*(2) 38–41.

Kohn, A. (1996). *Beyond discipline: From compliance to community.* Alexandria, VA: ASCD.

Kohn, A. (2001). Five reasons to stop saying "good job". *Young Children, 56*(5), 24–28.

Korf, R. (1999). Heuristic search. In R. Wilson & F. Keil (Eds.), *The MIT encyclopedia of the cognitive sciences* (pp. 372–373). Cambridge, MA: MIT Press.

Kounin, J. S. (1970). *Discipline and group management in classrooms.* New York: Holt, Rinehart & Winston.

Kounin, J. S. & Gump, P. V. (1958). The ripple effect in discipline. *Elementary School Journal, 59*, 158–162.

Kovalik, S. J. & Olsen, K. D. (2007). *Exceeding expectations: A user's guide to implementing brain research in the classroom* (3rd ed.). Washington: Books for Educators.

Krathwohl, D. R., Bloom, B. S., & Masia, B. B. (1964). *Taxonomy of educational objectives. Handbook II: Affective domain.* New York: David McKay.

Kriete, R. (2003, September). Start the day with community. *Educational Leadership, 61*(1), 68–70.

Krosnick, J. A. & Alwin, D. F. (1989). Aging and susceptibility to attitude change. *Journal of Personality and Social Psychology, 57*, 416–425.

Kuczaj, S. A. (1978). Why do children fail to overregularize the progressive inflection? *Journal of Child Language, 5*, 167–171.

Kuhn, D. (2006). Do cognitive changes accompany developments in the adolescent brain? *Perspectives on Psychological Science, 1*, 59–67.

Kuhn, D. & Dean, D., Jr. (2004). Metacognition: A bridge between educational psychology and educational practice. *Theory into Practice, 43*(4), 268–273.

Kuhn, D. & Franklin, S. (2006). The second decade: What develops and how? In D. Kuhn & R.S. Siegler (Eds.), *Handbook of child psychology: Vol. 1. Cognition, Perception and Language* (6th ed.). New York: Wiley.

Kulik, J. A. (1992). Ability grouping and gifted students. In N. Colangelo, S. G. Assouline, & D. L. Ambroson (Eds.), Talent development: Proceedings from the 1991 Henry B. & Jocelyn Wallace National Research Symposium on Talent Development (pp. 261–266). Unionville, NY: Trillium.

Kulik, J. A. (1992). *An analysis of the research on ability grouping: Historical and contemporary perspectives.* Storrs, CT: The National Research Center of the gifted & talented, University of Connecticut (RBDM 9204).

Kumar, M. (2006). Constructivist epistemology in action. *Journal of Educational Thought, 40*(3), 247–261.

Ladner, M. & Hammons, C. (2001). Special but unequal: Race and special education. In C. J. Finn, A. J. Rotherham, & C. R. Hokanson (Eds.), *Rethinking special education for a new century* (pp. 85–110). Washington, DC: Thomas B. Fordham Foundation: Progressive Plicy Institute.

Ladson-Billings, G. (2001). *Crossing over to Canaan: The journey of new teachers in diverse classrooms.* San Francisco, CA: Jossey-Bass, Inc.

Lage, M. J., Platt, G. J., & Triglia, M. (2000). Inverting the classroom: A gateway to creating an inclusive learning environment. Journal of Economic Education, 31, 30–43.

Lampert, M. (1986). Knowing, doing, and teaching multiplication. *Cognition and Instruction, 3*, 305–342.

Landrum, T. J., & Kauffman, J. M. (2006). Behavioral approaches to classroom management. In C. M. Evertson & C. S. Weinstein (Eds.), *Handbook of classroom management: Research, practice, and contemporary issues.* Mahwah: NJ: Erlbaum.

Larrivee, B. (1999). *Authentic classroom management: Creating a community of learners.* Boston, MA: Allyn and Bacon.

Larsen, O. N. (Ed.). (1968). *Violence and the mass media.* New York: Harper & Row.

Larson, R. W. & Crouter (2002). Continuity, stability, and change in daily emotional experience across adolescence. *Child Development, 73*, 1151–1165.

Larson, R. W. & Richards, M. H. (1994). *Divergent realities: The emotional lives of mothers, fathers, and adolescents.* New York: Basic Books.

Larson, S. A., Lakin, K. C., Anderson, L., Kwak, N., Hak Lee, J., and Anderson, D. (2001). Prevalence of mental retardation and developmental disabilities: Estimates from the 1994/1995 National Health Interview Survey Disability Supplements. *American Journal of Mental Retardation, 105*, 231–252.

Lazar, I., & Darling, R. (1982). Lasting effects of early education. *Monographs of the Society for Research in Child Development, 47*(No 2. 2–3, Serial No. 195).

Leavitt, H. J. (1951). Some effects of certain communication patterns on group performance. *Journal of Abnormal and Social Psychology, 46*, 38–50.

Lee, C. D. & Kahnweiler, M. (2000). The effect of a mastery learning technique on the performance of a transfer of training task. *Performance Improvement Quarterly, 13*(3), 125–139.

Lee, S. (1996). Unraveling the model minority stereotype: Listening to Asian American youth. NY: Teachers College Press.

Lehman, D. R., Lampert, R. O., and Nisbett, R. E. (1988). The effects of graduate training on reasoning: Formal discipline and thinking about everyday-life problems. American Psychologist, 43, 431–442.

Leonard, L. B. (1995). Phonological impairment. In P. Fletcher & B. MacWhinney (Eds.), *The handbook of child language.* Cambridge, MA: Blackwell.

Lepper, M. R. & Hodell, M. (1989). Intrinsic motivation in the classroom. In C. Ames & R. Ames (Eds.), *Research in motivation in education* (Vol. 3, pp. 73–105). San Diego, CA: Academic Press.

Levin, J. R., McCormick, C. B., Miller, G. E., Berry, J. K., & Pressley, M. (1982). Mnemonic versus nonmnemonic vocabulary learning strategies for children. *American Educational Research Journal, 19*, 121–136.

Lewin, K., Lippitt, R., & White, R. (1939). Patterns of aggressive behavior in experimentally created social climates. *Journal of Social Psychology, 10*, 271–299.

Li, J. (2003). U.S. and Chinese cultural beliefs about learning. *Journal of Educational Psychology, 95*(2), 258–267.

Li, Q. (2008). A cross-cultural comparison of adolescents' experience related to cyberbullying. *Educational Research, 50(3)*, 223–234.

Liberman, A. & Chaikin, S. (1992). Defensive processing of personally relevant health messages. *Personality and Social Psychology Bulletin, 18*, 669–679.

Lichtman, J. W. (2001). Developmental neurobiology overview: Synapses, circuits, and plasticity. In D. B. Bailey, Jr., J. T. Bruer, F. J. Simmons, & J. W. Lichtman (Eds.), *Critical thinking about critical periods* (pp. 27–42), Baltimore: Brookes.

Lickona, T. (1991). *Educating for character: How our schools can teach respect and responsibility.* New York: Bantam Books

Lickona, T. (2001). What is good character? And how can we develop it in our children? *Reclaiming Children and Youth, 9*(4).

Lilienfeld, S., Wood, J., & Garb, H. (2000). The scientific status of projective techniques. *Psychological Science in the Public Interest, 1*, 27–66.

Lindeman, M. & Koskela, P. (1994). Group size, controllability of group membership, and comparative dimension as determinants of intergroup discrimination. *European Journal of Social Psychology, 24*(2), 267–278.

Linderholm, T. & Zhao, Q. (2008). The impact of strategy instruction and timing of estimates on low and high working-memory capacity readers' absolute monitoring accuracy. *Learning and Individual Differences, 18*, 135–143.

Linn, R. L., Miller, M. D., & Gronlund, N. E. (2005). *Measurement and assessment in teaching* (9th ed.). Upper Saddle River, NJ: Pearson.

Lipman, M. (2003). *Thinking in education* (2nd ed.). New York: Cambridge University Press.

Locke, E. A., & Latham, G. P. (2002). Building a practically useful theory of goal setting and task motivation. *American Psychologist, 57*, 705–717.

Lockwood, J. H. & Cleveland, E. F. (1998). The challenge of detracking: Finding the balance between excellence and equity. U.S. Department of Education, Educational Resources Information Center (ED 422 436).

LoLordo, V. M. (2000). Encyclopedia of psychology, Vol. 2. Kazdin, Alan E. (Ed); pp. 91–95. Washington, DC, US: American Psychological Association; New York, NY, US: Oxford University Press, 2000.

Lopez, M. G., & Tashakkori, A. (2004). Narrowing the gap: Effects of a two-way bilingual education program on the literacy development of at-risk primary students. *Journal of Education for Students Placed At Risk, 9*(4), 325–336.

Lorch, R. F. (1989). Text-signaling devices and their effects on reading and memory processes. *Educational Psychology Review, 1*, 209–234.

Lovaas, O. I. (1987). Behavioral treatment and normal educational and intellectual functioning in young autistic children. *Journal of Consulting and Clinical Psychology, 55,* 3–9.

Lovaas, O. I. (1994). Presentation at Ohio State University Teleconference on Applied Behavior Analysis. Columbus, OH: Ohio State University.

Lovett, M. C. (2002). Problem solving. In H. Pashler & D. Medin (Eds.), *Stevens' Handbook of Experimental Psychology: Memory and Cognitive Processes.* New York: John Wiley & Sons.

Lucien, E. (2001). *Japanese education in grades k-12.* Washington, DC: Office of Educational Research and Improvement (ED). (ERIC Document Reproduction Service No. ED458185)

Luft, J. (1969). *Of human interaction.* Palo Alto, CA: National Press Books.

Lytle, S. L. & Cochran-Smith, M. (1992). Teacher research as a way of knowing. *Harvard Educational Review, 62* (4), 279–310.

Mace, F. C., Belfiore, P. J., & Hutchinson, J. M. (2001). Operant theory and research on self-regulation. In B. J. Zimmerman & D. H. Schunk (Eds.), Self-regulated learning and academic achievement: Theoretical perspectives (2nd ed., pp. 39–65). Mahwah, NJ: Lawrence Erlbaum.

MacWhinney, B. (2002). The gradual evolution of language. In B. Malle T. Givon (Eds.), *The evolution of language.* Philadelphia: Benjamins.

Madsen, C. H., Jr., Becker, W. C., Thomas, D. R., Koser, L., & Plager, E. (1968). An analysis of the reinforcing function of "sit down" commands. In R. K. Parker (Ed.), *Readings in educational psychology* (pp. 265–278). Boston: Allyn & Bacon.

Maehr, M., & Midgley, C. (1996). *Transforming school cultures.* Boulder, CO: Westview Press.

Mager, R. F. (1984). *Preparing instructional objectives* (2nd ed.). Belmont, CA: Pitman.

Malouff, J. (2008). Bias in grading. *College Teaching, 56*(3), 191–192.

Mandlebaum, L., Russell, S., Krouse, J., & Gonter, M. (1983). Assertive discipline: An effective classwide behavior management program. *Behavioral Disorders, 8,* 258–264.

Manning, M. A. (2007). Self-concept and self-esteem in adolescents. *Principal Leadership (Middle School Ed.), 7*(6), 11–15.

Mansfield, R. S., Busse, T. V., & Krepelka, E. J. (1978). The effectiveness of creativity training. *Review of Educational Research, 48,* 517–536.

Marchman, V. & Bates, E. (1994). Continuity in lexical and morphological development. A test of the critical mass hypothesis. *Journal of Child Language, 21,* 339–366.

Marcia, J. E. (1988). Common processes underlying ego identity, cognitive/moral development, and individuation. In D. K. Lapsley & F. C. Power (Eds.), *Self, ego, and identity: Integrative approaches* (pp. 211–225). New York: Springer-Verlag.

Marcia, J. E. (2002). Adolescence, identity, & the Bernardone family. *Identity: An International Journal of Theory & Research, 2*(3), 199–209.

Marcia, J. E. (1980). Identity formation in adolescence. In J. Adelson (Ed.), *Handbook of adolescent psychology.* New York: Wiley.

Mariano, J. A., Welteroth, S. J., & Johnson, J. E. (1999). Teachers' understanding of the effects of Japanese culture on social play with young children. *Early Childhood Education Journal, 26*(3), 189–194.

Markman, E. M. (1992). Constraints on word learning: Speculations about their nature, origins, and domain specificity. In M. R. Gunnar & M. P. Maratsos (Eds.), *Minnesota symposium on child psychology: Vol. 25. Modularity and constraints in language and cognition.* Hillsdale, NJ: Erlbaum.

Markman, E. M. & Wachtel, G. F. (1998). Children's use of mutual exclusivity to constrain the meaning of words. *Cognitive Psychology, 20,* 121–157.

Marland, S. (1972). Education of the gifted and talented (Vol. 1). Report to the U.S. Congress by the U.S. Commissioner of Education. Washington, DC: Office of Education, Department of Health, Education, & Welfare (ERIC document ED 056 243).

Marlatt, G. A. (1972). Task structure and the experimental modification of verbal behavior. *Psychological Bulletin, 78,* 335–350.

Marshall, R. E. (1978). The effect of classroom organization and teacher-student interaction on the distribution of status in the classroom. Unpublished doctoral dissertation, University of Chicago.

Marshall, S. P. (1995). *Schemas in problem solving.* Cambridge, UK: Cambridge University Press.

Martinez-Pons, M. (2002). Parental influences on children's academic self-regulatory development. *Theory into Action, 41,* 126–131.

Marzano, R. J. (2002). A comparison of selected methods of scoring classroom assessments. *Applied Measurement in Education, 14*(3), 249–267.

Marzano, R. J. (2003). *What works in schools: Translating research into action.* Alexandria, VA: Association for Supervision and Curriculum Development.

Marzano, R. J., & Marzano, J. S. (2003). The key to classroom management. *Educational Leadership, 61(1),* 6–13.

Marzano, R. J., Marzano, J. S., & Pickering, D. J. (2003). *Classroom management that works: Research-based strategies for every teacher.* Alexandria, VA: Association for Supervision and Curriculum Development (ASCD).

Maslow, A. H. (1970). *Motivation and personality* (2nd Ed.). New York: Harper and Row.

Mather, N. & Goldstein, S. (2001). *Learning disabilities and challenging behaviors.* Baltimore: Brookes.

Mautone, P., & Mayer, R. E. (2001). Signaling as a cognitive guide in multimedia learning. *Journal of Educational Psychology, 93,* 377–389.

Mayer, R. (1984). Aids to prose comprehension. *Educational Psychologist, 19,* 30–42.

Mayer, R. (1989). Models for understanding. *Review of Educational Research, 59,* 43–64.

Mayer, R. (2004). Should there be a three-strikes rule against pure discovery learning? The case for guided methods of instruction. *American Psychologist, 59*(1), 14–19.

Mayer, R. E. (1984). Aids to prose comprehension. *Educational Psychologist, 19*, 30–42.

Mayer, R. E. (1999). *The promise of educational psychology: Learning in the content areas.* Upper Saddle River, NJ: Merrill/Prentice Hall.

Mayer, R. E. (2001). *Multimedia learning.* NY: Cambridge University Press.

Mayer, R. E. (2003a). *Learning and instruction.* Upper Saddle River, NJ: Merrill/Prentice Hall.

Mayer, R. E. (2003b). Memory and information processes. In W. M. Reynolds & G.E. Miller (Eds.), *Handbook of psychology: Vol. 7. Educational psychology* (pp. 47–57). Hoboken, NJ: Wiley.

Mayer, R. E. & Wittrock, M. C. (1996). Problem-solving transfer. In D. C. Berliner & R. C. Calfee (Eds.), *Handbook of educational psychology* (pp. 47–62). New York: Macmillan.

Mayer, R. E. (1993). Illustrations that instruct. In R. Glaser (Ed.), *Advances in instructional psychology: Volume 4* (pp. 253–284). Hillsdale, NJ: Erlbaum.

Mayhew, M. J. & King, P. (2008). How curricular content and pedagogical strategies affect moral reasoning development in college students. *Journal of Moral Education, 37*, 17–40.

Mays, L. (2008). The cultural divide of discourse: Understanding how English language learners' primary discourse influences acquisition of literacy. *Reading Teacher, 61*(5), 415–418.

McAdams, C. R., & Schmidt, C. D. (2007). How to help a bully: Recommendations for counseling the proactive aggressor. *Professional School Counseling, 11(2),* 121–128.

McClelland, D. C. (1965). Toward a theory of motive acquisition. *American Psychologist, 20*, 321–333.

McClelland, D. C. (1985). *Human motivation.* Glenview, IL: Scott, Foresman.

McClleland, D. C., Atkinson, J. W., Clark, R. A., & Lowell, E. L. (1953). *The achievement motive.* New York: Appleton-Century-Crofts.

McConkie, G. (1977). Learning from text. In L. Shulman (Ed.), *Review of research in education* (Vol. 5). Itasca, IL: Peacock.

McConnell, J. L., & Hinitz, B. F. (2005). In their words: A living history of the Brown decision. *Journal of the American Educational Studies Association, 37*(1), 77–82.

McDaniel, M. & Pressley, M. (1984). Putting the keyword method in context. *Journal of Educational Psychology, 76*, 598–609.

McDermott, S. (1994). Explanatory model to describe school district prevalence rates for mental retardation and learning disabilities. *American Journal on Mental Retardation, 99*, 175–185.

McDevitt, T. M. & Ford, M. E. (1987). Processes in young children's communicative functioning and development. In M. E. Ford & D. H. Ford (Eds.), *Humans as self-constructing living systems: Putting the framework to work.* Mahwah, NJ: Erlbaum.

McDevitt, T. M. & Ormrod, J. E. (2007). *Child development and education* (3rd ed.). Upper Saddle River, NJ: Merrill/Prentice Hall.

McGerr, P. (1988). *Johnny Lingo's eight-cow wife.* Pleasantville, NY: Reader's Digest.

McKinley, N. (2004, September). Braving the bullies: What speech-language pathologists can do. *The ASHA Leader Online, 16–17.* Retrieved January 21, 2009, from http://www.asha.org/about/publications/leader-online/archives/2004/040921/040921d.htm

Meece, J. L. (2002). *Child and adolescent development for educators* (2nd ed.). New York: McGraw-Hill.

Meichenbaum, D. & Asarnow, J. (1979). Cognitive-behavioral modification and metacognitive development: Implications for the classroom. In P. Kendall & S. Hollon (Eds.), *Cognitive-behavioral intervention: Theory, research and procedures.* Orlando, FL: Academic Press.

Meier, C. R. & DiPerna, C. (2006). Importance of social skills in the elementary grades. *Education and Treatment of Children, 29*(3), 409–419.

Meier, S. L., Rich, B. S., & Cady, J. (2006). Teachers' use of rubrics to score non- traditional tasks: Factors related to discrepancies in scoring. *Assessment in Education, 13*(1), 69–95.

Meir, E. I., Keinan, G., & Segal, Z. (1986). Group importance as a mediator between personality-environment congruence and satisfaction. *Journal of Vocational Behavior, 28*, 60–69.

Mendes, E. (2003, September). What empathy can do. *Educational Leadership, 61(1),* 56–59.

Mendez v. Westminster, 64 F. Supp. 544 (S.D. Cal. 1946).

Merton, R. (1949). *Social theory and social structure.* New York: Free Press.

Meter, P. & Stevens, R. (2000). The role of theory in the study of peer collaboration. *Journal of Experimental Education, 69*(1), 113–127.

Metz, K. E. (1995). Reassessment of developmental restraints on children's science instruction. *Review of Educational Research, 65*, 93–127.

Meyer, B. J. F. (1975). *The organization of prose and its effect on memory.* New York: American Elsevier.

Meyer, B. J. F., Brandt, D. M., & Bluth, G. J. (1980). Use of top-level structure in text: Key for reading comprehension of ninth-grade students. *Reading Research Quarterly, 16*, 72–103.

Meyer, C. F. & Rhoades, E. K. (2006). Multiculturalism: Beyond food, festival, folklore, and fashion. *Kappa Delta Pi Record, Winter*, pp. 82–87.

Meyer, W. V., Folkes, V. S., & Weiner, B. (1976). The perceived information value and affective consequences of choice behavior and intermediate difficulty task selection. *Journal of Research in Personality, 10*, 410–423.

Milgram, S. (1963). Behavioral study of obedience. *Journal of Abnormal and Social Psychology, 67*, 371–378.

Miller, G. A. (1956). The magical number seven, plus or minus two: Some limits to our capacity for processing information. *Psychological Review, 63*, 81–97.

Miller, P. A., Eisenberg, N. Fabes, R. A., & Shell, R. (1996). Relations of moral reasoning and vicarious emotion to young children's prosocial behavior toward peers and adults. *Developmental Psychology, 32*, 210–219.

Miller, S. M. (1981). Predictability and human stress: Toward a clarification of evidence and theory. In L. Berkowitz (Ed.), *Advances in experimental social psychology* (Vol. 14, pp. 204–256). New York: Academic Press.

Miller, S. A. (2004). Tips for creating classroom rules. *Early Childhood Today, 19(3)*, 8–10.

Mintz, C., Wallace, M. D., Najdowski, A. C., Atcheson, K., & Bosch, A. (2007). Reinforcer identification and evaluation of choice within an educational setting. *Journal of Behavioral Education, 16*(4), 333–341.

Molenda, M. (2008). The programmed instruction era: When effectiveness mattered. *TechTrends: Linking Research and Practice to Improve Learning, 52*(2), 52–58.

Monroe, C. R. (2005). Understanding the discipline gap through a cultural lens: Implications for the education of African American students. *Intercultural Education, 16(4)*, 317–330.

Moomaw, S., & Jones, G. W. (2005). Native curriculum is early childhood classrooms. *Childhood Education, 82*(2), 89–94.

Moran, S. (2008). Creativity in school. In K. Littleton, C. Woods, & J. K. Staarman (Eds.), *Handbook of educational psychology: New perspectives on learning and teaching*. New York: Elsevier.

Moran, S., Kornhaber, M., & Gardner, H. (2006). Orchestrating multiple intelligences. *Educational Leadership, 64*(1), 22–27.

Morse, W. C. (1985). *The education and treatment of socioemtionally impaired children and youth*. Syracuse, NY: Syracuse University Press.

Moshman, D. (1998). Cognitive development beyond childhood. In D. Kuhn & R. S. Siegler (Eds.), *Handbook of child psychology, Vol. 2: Cognition, perception, and language* (5th ed.). NY: Wiley.

Moshman, D. (1999). *Adolescent psychological development: Rationality, morality and identity*. Mahwah, NJ: Lawrence Erlbaum Associates.

Mosston, M. & Ashworth, S. (1994). *Teaching physical education* (4th ed.) Columbus, OH: Prentice-Hall.

Motamedi, V. & Sumrall, J. (2000). Mastery learning and contemporary issues in education. *Action in Teacher Education, 22*(1), 32–42.

Mumford, M. D., Costanza, D. P., Baughman, W. A., Threlfall, K. V., & Fleischman, E. A. (1994). Influence of abilities on performance during practice: Effects of massed and distributed practice. *Journal of Educational Psychology, 86*, 134–144.

Murdick, N., Gartin, B., & Crabtree, T. (2002). *Special education law*. Upper Saddle River, NJ: Merrill/Prentice Hall.

Murray, H. (1938). *Explorations in personality*. New York: Oxford University Press.

Nangle, D. W., Erdley, C. A., Carpenter, E. M., & Newman, J. E. (2002). Social skills training as a treatment for aggressive children and adolescents: A developmental-clinical integration. *Aggression and Violent Behavior, 7*, 169–199.

Napier, R. W. & Gershenfeld, M. K. (2004). *Groups: Theory and experience* (7th ed) Boston: Houghton Mifflin.

National Assessment of Educational Progress (2007). National Center for Education Statistics, Washington, DC: U.S. Department of Education, Institute of Education Sciences.

National Center for Education Statistics (2002). *The condition of education 2002 (NCES 2002025)*. Washington, DC: U.S. Department of Education, Office of Educational Research and Improvement.

National Center for Education Statistics (2003). Percent of Students at or above Basic Level of Proficiency on the National Assessment of Educational Progress. Washington, DC: U.S. Department of Education, Institute of Education Sciences.

National Center for Educational Statistics (2008). *The condition of education 2008 (NCES 2008–031)*. Washington, DC: U.S. Government Printing Office. Available at: http://nces.ed.gov/pubsearch/pubsinfo.asp?pubid=2008031

National Center for Learning Disabilities (2006), www.ld.org

National Education Commission on Time and Learning. (1994). *Prisoners of time (archived)*. Washington, DC: U.S. Government Printing Office.

National Indian Education Association (2008). Native Education 101: Basic facts about American Indian, Alaska Native, and Native Hawaiian education. National Education Association, Washington, DC.

National Research Council. (2001). *Understanding dropouts: Statistics, strategies, and high-stakes testing*. Washington, DC: National Academy Press.

Nelson, K. (1996). *Language in cognitive development: The emergence of the mediated mind*. New York: Cambridge University Press.

Nelson, L. M. (1999). Collaborative problem solving. In C. M. Reigeluth (Ed.), *Instructional-design theories and models* (Vol. 2; pp. 241–267. Mahwah, NJ: Erlbaum.

Ngo, B. (2006). Learning from the margins: The education of Southeast and South Asian Americans in context. *Race, Ethnicity, and Education, 9*(1), 51–65.

Ngo, B., & Lee, S. J. (2007). Complicating the image of model minority success: A review of Southeast Asian American education. *Review of Educational Research, 77*(4), 415–453.

Nicholls, J., Cobb, P., Wood, T., Yackel, E. T., & Patashnik, M. (1990). Assessing students' theories of success in mathematics: Individual and classroom differences. *Journal for Research in Mathematics Education, 21*, 109–122.

Nicpon, M. F., Blanks, E. H., & Huser, L. (2006). The relationship of loneliness and social support with college freshmen's academic performance and persistence. *Journal of College Student Retention, 8*(3), 345–358.

Niemi, D., Baker, E. L., & Sylvester, R. M. (2007). Scaling up, scaling down: Seven years of performance assessment development in the nation's second largest school district. *Educational Assessment, 12*(3&4), 195–214.

Niguidula, D. (2005). Documenting learning with digital portfolios. *Educational Leadership, 63*(3), 44–47.

Nitko, A. J., & Brookhart, S. M. (2007). *Educational assessment of students* (5th ed.). Upper Saddle River, NJ: Pearson.

Nolen, J. L. (2003). Multiple intelligences in the classroom. *Education, 124*(1), 115–119.

Notar, C. E., Herring, D. F., & Restauri, S. L. (2008). A web-based teaching aid for presenting the concepts of norm referenced and criterion referenced testing. *Education, 129*(1), 119–124.

Nowack, A., Szamrej, J., & Latane, B. (1990). From private attitude to public opinion: A dynamic theory of social impact. *Psychological Review, 97*, 363–376.

Oakes, J., & Wells, A. S. (1998). Detracking for high student achievement. *Educational Leadership, 55*(6), 38–41.

Ogbu, J. (2003). *Black American students in an affluent suburb. A study of academic disengagement*. Mahwah, NJ: Lawrence Erlbaum Associates.

Olweus, D. (2003). A profile of bullying at school. *Educational Leadership, 60(6)*, 12–17.

Orbell, S., & Sheeran, P. (2000). Motivation and volitional processes in action initiation: A field study of the role of implementation intentions. *Journal of Applied Social Psychology, 30*, 780–797.

Orfield, G., & Frankenberg, E. (Spring, 2004). Brown v. Board: Where are we now? *Teaching Tolerance, 25*.

Oser, F. (1986). Moral education and values education: The discourse perspective. In M.C. Wittrock (Ed.), *Handbook of research on teaching* (3rd ed.). New York: Macmillan.

Overmier, J. B. & Lawry, J. A. (1979). Pavlovian conditioning and the mediation of behavior. In G.H. Bower (Ed.), *The psychology of learning and motivation* (Vol. 13), 1–55. New York: Academic Press.

Overskeid, G. (2008). They should have thought about the consequences: The crisis of cognitivism and a second chance for behavior analysis. *The Psychological Record, 58*, 131–151.

Owens, R. E. (1999). *Language disorders: A functional approach to assessment and intervention* (4th ed.). Boston: Allyn and Bacon.

Pace University Counseling Services (2008). *Learning styles and how to maximize your success in school.* New York: Pace University.

Page-Voth, V. & Graham, S. (1999). Effects of goal-setting and strategy use on the writing performance and self-efficacy of students with writing and learning problems. *Journal of Educational Psychology, 91*, 230–240.

Paivio, A. (1971). *Imagery and verbal processes.* New York: Holt, Rinehart & Winston.

Paivio, A. (1986). *Mental representations: A dual coding approach.* New York: Oxford University Press.

Palincsar, A. S. & Brown, A. L. (1984). Reciprocal teaching of comprehension-fostering and comprehension monitoring activities. *Cognition and Instruction, 1*, 117–175.

Park, H. S., & Bauer, S. (1999). Computational mathematical abilities of African American girls. *Journal of Black Studies, 30*, 204–215.

Pasnak, R., Brown, K., Kurkijan, M., Triana, E., & Yamamoto, N. (1987). Cognitive gains through training on classification, seriation, and conservation. *Genetic, General and Social Psychology Monographs, 113*(3), 293–321.

Patel, V. L. & Groen, G. J. (1986). Knowledge-based solution strategies in medical reasoning. *Cognitive Science, 10*, 91–116.

Pavlov, I. P. (1927). *Conditioned reflexes.* London: Oxford University Press.

Peacock, M. (2001). Match or mismatch? Learning styles and teaching styles in EFL. *International Journal of Applied Linguistics, 11*(1), 1–20.

Pedota, P. (2007). Strategies for effective classroom management in secondary setting. *The Clearing House*, 163–166.

Pepitone, A. (1964). *Attraction and hostility.* New York: Atherton Press.

Perkins, D. N. & Salomon, G. (1989). Are cognitive skills context-bound? *Educational Researcher, 18*(1), 16–25.

Perkins, D. N., & Unger, C. (1999). Teaching and learning for understanding. In C. M. Reigeluth (Ed.), *Instructional-Design theories and models (Vol.2). A new paradigm of instructional theory* (pp. 91–114). Mahwah, NJ: Lawrence Erlbaum Associates.

Perry, D. G., Kusel, S. J., & Perry, L. C. (1988). Victims of peer aggression. *Developmental Psychology, 24(6)*, 807–814.

Peterson, L. D., Young, K. R., West, R. P., & Hill Peterson, M. (1999). Effects of student self-management on generalization of student performance to regular classrooms. *Education and Treatment of Children, 19*, 170.

Petri, H. L. (1996). *Motivation: Theory, research and applications* (4th ed.). Pacific Grove, CA: Brooks/Cole.

Petrus, J. A. (1997). Bringing the shadow child into the light. *Learning, 26* (1), 36–40.

Petty, R. E., Wegener, D. T., & Fabrigar, L. R. (1997). Attitudes and attitude change. *Annual Review of Psychology, 48*, 609–647.

Phelps, R. P. (2006). Characteristics of an effective student testing system. *Educational Horizons, 85*(1), 19–29.

Phillips, J. (2003). Powerful learning: Creating learning communities in urban school reform. *Journal of Curriculum and Supervision, 18(3)*, 240–258.

Phinney, J. S. (1990). Ethnic identity in adolescents and adults: Review of research. *Psychological Bulletin, 108*(3), 499–514.

Phinney, J. S. (1993). A three-stage model of ethnic identity development in adolescence. In M. E. Bernal & G. P. Knight (Eds.), *Ethnic identity: ormation and transmission among Hispanics and other minorities* (pp. 1–79). Albany, NY: SUNY Press.

Phinney, J. S. (2000). Identity formation across cultures: The interaction of personal, societal, and historical change. *Human Development, 43*(1), 27–31.

Piaget, J. (1926). *The language and thought of the child.* New York: Harcourt, Brace & World.

Piaget, J. (1928). *Judgment and reasoning in the child.* (M. Warden, Trans.). New York: Harcourt Brace.

Piaget, J. (1932). *The moral judgment of the child.* New York: Harcourt, Brace & World.

Piaget, J. (1950). *The psychology of intelligence.* New York: Harcourt Brace Jovanovich.

Piaget, J. (1951). *Play, dreams and imitation in childhood.* New York: Norton.

Piaget, J. (1952). *The origins of intelligence in children.* (M. Cook, Trans.) New York: Norton.

Piaget, J. (1954). *The construction of reality in the child.* New York: Basic Books.

Piaget, J. (1958). Principal factors determining intellectual evolution from childhood to adult life. In E. L. Hartley & R. E. Hartley (Eds.), *Outside readings in psychology* (2nd ed., pp. 43–55). New York: Crowell.

Piaget, J. (1961). The genetic approach to the psychology of thought. *Journal of Educational Psychology, 52*, 275–281.

Piaget, J. (1964). Development and learning. In R. Ripple & V. Rockcastle (Eds.), *Piaget rediscovered* (pp. 7–20). Ithaca, NY: Cornell University Press.

Piaget, J. (1967). *Six psychological studies.* New York: Vintage Books.

Piaget, J. (1970). *Science of education and the psychology of the child.* New York: Viking Press.

Piaget, J. (1972). Intellectual evolution from adolescence to adulthood. *Human Development, 15*, 1–12.

Piaget, J. (1973). *To understand is to invent: The future of education.* New York: Grossman.

Piaget, J. (1977). *The development of thought: Equilibrium of cognitive structures.* New York: Viking Press.

Piaget, J., & Inhelder, B. (1969). *The psychology of the child.* New York: Basic Books.

Pine, K. & Messer, D. (2000). The effect of explaining another's actions on children's implicit theories of balance. *Cognition and Instruction, 18*(1), 35–51.

Pinker, S. (1984). *Language learnability and language development.* Cambridge, MA: Harvard University Press.

Pintrich, P. R. (2000a). An achievement goal theory perspective on issues in motivation terminology, theory, and research. *Contemporary Educational Psychology, 25,* 92–104.

Pintrich, P. R. (2000b). Multiple goals, multiple pathways: The role of goal orientation in learning and achievement. *Journal of Educational Psychology, 92,* 544–555.

Pintrich, P. R. (2003). A motivational science perspective on the role of student motivation in learning and teaching contexts. *Journal of Educational Psychology, 95,* 667–686.

Pintrich, P. R. & Schunk, D. H. (2002). *Motivation in education: Theory, research, and applications* (2nd ed.). Upper Saddle River, NJ: Merrill Prentice Hall.

Pintrich, P. R., & Schunk, D. H. (2008). *Motivation in education: Theory, research, & applications* (3rd Ed.). Upper Saddle River, NJ: Merill Prentice Hall.

Pintrich, P. R., Wolters, C. A., & Baxter, G. P. (2000). Assessing metacognition and self-regulated learning. In G. Schraw & J. C. Impara (Eds.), *Issues in the measurement of metacognition* (pp. 43–97). Lincoln, NE: The University of Nebraska Press.

Piotrowski, D., & Hoot, J. (2008). Bullying and violence in schools: What teachers should know and do. *Childhood Education, 84*(6), 357–363.

Polya, G. (1973). *How to solve it* (2nd ed.). Garden City, NY: Doubleday.

Pomerantz, E. M., Altermatt, E. R. & Saxton, J. L. (2002). Making the grade but feeling distressed: Gender differences in academic performance & internal distress. *Journal of Educational Psychology, 94*(2), 396–404.

Pomerantz, E. M., Saxton, J. L., & Kenney, G. A. (2001). Self evaluation: The development of sex differences. In G. B. Moskowitz (Ed.), *Cognitive social psychology. On the tenure and future of social cognition* (pp. 59–74), Mahwah, New Jersey: Erlbaum.

Popham, W. J. (2002). *Classroom assessment: What teachers need to know (3rd ed.).* Boston, MA: Allyn & Bacon.

Popham, W. J. (2006a). Needed: A dose of assessment literacy. *Educational Leadership, 63*(6), 84–85.

Popham, W. J. (2006b). Those [fill-in-the-blank] tests! *Educational Leadership, 63*(8), 85–86.

Premack, D. (1965). Reinforcement theory. In D. Levine (Ed.) *Nebraska Symposium on Motivation* (pp. 123–188). Lincoln, NE: University of Nebraska Press.

Pressley, M. (2002). *Reading instruction that works* (2nd. ed.). New York: Guilford Press.

Pressley, M. & Harris, K. (1990). What we really know about strategy instruction. *Educational Leadership, 48*(1), 31–34.

Pressley, M., & Woloshyn, V. (1995). *Cognitive strategy instruction.* Cambridge, MA: Brookline Books.

Prinstein, M. J. & La Greca, A.M. (2004). Childhood peer rejection and aggression as predictors of adolescent girls' externalizing and health risk behaviors: A six-year longitudinal study. *Journal of Consulting & Clinical Psychology, 72,* 103–112.

Punahou School web site available online at: http://www.punahou.edu/page.cfm?p=601.

Qualter, P. & Munn, P. (2002). The separateness of social and emotional loneliness in childhood. *The Journal of Child Psychology and Psychiatry and Allied Disciplines, 43*(2), 233–244.

Quilici, J. H., & Mayer, R. E. (1996). Role of examples in how students learn to categorize statistics word problems. *Journal of Educational Psychology, 88,* 144–161.

Rabinowitz, M. & Glaser, R. (1985). Cognitive structure and processin highly competent performance. In F. D. Horowitz & M. O'Brien (Eds.), *The gifted and talented: Developmental perspectives* (pp. 75–98). Washington, DC: American Psychological Association.

Rademacher, J. A, Callahan, K., & Pederson-Seelye, V. A. (1998). How do your classroom rules measure up? *Intervention in School & Clinic, 33*(5), 284–290.

Raffini, J. P. (1996). *150 ways to increase intrinsic motivation in the classroom.* Boston, MA: Allyn and Bacon.

Ramos, F. (2007). What do parents think of two-way bilingual education? An analysis of responses. *Journal of Latinos and Education, 6*(2), 139–150.

Randall, J., & Engelhard, G. (2009). Differences between teachers' grading practices in elementary and middle schools. *Journal of Educational Research, 102*(3), 175–185.

Reder, L. M. (1976). *The role of elaboration in the processing of prose.* Unpublished doctoral dissertation, University of Michigan, Ann Arbor.

Reed, P. & Best, S. (2001). Assessment for assistive technology. In J. L. Bigge, S. J. Best, & K. W. Heller Eds.), *Teaching individuals with physical, health or multiple disabilities* (4th ed.). Upper Saddle River, NJ: Merrill/Prentice Hall.

Reese, D. (2007). Proceed with caution: Using Native American folktales in the classroom. *Language Arts, 84*(3), 245–256.

Reich, P. A. (1986). *Language development.* Englewood Cliffs, NJ: Prentice Hall.

Reid, R. & Maag, J. W. (1998). Functional assessment: A method for developing classroom-based accommodations and interventions. *Reading and Writing Quarterly, 14,* 7–15.

Reiser, R. A. & Dick, W. (1996). *Instructional planning: A guide for teachers* (2nd ed.). Boston: Allyn and Bacon.

Renzulli, J. S. (1978). What makes giftedness? Reexamining a definition. *Phi Delta Kappan, 60,* 180–184, 261.

Renzulli, J. S. (1994). Research related to the Schoolwide Enrichment Triad Model. *Gifted Child Quarterly, 38*(1), 7–20.

Renzulli, J. S. (1996). The three-ring conception of giftedness: A developmental model for creative productivity. In R. J. Sternberg and J. E. Davidson (Eds). *Conceptions of Giftedness* (pp. 53–92). New York: Cambridge University Press.

Renzulli, J. S. & Reis, S. M. (1997). The schoolwide enrichment model: New directions for developing high-end learning. In N. Colangelo & G. A. Davis Eds.), *Handbook of gifted education* (2nd ed.) (pp. 136–154). Needham Heights, MA: Allyn and Bacon.

Renzulli, J. S., Smith, L., and Reis, S. M. (1982). Curriculum compacting: An essential strategy for working with gifted students. *Elementary School Journal, 82*(3), 185–194.

Resnick, L. B. (1987). Learning in school and out. *Educational Researcher, 16*, 13–20.

Rhode, G., Jensen, W. R., & Reavis, H. K. (1998). *The tough kid book: Practical classroom management strategies.* Longmont, CO: Sopris West.

Richardson, V. (2003). Constructivist pedagogy. *Teachers College Record, 105*(9), 1623–1640.

Roberts, T. (1991). Gender and the influence of evaluations on self-assessments in achievement settings. *Psychological Bulletin, 109*, 297–308.

Rogoff, B. (1990). *Apprenticeship in thinking: Cognitive development in social context.* New York: Oxford University Press.

Rogoff, B. (1995). Observing sociocultural activitiy on three planes: Participatory appropriation, guided participation, and apprenticeship. In J. V. Wertsch, P. D. Rio, & A. Alvarez (Eds.), *Sociocultural studies of mind* (pp. 129–164). Cambridge, UK: Combridge University Press.

Rogoff, B. (1998). Cognition as a collaborative process. In W. Damon (Series Ed.), & D. Kuhn, & R. S. Siegler (Vol. Eds.), *Handbook of Child Psychology: Cognition, perception, & language* (pp. 679–744). New York: Wiley.

Rogoff, B. (2003). *The cultural nature of human development.* Oxford, England: Oxford University Press.

Rose, R. J. (2002). How do adolescents select their friends? A behavior-genetic perspective. In L. Pulkinnen & A. Kaspi (Eds.), *Paths to successful development: Personality in the life course* (pp. 106–125). New York: Cambridge University Press.

Rosenberg, M. (1986). Self concept from middle childhood through adolescence. In J. Suls & A. Greenwald (Eds.), *Psychological perspectives on the self* (Vol. 3). Hillsdale, NJ: Erlbaum.

Rosenholtz, S. J. & Rosenholtz, S. M. (1981). Classroom organization and the perception of ability. *Sociology of Education, 54*, 132–140.

Rosenshine, B. (1979). Content, time, and direct instruction. In P. Peterson & H. Wahlberg (Eds.), *Research on teaching: Concepts, findings, and implications.* Berkeley, CA: McCutcheon.

Rosenshine, B. (1997). Advances in research on instruction. In J. W. Lloyd, E. J., Kameenui, & D. Chard (Eds.), Issues in educating students with disabilities (pp. 197–220). Mahwah, NJ: Erlbaum.

Rosenshine, B. (2002). Helping students from low income homes read at grade level. *Journal of Education for Students Placed at Risk, 7*(2), 273–283.

Rosenshine, B., Meister, C., & Chapman, S. (1996). Teaching students to generate questions: A review of the intervention studies. *Review of Educational Research, 66*(2), 181–221.

Rosenthal, R. (1974). The Pygmalion effect lives. *Psychology Today*, April, 56–63.

Rosenthal, R. & Fode, K. L. (1963). The effect of experimenter bias on the performance of the albino rat. *Behavioral Science, 8*, 183–189.

Rosenthal, R. & Jacobson, L. (1968). *Pygmalion in the classroom.* New York: Holt, Rinehart & Winston.

Rotberg, I. C. (2006). Assessment around the world. *Educational Leadership, 64*(3), 58–63.

Rothkopf, E.Z. (1966). Learning from written instructive materials: An exploration of the control of inspection behavior by testlike events. *American Educational Research Journal, 3*, 241–249.

Rothstein-Fisch, C., & Trumbull, E. (2008). *Managing diverse classrooms: How to build on students' cultural strengths.* Alexandria, VA: Association for Supervision and Curriculum Development (ASCD).

Rotter, J. B., Chance, J. E., & Phares, E. J. (1972). *Applications of a social learning theory or personality.* New York: Holt, Rinehart & Winston.

Rubin, B. C. (2006). Tracking and detracking: Debates, evidence, and best practices for a heterogeneous world. *Theory Into Practice, 45*(1), 4–14.

Runco, M. A. (2000). Creativity: Research on the process of creativity. In A. E. Kazdin (Ed.), *Encyclopedia of Psychology* (Vol. 2, pp. 342–346).

Russell, J. (2007). *How children become moral selves: Building character and promoting citizenship in education.* Portland, OR: Sussex Academic Press.

Rvachew, S., Chiang, P., & Evans, N. (2007). Characteristics of speech errors produced by children with and without delayed phonological awareness skills. *Language, Speech, and Hearing Services in the Schools, 38*, 60–71.

Ryan, A., Pintrich, P.R., & Midgley, C. (2001). Avoiding seeking help in the classroom: Who and why? *Educational Psychology Review, 13*, 93–114.

Ryan, R. M., & Deci, E. L. (2000). Intrinsic and extrinsic motivations: Classic definitions and new directions. *Contemporary Educational Psychology, 25*, 54–67.

Saab, N., van Joolingen, W., & van Hout-Wolters, B. (2005). Comminication in collaborative discovery learning. *British Journal of Educational Psychology, 75*(4), 603–621.

Sacks, P. (2001). *Standardized minds: The high price of America's testing culture and what we can do to change it.* Cambridge, MA: Da Capo Press.

Saddler, C. A. (2005). The impact of Brown on African American students: A critical race theoretical perspective. *Educational Studies, 37*(1), 41–55.

Sadker, M., & Sadker, D. (1994). *Failing at fairness.* New York: Macmillan.

Sadoski, M., Goetz, E. T., & Rodriguez, M. (2000). Engaging texts: Effects of concreteness on comprehensibility, interest, and recall in four text types. *Journal of Educational Psychology, 92*, 85–95.

Sampter, W. (2003). Friendship interaction skills across the life span. In O. J. Greene & R. B. Burleson (Eds.), *Handbook of communication and social interaction skills* (pp. 637–684). Mahwah, NJ: Erlbaum.

Sanders, M. (2004). Urban Odyssey: Theatre of the oppressed and talented minority youth. *Journal for the Education of the Gifted, 28*(2), 218–241.

Sapir, E. (2004). *Language: An introduction to the study of speech.* Mineola, New York: Dover Publications.

Sarason, I. G. (1980). *Test anxiety: Theory, research, and applications.* Hillsdale, NJ: L. Erlbaum Associates.

Sattler, J. M. (2001). *Assessment of children: Cognitive applications* (4th ed.). San Diego, CA: Jerome M. Sattler, Inc.

Scarr, S. (1997). Behavior-Genetic and Socialization theories of intelligence: Truce and reconciliation. In R. J. Sternberg & E. Grigorenko (Ed.), *Intelligence, Heredity, and Environment* (pp. 3–41), New York: Cambridge University Press.

Schacter, D. L. (2000). Memory: Memory systems. In A. E. Kazdin (Ed.), *Encyclopedia of psychology* (*Vol. 5*, pp. 169–172). Washington, DC: American Psychological Association.

Schaler, J. A. (2006). *Howard Gardner under fire: The rebel psychologist.* Peru, IL: Open Court Publishing Company.

Schaps, E. (2003). Creating a school community. *Educational Leadership, 60(6),* 31–33.

Schirmer, B. R. (2002). Hearing loss. In A. Turnbull, R. Turnbull, M. Shank, S. Smith, & D. Leal (Eds.), *Exceptional lives: Special education in today's schools* (3rd ed., pp. 516–554). Upper Saddle River, NJ: Merrill/Prentice Hall.

Schlaefli, A., Rest, J. R. & Thoma, S. J. (1985). Does moral education improve moral judgment? A meta-analysis of intervention studies using the *Defining Issues Test. Review of Educational Research, 55,* 319–352.

Schmuck, R. A. & Schmuck, P. A. (2001). *Group processes in the classroom* (8th ed.). New York: McGraw Hill.

Schoenfeld, A. H. (1985). *Mathematical problem solving.* Orlando, FL: Academic Press.

Schoenfeld, A. H. (1992). Learning to think mathematically: problem solving, metacognition, and sense-making in mathematics. In D. Grouws, (Ed.), *Handbook for Research on Mathematics Teaching and Learning.* New York: MacMillan.

Schon, D. A. (1987). *Educating the reflective practitioner.* San Francisco: Jossey-Bass.

Schon, D. A. (1991). *The reflective turn: Case studies in and on educational practice.* New York: Teachers College Press, Columbia University.

Schraw, G. (1998). Promoting general metacognitive awareness. *Instructional Science, 26,* 113–125.

Schunk, D. H. (1983). Ability versus effort attributional feedback: Differential effects on self-efficacy and achievement. *Journal of Educational Psychology, 75,* 848–856.

Schunk, D. H. (2004). *Learning theories: An educational perspective* (4th ed.). Columbus, OH: Merrill/Prentice Hall.

Schunk, D. H. & Miller, S. D. (2002). Self-efficacy and adolescents' motivation. In F. Pajares & T. Urdan (Eds.), *Academic motivation of adolescents* (pp. 29–52). Greenwich, CT: Information Age Publishing.

Schunk, D. H. & Zimmerman, B. J. (2003). Self-regulation and learning. In W.M. Reynolds & G.E. Miller (Eds.), *Handbook of psychology. Vol.7: Educational psychology* (pp. 59–78). Hoboken, NJ: Wiley.

Schwebel, M. (1975). Formal operations in first year college students. *Journal of Psychology, 91,* 133–41.

Scriffiny, P. L. (2008). Seven reasons for standards-based grading. *Educational Leadership, 66(2),* 70–74.

Seligman, M. E. P. (1990). *Learned optimism.* New York: Simon & Schuster.

Sellers, R., Smith, M., Shelton, J., Rowley, S., & Chavous, T. (1998). Multidimensional model of racial identity: Assumptions, findings and future directions. In R.L. Jones (Ed.), *African American identity* (pp. 275–302). Hampton, VA: Cobb & Henry.

Selman, R. L. (1980). The *growth of interpersonal understanding: Development & clinical analyses.* New York: Academic Press.

Selman, R. L., & Schultz, L. H. (1990). *Making a friend in youth: Developmental theory and pair therapy.* Chicago: University of Chicago Press

Sexson, S. B. & Dingle, A. D. (2001). Medical disorders. In F. M. Kline, L. B. Silver, & S. C. Russell (Eds.). *The educator's guide to medical issues in the classroom* (pp. 29–48). Baltimore: Brookes.

Shaker, P. S., & Heilman, E. E. (2008). Scapegoating public schools. *School Administrator, 65(6),* 27–29.

Shaklee, B., Whitmore, J., Barton, L., Barbour, N., Ambrose, R., & Viechnicki, K. (1989). Early assessment for exceptional potential for young and/or economically disadvantaged students. Washington, DC: Office of Educational Research and Improvement. U.S. Department of Education.

Sharan, S. (1980). Cooperative learning in small groups: Recent methods and effects on achievement, attitudes, and ethnic relations. *Review of Educational Research, 50,* 241–272.

Sharan, S. (1994). *Handbook of cooperative learning methods.* Westport, CT: Greenwood Press.

Shearer, B. (2004). Multiple intelligences theory after 20 years. *Teachers College Record, 106(1),* 2–16.

Short, J. F. (Ed) (1968). *Gang delinquency and delinquent subcultures.* New York: Harper & Row.

Shulman, S., Tuval-Mashiach, R., Levran, E., and Anbar, S. (2006). Conflict resolution patterns and longevity of adolescent romantic couples: A 2-year follow-up study. *Journal of Adolescence, 29(4),* 575–588.

Shweder, R. A., Mahapatra, M., & Miller, J. G. (1990). Culture and moral development. In J.W. Stigler, R.A. Shweder, & G. Herdt (Eds.), *Cultural psychology* (pp. 130–204). New York: Cambridge University Press.

Siegler, R. S. (1998). *Children's thinking* (3rd ed.). Upper Saddle River, NJ: Prentice-Hall.

Siegler, R. S. & Alibali, M. W. (2005). *Children's thinking* (4th ed.). Upper Saddle River, NJ: Pearson/Prentice Hall.

Simmons, N. E. (2004). (De)grading the standardized test: Can Standardized testing evaluate schools? *Education Canada, 44(3),* 37–39.

Sins, P. H. M., vanJoolingen, W. R., Savelsbergh, E. R., & van Hout-Wolters, B. (2008). Motivation and performance within a comparative computer-based modeling task: Relations between students' achievement goal orientation, self-efficacy, cognitive processing, and achievement. *Contemporary Educational Psychology, 33,* 58–77.

Sireci, S. G. (1998). Gathering and analyzing content validity data. *Educational Assessment, 5(4),* 299–321.

Skellenger, A., Hill, E., & Hill, M. (1992). The social functioning of children with physical impairments. In S.L. Odom, S.R. McConnell, & M.A. McEvoy (Eds.), *Social competence of young children with disabilities: Issues and strategies for intervention* (pp. 165–188). Baltimore: Brookes.

Skinner, B. F. (1953). *Science and human behavior.* New York: Macmillan.

Skinner, B. F. (1968). *The technology of teaching.* New York: Macmillan.

Slavin, R. E. (1987). Ability grouping and student achievement in elementary schools: A best evidence synthesis. *Review of Educational Research, 57,* 293–336.

Slavin, R. E. (1995). *Cooperative learning: Theory, research, and practice*. Boston: Allyn & Bacon.

Slotte, V., & Lonka, K. (1999). Review and process effects of spontaneous note taking on text comprehension. *Contemporary Educational Psychology, 24*, 1–20.

Smith, L. M. & Geoffrey, W. (1968). *The complexities of an urban classroom*. New York: Holt, Rinehart & Winston.

Snyder, C. R., Rand, K. L. & Sigmon, D. R. (2002). Hope theory: A member of the positive psychology family. In C. R. Snyder & S. J. Lopez (Eds.), *Handbook of positive psychology* (pp.257–276). New York: Oxford University Press.

Snyder, C. R., Shorey, H. S., Cheavens, J., Pulvers, K. M., Adams, V. H. III, & Wiklund, D. (2002). Hope and academic success in college. *Journal of Educational Psychology, 94*, 820–826.

Solley, B. A. (2007). On standardized testing: An ACEI position paper. *Childhood Education, 84*(1), 31–37.

Sonnenschein, S. (1988). The development of referential communication: Speaking to different listeners. *Child Development, 59*, 694–702.

Spearman, C. (1927). *The abilities of man*. New York: Macmillan.

Spears, R., Lea, M., & Lee, S. (1990. Deindividuation and group polarization in computer-mediated communication. *British Journal of Social Psychology, 29*(2), 121–134.

Spencer, S. J., Steele, C. M., & Quinn, D. (1999). Stereotype threat and women's math performance. *Journal of Experimental Social Psychology, 3*, 4–28.

Stahr, B., Cushing, D., Lane, K., & Fox, J. (2006). Efficacy of a function-based intervention in decreasing off-task behavior exhibited by a student with ADHD. *Journal of Positive Behavior Interventions, 8*(4), 201–211.

Stainback, S. & Stainback, W. (Eds.) (1991). *Teaching in the inclusive classroom: Curriculum design, adaptation, and delivery*. Baltimore: Brookes.

Stainback, S. & Stainback, W. (Eds.) (1996). *Inclusion: A guide for educators* (2nd ed.). Baltimore: Brookes.

Steeker, P. M. & Fuchs, L. S. (2000). Effecting superior achievement using curriculum-based measurement: The importance of individual progress monitoring. *Learning Disabilities Research and Practice, 15*, 128–134.

Steele, C. M. (1997). A threat in the air: How stereotypes shape intellectual identity and performance. *American Psychologist, 52*(6), 613–629.

Steele, C. M., & Aronson, J. (1995). Stereotype threat and the intellectual test performance of African Americans. *Journal of Personality and Social Psychhology, 69*, 797–811.

Steinberg, L. & Silk, J. S. (2002). Parenting adolescents. In M.H. Bornstein (Ed.), *Handbook of parenting, Vol. 1: Children and parenting* (2nd ed.) (pp. 103–133). Mahwah, NJ: Erlbaum.

Steinberg, L., Lamborn, S., Darling, N., Mounts, N., & Dornbusch, S. (1994). Over-time changes in adjustment and competence among adolescents from authoritative, authoritarian, indulgent, and neglectful families. *Child Development, 65*, 754–770.

Stensaasen, S. (1970). *Interstudent attraction and social perception in the school class*. Oslo, Norway: Universitelsforlaget.

Stephens, K. R. & Karnes, F. A. (2000). State definitions for the gifted and talented revisited. *Exceptional Children, 66*(2), 219–238.

Sternberg, R. (1985). *The triarchic mind: A new theory of human intelligence*. New York: Viking.

Sternberg, R. J. (1985). *Beyond IQ: A triarchic theory of human intelligence*. New York: Cambridge University Press.

Sternberg, R. J. (1988). *The triarchic mind*. New York: Viking.

Sternberg, R. J. (2000). Identifying and developing creative giftedness. *Roeper Review, 23*(2), 60–64.

Sternberg, R. J. (2001). What is the common thread of creativity? Its dialectical relation to intelligence and wisdom. *American Psychologist, 56*, 360–362.

Sternberg, R. J. (2006). Recognizing neglected strengths. *Educational Leadership, 64*(1), 30–35.

Sternberg, R., Ferrari, M., Clinkenbeard, P. R., & Grigorenko, E. L. (1996). Identification, instruction, and assessment of gifted children: A construct validation of a triarchic model. *Gifted Child Quarterly, 40*(3), 129–137.

Stiggins, R. (2007). Assessment through the student's eyes. *Educational Leadership, 64*(8), 22–26.

Stiggins, R., & Chappuis, J. (2006). What a difference a word makes: Assessment for learning rather than assessment of learning helps students succeed. *Journal of Staff Development, 27*(1), 10–14.

Stiggins, R., & Chappuis, J. (2008). Enhancing Student Learning. *District Administration, 44*(1), 42–44.

Stipek, D. (2002). *Motivation to learn: Integrating theory and practice* (4th ed.). Boston: Allyn & Bacon.

Stone, J. (1997). The preschool child. In H. Mason & S. McCall (Eds.), *Visual impairment: Access to education for children and young people* (pp. 87–96). London: Fulton.

Storandt, M., Kaskie, B., & Von Dras, D. D. (1998). Temporal memory for remote events in healthy aging and dementia. *Psychology and Aging, 13*, 4–7.

Strain, C. R. (2005). Pedagogy and practice: Service learning and students' moral development. *New Directions for Teaching and Learning*, Fall, 61–72.

Strrnberg, R. J. & Wagner, R. K. (1986). *Practical intelligence: Nature and origins of competence in the everyday world*. New York: Cambridge University Press.

Strickland, K., & Strickland, J. (1998). Reflections on assessment: Its purposes, methods, and effects on learning. Portsmouth, NH: Boynton/Cook.

Sugai, G. (2007). Promoting behavioral competence in schools: A commentary on exemplary practices. *Psychology in the Schools, 44*(1), 113–118.

Sugai, G., Sprague, J. R., Horner, R. H., & Walker, H. M. (2000). Preventing school violence: The use of office discipline referrals to assess and monitor schoolwide discipline interventions. *Journal of Emotional and Behavioral Disorders, 8*, 94–101.

Sutinen, A. (2008, January). Constructivism and education: Education as an interpretive transformational process. *Studies in Philosophy & Education, 27*(1), 1–14.

Taconis, R., Ferguson-Hessler, M. G. M. & Broekkamp, H. (2001) Teaching science problem solving: an overview of experimental work. *Journal of Research in Science Teaching, 38*, 442–468.

Tannenbaum, H. R., & Leaper, C. (2003). Parent-child conversations about science: The socialization of gender inequities? *Developmental Psychology, 39*(1), 34–47.

Taylor, B. M. & Samuels, S. J. (1983). Children's use of text structure in the recall of expository material. *American Educational Research Journal, 20*, 517–528.

Tharp, R. G. (1989). Psychocultural variables and constants. Effects on teaching and language in schools. *American Psychology, 44*(2), 349–359.

The Nobel Foundation (2008). *Ivan Petrovich Pavlov*. Retrieved July 8, 2008, from http://nobelprize.org/nobel_prizes/medicine/laureates/1904/pavlov-bio.html

Thompson, R. A. & Nelson, C. A. (2001). Developmental science and the media: Early brain development. *American Psychologist, 56*, 5–15.

Thompson, S. C., Gregg, L., & Niska, J. M. (2004). Professional learning communities, leadership, and student learning. *RMLE Online: Research in Middle Level Education, 28(1),* 1–15.

Thorndike, E. L. (1923). The influence of first-year Latin upon the ability to read English. *School Sociology, 17*, 165–168.

Thorndyke, P. W. (1977). Cognitive structures in comprehension and memory of narrative discourse. *Cognitive Psychology, 9,* 77–110.

Tikunoff, W. J., Berliner, D. C., & Rist, R. C. (1975). An ethnographic study of the forty classrooms of the beginning teacher evaluation known samples. San Francisco: Far West Laboratory for Educational Research and Development. (Tech. Rep. 75–10–5).

Tileston, D. W. (2004). *What every teacher should know about classroom management and discipline.* Thousand Oaks, CA: Corwin Press, Inc.

Tobias, S. (1985). Test anxiety: Interference, defective skills, and cognitive capacity. *Educational Psychologist, 20*, 135–142.

Tomlinson-Clarke, S., & Ota Wang, V. (1999). A paradigm for racial-cultural training in the development of counselor cultural competencies. In M. S. Kiselica (Ed.), *Confronting prejudice and racism during multicultural training* (pp. 155–167). Alexandria, VA: American Counseling Association.

Tomlinson, C. A. (2001). *How to differentiate instruction in missed ability classrooms* (2nd Ed.). Alexandria, VA: American Society for Curriculum Development.

Tomlinson, C. A. (2005). Grading and differentiation: Paradox or good practice? *Theory Into Practice, 44*(3), 262–269.

Topping, K. (2005). Trends in peer learning. *Educational Psychology, 25*(6), 631–645.

Torp, L. & Sage, S. (2002). *Problems as possibilities: Problem-based learning for K-12 education* (2nd ed.). Alexandria, VA: Association for the Study of Curriculum Development.

Torrance, E. P. (1984). *Torrance tests of creative thinking: Directions manual and scoring guide.* Bensenville, IL: Scholastic Testing Service.

Torres, V. (1999). Validation of the bicultural validation model for Hispanic college students. *Journal of College Student Development, 40*, 285–298.

Torres, V. (2003). Influences on ethnic identity development of Latino college students in the first two years of college. *Journal of College Student Development, 44*(4), 532–547.

Tuckman, B. W. (1988). *Testing for teachers.* San Diego, CA: Harcourt Brace Jovanovich.

Tuckman, B. W. (1989). Think out loud: Procrastination "busting." *Educational Technology, 29*(3), 48–49.

Tuckman, B. W. (1990). Group versus goal-setting effects on the self-regulated performance of students differing in self-efficacy. *Journal of Experimental Education, 58*, 291–298.

Tuckman, B. W. (1992). The effect of student planning and self-competence on self- motivated performance. *Journal of Experimental Education, 60,* 119–127.

Tuckman, B. W. (1995). The competent teacher. In A.C. Ornstein (Ed.), *Teaching: Theory into practice.* Boston: Allyn & Bacon.

Tuckman, B. W. (1996). The relative effectiveness of incentive motivation and prescribed learning strategy in improving college students' course performance. *Journal of Experimental Education, 64*, 197–210.

Tuckman, B. W. (1997). Using tests as an incentive to motivate procrastinators to study. *Journal of Experimental Education, 66*, 141–147.

Tuckman, B. W. (1999a). A tripartite model of motivation for achievement: Attitude/drive/strategy. Paper presented at the annual meeting of the American Psychological Association, Boston.

Tuckman, B. W. (1999b). *Conducting educational research* (5th ed.). San Diego: Harcourt Brace.

Tuckman, B. W. (2002). Evaluating ADAPT: A hybrid instructional model combining web-based and classroom components. *Computers & Education, 39*, 261–269.

Tuckman, B. W. (2003a). The effect of learning and motivation strategy training on college students' achievement. *Journal of College Student Development, 44*(3), 430–437.

Tuckman, B. W. (2003b). The Strategies-for-Achievement approach for teaching study skills. American Psychological Association, Toronto, CA.

Tuckman, B. W. & Bierman, M. (1971). Beyond Pygmalion: Galatea in the schools. Paper presented at the meeting of the American Educational Research Association, New York.

Tuckman, B. W. & Hinkle, J. S. (1986). An experimental study of the physical and psychological effects of aerobic exercise on school children. *Health Psychology, 5*, 197–207.

Tuckman, B. W. & Jensen, M. A. C. (1977). Stages of small group development revisited. *Group and Organizational Studies, 2*(4), 419–427.

Tuckman, B. W. & Kennedy, G. (2009). Teaching learning and motivation strategies to enhance the success of first-term college students. American Educational Research Association, San Diego, CA.

Tuckman, B. W. & Sexton, T. L. (1990). The relation between self-beliefs and self-regulated performance. *Journal of Social Behavior & Personality, 5*, 465–472.

Tuckman, B. W. & Sexton, T. L. (1991). The effect of teacher encouragement on student self-efficacy and motivation for self-regulated performance. *Journal of Social Behavior & Personality, 6*, 137–146.

Tuckman, B. W., Abry, D. A., & Smith, D. R. (2008). *Learning and motivation strategies: Your guide to success* (2nd ed.). Upper Saddle River, NJ: Pearson/Prentice Hall.

Tuckman, B. W. (2003a). The effect of learning and motivation strategies training on college students' achievement. *Journal of College Student Development, 44*, 430–437.

Tuckman, B. W. (2003b). The Strategies-for-Achievement approach for teaching study skills. American Psychological Association, Toronto, CA.

Tulving, E. (2002). Episodic memory: From mind to brain. *Annual Review of Psychology, 53*, 1–25.

Tuovinen, J. E. & Sweller, J. (1999). A comparison of cognitive load associated with discovery learning and worked examples. *Journal of Educational Psychology, 91*(2), 334–341.

Turiel, E. (1998). The development of morality. In W. Damon (series Ed.) & N. Eisenberg (vol. Ed.), *Handbook of Child Psychology* (5th Ed., vol. 3, pp. 863–932). New York: Wiley.

Turnbull, H. R. & Turnbull, A. P. (2000). *Free appropriate public education: The law and children with disabilities* (6th ed.). Denver: Love.

U.S. Department of Education (1999). Assistance to states for the education of children with disabilities and the early intervention program for infants and toddlers with disabilities: Final regulations. *Federal Register*, 64(48), CFR Parts 300 and 303.

U.S. Department of Education (2000). *Twenty-second annual report to Congress on the implementation of the Individuals with Disabilities Education Act*. Washington, DC: Author.

U.S. Department of Education (2002). *Twenty-fourth annual report to Congress on the implementation of the Individuals with Disabilities Education Act*. Washington, DC: Author.

U.S. Department of Education. (2004). The condition of education 2004. Washington, DC.

Underwood, M. K. (2003). *Social aggression among girls*. New York: Guilford Press.

Valencia, R. R. (2005). The Mexican American struggle for equal education opportunity in Mendez v. Westminster: Helping pave the way for Brown v. Board of Education. *Teachers College Record, 107*(3), 389–423.

van Merriënboer, J., Kirschner, P., & Kester, L. (2003). Taking a load off a learner's mind: Instructional design for complex learning. *Educational Psychologist, 38*(1), 5–13.

Van Riper, C. & Erickson, R. L. (1996). *Speech correction: An introduction to speech pathology and audiology* (9th ed.). Boston: Allyn & Bacon.

Vardill, R. (1996). Imbalance in the number of boys & girls identified for referral to educational psychologists: Some issues. *Support for Learning, 11*, 123–129.

Vasta, R. (1976). Feedback and fidelity: Effects of contingent consequences on accuracy of imitation. *Journal of Experimental Child Psychology, 21*, 98–108.

Verdinelli, S. & Gentile, R. (2003). Changes in teaching philosophies among in-service teachers after experiencing mastery learning. *Action in Teacher Education, 25*(2), 56–66.

Vermeer, H. J., Boekaerts, M., & Seegers, G. (2000). Motivational and gender differences: Sixth-grade students' mathematical problem-solving behavior. *Journal of Educational Psychology, 92*(2), 308–315.

Vernberg, E., Ewell, K., Beery, S., & Abwender, D. (1994). Sophistication of adolescents' negotiation strategies and friendship formation after relocation: A naturally-occurring experiment. *Journal of Research on Adolescence, 4*, 5–19.

Vernon, D. T. (1995). Attitudes and opinions of faculty tutors about Problem-Based Learning. *Medical Education, 23*, 542–558.

Viadero, D. (2007). Social-skills programs found to yield gains in academic subjects. *Education Week, 27*(16), 1–15.

Vicari, S., Caselli, M.C., Gagliardi, C., Tonucci, F., & Volterra, V. (2002). Language acquisitions in special populations: A comparison between Down and Williams syndromes. *Neuropsychologia, 40*, 2461–2470.

Vihman, M. M. (1992). Early syllables and the construction of phonology. In C.A. Ferguson, L. Menn, & C. Stoel-Gammon (Eds.), *Phonological development: Models, research, implications*. Timonium, MD: York Press.

Villegas, A., & Lucas, T. (2007). The culturally responsive teacher. *Educational Leadership, 64*(6), 28–33.

Vogel, S. (1990). Gender differences in intelligence, language, visual-motor abilities, and academic achievement in students with language disabilities: A review of literature. *Journal of Learning Disabilities, 23*, 44–52.

Vroom, V. 1964. *Work and motivation*. New York: Wiley and Sons.

Vygotsky, L. S. (1962). *Thought and language* (E. Haufmann & G. Vakar, Eds. and Trans.). Cambridge, MA: MIT Press.

Vygotsky, L. S. (1978). *Mind in society: The development of higher psychological processes* (M. Cole, V. John-Steiner, S. Scribner, & E. Souberman, Trans.). Cambridge, MA: Harvard University Press.

Vygotsky, L. S. (1987a). *Problems of general psychology*. New York: Plenum.

Vygotsky, L. S. (1987b). *The collected works of L.S. Vygotsky*. New York: Plenum Press.

Wadsworth, B. J. (1996). *Piaget's theory of cognitive and affective development* (5th ed., p. 132). New York: Longman.

Wadsworth, B. J. (2004). *Piaget's theory of cognitive and affective development* (5th ed.). Boston: Allyn and Bacon.

Wagner, R. K. (1987). Tacit knowledge in everyday intelligent behavior. *Journal of Personality and Social Psychology, 52*, 1236–1247.

Wakefield, D. (2007). NCLB keeps some great teaching candidates out forever. *Education Digest: Essential readings condensed for quick review, 72*(5), 51–57.

Walker, H. M. (1997). *The acting out child: Coping with classroom disruption* (2nd ed.). Longmont, CO: Sopris West.

Walker, H. M., & Buckley, N. K. (1974). Token reinforcement techniques: Classroom applications for the hard-to-teach child. Eugene, OR: E-B Press.

Walker, H. M., Colvin, G., & Ramsey, E. (1995). *Antisocial behavior in schools: Strategies and best practices*. Pacific Grove, CA: Brooks/Cole.

Wallach, M. A. & Kogan, N. (1965). *Modes of thinking in young children*. New York: Holt, Rinehart & Winston.

Wang, L., Beckett, G. H., & Brown, L. (2006). Controversies of standardized assessment in school accountability reform: A critical synthesis of multidisciplinary research evidence. *Applied Measurement in Education, 19*(4), 305–328.

Wang, M. C., Haertel, G. D., & Walberg, H. J. (1993/1994). What helps students learn? *Educational Leadership, 51*(4), 74–79.

Warren, W. Z. (2006). One teacher's story: Creating a new future or living up to our own history? *Phi Delta Kappan, 88*(3), 198–203.

Waterman, A. S. (1999). Issues of identity formation revisited: United States and The Netherlands, *Developmental Review, 19*, 462–479.

Watson, J. B. (1930). *Behaviorism*, revised edition. Chicago: University of Chicago Press.

Webb, N. M. (1982). Student interaction and learning in small groups. *Review of Educational Research, 52*, 421–445.

Webb, N. M. & Palincsar, A. (1996). Group processes in the classroom. In D. Berliner & R. Calfee (Eds.), *Handbook of educational psychology* (pp. 841–876). New York: Macmillan.

Weiner, B. (1980). A cognitive (attribution)-emotion-action model of motivated behavior: An analysis of judgments of help-giving. *Journal of Personality and Social Psychology, 39,* 186–200.

Weiner, B. (1986). *An attributional theory of motivation and emotion.* New York: Springer-Verlag.

Weiner, B. (1992). *Human motivation: Metaphors, theories, and research.* Newbury Park, CA: Sage.

Weiner, B. (1995). *Judgments of responsibility: A foundation for a theory of social conduct.* New York: Guilford Press.

Weiner, B. (2004). Attribution theory revisited: Transforming cultural plurality into theoretical unity. In D. M. McInerney & S. Van Etten (Eds.), *Big theories revisited: Research on sociocultural influences on motivation and learning* (Vol. 4, pp. 13–29). Greenwich, CT: Information Age.

Weiner, B., Russell, D., & Lerman, D. (1979). The cognitive-emotion process in achievement-related contexts. *Journal of Personality and Social Psychology, 37,* 1211–1220.

Weinstein, C. E. (1982). Training students to use elaboration learning strategies. *Contemporary Educational Psychology, 7,* 301–311.

Weinstein, C. E. & Mayer, R. E. (1985). The teaching of learning strategies. In M.C. Wittrock (Ed.), *Handbook of research on teaching* (3rd ed.) (pp. 315–327). New York: Macmillan.

Weinstein, C. S. (1996). *Secondary classroom management: Lessons from research and practice.* New York, NY: McGraw-Hill.

Weinstein, C. S., & Mignano, A. J. (2007). *Elementary classroom management: Lessons from research and practice (4th ed.).* New York, NY: The McGraw-Hill Companies, Inc.

Weinstein, C. S., Tomlinson-Clarke, S., & Curran, M. (2004). Toward a conception of culturally responsive classroom management. *Journal of Teacher Education, 55(1),* 25–38.

Weinstein, C., Curran, M., & Tomlinson-Clarke, S. (2003). Culturally responsive classroom management: Awareness into action. *Theory Into Practice, 42(4),* 269–276.

Weiss, R. S. (1973). *Loneliness: The experience of social and emotional isolation.* Cambridge, MA: MIT Press.

Weissberg, R., Caplan, M., & Harwood, R. (1991). Promoting competent young people in competence-enhancing environments: A systems-based perspective on primary prevention. *Journal of Consulting & Clinical Psychology, 59,* 830–841.

Wentzel, K. R. (2000). What is it that I'm trying to achieve? Classroom goals from a content perspective. *Contemporary Educational Psychology, 25,* 105–115.

Westby, C. E. & Clauser, P. S. (1999). The right stuff for writing: Assessing and facilitating written language. In H. W. Catts & A. G. Kamhi (Eds.), *Language and reading disabilities* (pp. 259–324). Boston: Allyn and Bacon.

White, R. W. (1959). Motivation reconsidered: The concept of competence. *Psychological Review, 66,* 297–333.

Whitty, M. (2002). Possible selves: An exploration of the utility of a narrative approach. *Identity, 2,* 211–228.

Wicker, A.W. (1969). Size of church membership and members support of church behavior settings. *Journal of Personality and Social Psychology, 13,* 278–288.

Wieczorek, C. (2008). Comparative analysis of educational systems of American and Japanese schools: Views and visions. *Educational Horizons, 86*(2), 99–111.

Wigfield, A. & Eccles, J. (1992). The development of achievement task values: A theoretical analysis. *Developmental Review, 12,* 265–310.

Wigfield, A. & Eccles, J. (2000). Expectancy-value theory of achievement motivation. *Contemporary Educational Psychology, 25,* 68–81.

Wigfield, A., & Eccles, J. S. (2002). *Development of achievement motivation.* San Diego, CA: Academic Press.

Wiggins, G., & McTighe, J. (2008). Put understanding first. *Educational Leadership, 65*(8),

Willingham, D. T. (2004). Practice makes perfect—but only if you practice beyond the point of perfection. *American Educator, 28*(1), 31–33.

Willoughby, B. (Spring, 2004). Brown v. Board: An American legacy. *Teaching Tolerance, 25.*

Willoughby, T., Porter, L., Belsito, L., & Yearsly, T. (1999). Use of elaboration strategies by students in grades two, four, and six. *The Elementary School Journal, 99*(3), 221–232.

Wilson, C. C., Robertson, S. J., Herlong, L. H., & Haynes, S. N. (1979). Vicarious effects of time-out in the modification of aggression in the classroom. *Behavior Modification, 3,* 97–111.

Windholz, G. (1997). Ivan P. Pavlov: An overview of his life and psychological work. *American Psychologist, 52*(9), 941–946.

Windschitl, M. (2002). Framing constructivism in practice as the negotiation of dilemmas: An analysis of the conceptual pedagogical, cultural, and political challenges facing teachers. *Review of Educational Research, 72*(2), 131–175.

Winger, T. (2005). Grading to communicate. *Educational Leadership, 63*(3), 61–65.

Winsler, A. & Naglieri, J. (2003). Overt and covert verbal problem-solving strategies: Developmental trends in use, awareness and relations with task performance in children aged 5 to 17. *Child Development, 74,* 659–678.

Wittrock, M. C., Marks, C., & Doctorow, W. (1975). Reading as a generative process. *Journal of Educational Psychology, 67,* 484–489.

Wixson, K. (1984). Level of importance of postquestions and children's learning from text. *American Educational Research Journal, 21,* 419–433.

Wolf, P. J. (2007). Academic improvement through regular assessment. *Peabody Journal of Education, 82*(4), 690–702.

Wong, K. C. (2001). Chinese culture and leadership. *International Journal of Leadership in Education, 4*(4), 309–319.

Wood, E., Pressley, M., & Winne, P. (1990). Elaborative interrogation effects on children's learning of factual content. *Journal of Educational Psychology, 82,* 741–748.

Woodward, A.L., Markman, E.M., & Fitzsimmons, C.M. (1994). Rapid word learning in 13- and 14-month-olds. *Developmental Psychology, 30,* 553–566.

Woolfolk Hoy, A. E., & Burke-Spero, R. (2005). Changes in teacher efficacy during the early years of teaching. *Teaching and Teacher Education, 21*(4), 343–356.

Worchel, S., Andreoli, V. V., & Folger, R. (1977). Intergroup cooperation and intergroup attraction: The effect of previous interaction and outcome of combined effort. *Journal of Experimental Social Psychology, 13,* 131–140.

Wormeli, R. (2006). Accountability: Teaching through assessment and feedback, not grading. *American Secondary Education, 34*(3), 14–27.

Wraga, W. G. (2006). The heightened significance of "Brown v. Board of Education" in our time. *Phi Delta Kappan, 87*(6), 425–428.

Wright, T. L. & Duncan, D. (1986). Attraction to group, group cohesiveness, and individual outcome: A study of training groups. *Small Group Behavior, 17,* 487–492.

Yamarik, S. (2007). Does cooperative learning improve student learning outcomes? *The Journal of Economic Education, 38*(3), 259–277.

Yilmaz, K. (2008). Constructivism: Its theoretical underpinnings, variations, and implications for classroom instruction. *Educational Horizons, 86*(3), 161–172.

Yussen, S. R. (1974). Determinants of visual attention and recall in observational learning by preschoolers and second-graders. *Developmental Psychology, 10,* 93–100.

Zenasni, F., Besancon, M., & Lubart, T. (2008). Creativity and tolerance of ambiguity : An empirical study. *The Journal of Creative Behavior, 42*(1), 61–73.

Zhao, Y. (2006). Are we fixing the wrong things? *Educational Leadership, 63*(8), 28–31.

Zimmerman, B. J. (1990). Self-regulating academic learning and achievement: The emergence of a social cognitive perspective. *Educational Psychology Review, 2,* 173–201.

Zimmerman, B. J. (1998). Developing self-fulfilling cycles of academic regulation: An analysis of exemplary instructional models. In D. H. Schunk & B. J. Zimmerman (Eds.), *Self-regulated learning: From teaching to self-reflective practice* (pp. 1–19). New York: Guilford Press.

Zimmerman, B. J. (2000). Attaining self-regulation: A social cognitive perspective. In M. Boekaerts, P. R. Pintrich, & M. Zeidner (Eds.), *Handbook of self-regulation* (pp. 13–39). San Diego, CA: Academic Press.

Zimmerman, B. J. (2002). Becoming a self-regulated learner: An overview. *Theory into Practice, 41,* 64–70.

Zimmerman, B. J. & Dibenedetto, K. (2008). Mastery learning and assessment: Implications for students and teachers in an era of high-stakes testing. *Psychology in the Schools, 45*(3), 206–216.

Zimmerman, B. J. & Schunk, D. H. (2004). Self-regulating intellectual processes and outcomes: A social cognitive perspective. In D. Y. Dai & R. J. Sternberg (Eds.), *Motivation, emotion, and cognition: Integrative perspectives on intellectual functioning and development* (pp. 3223–349). Mahwah, NJ: Lawrence Erlbaum.

Zimmerman, B. J., Bandura, A., & Martinez-Pons, M. (1992). Self-motivation for academic attainment: The role of self-efficacy beliefs and personal goal setting. *American Educational Research Journal, 29,* 663–676.

Zirkel, S. (2005). Ongoing issues of racial and ethnic stigma in education 50 years after Brown v. Board. *The Urban Review, 37*(2), 107–126.

Zoeckler, L. G. (2007). Moral aspects of grading: A study of high school English teachers' perceptions. *American Secondary Education, 35*(2), 83–102.

Author Index

Page references followed by the letter 'f' indicate figures; page references followed by the letter 't' indicate tables

Subject Index

Pages in bold indicate definitions of terms; page references followed by the letter 'f' indicate figures; page references followed by the letter 't' indicate tables